GROWING MEDIA

for ornamental
plants and turf

GROWING MEDIA

for ornamental plants and turf

KEVIN A. HANDRECK BSc, MAgrSc
Division of Soils, CSIRO, Adelaide, South Australia

NEIL D. BLACK BScAgr, DipEd(Tech)
Rural and Mining Industry Training Division, TAFE (NSW)

UNSWP

Published by
UNIVERSITY OF NEW SOUTH WALES PRESS
22–32 KING STREET,
RANDWICK NSW Australia 2031

Telephone (02) 398 8900
Fax (02) 398 3408

© K. Handreck, N. Black

First published 1984
Reprinted 1986, 1989, 1991
Revised edition 1994

National Library of Australia
Catalogue-in-Publication entry:

Handreck, Kevin, 1938–   .
  Growing media for ornamental plants.

  Rev. ed.
  Bibliography.
  Includes index.
  ISBN 0 86840 333 4

  1. Plants, Ornamental - Soils. 2. Plant growing
  media. I. Black, N. D.(Neil D.),
  1946–   . II. Title.

635.914

Typeset in Sabon 8.5/10 by DOCUPRO, Sydney
Printed by McPherson's Printing Group

Available in North America through:
ISBS Inc
Portland Oregon 97213-3644
Tel: (503) 287 3093
Fax: (503) 280 8832

CONTENTS

PREFACE

Much has happened in the nursery and turf industries in the years since the first edition of *Growing Media* appeared in 1984. Research has provided new information and new ways of doing things, and new products have changed management practices. Some of the more important of these happenings were included in the reprints of 1986, 1989 and 1991. However, such inclusions were inevitably brief because they could only replace existing material of equal length. The need to reset the text for this edition has allowed complete revision and the inclusion of much new information. The basics have not changed, but as needed we have clarified their presentation.

Major additions have been made to the sections on wetting agents, air-filled porosity in potting media, and the measurement and adjustment on pH. The very considerable developments in the technology of composting, brought about largely by the need to recycle huge mountains of 'waste' organic materials in cities, have been interpreted for use in situations where 'high-tech' solutions are too expensive.

The availability of reliable methods for determining the physical and chemical properties of potting media, as summarized in the Australian Standard for Potting Mixes, has radically improved the way in which manufacturers operate. High quality can be consistently delivered. These and related developments in fertilizer practice have led us to completely revamp our treatment of the production of potting media and the use of fertilizers in nurseries. We have expanded our discussion of ways of reducing the export of plant nutrients in water leaving nurseries, in anticipation of action by Environmental Protection Agencies. Much development is likely in this area over the next few years.

Major changes have also been made to the turf chapters. These changes summarize and interpret for Australian conditions the considerable body of research results produced in recent years, mainly in the UK, the USA and New Zealand. They also reflect the developing expertise of local advisory bodies, particularly in optimizing the physical properties of root zone mixtures and constructions for intensively used turf. Some guidelines on the use of slow-release fertilizers on turf are provided, but unfortunately the lack of local research has limited our discussion of this topic.

Drought and the increasing cost of water have made us all conscious of the need to minimize our use of water. They have also stimulated major advances in methods of monitoring soil water and delivering irrigation water. Turf and landscape managers now have several excellent aids that allow them to minimize water use without impairing plant quality. We have catalogued these advances, and have provided some guidelines for choosing between different systems. However, we fully realize that the next few years are likely to produce many more innovations.

Finally, the 'self-help' chapter of simple tests that can be used by nursery, landscape and turf managers has been expanded by the inclusion of many additional tests.

We hope that lecturers, students and industry personnel find much of interest and practical help in this new edition. We welcome feedback that will enable us to eliminate errors and to continually improve *Growing Media*.

K.A.H. and N.D.B.
Adelaide and Orange, 1994

Note

For simplicity, some trade names are used in the text of this book or can be seen on illustrations. No endorsement of these products is intended, nor is criticism implied of similar products that are not mentioned or illustrated.

INTRODUCTION

You are confronted with:

- a rubble-strewn yard that you want to make into a garden;
- a pile of pine bark, sand or composted sawdust that is said to be of suitable quality for use in potting mixes;
- four sand samples for possible use in topdressing a bowling green;
- a mountain of mine overburden that has to be revegetated;
- a batch of potted plants that have suddenly gone 'off-colour';
- a need to buy fertilizer;
- a need to save water by reducing irrigation to a minimum acceptable level;
- an area of poor quality turf that must be improved—at minimal cost;
- a need to decide what sort of growing medium to use in large planter tubs.

You must make a decision quickly. The customer is impatient, the boss is breathing down your neck, the season is already far advanced or the weather is about to break. You know that mistakes can lose you customers, your job or income. Your assessment has to be made quickly and accurately. How do you go about deciding what to do?

First, you *look*, closely and carefully. No matter what knowledge you may have or may get from this book, we cannot do your looking for you. Use your eyes to look at the problem area, plants, medium or whatever. Look at it from different directions and in different ways.

Then, *get your hands dirty*. Feel the medium: let it run through your fingers, feel it between fingers and thumb. And while feeling *look*. Beauty or ugliness is not skin deep, so dig some holes. A spade and auger are essential tools for anyone working with soils.

Left: What has the builder buried here? *Photograph J Coppi*

Right: Which sand is best? *Photograph J Coppi*

While *looking* and *feeling*, talk to yourself. *Ask* yourself *questions* about what you see and feel. Ask what they mean, how they affect what you might do, what problems they might cause. Of course, for you to be able to ask the *right* questions, you need to have some knowledge of the properties of growing media.

OUR AIM

An important aim of this book is to provide a background of knowledge about growing media. As your knowledge increases, your questions during looking and feeling will begin to get more useful answers.

Another aim of this book is to encourage readers to think about the bottoms of plants—their roots—and the materials those roots are growing in—soils and other growing media. We do this by describing those properties of growing media of importance to plants, at each step showing the relevance of the information to practical growing situations. The emphasis is on providing information for solving practical problems. We deal with all that is below the surface of growing media. That above the surface of growing media is mentioned only as it affects or is affected by that below.

This book has been written mainly for those who earn, or hope to earn, their living from working with soils and other growing media, or who have a keen hobby interest. Students in schools and colleges of horticulture are the main group we have had in mind. The employment destinations of these students will be in nurseries and as landscape gardeners and designers, horticulturists, green-keepers, general gardeners, and their suppliers. We hope that the book will also be found useful as an aid to problem solving by people already in these trades and professions.

GENERAL REMARKS

We find growing media fascinating. We hope that readers will come to share this fascination with us. We hope, too, that as you learn and begin to apply your new knowledge you will increasingly look on natural soils not as 'dirt' to be pushed around and exploited, but as a basic irreplaceable resource—to be used, certainly, but also to be conserved and improved for future generations. 'Dirt' implies something nasty to be washed away. Don't ever use that word for the basis of our survival.

The title of the book highlights the fact that many plants in current urban environments are not grown in 'natural' soils. Many media used in the nursery trade and for indoor plants do not contain soil at all. Root zone mixes for specialized turf often also have little natural soil. This creates problems for those who write about both landscape and 'artificial' situations in one book: the phrase 'soils and other growing media' becomes wearying to writer and reader alike if repeated too often.

We use the word 'soil' for all natural, outdoor situations and for some others too. Where the stuff plants are growing in is not a natural soil, we tend to use the words 'growing medium' or simply 'medium'. We also use 'growing medium' where the application is to everything in which plants can be grown.

Finally, two notes of explanation. We use the words 'medium' and 'media', not 'mediums'. The first is singular (This medium . . .), the second is plural (These media . . .), the last are spiritualists. We are aware that dictionaries allow both forms of the plural. We are also aware that some horticultural writers use 'mediums' as their plural. Here, we prefer to leave that term to the spirits.

Also, we use the word 'compost' only for the residues of organic materials that have been decomposed biologically in heaps. Its use to describe materials commonly called potting mixes or container growing media is confusing. We also prefer not to use the term 'potting soil' for mixes that do not contain soil.

1 PLANTS: NEEDS FOR GOOD GROWTH

You will be reading this book because you are already growing plants, or because you want to—be they ornamentals, nursery stock, indoor plants, flowers, turf, vegetables or fruit trees. A thumbnail sketch of plants, the way they grow and what they need from a growing medium, will help to set the scene for providing those needs.

WHAT WE SEE

Plants have tops and bottoms. The bottoms are called roots. Unless they belong to plants such as *Wisteria* or poplar and are able to produce new tops (suckers), beheaded roots soon die. Tops alone either grow new roots, as during propagation by cuttings, or they die. Each needs the other for survival.

The tops of most plants consist of stems, leaves, flowers and fruit (seeds or spores). Stems provide a framework that holds leaves where they can get the right amount of sunlight (Fig. 1.1(a)). Roots anchor the plant in some sort of growing medium, usually soil, but also potting mixes, water (e.g. water hyacinth) and organic residues (e.g. orchids in tree clefts).

With a microscope we can see that both tops and roots consist of thousands of cells joined together in regular and beautiful patterns (Figs 1.2 and 1.3). Most

Figure 1.1(a)
The main parts of a typical plant

Figure 1.1(b)
Detail showing the pathway of water through plants

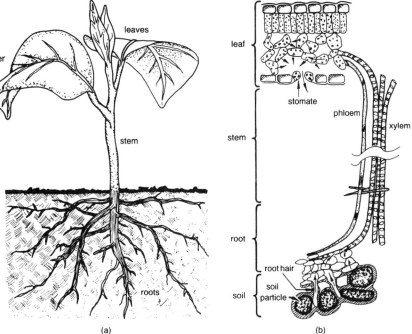

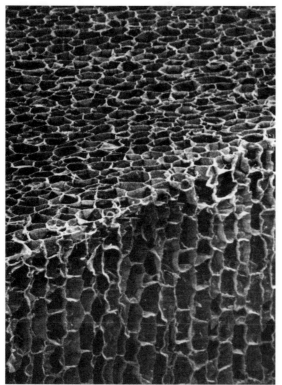

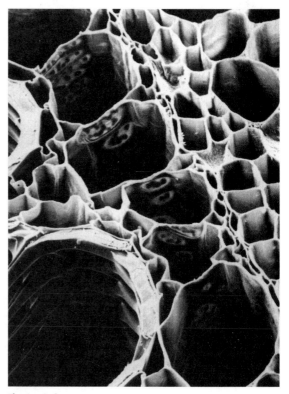

Figure 1.2
Cells of cork (the bark of *Quercus suber*). Magnification: x 3450.
Courtesy of J H Troughton, Physics and Engineering Laboratory,
DSIR, New Zealand

Figure 1.3
Part of the cellular structure of the stem of a bracken fern
frond. Magnification: x 2150. *Courtesy of J H Troughton,*
Physics and Engineering Laboratory, DSIR, New Zealand

cells are very small—from 0.001 to 0.04 mm in diameter and from 0.001 to 30 mm long. There are many types of cells, each having its own special role:

- In leaf surfaces (mainly the lower surface), there are small openings, called stomata, into the interior of the leaf (Figs 1.4, 1.5 and 1.6). Stomata are opened and shut as the cells around them shrink and swell in response to changes in light intensity and water supply.
- Near the tips of roots, some cells have long extensions going out from them. These are called root hairs. They greatly increase the total surface area and length of roots. They can fit into tiny nooks and crannies in the medium.
- In roots and stems there are long strings of cells, like pipes, that bring water from roots to leaves (see Fig. 1.1(b)). Other strings of cells carry flow from tops to roots.
- Different types of plants have varying proportions of their total mass as roots. Alpine and desert plants are 80–90% roots, heathland plants 60–70%, grasses 50–60% and evergreen trees about 20% roots.

Inside workings

Roots take up water and nutrients from the medium for the whole plant. Tops provide the organic 'food' needed for making new cells and maintaining old ones throughout the plant.

Leaves are like food-producing and food-processing factories. Carbon dioxide enters them through the stomata. Eventually it gets to the chloroplasts—the small

Figure 1.4
Surface of a cabbage leaf, showing stomata and a heavy coating of wax. Magnification: x 1200.
Courtesy of J H Troughton, Physics and Engineering Laboratory, DSIR, New Zealand

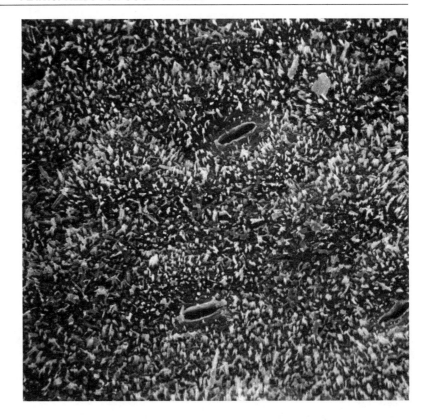

bodies inside leaf cells that give them their green colour. There, together with water, various chemicals and the energy of sunlight, the carbon of the carbon dioxide is used to make sugars. Oxygen gas is released. This process is called photosynthesis. Sugars are the basic building blocks for all the other compounds of which plants are made:

- carbohydrates such as cellulose for cell walls and starches for energy reserves;
- lignin for cell walls;
- proteins and vitamins for cell contents and seeds;
- flavours for fruit;
- enzymes and hormones to make it all happen.

The sugars and other compounds are moved to wherever in the plant they are needed. A temporary excess of sugar is stored as starch in cells throughout the plant. The starch is reconverted to sugars for use as energy in times of need. One such time is during propagation by cuttings. Formation of new roots tends to be easiest when the cutting has a good reserve of starch. Another time of need is in early spring when winter dormancy is being broken.

The stomata of most plants open in response to daylight. This time of opening allows them to process carbon dioxide into sugars as soon as it enters their leaves. But, of course, opening during the day results in greater loss of water than would opening during the cool and higher humidity of the night.

Some plants that grow in arid areas, notably the cacti and plants in genera such as *Crassula, Echevaria, Kalanchoe* and *Sedum*, survive because their stomata open only at night. Carbon dioxide that enters the plant is temporarily held as malic acid (as in green apples). During the next day, behind closed stomata, the malic acid is processed into sugars.

Light is essential for photosynthesis, but light—or rather lack of it—has

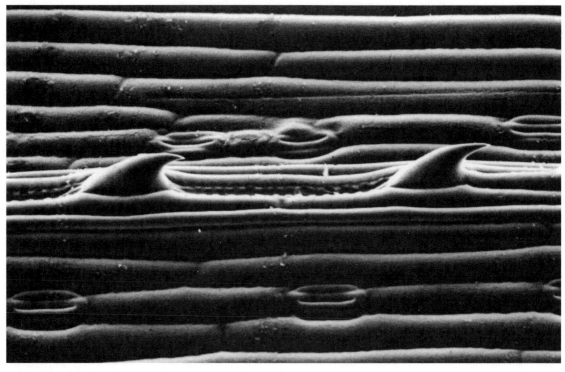

Figure 1.5
Surface of an oat leaf, showing closed stomata. The hooks can be felt as a roughness when the leaf is pulled between the fingers.
Magnification: x 420. *Photograph P E Kriedemann*

another important influence on plants. Flowering in many plants is controlled by the length of the period of darkness. Some plants flower only after they experience one or more short nights. Botanists refer to these as long day plants. Other plants flower only after they experience one or more long nights, so they are called short day plants. Some plants are day-neutral.

Loss of water from leaves is called transpiration. It is really evaporation of water from plants. The energy used to evaporate this water comes from the sun.

When water is transpired from leaf surfaces, a deficiency of water is created inside them. This deficiency gives the necessary 'pull' to raise water up through the plant.

Transpiration is essential because it cools leaves and helps to bring nutrients from roots to tops. But otherwise it is a nuisance to us because it means that we must continually supply more water to roots for continued plant growth.

Sometimes a growing medium appears to have plenty of water for transpiration, yet plants will be seen to wilt. One cause of this apparent contradiction is that the medium is completely saturated with water. This water reduces the supply of oxygen to plant roots, and so reduces their ability to take up water and nutrients. Both water and oxygen are needed by plant roots if they are to thrive.

Another important influence on plants is temperature. Plants from different areas have evolved to have different optimum temperature ranges for their roots. For example, plants from the lowland tropics grow little until the temperature of the medium is at least 12–16°C. Prolonged temperatures over 35°C in the medium kill the roots of many plants. Plants from tropical highlands and temperate areas often show reduced growth if the temperature around their roots goes much over 25°C. Twenty minutes at 45°C is enough to kill most young roots.

Yet another important influence on plants is attack on their roots by disease-causing organisms in the growing medium. Most media contain some such

Figure 1.6
Cross-section of a broad bean leaf. Guard cells (G) around a stomatal opening are shown. Palisade mesophyll cells (P), packed with chloroplasts, have large surfaces for absorbing carbon dioxide from the large air-filled cavities (C) inside the leaf. Magnification: x 200. *Courtesy of J H Troughton, Physics and Engineering Laboratory, DSIR, New Zealand*

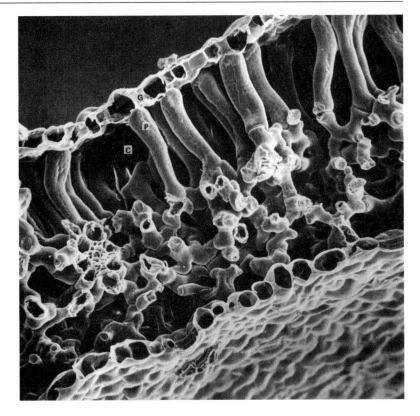

organisms, but their ability to damage a plant depends on the susceptibility of the plant and on whether or not the root environment allows attack.

In summary, then, growing media must provide plants with nutrients, water, oxygen, room to develop and minimal risk of disease. Our task is to learn how to provide these requirements.

2 THE BASICS

Figure 2.1
The proportions of the several components of soils are often shown in diagrams such as these

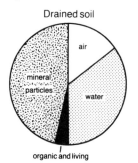

Drained soil

air
mineral particles
water
organic and living

Soil dried in the sun

mineral particles
air
organic and living
water

Whether a growing medium is a natural soil or a made-up 'mix' for containers or turf, it will usually have five main components:

- mineral particles—the inorganic fraction;
- organic matter—the remains of living organisms;
- water—the 'soil solution' in which nutrients for plants are dissolved;
- air—which fills the space between solid particles not filled with water;
- living organisms—small animals and microbes.

We can represent their proportions as in Fig. 2.1. Of course the proportions of each will vary widely:

- most natural soils will have only a few percent organic matter;
- many potting mixes are more than 60% organic matter;
- subsoils have less organic matter than do topsoils;
- proportions of water and air depend on rainfall or watering patterns, drainage, evaporation, etc.;
- living organisms are most abundant where there is ample food for them— around roots and in topsoils;
- if we mistreat a growing medium we can easily alter the proportions of air and water—to the detriment of plants.

We can grow plants in media that have no organic matter and no living organisms. We can grow plants in media such as pine bark or peat that contain no solid mineral particles. We can even grow plants in media that contain no solid mineral particles, organic matter or living organisms—hydroponics solutions. But we cannot grow plants without water, and that water must contain dissolved air and nutrients.

WHAT GROWING MEDIA SUPPLY

Good growing media will continuously supply plant roots with the following, in balanced proportions:

- water;
- air;
- nutrient elements.

Plant growth suffers when:

- air and water in the medium are out of balance with one another (too much air equals drought; too much water equals waterlogging);
- the nutrient supply rate is too low or too high;
- there is imbalance in supply between the different nutrients;
- the medium is too 'strong' (compacted) for roots to easily push through it;
- there are not enough beneficial living organisms of the right sort;
- disease-causing organisms grow unchecked;
- the medium is hotter or colder than preferred by the species being grown.

THE PROPERTIES OF GROWING MEDIA

Growing media have many different properties, but all can be put into one or other of three groups:

Physical properties are those properties we can see and feel. Included are colour, structure, texture, and behaviour towards air and water.

Chemical properties are properties that involve chemical reactions and the supply of plant nutrients.

Biological properties have to do with living organisms, both visible and invisible to the unaided eye.

These are not watertight groups. Biological activity changes chemical and physical properties, and vice versa. Chemical properties often have a major effect on physical properties.

3

TEXTURE AND PARTICLE SIZE

When friends meet they first look at one another, then touch. An encounter with a new growing medium should go the same way. Look carefully, then feel ('shaking hands' will do). We have already encouraged you to look. Here we concentrate on feeling.

DETERMINING SOIL TEXTURE

If you take small samples of soils from different places, knead them with water in your hands and then press them out between thumb and forefinger, you will find that they feel and behave differently from one another. At one extreme are soils in which no individual particles can be felt. They are smooth and slippery and can be pressed into long ribbons—the clays. At the other extreme are soils that cannot be pressed into ribbons; the particles in them can be easily felt and seen—the sands. Most soils lie in between these extremes. We can feel sand in them, but they also contain finer material and they can be pressed into short ribbons—these soils are called loams.

This simple test, finding the *texture* of a soil, tells us much about the interaction of the soil with water and its likely behaviour during cultivation. Soils with much clay are often called 'heavy' because it takes much effort to pull cultivation implements through them. Sandy soils are said to be of light texture. It is the size distribution of particles in the soil that determines its texture.

The technique of texture determination is given in greater detail below. Those who often have to assess soils should master the technique and learn to interpret the results.

Figure 3.1
Determine the texture of a soil by kneading about this amount of soil with water. *Photograph J Coppi*

1. Take a small sample of soil sufficient to fit comfortably in the palm of one hand (Fig. 3.1). Discard obvious pieces of gravel.
2. Moisten the soil with water, a little at a time, and knead until there is no apparent change in the way it feels. Kneading will break aggregates so that they are no longer felt. This may take several minutes. The moisture content should be such that the soil just fails to stick to the fingers.
3. Inspect the sample to see if sand is visible; if not, it may still be felt and heard as the sample is worked.
4. Next squeeze the sample hard to see whether it will form a ball or cast, and if so, whether the cast is durable or falls apart readily.
5. Finally, squeeze it out between the thumb and forefinger with a sliding motion and note the length of self-supporting ribbon that can be formed.

Figure 3.2
The kneaded soil is pressed out in a ribbon between thumb and forefinger. The longer ribbon is of a heavy clay; the shorter ribbon is of a sandy loam.
Photograph J Coppi

No coherence; cannot be moulded; single grains stick to fingers.	Sand
Forms a fragile cast that just bears handling; gives a short (6 mm) ribbon that breaks easily; discolours fingers.	Loamy sand
Forms a fragile cast; sticky when wet; many sand grains stick to fingers; discolours fingers with clay stain; forms minimal ribbon 5–15 mm long.	Clayey sand
Forms a cast that will just bear handling; individual sand grains can be seen and felt; gives a ribbon 15–25 mm long.	Sandy loam
As for sandy loams, except that individual sand grains are not visible, although they can be heard and felt; gives a ribbon 15–25 mm long.	Fine sandy loam
Forms a coherent cast that feels spongy but with no obvious sandiness or 'silkiness'; may feel greasy if much organic matter is present; forms a ribbon about 25 mm long.	Loam
Coherent but will crumble; very smooth and silky; will form a ribbon 25 mm long.	Silty loam
Forms a strongly coherent cast in which sand grains can be felt; forms a ribbon 25–40 mm long.	Sandy clay loam
Forms a coherent cast with a rather spongy feel; plastic when squeezed between thumb and forefinger; smooth to manipulate; will form a ribbon 40–50 mm long.	Clay loam
Forms a plastic cast, except that sand grains can be seen, felt or heard; forms a ribbon 50–75 mm long.	Sandy clay
Smooth plastic cast; slight resistance to shearing between thumb and forefinger; forms a ribbon 50–75 mm long.	Light clay
Smooth plastic cast, handles like plasticine and can be moulded into rods without fracture; some resistance to ribboning; forms a ribbon 75 mm or more long.	Medium clay
Smooth plastic cast that handles like stiff plasticine; can be moulded into rods without fracture; firm resistance to ribboning; forms a ribbon at least 75 mm long.	Heavy clay

PARTICLE SIZE ANALYSIS

Soils behave and feel differently during texture determination mainly because they contain different proportions of mineral particles of different sizes. This can be seen in a simple test:

1. Use three tall screw-top glass jars of about 600 mL capacity. Into each place two heaped tablespoons of one of three soils of different textures; a sand, a loam and a light clay would be suitable.
2. Add ¼ teaspoon of 'Calgon' or 'Aqua Soft' and enough water to make thick slurries. Gently work the slurries with a flat piece of wood until all crumbs of soil are broken apart.
3. Add water to the ¾ mark and shake vigorously for a few minutes.
4. Allow the jars to stand undisturbed while you carefully observe what happens (Fig. 3.3).

Figure 3.3
The largest particles settle first from suspensions of soils in water

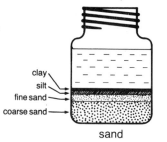

sand   loam   clay

clay
silt
fine sand
coarse sand

First you will notice that in the jars containing the sand and the loam, layers of large particles (sand) quickly settle to the bottom. In fact, soon almost all of the contents of the sand jar will have settled out, leaving the water more or less clear. In both the sand jar and the loam jar, many of the sand particles at the very bottom will be larger (coarse sand) than those that settle later (fine sand).

In the loam jar, the sand is slowly covered by finer and finer particles, some of which will still be settling out in a couple of days. These finer particles are called silt.

In the clay jar, some very fine sand and silt will settle out over a day or so.

The water in the loam jar and the clay jar may remain murky for days or weeks because of the very small particles of clay suspended in it. (Even after they have settled out, the water may still be discoloured by dissolved organic matter.)

The mineral particles in soils have a continuous range of sizes, but it has been found convenient to separate them into named groups with definite size limits. Two systems are in common use (Tables 3.1 and 3.2). Note that clay and gravel are given the same size ranges in each system. Silt is the main difference. The greater number of sand fractions in the USDA system makes it the more useful system to use in horticulture.

Table 3.2
Sizes of soil particles according to the United States Department of Agriculture (USDA) system

Name of fraction	Size range (effective diameter) mm
Clay	less than 0.002
Silt	0.002–0.05
Very fine sand	0.05–0.1
Fine sand	0.1–0.25
Medium sand	0.25–0.5
Coarse sand	0.5–1.0
Very coarse sand	1.0–2.0
Gravel	more than 2.0

Table 3.1
Sizes of soil particles according to the International Soil Science Society system

Name of fraction	Size range (effective diameter) mm	Visible by
Clay	less than 0.002	electron microscope
Silt	0.002–0.02	light microscope
Fine sand	0.02–0.2	hand lens/eye
Coarse sand	0.2–2.0	eye
Gravel	more than 2.0	eye

Table 3.3
Typical particle size composition of soils of different textures

Texture grade	% sand	% silt	% clay
Medium clay	35	10	55
Sandy clay	60	2	38
Clay loam	45	20	35
Loam	60	20	20
Sandy loam	75	10	15
Silty loam	35	55	10
Loamy sand	75	20	5
Sand	95	2	3

Standard methods of laboratory analysis (called particle size analysis), similar to our glass jar test, are used to determine the proportions of clay and silt in soils. The sand fractions are separated from one another on sieves.

Some typical results of analysing soils of different textures (feel) are given in Tables 3.3 and 3.4. Several soils that feel alike can have a fairly wide range of proportions of clay, silt and sand. Usually this need cause no concern. Only where it is important to know the actual proportions of particles of different size should one go further than determining soil texture by hand. The main such situation is in checking sands and soils for use as root zones and topdressings for turf (see Chapter 17).

Table 3.4
Clay contents of soils of different textures

Texture grade	% clay
Heavy clay	50 or more
Light clay	40–50
Silty clay	40–60
Sandy clay	35–45
Clay loam, silty clay loam	25–40
Silty loam	0–25
Sandy clay loam	20–30
Loam	10–25
Sandy loam	10–15
Sand	less than 5

USING INFORMATION ABOUT SOIL TEXTURE

If we know the texture of a soil, we can make some shrewd guesses about some of its other properties.

A *clay* will probably be difficult to cultivate. It will be sticky when wet and 'tough' and cloddy when dry. Water will move into (infiltrate) it and percolate through it slowly. It may easily become waterlogged. A clay topsoil will probably have a moderate organic matter content and a good supply of most nutrients. But there are exceptions. Some clays crack deeply and so allow rapid and deep water penetration until the cracks close. In others, such as the black soils of northern New South Wales and the Darling Downs and those used for cricket pitches, clods spontaneously break into small crumbs. Traffic compacts clay soils, so that they become less suitable for plants.

Sandy soils will probably have little organic matter, allow rapid infiltration and drainage of water, hold little water for plants, and be easy to cultivate. They will usually be poor suppliers of plant nutrients. However, some sandy soils are water repellent (see Chapter 6).

Loams are supposed to be ideal for growing plants. That's what gardening books say. They are easy to dig, give a fine seed bed and good conditions for root growth. They drain freely, yet hold moderate amounts of water and nutrients for plants. The best are like that. But loams have a wide range of compositions and an even wider range of properties. Some set like concrete; some are like fine powder. Crusts that form on some reduce water entry to near zero. Some are very poorly endowed with nutrients.

Soil textures gives information only about the sizes of the particles in the soil. Usually these particles are grouped together into aggregates or crumbs. The arrangement of these crumbs gives a soil its characteristic structure (see Chapter 8). Structure is often more important than texture in determining how a soil behaves towards water and plant roots.

Despite this, finding the texture of a soil is a good starting point in understanding a soil. It takes only a few minutes. Numerous examples of the effect of texture on other soil properties are given throughout the book. Here, we give just a few general uses of textural information.

Figure 3.4
Number of volumes of sand to add to one volume of 1:1 soil/peat blends of different sand contents to obtain mixtures with total sand contents (% by weight) in the range 85–95%. *From* D H Taylor and G R Blake *Agron. J.* 76: 583, 1984

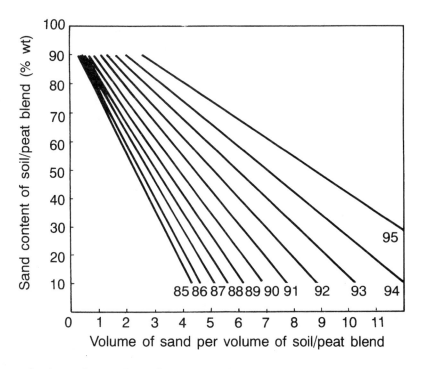

Checking the quality of commercial 'loam'

Sand, soil and gravel merchants usually have 'garden loam' available for sale. Some of the 'loam' is that, some isn't. A simple texture determination on the spot will at least tell you whether the soil has too much clay or not. Other tests (Chapter 33) are needed to fully assess a soil.

Assessing soil response to water

Generally sands hold less water than clays. Loams, especially silty loams, hold the greatest amounts of plant-available water (p.64). Ability to accept rain or irrigation water is usually greatest for sands and loams. A layer of clay down a soil profile may point to waterlogging problems.

As a guide to changing soil texture

Adding sand to a clay soil can 'open it up', making it easier to cultivate and improving its ability to accept water. Adding clay to a sand will enable it to hold more water and plant nutrients, but mixing is very difficult. The clay must be dry and mixing should be by rotary hoe.

The following example is to be taken only as a rough guide to the proportions of different soils needed to give a mixture of a particular texture. Mixing will give a mixture with a particular texture. However, this mixture will not behave like a natural soil of that texture until the natural forces that form soils have acted on it for some years.

Example

We have a clay with a composition 35% sand, 10% silt and 55% clay. How do we make it into a loam? Firstly we can try using an equal volume of a sand of composition 95% sand, 2% silt and 3% clay.

If we want a true loam, it would be necessary to add a soil with less sand and more silt.

	% sand	% silt	% clay	
(Clay) +	35	10	55	
(Sand)	95	2	3	
	130	12	58	
÷ 2 =	65	6	29	(Sandy clay loam)

To achieve the composition of loam closer to that given in Table 3.3, we need to add more loamy sand.

	% sand	% silt	% clay	
(Clay) +	35	10	55	
(Loamy sand)	75	20	5	
	110	30	60	
÷ 2 =	55	15	30	(Clay loam)

	% sand	% silt	% clay	
(Clay) +	35	10	55	
2 × (Loamy sand)	150	40	10	
	185	50	65	
÷ 3 =	62	17	22	(Loam)

Clearly, very large amounts of sandy soils are needed to make clays into loams.

A caution: Adding a small amount of sand to a clay soil will make almost no difference to its texture and properties. Adding a bit more may make it worse than it was. Mixing destroys the structure of the clay. The clay particles can then fill in all the gaps between the added sand particles, leaving only tiny spaces for water and air. Infiltration of water will be slow. This happens all too often with sports fields. Only when much large amounts of sand are added, as in the example, will worthwhile changes to soil properties be made.

Conversely, it will take only 20–30% of a clay soil to convert a very sandy soil into a loam. Getting an even mixture is difficult. Comments on the effects of creating layers are given in Chapter 9. One very special situation in which soil is added to sand is when golf and bowling greens are constructed according to the exact specifications of the US Golf Association (USGA). The aim is for the final mixture to have a few percent each of particles of silt and clay size (Chapter 17). That means that these mixtures are usually at least 90% sand. From Fig. 3.4, it can be seen that to make a mixture that will contain 90% sand using a soil with only 20% sand, it will be necessary to use over 6 volumes of

Table 3.5
Sieves used to separate sands into named fractions

Name of fraction	Size range (mm)	Sieve mesh number (approximate)
'Fines' (silt and clay)	less than 0.05	passes through 300
Very fine sand	0.05-0.1	passes through 150, retained on 300
Fine sand	0.1-0.25	passes through 60, retained on 150
Medium sand	0.25-0.5	passes through 30, retained on 60
Coarse sand	0.5-1.0	passes through 16, retained on 30
Very coarse sand	1.0-2.0	passes through 8, retained on 16
Gravel	more than 2.0	retained on 8

Figure 3.5
Set of sieves and a mechanical shaker used to determine the proportions of particles of different sizes in sands *Photograph J Coppi*

sand to each volume of soil. This information is to be used as a rough guide only. *We want to state very strongly that root zone mixtures must be formulated only on the basis of laboratory analysis.*

TEXTURE IN OTHER GROWING MEDIA

Most potting mixes and root zone soils under intensively used turf have only small proportions of clay and silt. Their texture is, respectively, 'gravelly sand', and sand or loamy sand—all at one end of the texture range. Looking at and handling them will give us only a limited amount of information about them. For both materials it is essential that their physical properties are assessed by tests specifically designed for them (Chapters 10, 13 and 33).

'Fine' and 'Coarse'

'Fine' and 'coarse' are not very precise terms, unless they are carefully defined. What is a coarse sand to one person may be called gravel by another or fine sand by yet another. The 'fine pine bark' used by some nurserymen is only 'fine' by comparison with the chunks used as a mulch on garden beds. Compared with 'coarse sand', much of it is very coarse indeed. All this leads to some confusion and difficulty in communicating. In the interests of greater clarity, we urge readers to use the precise definitions of coarse and fine of the USDA system of classification (Table 3.2).

Sieves may be used to determine the proportions of particles of different sizes in materials such as sands and components for use in potting mixes (Table 3.5). These sieves are very expensive, so most readers won't have access to them or won't want to buy a full set.

Potting mix manufacturers might find it useful to have sieves that can show the proportions of particles smaller than 1 mm and larger than 5 mm. Those with a major interest in sands for turf root zones will have most need for sieves that show the proportions in fine, medium and coarse fractions. Laboratories that specialize in turf soils carry a full range of sieves (Fig. 3.5).

Sieve analysis is only the beginning of an assessment of sands for turf root zones. Much more important are determinations of the rate at which water enters and moves through a sand or mixture of sand(s)/soil/organic materials after they have been compacted, and their moisture release curves. Laboratories use these tests and others as a basis for deciding on the proportions of materials to use for specific turf situations. By all means use sieves as a first level of assessing sands, but realize that only laboratory testing can produce a recipe for a root zone mixture that will not give problems during use.

4 SOME SIMPLE CHEMISTRY

Table 4.1
Elements of most importance to those interested in plants and growing media. Each name is followed by the shorthand symbol used for it

Element (symbol)	Atomic mass*
Aluminium (Al)	27.0
Boron (B)	10.8
Calcium (Ca)	40.1
Carbon (C)	12.0
Chlorine (Cl)	35.5
Cobalt (Co)	58.9
Copper (Cu)	63.5
Hydrogen (H)	1.0
Iron (Fe)	55.8
Magnesium (Mg)	24.3
Manganese (Mn)	54.9
Molybdenum (Mo)	95.9
Nitrogen (N)	14.0
Oxygen (O)	16.0
Phosphorus (P)	31.0
Potassium (K)	39.1
Silicon (Si)	28.1
Sodium (Na)	23.0
Sulphur (S)	32.1
Zinc (Zn)	65.4

*Atomic masses are discussed towards the end of this chapter.

Some understanding of chemistry is essential to an understanding of growing media. This chapter gives a brief introduction to chemistry, or it can be used to refresh rusty memories. We simply present the conclusions of a couple or centuries of research. Those who want detail about the experiments that led to these conclusions should consult standard textbooks on chemistry.

ELEMENTS AND ATOMS

Gold, silver, zinc, copper, iron, aluminium, sulphur, nitrogen and oxygen are materials with which we are all familiar. They are different in many ways, but they have one thing in common—they are all elements. The main property that sets an element apart from other materials is that the tiniest pieces we can break it into—whether we use a file, knife, heat, acids, electricity, magnets or our teeth—are all exactly the same as one another.

These tiniest pieces of an element are called atoms. All the atoms of an element are the same, but they are different from the atoms of all other elements. Atoms are very small: between 2 and 16 million would fit one high on a line 1 mm long, depending on the element. Atoms are indestructible by all means commonly available to us. Only in the sun and other stars, atomic bombs, atomic reactors and similar machines can atoms be destroyed.

There are more than 100 elements, but we can forget about most of them. Table 4.1 lists the important ones for those interested in growing media and plants. Each name in the table is followed by the shorthand way of writing it used by chemists. Chemistry is the study of elements, the ways they behave, the ways they combine with one another and the properties of these combinations.

Before we look at some of these combinations it is necessary to delve a little more deeply into the nature of elements and their atoms. This delving will set the scene for an understanding of many aspects of growing media and plant nutrition.

STRUCTURE OF ATOMS

All atoms have a central core—the nucleus—which is composed of neutrons and protons. Whirling around the nucleus are one or more electrons. The lightest of all elements—hydrogen—has just one proton and one electron (Fig. 4.1) Oxygen has 8 neutrons, 8 protons and 8 electrons. Sodium has 11 protons and electrons and 12 neutrons (Fig. 4.1). Gold has 79 protons and electrons and 118 neutrons. The atomic number of an element is defined as the number of protons in its nucleus.

A proton from hydrogen and a proton from gold each weigh exactly the same. A neutron from oxygen and a neutron from gold also weigh exactly the same as one another and almost the same as a proton. It follows from this that the greater the atomic number of an element the greater will be the mass of each of its atoms and the greater the density of the element. Electrons are midgets

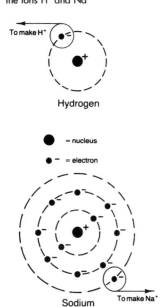

compared with protons and neutrons. It takes 1840 electrons to make the mass of one proton.

It has been found that protons and electrons are electrically charged. By convention it is said that protons are positively charged and electrons negatively charged. Neutrons are neither positively nor negatively charged and so are said to be electrically neutral. In the atoms of an element in its pure state the number of protons is the same as the number of electrons and so the numbers of positive and negative charges are equal; the element is electrically neutral.

The electrons surrounding the nucleus are continuously revolving around it, in much the same way as the Earth and the other planets of our part of the universe revolve around our sun. And just as each of these planets has a set orbit around the sun, so each electron has a set orbit around the nucleus. But unlike the planets, electrons are arranged in shells or layers, each of which contains from 1 to 14 electrons. Those in the shells closest to the nucleus are held much more firmly than are those in outer shells. In fact, it is relatively easy to remove one or several electrons from the outer electron shells of atoms in many elements.

IONS—CATIONS AND ANIONS

When one electron is removed from an atom, that atom becomes positively charged, with a charge of plus one (Fig. 4.1). Adding an electron to an atom gives it a charge of minus one. *These positively and negatively charged atoms are called ions.* Positively charged ions are called cations (*cat*-eye-ons) and negatively charged ions are called anions (*an*-eye-ons). The shorthand way of writing a cation such as that of sodium (Na) is to give it a superscript '+'—Na^+. Loss of two electrons is designated as follows: Ca^{2+}, Mg^{2+}. Similarly, anions are written Cl^- (chloride), F^- (fluoride) and so on. Table 4.2 lists the main ions of interest to us.

Table 4.2
Some common cations and anions

Cations		Anions	
Hydrogen	H^+	Chloride	Cl^-
Potassium	K^+	Fluoride	F^-
Sodium	Na^+	Hydroxide	OH^-
Calcium	Ca^{2+}	Sulphate	SO_4^-
Magnesium	Mg^{2+}	Nitrate	NO_3^-
Copper	Cu^{2+}	Bicarbonate	HCO_3^-
Aluminium	Al^{3+}	Phosphate	PO_4^{3-}
Ammonium	NH_4^+	Molybdate	MoO_4^{2-}

Atoms gain and lose electrons because by doing so they become more stable. The most stable elements are the so-called noble gases such as helium, neon and argon. Each of these has its outer electron shell completely filled. For example, argon (Ar) has three shells with 2, 8 and 8 electrons. It has an atomic number of 18. Potassium and calcium of atomic numbers 19 and 20 have the 2, 8, 8 configuration plus an extra one or two electrons, respectively. By losing these electrons they acquire the configuration of Ar, becoming the ions K^+ and Ca^{2+}. Chloride and sulphur have atomic numbers of 17 and 16, respectively. Their electronic configurations are 2, 8, 7 and 2, 8, 6. They increase their stability by gaining electrons to form Cl^- and S^{2-} (sulphide). The number of electrons gained or lost is called the *valence* of the element.

It is mainly as ions that plants take up nutrients from growing media (Chapter 14). It is mainly as ions that these nutrients are present in hydroponics solutions

Table 4.3
Some common mixtures of elements

Mixture	Elements in the mixture
Air	nitrogen, oxygen, helium, argon, etc
Brass	copper, zinc
Bronze	copper, tin
Steel	iron, carbon, silicon, etc

Figure 4.2
Arrangement of atoms in two simple molecules

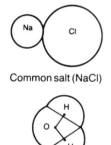

Common salt (NaCl)

Water (H$_2$O)

and in the water surrounding roots in solid growing media (Chapters 21 and 27). It is mainly as ions that these nutrients are held in available form on the surfaces of particles in growing media (Chapter 7). Some important physical properties of soils (Chapter 7 and 21) are heavily influenced by the types and proportions of cations present on particle surfaces.

COMPOUNDS

Sometimes we meet an element by itself—a bag of sulphur, a bar of gold bullion, a cylinder of oxygen. Sometimes we meet elements in the form of mixtures (Table 4.3). More often, however, we meet elements in combination with one another. These combinations are called compounds.

The difference between compounds and mixtures can be seen from the following example. Powdered sulphur and iron filings stirred together in any proportion will make a mixture; individual pieces of sulphur and iron can still be seen and can be separated from one another by, for example, removing the iron with a magnet. If, however, we mix 7 parts by mass of iron filings with 4 parts of sulphur and heat them, we end up with a compound called iron sulphide. It is not possible to separate the iron and sulphur in this compound with a magnet. Iron sulphide always contains iron and sulphur in the same proportions—one atom of iron for each atom of sulphur. The formula for iron sulphide is therefore written Fe_1S_1, shortened to FeS, using the symbols given in Table 4.1. Common salt (sodium chloride) is a compound in which there is one atom of sodium for each atom of chlorine in the crystal (Fig. 4.2); it is therefore written NaCl.

The smallest portion of a compound that can exist as a stable discrete particle is called a molecule. Methane, the main ingredient of natural gas, consists of one atom of carbon chemically combined with four atoms of hydrogen. Methane, therefore, has a molecular formula of CH_4. Water molecules each contain two atoms of hydrogen combined with one atom of oxygen; water is therefore written H_2O. Table 4.4 gives some other examples.

It is not possible to have a bottle of, say, calcium ions, but we can have a bottle of calcium and nitrate ions; it will be labelled calcium nitrate. Most of the 'salts' that we are familiar with are combinations of ions (see Table 4.5).

Compounds that have carbon (C) as a main element, together with oxygen (O) and hydrogen (H), and often other elements, are called organic compounds. There is an extremely large number and wide variety of this type of compound. Some simple examples are butane (C_4H_{10}), ethanol (alcohol) (C_2H_5OH), urea (CON_2H_4). The term 'organic' was derived from the original belief that these types of compounds were found only in living organisms. While the sugars, carbohydrates and proteins of living organisms are organic compounds, the term now includes a vast range of synthetic materials such as plastics, drugs, dyes, explosives and detergents, all based on carbon.

The many thousands of compounds not based on carbon are referred to as inorganic. Examples include sulphuric acid (H_2SO_4), gypsum crystals ($CaSO_4$. $2H_2O$) and potassium nitrate (KNO_3).

There are millions of different compounds. Sometimes we can see them in relatively pure form, but more often we meet them in mixtures with other compounds (Table 4.6). Different compounds in different mixtures and arranged in different ways within those mixtures give the enormous variety that we see all around us.

BONDING

The molecules of compounds are held together—bonded—by two main means: ionic and covalent. Ionic bonding refers to the bonding between two ions and is the main type of bonding present in many of the fertilizers and other compounds collectively referred to as 'salts'. Here are two examples of ways in which ionic compounds are formed.

Table 4.5
Some readily available salts

Common name	Chemical name	Ions present	Chemical formula
Common salt	sodium chloride	Na^+, Cl^-	$NaCl$
Baking powder	sodium bicarbonate	Na^+, HCO_3^-	$NaHCO_3$
Washing soda	sodium carbonate	Na^+, CO_3^{2-}	Na_2CO_3
Calgon	sodium hexametaphosphate	Na^+, HPO_3^-	$Na_6(HPO_3)_6$
Sulphate of ammonia	ammonium sulphate	NH_4^+, SO_4^{2-}	$(NH_4)_2SO_4$
Muriate of potash	potassium chloride	K^+, Cl^-	KCl
—	calcium nitrate	Ca^{2+}, NO_3^-	$Ca(NO_3)_2$
Epsom salts	magnesium sulphate	Mg^{2+}, SO_2^{2-}	$MgSO_4$
Superphosphate	calcium dihydrogen orthophosphate +	Ca^{2+}, $H_2PO_4^-$	$Ca(H_2PO_4)_2$
	gypsum (calcium sulphate)	Ca^{2+}, SO_4^{2-}	$CaSO_4$

Table 4.4
Examples of chemical compounds

Compound	Elements present
Carbon dioxide	carbon, oxygen (CO_2)
Quartz	silicon, oxygen (SiO_2)
Ammonium sulphate	nitrogen, hydrogen, sulphur, oxygen ((NH_4)SO_4)
Urea	carbon, hydrogen, oxygen, nitrogen ($CO(NH_2)_2$)
Sugar	carbon, hydrogen, oxygen ($C_{12}H_{22}O_{11}$)
Protein	carbon, hydrogen, oxygen, nitrogen, sulphur (many different compounds)
Malathion®	carbon, hydrogen, oxygen, phosphorus, sulphur ($C_{10}H_{19}O_6PS_2$)
2,4–D	carbon, hydrogen, oxygen, chlorine ($C_8H_{12}O_3Cl_2$)
Clay minerals	silicon, oxygen, aluminium, iron, magnesium, potassium, hydrogen, etc. (many different compounds)

When a piece of sodium is dropped into water, there is a violent reaction in which the sodium atoms lose electrons: $2Na + 2H_2O \rightarrow 2Na^+ + 2OH^- + H_2$.

The hydrogen molecules (H_2) either burn or escape into the air. We are left with sodium cations (Na^+) and hydroxide anions (OH^-). Together these are sodium hydroxide (caustic soda). Solid sodium hydroxide crystals would be obtained if the water was evaporated. In the crystals, sodium and hydroxide ions are arranged together in a regular pattern (Fig. 4.3).

Zinc chloride is formed through the reaction of zinc metal and hydrochloric acid: $Zn + 2HCl \rightarrow Zn^{2+} + 2Cl^- + H_2$.

The molecules of hydrogen bubble from the solution. Evaporation of the water from the hydrochloric acid will leave crystals of solid $ZnCl_2$.

Most compounds that are combinations of ions are able to dissolve in water; there the ions separate from one another. If two such compounds are dissolved in the same water we can end up with a mixture of the two or ions can be swapped. Thus the swapping of chloride in a mixture of NaCl and KCl still leaves sodium and potassium chlorides.

But if calcium chloride and potassium sulphate are mixed, most of the calcium and sulphate will precipitate out of the solution as calcium sulphate, which is only slightly soluble in water, leaving potassium and chloride ions in the solution: $CaCl_2 + K_2SO_4 \rightarrow CaSO_4 + 2K^+ + 2Cl^-$.

Ionic compounds are called electrolytes because when they are dissolved in water they allow the passage of electricity if two electrodes connected to a source of electrical power are placed into the solution. This phenomenon is used industrially to produce very pure copper by plating it out from a solution of copper sulphate. It is also used when we estimate the concentration of salts in a fertilizer solution or the salinity of a water supply using a conductivity meter (Chapters 21 and 33).

The second very common form of bonding is called covalent bonding. In this, the electron in the outer shells of two or more atoms are shared between those atoms. We can think of this bonding as attraction between electrons of one atom and protons of another atom, and vice versa. Water (H_2O), oxygen (O_2), urea ($CO(NH_2)_2$) and ammonia (NH_3) are examples of compounds in whose molecules the atoms are covalently bonded. Covalently bonded compounds that dissolve in water do not conduct electricity (unless the compound reacts with water to form ions, as when NH_3 forms ammonium ions—NH_4^+) so they are not detected by conductivity meters. Note that in complex cations such as of ammonium

Table 4.6
Examples of mixtures of compounds

Material	Main compounds present
Wood	cellulose, lignin, hemicellulose, sugars, protein, waxes, resins, tannins, etc.
Soil	quartz, iron oxide, aluminium oxide, kaolinite, halloysite, smectite, 'humus', etc.
Rubber (tyres)	isoprene polymer, sulphur, carbon black, zinc oxide, silica, etc.
Paper	cellulose, kaolinite, dyestuffs, etc.
Plastics	polymer (e.g. polyethylene), dyestuffs, fillers, plasticisers, etc.

Figure 4.3
Atoms in crystalline compounds arrange themselves in regular patterns

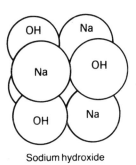

Sodium hydroxide

(NH_4^+) and nitrate (NO_3^-) the atoms within each ion are covalently bonded with one another.

ATOMIC AND MOLECULAR MASSES

A brief look at atomic and molecular masses will help in understanding fertilizers and the meaning of pH. An atom of hydrogen has a mass of 0.167×10^{-23} g; an atom of oxygen has a mass of 2.66×10^{-23} g, while an atom of carbon has a mass of 1.99×10^{-23} g. It would be very cumbersome to use numbers like these all the time. Instead, by international agreement, carbon has been chosen as the reference standard and assigned the number 12.00 as its atomic mass (formerly atomic weight). The atomic masses of all other elements are calculated in relation to carbon = 12.00.

Thus the atomic mass of hydrogen is $12 \times \dfrac{0.167 \times 10^{-23}}{1.99 \times 10^{-23}} = 1.008$

The atomic mass of oxygen is: $12 \times \dfrac{2.66 \times 10^{-23}}{1.99 \times 10^{-23}} = 16.0$

Some atomic masses were given in Table 4.1. When atoms combine to form molecules, the atomic masses of the elements are added together to give the molecular mass of the compound. Thus water (H_2O) has a molecular mass of: $2 \times 1.008 + 1 \times 16.0 = 18.016$.

This means that 2.016 g of hydrogen will combine with exactly 16 g of oxygen to form 18.016 g of water (or 2.016 kg of hydrogen combine with 16 kg of oxygen to form 18.016 kg of water). The term 'mole' is a short way of saying 'molecular mass in grams' (and is often abbreviated further to the symbol 'mol'). The molecular masses of some fertilizer materials are given in Table 15.3.

When dealing later with cations in soils, it will be useful to use the term 'equivalent mass'. This is the atomic mass of the element divided by the number of positive charges its ions carry. For example, the equivalent mass of calcium (Ca^{2+}) is $40.1 \times \frac{1}{2} = 20.05$. A milliequivalent is one thousandth of an equivalent. A milliequivalent (m.e.) of calcium has a mass of 20.05 mg.

ACIDITY AND ALKALINITY

Finally, one important aspect of water—that universal solvent and essential component of all media supporting plant growth—must be briefly mentioned. As we saw earlier, water is a compound in which each molecule contains two hydrogen atoms and one oxygen atom. In pure water, almost all molecules remain intact, but one in about 600 million split into hydrogen and hydroxide ions:

$$H_2O \rightarrow H^+ + OH^-$$

This is usually given in another way. In a litre of pure water, at any one time 1×10^{-7} mole of that water has split into hydrogen and hydroxide ions. This might appear to be an odd way of saying it, but there is a good reason for doing so, as we shall see below.

In pure water, the number of hydrogen ions equals the number of hydroxyl ions. That water is said to be neutral. If, by some means, we increase the proportion of hydrogen ions, the water is said to become acid. If the proportion of hydroxyl ions is increased, the water is said to become alkaline. Some examples will help make this clear.

1. If we bubble carbon dioxide through water, some of it will dissolve as follows:

$$H_2O + CO_2 \rightarrow H^+ + HCO_3^- \rightarrow 2H^+ + CO_3^{2-}$$

Thus we have released extra hydrogen ions from water molecules, increasing their concentration to perhaps 1×10^{-6} mole per litre. Rain water has carbon dioxide dissolved in it and so is slightly acid.

**Table 4.7
Terms used for describing
solutions of differing pH
values**

pH	Terms used
Below 4.0	extremely acid
4.0 to 5.0	very strongly acid
5.0 to 5.5	strongly acid
5.5 to 6.0	moderately acid
6.0 to 6.7	slightly acid
6.7 to 7.3	neutral range
7.0	neutral
7.3 to 8.0	weakly alkaline
8.0 to 8.5	moderately alkaline
8.5 to 9.0	strongly alkaline
9.0 to 10.0	very strongly alkaline
Above 10.0	extremely alkaline

2. If we bubble nitrogen dioxide through water we get the following reaction:

$$H_2O + 3NO_2 \rightarrow 2H^+ + 2NO_3^- + NO$$

| nitric acid solution | nitrogen monoxide gas |

Nitrogen dioxide has a greater ability to do this than has carbon dioxide, so more hydrogen ions are formed, perhaps as many as $1 \times 10^{-1} = 0.1$ mole per litre. The solution is called nitric acid. The nitrogen monoxide gas bubbles out of the solution.

3. If we pass an electric current through salty water, we get the following reaction:

$$2H_2O + 2NaCl \rightarrow 2Na^+ + 2OH^- + H_2 + Cl_2$$

Hydrogen and chlorine bubble from the solution, leaving sodium hydroxide. The concentration of hydrogen ions may be only 1×10^{-11} mole per litre because of the increase in the concentration of hydroxide ions. The solution is highly alkaline.

Instead of using 1×10^{-11}, 1×10^{-7}, 1×10^{-6} etc. for the concentration of hydrogen ions, it has been found convenient to write the reciprocal of these numbers (10^{11}, 10^7, 10^6) and then the logarithms of them (11, 7, 6). This is called the pH of the solution. It should be noted that a solution with a pH of, say, 5, has *10 times* the concentration of hydrogen ions in a solution of pH 6, 100 times the concentration at pH 7, and so on.

The more *acid* the solution, the *lower* its pH; the more *alkaline* the solution, the *higher* its pH. Terms used are given in Table 4.7.

Soils, too, contain hydrogen ions. Different soils contain different concentrations and therefore are of differing pH. Reasons for the importance of soil pH, and ways of using this information, are given in Chapter 11. Measurements of pH are made either with organic dyes whose colour changes with pH or, more accurately, with a gadget called a pH meter (see Chapter 33).

More information about chemistry

BUCAT R B *Elements of Chemistry* Vols 1 and 2 Australian Acad. Sci. 1984
CARWELL D J, NEWMAN B C and MIHKELSON A E *Fundamentals of Senior Chemistry* Heinnemann 1988
GALLAGHER R and INGRAM P *Chemistry Made Clear* Oxford Univ. Press 1987
SMITH R *Conquering Chemistry* McGraw Hill 1987
WIECEK C *Chemistry for Senior Students* Brooks Waterloo 1989

5 ORGANIC MATTER —THE VITAL COMPONENT

Organic: As used here, the term 'organic' refers to materials that contain carbon, in combination with a variety of other elements (notably hydrogen, oxygen, nitrogen and sulfur), and that are or were parts of plants or animals.

Soil organic matter: This term embraces the remains of plants and animals at various stages of decomposition, the cells and tissues of soil organisms, and substances such as humus made by these organisms. (Some definitions include living organisms in soil organic matter. Living organisms are organic, but here we have chosen to keep them separate from the materials they produce or use as food.)

The aim of this chapter is to show that organic matter is an essential part of most growing media. Certainly soils would not be soils if it were not for organic matter; some organic matter is essential in special root zone sands for turf; potting media usually contain much organic matter. Only the media for various hydroponics systems—rockwool, scoria, sand, gravel, nutrient solution—need not have organic matter in them. But even in them, a small amount of humus (100 to 300 mg/L solution) will improve plant growth.

This chapter is mainly about field soils, and emphasis is on the cycling of organic matter in them. Many of the remarks apply to sandy root zones for turf. The main benefits given by organic matter—improved structure, increased ability to supply nutrients to plants and an aid to disease control—are discussed in later chapters.

CRUSHED ROCK, OR SOIL?

Rock quarries produce many different grades of crushed rock, ranging from large stones to the finest of quarry dust. With a bit of effort we could screen some of this quarry dust to give a material with the range of particle sizes of loam.

But if we determine the texture of this 'loam' by the method given in Chapter 3, we soon find that it neither feels nor behaves like a loam. For one thing, the particles feel harsh and jagged; for another, it is possible to form only a short, fragile ribbon.

There are several reasons for our 'loam' not behaving like a loam. One is that it has not been subjected to the slow, centuries-long changes that take place in moist, oxygen-rich soils. It therefore does not contain the range of minerals found in any normal soil (p.42). Also, it has not had living things growing in it, so it contains no organic matter. It is only crushed rock. It will become a soil only after it has weathered for many years and has accumulated some organic matter.

BENEFITS OF ORGANIC MATTER

Organic matter has several important effects on soils and the plants growing in them. We summarize these effects here and discuss them more fully on later pages.

Organic matter:

- Binds together the mineral particles of soils into aggregates. In other words, organic matter improves soil structure and therefore the supply of oxygen and water to plants.
- Is a source of nutrients for plants. These nutrients are released as the organic matter slowly decomposes.
- Regulates the supply of nutrients, by holding them in readily available forms and reducing losses in drainage waters.
- Helps to buffer soils against rapid changes in pH.
- Helps to control root diseases, in part through a general reduction in the level of disease-causing organisms by microorganisms that are decomposing the organic matter.
- May stimulate seed germination, root development and general plant growth through the plant hormone-like activity of some of its components.

AMOUNTS OF ORGANIC MATTER IN SOILS

Most topsoils (the top 10 cm) contain less than 10% organic matter. Cultivated soils, such as those of the Wheat Belt, typically contain only 0.5–2.5% organic matter. Soils under long-established pastures may contain 5–8%. Natural bushland soils may range from less than 1% in dry inland areas, through 2–4% for sclerophyll forests, to about 25% for alpine mountain ash and tropical rainforest soils. Peats contain between 30 and 90% organic matter.

Subsoils almost always contain less organic matter than do surface soils. One metre under cereals and pastures, the levels are about 0.2–0.5%. Many commercial 'loams' contain less than 1%.

ORIGINS OF ORGANIC MATTER

Figure 5.1
The origins of soil organic matter

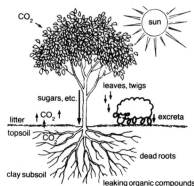

Plants are the primary source of all soil organic matter (Fig. 5.1). Parts of plants reach the soil in the following ways.

From plant tops

- Various parts of plants—leaves, bark, twigs, branches, flowers, fruit—fall from them during normal life cycles. They become part of the litter on the soil surface.
- Rain washes some soluble organic materials from leaves and stems.
- Animals and insects eat plant tops and their excreta falls to the soil surface.
- Eventually plants die and all remaining parts of the tops fall to the soil surface.
- Farmers and gardeners add plant materials to soils by ploughing or digging in weeds, cover crops or residues, or as composts, blood-and-bone, peat moss, animal manure and other organic fertilizers.

From roots

- As root tips move through soil, the outer layers of cells at the tip are scraped off against soil particles.
- Organic materials are continually leaking from living root cells.
- Young roots are coated with a jelly-like material that aids the uptake of water and nutrients from the soil. As the roots age this material becomes part of the organic matter of the soil.
- Some roots are eaten by small soil animals (e.g. parasitic nematodes and scarab beetle larvae).
- Eventually all roots die.

The total amount from roots is often about the same as or a little more than the mass of new top growth each year.

Table 5.1
Relative rates of decomposition of organic compounds

Rate of decomposition	Compound
Rapid	sugars, starches, protein, hemicelluloses, cellulose
Slow	lignin, fats, waxes

DECOMPOSITION

All plant parts reaching soils eventually become unrecognizable as plant parts. They become smaller in size and eventually seem to disappear. The rate of 'disappearance', usually called decomposition, is most rapid for the softer parts—small roots, leaves, flowers—which are usually unrecognizable after a few months in moist soil or on its surface. Harder, woodier parts take longer to become unrecognizable. At the extreme, large tree trunks may remain recognizable for a century or more in cold areas such as the highlands of Tasmania.

Decomposition is caused by millions of living things that use the plant parts as food. Vegetarian insects and small animals chew into the plant parts, breaking them up and leaving the residues in their excreta. Other small animals and insects use this excreta as food. Carnivorous animals and insects use the vegetarians, and one another, as food. These animals and insects are important in reducing the size of plant materials, and in mixing microorganisms with the residues.

Microorganisms—mainly fungi, bacteria and actinomycetes—are responsible for much of the decomposition of plant parts in soils. Some of them attack living plants, but most live on the dead remains of plants, animals and insects and their excreta, and one another. They do an excellent job of recycling those remains.

CHANGES DURING DECOMPOSITION

Dry plant material is about half carbon (C), derived originally from the carbon dioxide (CO_2) of the air. In the plant it is combined with hydrogen (H), oxygen (O), nitrogen (N), and smaller amounts of 12 other elements essential to plant life. There are many thousands of different combinations of these elements in plants. The names given to some of the most abundant ones are sugars, protein, cellulose, hemicellulose and lignin. The relative ease of their decomposition is given in Table 5.1

During decomposition, much of the carbon is 'burnt' to carbon dioxide and so returns to the atmosphere for re-use by living plants. Much of the hydrogen is 'burnt' to water. Of the carbon taken by microorganisms at each 'bite' about 20–40% goes to make more microorganisms. A few percent is converted to humus. The rest is given off as carbon dioxide.

Release of Nutrients

'Organic matter is the original slow-release fertilizer.' The nutrients in plant materials first become part of the bodies of microorganisms. Then, as these are eaten by others, some are released as 'wastes'. They are thus available for reuse by living plants. Eventually, most of the nutrients are released. The cycle has been completed (Fig. 5.2).

In an ecosystem in which losses of nutrients are very low—in grassland or forest, for example—plant growth can be sustained almost indefinitely through recycling. Here, the rate of release of nutrients can support adequate plant growth. (Some extra nutrients come from the decomposition of soil minerals.)

But if we want *vigorous* growth, we must increase the rate of supply of nutrients. The usual way of doing this is to use a fertilizer. If there is a high level of organic matter in the soil, however, the amount being decomposed each day may be able to supply enough nutrients. For this to happen, much of the organic matter in the soil needs to be residues of large amounts of young plant materials added over the previous few years. The rate of decomposition of older organic matter—humus and woody materials—is too low to provide enough nutrients (see below). At the other end of the scale, few nutrients are released from newly added plant materials until they have been decomposing for a few weeks or months. Composting (discussed in Chapter 12) shortens this lag time.

The rate of decomposition of organic materials various enormously (Table 5.2), but typically goes something like Fig. 5.3. The time taken until only 10%

Figure 5.2
The organic matter cycle

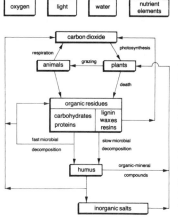

Figure 5.3

Some parts of organic materials added to moist, oxygen-rich soils decompose rapidly. Others are only slowly decomposed over many years

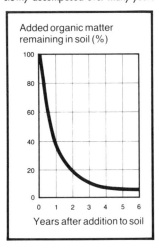

Added organic matter remaining in soil (%)

Years after addition to soil

Figure 5.4

Piece of soil organic matter protected from microbial attack through being coated with clay mineral particles. Also in the picture is a fractured quartz grain (Q). Magnification: x31000 *Photograph R C Foster*

is left might be months in a tropical rainforest, through three or four years in a cool moist pasture, to tens or hundreds of years in very cold, mostly waterlogged soils. In most soils there are only a few percent left after five or six years. That remaining is mainly microorganisms and humus.

Humus formation

Humus is microorganism excreta. To put it more technically: Humus is the more-or-less stable part of soil organic matter remaining after the major portions of plant and animal remains have been decomposed. Humus is dark-coloured and consists of large organic molecules containing mainly carbon, hydrogen and oxygen but also considerable amounts of nitrogen and sulphur and smaller amounts of other elements. A large proportion of humus is probably formed from the lignin of plants—the material that gives stems and wood their rigidity. Micro-organisms rearrange the atoms, forming them into very large conglomerates—humus.

Humus gives soils their dark brown or black colour. It has a major effect on many soil properties. Especially important are its effects on soil structure (Chapter 8) and the ability of a soil to hold and supply plant nutrients (Chapter 7).

Humus can last a long time in soils. In one study, the *average* age was found to be more than 2500 years. This means that microorganisms either do not find humus a palatable food, or that they are unable to get at it. Both seem partly true. Humus has already been discarded by microorganisms as a waste product. But perhaps more importantly, much humus is sandwiched between mineral particles (Fig. 5.4). It is protected from attack, at the same time helping to hold the particles together into the stable crumbs that make for good soil structure.

Figure 5.5 gives a typical elemental composition of humus. When humus is broken down in a soil, the nitrogen, sulphur, phosphorus, etc., it contains can re-enter the microbe–living plant–microbe cycle again. This seems to happen to a few percent of the humus in a soil each year.

In situations where nutrients are repeatedly removed in crops, relying on humus decomposition for plant nutrients is like living on capital; it soon runs out. Then a soil becomes difficult to cultivate, it has a poor structure, does not readily accept water, stores less water and will be referred to as infertile. It is

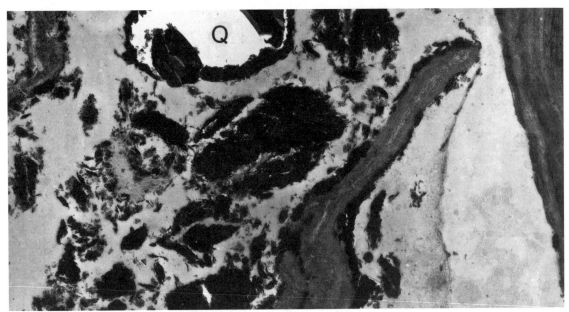

Table 5.2
Decomposition of some organic materials when mixed with soil and stored moist for 6 months. Ample oxygen was supplied. (*From J P Martin et al. Agrochimica 22: 248, 1978*)

Material	% decomposed
Cattle droppings (fresh)	54
Compost	51
Poultry manure (fresh)	46
Horse manure	38
Ponderosa pine sawdust	29
Poultry manure (composted)	26
Ponderosa pine bark	20
Redwood sawdust	19
Canadian peatmoss	18
Black peat	2
Soil humus	2

Figure 5.5
Approximate proportions of the main elements in humus

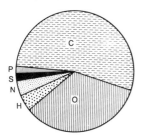

essential for the well-being of a soil and for its ability to support plant life that its pool of humus is maintained and that as much plant litter as possible is left where it falls. If the 'mess' this causes is unacceptable, the materials should be composted (Chapter 12) and the compost returned to the soil.

A compost heap is a *must* for all parks, recreation areas, reserves, ovals and gardens. Never burn anything that can be composted. Chip the larger pieces and return them as a mulch.

Repeated removal of plant litter from under trees, or the inability of nutrients from decomposing litter to get to plant roots through concrete and asphalt means that many trees in carparks and city streets decline in vigour. They often need to be helped with fertilizers to make up for the lack of recycling.

CHANGING THE LEVEL OF ORGANIC MATTER IN A SOIL

Left to itself, a soil will have about the same level of organic matter year after year. The rate of decomposition of plant residues equals, on average, the rate at which organic materials are produced by plants. The soil is said to be in equilibrium with its environment. But any change to that environment will begin slowly to change the level of organic matter in the soil.

Increasing

- Adding fertilizer that increases plant growth will increase the amounts of organic materials reaching the soil and so increase soil organic matter levels.
- Adding extra plant residues (compost, mulching materials, animal manures) will increase soil organic matter levels.

The rate of increase is quite slow unless very large amounts are added. For example, it took 39 years for the level of organic matter in a soil in the south-east of South Australia to rise from 1.4% to 5% in a fertilized pasture. The effects of adding 35 tonnes of farmyard manure per hectare each year to a soil in England are shown in Fig. 5.6. Eventually both soils will reach a new equilibrium level of organic matter, which will be maintained so long as conditions remain unchanged.

- Adding clay to a sandy soil will enable it to retain more of any organic materials coming its way.
- Decreasing soil pH will increase the amount of organic matter retained. We want to make it clear that we are *not* saying that soils should be deliberately made more acid so that they will have a higher level of organic matter. Acidity brings other problems (see Chapter 11). But if a soil does become more acid, it is likely to retain more organic matter.

  This happens in peat bogs. They are acid and waterlogged; this all but eliminates soil animals and many microorganisms (notably bacteria). Plant residues are only partly decomposed before becoming part of the peat. Draining peat bogs and adding lime greatly accelerates the decomposition of the peat.

  Peat used in potting mixes will also begin to decompose more rapidly once its pH is raised. However, most peats are so stable that the amount of decomposition will usually not have much effect on the properties of the mix over periods of up to six months (Table 5.2).

  When turf soils become strongly acid (less than about pH 5) through the effects of adding ammonium-based fertilizers, and leaching, the decomposition of residues is retarded and thatch build-up is increased. Applying lime to keep soil pH near 6 is one way of reducing thatch build-up.

Figure 5.6
Effect of farm-yard manure on the organic matter content of a cropped soil in England. *From* D S Jenkinson and A E Johnston *Rothamsted Report* Part 2: 94, 1976

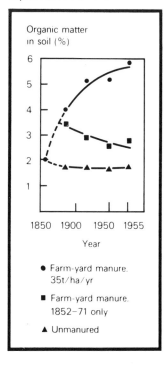

Decreasing

- Removing all plant litter will gradually reduce the level of organic matter in a soil. The recycling of plant nutrients will also be reduced and, eventually, plants may suffer from deficiencies.
- Extending the time that a soil remains moist will increase total decomposition of soil organic matter. Thus irrigation may lower soil organic matter levels, unless the extra water increases plant growth and litter return.
- Fire will reduce the return of organic materials to a soil. But often fire reduces attack by diseases and may lead to better plant growth and a greater litter fall. It seems that the effect of fire on soil organic matter levels is small.
- Cultivation is the most aggressive and 'successful' method of reducing soil organic matter levels. Cultivation shatters the protective bonds between clay minerals and organic matter, allowing attack by microbes. Soil organic matter levels are halved by 25–50 years of cultivation. Wherever possible, soils should be left uncultivated, with their surfaces protected by organic mulches. Except for the build-up of thatch in turf, increasing the level of organic matter, or at least maintaining it, should be an aim of all who work with soils.

6
PROBLEMS WITH ORGANIC MATERIALS

Organic matter is generally beneficial in any growing medium. But there are situations in which some types of organic matter can cause problems for us or our plants.

WATER REPELLENCE

Field and turf soils

The sand grains in some sandy soils (sands to sandy clay loams) sometimes become water repellent (hydrophobic) by being coated with organic residues from some, but not all, plant materials. In severe cases, water sits in droplets on top of the dry soil (Fig. 6.1). Water repellence in turf shows up as areas of dead grass or poor growth (Fig. 6.2). The grass cannot get enough water. Germination of seeds planted into water-repellent sandy soils is usually poor.

Several strategies are available for coping with water repellence. Mechanical agitation of the soil–water mixture will encourage wetting. Then, preventing the soil from drying out—by mulching and frequent watering—will usually prevent redevelopment of the problem.

Where possible, a long-term cure for a water-repellent sandy soil is to increase the clay content of the soil to above 10–15%. Add clay to give a layer about 20 mm thick on the surface. This will require about 10–13 kg/m². Mix it into the top 100 mm of sand. A dispersive sodic (Chapter 21) clay appears to give best results. This converts the soil to a sandy loam or loam. It seems that the higher clay content gives soil conditions that prevent the coating of sand grains with water-repellent organic materials.

Seeds planted at the bottom of furrows have a better germination rate than those sown in the same soil with a flat surface. Water shed from the hills sits longer in the furrows and so has a better chance of wetting the soil, and the seeds.

Wetting agents (Figure 6.5) give excellent results in both field and turf soils. As little as 1 litre of concentrate per hectare of field soil, applied in a narrow band over the furrow in which the seed has been dropped, has allowed sufficiently better water penetration to produce severalfold increases in wheat yields on sandy soils.

The addition of lime to acid water-repellent soils has sometimes been found to reduce, even eliminate, water repellence. It is speculated that raising soil pH alters the properties of the organic substances that are responsible for repellency.

The existence or severity of water repellence may be simply assessed by placing a drop of water on the dry soil. If the drop stays on the surface (Fig. 6.1) the soil is water repellent. The severity of water repellence is given by the time taken for the drop to disappear. See Chapter 33 for details of this test and an interpretation of readings.

Figure 6.2
Water-repellent sand under turf. The darker soil is damp; the lighter is dry because water has not been able to penetrate into it.   *Photograph R Bond*

Figure 6.3
Shallow coring gives better wetting of dry patches in turf than does deeper coring

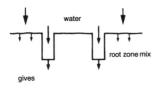

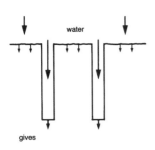

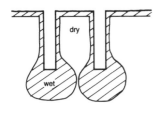

Dry Patch

Dry patches in turf are often caused by water repellence. Very sandy materials are commonly used for the root zone mixes of bowling and golf greens and major football fields. Materials with more than a few percent clay and silt cannot be used, because heavy use will ruin their physical properties (Chapter 17). Decomposition of the thatch produced during normal turf growth can produce hydrophobic organic materials that accumulate in the thatch and the upper part of the root zone. This is particularly noticeable within fairy rings.

The best way of overcoming dry patch is through the use of wetting agents, as follows:

1. Towards the end of the wet season (September in southern Australia), apply the chosen wetting agent at about 150–200 mL concentrate per 100 m², or as recommended by the manufacturer. Dilute liquid concentrates into about 50 times this volume of water.
2. Repeat the addition in November and March, if your experience suggests that dry patch is likely to develop. It has been found in Western Australia that three light applications, spread through the dry season, give better results than one large application early in the season.
3. After each application, irrigate at a low rate—say 5–10 mm per hour—so that the water can penetrate deeply into the affected area.
4. Especially bad patches may need to receive additional treatments.
5. The shallow coring recommended in the 1980s by the Western Australian Department of Agriculture (Fig. 6.3) has been found to be unnecessary in all but the most stubborn patches. There is also no need to add pelleted poultry manure.

Note: Dead patches or poor growth in turf may have causes other than water repellence. Check for soil compaction, waterlogging, salinity (including from dog urine), thatch build-up, insect attack, diseases, underwatering, and too much or too little fertilizer.

Water repellence in potting mixes

Many peats, barks and sawdusts, and potting media made from them, are difficult to re-wet if they dry out either before potting or when in pots. The development of a water-repellent condition in pots allows much of the water applied to run around the outside of the rootball and through large channels within it. The

Figure 6.4
Retention of water poured onto the surface of dry potting medium containing various wetting agents, as a proportion of the water retained following dunking. □ Aquasoil Wetter (Dolmar Dynamic, Canning Vale, WA), △ Wetta Soil (Wetta Chem Products, Bunbury, WA), ▽ Agral 600 (ICI, Melbourne), ◇ Hydraflo Liquid (Grace Sierra), ○ dishwashing detergent. C = control medium. *From* K A Handreck *Australian Hortic.*, August: 23, 1992

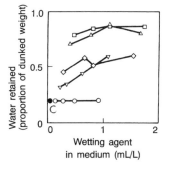

medium itself is hardly any wetter than before watering. Plants in such a medium suffer from water stress and will grow poorly.

Water repellence is reduced in severity, but sometimes not prevented, by including at least 30% sand in otherwise organic media. Prevention is achieved through the use of wetting agents.

Wetting agents

Wetting agents are synthetic chemicals that allow easier spreading of water across surfaces. Common dishwashing detergents are one type of formulation of wetting agents. They are, however, useless for overcoming water repellency: they are much less effective than the best wetting agents; they are decomposed in seven days in soils and potting media, as they are required to be biodegradable. Laundry detergent powders contain high percentages of sodium compounds that can severely damage growing media and plants alike. Some have very high levels of boron.

Table 6.1
Wettability in seconds of potting mixes containing wetting agents, after storage moist in bags for 8 months, as measured by the Australian Standard method (Chapter 33). (*From* K A Handreck *Australian Hortic.* August: 29, 1992)

| | Wetting agent addition rate (mL/L mix) | | | | |
Wetting agent	0.1	0.2	0.4	0.8	1.2
Aquasoil Wetter	174	145	55	45	33
Wetta Soil	180	158	104	54	55
Control	197				

At 8 months all other wetting agents included in the test gave test results that were not significantly different from control.

Research on soils by the Western Australian Department of Agriculture and on potting media by CSIRO showed that of all the wetting agents on sale in the

1980s and early 1990s two—Wetta Soil and Aquasoil Wetter—were outstanding in their ability to overcome water repellency (Fig. 6.4), for longevity of the effect (Table 6.1) and for low toxicity. In early 1993, as this edition was going to press, two newly released wetting agents named Drygone and Saturaid were being shown to be very effective. A considerable number of other products had been shown to be inferior. During decomposition in soils and potting mixes, some inferior products actually increase water repellency! Use the test methods in Chapter 33 to compare new and older products with one another.

Adding an effective wetting agent at a rate of 400 mL of concentrate per cubic metre of medium will prevent the occurrence of water repellency for 8 to 12 months. To include wetting agent in a potting mix before potting, dilute the concentrate in about 10 times its volume of water. Granular formulations (Fig. 6.5) are easier to add. There are unpublished reports that they give longer protection than do the same chemicals in liquid form. Where shorter periods of protection are acceptable, as in media for plugs and bedding plants, amounts of wetting agent needed can be less than one-quarter of that suggested above.

Medium that has become water repellent in pots can be treated in two ways. Small numbers of pots can be treated by dunking them into a solution containing 1 mL/L of the wetting agent. For large numbers of pots, pour onto each a volume of a solution (containing 1.5 mL/L concentrate) equal to about one-quarter of the volume of medium.

Figure 6.5
The top two wetting agents illustrated have a good track record, but in early results available at the time of writing, the wetting agent illustrated below them was also performing well. Choose among them (and other new ones) on the basis of local trials extending over a year.

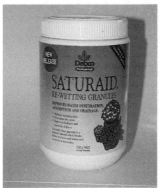

PHYTOTOXICITY

Some parts of organic matter in growing media are able to injure, even kill, plants. These parts are lumped together under the term 'phytotoxins', which literally means plant poisons.

Natural soils

In soils, phytotoxins can come from:

- plant residues newly dug into the soil;
- microbes as they decompose residues;
- living plants themselves.

Some examples are:

- Reduced yields of apples caused by toxins produced by some grasses growing under them and by interplanted potatoes.
- Poor growth and death of young peach trees planted into old peach orchards, caused by toxins released during the decomposition of old peach roots.
- Reduced growth of a second crop of such plants as stocks, chrysanthemums, cabbages, broccoli, turnips and swedes quickly following a first crop.
- Poor germination and/or growth of nearby plants caused by many weeds, including thistles, wire weed, summer grass, fat hen, pigweed, Chinese lantern, barnyard grass, evening primrose, wild oats and tussock grasses, and couch grass used for lawns.
- Poor germination of some seeds caused by organic materials leaching from the leaves of plants of the same or other species. Examples of species producing such toxic chemicals include some eucalypts, *Prunus* species, some *Pinus* species, junipers, etc. For example, the soil under the drip circle of *Eucalyptus globulus* (Tasmanian blue gum) is usually devoid of small plants: lawn cannot be grown there.
- Poor growth or death of lettuce and other seedlings planted into soil immediately after plants such as broad beans previously growing there had been chopped into the soil.
- Poor germination of seeds and retarded early growth of plants in soil containing newly decomposing straw (Fig. 6.7).
- Indifferent growth of plants in recycled potting mix. This is sometimes due to mild toxicity produced during the decomposition of roots from the previous crop.
- Another example is listed on p. 34.

Overcoming the problem: Toxicity from rotting residues usually reaches a peak between 5 and 25 days after the start of decomposition. Thereafter, it declines rapidly and usually disappears 10 to 15 days later. That is why it is advisable to wait for about five weeks before planting seeds in a soil into which mature plant residues have been mixed. Young, succulent material is less toxic than older materials. Green manure crops are usually dug in when relatively young, so toxicity from them is usually slight. (Sudan grass appears to be an exception (Fig. 6.8).) Nevertheless, it seems best to be on the cautious side and wait a few weeks before planting. If nothing else, this delay will allow rotting to break down bulky material that might otherwise interfere with planting.

Damage by phytotoxins is often less when residues are retained on the surface as a mulch than when they are mixed into the soil. Gardeners can use residues as mulch under established plants.

A preferred alternative is to compost residues. The high temperatures in a compost heap speed decomposition so that phytotoxins are quickly decomposed too. By the time the compost is ready to use—two weeks to a year, depending on the method used—few, if any, phytotoxins will remain.

Figure 6.6

Effect of lucerne root residues in a sand/soil medium on root growth of cucumber seedlings. + number of roots; △ weight of roots. *From J E Ells and A E McSay HortScience 26: 368, 1991*

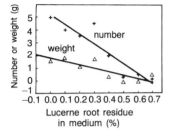

Figure 6.7

Phytotoxicity caused by rotting wheat straw. A: healthy wheat seedlings. B and C: poor germination and growth caused by toxins released from the rotting straw.

Photograph R L Kimber

Potting media

Most of the barks and sawdusts used in potting media contain natural chemicals that are toxic to plants (Fig. 6.9). Presumably the chemicals are there to protect living trees against attack by animals and microorganisms. Plants can only be grown successfully in these materials after the level of toxins has been reduced. Young plants—seedlings and cuttings—are more easily and severely damaged than older plants.

Different barks and sawdusts contain different levels of phytotoxins. At one end of the range are *Eucalyptus marginata* (jarrah) and *E. diversicolor* (karri) whose sawdusts are relatively free of toxins. They can be used in mixes without treatment.

As far as is known, all other sawdusts available in Australia need composting to reduce the level of phytotoxins (and to decrease later nitrogen draw-down). The conditions needed are given in Chapter 12. A minimum of six weeks is needed for most sawdusts (Table 6.2). Aerated steaming of mixes containing hardwood sawdusts has been shown to further reduce phytotoxicity. Meranti sawdusts are particularly toxic and may not be fully detoxified by six weeks of composting.

Pine barks can be detoxified by moist storage in windrows for 4 to 6 weeks. Composting (Chapter 12) makes detoxification more certain and gives a better product because of diminished nitrogen hunger and increased humus content. Further ageing or composting will be needed if the bark is hammer milled, as this releases more toxins from inside large pieces. Sawdust and ground pine bark stored in very large heaps (height and width each greater than about 3 m) can become anaerobic and very toxic through the formation of organic acids, nitrite ions and compounds with hormone-like activity. The possibility of such toxicity developing is enhanced during prolonged wet weather and by the absence of daily to weekly turning of the heap. Sometimes toxicity can develop in composted materials being stored after composting has apparently been completed. In reality, composting has not finished, and lack of the oxygenation provided by turning can produce all of the problems listed above.

The anaerobic condition is usually obvious from the sour smell of the materials and their low pH (often lower than pH 4.5). Liming such materials will raise pH, but it may not remove all of the toxic compounds. It is strongly recommended that you do not use materials from anaerobic heaps, or accept loads of potting mix that smell as if they have been made from such materials.

Figure 6.8
A: Healthy 2-week old *Pinus strobus* seedlings. B: *P. strobus* seedlings of similar age growing in soil containing the residues of two crops of sorghum-sudan grass green-manure. *From J G Lyer Plant and Soil 54: 159, 1980; courtesy of Martinus Nijhoff Publishers*

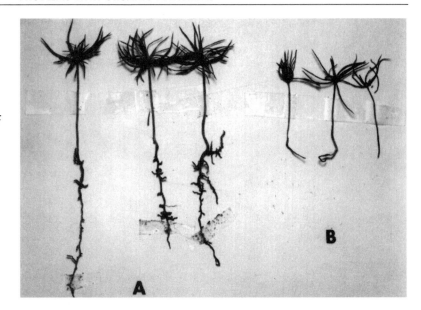

Figure 6.9
Root growth on cuttings of *Impatiens linearifolia* one week after transplanting into *Pinus radiata* bark aged for 6 weeks (L) or fresh (R). *From D G Nichols Scientia Horticulturae 15:291, 1981; courtesy of Elsevier Scientific Publishing Co*

Large heaps of moist, lightly decomposed and newly dug peat (perhaps >30 m³) can self-heat to above 70°C. This leads to charring, the production of high concentrations of ammonium ions and compounds that inhibit plant growth. Potting media prepared from such peat has also been shown to have a high rate of nitrogen drawdown. Do not accept deliveries of peat that has a charred/musty smell which probably indicates that it has suffered from self-heating.

Composted materials produced with additions of organic forms of nitrogen (offal, food wastes) that raise the nitrogen content of the heap to more than 1% can contain toxic concentrations of ammonium and ammonia. Such heaps must be composted for at least six weeks and often matured for several months before they can be considered free from toxicity.

Aerated steaming has been reported to temporarily increase the toxicity of young, fresh *P. radiata* bark. The effect is eliminated by moist ageing as described above.

Not all phytotoxic chemicals in sawdusts are natural. Some sawdusts are from

Table 6.2
Germination of cabbage seeds as affected by sawdusts and bark from different tree species and composted for different times. The propagation medium was 1:1 fine sand/sawdust or bark. Figures are percentages relative to that in vermiculite/fine sand being rated at 100% germination. (*From R J Worrall Acta Horticulturae 82: 79, 1978*)

Tree species	Days composted				
	3	**11**	**17**	**34**	**44**
Sawdusts					
Eucalyptus andrewsii	52	76	86	84	98
E. microcorys	24	78	78	90	93
E. pilularis	17	86	90	85	85
E. radiata	59	73	89	95	94
E. saligna	47	55	81	95	93
Bark					
Pinus radiata	91	90	99	–	–

timber treated with preservatives such as creosote and CCA (copper-chrome-arsenic) or with boric acid. Creosote can be detected by its smell, CCA by its green colour. The toxicity of these sawdusts cannot be removed. They must never be used in potting mixes.

A simple test for the presence of phytotoxins is given in Chapter 33.

Phytotoxins and microorganisms

Harmful effects: Damage caused to roots by phytotoxins greatly increases the risk of pathogens successfully attacking plants. For example, bush beans are more severely attacked by *Fusarium* root rot fungi after coming in contact with toxins washed from decomposing residues of barley, rye, timothy grass, broccoli or broad beans. Often, too, the resistance of varieties that are otherwise resistant to *Fusarium* is completely broken down.

Beneficial effects: Toxins from plant materials do, however, have their uses. Toxins given off by germinating seeds help to protect them from attack by microorganisms that would otherwise destroy them. Toxins leaching from plant litter and produced during decomposition in the soil suppress many parasitic nematodes. Applying organic materials to a soil will usually reduce the level of pathogens in it. Toxins help in this reduction, but there are other causes too (Chapter 25). Some organic compounds present in composts and organic potting mixes help suppress pathogens, but other microorganisms are usually more important (Chapter 26).

Conclusion

It is safe to say that most plants affect the growth of nearby plants through the organic chemicals they give off from their roots or tops. Many of these effects are small. But sometimes the effects can be large. If you are having problems establishing a particular plant in a soil in which another of that or another species has been growing, or near another well-established plant, suspect that it might be getting poisoned.

TOO LITTLE WATER

Soils

Often seedlings need frequent watering and grow poorly during early growth in a soil 'fluffed up' through having large amounts of partly decomposed organic materials recently mixed into it. Root damage during transplanting can be a cause, but there is another one too.

A 'fluffed up' soil has many large pores that are unable to retain water against gravity. Most water from sprinklers or rain drains beyond the reach of young roots. Few small pores means little water held for plants. Only when the young roots have grown to penetrate a large volume of soil are they able to contact enough water to supply daytime needs. These soils can be as 'droughty' as coarse sands.

Eventually, as the bulky materials are decomposed, the large pores collapse, the number of smaller pores increases and the ability of the soil to hold water increases. In fact, once this has happened, the ability of the soil to hold water will usually be greater than that of the same soil without the extra humus.

Farmers sometimes roll seedbeds to collapse large pores. Gardeners usually press the soil firmly around the seedlings. They can also lightly tamp the soil beneath where seeds are to be planted. But too much tamping can compact a soil so much that roots have difficulty in getting through it. Somewhere in the middle is best.

Delaying transplanting or seed sowing until bulky organic materials have decomposed may sometimes be necessary.

If a soil is already well endowed with humus, extra organic amendments might be better left as a mulch on the surface rather than mixed in. The trade-off is that more nitrogen is usually lost from mulched high-nitrogen organic materials than from those incorporated into the soil.

Turf

Some organic matter is necessary in soils under turf. Deep accumulation on the surface (thatch) is another matter. If the soil is so compacted that the turf roots penetrate it with difficulty, many of them will be growing in the thatch layer. As thatch has mainly large pores, it holds little water. Frequent watering will be necessary in hot weather. Remedies are given in Chapters 17 and 19.

EXCESSIVE RELEASE OF MINERAL SALTS

Mineral salts are always released from decomposing organic materials. This is a main natural way that living plants are kept supplied with nutrients. In most situations the rate of release of mineral salts is about the same as the rate of uptake by plants so there is never an excessive build-up.

But in some situations the amounts of soluble salts released can cause problems unless we make allowances.

Composts made from materials that decompose easily and that have not been leached by rain can have a high level of soluble salts. As explained in Chapter 21, electrical conductivities (saturation extract) of 3 dS/m are common. Sensitive plants are harmed at values above about 1.5 dS/m and even moderately tolerant plants suffer about 20% growth reduction at 3 dS/m (Table 21.13).

Mushroom composts are usually very salty indeed. The salts are mainly of plant nutrients, so such composts make excellent mulches when applied lightly. Disaster can follow their use at anything more than 10% of a potting mix. Check both pH and electrical conductivity (EC) before using them.

The level of salinity can be very high in compost made in summer with large additions of salty tap water. Salts in the water remain in the compost after the water has evaporated. The more saline the water, the higher the salinity of the compost.

Such composts should not make up more than 25% of any potting mix. Alternatively, leaching the compost with about 2 volumes of water will reduce the salinity to less than a quarter of its original value. Excessive leaching is to be avoided, however, as it will unnecessarily decrease the level of soluble nutrients in the compost.

Composts stored moist for long periods may have especially high levels of salts. This is because decomposition continues slowly during storage. If composts are to be stored for long periods, it is better that they are dried in the air first. They don't have to be bone-dry; just dry enough so that they look and feel dry and do not heat in storage. That means less than about 35% moisture.

UNDESIRABLE CHANGES IN SOIL pH

Plant growth tends to make soil more acid (lower pH) through the release of organic acids and hydrogen ions from living roots. But in a natural, long-established plant community where the amount of organic materials decomposed is the same as the amount produced, the pH of the soil remains about the same from year to year. Only if there is leaching of soluble materials from the soil, out of reach of plant roots, will the soil become (over many years) more acid. Leaching is most likely in areas of high rainfall, so soils in these areas tend to be more acid that those in drier areas.

Human activity can accelerate or change the direction of these natural processes. If a tropical rainforest is cleared, there will be more run-off of water and more leaching of the soil. It will inevitably become more acid, and impoverished through lowered organic matter levels.

In other, more temperate areas, the establishment of improved pasture (of clovers and imported grasses), made possible through the correction of nutrient deficiencies, leads to greater total plant growth and a build-up of soil organic matter levels. In soils that are already acid and that have little ability to resist a change in pH, the accumulation of acidic organic matter, and leaching, cause a steady decline in soil pH to the point where plant growth is seriously reduced. After 40–50 years soil pH may decrease from 6 to 4.9.

It is not the accumulation of organic matter that is the real problem, but the lack of balancing alkaline materials. Adding them—lime or dolomite—will correct the imbalance.

These same trends occur in gardens, too, and may in fact be more rapid there because of the extra leaching caused by irrigation in dry weather. The use of urea and ammonium fertilizers will hasten acidification (Fig. 11.5). Wherever plant growth is increased, soil pH should be monitored and lime or dolomite applied as needed.

TEMPORARY DECREASE IN NUTRIENT SUPPLY

In Chapter 5 we said that decomposing organic materials supply nutrients to plants. So they do, but in the early stages of decomposition, the supply of some nutrients can be greatly reduced. In order to use the organic part of the added materials (the sugars, cellulose, hemicellulose, etc.), microorganisms must have a readily available supply of nutrient elements. They can get these from the added materials or from reserves in the medium. All is well if the added materials contain ample supplies of nutrients. Young plant materials such as lawn clippings, weeds, green-manure crops and most animal manures are like this. All can be well, too, if the medium has large reserves of readily available nutrients—as from controlled-release fertilizers.

But if the added materials contain only small amounts of nutrients, the microorganisms must use nutrients dissolved in the water in the medium. They therefore compete, successfully, with any plants growing there. If the amount of materials added is large, plant growth is retarded. Nitrogen is the nutrient element in greatest demand, but supplies of sulphur and phosphorus may also be stretched.

Nitrogen deficiency

The tissues of microorganisms contain carbon and nitrogen in the ratio of about 30:1. If they are to decompose materials with a higher C/N ratio (Table 6.3), they must get extra nitrogen from elsewhere. They therefore quickly use up any soluble nitrogen present around them. Plants growing in soils or potting mixes containing materials such as sawdust will soon have little soluble nitrogen available to them unless more is continually supplied.

Approximate times that it takes for soluble nitrogen to be released to plants from added organic materials are given in Table 6.4. Clearly it can take several years for the effects of mixing sawdusts and barks into soils to disappear.

Nitrogen deficiency soon after adding low-nitrogen materials can be much more severe with materials that are readily decomposed than with those that resist decomposition. Thus chopped straw is decomposed quickly, and deficiency is severe but short-lived. Sawdust resists decomposition, so early deficiency is not as severe, but it lasts a long time.

The main reason for wanting to add sawdust and bark to soils is to increase the level of organic matter, so improving their physical properties. For success, plants growing in the soil must be supplied with extra soluble nitrogen. When deciding what to do, the benefits to soil structure must be weighed against the hassles of fertilizing or composting.

Table 6.3
Approximate nitrogen contents of some dried organic materials

Material	N in dry material (%)	C/N ratio*
Bagasse	0.4	120
Brown coal	0.5	130
Clovers	2.2	18
Corn stalks	1.2	33
Cow manure	2.6	15
Eucalypt bark	0.2	250
Eucalypt sawdust	0.1	500
Eucalypt sawdust, composted	0.45	100
Grasses	1.8	22
Leaves, mature	0.7	60
Lignite	1.8	27
Lucerne hay	3.1	13
Paper	0.2	170
Peanut shells	4.4	12
Peat	1.5	30
Pinus radiata bark	0.1	500
P. radiata bark, composted	0.40	100
P. radiata sawdust	0.09	550
Poultry droppings	5.5	7
Poultry litter	2-4	10-11
Rice hulls	0.3	140
Seaweed (kelp)	1.5	25
Sphagnum moss	1.0	54
Straw, oats, wheat	0.4	100
Weeds, mixed	2.0	19

*If a material contains 54% C and 1.2% N, its C/N ratio is 54/1.2=45.

**Table 6.4
Approximate time it takes
for nitrate to be released
from organic materials of
various nitrogen contents**

1.2% N	12 months
1.5% N	9 months
1.8% N	6 months
2.0% N	3 months

An easier alternative is to use the bark or sawdust as a surface mulch. Only the material in contact with the soil will be decomposing. Draw-down of nitrogen will be minimal. Biological activity will gradually and painlessly mix the decayed organic matter into the soil.

Little soil nitrogen will be removed by chunky pine bark mulches. But if the bark contains a high proportion of fines, which settle to the soil surface, there can be some draw-down (and temporary toxicity problems).

Nitrogen drawdown in potting mixes

Sawdust, bark, rice hulls and other low-nitrogen organic materials will behave in potting mixes in exactly the same way as they do when mixed into soils. As they decompose, soluble nitrogen will be removed from the water in the mixes, and from the reach of plant roots (Fig. 6.11).

Nitrogen drawdown in potting mixes is discussed in detail in Chapter 16. It is sufficient here to note that a knowledge of the Nitrogen Drawdown Index of a potting mix allows the application of enough fertilizer nitrogen to ensure adequate plant growth even in mixes composed mainly of sawdust.

Figure 6.10
The nitrogen cycle. The main cycle is indicated by the darker lines

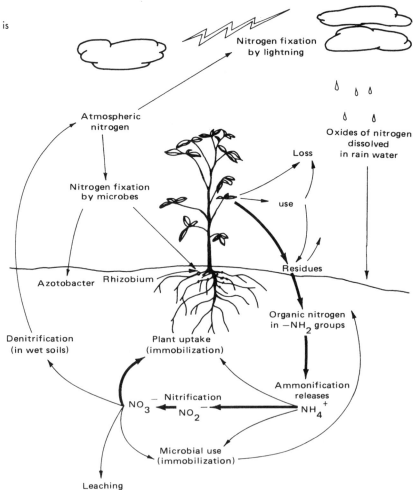

Figure 6.11

Pinus radiata bark and wood shavings use (draw-down) more soluble nitrogen than does peat in potting mixes. *From M Prasad Scientia Horticulturae* 12: 203, 1980

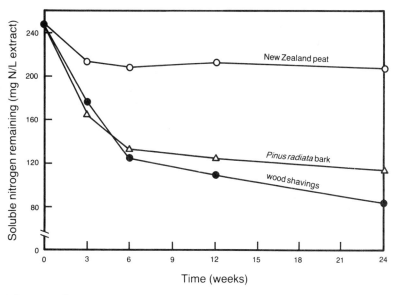

Other nutrients

Decomposition of woody materials can also cause a temporary decline in the levels of soluble sulphur and phosphorus. Whether deficiencies actually occur will depend on the levels in the medium. It seems, though, that nitrogen drawdown dominates. Soluble sulphur and phosphorus appear to become available to plants long before nitrogen does.

RELEASE OF CARBON DIOXIDE

Carbon dioxide is released during the decomposition of organic materials. It was once thought that this release could harm plant roots. However, it is now known that such damage is rare. Almost always, root growth is slowed more by reduced oxygen supply than by build-up of carbon dioxide.

REDUCED EFFICIENCY OF CHEMICALS

Figure 6.12

Microbes in the thatch (. . . .) or soil (– – –) rapidly decompose diazinon insecticide applied to turf. *From B E Branham and D J Wehner Agron. J.* 77: 101, 1984

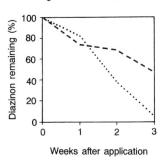

The effectiveness of at least some herbicides and fungicides is reduced when a growing medium contains high proportions of organic matter. Part of this loss of efficiency is due to the chemicals being absorbed into organic matter particles and so removed from circulation. Adsorption onto the surfaces of humified organic matter is another mechanism by which efficiency is reduced.

In addition, the usually larger populations of microorganisms present in organic materials, as compared with mineral materials, speeds the rate of decomposition of many chemicals. In some situations, notably heavily thatched turf, the often large population of pathogens harboured requires more chemical for effective control. In extreme situations the combined effects of lowered efficiency and larger population make control impossible.

As an example, in one trial, as soil organic matter content increased from 8 to 19%, the rates of application of the herbicides Linuron, Trifluralin, Terbacil, Atrazine and Alachlor needed for 80% weed control had to be increased by 1.7–2.8 fold. In another trial, the insecticide diazinon was decomposed more rapidly in the thatch layer on a turf soil than in the soil itself (Fig. 6.12).

7

CLAY AND HUMUS: SOIL COLLOIDS

State anything about soils that you think is important. Go on, think! And don't read on until you have!

Our bet is that the sorts of things going through your mind have something to do with providing plants with food and drink, with the way soils of wet playing fields behave, or with the starkness of an area where soil has been lost by erosion. Whatever you thought of, it is certain that its importance is somehow linked with the very smallest of soil particles—those called clay and humus.

Early soil scientists found that particles smaller than about 0.002 mm diameter were very different from those even a little larger. These small particles were found to be especially important in enabling soils to supply plant nutrients. A small amount of these particles had a much bigger effect on soil behaviour than did the same mass of larger particles.

Small mineral particles are called clay and small organic particles humus. Together, they make up what is often called the colloidal fraction of soils. The word 'colloid' describes their ability to remain suspended in pure water for long periods.

HOW SMALL?

Some rock splitting will give us a good introduction to colloids. Suppose we take a cube of quartz rock with sides 10 mm long. This is the size of a piece of gravel. Its surface area is 0.000 6 m^2 and it will weigh 2.65 g.

Let us slice it up systematically into smaller cubes. The first slices give 8 cubes of side 5 mm; the total surface area is 0.001 2 m^2. Continued slicing of each cube into 8 gives the situation summarised in Table 7.1

This rock splitting exercise highlights some important aspects of colloids.

- A gram of clay contains an enormous number of particles.
- The particles of a gram of clay have an enormously larger surface area than a gram of, say, sand particles. In this example, all the particles were made cubic, but actual clay particles are often shaped like flat plates (Fig. 7.1). A plate of a given volume has a much bigger surface area than a cube of the same volume. (If our 10 mm cube of quartz had been $100 \times 10 \times 1$ mm, its surface area would have been 0.002 22 m^2, not 0.000 6 m^2.)

Actual measurements on soil colloids give surface areas of from 10 to 800 m^2/g for clay and 800 to 900 m^2/g for humus, as against 0.01 m^2/g for coarse sand.

- It must be realised that clay is not just small bits of rock. To be sure, a few clay particles are just that, but most are completely different minerals. They are of two main groups: the clay minerals, and the metal oxides.

Some readers may find this chapter to be the hardest to understand in the whole book. We hope that you persevere with it because as you grow in your understanding of its contents you will really begin to understand soils.

Table 7.1
Effect of repeated slicing up of a 10 mm cube of rock into smaller particles

Slicing	Number of particles	Length of cube side (mm)	Size name	Surface area (m²) Total	Per gram
	1	10	gravel	0.000 6	0.000 2
1	8	5	gravel	0.001 2	0.000 5
2	64	2.5	gravel	0.000 24	0.000 9
3	512	1.25	very coarse sand	0.004 8	0.001 8
4	4 096	0.625	coarse sand	0.009 6	0.003 6
5	32 768	0.312 5	medium sand	0.019 2	0.007 2
6	262 000	0.156 2	fine sand	0.038 4	0.014 4
7	2.1 million	0.078 1	very fine sand	0.076 8	0.029
8	16.8 million	0.039 1	silt	0.154	0.058
9	134 million	0.019 5	silt	0.307	0.116
10	1 075 million	0.009 76	silt	0.614	0.231
11	8 600 million	0.004 88	silt	1.23	0.46
12	69 thousand million	0.002 44	silt	2.46	0.93
13	550 thousand million	0.001 22	clay	4.92	1.86
14	4 million million	0.000 61	clay	9.84	3.78
15	32 million million	0.000 305	clay	19.7	7.4
16	256 million million	0.000 152	clay	39.4	14.9
17	2 thousand million million	0.000 076	clay	78.7	29.7
18	16 thousand million million	0.000 038	clay	151	59
19	128 thousand million million	0.000 019	clay	315	119
20	1 million million million	0.000 009 5	clay	630	238
21*	8 million million million	0.000 004 8	clay	1250	471

* About the size of the smallest clay particles

- It is quite impossible for us to see particles of clay and humus with our unaided eyes. All our eyes show us are the effects of large numbers of particles bunched together: mud on our shoes, dirty hands in pottery classes, or muddy waters in dams. But it is possible to see these particles with the aid of an electron microscope (Fig. 7.1).

Figure 7.1
Particles of the clay mineral kaolinite. Magnification: × 10 000.   *Photograph S McClure*

Figure 7.2
Arrangements of the sheets of atoms in some minerals: (a) The clay mineral kaolinite. (b) The clay mineral smectite. Soils containing a high proportion of smectite swell and shrink markedly because the layers of atoms in smectite particles move as water molecules enter between them or leave.
(c) Vermiculite. Some vermiculite, but not all, has much exchangeable potassium as well as magnesium.
(d) The clay mineral illite

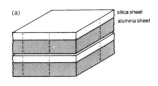

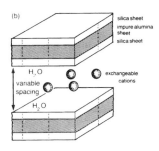

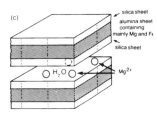

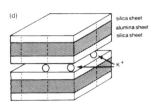

CHEMISTRY (SIMPLIFIED) OF SMALL SOIL PARTICLES

Clay minerals

Clay minerals are formed from rocks by the processes of weathering. The main building blocks of clay minerals are atoms of silicon (Si), aluminium (Al), oxygen (O) and hydrogen (H), but many also contain iron (Fe) and magnesium (Mg), plus other elements. These atoms are arranged together in repeating patterns, as follows.

A clay mineral particle consists of a series of layers (Fig. 7.2). Within each layer there are either two or three sheets of atoms. One type of sheet (the silica sheet) contains Si and O, with each Si atom surrounded by four O atoms. The other type of sheet (alumina sheet) contains Al and O (or OH) with each Al atom surrounded by six O atoms (or OH groups).

In minerals of the kaolinite group of clay minerals, each layer contains one silica sheet and one alumina sheet, as depicted in Fig. 7.2(a). These minerals—kaolinite and halloysite mainly—are often referred to as 1 to 1 minerals.

In the other group of minerals, each layer contains an alumina sheet sandwiched between 2 silica sheets. They are often referred to as 2 to 1 minerals. Some of the more common minerals of the group are smectite (previously called montmorillonite) (Fig. 7.2(b)), vermiculite (Fig. 7.2(c)), illite (Fig. 7.2(d)), and the chlorites.

Clay minerals are different from one another partly because the layers are stacked together differently. In some they are only loosely held together (e.g. kaolinite); in others, they are held together by ions of potassium (e.g. illite) or magnesium and calcium (e.g. smectite).

But most differences are due to atoms of Al or Fe being substituted for Si in Si sheets, and/or atoms of Fe, Mg and other elements for Al in Al sheets, during the formation of the clay minerals. This substitution is a main reason for the small size of clay mineral particles. Aluminium and silicon sheets must be distorted slightly to fit together. Substitution increases this distortion, leading to cracking and breaking.

Another important effect of substitution is that clay mineral particles are left with negative electrical charges. For example, substituting Mg^{2+} for Al^{3+} reduces the positive charge by one, so leaving a surplus of one negative charge. This negative charge is always balanced by cations being attracted to the clay mineral surface (Fig. 7.5).

Iron and aluminium minerals

Under prolonged weathering, silicon and cations such as Ca^{2+} and Mg^{2+} are dissolved from clay minerals. All that is left are oxides and hydroxides of iron and aluminium. Tropical soils often have high proportions of these minerals. The red, orange, yellow and brown colours of many soils are due to the presence of different iron minerals in different proportions; goethite and hematite are the names of two common iron minerals. Gibbsite and boehmite are the commonest aluminium minerals.

These minerals are often seen as very small particles in amongst clay mineral particles (Fig. 7.3) or as coatings on their surfaces.

Humus

Humus is produced by soil microorganisms as they consume organic materials. It consists of large numbers of atoms of C, H and O, and smaller numbers of atoms of N and S, joined together in complex ways. The number of atoms per particle (i.e. per molecule) ranges from several hundred to several million. The chains of atoms are coiled around one another so that humus particles end up,

Figure 7.3
Much of the colour of red, yellow, orange and brown soils comes from small particles of iron oxide and iron hydroxide compounds, here shown coating clay minerals.
Magnification: × 40 600.
Photograph A W Fordham

more or less, as spheres, but with lots of holes in them. A ball of plastic sponge gives some idea of what a humus particle might look like when magnified.

Most humus particles are at the smaller end of the clay size range, with diameters between 0.000 004 and 0.000 04 mm. Surface areas are enormous, being usually in the range 800–900 m²/g.

Humus particles are usually negatively charged.

WHY SURFACE AREA IS IMPORTANT

Actually, surface area by itself is not all that important. To explain: imagine a person and a life-size statue of that person. Both will have exactly the same surface area, yet they will interact very differently with their environment. One just sits and stares; the other is able to make contact with that environment in a variety of ways. The difference between statue and person comes partly from the types and arrangement of atoms 'inside' and at the surface.

Soil particles are a bit like statues and people. Some, such as quartz, just sit around taking up space, even though they may be of colloidal size. The different types and arrangements of atoms in clay minerals and humus enable them to be more active. Of course they cannot move themselves, but they can be moved by water, soil animals and plant roots and by human activity. They group together; they attract ions from the water around them. And just as there are differences between people, so some types of clay and humus are more active than others.

The combination of activeness and large surface area means that a small amount of clay or humus in a soil has a large effect on the properties of that soil. That is the real importance of large surface area. 'Activeness' goes hand-in-hand with the density of negative charges at their surfaces.

COLLOIDS AND THE PROPERTIES OF GROWING MEDIA

Many important properties of growing media are linked with the colloids in them. First is the link with the ability of growing media to supply nutrients to plants. Nutrients come from the breakdown of minerals and organic matter and from fertilizers, but colloids are very important in regulating the supply (see 'Exchangeable cations', below).

Another link is with pH. This most commonly tested property of growing media has links back to nutrient supply (p. 86). It is also important to life other than plants in growing media (p. 90). A related link is with buffer capacity—the ability of a medium to resist changes in its chemical properties (p. 98).

A major link is with the physical properties of growing media (Chapter 8). These properties have to do with the response of soils to cultivation, the ability of media to hold water and to supply water and air to plant roots, the colour of soils, the shrinking and swelling of some soils as they dry and become wet, the stability of earth dams, and the ability of media to allow good root growth. Particles other than colloids affect these properties, but small amounts of colloids often have large effects.

The links don't end there: they will pop up here and there throughout the rest of the book. And as you will see, in some media the effects of colloids are not always welcome. Large proportions of them in potting media and in heavily trafficked turf soils can have disastrous effects on plant growth. But usually, when they are present in the right proportions, their effects are beneficial.

Figure 7.4
The rhizosphere of a peanut root has a much lower pH than the surrounding soil. *From G Schaller Plant and Soil 97: 439, 1987*

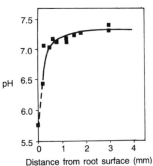

EXCHANGEABLE CATIONS

We can get some idea of exchangeable cations in growing media if we first consider what happens at a stock exchange. At a stock exchange, shares are continuously being passed from one person to another. Sometimes one type of share is exchanged for another; sometimes there is an exchange of shares and

Figure 7.5

Ions cluster near colloid surfaces somewhat like this

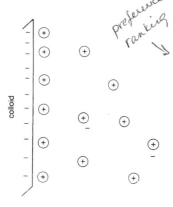

money. There are many different types of shares and some are worth more than others. At the exchange, shares are continually moving on and off the trading boards. Sometimes there is hectic swapping; at other times there is little activity. The size of the trading boards can set a limit to the capacity of the stock exchange to exchange shares.

In growing media, cations are like shares and the surfaces of clay and humus particles are like trading boards. There are seven main cations involved—H^+, Al^{3+}, Ca^{2+}, Mg^{2+}, K^+, NH_4^+ and Na^+—together with many others present in tiny amounts.

Cations, being positively charged, are attracted to the negatively charged surface of colloid particles, where they are held loosely. Often they swap (exchange) places with other cations in the soil water nearby. The capacity of the particles to hold cations is limited to the number of negative charges on their surfaces. Changes in the concentration of cations in the water bathing the surfaces can lead to hectic exchange, just as changing expectations can encourage stock-brokers to push shares on to the trading boards or rapidly remove them.

An increase in the concentration of a cation in the water in a medium will allow that cation to displace other cations from colloid surfaces.

- If we apply the fertiliser ammonium sulphate to a soil, some of the ammonium ions (NH_4^+) will exchange places with cations such as Ca^{2+} and Mg^{2+} that are already on colloid surfaces.
- The roots of some plants give off H^+ ions, so colloid surfaces near roots gain H^+ (Fig. 7.4) and lose other cations. These can then be taken up by the roots.

The picture we want to get across is one of colloid particles surrounded by a cloud of rather loosely held cations, as in Fig. 7.5. When the numbers and types of cations in the surrounding soil water change, there is an exchanging of places with some of the cations around the particles. The total number of cations held is limited by the number of negative charges on the colloids.

Table 7.2

Clay and organic matter contents and cation exchange capacities of topsoils from all main soil groups in the Canberra area (From J R Sleeman and P H Walker, CSIRO Division of Soils, Soils an Land Use Series No. 58, 1979)

% clay	8	9	10	10	11	11	11	14	16	18	20	23	23
% organic matter	1.9	1.6	1.8	2.9	1.3	3.3	7.9	3.1	4.2	4.2	3.6	7.3	5.8
Cation exchange capacity (m.e./100 g)	9.6	8.7	8.6	10.7	8.1	9.1	16.3	11.8	15.8	15.3	15.3	22.5	26.5

Table 7.3

Approximate cation exchange capacities of some soil colloids

Colloid	CEC (m.e./100 g)
Smectite	100
Kaolinite	5
Illite	30
Iron oxides, pH 6	0
Iron oxides, pH 9	some
Humus, pH 5	120
Humus, pH 7	160
Humus, pH 8	210

Terminology

A common way of giving the amounts of exchangeable cations held in growing media is in milliequivalents. One milliequivalent is the atomic mass of the particular element expressed in grams (Table 4.1), divided by 1000 and by the number of positive charges on the cation. Milliequivalent is abbreviated to either m.e. or meq.

Example: The atomic mass of calcium is 40 (g). One m.e. of calcium is

$$\frac{40}{1000 \times 2} = 0.02 \text{ g} = 20 \text{ mg}$$

The total amount of cations held by a material is called its cation exchange capacity (CEC for short). If 100 g of a soil can hold 10.5 m.e. of exchangeable cations, it is said to have a cation exchange capacity of 10.5 m.e./100 g.

The cation exchange capacities of potting media are usually given on a volume basis—for example, 65 m.e./L.

Another common way of giving the amounts of exchangeable cations held in

Figure 7.6

Approximate cation exchange capacities, in m.e./L, of some materials used in potting media. The hatched parts of the columns indicate the range of values found. To convert to a mass basis use:

m.e./100 g =

$$\frac{\text{m.e./L}}{10 \times \text{bulk density in g/mL}}$$

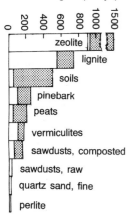

Cation exchange capacity (m.e./L)

a growing medium is in parts per million (ppm). Multiply m.e./100 g by 10 times the atomic mass, divided by the number of positive charges on the cation, to get ppm. For example,

$$4.1 \text{ m.e calcium/100 g} = 4.1 \times \frac{40}{2} \times 10 = 820 \text{ ppm}$$

Many analytical laboratories report exchangeable cation levels in media in ppm.

Amounts of cations held

Sand and silt particles have small surface areas and few negative charges, so hold few cations. Most of the exchangeable cations held in growing media are held by colloids—clay and humus. This means that soils with higher proportions of clay and humus hold more cations than do sandy soils. This is shown in Table 7.2 for the main soils of the Canberra area.

There is a general increase in cation exchange capacity as clay content increases. Variations are due mainly to changes in organic matter content, as is shown in Table 7.2 for the three soils with 11% clay. Measured cation exchange capacities for Australian soils range from 2 m.e./100 g for a 'soil' from coastal Queensland containing 90% sand and 2% clay, to 74 m.e./100 g for a peat from Tasmania containing 55% organic matter.

Different clay minerals have different cation exchange capacities, so two soils having the same clay and organic matter contents can have very different exchange capacities. Table 7.3 gives some exchange capacities for some common soil colloids.

The importance of humus in soils

A small increase in the level of humus in a soil will greatly increase its exchange capacity.

Example: A soil has 1% humus and a cation exchange capacity of 8 m.e./100 g. Let us assume that the humus has an exchange capacity of 160 m.e./100 g. The humus holds $\frac{1}{100} \times 160 = 1.6$ m.e. cations/100 g soil. It accounts for $\frac{1.6}{8} \times 100 = 20\%$ of the exchange capacity. Over several years we add large amounts of organic manures, increasing the humus content to 5%. If the new humus has an exchange capacity of 160 m.e./100 g, it holds $\frac{4}{100} \times 160 = 6.4$ m.e. cations/100 g soil. The soil will now have a cation exchange capacity of $(8 + 6.4) \frac{100}{104} = 13.8$ m.e./100 g.

Humus now accounts for $(1.6 + 6.4) \frac{100}{104} \times \frac{100}{13.8} = 56\%$ of the cation exchange capacity.

Cation exchange in potting mixes

When plants in containers are fed by liquid feeds or slow-release fertilisers, the growing medium need have only a low CEC. However, a moderate CEC (say 50–100 m.e./L) is desirable. The supply of cations will be more even, and losses in drainage waters will be minimised.

Media that are at least half peat, composted pine bark, composted sawdust or vermiculite (by volume) have moderate CECs (Fig. 7.6). Undecomposed organic matter has a low cation exchange capacity. During decomposition the cation exchange capacity of the remaining material gradually increases as humus is formed (Fig. 7.7).

A higher CEC may be achieved most cheaply by using materials that are highly humified. Thoroughly matured composted tree barks, fine dark-coloured peats and lignite (brown coal), vermicomposts and other composts made from garden wastes can all be used, subject to the limitations imposed by their rate of decomposition and the need for good aeration discussed in Chapters 10 and 13. A CEC of 200 m.e./L is fairly easily achieved, and 300 m.e./L is possible. Among the minerals, zeolite has the greatest ability to increase CEC; a 5% by

Figure 7.7
The cation exchange capacity of
sawdust increases greatly during
composting (here with poultry
manure) and moist storage. The
arrow indicates the end of the hot
phase of composting. *From* W S
Galler and C B Davey *Livestock
Waste Management and Pollution
Abatement* Amer. Soc. Agric. Eng.
1971, p.161

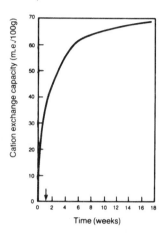

Figure 7.8
Pinus radiata bark retains a greater
proportion of added phosphorus
than does peat, or pine sawdust
aged for 3 months. *From* M Prasad
Scientia Horticulturae 12:203,1980

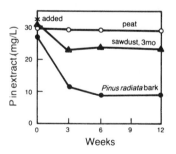

volume addition will increases CEC by about 60 m.e./L. The inclusion of soils of loam or sandier texture in otherwise humified organic potting mixes will probably reduce CEC.

ANIONS—EXCHANGEABLE AND OTHERWISE

Like male and female, ions come in pairs. For every cation there is an anion nearby; no 'homoionics' is possible here. When an anion such as nitrate (NO_3^-) approaches a negatively charged colloid surface, it is repelled.

Where, then, do anions end up? Partly in the water, partly attached to positively charged sites, and partly combined with minerals and humus.

The importance of this? Anions are important because they are the main or only soluble source of several nutrient elements. Those elements are phosphorus, sulphur, nitrogen and molybdenum; the anions are phosphate (PO_4^{3-}, HPO_4^{2-}, $H_2PO_4^-$), sulphate (SO_4^{2-}), nitrate (NO_3^-), and molybdate (MoO_4^{2-}). Other anions commonly present are chloride (Cl^-), bicarbonate (HCO_3^-) and fluoride (F^-). Boron is present mainly as boric acid ($B(OH)_3$); it is included here because it behaves somewhat like some of the anions.

The number of positively charged sites in soils in usually no more than 5% of the number of negatively charges sites, and is often less than 1%. Combination with colloids, mainly iron and aluminium oxides, is therefore the main way that phosphate, molybdate, boric acid, sulphate (and fluoride) are held in soils. They are slowly released into the soil water, as those already there are removed by plants. The firmness with which they are combined is phosphate > molybdate > sulphate = boric acid > chloride > nitrate (the symbol '>' means 'greater than').

Some practical consequences of this are as follows:

- Because most nitrate ions remain in the water, heavy leaching caused by heavy rain or excessive irrigation will quickly remove them from growing media. Plants with deep roots may still be able to get them in soils, but those with shallow roots and those that are in pots may run short unless there is a constant replacement.
- When anions are leached from a medium, they take cations with them. Calcium is usually taken in the greatest amounts, followed by sodium (if present), potassium and magnesium. An extreme of this situation is when excessive amounts of fertilisers such as ammonium sulphate and ammonium nitrate are used. Conversion of ammonium to nitrate, and loss of nitrate by leaching, can remove as much as 200 g Ca/m^2 from a soil in one year. Loss of Ca and Mg leaves the medium more acid.
- The reaction of arsenate (AsO_4^{3-}) with colloids allows a soil to detoxify arsenic from applications of lead arsenate—as far as plants are concerned, but not as far as earthworms are concerned.
- Soil colloids have a large capacity for removing fluoride (F^-) from water, so repeated use of fluoridated water has little effect on the uptake of fluoride by plants from soils.
- Phosphate ions are held quite firmly by soil colloids and so are protected from leaching from soils. However, they are not held with anywhere near the same firmness by most of the materials used in soilless potting mixes. (Exceptions are clay pellets, attapulgite and shale.) Much of any soluble phosphate in a pre-plant addition will remain in solution in the mix. Phosphorus toxicity (Chapter 14) can be one result. Losses by leaching can be considerable (Fig. 7.8). For a given level of phosphate addition, toxicity and losses will be greater from mainly peat-based mixes than from pine bark-based mixes.
- Boric acid and sulphate ions are held fairly loosely. Between 30% and 50% of an addition of boric acid, and close to 100% of an addition of finely ground gypsum are lost from soil-less media during 50 days of leaching similar to that experienced in nurseries. Losses must be replaced via the water used

or through additions from humus or fertilizers. Coarse particles (1–5 mm) of gypsum are an excellent long-term slow-release source of sulphur.

COLOUR

Much of the colour in soils comes from its colloids.

- Humus always darkens any underlying mineral colour.
- Reds, oranges, yellows and browns are caused by varying proportions of several iron oxides/hydroxides.
- Yellow soils and subsoils are generally considered to have been formed under wetter conditions than have red soils.
- Green-blue colours in subsoils are caused by iron hydroxy-carbonates, formed only under waterlogged conditions.
- Grey and whitish colours usually mean a lack of organic matter and long periods of leaching.
- Pale colouration of clay minerals is usually caused by the presence of small amounts of substituting atoms: green—magnesium and different forms of iron; purples, reds and pinks—manganese; blue—chromium.
- Pale colour in potting mixes can indicate an absence of humus due to rawness of bark or sawdust, an inadequate supply of iron or a pH value well below 5.

8

STRUCTURE AND PORE SPACE

Imagine concrete. Gravel forms a framework; the holes between are completely filled with sand grains and smaller particles. Little space for air here, and few holes through which water can move. Hard, solid, immovable.

Most soils contain large and small particles. The small ones are easily able to fit into the spaces between the large ones. If there are enough of them they could completely fill the spaces to make the soil into something like concrete. Why is it then that most natural soils are not like that?

Part of the answer is that soils are crumby, fortunately. In most, the particles are grouped together into small aggregates, or crumbs. These are then arranged together in ways that leave some spaces, or pores, between them. This arrangement of crumbs gives a soil its characteristic structure.

In this chapter we provide information about:

- why crumbs form in natural soils;
- how we can encourage them to form (and hence how to improve soil structure);
- the basis of good structure in other growing media;
- the critical importance of good structure to the supply of air and water to plant roots.

Good structure cannot be bought in a bag as can good nutrition. We must manage our growing media so that structure is maintained or improved.

CRUMBS

Crumbs come in all sizes. The smallest might be a few clay mineral particles clumped together. At the other extreme are clods—anything more than about 5 mm across. A soil with a good structure for plants will have many crumbs from about 0.2 to about 3 mm across. Like bread crumbs, soil crumbs come in all shapes (Fig. 8.1). In undisturbed soils, many crumbs fit loosely together into larger units that can easily be broken apart between the fingers or during cultivation. Gently crumble some garden soil and see for yourself. Soil scientists call natural soil crumbs 'peds'. If a soil is composed mainly of peds when it is moist, it is said to be highly pedal. If peds cannot be recognised in the moist soil it is said to be apedal.

Crumb formation is enhanced with increasing:

- organic matter
- iron and aluminium
- clay
- exchangeable calcium.

It is seriously decreased by increasing levels of exchangeable sodium (and to a lesser extent, magnesium).

Figure 8.1
Typical soil crumbs. Magnification:
× 4.   *Photograph J Coppi*

Organic matter

Organic matter is essential to the formation of soil crumbs, and so are soil microbes. Just mixing some leaves into a soil will not produce crumbs. But allow soil microbes to feed undisturbed on those leaves and they will begin to produce crumbs.

As they feed, soil microbes secrete slimes similar to those we can feel on rotten meat or on the outsides of slugs and earthworms. These slimes stick mineral particles together loosely. Worm casts are held together mainly by slimes produced by bacteria in the worm's gut.

Soil fungi get their food through sticky strands called hyphae. As hyphae weave through the soil they behave like sticky string bags in holding particles together (Figs. 8.2 and 25.5).

Therefore, anything that encourages microbes to multiply rapidly in a soil will encourage crumb formation. Obviously, we must provide plenty of easily digestible food for them by growing plants and adding easily decomposable organic matter.

Figure 8.2
Electron scan picture of a water-stable soil aggregate, with the particles held together mainly by fungal hyphae. Especially noteworthy are the many particles of clay size (less than 0.002 mm) firmly adhering to the hyphae in the lower right-hand corner. Magnification: × 800.   *Photograph J Tisdall*

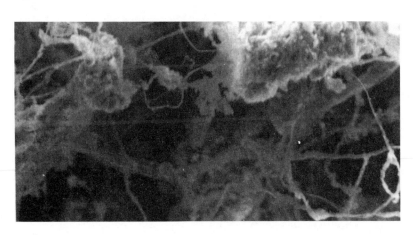

Figure 8.3

Soil crumbs are probably held together in this way. O = organic matter, C = clay mineral particles. *After W W Emerson J. Soil Sci.* 10: 235, 1959

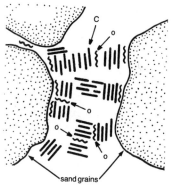

Growing plants mean litter falling to the soil surface and roots growing and dying in the soil. The soil immediately around living roots (the rhizosphere) is always much richer in microbes than is the rest of the soil. This means that plants with many fine roots closely exploring the soil will support large populations of microbes. Grasses and cereals are like this, so crumb formation is high and soil structure good under pastures that have not been cultivated for many years and under turf that has not been compacted by heavy use. A gram of old pasture soil may have 2 to 5 km of fungal hyphae!

The structures of the soils of orchards and plantations are much better if cover crops of grasses and legumes are grown rather than when the soil is repeatedly cultivated to control weeds. The disadvantage of applying extra water and mowing the grass can be small compared with the advantages.

Anything that increases plant growth will tend to increase crumb formation. Overcoming nutrient deficiencies, providing extra water, draining boggy soils and reducing sodicity (see below) will all work in that direction. Time, too, is necessary. Disturbing a soil every few months will damage roots and can easily break up newly formed crumbs. Stable crumbs and excellent structure take several years to develop.

Adding easily decomposable organic matter by digging in a green-manure crop or partly matured compost will cause an explosion in microbial activity in a soil. Crumb formation will be extensive, but the binding will be loose and easily destroyed by further cultivation. The soil will be 'fluffed up', but the crumbs need the influence of plant roots and time for them to become stable.

Organic materials such as straw and sawdust, being of low nitrogen (and phosphorus and sulphur) content, are not quickly decomposed and so take much longer to produce crumbs. Supplementing them with nutrients will hasten decomposition and crumb formation.

Slimes and 'sticky string bags' can themselves be eaten by other microbes, so breaking up loosely made crumbs. But with the passage of time, several things can happen to stabilise crumbs. Roots pushing through the soil, and getting thicker, compress the crumbs, forcing the mineral particles and organic matter close together. Wetting causes soils to expand a little or a lot; drying causes them to shrink. Repeated wetting and drying seem to squeeze crumbs and so stabilise them. As microbes eat organic materials they produce humus, for them a waste product not unlike faeces for animals. It resists microbial attack and, when sandwiched between mineral particles, resists it even more. Humus may also stabilise crumbs by forming coatings around them.

In summary, for organic matter to help form stable soil crumbs, we need microbes, food for them, plant roots, and time—time to allow the other three to interact undisturbed.

Clay, iron and aluminium

Organic matter can hold sand and silt particles together, but the resulting crumbs are easily broken up. Some clay is also necessary before stable crumbs are formed. The 'inside' of a typical soil crumb looks something like Fig. 8.3. The organic matter joining mineral particles is itself partly held together by iron and aluminium atoms. If they are removed, soil crumbs are less stable.

Clay particles can also form 'skins' around crumbs. A soil with a high clay content may have a very poor cloddy structure unless it also contains organic matter. The organic matter, in binding particles into crumbs, also limits their size to below that of clods.

Exchangeable cations

Exchangeable cations have big effects on the stability of soil crumbs. If most of them are H^+, Al^{3+} and Ca^{2+}, crumbs will usually be stable. But if the percentage that is exchangeable sodium (ESP for short!) goes above about 6, crumbs become

Figure 8.4
Poor seedbed produced by cloddy soil

increasingly unstable when wet. Such soils are called 'sodic' because of their sodium content.

Exchangeable magnesium also has an effect on soil crumbs. If calcium is the main exchangeable cation and magnesium makes up only 10–15% of total cations, its effect is small. But as Ca^{2+} goes down and Mg^{2+} goes up, its effect becomes noticeable. In general, a high proportion of exchangeable magnesium imparts a 'toughness' to a soil. This can make the soil difficult to cultivate. Soils with high sodium and high magnesium have an especially poor structure.

Sodic soils tend to waterlog easily and are either slippery and sticky or like concrete. They erode easily and are difficult to manage. Crusts form on their surfaces. Detail is given in Chapter 21. They are improved by replacing the sodium with calcium.

GOOD SOIL STRUCTURE

Soils with good structure will have moderate organic matter contents (perhaps 3% or more), some clay, and calcium as the main exchangeable cation. They will probably have been left undisturbed (uncultivated and not subjected to the repeated traffic of machinery or feet) for several years or more. They will therefore be growing pasture, bushland or forest, or they will be in gardens to which large amounts of organic materials have been added.

Good structure means that the mineral particles are bound together into crumbs that are then loosely arranged into larger groupings. Cultivation breaks these groupings to give a seedbed of soil crumbs or smaller groupings of crumbs. Such a soil is said to be *friable* and when cultivated to have good *tilth*. A soil of poor structure may break down either into a powder of individual particles and very small crumbs or into large clods (Fig. 8.4). Tilth is poor, and so may be seed germination. The crumbs in a soil of good structure resist being broken by cultivation or rain.

Good structure means that there are spaces between crumbs. The larger spaces may be animal burrows, the channels left by dead and decayed roots, or cracks caused by shrinkage of the soil on drying. But there are also smaller spaces, with a soil of good structure having a wide range of space sizes. The importance of these spaces is given below.

STRUCTURE IN OTHER GROWING MEDIA

Potting mixes

Most potting mixes contain little or no soil. Crumbs of the type found in well-structured natural soils cannot be formed. Their place is taken by particles of sand, other minerals and organic materials. Structure is determined mainly by the range of particle sizes present. In other words, structure is determined mainly by texture.

Therefore, most of the particles need to be in the size range of soil crumbs— 0.2–3 mm diameter. A high proportion of smaller particles will clog pores between the bigger particles (see Table 13.4), giving a poor structure.

The structure of potting mixes can deteriorate if particles break down or collapse. For example, decomposition of organic materials such as sawdust and bark will reduce particle size; collapse of vermiculite particles through rough handling can cause them to clog pores. The particles of materials used in potting mixes must be stable enough for the structure to be maintained during the expected time plants are to be held in them.

More detail on the physical properties of potting mixes in Chapter 13.

Root zone mixes for intensively used turf

The crumb structure of natural soils is easily destroyed by heavy traffic. One way of avoiding this under intensively used turf is to grow the grass in a specially prepared sandy soil. The low clay and silt content of these root zone mixes means that crumbs are not formed. Structure depends on texture. Sands for these mixes are chosen carefully so that even under heavy traffic there is still enough pore space between the sand grains for water, air and roots.

More detail about root zone mixes is given in Chapter 17.

DO NOT DO THESE THINGS TO YOUR SOIL

Do not:

- Drive heavy machinery over the soil, especially when it is wet.
- Allow quagmire conditions to develop on playing fields by allowing play under all conditions and refusing to install a drainage system.
- Ignore the signs of developing problems and take no remedial or preventive action.
- Destroy all microbial and small animal activity in a soil with heavy and repeated applications of chemicals.
- Carefully remove all organic materials in the interests of tidiness.
- Irrigate heavily so that the soil is frequently waterlogged.
- Irrigate with high-sodium water and don't bother about taking any precautions.
- Bash the soil about with cultivating implements, push it around wet with dozer blades, pulverise it with rollers.
- Never bother to get expert help when constructing areas for turf. What has been done in the past is good enough. Use what you have on hand. She'll be right.
- Throw any old thing, especially easily decomposed organic materials, into a potting mix and ram them down firmly into the pot.

Do the opposite of these practices, and your management of your soil's structure will be good.

PORE SPACE

Holes are important. What would we do if there were no mouths or nostrils? How would intending passengers fare if trains and buses had no holes into or inside them? Where would we put posts, building foundations, lake waters or the sea?

So it is in growing media: the solid bits are there only to provide holes of shapes and sizes that suit plant roots. Well, that's one way of looking at it. And as we shall see, that way has a lot of truth.

In this section we encourage readers to look at growing media as plant roots find them. We encourage you to look from the inside, out—from the insides of holes to the outer walls of those holes, which are the surfaces of particles and crumbs.

Holes in growing media are called *pores*. Some pores are between particles and crumbs; some are inside them. Together, all pores in a medium are called the *pore space*, or total pore space.

Total pore space

The total pore space of a medium is the percentage of its volume that is not filled with solids. A total pore space of 40% means that in every litre there is 400 mL of pore space and 600 mL of solids (Fig. 8.5).

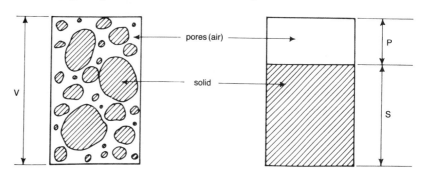

Figure 8.5
The total volume (V) of a growing medium is made up of the volume of solids (S) and the volume of pore space (P)

Percent pore space = $\frac{P}{V} \times 100$

The total amount of pore space varies from as little as 30% in a heavily trafficked field and turf soil to about 95% in some peats. Good garden, field and turf soils contain about 50% pore space and good potting mixes about 60–80%. The reason for the extra pore space needed in containers is explained on p. 64.

Compaction reduces total pore space. Total pore space is important, but pore shape and size is even more important.

Pore space and size

Life for small soil animals must be something like cave exploring for humans. Sometimes movement is rapid through enormous caverns; at other times progress can be made only by squeezing through the narrowest of cracks. Frequent dead-ends makes progress slow. Pore space is like a huge 3-D maze.

We can get some idea of the shape of pore space in growing media by looking at a stack of tennis balls, glass beads, marbles or Christmas tree decorations. A plaster cast of the spaces would look something like Fig. 8.6. Here the pattern is regular, but it is anything but regular in most media (Fig. 8.7). Only in root zone mixes composed mainly of rounded sand grains, all of about the same size, will the pore space have anything like a regular pattern.

Perhaps one of the most important messages we want to get across is that pore space has a wide range of sizes. At one end of the range are small ('thin', narrow) pores within crumbs and particles, between small particles closely packed together and between larger particles meeting at sharp angles. Grading up from these are every possible size to the largest ('thickest', widest) between large

Figure 8.6
The shape of the 'pores' between stacked tennis balls

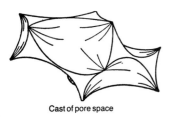

Cast of pore space

Figure 8.7
Soil pores (and crumbs).
Magnification: × 1000. *Photograph*
A D Rovira

particles and loosely packed aggregates. Animal burrows, old root channels and cracks make up a system of even larger pores.

It follows that the average size of pores will be greatest for:

- gravels and coarse sands;
- loosely packed media;
- soils with well-developed structure, especially if laced with cracks and animal burrows.

Importance of pore shape and size

Largeness ('thickness') and smallness ('thinness') of pore space is of the utmost importance to how well a growing medium is able to satisfy the needs of plants. The following summary will serve as an introduction to the detail to be given in later chapters.

- In a 'just-drained' medium, water is held in the smallest pores and as a coating on particle surfaces.
- In a 'just-drained' medium, the larger pores are filled with air.
- If most pores in a medium are small, it will hold much water but have very little air when 'just-drained'.
- On the other hand, a medium with mostly large pores will hold very little water.
- A medium with a wide range of pore sizes can hold water and air in nearly equal amounts.
- Movement of water will be more rapid through a medium with many large pores than through one with few large pores.
- Plant roots may find it more difficult to push through a medium with mainly small pores than through one with larger pores.

Figure 8.8
Diagrams showing the proportions
of solids, air and water in a soil
under different conditions:
(a) Approximate proportions of
solids and pore space in a good top
soil.
(b) Waterlogged.
(c) Completely dried.
(d) Minimum air-filled porosity for
good growth of many plants. (e)
'Ideal' proportions of air and water
for excellent plant growth. (f) Effect
of severe compaction.

Pore space, water and air

We can summarise information about the proportions of solid particles, air and water in growing media in diagrams such as those of Figure 8.8. A natural soil of excellent porosity may have 45% solids and 55% total pore space (Fig. 8.8(a)). Waterlogging is given by Fig. 8.8(b); the soil after baking in the summer sun is given by Fig. 8.8(c). A just-drained soil may have the composition given by Figs 8.8(d) or (e). Transpiration by plants or evaporation from the surface will take it back towards Fig. 8.8(c).

The volume percentage of a medium filled with air when 'just-drained' is usually called its air-filled porosity. Other terms used include air capacity, air space and air porosity.

Bulk density

Bulk density is a kind of opposite to the total pore space of a soil. It is defined as the mass in grams of a dried cubic centimetre (cm^2) or millilitre (mL) of soil. Obviously, the more pore space there is in that mL, the less will be the bulk density (Table 8.1; Fig. 8.9). But also, as the density of the actual particles increases, bulk density will also increase.

Table 8.1
Total pore space in a fine sandy loam soil compacted to different bulk densities (*From* W J Flocker et al. *Soil Sci. Soc. Amer. Proc* 23: 188, 1959)

Compaction level	Total porosity (volume %)	Bulk density of dry soil (g/mL)	Air filled porosity (volume %)	Water (volume %)
Nil	58	1.13	42	16
	54	1.23	37	17
	50	1.33	30	20
	46	1.43	28	18
	42	1.54	24	18
	38	1.64	19	19
Greatest	34	1.74	9	25

Different minerals have different particle densities, but for most practical purposes we can assume that they weigh 2.6 g/mL, a little below the density of quartz at 2.65 g/mL. Different organic materials also have different particle densities, but 1.55 g/mL is a good average.

Example: A solid lump of quartz 1 cm × 1 cm × 1 cm will have a mass of 2.65 g. If it is smashed up into sand, it might have a volume of 1.6 mL and so have a bulk density of $^{2.65}/1.6$ = 1.65 g/mL. Total pore space will be 0.6 mL or $^{0.6}/1.6$ × 100 = 37.5%.

Mineral soils commonly have bulk densities in the range 1.0–1.9 g/mL (Table 8.2). This means that a cubic metre of soil (dry) will have a mass of between 1000 and 1900 kg. As moist soil can contain from 0.1 to 0.5 g water per mL, the total mass of a cubic metre of moist soil could range from 1100 to 2400 kg.

Organic materials such as sawdust, milled bark and peatmoss commonly have bulk densities in the range 0.05–0.2 g/mL. A cubic metre (dry) will have a mass of 50–200 kg. This is between 3 and 20% of the mass of the same volume of sand or soil. Even with water contents of 0.3–0.5 g/mL, total moist masses of 350–800 kg/m^3 are still well below those of sand or soil.

The difference in density between minerals and organic materials means that soils and potting mixes rich in organic materials have lower bulk densities than those rich in minerals. In soils, increasing organic matter further reduces bulk

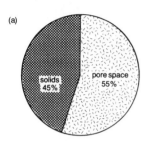

(a)

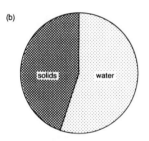

(b)

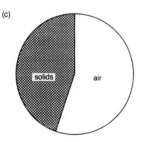

(c)

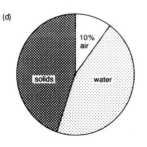

(d)

(e)

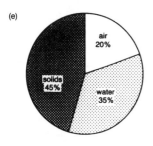

(f)

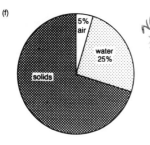

density by giving crumbs with more pore space inside them.

In potting mixes, 'lightness' (low bulk density) can have advantages and disadvantages. The advantages include less staff fatigue and lower transport costs. A disadvantage is that pots can more easily tip over, especially with older, taller plants. Sand is added to organic mixes as ballast and to aid wetting.

How to avoid hassles when ordering bulk materials

Information about bulk density is essential when materials such as sand and soil mixes are being ordered. These materials are often sold by volume, as they have to fit a hole of known volume. However, just ordering, say, 1000 m³ of soil, without qualification, will lead to dispute. A volume of 1000 m³ at the time the soil is loaded into trucks will settle to perhaps 700–750 m³ during transport and packing into a planter bed. The final volume is often specified on the basis of 85–90 % of heavily compacted (rodded) volume.

To reduce hassles, some contracts specify soil by mass, with a measure of bulk density being used to decide how much mass is needed to give the required volume. In the example above, soil with an in-place bulk density of 1.5 would have had a loose bulk density of 1.05–1.13 kg/L. It is necessary to state the water content of the soil because of the effect of water content on mass of a given volume of soil (see below). Considerable care is needed in writing contracts so that all parties concerned know and agree on exactly what is being agreed.

Compaction

To compact is to press together, to compress, to fill in, to make firm. And that is exactly what happens when growing media are compacted: the crumbs and particles are pressed together so that the spaces between them are reduced in size. As we shall see below, this usually has a big effect on plant growth. For soils the effects of compaction are usually more severe with those of fine texture (clays) than with those of coarser texture (loams and sands).

Detecting compaction

- Through poor plant growth. Compaction is only one cause of poor growth; poor nutrition, disease, lack of light, low temperatures, may all contribute. If you suspect that compaction is at least a part cause of poor growth ask yourself: 'Has there been any recent or long-past event that could have compacted the soil?' You will be asking about heavy foot or vehicular traffic. If the answer is 'yes' or 'maybe', do some measuring (see Fig. 8.10 and Chapter 33).
- A compacted layer will be most easily seen if the soil is moistened.
- Measure the bulk density, because compaction increases the bulk density of a soil (as shown in Table 8.1). Compare the bulk density of the soil in the area of poor growth with that of soil under more vigorous plants nearby. Otherwise interpret bulk density readings for soils according to the information in Table 8.2.
- Measure (roughly) soil strength. A couple of days after the soil has received soaking rain or irrigation, push into the soil a screwdriver, sharpened length of metal rod, or a sharpened pencil (Fig. 8.10). The greater the strength of the soil, the more you will have to push, and the more your palm will hurt. If your pushing hurts more, and penetration is less into the soil under the stunted plants than under nearby more vigorous plants, suspect that compaction is contributing to the poor growth.

Effects of compaction

Reduced infiltration rate: Compaction collapses the larger pores—those that are filled with air in a medium that has just drained (Table 8.1). These are the pores

Figure 8.9

Example of the effect of compaction on the bulk density of a soil

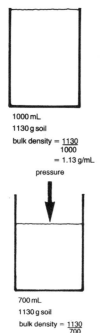

Figure 8.10

Compaction can be detected by trying to push a pencil or sharpened piece of steel rod into *moist* soil. If you cannot push the pencil or rod in, the strength of the soil is high enough to seriously reduce root growth

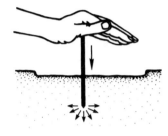

Table 8.2

Guidelines for interpreting figures for the dry bulk densities of soils

Bulk density (g/cm³ or g/mL)	Sandy soils	Loams	Clay soils
<1.0	—	seedbed conditions	satisfactory
1.0–1.2	—	satisfactory	satisfactory
1.2–1.4	very open	satisfactory	some too compact
1.4–1.6	satisfactory	some too compact	very compact
1.6–1.8	most too compact above 1.7	very compact	extremely compact
>1.8	very compact	extremely compact	—

that allow rapid movement of water through a medium. Compaction, therefore, slows water movement into a medium (infiltration rate) and its ability to drain quickly (Fig. 8.11). This means increased surface runoff from soils, with increased risks of erosion and less water in the soil for plants. Poor drainage often means waterlogging in and above a compacted layer of soil and hence reduced root growth.

Reduced availability of water: A small amount of compaction of a 'fluffy' medium often increases the amount of available water (p.69) held in it. Hence the need to slightly compact the soil around newly planted seedlings in recently dug soil or to gently 'dump' newly filled pots.

But more severe compaction usually decreases the proportion of water in the medium that is readily available to plants. This is because compaction reduces

Figure 8.11

Effect of compacting a soil/peat/coarse sand (60:25:15) mix on the growth of tomatoes and on the rate of water movement through the mix. *From A C Bunt Plant and Soil* 15: 228, 1961

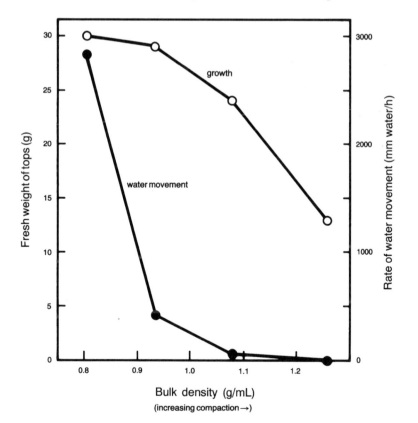

Figure 8.12
Barley roots become thicker and shorter as the strength of the soil they are trying to grow in is increased. *From M J Goss J. Experimental Botany* 28: 96, 1977; *Courtesy of Oxford University Press*

0 bar

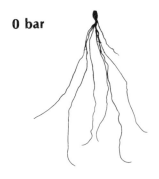

0.07 bar

0.14 bar

0.25 bar

the average size of the pores. Water is held more tightly in small pores than in larger pores (p. 62), so plants must use more force to get enough water.

Reduced air supply to roots: Compaction reduces the average size of pores. More water is held in the medium after drainage has stopped. This means that the proportion of air in the medium is reduced. Often compaction has a bigger effect on air-filled porosity than on total pore space (Table 8.1). Oxygen supply to roots should still be adequate if air-filled porosity is still 10% of the volume of the topsoil. More detail is given in Chapter 10.

Increased soil strength: Compaction increases the strength of a soil as far as plant roots are concerned. We can see this as follows:

We all know what it is like to walk head on into a very strong wind. We have to use a lot of energy to move a short distance; we soon feel exhausted, and have little energy for other activities. So it is with roots. They find a compacted soil to be 'strong' and so use a lot of energy in trying to push their way through it. There are few large pores for the roots to move through. Even those that there are, in a compacted soil, have walls that cannot easily be pushed aside by the growing root. The plant has less energy for producing leaves and flowers, so plants in compacted soils are usually stunted by comparison with nearby plants in less compacted soil (Fig. 8.11). They are in a state of permanent exhaustion.

High soil strength is especially damaging to those young roots that are to form the main underground network. They are larger than those that branch from them. Few large pores means that the plant cannot develop an extensive network of main roots (Fig. 8.12). The whole root system tends to be shallow and small. With less soil being explored, the plant is less well supplied with nutrients and water. It wilts sooner than a plant in less compacted soil.

But compaction is not the only reason why soil strength increases. It increases as a soil dries out (Fig. 8.13). Roots really have a tough time in a dryish, heavily compacted soil. Often they just give up.

Water aids compaction of soils

A dry soil compacts little, even under heavy traffic. There is no water to lubricate particle surfaces so they remain where they are. All that happens is a powdering of the surface soil.

Compaction becomes easier and easier as soil water content increases. It is easiest when the soil is a little wetter than field capacity. As the soil becomes even wetter, compaction again becomes less, but then intense traffic can make a slurry of the surface soil. On drying, the slurry may set into a hard crust that can be just as poor for plant growth as compacted soil.

This means that traffic—foot or vehicular—damages soils most easily for one or two days immediately after rain or irrigation, that is, until the soil has drained to about field capacity. Traffic should be kept to a minimum on soils during that time. Of course waiting for a day or two after each rain is totally unacceptable for sports turf. Root zone mixes for turf must drain rapidly even when compacted. Hence the use of special sands for sports turf.

Overcoming compaction

Prevention is the best cure:

- In soils, wherever possible maintain and improve structure. Restrict or ban movement of vehicles or people within two days of rain or irrigation.
- For intensively used turf, use only the very best materials during construction (Chapter 17).
- For media in containers, use materials giving an appropriate particle size range (Chapter 13). Allow for decomposition during the life of the plants in the container. Don't compress the mix during pot filling or planting.

Figure 8.13

The strength of a soil increases as it becomes drier and as it is compacted. *From* B W Eavis *Plant and Soil* 36: 613, 1972

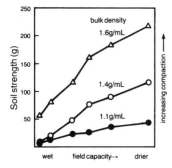

Proceed as follows when compaction is already present:

- Cultivate deeply enough to break up the whole of the compacted part of soil. This will usually be no more than the top 15 cm. Deeper cultivation may be needed where there is a natural clay pan or where repeated ploughing at the same depth has compacted the soil just under that depth. Use implements such as chisel ploughs for large areas and forks for small areas (Chapter 31).
- Cultivate when the soil is rather drier than field capacity so that the compacted soil is shattered into small clods.
- Follow cultivation with every possible means of maintaining and improving structure.
- Cultivation to relieve compaction should always be the final action after heavy construction machinery has left a building site and one of the first actions in preparing a site during landscaping.

Special procedures for relieving compaction in turf soils are given in Chapter 19.

9 GROWING MEDIA AND WATER

No water: no plants. We must all live with that fact. No matter how perfect a growing medium may be in all other ways, unless it contains, and continues to contain, enough water for plant growth, it is useless.

Nature is not especially good at providing water in just the right amounts for the plants most of us want to grow. Either we must live with this and plan accordingly, or we must provide extra or remove excess.

The technology of providing more (irrigation) and of removing excess (drainage) is dealt with in later chapters. Here we are concerned with what really goes on as a growing medium becomes wet and then is dried out by plants or evaporation. When we understand what goes on 'down below', looking after the water needs of the plants in our care will be easier.

Background summary

We have already learnt that growing media consist of large numbers of small inorganic and organic particles. In sands and most potting mixes many of the particles are relatively large. Even when packed together there are spaces (pores) between them. In natural soils, the particles are usually arranged together into groups called crumbs or aggregates. There are pores between crumbs and also inside them. Pores contain either air or water. It is through pores that air and water move into and through growing media.

INFILTRATION

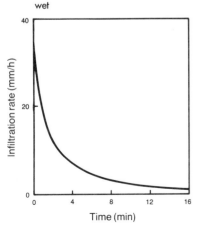

Figure 9.1
Example of the fall in infiltration rate to a steady value as a soil becomes wet

The first contact between a growing medium and water is usually at the surface of the medium. Water arriving there will either soak in, remain on the surface, or run down-slope. Only that water which actually soaks in is going to be of much benefit to plants.

An important property of a growing medium is the rate at which water soaks into it. This is called its *infiltration rate*; it is most easily measured as mm (height) of water soaking in per hour. Infiltration rate can vary from zero for water-repellent sands or closely packed, dry organic potting mix, to many hundreds of mm per hour for coarse sands and mixes such as those used for growing epiphytic orchids.

The infiltration rate of any medium decreases as it becomes wetter (Fig. 9.1), finally reaching a steady value that is maintained until a drainage system clogs up or the water table comes near the surface. It is this steady infiltration rate that is most important.

If the steady infiltration rate is very low, say less than 5 mm per hour, even very gentle rain falling on moist medium will cause surface ponding or runoff of water.

- The surfaces of playing fields will remain mushy for days after rain, allowing play to cause much damage to the turf.
- In areas of low rainfall, full use will not be made of the rain that does fall.

- Much irrigation water will run to waste because few irrigation systems are able to supply water at such low rates.
- Plants in containers may grow poorly because too little water is able to reach their roots.

In these situations the only solution is to increase infiltration rate.

Table 9.1
Effect of slitting at 37 slits/m² on the rate of infiltration of water into compacted turf soils. The measurements were made one year after slitting had started. (*From* H A Kamp *Zeitschrift Vegetationstechnik* 2: 17, 1979)

Treatment frequency/month	Infiltration rate (mm/hour)	
	Training area	Main pitch
1	35	46
2	60	115

Increasing infiltration rate

An analogy will show how to increase infiltration rate. To quickly pour a lot of water into a drum, we need a funnel with a wide spout, not a tiny kitchen funnel. Replace the drum with soil, and the funnels with pores, and we are back where we belong: Many large pores are needed for a high infiltration rate.

Therefore, infiltration rate is increased by:

- Increasing permeability. The amount of water percolating through a medium is determined by the permeability of the least pervious part. The number of large pores through that part must be increased. In practice that means:
- Opening up the surface. Crusts on the surface of soils greatly reduce infiltration rate, as can a compacted mat of dead organic matter that has been stuck together with microbial slimes. Crusts are common on sodic soils (Chapter 21); their permeability can be improved with gypsum. Often, crusts and mats must be broken up mechanically.
- Relieving compaction. This will mean digging or some other form of cultivation where this is possible. Otherwise deliberately providing large 'pores' by coring, spiking or slitting can greatly increase infiltration rate (Table 9.1).
- Improving structure. Well-structured soils automatically have many large pores that give high permeability (Chapters 8 and 25).
- Using another medium. For turf this will mean remaking the area with a more suitable (sandier) material (Table 9.2). For containers, this means decreasing the amount of 'fines' in the medium (Chapter 13).
- Overcoming water repellency.
- Breaking up any heavy, impermeable clay layer.
- Use liquid soil conditioners? Some scientific research has found that they did not improve the hydraulic conductivity of the soils used. On the other hand, a recent report showed that one product reduced bulk density, water runoff and erosion of a sandy loam soil (Table 9.3).

Decreasing infiltration rate

The need to increase infiltration rate is much more common than is the need to decrease it. But sometimes potting media let water run through too quickly; they hold too little water. Increasing the proportion of particles of 0.1–0.25 mm and smaller will decrease infiltration rate and increase the amount of water held.

Figure 9.2
There is a mutual attraction between water and the surfaces of many materials

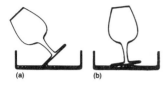

(a)   (b)

Table 9.2
Approximate steady infiltration rates for different soils

Soil	Steady infiltration rate (mm/hour)
Deep sands, aggregated silts	more than 20
Deep sandy loams	10–20
Clay loams, shallow sandy loams, soils low in organic matter	5–10
Clays	1–5
Sodic clay soils	less than 1

Table 9.3
Effect of the soil conditioner Agri-Sc® on the effects of heavy rain on a loamy sand soil. (From M A Fullen, A M Tye, D A Pritchard and H A Reynolds *Soil Use and Land Management* 9:21 1993)

	Relative	
Treatment	Runoff	Erosion
Untreated	1.6	2.9
Treated (0.5 mL/m²)	1.0	1.0

Figure 9.3
The narrower the column of water, the higher its rise against the pull of gravity. This demonstrates that water is held more tightly as the size of the space it is in decreases.

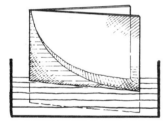

WATER AFTER INFILTRATION

Water wets media. That's obvious. But why is it that some of the water percolating through a medium remains in it to give it the feeling of wetness? For the answer to that and for an understanding of many other things about water in growing media, read on.

Water and surfaces

Run water into a flat-bottomed dish or plate to a depth of 1–2 mm. Now take a wine glass and gently touch its base to the water, as shown in Fig. 9.2(a). Notice that as you raise it a little a column of water is drawn up from the dish. Now tilt the glass so that its base is more nearly horizontal, (as shown in Fig. 9.2(b)). Notice that a film of water runs along the base of the glass as the space between it and the water surface narrows (becomes smaller). A thin column of water is held above the surface of the water in the dish by the combined effects of the ability of water molecules to 'stick together' (cohere) and attraction between water and other solids, in this case the base of the glass.

These effects can be seen in action even more dramatically:

- When two sheets of clean glass arranged to form a wedge are dipped into water, the result is as shown in Fig. 9.3. The smaller the space between the sheets, the greater the height of water supported.
- The narrower the bore of a capillary tube, the greater the height of water column supported (Fig. 9.4).

Figure 9.4
The narrower a capillary tube, the greater the height to which water rises in it. *Photograph J Coppi*

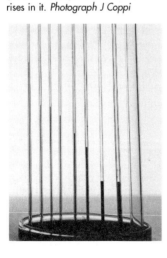

These examples show that water is attracted to glass surfaces with a 'pull' large enough to support quite a mass of water against the 'pull' of gravity, with the smaller cohesive 'pull' between water molecules holding the column of water together. The narrower the space, the greater the height of water held to reach this mass. It follows that water in small (narrow) spaces is held more firmly than that in larger (wider) spaces.

Water in pores in growing media

Water is attracted to the surfaces of particles of (most of) the materials in growing media. (Those few with water repellent properties are the exception.) It is held on those surfaces and in the pores between them. Some proof is as follows:

- A small clod of dry soil will easily soak up a drop of water. This is the way in which water moves sideways in soils.
- Water can be seen glistening at the surface of medium in a pot watered only by standing it in a dish of water, or on a capillary mat.
- Water dripping onto dry soil can be seen to slowly move sideways through the soil.
- Growing media that have been allowed to drain after being made wet still retain much water.

It can also be shown that the smallest (narrowest) pores in growing media hold water more firmly than larger (wider) pores. In a medium that has been saturated with water and allowed to drain, the water remaining is held in the smaller pores. They are often referred to as capillary pores, because they are narrow like capillary tubes. The larger ones filled with air are called non-capillary pores.

FIELD CAPACITY IN NATURAL SOILS

Figure 9.5
Where water is held in a growing medium

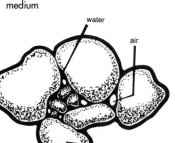

A day or two after rain or irrigation, most drainage down through a soil will have stopped. The soil is now said to be at field capacity. It is able to hold about this amount of water for some time, if evaporation from its surface and transpiration by plants is prevented. The soil feels moist. It is easy to crumble. Cultivation is easiest when a soil is at field capacity or a little drier.

In a soil at field capacity, all the smallest pores and some that we might call medium-sized are filled with water. They are able to hold the water against the pull of gravity. It has been found that pores up to 0.03 mm across—the capillary pores—are filled with water at field capacity. There is also a film of water on the surfaces of particles bordering large pores (Fig. 9.5).

Soil texture and the amounts of water held

A quick look at the sizes of pores in a stack of tennis balls and in a stack of marbles will soon show that they are much smaller between the marbles than between the tennis balls. The same is true at the scale of sizes of soil particles: on average, pores in coarse sands are bigger than those in, for example, fine sands or clay loams. Figure 9.5 illustrates this.

Figure 9.6 summarises information about the *approximate* amounts of water held in soils of various textures. We say that these are approximate figures because the way soil particles are arranged together—the structure of the soil—has a big effect on the amount of water that can be held. The figures for sandy loam with and without organic matter, and the two clays, are examples. A well-structured soil will usually hold more water at field capacity than will a soil of similar texture but poor structure. Put another way, good structure gives soils more pores of the size that hold water against the pull of gravity.

Texture, therefore, is a useful but only approximate guide to the ability of natural soils to hold water.

CONTAINER CAPACITY

Underneath topsoils are subsoils. Underneath pots is air, and underneath the root zone sand of most bowling greens is gravel containing large pockets of air. That difference makes a very big difference to the amount of water that is held in just-drained media in pots and root zones over gravel. Just-drained potted media are said to be at 'container capacity' instead of 'field capacity'. As a root zone

Figure 9.6

Approximate amounts of available and unavailable water held by soils of different textures

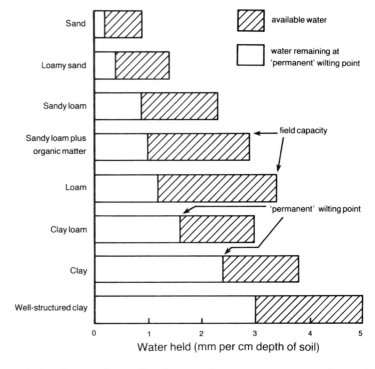

Figure 9.7

A sponge being used to show the effect of change in height on the amount of water held in a container

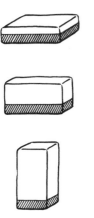

underlain by gravel is really a big pot, the term container capacity can be used for it too.

We show what happens by three simple experiments.

1. Saturate a thick towel with water and peg it on the clothes line. Watch what happens. First, water drains rapidly from the higher parts of the towel, flowing freely from the lowest edge. The flow gradually lessens and finally stops. Now feel the towel from top to bottom. The top feels relatively dry, although it is still damp. As you move down, you will find that gradually, and then more rapidly, it becomes wetter. The bottom few centimetres will still be saturated and water can easily be squeezed from that part of the towel.

2. From offcuts of plastic foam (or mattress overlay) 12 mm thick, cut seven squares about 80 × 80 mm. Submerge them in a bucket of water and, while submerged, squeeze them until all air has been removed. Make a stack of them while they are still submerged. Then carefully lift the stack from the water and place it on a wire mesh base. Leave until all drainage has stopped.

 Now remove the pieces of foam one at a time, starting at the top. Carefully squeeze as much water as possible from each into a container. Measure the volume or mass of water from each piece. (Remember that 1 mL of water weighs 1 g.) You will notice an increase in water content as you go down the stack. In fact, the bottom piece of foam will be almost saturated. The volumes of water removed will be something like those in Table 9.4.

 If the stack is made taller, there is no change in the proportions of water and air in the lower sponges. The same applies when the stack is shorter; all pieces of foam in a stack three high will be quite wet.

3. Saturate a sponge by squeezing and letting go while it is under water. Carefully remove it with its largest surface horizontal and place it on a wire screen. After drainage stops, note the height of the saturated portion of the sponge.

 Now tip the sponge onto its longest side (Fig. 9.7). More water will immediately drain from it. After drainage has stopped, note that the height

Table 9.4
Water held in a stack of pieces of plastic foam after drainage has stopped. The pieces were each 12 mm high, had pore holes about 0.8 mm across. Foam with pores of a different size would have given different proportions of air and water

7 pieces of plastic foam	Volume of water held (mL)	Water (volume %)	Air (volume %)
—	6.5	13	82
—	6.8	14	81
—	7.3	15	80
—	16.4	33	62
—	43.2	87	8
—	44.3	89	6
—	47.3	95	0

of the saturated portion is the same as was the height in the flat sponge, but of course the total volume of water held is less.

Finally, tip the sponge onto its end. More water will drain out, but again the height of the saturated portion remains the same.

In going from a shallow sponge to a deep sponge, the average water content of the sponge has decreased. These observations apply directly to media in containers.

Explanation

Why is it that water doesn't simply run right out the bottom of a sponge or wet towel? After all, there is no soil barrier there, just air.

For an answer we go back to the basics at the beginning of the chapter; water is attracted to many solid surfaces, and small pores in materials hold water more firmly than larger pores. Our sponge and towel have many small pores. Below them there is only one large pore—the whole of the atmosphere. Its surfaces can exert no pull on the water in the sponge.

Water can flow from the sponge only when all the suction ability of the pores in it is fully met. This happens only when the bottom pores in the sponge are completely saturated and there is a slight 'head' or weight of water above. Then water can flow under gravity from the sponge, but not beyond the point where the suction ability of pores in the sponge is still fully met.

If, by squeezing, we removed some water from a just-drained sponge, the suction ability of its pores would be less than fully met. Water would be sucked into it if it is touched into a pool of water. We do it every day in mopping up spills!

LAYERS

Now suppose we put our sponge on a layer of gravel with particles that just pass through a sieve with 10 mm holes. The pores in the gravel are all large. They have very little ability to hold water. No more water moves from the sponge than if it were still sitting on the wire screen. Reducing the size of the gravel would make little difference until at least some of the pores in it reached the size of those in the sponge.

This information has application in many practical situations in the nursery, turf and landscaping industries.

Figure 9.8

Proportions of air and water at different depths in 'potting mixes' with different particle size ranges, and hence different sizes of pores

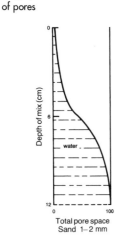

Total pore space
Sand 1–2 mm

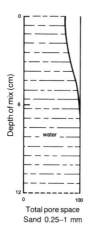

Total pore space
Sand 0.25–1 mm

Total pore space
Sand <0.1 mm

Application to containers

Growing media in containers behave towards water in the same way as do drying towels and stacked sponges.

- Immediately after drainage has stopped, the medium at the very bottom of a container remains saturated unless it is sitting on an absorbent surface. The water content decreases to be least at the top.
- The actual proportions of water and air in the pore space of media in containers of the same height will depend on the sizes of those pores. As with natural soils, media with large pores will hold less water (and have a higher air-filled porosity) than media with mainly small pores. Figure 9.8 gives some examples. More detail on the effects of texture on air-filled porosity is given in Chapter 13.
- The height of saturated and very wet medium is the same no matter what the height of the container (Fig. 9.9). This means that a medium in shallow containers will have a higher average water content (and a lower air-filled porosity) than the same medium in taller containers (Fig. 10.8).
- This also means that the average percent water in tapered pots is lower than the percent in vertical-sided pots of the same height (Fig. 9.10).
- The proportion of water in just-drained medium in a typical nursery pot will always be greater than the proportion in a similar depth of the medium if it formed the upper part of the natural soil of an area.
- In other words, container capacity is always greater than field capacity for the same medium. This means that if we put a soil having 35% water at field capacity into a container, we could find that its container capacity is nearer 40–45%. That would leave very little space for air. Only in very tall containers (perhaps more than 0.8–1m tall) is container capacity much the same as field capacity.
- Media for use in containers must have a higher proportion of large pores than do natural soils if the roots of plants in pots are to get enough oxygen.

Application to 'special' turf

By 'special' turf we mean areas of turf that have been specially constructed with a layer of gravel, equipped with drains, underlying the whole of the constructed area. Such an area behaves like a giant pot. The root zone mix immediately above the gravel remains saturated after all drainage has stopped. It is said to have a perched or suspended water table.

Table 9.5 gives some data for a root zone mix consisting mainly of fine sand (0.1–0.25 mm diameter). Container capacity totals 118 mm for the 400 mm depth. The top 400 mm of this sand in a natural soil situation holds less than 40 mm of water. The gravel layer therefore allows a trebling of the amount of water held in the root zone mix. This will allow a decreased frequency of irrigation. Note, however, that this effect applies only to level areas. When the top of the gravel layer slopes, the only part of the area with a perched water table will be the very lowest part of the slope. In contrast to sand, a clay soil placed over gravel could easily remain so wet that the air-filled porosity of the root zone could be too low for good plant growth. Gravel 'drainage' layers are a means of increasing the amount of water held in sandy root zone materials, and of conducting excess water away rapidly. They do not improve the drainage of heavy soils—quite the contrary.

Layering—beneficial and otherwise

A layer of gravel under properly constructed sandy root zone mixes is beneficial to turf (and the turf manager). Most other layering has unwelcome effects.

Only rarely are distinct layers of coarse materials found at shallow depths in natural soils. If they had been there, perhaps as alluvial deposits, movement of

Figure 9.9
The height of saturated medium is the same no matter what the height or width of a container

Figure 9.10
Containers of the same height have increasing air-filled porosity and decreasing water content as they taper more sharply at their bases. *From* T M Bilderback and W C Fonteno *J. Environ. Hortic.* 5(4): 180, 1987

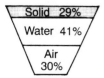

finer particles into them over tens or hundreds of years, and mixing by soil animals, has usually bridged them long ago.

Undesirable layering is usually the result of recent human activity, or inactivity:

- Layers are often produced during construction operations, especially during clean-up operations with scraper blades.
- Uneven layering is common in filled sites.
- The topdressing of turf with materials of different texture will produce a series of layers (Fig. 9.11).

Whatever its origin, a layer of coarse material underlying a soil of finer texture will cause that soil to remain wetter than if the layer were not there (Fig. 9.12).

Serious problems can result if the layer occurs at depths of about 10 cm or less.

- Plant growth will suffer in prolonged wet weather.
- Heavily used turf will become a quagmire.
- If this doesn't happen, traffic can more easily compact the wet soil than if it were drier.
- Turf grass roots and stolons will tend to grow nearer the surface, or on it. Thatch buildup is often hastened.

Layering is overcome by mixing all the layers together—where possible—or providing channels down through the layers. Coring and sand slitting are two techniques available for turf (Chapter 19).

Table 9.5
Variation of air-filled porosity and water content of a sandy root zone mix of near ideal particle size composition, according to the University College of Wales (*From* W L A Adams et al. *The Construction and Drainage of Sportsfields for Winter Greens in Britain* University College of Wales, Aberystwyth)

Root zone depth (mm)	Air-filled porosity (volume %)	Water (volume %)	Water held (mm)
Turf			
Root zone mix			
0–			
50–	29	11	5
100–	20	20	10
150–	13	27	13.5
200–	8	32	16
250–	7	33	16.5
300–	5	35	18
350–	2	38	19
400–	0	40	20
Gravel layer		Total water held: 118 mm	

Gravel 'drainage' layers in pots

Many popular gardening and indoor plant books still tell readers to put a layer of broken brick, gravel or other coarse material in the bottom of pots. As we have just seen, all this will do is decrease the height of medium in the pot, so *increasing* its wetness. The surest way of ensuring good drainage in pots is to use a medium with a high enough air-filled porosity (p. 80).

Figure 9.11
Manuka Oval, Canberra, before remaking. The surface was a quagmire in winter because of the perched water table effect of the layers of coarse sand near the surface and the low rate of percolation of water through the silty clay loam. *From* D S McIntyre and C L Watson CSIRO Division of Soils, *Divisional Report* No. 4, 1975

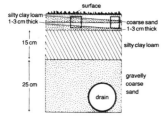

REMOVING WATER FROM MEDIA

Water can leave a medium by drainage, evaporation from its surface or through plants (transpiration). In this section we assume that drainage has stopped and that a mulch prevents evaporation. We want to look at the removal of water by plant roots.

Water in a just-drained medium is held firmly enough to resist removal by the pull of gravity. If plant roots are to get water from the pores, they must pull at least a little harder than this. The necessary pull or suction comes mainly from the transpiration of water from leaves. The deficiency of water created in leaf cells by transpiration is transmitted down through the plant to cells in the root. These are then able to draw water in from the medium around them.

With plenty of water in the pores of a just-drained medium, the demands of the roots are easily met. Water removed close to them is rapidly replaced from nearby pores by flow through thick films of water on particle surfaces (Fig. 9.13).

The easiest water to remove is that in the largest pores, so they are depleted first. As removal continues, the remaining water is held in smaller and smaller pores. Higher and higher suctions are needed to remove it. The extra suction comes from a further decrease in water content of cells in the plant (= slight wilting). Because the films of water connecting the pores are thinner, the rate of flow to the roots decreases.

Permanent wilting point

As more water is removed from the medium, greater and greater suctions are needed to remove that remaining. The plant may be seen to wilt during the heat of the day, and to recover after dusk.

But eventually the plant does not fully recover at night. There is either too little water in the medium, it is held too tightly, or it is too far from roots to get there quickly enough. The plant wilts permanently. Unless water is soon supplied, the plant begins to shed leaves in an effort to survive. Eventually it dies.

A growing medium in which a plant has just wilted permanently is said to be 'at the permanent wilting point'. It still contains some water in the tiniest pores (less than 0.0002 mm diameter) and as an even thinner film on particle surfaces, but this water is too slowly available to plants to be of much use to them. The soil will look and feel slightly damp, but won't be dusty. Figure 9.6

Figure 9.12
A thin layer of coarse material close to the surface keeps the soil above it wet. *Photograph J Coppi*

Figure 9.13
The thicker the film of water around the solid particles in growing media, the greater the rate at which water can move towards roots

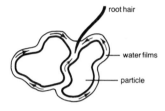

gives the approximate amounts of water held in soils of different textures at the permanent wilting point.

AVAILABLE WATER

The water held in soils between field capacity and permanent wilting point is called *available water*; it is the maximum amount of water that that medium can supply to plants growing in it. Figure 9.6 gives the approximate amounts held in soils of various textures. Note that soils with good structure hold more available water than do similar soils of poorer structure (Fig. 9.6 and Table 9.6). The amount of available water able to be held by a medium is a reasonable guide to the ability of that medium to sustain plant growth. A low amount of available water—as in sandy soils—affects plants and us as follows.

Where applying extra water is not possible:

- Only drought tolerant plants survive. Extensive root systems, ability to store water, and an ability to 'shut down' to wait out the drought, all help.
- Revegetation of sandy soils should be attempted only with drought tolerant plants. Some of the publications listed in the 'Further Reading' appendix include names of suitable species.
- Planting out or seeding has the greatest chance of success at the wettest time of the year.
  Where irrigation is possible:
- Frequent watering will be necessary if plants of low drought tolerance are to survive.
- The low water storage capacity of sands means that only relatively small amounts of water should be applied at each irrigation.
- Even where irrigation is possible, time and money are saved when plants adapted to the soil and climate are grown.
  For plants in pots:
- A low amount of available water makes frequent watering necessary.
- Where care may be erratic—as in some indoor situations—a low amount of available water may mean that plants are frequently stressed.
- Deterioration of potted plants on the retail store shelf is often caused by the combination of media that hold little available water, and infrequent watering.

At the other end are media that hold 'too much' water. This is only a problem if it reduces the supply of air to plant roots. Such can be the case when bedding plants, typically grown in shallow containers, are watered too frequently in winter (Fig. 10.5).

Table 9.6
Decreases in soil organic matter content (and degradation of soil structure) brought about by cultivation decrease the amount of available water held in soils. In this example, the three pairs of soils were from nearby old pastures and plots cultivated for 30+ years (*From* A P Hamblin and D B Davies *J. Soil Sci*. 28: 11, 1977)

		Available water	
Soil	Organic matter %	Volume %	% increase due to organic matter
1	5.3	18	20
	3.6	15	
2	6.3	20	33
	3.8	15	
3	5.7	22	47
	3.2	15	

Putting numbers to available water

Water in growing media is most simply described by the amount of suction needed to remove it. (But see 'SOME EXTRA SCIENCE' p. 72.) That suction is given in units called kiloPascals (kPa). Any reader who has pumped up car tyres recently will be aware that the pressure needed is given in kPa. Most car tyres need an air pressure in the range 120 to 300 kPa. Suction is negative pressure (think of sucking on a straw or blowing down it) so it can be measured in the same units.

Experiments have shown that:

- A suction of less than 0.5 kPa is enough to remove the first water from a saturated medium. If the medium is barely damp, a suction of 70 kPa or more may be needed.
- A suction of about 10 kPa is needed to pull the first water from a soil at field capacity.
- By the time about 70 kPa is needed, the soil will be too 'tough' to cultivate easily. It will break into clods.
- A suction of at least 1500 kPa is needed to get water from a soil at the permanent wilting point.
- Between these two suctions, extra water can only be removed from a medium by increasing suction (Fig. 9.14). In other words, the smaller the remaining amount of 'available' water in a medium, the lower is the availability of that water. Some effects of this on plant growth are given in Chapter 22.

Media in containers

Remember that the very bottom of a medium at container capacity is saturated with water, with the water content decreasing with height.

- The suction needed to remove water from the bottom of the container will be only a little above zero kPa. Roots will remove that water first and then exert greater suction to get some of the rest.
- The suction required to remove water from the top part of the medium depends on the height of that part above the bottom of the pot. If the medium is 20 cm high, then the suction needed is just a little more than 20 cm of water suction, which is 2 kPa.
- Therefore, the *average* suction needed to remove water from a pot 20 cm high is (0 + 2)/2 = 1 kPa. For medium in 12 cm tall pots, the average suction will be (0 + 1.2)/2 = 0.6 kPa.

Figure 9.14
Curves showing that sands release much of their water at quite low suctions (less than 20 kPa), while heavier soils retain much water at the 'permanent wilting point' (1500 kPa)

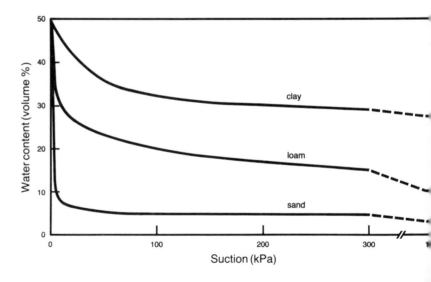

Figure 9.15
Explanation of water release curves for potting mixes, showing that as extra suction is applied to the mix, the volume percent of water in it decreases and the volume percent of air increases

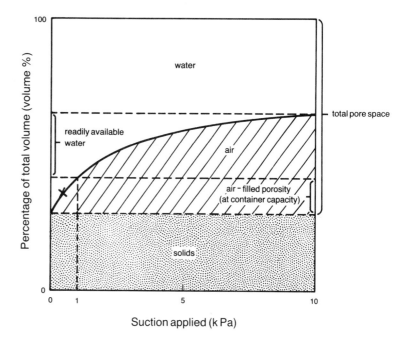

- A standard way of describing the water and air contents of potting media at container capacity, used mainly in Europe, is illustrated in Fig. 9.15. The water in saturated medium is removed by carefully applied standard suctions of 1, 5 and 10 kPa. Container capacity is taken to be simulated by the 1 kPa suction, so this method actually gives figures for medium in pots 20 cm high.
- The percentage of the total volume of medium that is water held at 1 kPa, but removed at 5 kPa, is referred to as *easily available* water. Water held at 5 kPa, but removed by a suction of 10 kPa, is referred to as the *water buffer capacity* of the medium. This latter percentage is usually quite small, so in this book we add these two together and call the sum *readily available* water.
- Note that the percent readily available water of a medium in pots that are shallower than 20 cm will be rather higher than that measured by this method. For example, the medium used to produce the curve of Fig. 9.15 would have a container-capacity water and air content as given by the 'x' in a 12-cm tall pot. But of course the total volume of water could well be less because the container is likely to be smaller.
- If plants in containers are to continue to grow vigorously, the medium around their roots should never dry beyond about 10 kPa (Table 9.7). In fact, for open mixes, the limit should be 5 kPa. Many European growers place the

Table 9.7
Effect of extent of drying of the medium on yields and bud weight of roses *(From Z Plaut et al. Scientia Horticulturae 5: 277, 1976)*

Tensiometer reading at start of irrigation (kPa)	Saleable flowers	Flower bud weight (g)
2–3	282	7.0
4–6	284	6.4
10–15	263	6.0

Figure 9.16
Water release curves, modelled on the style of Fig. 9.15, for some components often used in potting mixes

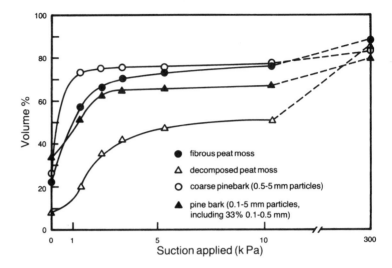

limit at 3.5 kPa. These very low limits are set mainly because of the small volume of most containers and the coarse texture of most media used in containers. Coarse texture is needed to avoid waterlogging when the 'overkill' method of irrigation is used. This involves frequent, heavy irrigation to ensure that the plants are never short of water. See Chapter 22. Removal of just a little more of the water remaining at 10 kPa will send the suction needed to remove more well beyond 10 kPa (Figs 9.15 and 9.16). Growth rate will soon suffer.

- An example of the effect of the volume of readily available water on irrigation frequency is given in Table 9.8.

Table 9.8
Approximate maximum times allowable between irrigations, at two rates of evaporation, if maximum growth rate of plants in containers is to be maintained.* The containers were of 1 litre capacity.

Readily available water (volume %)	Days between irrigations at evaporation rates of:	
	3 mm/day†	15 mm/day†
5	1.5	0.3
10	2.9	0.6
15	4.4	0.9
20	5.9	1.2
25	7.4	1.5

* When a low growth rate is acceptable and the plants are in large containers of medium with a high capacity to hold water, drying to around 70 kPa is acceptable. This applies mainly to plants in large containers indoors.
† Typical rates for early spring and mid-summer

SOME EXTRA SCIENCE

The standard scientific way of describing water in growing media and plants is in terms of its 'potential' (to do work). Water in a high dam has the potential of doing much work. Some of this potential is realised when the water runs through a hydroelectric power station. After leaving the station, the potential of the water is greatly reduced.

Pure water in a saturated medium is defined as having a potential of zero. The water in a barely moist medium has a negative potential. Work must be done by plants or us to extract the water. The drier the medium, the more negative the potential of the water in it. The water in a soil at field capacity will have a potential of about −10 kPa; at wilting point it will be about −1500 kPa.

Salts dissolved in water make its potential more negative. For example, a saturation extract having an electrical conductivity (EC) of 3 dS/m (Chapter 21) will have a potential of about −100 kPa. A plant must overcome this negative potential, in addition to that due to the medium itself, if it is to take up water.

10 SUPPLYING AIR TO ROOTS

Some plants grow in soils that are permanently under water. Their names might be rice, reed, or water lily. Other plants grow best in soils that are very wet for parts of the year, but dry out somewhat in summer. Their names could be *Boronia*, poplar, *Melaleuca* or willow. Given drier conditions these plants do not grow very well.

Far removed are the epiphytes that in natural conditions have most of their roots dangling in moist air. Put them in a medium with a lot less air and they grow poorly.

Most plants are somewhere in between these two extremes: for good growth they need plenty of water in the medium around their roots, but also some air or, to be more exact, oxygen.

ALL ROOTS NEED OXYGEN

All roots need oxygen, but they get it in different ways. Water-loving plants are able to supply their roots with oxygen brought down from their leaves through special cells in their stems. When faced with a crisis, others are able to develop this ability to some extent. Most plants probably have some ability to do this, but their growth is less than if they were able to get more oxygen from air in the growing medium itself.

Roots are just like us. They need oxygen to make new cells (grow), repair cells and take up nutrients and water. In using the oxygen, they produce carbon dioxide, releasing it into the medium around them.

Changes take place in roots within minutes of oxygen supply being completely cut off. We cannot see these changes, but sensitive instruments can. Root growth stops (Fig. 10.1). Uptake of nutrients (especially potassium and phosphorus) is almost stopped and the ability of water to move into the roots is reduced perhaps three-fold. Alcohol and ethylene are produced in the roots; hormone production is upset. After hours and days, the combined effects of these changes become increasingly easy to see in dying roots and stunted or wilted tops.

Getting oxygen into growing media

Consider the following everyday scene: You are sitting in a part of your home that is furthest from the kitchen. There are no drafts; the air is still. Someone starts to percolate coffee in the kitchen. If the doors are open, within minutes you can smell the aroma of the coffee where you are sitting. An almost-closed door slows down the arrival of the aroma and reduces the amount you get. Molecules of the aroma compounds have not been blown to you: they have diffused there. They have gone from a place where their concentration is high (the kitchen) to where it is lower.

Diffusion is also the main way that oxygen gets into growing media. The larger pores in a drained medium will be in contact with the atmosphere (Fig. 10.2). Of course the contact is through the maze of pores, so the distance for oxygen molecules to diffuse 10 cm into a medium could be many times that.

Figure 10.1
The growth of roots (here of *Capsicum annum*) stops when the concentration of oxygen in the soil air around them is reduced to zero. *From B E Janes Mechanisms of Regulation of Plant Growth* eds R L Bieleski et al. Bulletin No. 12 Royal Soc. New Zealand 1974 p 379

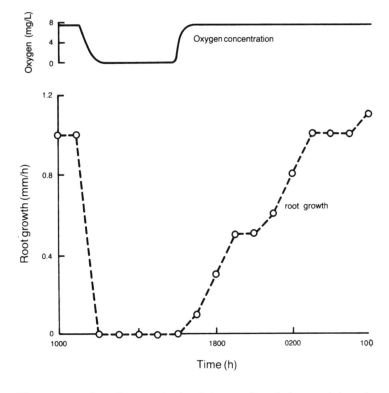

Figure 10.2
Gases diffuse into and out of growing media most rapidly through the larger pores

The concentration of oxygen in the air in a medium is decreased through use by roots and microorganisms. More is then able to diffuse in from the atmosphere. The rate at which it moves in depends on the size of the pores. Small pores are like almost-closed doors. Many large connected pores give rapid entry of oxygen.

Other, usually minor, ways in which oxygen enters media are:

- During heating and cooling. Heating causes some air to leave; cooling allows new air to be pulled in.
- Wind gusts can increase entry into the top part of a medium.
- Some air is pushed and pulled in as water moves into and through a medium.

Carbon dioxide and other gases produced in the medium leave it in the same ways that oxygen enters.

WATERLOGGING

Oxygen diffuses through air at about 10 000 times the rate it diffuses through water. That is about the difference between a jet aircraft and a rather slow turtle. This means that oxygen movement to roots through pores filled with water (a waterlogged soil) is very slow indeed. Unless the plant has an ability to move oxygen down from its leaves to its roots, its growth will suffer.

However, lack of oxygen is not the only cause of poor growth in waterlogged media. Others include:

- Various organic toxins. The list is long, but the main ones are organic acids, methane and ethylene.
- Hydrogen sulphide (rotten egg gas) may cause injury in some media.
- Soluble iron and manganese. Toxic levels of iron and manganese may be dissolved from minerals in some soils.
- Loss of nitrogen. Soluble nitrogen (nitrate) is quickly converted to nitrogen

oxides and nitrogen gas in waterlogged media. Plants cannot use these, so nitrogen deficiency can result.

- Salinity is made worse by waterlogging. Uptake of sodium, if present, is enormously increased because of disruption of root cell membranes caused by the waterlogging.
- If leaching accompanies waterlogging, loss of soluble nutrients adds to the plant's problems.
- Attack by pathogens can be increased by waterlogging.
- Lack of oxygen decreases the ability of beneficial microorganisms to be of benefit to plant roots.

Detecting waterlogging and poor aeration

Obviously a lot of water is one clue. Free flow of water from a sample taken more than two days after rain or irrigation will suggest waterlogging.

Suspect poor aeration if roots are formed on the stems of cuttings near the surface of a propagating medium, but not at the base.

Become a sniffer. If you suspect that a medium is poorly aerated, dig some up and sniff it. A dank, musty smell, tinged with rotten eggs or worse, will tell that oxygen is needed. A well aerated medium has a pleasant 'earthy' smell—the smell of new rain on hot, long-dry soil. Then look at the plants.

Effects of severe waterlogging

In susceptible plants the first visible symptom is often wilting of leaves and downward bending of leaf petioles (Fig. 10.3). As poor aeration continues, root growth becomes restricted to those remaining pores that still contain some oxygen. Soon the effects are clearly visible in the root system. Healthy root tips are white and have a profusion of root hairs just back from the tip. Branching is prolific. With poor aeration, the tips turn brown, later black. There are few or no root hairs. With severe lack of oxygen, they smell sour.

By the time roots tips are black, the tops are really beginning to show signs

Figure 10.3
Typical effects of waterlogging (right) on sunflowers. *Photograph J Coppi*

of stress too.

Compared with well oxygenated plants, they are stunted. Older leaves are paler, often with a mottled appearance. With prolonged lack of oxygen the oldest leaves become quite yellow, with dead, brown or blackened margins. Soon they die. Those leaves left on grasses tend to be short and pale and to stick straight up into the air. They are too short to curve over naturally. Leaves of shrubs may droop, giving the plants a 'hang-dog' look.

With prolonged poor aeration there will be increasing disease problems, with most roots being rotted away. Eventually plants may die.

The effects of waterlogging show up faster and are more severe as temperature rises. Summer waterlogging can be rapidly lethal to some plants.

Figure 10.4
A short period of restricted aeration severely reduces flowering in tulips. The air-filled porosity of the soil was 20% for 45 days, then as shown by the bars. *From G G M van der Valk Acta Horticulturae 23: 333, 1971*

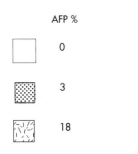

AFP %

0

3

18

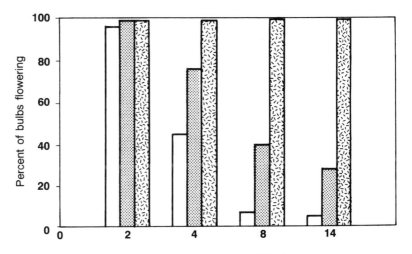

Length of period of restricted aeration (days)

A short burst of waterlogging

A short burst of waterlogging can have little or severe effects on plant growth, depending on plant species and growth stage. Germinating seeds are especially severely affected; they have no ability to transfer oxygen from their leaves, as they have none. In annuals, just before flowering starts is another period when injury can be particularly severe in its effects on later growth. Just a few days of restricted aeration can seriously reduce flower production (Fig. 10.4).

Effects of mild lack of oxygen

More often than not, the effects on plant growth are not as severe as listed above. Affected plants look smaller than well aerated plants nearby. They grow more slowly. Elongation of stems is affected before weight gain. Nursery plants take longer to reach saleable size. Colour may be different too.

This may not be a cause for concern. Not everyone wants their plants belting along at full speed. But wherever maximum growth rates are needed, it is important to make sure that the medium has a continuing high level of oxygen.

Table 10.1
Effect of irrigation interval on shoot extension and number of leaves on *Photinia* x *fraseri* during winter and summer. *From* D F Welsh et al. *J Environ. Hortic.* 9: 79, 1991

Irrigation interval (days)	Shoot extension (cm)	Number of leaves
	Winter	
3.5	16.46	19.6
7.0	21.21	27.2
	Summer	
3.5	26.33	25.7
7.0	26.81	26.0

Figure 10.5
Daily watering of salvia seedlings in punnets of a mix with an AFP of 10% (as measured by the standard method) markedly reduced growth compared with less frequent watering. Rating: 0 = dead; 5 = excellent quality. *From* D Nichols Australian Hortic. June: 40, 1990

GAS LEAKS

Gas, whether natural or 'coal', can severely damage or kill plants when it leaks into the soil around their roots. Effects are particularly severe where plants are surrounded by asphalt or other impervious paving. Symptoms of injury by natural gas are the same as those caused by waterlogging. They usually show up first in the youngest leaves. The margins of these leaves scorch and turn under. Interveinal areas die, leaving the midrib and veins green for a while. Then limbs die back from the tips; whole branches die. Of course roots are severely damaged.

The leak(s) must be repaired. Vent holes cut into asphalt will allow gas to escape and oxygen to enter the soil. There is no need to cut vent holes into soil that is not covered by concrete or asphalt. It takes a year for the oxygen level in a clay soil to return to an adequate level, and perhaps several months for sandy soil. Light pruning of dead and dying branches will help the recovery of trees only slightly affected. Severely affected trees usually die. Wait a year before replanting.

Ask your gas supply company to check the soil if you suspect that poor growth is due to a gas leak.

AIR-FILLED POROSITY REQUIREMENTS

Aeration depends mainly on the sizes of pores in a medium. If all the pores are very small (as in a heavy clay soil of poor structure) drainage will not remove water from them and allow air in. Increasing the proportion of larger pores will allow more of the medium to be air after drainage has stopped.

The question is: 'What proportion of a medium must be air for it to supply enough oxygen for plant growth?' Before giving an answer, we emphasize again that different species of plants have very different abilities—from complete to none—to cope with waterlogged conditions. Most land plants have a limited ability to cope with waterlogging. It is for this broad mass of plants that we mainly write.

Air-filled porosity and irrigation frequency

We must further delay an answer to the question about optimum air-filled porosity, so that we can consider the effect of irrigation frequency. We use potting mix as an example, but exactly the same argument holds for compacted turf soils that are irrigated at too great a frequency or too heavily.

Let us suppose that we have a mix that has an air-filled porosity that is barely adequate for the plant growing in it. The roots might be a bit short of oxygen for some hours after watering, but if losses through transpiration are rapid, the effective air space will soon increase to an adequate level. If we delay watering until much of the water has been used, most of the time the plant's roots will have plenty of oxygen.

However, the roots could be short of oxygen for most of the time if irrigation is so frequent that there is very little increase in air space between irrigations. A low transpiration rate will extend the time of inadequate oxygen supply. Therefore, irrigation frequency must match the rate of water loss, but must also take into account the air-filled porosity of the mix in the container being used. As a general rule, choose a medium with a high water-holding capacity for plants that use water rapidly and one with a higher air-filled porosity for plants with lower water needs. Two examples are given in Table 10.1 and Fig. 10.5 of the damaging effects of too-frequent irrigation in winter.

It is possible to 'get away with' an air-filled porosity that is rather low if irrigation is carefully scheduled according to the weather. If you want to irrigate 'by the clock' you should make very sure that irrigation frequency matches the air-filled porosity of your mix or soil. Readers with an interest in turf will, we are sure, find that the various devices described in Chapter 22 will enormously improve their ability to deliver water when it is really needed.

Always remember that the person who irrigates your plants controls their appearance and your profit.

Soils

Many experiments with agricultural crops have shown that topsoils need about 10% or more air-filled pore space (air-filled porosity) if the crops are to grow vigorously. This means that one or two days after soaking rain or irrigation, the top 15 cm or so of the soil should have at least 10% of its volume as air. In other words, an air-filled porosity of at least 10% at field capacity seems essential. A method of measuring air-filled porosity is given in Chapter 33.

No doubt there are many species that will grow well with less air and many that need rather more.

Turf soils

The turf literature contains statements that an air-filled porosity of 10% is necessary for stress-free growth of turf grasses. The data of Table 10.2 suggest

Table 10.2
Some properties of soil samples from soccer pitches (means of 10 British pitches) *From P M Canaway J. Sports Turf Res. Inst. 56: 128, 1980*

Area sampled	Bulk density (g/cm³)	Total porosity (volume %)	Air-filled porosity (volume %)	Water held (volume %)
Behind the goal line (good grass cover)	0.98	59.0	8.0	51.0
Goal area (worn turf)	1.20	50.3	6.5	43.8

that 8% air-filled porosity is enough. But turf root zones are too complicated for simple assessment using air-filled porosity. The lower part of a turf root zone may have an air-filled porosity above 10%, but a heavily compacted surface may totally prevent oxygen from diffusing into the lower soil, especially if that surface is saturated because of layering. Also, slow drainage from the base of the root zone can allow it to remain saturated for extended periods. A measure of air-filled porosity is of limited use for assessing turf soils. Various methods of measurement of oxygen diffusion rate and oxygen concentration in the root zone have been made but are of no practical use.

Infiltration rate is a more useful indicator of aeration. Good aeration is probable if the steady infiltration rate is greater than 20 mm/h. Whether 10 mm/h is enough will depend on rainfall and irrigation intensity.

The occurrence of black layers in some turf root zones is a sure indication of near total lack of oxygen in them. This blackness is iron and manganese sulphides, which are formed only under waterlogged conditions. The cause may be a shallow water table, a blocked drainage system, compaction or layering that keeps the upper part of the root zone saturated, clogging of pores by roots and/or excessive irrigation. An anaerobic condition in the root zone can be made worse if a rapidly decomposing thatch/mat layer reduces the entry of oxygen into the soil below.

Poor turf growth, often ascribed to poor aeration, may be due in part to wear by traffic, high soil strength that restricts root growth, excessive use of nitrogen, or drought produced by slow infiltration of water into compacted soil. Renovation operations—referred to in the USA as cultivation, aeration or aerification—may improve air supply to roots, but often their main effects will be to relieve compaction, reduce soil strength and increase infiltration rate. We prefer therefore to use terms that describe what is being done—coring (hollow tining), spiking, slitting, etc.

Figure 10.6

Growth of overwatered tomatoes, as a percentage of the growth of those not overwatered. The medium had to have an air-filled porosity of at least 10% at container capacity if overwatering were not to reduce growth. *From A C Bunt Media and Mixes for Container-Grown Plants* Unwin Hyman, London, 1988

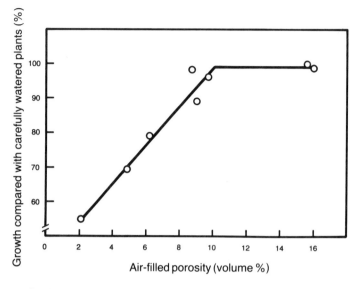

Media in pots

We stress again the facts that different plants have different air-filled porosity (AFP) requirements (Figs 10.6 and 10.7) and that frequent irrigation can override any benefits of good AFP (Fig. 10.5, Table 10.1).

There is another complication in interpreting published AFP data. Different measurement methods are used in different countries. The effective heights of containers used range from 7.6 cm to 20 cm. As shown in Fig. 10.8, the AFP of a mix in a 20 cm high pot is double its porosity in a 7.6 cm high pot! Data from different places can be compared only if the height of the mix during measurement, or the applied suction, is known.

The standard height of measurement in Australia, New Zealand, the UK and Ireland is 12 cm, this being about the height of mix in the most commonly used

Figure 10.7

Effect of increasing air-filled porosity of a medium on the fresh weight of chrysanthemum tops 30 days after planting rooted cuttings. *From J L Paul and C I Lee J. Amer. Soc. Hort. Sci.* 101: 500, 1976

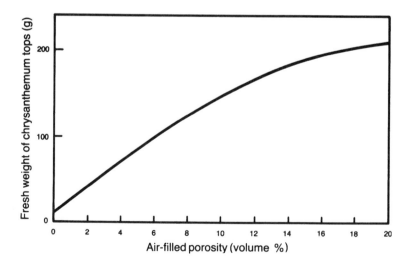

Figure 10.8
Effect of changing container height on the AFP of six pine-bark-based potting mixes with Australian standard AFPs (at 12 cm) in the range 8 to 21%. *From K A Handreck Australian Hortic.* April: 28, 1993

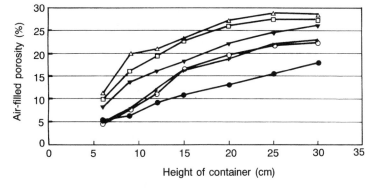

Figure 10.9
In a medium inoculated with *Phytophthora cinnamomi*, the roots of *Heteromeles arbutifolia* were more severely attacked as the air-filled porosity of the medium was decreased. Adapted from C L R Filmer et al. *Hort-Science* 21: 1010, 1986

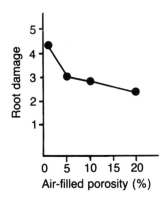

production pots. *The guidelines that follow are based on measurements on mix 12 cm deep.* Use Fig. 10.8 to get an idea of what the AFP of a mix might be in pots of different height. The Standard Australian method for determining AFP is given in Chapter 33.

5% air-filled porosity (AFP): This is too low for plants in most containers used in nurseries, unless the plants are adapted to waterlogged conditions. A medium testing at 5% could be used in tubs and planters over 40 cm deep.

5–7% AFP: Suitable for use in containers over 30 cm deep. Media testing at 7% AFP can be used when total water content must be high so that shelf life or survival after planting out is maximized. Such media can be used in tubes when production is mainly during summer.

7–10% AFP: Suitable for use in containers over 25 cm deep and in containers 20–25 cm deep for plants that transpire rapidly (mainly those with large leaves and with open, upright growth habits). Media testing at about 10% AFP can be used for bedding plants but irrigation frequency must allow the medium to dry between irrigations (Fig. 10.5).

10–13% AFP: Suitable for use in containers at least 15 cm deep and in shallower containers in hot areas. Watering frequency still needs to be managed carefully in cooler areas.

13–20% AFP: For use in all containers up to 20 cm deep. Use media testing in the upper end of the range for plants that transpire slowly, because of either their size or environmental conditions. Watering frequency must be higher for media at the upper end of the range than at the lower end. Media testing at the upper end of this range is useful for indoor plants in situations where 'overwatering' is probable.

20–25% AFP: Media with porosities in this range, and higher, are needed when *Phytophthora* fungal diseases are potentially a problem (Figs 10.9 and 10.10). High growth rates are possible at these levels of AFP, but only if watering is frequent enough to prevent drought stress. Start in this range with media whose components decompose readily, thereby reducing AFP (Table 10.3). Cymbidium orchids grow well in the drier and warmer parts of Australia in media testing in this range, but in cooler and wetter parts the AFP of media for cymbidium orchids should be 35–40% if root rotting in winter is to be prevented.

25–35% AFP: Media testing in this range will be suitable mainly for semi-epiphytic plants. Rapid growth is possible only if watering is frequent.

35–50% AFP: These very open media are needed for epiphytic plants. Such media may contain as little as 5 volume % available water, so the plants must be irrigated at least daily if rain is not doing it for you. These media will have little ability to hold nutrients so use a controlled-release fertilizer or liquid feed daily or several times each week.

Don't be tempted to use fertilizers that claim to improve oxygenation of potting mixes via the peroxides they contain. Such chemicals do release oxygen, but will raise the oxygen level in the medium for no more than an hour.

Figure 10.10
Rotting of *Rhododendron* 'Nova Zembla' roots was much less severe when the plants were grown in mixes, heavily infected with *Phytophthora cinnamomi*, with high AFP values than in one with a lower AFP. *From* B H Ownley et al. *J. Amer. Soc. Hortic. Sci.* 115: 564, 1990

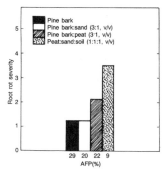

Legend:
- Pine bark
- Pine bark:sand (3:1, v/v)
- Pine bark:peat (3:1, v/v)
- Peat:sand:soil (1:1:1, v/v)

Y-axis: Root rot severity
X-axis: AFP(%) — 29 20 22 9

Table 10.3
Effect of air-filled porosity and the stability of the medium on growth of *Rhododendron* 'Nova Zembla' and *Ilex* 'Blue Angel' (*From* B Scarborough *Proc. Intern. Plant Propagators Soc.* 26: 80, 1976)

Medium	Air-filled porosity (volume %)		*Rhododendron* growth (% culls*)	*Ilex* growth (% culls*)
	At start	After 15 months		
Peat/sand (3:2)	12.7	9.5	47	97
Coarse (hardwood) bark/ peat/sand (2:1:1)	36	19	10	26

*% culls = % under marketable size

Media for rooting cuttings

Earlier editions of this book used research results then available (e.g. Table 10.4) to show that propagation media should test at AFP values in the range 25–30%. This conclusion is still valid if the testing has been done by the Standard method, because the AFP of the mix in the typically shallower propagation containers could be less than 10% (Fig. 10.8). For example if cuttings are inserted into 30 mm deep medium, their bases will probably be no more than 10–15 mm from the bottom of the container, so they will be in a zone of high water content.

Recent research results indicate the need for some reassessment of the 'need' for a high AFP for some situations, particularly when the environment around the cuttings is maintained by fog rather than mist. Under frequent misting, many media in shallow containers (typically less than 70 mm deep) will have poor aeration. But under fog the medium itself receives little water and may come to be too dry for the cuttings.

Wilting (loss of turgor) reduces the ability of any plant to grow (Chapter 22). The greater the loss of turgor and the longer it lasts, the greater will be the loss of growth. Cuttings inevitably lose turgor during preparation for propagation. They will have diminished ability to form callus and new roots until they regain turgor. Water can enter cuttings through their leaves or through their cut bases. Entry through leaves is slow compared with the early (first two days) rate of entry through cut bases. But by seven days after insertion little water is able to enter through cut bases. Turgor is maintained by minimising losses—by having the relative humidity of the air around them at 90–99% (see below)—and by wetting the leaves.

Fog provides a more humid atmosphere around the cuttings than does mist,

Table 10.4
Example of the effect of increasing air-filled porosity on root formation by carnation cuttings (*From* S P Monselise, and J Hagin *Plant and Soil* 6: 245, 1955)

	Particle size range		Air-filled porosity	Callus grade *
	>1 mm (%)	>0.25 mm (%)	(volume %)	
Coarse	88	93	36	4.0
Medium	35	61	23	1.3

*0 = no callus, 5 = excellent callus formation.

Figure 10.11
Variation in saturation deficit with distance from a fogging nozzle in a tunnel, and its effect on % rooting of four species during summer and winter. *From* K Loach *Acta Horticulturae* 226: 403, 1988

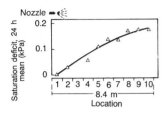

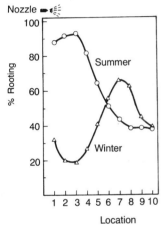

Table 10.5
Rooting response of *Eucalyptus grandis* cuttings in four media with different air porosity and moisture contents. (*From* A Carter *Proc. Intern. Plant Propag. Soc.* 41: 39, 1991)

Media	Rooting (%)	Primary root number per rooted cutting	Root mass per rooted cutting (mg)	Volumetric air porosity (%)	Moisture content (%)
Peat/perlite/sand	83	2.3	44	11	55
Peat	40	1.9	42	20	60
Perlite	25	1.4	22	39	42
Sand	20	0.4	19	8	25

but it is less able to wet leaves than is mist. In the first few days after insertion, the cuttings must rely mainly on water uptake through the basal cut. Close contact with water in the medium is essential for this to happen. Such contact will be less in an open medium than in one with lower AFP. Table 10.5 shows that for *Eucalpytus grandis* cuttings, rooting was best in media with the highest water content, and was not related to AFP. Similar results were obtained with juniper and azalea cuttings (Table 10.6). Other experiments have shown that percent rooting is greatest when the cuttings are 'suffering' from a very slight water deficit (Fig. 10.11).

From these experiments it can be concluded that volumetric water content is more important than AFP for rooting the cuttings of at least some species. The atmosphere around the cuttings is critically important, with a relative humidity of 98–99% being needed in summer and perhaps 90% in winter, at least in areas well away from the tropics. The rapid drop in relative humidity with distance from a fogging nozzle (Fig. 10.11) suggests that gentle stirring of the air in the propagation house is desirable.

Table 10.6
Survival, basal rot and rooting percentages of stem cuttings of two species propagated in peat–perlite medium at five moisture levels. (*From* W H Rein et al. *J. Amer. Soc. Hortic. Sci.* 116: 632, 1991)

Medium moisture (% dry out)	Survival (%)	Basal rot (%)	Rooting (%)
Blue Rug juniper			
125	77	43	0
250	95	24	0
375	100	43	10
500	100	43	5
625	100	33	48
Hino-Crimson azalea			
125	13	0	0
250	19	0	0
375	81	0	19
500	100	0	38
625	100	0	75

PROVIDING AND MAINTAINING GOOD AERATION

Ways of providing good aeration are given in Chapter 2 (soils), in Chapter 13 (potting media) and in Chapter 17 (sports turf). The special methods needed for maintaining aeration in turf soils are covered in Chapter 19.

11 pH

'I like to have my mix at pH 6.'
  'The pH is too high for azaleas.'
  'We had better add more dolomite next time. That new peat has a lower pH than the old batch.'
  'We've had problems ever since we started using effluent water. The pH of the soil keeps drifting up.'

These sorts of statements can be heard wherever those who grow plants meet. Judging by the amount of talk and writing about pH, it must be an important property of growing media. It is, and it's important enough for us to devote a whole chapter to it.

WHAT IS pH?

In plain words it is about acidity and alkalinity. A growing medium with a pH of less than 7 is said to be acid; above 7, alkaline, and about 7, neutral.
  Some use the word 'sour' to describe media that are very acid, perhaps because such media sometimes smell like sour cream, silage or vinegar, all of which are acid. The word 'sweet' is sometimes used for slightly alkaline media.
  In more technical language, pH refers to the concentration of hydrogen ions in the medium (Chapter 4). The higher this concentration, the lower the pH.

WHY pH IS IMPORTANT

Very low and very high pH can cause direct damage to plant roots, but slightly less low or high pH can also decrease plant growth through effects on:
- availability of nutrients to plants;
- amounts of nutrients held in soils;
- toxicities;
- microorganisms.

Different plant species (and cultivars) have different optimum pH ranges. For example, plants that evolved on very acid soils can grow well in soils with pH values considerably less than 4, while those that grow well on highly calcareous soils (pH over 8) may be harmed at pH 6.
  In growing media, the hydrogen ions are mainly associated with the surfaces of colloids. If a high proportion of the cation exchange capacity of the medium is taken up with hydrogen ions*, that medium will be acid. If most of the exchangeable cations are other than hydrogen, the medium will be alkaline. A glance at the figures in Table 14.4 shows this for a range of soils.

---

*Actually, in soils that are measured as being acid, aluminium ions (Al^{3+}) are much more common than H^+ on colloid surfaces. Reactions such as the following:
  $$Al^{3+} + H_2O \rightarrow AlOH^{2+} + H^+ \; ; \; AlOH^{2+} + H_2O \rightarrow Al(OH)_2^+ + H^+,$$
release hydrogen ions into the water around the colloid particles and it is these that give the measurement of acidity.

A caution: Measuring pH is probably the most common test done on growing media. This is partly because it is very easy to do, but also because pH is important. However, it is not so important that we must at all costs keep it within 0.1 of a unit of some 'ideal' value. For most practical situations, being within 0.5 of a value known to give good plant growth is sufficient. Some might consider this sloppy practice; we hope that the information on the next few pages will convince you that it is just being realistic.

EFFECT OF pH ON THE AVAILABILITY OF PLANT NUTRIENTS IN SOILS

The availability to plants of nutrients in growing media changes as pH changes. Figure 11.1 gives the information for mineral soils—that is, those containing only a few percent organic matter. That's most Australian soils.

It is clear that in the range pH 6 to 7.5 most nutrients are reasonably available to plants. Almost all have maximum availability in the range 6 to 7, so somewhere between the two is generally considered to be the ideal pH for the soils of gardens, sports fields and the general landscape. Many books suggest that we should aim for a pH of 6.5.

We want to stress here that there is no point in making a fetish of trying to get all soils to *exactly* pH 6.5, and keeping them there. Because:

- The data used to construct Fig. 11.1, and that on which the 'pH 6.5' statement has been based, were obtained using a variety of measurement methods, but mainly the saturated paste method. (See Chapter 33 for methods of measuring pH.) If we use a method that gives a higher pH for the same soil, we should aim at a higher 'ideal' pH. Approximate conversions between methods are given on (p. 414).

Figure 11.1 (left)
The availability to plants of nutrient elements varies with pH in this manner in mineral soils. The wider the bar, the greater the availability. *From* E Truog *US Dep. Agr. Yearbook*, 1941-47, pp 566-576.

Figure 11.2 (right)
The availability to plants of nutrient elements in organic potting mixes varies with pH in this manner. Based on experimental data of K A Handreck for Australian potting mixes

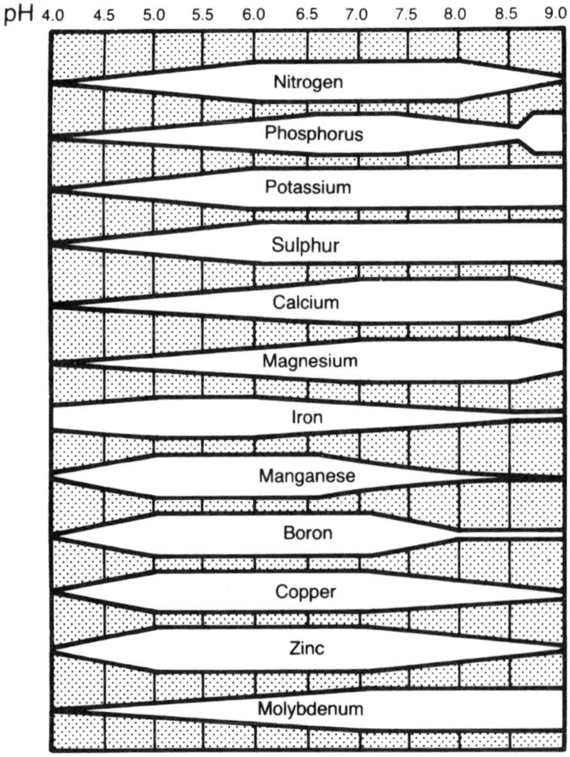

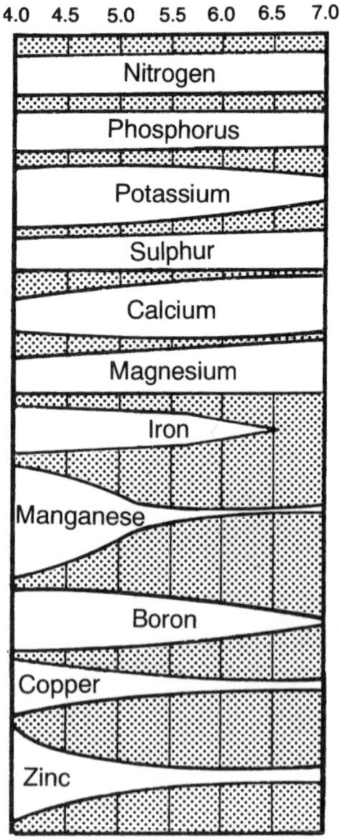

Figure 11.3

Eucalyptus macrorrhyncha growth in a pine bark medium containing 2 kg/m³ ferrous sulphate, as affected by pH. From left to right, pH: 4.5, 5, 5.5, 6, 6.5, 7, 7.25, 7.5. From K A Handreck Commun. Soil Sci. Plant Analysis 20: 1297, 1989 Photograph J Coppi

- Plants vary greatly in their abilities to extract nutrients from soils. Some are poisoned by high levels of soluble manganese in acid soils; others cannot get enough iron from alkaline soils. This variation comes from the way plants have evolved to grow in different soils. If we can't change the pH of a soil, we can soon find plants that will grow in it as it is.

  But apart from that, the 'ideal' pH is really an ideal range which is fairly wide. Most of us would be hard pressed to find much difference between plants growing in garden soils of pH 5.5 and pH 6.5. Coniferous shrubs and trees need rather lower soil pH levels—about 5.0 to 5.4 (saturated paste). This is about the range preferred by acid-loving plants such as azaleas, rhododendrons and ericas, although soils with pH values as low as 4.3 are acceptable.

- Plant roots change the environment immediately around them. Hydrogen ions are released as cations such as NH_4^+, Ca^{2+} and K^+ are taken up. This makes the medium more acid. Bicarbonate ions are released during the uptake of anions such as NO_3^- and SO_4^{2-}. This makes the medium more alkaline. The final effect depends on the relative amounts of cations and anions being absorbed. Some plants are able to change the pH around their roots and so modify or overcome the effects of unfavourable pH: others are less able to do this.

- Carbon dioxide released from plant roots and the large numbers of microorganisms living on or near them will further acidify the soil water nearby.

$$[CO_2 + H_2O \rightarrow H^+ + HCO_3^-]$$

  This acidification can be masked by measurement methods using dilution with water. The amount of CO_2 in the air of a soil containing many living roots plus decomposing organic matter can easily lower the pH of a slightly alkaline soil by a full pH unit.

- The effect of pH on nutrient availability is particularly important when the supply of nutrients is poor. Changing pH can then improve availability. Examples are given in Chapter 14. However, if nutrients are continuously supplied in adequate amounts, pH is far less important.

Conclusions for soils

As far as nutrient supply is concerned for natural soils, a pH somewhere in the range 5.5 to 7 should be suitable for most plants. Soils with pH values at the bottom end of this range are needed for the so-called acid-loving plants (Table 11.1)

Generally, raising the pH of very acid soils is more necessary than lowering the pH of even moderately alkaline soils. But note that changing pH will not automatically mean an ample supply of nutrients. If a soil contains little of an element, no amount of pH change will improve supply enough for good growth. On the other hand, if a soil contains a large amount of a nutrient, it may still supply enough at what appears to be an unfavourable pH.

EFFECT OF pH ON THE AVAILABILITY OF PLANT NUTRIENTS IN ORGANIC POTTING MEDIA

The effect of pH on nutrient availability in highly organic media such as potting mixes is different from that in natural soils. The optimum pH range for such media is something like 0.5 to 1 pH units lower than for soils (Fig. 11.2). This is mainly because of the effect of pH on the trace element iron. Its availability to plants in organic media decreases markedly as pH is increased, until it is vanishingly small to many plants at pH 6.5 (Figs 11.2 and 11.3).

The great majority of the many thousands of species and cultivars of plants produced by nurseries can be grown in organic potting media with pH values in the range 5.5 to 6.3. This statement is true only if the supply of trace elements is balanced (Chapter 16), that N, P, K and S are supplied in fertilizers and that

Table 11.1
Some plant genera that need acid soils

Abelia	Nandina
Camellia	Persea
Catalpa	Photinia
Citrus	Pyracantha
Dichondra	Quercus
Gardenia	Raspberry
Gladiolus	Rhododendron
Hibiscus	Spirea
Hydrangea	Stawberry
Iris	Syringa
Juniper	Verbena
Ligustrum	Vinca
Liquidambar	Willow
Lonicera	Wisteria
Magnolia	

Table 11.2
Quality score of two ferns said to need alkaline soil conditions, as affected by the pH of a soil-less potting medium, and by the Ca/Mg ratio of the sources added to the medium. (From K A Handreck *Scientia Horticulturae* 50: 115, 1992)

Ca/Mg ratio	Medium pH			
	4.5	**5.5**	**6.5**	**7.5**
Asplenium ceterach				
0	2.8*	1.0*	0*	0*
0.33	4.4*	5.8*	4.8*	6*
4	5.0	9.0	8.8	9.0
Infinity	6.0	10	10	10
A. scolopendrium				
0	4.0*	7.2*	0*	0*
0.33	5.1*	9.3	8.5	9.5
4	7.0	10	10	10
Infinity	4.5†	8.0†	7.8†	7.2†

* Calcium deficiency
† Magnesium deficiency
0 = dead; 10 = excellent quality

the Ca/Mg ratio is in the range 2–10. For example, ferns that evolved on alkaline soils grow well in potting media with pH values as low as 5.5 so long as there is balance between calcium and magnesium (Table 11.2). But note that they also grew equally well in the same medium at pH 7.5.

In contrast, lisianthus grew best in a peat-based mix at pH 6.4 (Table 11.3). Another type of behaviour is shown by geranium (*Pelargonium*), *Salvia*, asters and a number of other plants (see Chapter 14) in organic media. They tend to show symptoms of iron toxicity in organic media of pH 5.5, even when apparently 'normal' levels of these elements are present. These plants grow best in potting media of pH 5.8–6.3.

Table 11.3
Fresh weight and flower number of *Eustoma grandiflorum* 'Saga Purple' (lisianthus) as affected by the pH of the peat/vermiculite/sand/perlite growing medium. (From B K Harbauch and S S Waltz *HortScience* 26: 1279, 1991)

pH	Fresh weight (g)	Number of flowers and buds
5.0	7.6	0
5.4	31.0	52
6.4	68.8	69
7.1	52.5	75
7.5	38.0	63

Another type of behaviour is shown by species that evolved on very acid soils. Thus *Macadamia*, azalea, *Ilex crenata* and *Juniperus chinensis* are reported to grow best and are propagated most easily, in organic potting media with pH values in the range 4–5. Pecan seedlings developed severe 'mouse ear' symptoms when medium pH was 5.4 and higher (Table 11.4).

Table 11.4
Effects of liming rate on the severity of mouse ear in pecan trees (*Carya illinoensis*) grown in a pinebark/sand medium. (*From* W D Goff and G J Keever *HortScience* 26: 383, 1991)

Lime rate (kg/m³)	pH	Severity rating
0	3.9	4.9
5.4	5.4	2.9
10.7	5.8	2.4

Rating: 1 = severe mouse ear; 5 = normal

pH AND THE AMOUNTS OF NUTRIENTS HELD BY SOILS

Different soils hold different amounts of nutrient cations, as is shown in Table 14.5. Amount of colloid and type of colloid are the main reasons.

But altering soil pH can also change the amounts of nutrients that can be held: as the pH of a soil is raised, more negative charges are produced on some colloid surfaces. They are therefore able to hold more cations (Table 7.3).

Liming, therefore, not only supplies an acid soil with Ca and Mg, and improves the availability of other elements; it also enables the soil (or potting mix) to hold larger supplies of them for plants.

pH AND TOXICITIES IN SOILS

Plants can be poisoned in soils of low pH. First, toxic amounts of soluble manganese can be released into soil water. Then, as pH is further lowered, toxic amounts of aluminium can be released. In soils heavily polluted with copper or zinc (e.g. from sprays and galvanizing), these, too, may add to the toxicity.

Manganese toxicity will only be produced in soils that have enough manganese to dissolve, and that's not all soils. But most soils can be driven to aluminium toxicity as the pH is decreased.

Manganese is toxic mainly because it destroys root and leaf cells. Aluminium can do this too, especially to root cells. But the main effect of excess aluminium is that it stops plant tops from getting enough phosphorus. The symptoms of phosphorus deficiency show up only after the roots have been damaged. Roots provide an early warning system for detecting toxicities.

The pH levels at which these toxicities appear will vary with the soil. However, for manganese, toxicity becomes possible when the pH falls below 5.5. Aluminium toxicity starts to become a problem when the pH falls to about 5.0.

pH AND TOXICITIES IN POTTING MEDIA

Manganese and iron are the elements most likely to become available in toxic amounts in organic media. Only a small number of species is likely to be affected by iron toxicity (see above), but manganese toxicity is more widespread, probably because of the dramatic increase in manganese availability as pH drops below 5 (Fig. 11.2). A primary cause of manganese toxicity is heavy applications of ammonium-based fertilizers to media that contain sources of Mn that can be dissolved at low pH. Boron toxicity may be produced by use of fertilizers that contain boron, especially if the water used contains more than 0.5 mg/L boron. Repeated irrigation with water caught on a galvanized roof or stored in galvanized tanks is likely to produce zinc toxicity if pH drops to 5 and below (Fig. 11.4). Copper toxicity is unlikely, even when a potting mix contains more than 50% composted sewage sludge.

Figure 11.4
A high level of zinc in a soil-less potting medium is tolerated better at pH 6.5 (right) than at 5.5 (centre) or 4.5 (left). *From* K A Handreck unpublished, 1992 *Photograph J Coppi*

EFFECT OF pH ON MICROORGANISMS

All microorganisms have a pH range in which they survive and grow best. The range is different for each. Outside that range they survive but they do poorly.

Table 11.5
Ranges of soil pH preferred by various beneficial soil microorganisms

Microorganisms	pH range preferred	Comments
Rhizobium bacteria	Above 5	H+ is toxic to them; inoculation of legume roots requires Ca
Ectomycorrhizal fungi	4 to 6, some to 7	higher pH inhibits their spread to seedlings and inhibits seedling infection
Endomycorrhizal fungi	4.5 to 8	some species still effective at higher pH levels
Decomposers of organic matter	5 to 9	bacteria and actinomycetes become less numerous as pH declines; fungi, which are slow decomposers, dominate at low pH
Bacteria that convert ammonium to nitrate	above 6	ammonium from fertilizers is only slowly converted to nitrate in media below about pH 6
Bacteria that attack fungi	6.5–7.5	some are active at higher or lower pH levels but effectiveness is greatest near neutrality

Beneficial microorganisms

Table 11.5 summarizes the pH ranges that best suit the different microorganisms that are beneficial to plants.

Pathogenic microorganisms

Pathogenic means disease starting. Pathogenic microorganisms start diseases in plants, or at least they try to. Some plant pathogens attack plants through their leaves. Here we are concerned only with those that attack roots. Most are fungi. From the point of view of the fungi, roots are food; attack is eating.

Although most fungi prefer acid conditions, some don't mind a neutral or alkaline soil. Thus *Rhizoctonia* attack on turf grasses is greatest in acid soil (below pH 6). On the other hand, *Ophiobolus* and *Fusarium* are more virulent in neutral to alkaline soils. Damping off (rotting of seedlings at ground level because of fungal attack) in coniferous nurseries increases as soil pH rises above about 5.9.

Trying to control diseases through modifying pH alone seems to be like trying to pull ourselves up by our own shoelaces. Preventing infection, pasteurization or fumigation, or using chemicals such as fungicides, are often also necessary. But where it is possible to change pH, and where a change is known to help control a disease, pH change can be a useful tool to have.

If a plant is weak through growing in a medium with a pH not to its liking, it will be more susceptible to attack than if it were growing more vigorously. Changing pH can then indirectly help prevent or control disease (Table 11.6).

RAISING pH

Raising pH is simple. All we need to do is add a liming material. But how much? That's where the answer starts to get a bit more complicated.

Liming materials

Any material that will soak up hydrogen ions will raise pH. Caustic soda (NaOH) will do this (NaOH + H+ → Na+ + H_2O) but it is *never* used because of the

Table 11.6
Effect of the pH of a sandy loam/peat/pine bark medium, inoculated with *Thielaviopsis basicola*, on the severity of root rotting in *Ilex crenata* 'Helleri'. (From L E Merrill et al. *J. Amer. Soc. Hortic. Sci.* 111: 102, 1986)

	Root rot rating	
pH	Non inoculated	Inoculated
5.0	1.4	2.3
6.0	1.4	2.8
6.5	1.1	3.4

Rating: 1 = all roots healthy; 5 = all roots dead.

harm done to soils by sodium ions (Chapter 21). What we need are compounds that supply useful cations as well as something to soak up H^+. This means Ca^{2+}, Mg^{2+} and K^+. Compounds of Ca and Mg are much cheaper than those of K, so they are used.

Limestone—calcium carbonate ($CaCO_3$)—is the most widely used liming material. It is never pure. Most limestones contain some magnesium carbonate, silicate minerals (sand, clay minerals, etc.) and other materials in minor amounts. These other materials reduce the effectiveness of the limestone.

Dolomite—mixed calcium and magnesium carbonates ($CaCO_3.MgCO_3$)—is commonly used in potting mixes because it supplies magnesium as well as calcium. Again, no dolomite is an absolutely pure mixture of calcium and magnesium carbonates in equal quantities.

Occasionally, calcite—pure crystalline calcium carbonate—and magnesite—pure magnesium carbonate—are used.

A commonly used classification of limestones and dolomites is given in Table 11.7.

It is also possible to use calcium oxide (CaO) (burnt lime, quicklime) and calcium hydroxide ($Ca(OH)_2$) ('Limil', builder's lime), and their magnesium equivalents, but they are much more expensive. Because they are more 'concentrated' than limestone or dolomite (Table 11.8) it is easier to overshoot the required pH with them. The oxides are dangerous to use, but builder's lime can be useful where a quick result is needed on a small scale.

Table 11.8
Relative abilities of pure liming materials to change pH (*From* R W Pearson and F Adams eds *Soil Acidity and Liming* Agronomy Series No. 12, American Soc. Agronomy 1967)

Material	Value (%)	kg equivalent to 1 kg of calcium carbonate
Calcium carbonate	100	1.0
Magnesium carbonate	119	0.84
Dolomite (pure)	109	0.92
Calcium hydroxide	135	0.74
Magnesium hydroxide	172	0.58
Calcium oxide	178	0.56
Magnesium oxide	250	0.40

Most Australian crushed limestones have at least 1% Mg. The liming reaction with these materials can be written:

$$CO_3^{2-} + 2H^+ \rightarrow H_2O + CO_2$$

The Ca^{2+} and Mg^{2+} of the liming materials take the place of the H^+ on colloid surfaces. The strength of a liming material depends on its ability to remove H^+ ions. This ability varies as follows: O^{2-} (oxides) > OH^- (hydroxides) > CO_3^{2-} (carbonates). Sulphates (SO_4^{2-}) such as gypsum have no liming value unless they are contaminated with carbonates.

Slags from iron and steel production can have around 80–100% of the liming ability of calcium carbonate.

Wood ash, composed mainly of the oxides/hydroxides/carbonates of Ca, Mg and K, can be used as a liming material. Its liming ability will vary according to the materials burnt to make it, but a figure of 50% of that of the same weight of calcium carbonate is common. The figure for ash from burnt straw or hay is more like 5 to 15%.

Black coal ash has some liming ability, but brown coal ash has little. The

Table 11.9

Approximate amounts of calcium carbonate needed to raise the pH of the top 10 cm of soils of different texture (g/m²) (*From* R W Pearson and F Adams eds *Soil Acidity and Liming* Agronomy Series No. 12, American Soc. Agronomy 1967)

Soil texture	pH 4.5 to 5.5	pH 5.5 to 6.5
Sand, loamy sand	85	110
Sandy loam	130	195
Loam	195	240
Silty loam	280	320
Clay loam	320	410
Organic soil	680	790

Figure 11.5

Changes in the pH of a clay loam soil following application of crushed limestone. *From R Roe Field Station Record* CSIRO Division of Plant Industry 1: 10, 1962

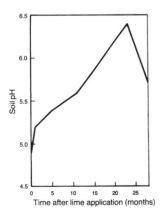

toxicity of some components of some ashes makes it unwise to add them to growing media without prior testing.

The liming value of a commercial limestone or dolomite will depend on how pure it is. High proportions of siliceous materials will lower its value. If you are going to need a large amount of liming material, you should send a sample to a laboratory for analysis or get a written guarantee of purity and liming value.

Amounts of liming material to use: soils

The amount of liming material to use depends on:

- initial soil pH;
- colloid content of the soil;
- types of colloids present;
- final pH needed;
- neutralizing value of the material to be used.

The range might be from 1.5 kg/m² (15 t/ha) to bring the top 10 cm of an acid organic clay soil to pH 6.5, to 0.1 kg/m² (1 t/ha) to achieve the same result with an acid sandy loam with less than 1% organic matter.

Obviously, the lower the starting pH and the higher the pH required the greater the amount of liming material needed. Table 11.9 gives an *approximate* guide to the amounts of calcium carbonate needed to raise the pH of soils of different texture.

If you have only a pH value and an approximate texture to go by, it would be wise to start off with no more than half the amounts given in Table 11.9. You can always add more later, but overshooting can cause problems.

Otherwise, there are laboratories that will, for a fee, test soils for lime requirement and test the liming value of available materials.

Time for liming to be effective

Liming changes pH most rapidly as:

- the particles of the liming material become smaller;
- temperature rises;
- moisture content increases (up to field capacity);
- the liming material is mixed more thoroughly through the medium;
- the magnesium content of the material decreases.

Thus, pH change is most rapid when very finely ground, high-calcium limestone is mixed thoroughly through moist, warm medium.

Example 1: Almost all of a typical addition of 2 kg finely ground dolomitic limestone to a cubic metre of potting mix will dissolve in half an hour of aerated steaming at 60°C.

Example 2: In one experiment, crushed limestone of unspecified grade was mixed at the rate of 650 g/m² into the top 8 cm of a clay loam soil from near Dorrigo, New South Wales. Soil pH changed as shown in Fig. 11.5. Time to reach maximum pH would have been longer if the lime had simply been spread on the surface.

Grade of liming material to use

The finer the grinding, the quicker the result. But grinding takes energy and energy costs money, so the finer the powder the higher the cost. It would be uneconomical to use lime of silt size (about 0.02 mm) on a 100 hectare paddock. But then it would not be sensible to use gravel size either. Table 11.10 summarizes some simplified recommendations.

Anything that won't pass 10 mesh (i.e. bigger than 2 mm diameter) is of little or no value as a liming material. While Table 11.6 gives size ranges within which most particles should fall, there is really no lower size limit, hence the '+' signs.

Figure 11.6
Rate of change in the pH of a peat/perlite (2:1) mixture after addition of various amounts of dolomite (kg/m³) or irrigation with water having a total alkalinity of 317 mg/L calcium carbonate (– – –). *From B J Williams et al.* HortScience *23: 168, 1988 and* J. Amer. Soc. Hortic. Sci. *113: 210, 1988*

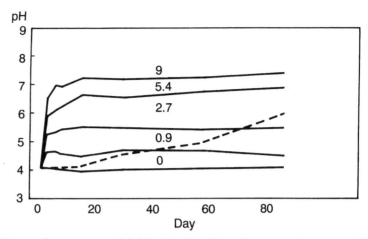

Table 11.10
Grades of liming materials to use in different situations

Situation	Maximum size	
	Mesh*	mm
Large areas rehabilitation sites, large areas of landscape, fairways, fields	30	0.6
Gardens	40	0.4
Greens	40	0.4
Potting mixes	60	0.25

* See Table 3.5 for more information about mesh sizes.

Table 11.11
A ground limestone that will give both short- and long-term change in soil pH

Particle size range		Percentage of total
Mesh	mm	
50-60	0.32-0.25	20
60-80	0.25-0.18	20
80-100	0.18-0.15	30
<100	<0.15	30

For gardens, greens and fields, it is desirable to have some fine material for a rapid start to pH change, plus some coarser material that will dissolve slowly over several years. Table 11.11 gives the composition of a reasonable mixture, but it is stressed that many other mixtures with different proportions of the different particle sizes will probably be just as effective.

Frequency of application to soils

Golf and bowling greens usually need an application every 3–5 years, but the decision to lime should always be based on pH and other test data. The more intense the fertilization program, the more frequently must lime be applied. Greens should be tested at least once a year. Note that some irrigation waters increase soil pH. The opposite of liming may then be necessary.

Applications to larger areas can be less frequent than every five years, but it all depends on growth, changes in soil pH and the desired result.

Amounts of liming material to use: potting mixes

The organic materials used in potting mixes usually have a low pH, often in the range 4 to 5. This is too low for all but acid-loving plants, so it is usually necessary to raise pH with liming materials. These should contain about 6% Mg, so that Ca and Mg are in good balance for plants. Several suitable mixtures are suggested in Chapter 16. You need to do a little experiment to find out how much liming material to add per cubic metre of materials. Do it as follows.

1. Make up about 40 L of the mixture of components that you have decided to use.
2. Add any other amendments, such as superphosphate, potassium sulphate, ammonium nitrate, iron sulphate and other trace elements.
3. Divide the mix into four samples, each of 10 L.
4. Add the chosen liming material at rates of 1, 2, 4 and 6 g/L. Mix thoroughly.
5. Add water to the four samples of mix until they are a little wetter than you normally have at potting. Mix thoroughly.
6. Store the samples in the shade in plastic bags.
7. Remix the samples after a few days and again a week later. The pH should reach equilibrium in about two weeks (Fig. 11.6).
8. Two weeks after starting, thoroughly mix the samples and remove small amounts for pH determination.
9. Plot the pH readings on a graph similar to that shown in Fig. 11.7. Read off the amount of liming material needed to give the pH you want. Convert it to the amount needed for each batch handled by your machinery.

Figure 11.7

A typical lime response curve for a potting mix

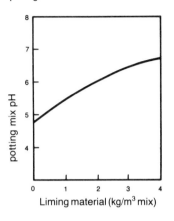

Figure 11.7

A typical lime response curve for a potting mix

10. Just to make sure, check the pH of the first large batch you make. Recheck from time to time and certainly if there is a change in any of the component materials.

If you buy your mix, you should check the pH of each load, 'just in case'.

Frequency of application to potting media

It is usually assumed that the liming materials added before potting will maintain the pH of a medium for the whole of a typical production period in nurseries. That ideal is often achieved, but sometimes the pH can come to be lower than the preferred range well before the end of production. A main cause is the use of fertilizers based on urea and ammonium salts. See point 2 on p. 97.

It can take several months for the corrective action given below to show results. Even then, if your plants have been subjected to some months of very acid medium, they may never recover their full vigour. You should seriously consider cutting your losses by composting the plants. However, if you do have the space and time to attempt correction, you need to do one of the following.

- Make a slurry of hydrated lime (10 g/L). Apply this at a rate of 100 to 200 mL per litre of medium. Repeatedly stir the slurry to keep the solid in suspension. All of the applied slurry will remain in the pot if the medium is slightly dry when you start. Some extra magnesium sulphate may need to be included in your fertilization program to balance the calcium of the hydrated lime.
- An alternative that takes somewhat longer to have an effect is to sprinkle a ground limestone/dolomite mixture onto the surface of the medium. Add 1-3 g/L medium. This alternative works only if irrigation is through the top of the rootball.

ACIDIFYING GROWING MEDIA

Growing media are alkaline because they contain few exchangeable hydrogen ions and much exchangeable calcium and magnesium and, sometimes, sodium. Usually, they contain solid calcium and magnesium carbonates and, above about pH 8.4, sodium carbonate as well. These carbonates must be dissolved if alkaline media are to be made acid.

Acidifying materials

Any material that provides hydrogen ions or that causes them to be formed in the medium could be used. However, cost, availability and toxic side-effects limit the choice to a few materials.

Sulphur is the cheapest and most commonly used material. In the medium, microorganisms convert it into sulphuric acid.

$$2S + 3O_2 + 2H_2O \rightarrow 2H_2SO_4 \rightarrow 4H^+ + 2SO_4^{2-}$$

This then combines with the carbonate materials:

$$H_2SO_4 + CaCO_3 \rightarrow CaSO_4 + H_2O + CO_2$$

When all the carbonate materials have been dissolved, the sulphuric acid can react with cations on colloid surfaces:

$$\text{colloid} = Ca^{2+} + H_2SO_4 \rightarrow \text{colloid} = \frac{H^+}{H^+} + CaSO_4$$

It takes about 6 to 8 weeks for sulphur to act during summer and perhaps double this time in cooler weather.

For a quick response, use iron (ferrous) sulphate or phosphoric acid solution. Routine use of ferrous sulphate is discouraged because large amounts of iron will reduce the availability of phosphorus. However, this reduction may be beneficial for turf soils that have received large applications of phosphorus. The

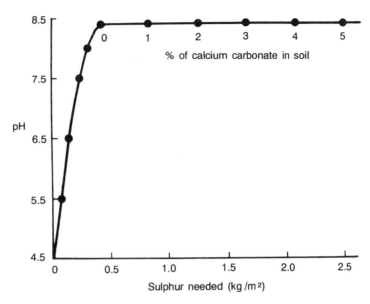

Figure 11.8
Adding sulphur to a soil will not
alter its pH until after all of the solid
calcium carbonate in it has been
dissolved.

iron may also prevent phosphorus toxicity in sensitive plants being established
in farmlands.

Aluminium sulphate, sometimes recommended for reducing pH, is to be used
only for reducing pH around hydrangeas. They need aluminium if their flowers
are to be blue. Soluble aluminium seriously interferes with phosphorus supply.

Peat has a considerable acidifying ability. It is especially useful in creating
acid potting mixes or in reducing the pH of the root zone mix used in making
greens.

Some fertilizers acidify soils (p.97), but to use only a fertilizer such as
ammonium sulphate to make a large change in soil pH would not only be
expensive, but could also cause problems for plants through ammonium toxicity
and salinity.

Amounts of acidifying materials to use

Figure 11.9
Hydrochloric acid is readily
available in hardware stores.
Photograph K A Handreck

It is very expensive to lower the pH of a soil that contains more than a few per
cent lime (Fig. 11.8).

Example: According to the chemical equations above, and the atomic and
molecular masses given on p. 17 and in Table 15.3, we find that:

32.1 g of S will neutralize 100.1 g $CaCO_3$

A slice of soil 1 m square by 100 mm thick weighs about 130 000 g.

A 1% lime content would give 1300 g lime.

This would need $1300/100.1$ x 32.1 g S = 417 g S to neutralize it.

A 5% lime content would need 5 x 417 = 2.09 kg per square metre.

In 1993, agricultural sulphur cost about 81c per kg. An average garden of
500 m² of soil with 5% lime would cost $846 for sulphur just to acidify the
top 10 cm. This may be acceptable for such a relatively small area, but clearly
the cost for larger areas is prohibitive unless the advantages make acidification
worth the expense.

Before attempting to acidify soils known to contain some lime, it is best to
have a sample analysed for lime content. Lime is present if pouring strong
hydrochloric acid (30 mL concentrated plus 70 mL water—sold in hardware
stores for acidifying swimming pool water (Fig. 11.9)) onto the soil produces
bubbles (of carbon dioxide).

For soils that are neutral or only slightly alkaline (say pH 7.5) between 25
and 100 g S per m² should reduce the pH of the top 10 cm to between 6.0 and

6.5. The smaller amount is for sands, the larger for clays. Loams would be somewhere in between.

The amount of peatmoss needed to give a 1 unit drop in pH will vary with the type used. A cubic metre of peatmoss will need between 1 and 2 kg of lime to raise its pH by 1 unit. Thus, a cubic metre of peatmoss has the same acidifying power as 321–642 g of sulphur.

Ferrous sulphate ($7H_2O$) can be initially applied at 50–150 g/m² of soil, that is, at about double the rate of application of elemental S.

Calculation: Suppose we have a loamy sand that we want to use in a potting mix. It has a pH of 6.2 and we want a pH of 5.2. According to the information above, perhaps 40 g S would be enough for 1 x 1 x 0.1 = 0.1m³, so 400 g S would be needed for 1 m³ of soil. We would need about 1 m³ of peat to do the same job, giving a 50:50 mixture. That may or may not be commercially acceptable.

Readers are reminded that all the figures given here can only be taken as an approximate guide. You should always do some trials of your own with the materials you propose to use.

Grade of sulphur to use

Agricultural sulphur, having a mixture of particles in the coarse sand to fine sand range, is the cheapest material to use. The finer particles work within a couple of weeks in moist soil and the coarser ones up to a few months.

Air-floated dusting sulphur, being a very fine powder, works faster but it is not as easy to apply. It is twice as expensive as agricultural sulphur.

Change in pH is most rapid if the sulphur is thoroughly mixed through the medium. Where it can only be spread on the surface, it should be watered in thoroughly, but even so the effect on pH will not be as rapid as if it could have been mixed in.

General comments given for 'liming' apply equally well here.

Acidifying media in containers

Irrigation with water with a high total alkalinity can raise medium pH, even when acidifying fertilizers are being used. Prevention is discussed under point 1, below. A cure, once the pH has risen over 7, is very difficult. Applying sulphur is messy, inaccurate and time-consuming. A useful amount of acidification may take months. The alternative of applying large volumes of dilute sulphuric acid and/or ferrous sulphate solution may damage the plants and has been found to be ineffective. Repotting into an acid medium, after removal of half the rootball, may be more effective, but composting the plants might be the most sensible action with other than very valuable plants.

CHANGING pH 'BY ACCIDENT'

The pH of a growing medium can be changed 'by accident' in the following ways:
1. Watering with hard water   ⇒ more alkaline
2. Repeated use of fertilizers containing ammonium salts   ⇒ more acid
3. Heavy fallout of acid in urban and industrial areas   ⇒ more acid
4. Drift of dust from roads surfaced with crushed limestone ⇒ more alkaline
5. Overwatering and excessive leaching with soft water,
   especially in hot areas   ⇒ more acid
6. Repeated use of the same organic fertilizers   ⇒ Either more
                                                                    acid, or no
                                                                    change
7. Builders leaving mortar residue behind   ⇒ more alkaline

Figure 11.10

Example of the effect of applying ammonium sulphate (here at about 34 g/m² annually) on the pH of a loam soil. *From J R Escritt and H J Lidgate J. Sports Turf Research Institute 40: 7, 1964*

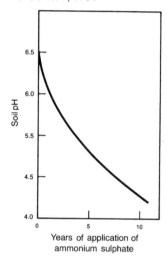

Years of application of ammonium sulphate

8. Watering with laundry effluent or septic tank effluent containing laundry detergent residues   ⇒ more alkaline
9. Disposal of ash and incinerator ash on garden soils   ⇒ more alkaline
10. Repeated removal of plant tops   ⇒ more acid
11. Applying mud from the bottom of lakes and dams   ⇒ more acid

Notes

1. 'Hard' waters contain moderate to high concentrations of calcium, magnesium and sodium ions. These ions are often accompanied by bicarbonate and carbonate ions, so they increase the pH of the medium just as does limestone. Their total alkalinity is in fact given as the amount of calcium carbonate that would have the same ability to react with acid. Thus, in the example given in Fig. 11.6, the water used had a total alkalinity of 317 mg/L calcium carbonate. In other words, the equivalent of 317 mg of calcium carbonate is added to a growing medium every time a litre of this water is applied. It does not take long for such additions to raise the pH of the medium.

Waters with modest levels of total alkalinity (say, up to 100 mg/L of calcium carbonate) are very useful in horticultural situations. They usually supply the nutrients calcium and magnesium, which are often absent from concentrated fertilizers. Also, their alkalinity can completely counteract the acidifying effects of ammonium-based fertilizers.

But as total alkalinity rises above 150 mg/L calcium carbonate, there is an increasing possibility that the pH of the growing medium will rise. Where such a rise is not acceptable—as, for example, when acid-loving plants are being grown—preventative or corrective action must be taken.

In nurseries, the easiest preventative action is to acidify all water used. Use nitric acid, unless you do not want to provide nitrogen. Phosphoric acid does not work very well and provides too much phosphorus. Sulphuric acid can be used but is more dangerous to handle. Aim for a water pH of 5.8–6.0 and use an automatic acid dosing pump and a mixing tank to ensure even acidification. You may need to dilute the acid 1:100 to ensure accurate injection. It will take about 130 mL of 60% nitric acid to acidify 1000 L of water with a hardness of 225 mg/L calcium carbonate. The water will contain about 25 mg/L N.

If water with a total alkalinity of 100–150 mg/L causes an unacceptable rise in pH, you should be able to strike a balance by increasing the ratio of ammonium to nitrate forms of N in the fertilizers used, rather than through use of acid. For short-term crops, starting with a pH that is at the lower end of the acceptable range will give you some extra breathing space.

An unacceptable pH rise in soils and turf root zones is most easily corrected through the use of agricultural sulphur, as outlined above.

2. Fertilizers whose nitrogen is more in the ammonium and urea form than in the nitrate form will acidify media through the following reaction:

$$NH_4^+ + 2O_2 \rightarrow NO_3^- + H_2O + 2H^+$$

Urea behaves as an ammonium salt because it is totally converted to ammonium carbonate within two days of addition to most media. Repeated application of these fertilizers to an already acid medium will increase its acidity (Fig. 11.10). Lime must eventually be applied. The approximate amounts needed are given in Table 11.12.

A fertilizer whose N is equally in ammonium and nitrate forms should not change the pH of a medium, whether or not the ammonium is converted to nitrate before use by a plant. This is because the bicarbonate ions released by plant roots as they take up nitrate ions balance the acidity produced when ammonium is taken up or converted to nitrate.

However, in normal nursery practice it is common to find that medium pH drifts down even when equal amounts of ammonium and nitrate are supplied.

Table 11.12
Calcium carbonate needed to restore pH after using fertilizers

Fertilizer	Calcium carbonate needed (kg per kg of fertilizer)
Ammonium sulphate	1.1
Urea	0.75
Ammonium nitrate	0.6
Ammonium phosphate	0.5
Dried blood	0.2
Superphosphate	0.2

Figure 11.11
Buffer capacity may be understood by looking at liquid in a hollow-handled mug (A). If the handle is almost emptied of liquid (B), the overall drop in height of liquid in the mug is small (C). The large volume of the mug has acted as a buffer that has kept change to a minimum

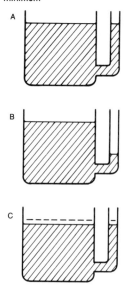

This is because of leaching. Loss of nitrate added as nitrate will not alter pH, but loss of nitrate produced from ammonium in the medium will do so. Acidification in nurseries is probably more due to this effect than to a direct effect of ammonium. Such acidification can be prevented by use of fertilizers with nitrate to ammonium-N ratios of 2 or 3:1.

Resin-coated ferrous sulphate is another source of acidity. Each kg of ferrous sulphate added to a potting mix needs an extra 0.6 kg of calcium carbonate to neutralize its acidity. Potting mix manufacturers automatically compensate for additions of ferrous sulphate powder added during manufacture. However, the acidity produced around granules of resin-coated ferrous sulphate included in media will not usually be compensated for. The very low pH (less than 3) close to granules may be useful to acid-loving plants but it can kill seedlings of many plants that were originally from less acid soils.

Ammonium-based fertilizers will not change the pH of an alkaline soil for many years. Only when all the lime in it has dissolved will the pH begin to fall. Soils with more than a few percent lime may never get to this point.

Calculation: A slice of lawn soil 1 m square and 10 cm deep contains 100 000 mL of soil; 1 mL may weigh 1.3 g, therefore the slice weighs 1.3 x 10^5 g. If it contains 1% lime it will contain 1/100 x 1.3 x 10^5 g lime. A maximum annual application of ammonium sulphate to turf is about 100 g/m². This will need 100 g calcium carbonate to neutralize the acidity. Our soil containing 1300 g lime per square metre will not need lime for at least 13 years. A soil with 10% lime will take 130 years to get to the same point.

The figure for superphosphate in Table 11.12 is a 'best guess' figure obtained for farm soils. It may apply to turf that receives regular applications of super-phosphate.

Calcium and sodium nitrates tend to make media more alkaline. The effect is small; 0.2 and 0.3 kg of sulphur, respectively, would neutralize the alkalinity produced by 1 kg of these fertilizers.

Information about other fertilizers is given in Chapter 15.

Those who look after areas of turf should keep a running tally of all fertilizers applied to each area under their care. This will be a useful aid in deciding when to apply lime, and how much to apply. But of course this information should always be checked against a soil pH measurement, and occasionally, a lime requirement test.

The opposing effects of different fertilizers on pH can be used to adjust pH in potting media.

3. Sulphur dioxide produced during the burning of fossil fuels and nitrogen oxides produced by cars are converted in the atmosphere into sulphuric and nitric acids. These fall to the ground in tiny droplets or are washed there in rain. Acid rain is causing serious damage to soils and waters in Europe and North America. The rain in some inner suburbs of Sydney is acid enough to reduce the pH of a sandy soil by 1 unit in about 40 years. It is obviously worth checking soil pH regularly in such areas of high pollution. Apart from a few other similar areas, acid rain is unlikely to be of any significance in Australia.

4. Crushed limestone and dolomitic rock are extensively used in some parts of the country for road construction and in the surfacing of gravel paths. Dust blown from them, or fines washed onto nearby soil, can make these soils quite alkaline. Lime chlorosis in plants is a common sign of this. Acidifying materials may help, but in the most severely affected situations the opportunity to grow lime-tolerant species can be welcomed.

5. Soft water—water containing little dissolved calcium and magnesium salts—is usually slightly acid. As it moves through soils it dissolves some calcium and magnesium (and other elements too), leaving hydrogen ions behind. Topsoils slowly become more acid. If deep rooted trees 'catch' most of the leached nutrients and return them to the surface in litter, the change in pH is negligible.

But *if* only shallow-rooted plants are grown (e.g. turf), *if* the soil is sandy, *if* excessive amounts of rain or irrigation water soak through the soil, and *if* soil temperature is high for most of the year, then much calcium and magnesium is lost and soil pH can fall. In cool areas the equivalent of about 50 g $CaCO_3/m^2$ can be lost in one year. This could change soil pH by as much as half a unit, although 0.1 to 0.2 of a unit might be more common. In tropical areas, leaching has been known to remove 10 times this amount of lime. Checks of soil pH need to be frequent in the tropics. Massive overwatering is to be avoided.

6. Organic materials such as compost are often neutral, but some, such as composts made from oak leaves, can be acid. Adding lime or dolomite to a compost heap will often give an alkaline compost. Almond shells are highly alkaline. Repeated use of the one type of material may eventually affect soil pH. Check.

7. Builders rarely clean up properly. They leave mortar rubble lying around; washings from cleaned brick-laying tools soak into the soil. Often the evidence is covered by a thin veneer of imported soil. The lime in these patches may cause problems later. A few inspection holes will point to the remedy needed—deep mixing of the soil, the addition of sulphur, or a change of plant species grown.

8. Laundry detergent powders give alkaline wash waters with very high levels of sodium. This sodium will cause problems by itself (Chapter 21), but otherwise these waters can quite quickly make soils alkaline. Either neutralize these waters first or, preferably, don't run them onto garden soils. The sodium problem can be avoided through the use of liquid detergents.

9. The liming ability of ashes has been dealt with on p. 91–2.

10. Repeated removal of plant tops—lawn clippings, trimmings from shrubs and trees, leaf litter—from a soil will also repeatedly remove large amounts of cations, notably calcium, potassium and magnesium. The effect of this removal on soil pH will be similar to that caused by removal by leaching (No. 5, above). This effect is relatively small, but wherever possible, leave clippings and litter where they fall and reduce the need to add lime (and fertilizers).

11. There is little oxygen in the muds at the bottom of lakes and dams. Any sulphur in the mud is converted to sulphide ions (S^{2-}). These can react to form various sulphides, especially iron sulphides and hydrogen sulphide (rotten egg gas). This latter can be smelt in water taken from the bottom of a dam. When this mud is exposed to the air, as when it is spread on soil, sulphuric acid is produced from the iron sulphides:

$$4FeS + 9O_2 + 4H_2O \rightarrow 4H_2SO_4 + 2Fe_2O_3$$

Such muds can have a pH of less than 3 and can require 20 kg lime/m^3 to bring them up to pH 6.5. Beware!

COLLOIDS AND BUFFER CAPACITY

If we mix 100 mL of battery acid into a litre (= 1 kg) of water of pH 6, the pH of the mixture might end up at 2. The same amount of acid might drop the pH of 1 kg of soil of pH 6 to perhaps 5.7. There would be no change in a soil of pH 8.5.

The ability of growing media to resist changes in pH is called their buffer capacity. Media are able to cushion or buffer themselves against the 'shock' of added acid (or alkali). This ability comes about in two ways. In media of high pH, the acid simply dissolves a small amount of carbonate mineral (limestone, etc.). In neutral and acid media, the added hydrogen ions will exchange places with some of the cations on colloid surfaces. The number added is usually small compared with the number already there, so pH changes little. The analogy in Fig. 11.11 helps explain this.

It follows that media with high cation exchange capacities—those with much clay and, especially, humus—have the greatest ability to withstand pH change.

Table 11.13
Buffer capacity, relative to vermiculite = 100, of various components used in potting mixes. The figures are for the range pH 4 to pH 8.

Component	Relative buffer capacity	
	Weight basis	**Volume basis**
Peatmoss		
Canadian	150	123
Finnish	62	78
Irish	92	101
New Zealand	86	100
German	96	61
Swedish	108	29
NSW sedge peat	22	51
Sawdust, composted		
Eucalyptus camaldulensis	11	23
Pinus radiata bark (aged moist for 2 months)		
2-5 mm	2	3
1-2 mm	3	7
0.5-1 mm	5	9
less than 0.5 mm	16	43
Garden compost	38	122
Lignite		
0.5-1 mm	21	90
0.1-0.5 mm	65	273
less than 0.1 mm	85	338
Vermiculite, exfoliated, 1-2 mm	<u>100</u>	<u>100</u>
Perlite 2-5 mm	0	0
Quartz sand 0.5-1 mm	0	0
Diatomite 0.25-2 mm	2	9
Attapulgite, calcined, 0.25-1 mm	22	106
Illite clay	42	450
Scoria 0.5-2 mm	0	0
Potting mixes (a selection from around		
Australia) range	3-13	20-74
mean	8	43

This means that the acidifying effects of fertilizers is greatest on quartz sands and least on peats.

Ability to resist pH change is a desirable property of any growing medium. Decomposed organic matter in sandy turf soils provides much buffer capacity. The organic components of potting mixes also provide buffer capacity. Table 11.13 gives the relative buffer capacities for a range of commonly used materials. Note that humified organic materials have high buffer capacities. There is no buffer capacity that *must* be achieved. But the higher the buffer capacity of a mix, the lower the risk of undesirable pH changes.

Another effect of very acid or very alkaline water

We saw on p. 97 that water with a very acid or very alkaline pH value can alter the pH of growing media. Another effect of this water is that it can reduce the effectiveness of some pesticides. For example, half the carbaryl in a solution will be inactivated in 300 weeks in water of pH 4.5, but in just a day in water of pH 8. The effectiveness of malathion is halved in 18 weeks at pH 4.5 and in 3 days at pH 8. On the other hand diazinon half disappears in 3 days at pH 4.5, in 10 weeks at pH 7 and in 8 weeks at pH 8.

12 COMPOSTING

Composting is a method of speeding up the decomposition of organic materials. The ingredients are made into a heap of at least 1 cubic metre. Heat given off by microorganisms inside the heap is trapped there by the insulation provided by the outer few centimetres. Inside temperature rises and so does the rate of decomposition. Composting is most rapid when the heap is made with the 'right' ingredients and turned frequently.

Composting is most useful in three situations:

- recycling 'wastes' from gardens and parks;
- making soil conditioner from municipal wastes;
- preparing sawdusts and barks for use in potting mixes.

The principles are the same for all three, although some details of practice differ. After a brief overview of the principles of composting, we will give practical detail for the composting of general organic wastes, sawdusts and barks.

PRINCIPLES

A compost heap can be thought of as an enormous number of microorganisms having a fantastic time consuming a mountain of food. If they are provided with the right conditions they will do the rest. 'Right' conditions are:

- plenty of organic matter for energy;
- enough nutrient elements, especially nitrogen;
- oxygen—those microorganisms that are best at decomposing plant materials need plenty of oxygen;
- moisture—not too much, not too little;
- a source of cations, especially calcium, to stabilize the compost;
- sometimes, adjusted pH.

Decomposer microorganisms

Some hundreds of species of microorganisms, mostly bacteria, fungi and actinomycetes (branching bacteria), are involved in decomposing organic materials. They and their spores are everywhere—in the air, on this page, on living plants. They remain inactive until conditions for their growth and reproduction are favourable. As a plant begins to age and die, they invade it, beginning the process of decomposition.

Almost always, there are ample numbers and types of microbes already present on organic materials for composting to start quickly. 'Accelerators' or 'activators', supposedly containing large numbers of microbes, are almost always of no benefit. It is probably the nitrogen in some activators that is responsible for any apparent improvement in composting that might be seen. Urea and ammonium nitrate are much cheaper sources of nitrogen. Even if there are microbes in the 'activators', they may be quickly overwhelmed by the native population. A compost heap comes to be dominated by those species of microbes that particularly like the food and conditions provided.

Many millions of cubic metres of compost are produced worldwide each year

Figure 12.1
Chunky bark being separated from a composted mixture of bark and sewage sludge for return as bulking agent and inoculum for a further batch of sludge. *Photograph K A Handreck*

with just the microbes that are naturally present on the materials used. Carefully controlled experiments have shown that 'activators' have no effect on the decomposition of correctly prepared compost heaps.

Sawdusts and some other wastes from manufacturing industries may initially have very low microbial populations, and so their composting can take a week or so to really get going. The best way of ensuring a very rapid start to their composting is to add to them a few percent of a previous heap. It will have millions of times more microbes than any typical application of 'activator', and they will be the right sort for that particular mixture of materials. The chips and coarse bark used as bulking agent when sewage sludges are composted (Fig. 12.1) are screened from the compost and returned to the next heap, carrying with them huge numbers of microbes.

Organic materials and nutrients

Any organic material that is of plant or animal origin can be composted, but it is first necessary to reduce it to the right size and to adjust the level of nutrients. Small tree branches, corn stalks, dead bedding plants, etc., all need to be shredded to pieces shorter than 50–100 mm. Pine bark has to be milled to the required particle size range. Glass, metals and plastics should be removed from municipal solid wastes (MSW) before they are composted, if composts made from them are to contain acceptably low levels of contaminants. At the very least, non-separated MSW should be no more than lightly teased apart before composting. Harsh grinding gives composts with unacceptably high amounts of contaminants.

An adequate level of nutrients can be supplied either by adding materials of different composition, or fertilizers, or both. The most important requirement is the ratio of the percent carbon (C) in the materials to the percent nitrogen (N). This is called the CN ratio and is written C/N (or C:N) ratio. If a material contains 54% C and 1.2% N, its C/N ratio is 54/1.2 = 45. Guidelines on the use of the C/N ratio are given below.

Moisture and oxygen

All microorganisms need water. A compost heap of about 30% moisture (30 g water per 100 g moist materials; 30 g water + 70 g dry materials) is too dry for most microorganisms; decomposition will be very slow. At 40% moisture there will be some activity but less than that normally needed for rapid composting. Rapid decomposition is possible only when the moisture content is at least 50%. The upper limit is about 65% moisture; above that level the heap contains too little air. The ideal moisture content is usually in the range 50–65% (Fig. 12.2). This is the moisture content of a squeezed sponge. It feels damp, but is not soggy.

Figure 12.2
The rate of decomposition of hardwood bark (mixed northern hemisphere species) is much less at 40% moisture content than at 60%. The bark had received 0.75% nitrogen.

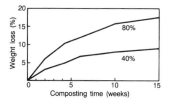

The best moisture content for a particular heap is determined by the bulk density of the materials in it, and the need by decomposer microbes for a continuous supply of oxygen. It has been found that a minimum of 50% of the volume of a heap must be air if composting is to be rapid. This means that the heap should be 'fluffed-up', with a low bulk density. Never trample a heap or run machines over it—it would become compacted (bulk density increases) and the spaces between particles would become smaller. Adequate aeration is then possible only if water content is reduced to a point where composting is slowed (Fig. 12.3). In contrast, if the heap is kept 'fluffed-up' by frequent turning, the moisture content can be kept high. With ample oxygen and water, decomposition is very rapid.

Water can easily be added at turning if a heap becomes too dry. In very wet areas heaps may have to be sited under shelter. Too much water in a heap automatically means too little air space. Too little air space means not enough oxygen for decomposer microbes. Those that need oxygen (the aerobes) die out or enter a resting stage. Those that do not need oxygen (the anaerobes) increase

Figure 12.3
Figure 12.3
Use this graph to find out how wet
to make a heap of composting
organic materials so that it still
contains between 50% and 60% air
space. *From J Cappaert et al.*
Compost Sci. 17: 6, 1976

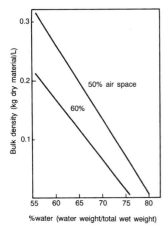

Figure 12.4
Turning windrows of composting
bark and sawdust/sewage sludge.
Courtesy of P Soars, *Australian*
Native Landscapes, Sydney

in numbers. However, anaerobes can only partly decompose plant materials, so when a compost heap becomes anaerobic the rate of decomposition drops markedly.

Another effect of a heap becoming anaerobic is that its pH drops because of acids produced by anaerobes. The pH can drop to less than 2. It will then be highly toxic to plants. Besides, it stinks—something like rotting pig manure. The neighbours tend to complain. Losses of nitrogen can be high.

Compost heaps can be kept aerobic by keeping the moisture content down to about 55–65% and by frequent turning or forced aeration. The amount of air needed each day is about 27 m^3 per cubic metre of heap.

GENERAL ORGANIC 'WASTES'

The 'wastes' covered here include animal manures, agricultural and food processing industry wastes, and garden and kitchen wastes. Most contain plenty of microbes for decomposition to start as soon as moisture and oxygen levels are right. There is absolutely no need to add any special microbial preparation to compost heaps made from these 'waste' materials.

Decomposition will take place in heaps of any practical size. However, the volume should be at least 1 m^3 and preferably 5 m^3 if the temperature inside is to become high enough to kill pathogens and most weed seeds.

It is possible to make compost simply by mixing the materials, adding water as needed, and letting the heap look after itself. Depending on air temperatures and the size of the heap, finished compost should be available in 1–3 years.

However, turning as little as a couple of times will greatly reduce composting time by improving the aeration of the heap. Regular turning allows garden compost to be finished in a few weeks.

Windrows

More rapid (and better and more expensive) composting of general organic wastes is achieved by forming the coarsely-ground material into windrows about 2–4 m wide and 1.5–3 m high, with addition of water as needed. (Aeration in the middle of wider heaps is usually so poor that foul odours are readily produced.) Adequate aeration is provided either by frequent turning or by blowing air into the heap. The fans and pipes needed for air blowing make this method of aeration too expensive for general organic wastes. Turning is done with a front-end loader or with special turning machines (Fig. 12.4).

The frequency of turning the windrow depends on what is happening in it. Rapid early heating will call for turning every 1–3 days. Frequency can be gradually reduced until it can be once a week or even less. Temperature is the main indicator of a need to turn. A fall below 45°C may indicate a need to provide more oxygen. A rise to over 60°C indicates a need to turn to cool the heap down. (An exception is when you want to kill pathogens in the heap. This is achieved by maintaining heap temperature above 55°C for at least 3 days.) Active composting should be completed in about 8 weeks.

The compost should be cured for another month or so. During this time, humus continues to be formed, and most of any residual ammonium is converted to nitrate. Aerobic conditions should be maintained by turning as required. The compost can then be screened, and the oversized material either returned to new compost heaps as bulking agent or sold as mulch.

A popular method of composting sewage sludges and green wastes in the USA and Europe is to compost in concrete troughs 2–3 m wide, about 2 m high, and up to 100 m long. The whole operation can be enclosed in a shed (very expensive), or each trough can be covered with a plastic canopy much like a poly tunnel. The composting materials are turned by a machine that runs along the upper edges of the trough (Fig. 12.5). An advantage of this system is that gases given off can be caught and deodorized by being blown into a biofilter

Figure 12.5
Trough system being used to compost a mixture of sawdust, raw sewage solids and sewage sludge.
Photograph K A Handreck

Figure 12.6
Pinebark biofilter for deodorizing gases given off by municipal solid wastes being composted in a nearby building. Note the sprinkler lines for keeping the bark moist. *Photograph K A Handreck*

Figure 12.7
Adding crushed limestone to a compost heap increases the loss of nitrogen from it. *From C Golueke Reclamation of Municipal Refuse by Composting Sanitary Engineering Project, University of California, Berkeley Tech. Bull. No. 9, 1953*

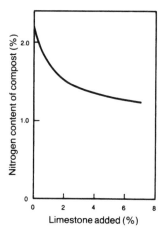

bed (Fig 12.6). Any foul odours produced do not then encourage neighbours to ask for your operation to be shut down.

C/N ratio

The ideal C/N ratio of materials for composting is in the range 25–40. Composting is slower at higher C/N ratios. Heaps with ratios below 25 tend to be smellier than those with higher C/N ratios, and they lose more ammonia. They need more frequent turning than do heaps of higher C/N ratio if they are not to develop foul odours.

These statements apply to components of the heap that will decompose in 8–10 weeks. The presence of coarser pieces with a higher C/N ratio will have only a limited effect on what happens, because the microbes will decompose only their outer layers. In estimating the effective C/N ratio of a heap of general organic wastes, you can concentrate on the finer materials. The biodegradable fraction can be calculated by the following formula:

Biodegradable fraction = 0.83 − (0.028 × lignin content)

Lignin content is expressed as % dry mass. As the lignin content of wood is much higher than that of soft tissues, this formula really gives a method of allowing for slow decomposition of wood.

Use the C/N ratios of Table 6.3 to get a first approximation of the proportions of materials to use in a compost heap. Those involved in large-scale composting should check their chosen mixture through laboratory analysis.

Other nutrients

Achieving a C/N ratio of about 30 with general organic wastes will usually provide enough of all other nutrients, with the possible exception of Phosphorus (P). Manure from grain-fed animals (e.g. poultry) will supply P, as will a light dusting of superphosphate. The amounts added could be about 7 and 0.7 kg/m^3, respectively. Some of the P of rock phosphate will be made more soluble, and therefore more available to plants, during composting. The need to add extra P is probably rare.

At the end of composting the C/N ratio of the compost will usually be less than 15. There will still be partly decomposed plant cells, but much of the compost will be humus and microorganism bodies.

Humus is a main product formed in a compost heap. For it to be friable, its main exchangeable cation should be calcium. Of course some calcium will come from the plant materials added to the heap. Some more will come from any superphosphate added. Soil will supply some too.

It has been traditional to add extra calcium in the form of ground limestone. The main reason given for adding limestone (or dolomite) has been to ensure that the compost is not acid. This is not usually a valid reason, because most general organic composts end up at about neutral pH without lime or dolomite. Adding liming materials increases losses of nitrogen from the heap (Fig. 12.7) because it becomes too alkaline. There is always some loss of nitrogen from compost heaps, with losses being greater for materials of low C/N ratio than for those of higher C/N ratio (Fig. 12.8). Addition of lime does tend to increase composting rate, but losses of nitrogen can be 50% or more from a limed heap. Use lime only if the materials being composted are of very low pH (e.g. fruit wastes) and the pH of the matured compost is too low.

A more desirable way of adding calcium—if it is indeed needed—is via gypsum. Mushroom growers have been using it for more than 60 years. There is no precise information about how much to use with other materials, but 1–2 kg/m^3 of materials used seems a reasonable amount. Both gypsum and superphosphate reduce the level of undesirable odours coming from heaps and also reduce losses of nitrogen.

Figure 12.8
Losses of N during composting are much greater from materials with a C/N ratio of 12 (turf clippings) than from materials with a higher C/N ratio (85; hay). *From G H H Hammouda and W A Adams in Compost Production, Quality and Use, M de Bertoldi, et al. eds Elsevier, London, 1987*

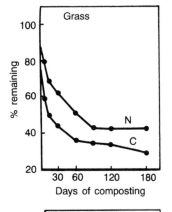

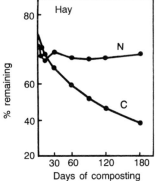

If newspaper is to be used in a compost heap, it must be shredded and mixed among other materials. Otherwise it will mat and give poor aeration.

COMPOSTING SAWDUSTS AND BARKS FOR USE IN POTTING MIXES

Sawdusts have C/N ratios in the range 250 to 800. A fair average seems to be about 500 for many trees, including eucalypts and *Pinus radiata*. When sawdusts are being composted for use in potting media, it is *not* necessary to bring the C/N ratio down to 30. This is because of the types of organic compounds present in greatest quantities in sawdusts.

All plant materials contain a large number of compounds. Some, such as sugars and proteins from inside cells, are easily decomposed by microbes. Others, such as the cellulose and hemicellulose of cell walls, are reasonably easily decomposed. (The relative rates of decomposition are given in Table 5.1.) But lignin, a major component of cell walls in woody materials, resists microbial attack. Much of it is left behind, more or less untouched, after the other compounds have been decomposed. The lignin also protects some of the cellulose from decomposition. Nitrogen added to balance the carbon of this lignin and cellulose is simply wasted. The C/N ratio will typically be about 140 at the beginning of composting and perhaps 80–100 at the end. There will be a continuing need for nitrogen as decomposition continues when the sawdust or bark is part of a potting mix. This nitrogen drawdown is discussed in Chapter 16.

Eucalyptus marginata (jarrah) sawdust need not be composted, but its hunger for N will be reduced if it is. For it and *E. camaldulensis* (river redgum), use 0.5–1.0 kg N/m³ (1-2 kg urea/m³) for composting. Experiments indicate that other eucalypt sawdusts should receive 0.5–0.6% N (dry weight basis) and *Pinus radiata* bark and sawdust 0.3% N. These amounts work out at about 1.1–1.3 and 0.7 kg N per cubic metre, respectively (2.3–2.7 and 1.5 kg/m³ urea). Urea has been considered to be the best source of N, but adequate curing is needed to ensure that the ammonium level in the composted material is low enough to prevent toxicity to sensitive plants. Ammonium will be less of a problem when ammonium nitrate is used. Calcium ammonium nitrate is even safer. Ammonium sulphate must not be used. Maximum temperature in the heap tends to be a little lower with nitrate than with urea.

Higher amounts of nitrogen than those given are wasteful and can be harmful. Much of the extra nitrogen is lost to the atmosphere as ammonia. Carry-over of ammonium into the potting mix can seriously harm plants. (An immature compost in which both ammonium level and pH are high is especially harmful.) Some bedding plants growing under the low-light conditions of a southern Australian winter are harmed in media giving 50 mg/L ammonium in a 1:1.5 water extract.

Poultry manure and litter can be used instead of urea. Use enough to give the same amount of nitrogen. The manure to be used should be analysed as nitrogen content can vary widely. Manures containing 2.5–5.5% nitrogen on a dry basis would be used at rates of 44–20 kg/m³ to supply 1.1 kg N/m³. This works out at 150–70 litres/m³, or 15–7% by volume. These amounts give wastefully high concentrations of phosphorus (equivalent to 2–5 kg superphosphate/m³) which will pollute drainage waters and harm some plants (Chapter 16). More than about 10 volume % of actual manure will give enough salts to make it necessary to leach the compost immediately after potting. The hassles involved in using poultry manure have encouraged many to prefer urea or ammonium nitrate.

There is controversy about the need for other nutrients. Some overseas experiments found a need for some phosphorus, others did not. On the basis of those that did, superphosphate has often been added at 1.5 kg/m³ to composting

Table 12.1
Fertilizers to be added to hardwood sawdusts before composting* (R Worrall, NSW Dept. Agric., Gosford)

Fertilizer	Amount (kg/m^3)
Urea	2.6
Superphosphate	1.5
Potassium sulphate	0.5
Copper sulphate	0.2
Zinc sulphate	0.06
Manganese sulphate	0.06
Ferrous sulphate	0.5-1.0
Boric acid	0.002
Ammonium molybdate	0.002
Dolomitic limestone	up to 9

* Note that the potassium sulphate is not necessary for composting; the additions of copper and zinc are unnecessarily high; and the other trace elements may not be needed if other components bring them to a potting mix in which the sawdust is being used.

sawdusts. Eucalypt and pine sawdusts have a very low phosphorus content, so a small amount of extra phosphorus may be useful, but 1.5 kg/m^3 seems excessive. The superphosphate addition should be cut to less than 0.5 kg/m^3 (Chapter 16), and to zero if the compost is to be used for plants sensitive to P.

Extra trace elements are not needed for composting to proceed, but it is normal practice to add a moderate amount of ferrous sulphate (0.5 kg/m^3) to aid detoxification of phenolic materials. When other trace elements are added in sufficient amounts before composting, further additions will probably be unnecessary when potting mix is being made.

The recipe given in Table 12.1 has been found to give satisfactory results in New South Wales with mixed eucalypt sawdusts. The potassium is unlikely to affect composting, but it will remain as a pre-plant fertilizer. However, the additions of copper and zinc are unnecessarily high; none of either is needed if composted sewage sludge is to form part of a potting mix made with the sawdust. Some sawdusts already have high concentrations of manganese. Adding more increases the possibility of manganese toxicity in plants should the pH of a potting mix made with the sawdust drop below 5 (Fig. 11.2).

We strongly recommend that additions of trace elements be made on the basis of analysis of the finished compost or of potting mixes made with it.

Most manufacturers add some liming material before composting to speed up composting and detoxification. Use a lower rate than is needed to give the desired pH to mixes made with the finished compost. This will allow some leeway for producing mixes of different pH from the same compost.

Windrows and heaps of sawdusts and pine barks being composted should not be larger than the sizes listed above for general organic wastes.

Sawdusts need to be composted for at least 6 weeks, and usually longer. Turning is essential, and frequency should be based on measurements of temperature and pH. It is essential that aerobic conditions are maintained throughout the heap. The composted sawdust is ready for use when water leached through it does not come out black. Turning is less necessary with coarse sawdusts than with fine ones. Pine barks are typically composted for 5–7 weeks. Frequent turning based on the temperature and pH of the heap is needed if a stabilized material of low ammonium content is to be produced in 5 weeks. Four to five weeks of maturation after the hot phase of composting will produce a compost with a lower hunger for N, and possibly better disease suppression (Chapter 26).

At the end of the main composting period for sawdust (i.e. when the heap has cooled to below 40°C), the C/N ratio could still be about 100. This means that decomposition will continue. After some months to a year the C/N ratio might have fallen to perhaps 30–40. Clearly, during this time and beyond, the sawdust will continue to remove soluble nitrogen from its surroundings. In a potting mix, it is *essential* that nitrogen be supplied continuously (from slow-release fertilizers) or frequently (as by liquid feeds) to supply both microbes and plants.

It is possible to produce potting mixes from pine bark that has been aged rather than composted. Ageing involves stacking the ground, moistened bark into heaps. These heaps must not be larger than is given above if anaerobic conditions that produce toxins are to be avoided. Heaps of ageing bark are usually not turned more than a couple of times during a typical 2–4 week ageing period.

Ageing is of course cheaper than composting, but aged bark has less humus and a greater nitrogen drawdown rate than has composted bark. While excellent plants can be grown in mixes based on both aged and composted barks, management is often found to be easiest with composted bark. It is much more difficult to produce bedding plants of high quality with aged than with composted bark.

During composting or ageing, the proportion of small particles in the bark or sawdust increases. As shown in Tables 12.2 and 12.3, this affects other properties of the composted or aged materials. These trends will continue in potting mixes containing these materials. The mix can shrink in the pot, leading to higher water content and poor aeration. One reason for mixing sand and other inert materials into mixes is to help maintain the physical properties of the mix.

Table 12.2
Properties of fresh and aged *Pinus radiata* bark

Property		Fresh	Aged 3 months
Particle size (mm)	>5	6	7
(% by volume)	2-5	23	17
	1-2	42	29
	0.5-1	17	16
	0.25-0.5	6	10
	0.1-0.25	4	9
	0.05-0.1	1	4
	<0.05	1	8
Bulk density (g/mL)		0.25	0.27
Total porosity (volume %)		70	71
Air-filled porosity (volume %)		30	20
Readily available water (volume %)		9	16
Cation exchange capacity (m.e./L)		140	210

Table 12.3
Properties of fresh and composted *Eucalyptus camaldulensis* (river redgum) sawdust

Property		Fresh	Composted 3 months
Particle size (mm)	>5	1	1
(% by volume)	2-5	3	2
	1-2	31	26
	0.5-1	37	40
	0.25-0.5	21	19
	0.1-0.25	7	10
	0.05-0.1	1	2
	<0.05	0	1
Bulk density (g/mL),		0.18	0.23
Total porosity (volume %)		86	84
Air-filled porosity (volume %)		51	42
Readily available water (volume %)		15	19

Eucalypt barks are little used outside Western Australia, where *Eucalyptus diversicolor* (karri) and *E. calophylla* (marri) barks are used. Excessive grinding or ageing produces a material which is too fine for use without amendment with coarser materials. Composted karri and marri barks have been found to be highly suppressive of pathogens such as *Phytophthora cinnamomi* and *P. dreschleri*, as has composted whole (wood and bark) acacia. There is every reason to expect that barks from other species will be similar. These composts remain suppressive for at least three years. As little as 10% by volume imparts suppressiveness to other materials. Testing for possible trace element toxicities should be carried out on any new materials.

Figure 12.9

Changes in the temperature of a
typical garden compost heap that is
turned frequently

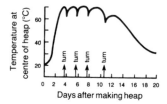

CHANGES IN THE COMPOST HEAP

Changes in compost heaps are similar to those that happen to organic materials added to a soil (Chapter 5), plus a few special ones.

Volume change

Of the carbon in each 'bite' taken from the materials by microbes, about 60% is converted to CO_2, about 33% is made into microbial cells, and the rest is discarded as solid wastes. When these microbes are used by others as food about 60% of their carbon is converted to CO_2, and so on. The CO_2 diffuses into the atmosphere. The heap gets smaller. Heaps made from general wastes may end up at about one-third of the original volume. Shrinkage of bark and sawdust heaps is less because total decomposition is less.

Loss of carbon means that the concentrations of other elements in the remaining materials increase. This means that the compost becomes a richer source of these elements. It can also mean that the salinity of the compost increases as decomposition continues.

Temperature

Much of the 'body' heat given off by microbes in the heap is trapped inside it by the insulating ability of the outer few centimetres of materials. The temperature inside the heap rises, as shown in Fig. 12.9. Turning causes temporary cooling. Peak temperatures inside sawdust heaps are usually in the range 50–65°C. They can be as high as 75°C inside some heaps. As some microbes die at these temperatures, the temperature of the heap can be self-regulating, unless low moisture content allows charring and spontaneous combustion.

Decomposition is most rapid at temperatures in the range 45–50°C. Control to within this range is possible only in heaps that have air blown through them or which are turned on the basis of temperature.

Eventually the amount of undecomposed material decreases, so microbial numbers and the temperature of the heap fall. Composting is more or less over by the time it has fallen to 40°C, although further decomposition will continue slowly.

Microorganisms

Decomposition is carried out by wave after wave of different microbes. First, fungi and acid-producing bacteria use readily available foodstuffs such as amino acids, sugars and starches. As the temperature rises, these first microbes are killed, except in the outer part of the heap. Inside, microbes that thrive at high temperatures increase in numbers. They decompose proteins, fats, cellulose and hemicellulose. Heat-loving actinomycetes are especially good at decomposing cellulose. They can be seen as a greyness covering materials in the heap. They are called 'fire-fang' by those who make mushroom composts.

After food supplies fall and the heap begins to cool, fungi and bacteria sheltering from the heat in the outer part of the heap re-invade the inner parts, presumably using the cells of other microbes as their main food.

Eventually, all that is left are microbial cells, resistant parts of the original materials, and humus.

Killing pathogens and weed seeds

The moist, hot, oxygenated conditions in an active compost heap are just right for killing plant (and animal) pathogens and parasites. Either they are killed outright by the heat or they become food for other microbes. Most weed seeds are also killed if the temperature is high enough (Fig. 26.4).

It is essential that *all* materials spend at least three days in the interior of a

Figure 12.10
The pH of a typical garden compost heap that is regularly aerated varies in this manner

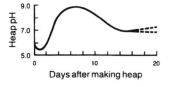

hot heap. This means that outer materials must be put on the inside at each turn.

Composts are not free of microbes, far from it. But they can be free from pathogens and, after a some weeks of maturation, will often come to have a high population of microbes that are able to suppress pathogens. They can have a built-in protection against re-infection (Chapter 26).

pH

Plant sap is acidic, so compost heaps start off acidic. General garden materials may start off at about pH 6. Sawdusts and barks are often more acidic, in the range pH 3–5.

Without lime, the pH of a garden compost heap first drops. Then, as the organic acids are decomposed, ammonia is released. The ammonia combines with hydrogen ions to form ammonium ions; the pH rises (Fig. 12.10). Later, the ammonium is used by microorganisms, and some hydrogen ions are again released. The pH falls and usually stabilizes at about 7. If the compost is stored moist for some months, its pH may fall because of the conversion of organic nitrogen to nitrate. Lime would prevent this fall or reduce its extent.

The pH 3–5 range of sawdusts and barks retards composting, so liming materials are essential for rapid decomposition. Otherwise the changes in pH follow the pattern of Fig. 12.10, with the final pH depending on the amount of lime added.

The warnings about large heaps, excessive wetness, infrequent turning that leads to anerobic conditions and the dangers of high ammonium levels in immature compost are emphasized again.

STORING COMPOSTED MATERIALS

Compost dried to less than 40% moisture can be stored indefinitely under cover. There will be a small amount of decomposition until it dries to about 30% moisture.

Decomposition will continue slowly in composts stored at higher moisture contents. Weight and volume will be lost. Any fertilizer added will increase the rate of decomposition. The compost will heat up and may become anaerobic. Its pH can fall to 2 or less. It will probably then be toxic to plants because of the organic acids in it.

Particular care has to be taken to ensure that compost filled into plastic bags is well matured. Bags need to have ventilation holes in them. Pallets of bags should have air spaces between them.

Figure 12.11
A simple method of producing vermicompost. Tiger worms are introduced into a window (1) of organic materials. Additional materials are added (2, 3, etc.) as they become available. The worms eventually separate themselves from their castings in the first window, etc., as they move to the newer materials

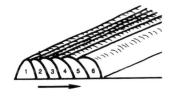

Table 12.4
Concentrations of nutrient elements in some vermicomposts, and their pH values (K A Handreck, unpublished data)

Source	N	P	K	S	Fe	Mn	Zn	Cu	B	Mo	pH
	% in dry matter				ppm in dry matter						
Cow manure	1.5	0.8	0.6	0.7	16400	950	205	45	16	21	6.7
Pig manure	2.1	2.5	0.3	0.4	7600	390	910*	380	6	72	5.8
Sheep manure	2.7	1.9	0.2	0.6	4600	325	865	100	46	68	6.9
Poultry manure	2.4	3.2	0.1	0.4	3700	500	580	41	9	47	6.7
Kitchen scraps	1.1	0.4	0.3	0.2	8300	520	185	22	14	18	5.9
Domestic wastes	2.2	1.1	1.2	0.4	6900	270	1005*	117	43	78	7.8

* These amounts gave toxicity symptoms in test plants.

Matured garden-type composts should not be left in the rain. Plant nutrients, especially nitrogen as nitrate ions, can be lost by leaching.

VERMICOMPOSTING

Although not strictly composting, vermicomposting is mentioned here because it is an alternative method of converting organic wastes into a useful material. In vermicomposting, earthworms, usually tiger worms (*Eisenia fetida*), are allowed to eat their way through heaps of organic wastes such as pig manure, poultry manure and food scraps. A typical arrangement is shown in Fig. 12.11. Vermicompost is a mixture of worm castings and uneaten food. Some producers allow the worms to work the beds until all that is left is pure worm castings.

Vermicomposts and castings have a very wide range of compositions, reflecting their varied sources (Table 12.4). The high levels of some trace elements in some vermicomposts may produce toxicities in some plants in soil-less media if their pH drops below 5. Apart from this, the trace elements in vermicomposts can overcome deficiencies in soils and in potting mixes. Phosphorus levels may be too high for some plants. Most vermicomposts will not supply enough soluble N to satisfy the demands of plants and microbes in sawdust and bark-based potting media.

13 CHOOSING MATERIALS FOR POTTING MIXES

It is possible to grow plants in containers filled with a very wide range of materials. It is even possible to adjust the properties of most of these materials so that excellent plants can be produced. However, the hassles and difficulties of producing plants in potting mixes chosen mainly on the basis of low cost can be very great indeed. We urge all who grow plants in potting mixes to be kind to themselves and buy components or mixes on the basis of quality rather than price. Even though environmental and other factors play a part, a high-quality mix is vital for success in any nursery.

This chapter summarizes information about materials available for use in potting mixes and gives guidelines for formulating them.

MATERIALS AVAILABLE

Pine bark

Figure 13.1
Pine barks and sawdusts are most efficiently composted when they are turned as need is shown by heap temperature. *Courtesy of Debco Pty Ltd, Tyabb, Victoria*

Of all the materials widely available in Australia for potting mixes, composted pine bark (Fig. 13.1) is considered by many to be the best. It can be produced with a range of particle sizes, so that mixes with any desired air-filled porosity can be produced. Mixes based on it shrink little as they dry. Self-mulching of the surface minimizes evaporation of water. Bark particles have about 40% pore space, much of which can hold water. Roots penetrate particles and so have access to water held in them. The humus produced during composting gives them as much cation exchange capacity as many peats. Decomposition rate is lower than that of sawdusts and white peats. Many composted barks have an ability to suppress pathogens.

Barks are available from several species—*Pinus radiata, P. pinaster* and *P. elliotii. P. radiata* and *P. elliotii* barks must be at least aged moist for 4–6 weeks to inactivate toxins. A week or so is enough for *P. pinaster*. Chunky bark from old trees is much easier to grind and handle than is the stringy bark from young trees. Another disadvantage of young bark is that it decomposes more rapidly than does older bark.

While excellent mixes can be made from aged bark, the lower requirement for nitrogen (Chapter 16), the greater buffer capacity and enhanced nutrient-holding capacity of composted bark (Chapter 12) have led to its increasing use. Suppressiveness to pathogens (Chapter 26) will be enhanced if composted bark is matured for some weeks before use.

Sawdust

Hardwood and softwood sawdusts often have to be used as a main component of potting mixes wherever pine barks are unavailable or in short supply. Rapid decomposition of whitewood sawdusts in pots—volume loss can be as much as 50% in one year—causes slumping and sometimes a catastrophic loss of air-filled porosity. The microbes causing this decomposition have a high demand for soluble nitrogen, so that very heavy applications of fertilizer nitrogen are usually

Figure 13.2

Growth of *Cuphea hyssopifolium* 'Violet' in media containing the same concentration of controlled-release fertilizer, but with NDI values ranging from NDI_{75} = 1.1 (left) to NDI_{150} = 0.36 (approx NDI_{75} = −0.64; Fig. 16.10) (right). *From K A Handreck Australian Horticulture* August: 24, 1993

necessary if plants are to receive their requirements (Fig. 13.2). Management is much trickier in sawdust than in pine bark mixes, but with careful attention to nutrition it is possible to grow excellent plants in sawdust-based mixes.

Sawdusts are occasionally from the one species of tree but are more usually mixtures from several species. All hardwood sawdusts, with the exception of jarrah, must be detoxified by composting before use in potting mixes. Composted coarse sawdusts initially have good physical properties; finer sawdusts need amending to improve aeration. A main cause of problems experienced in nurseries with sawdusts is variation in nitrogen drawdown between batches. This presumably is caused by inadequate control of the composting process, leading to varying degrees of stabilization and maturity in the composted sawdust. Composting should be done in windrows that have cross-sections no larger than those given in Chapter 12, and with a turning frequency that maintains adequate aeration and moisture content throughout the whole sawdust mass.

Composted hardwood sawdusts have too high a nitrogen drawdown rate for successful inclusion in mixes for bedding plants or propagation by cuttings. Their inclusion in general potting mixes should generally be limited to 20% by volume, but higher proportions can be used so long as you are prepared to increase nitrogen supply in line with the nitrogen drawdown index (NDI) of the mix (Chapter 16). Pine sawdusts may be used in propagation media without composting, but they will give better results if they are composted before inclusion in general potting mixes.

The peats and peatmosses

Peatmoss, sphagnum peat, sedge peat, sphagnum peatmoss, hypnum peat, white peat, black peat. These names cover many materials that have similar origins, yet can be very different from one another. All peats are dug from swampy areas in cool climatic zones. They are the partly decomposed remains of plants that grow in swampy conditions. The most common plants are the *Sphagnum* mosses and the sedges *(Caryx* species). Under cool waterlogged conditions, sugars and celluloses are decomposed, leaving behind the lignified cell walls and humus. The cellular structure of the plants is more or less preserved in the peat. It is this cellular structure (Fig. 13.3) that gives *Sphagnum* peats their unique properties.

Much of a *Sphagnum* moss leaf is made up of large cells about 0.1 to 0.2 mm long. These cells are internally 'buttressed' so that they resist pressures that would otherwise collapse them. The many holes in the cell walls allow entry and exit of water. Partial decomposition of cell walls means that the whole structure is 'fluffed up' during milling. Water can be held in the cells and in the many medium-sized pores formed between them. The total amount of water held is as much as eight times the dry weight of the moss. The size of the pores is such that a high proportion of the water in the best peatmosses is readily available to plants.

Peats differ from one another for several reasons:

- They contain the remains of different species of plants. Generally, those formed from *Sphagnum* mosses provide better aeration when wet than do the sedge peats.
- They vary in their degree of decomposition. In the most decomposed the particles are very small. Water-holding ability is high, but aeration is poor in containers.
- Variable proportions of mineral matter may be present. High proportions will give poor aeration in containers. Those peats (sphagnum) most readily available in Australia come from Germany, Canada, New Zealand, Russia, Ireland and Tasmania. Variation in quality between brands and batches makes it impossible to make more than general comments about their properties.
- The term 'sphagnum peatmoss' is reserved for dried, recently alive *Sphagnum*.

Figure 13.3
Detail of a *Sphagnum* leaf showing the large water-holding cells opening to the outside through pores. The cells are prevented from collapsing when they dry by thickened bands of cell wall material that can be seen through the cell surface and through the pores. Magnification: x840.   *Photograph R C Foster*

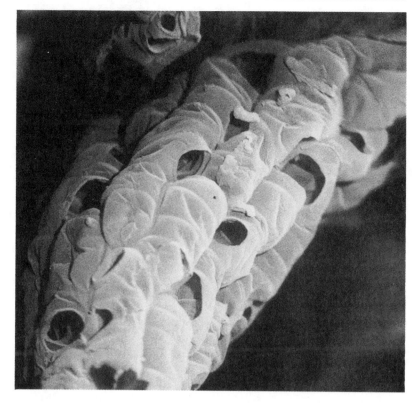

It is the most open of all peatmosses. It decomposes more rapidly in pots than peats that are already more highly decomposed.

- The term 'white peat' refers to light-coloured sphagnum peat of large particle size and limited decomposition. It is more expensive than the more decomposed, black peats. Its importance is in its ability to provide excellent aeration plus moderate water-holding capacity. It decomposes more rapidly than black peats.

- The more highly decomposed 'black peats' are not suitable for use in growing media until they have been frozen in the peat bogs for at least a week. During freezing, cells are expanded as ice crystals grow inside them. Black peat quality is poor in years when northern hemisphere winters are mild.

- European peats vary in quality according to source, season and even container load, so only general comments can be made. Coarser, lumpy types are of no use in plugs and small cells, but can be used to increase the air-filled porosity of a fine mix. Fine grades are useful for increasing the amount of water held in otherwise very open bark and sawdust-based mixes. You *must* measure the air-filled porosity of your mix with every change in batch or brand of peat, if you are to avoid drowning or droughting your plants.

- Mixes containing high proportions of peat (more than 60–70%) shrink as water is removed from them. Water must be applied before shrinkage is so great that it just runs down between container wall and mix and does not stop long enough to wet much mix.

- High-peat mixes rapidly lose water by evaporation from the surface. A mulch of coarse bark, bagasse, or similar materials will greatly reduce the rate of loss. These last few points lead us to conclude that high peat mixes are generally inferior in physical properties to mixes based on the best composted pine barks.

- Australian peats are a mixed bag. The only true sphagnum peat with good physical properties comes from Tasmania. Sedge peats from southern New South Wales tend to be somewhat stringy but can be useful. All other peats are highly decomposed black peats. Including 5-10% in a mix will give a useful boost to cation exchange capacity (CEC) and will provide some available iron. Many of them are saline as mined and must be washed before use. A few from Western Australia have an acceptably low salinity as mined. A coarse grade of one is useful for providing high CEC without reducing air-filled porosity unacceptably.
- All peats are acid. They have a low bulk density (Table 13.1), a high level of readily available water, variable air-filled porosity at container capacity, and high buffer capacity (p. 99).

Table 13.1
Approximate **dry bulk densities of some materials used in growing media**

Material		Bulk density (g/mL)
Peatmosses		0.03–0.14 (mostly about 0.1)
Pine bark	2-5 mm	0.12
	0.5-1 mm	0.21
	<0.5 mm	0.30
	mixed	0.25–0.27
Coir dust		0.16–0.25
Sawdust (*Eucalytus camaldulensis*)		0.23
Sand	0.5-1 mm	1.28
Clay		1.2
Diatomite		0.42
Attapulgite (calcined)		0.53
Lignite	0.5-1 mm	0.47
	0.1-0.5 mm	0.46
Vermiculite, exfoliated	1-2 mm	0.11
Clay pellets		0.3–0.6
Perlite	2-5 mm	0.21
Scoria	0.5-2 mm	0.85

All imported peat is expensive, but it can be a very useful component in mixes where lightness, ability to hold water and high buffer capacity are essential.

Concern about the destruction of peat bogs has led to successful campaigns in Europe for a halt to the use of peat in horticulture. We consider these campaigns to be somewhat misinformed, in view of the fact that most mined peat is burnt in power stations. Nevertheless, they have caused a reduction in the use of peat in Europe and a considerable increase in the use of other materials.

Eucalypt bark

Research in Western Australia has shown that bark from *Eucalyptus diversifolia* and *E. calophylla* that has been composted and aged for about 12 months, when included at about 10% in a mix with coarser materials, suppresses a range of root-rotting diseases (Chapter 26). This composted material is too fine to use alone. Bark from these same species is now milled to a physical consistency that makes it an excellent component (20–30%) of potting mixes without composting. Mixing of media containing it is to be done in shredder-blenders, as the bark tends to 'ball' in concrete mixers. These positive results with bark from two species should not be transferred without testing to bark from other species. For

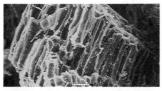

Figure 13.4
Scanning electron micrograph of coir fibre dust, showing the multitude of pores that hold water in a form that is readily available to plants. Magnification: × 87 *Photograph S McClure*

example, the very high manganese content of some eucalpyt barks (up to 3900 ppm Mn) could cause toxicity if more than a small proportion were to be used.

Rice hulls

Whole rice hulls are moderately resistant to decomposition. They hold little water and improve aeration; they are a useful lightweight component of mixes for orchids and are also used to increase the porosity of bedding plant mixes based on peat. An upper limit of use is about 25% by volume, mainly because their large particles reduce the water-holding capacity of the mix. Their high manganese (Mn) content means that fertilizers used should not contain Mn, and the pH of the mix must not be allowed to fall below 5 if Mn toxicity is to be avoided.

Rice hulls that have been composted with other materials and hammermilled are also available. Severe nitrogen drawdown (NDI_{150} of about 0.2) will limit the usefulness of this product. Ferrous sulphate addition should be at least 1 kg/m^3. There is a possibility of Mn toxicity if pH falls below 5. An upper limit to its inclusion in a mix is about 50%.

Bagasse

This is the fibrous residue left after juice has been extracted from sugar cane. It decomposes rapidly when used as a component of potting media. Its stringiness makes it difficult to handle. Composting gives a fine material that can make up only a small proportion of a mix. Quite a few nurseries use it, but if other materials are available they are usually preferred.

Coir dust

Since about 1990 there has been a dramatic increase in interest in the use of coir fibre dust in potting media, mainly as a direct substitute for peat. Coir fibre dust is the pithy material left after coir fibre is extracted from coconut husks. It is produced in Sri Lanka, Malaysia, Indonesia, the Philippines and potentially in other tropical countries with extensive coconut plantations. The husks must be soaked in water before fibre extraction, so the residual pith is produced in a wet state. It is dried and often compressed into blocks before being exported.

Coir dust has excellent physical properties. It does not suffer from the water-repellency problems of other organic materials. Its water-holding characteristics are better than those of most peats, because of its finer pore structure (Fig. 13.4). However, most coir dusts are too fine to make up the majority of a

Table 13.2
Concentrations of chloride found in some samples of coir dust and other materials being sold in Australia. (*From* K A Handreck *Australian Hortic.* November: 54, 1992 and unpublished data)

Sample and origin	Chloride concentration in 1:1.5 extract (mg/L)
Malaysia	886
Sri Lanka	280
Sri Lanka	250
Sri Lanka	14
Thailand	411
Peat from Russia	35
Pine bark, Australia	25

mix. Coir dust's main potential use is in increasing the water-holding capacity of barks and sawdusts without unacceptable reduction in air-filled porosity.

A major problem with coir dust is its often high chloride content (Table 13.2). Plant growth is inevitably reduced by the concentrations in some products. Coir dust with an acceptably low chloride content can be produced. You should check any product offered or get a guarantee that all of the batch is uniformly low in chloride. Fertilizers used should not contain chloride. There are other nutritional problems, but these are easier to overcome than is a high chloride content.

All coir products tested have very high K contents and very low calcium contents. Their pH is generally close to 6 so there is no possibility of using liming materials to supply calcium. Therefore, all coir-based media must be amended with gypsum, which also overcomes their low sulphur status. Iron and copper must be added at the rate commonly used for bark media (Chapter 16). Coir dust has an NDI of about 0.7 (Chapter 16), which means that liquid feeds need to contain an extra 50 mg/L N above the concentration needed by the same plants growing in peat-based media. Nitrogen requirements are therefore similar to those for plants in composted pine bark mixes.

Peanut shells

Coarser grades of peanut shells improve aeration and drainage. Finer grades increase readily available water content. Extra nitrogen is needed. Decomposition leading to slumping of the mix can cause problems in pots held for a year or more. High salinity in some batches has caused problems. Any nematodes and weed seeds should be killed by pasteurization or with methyl bromide.

Composts

Composts and leaf moulds were once a major component of potting mixes. (The very use of the term 'potting compost' in Britain for materials for pots shows what was once used.) 'Organic' growers still use them, but unless one has access to a ready supply of raw materials of consistent quality, the expense and effort of preparing them makes them dearer than alternatives. Matured composts contribute nutrients and increase the readily available water content of otherwise very open mixes. Salts content can be high before leaching. Cation exchange capacity is high.

Increasing volumes of composts made from general organic wastes (mainly of garden origin), from sewage sludges (sometimes now referred to as biosolids) and from municipal solid wastes (MSW) will be produced as we go through the 1990s. All can be used in potting mixes, but with caution and with volume additions being based on physical and chemical analysis. It is essential that you at least test for pH, salinity and ammonium content.

Sewage sludge material with a total zinc content of about 1000 mg/kg should not make up more than about 50% of a mix, unless you can be sure that the pH of the mix will remain above 6. A drop in pH to below 5 may produce zinc toxicity in some plants.

- Composts made from general organic wastes have been successfully used at up to 50% by volume. Caution is needed in transferring these results to all such composts. Thus some composts are fine and decompose rather quickly; they should probably make up no more than 30% of any mix.
- MSW composts are usually fairly fine and typically contain levels of boron that will be toxic to plants if they make up more than about 20% of a mix. These composts must be thoroughly matured. At least 90 days of composting plus maturing is needed to produce an acceptable product.
- Mushroom composts are usually of very high pH and salinity (EC of a 1:1.5 extract can be 12–15 dS/m; compare this with Table 21.13). They can make up about 10% of a mix, but only if analysis of the mix shows no problems.

A disadvantage is the appearance at the pot surface of fruiting bodies ('toadstools') of the fungi that decompose it.

- Sewage sludge composts are being used in potting media in some states. Their fineness limits use rate to around 20%. The levels of copper and zinc in sludge composts mean that neither of these elements should be added in fertilizers. Most sludges have low levels of available manganese, so this element must be added in amounts indicated by analysis. The use of these composts is subject to strict government control. Much of the high total P content of sewage sludge composts is poorly available to plants, but the ability of proteoid roots to dissolve some of this P suggests that proteaceous plants should not be grown in media containing this material.
- Composted poultry litter has been used, but its often high and variable salinity, and the strong possibility of ammonium toxicity, suggest that it is of very limited use. These factors restrict its use to no more than 2–5% of a mix by volume.
- In some areas, waste products such as poppy straw and cotton gin trash are composted to make useful components of potting mixes.
- Composts are excellent sources of trace elements, and they can suppress pathogens (Chapter 26).

Vermicompost and worm castings

Vermicompost is a mixture of the castings and unused bed materials produced when earthworms are fed exclusively on organic materials such as animal manures and vegetable and fruit wastes. Some producers allow sufficient time for the beds to become pure worm castings. Vermicomposts produced from different materials have widely differing compositions (Table 12.4). At 30% by volume in a pinebark/sand-based mix they are usually unable to supply more than a minute amount of soluble nitrogen (Fig. 13.5). Most supply enough phosphorus and potassium for some months of growth. The trace element content of most vermicomposts is high and readily available to plants. Some contain levels of zinc (Table 12.4) that make them potentially toxic to plants if mix pH drops below 5. As for other composts, additions must be based on a measurement of air-filled porosity. The granular nature of worm castings gives them a better structure than that of ordinary compost made from the same materials, but otherwise there is little difference between them.

Fern fibre

The ground trunks and fronds of tree ferns—rescued from the seemingly relentless march of destruction in some Australian native forests or from *Pinus radiata* plantations in New Zealand—and ground bracken ferns, make excellent potting mixes. All that is needed is the addition of liming materials to raise pH from a natural value typically around 4, ferrous sulphate at about 800 g/m^3 and copper sulphate at about 20 g/m^3.

Grape marc

Grape marc consists of the skins, stems and seeds of grapes that have been crushed for winemaking. When stacked in heaps, the skins and parts of the stems decompose, leaving seeds the size of very coarse sand plus compost. Before you use it, make sure that it is composted until it no longer heats up on being turned. It is useful as a component of 'light' mixes in grapegrowing areas. Unleached, it is very saline. The nutrients in it are somewhat imbalanced, with the level of potassium being very high and the levels of calcium, magnesium, copper and zinc being very low. It seems best to use no more than about 20% in a mix, but analysis will soon show what level is possible.

Figure 13.5
Response of stocks (*Matthiola incana*) to the incorporation of 30% by volume of vermicomposts into a pinebark/sand mix. Left pot in each photograph = control (no vermicompost; complete liquid feed at each watering). (a) No N in the liquid feed to V3 pots (containing vermicompost based on poultry manure); (b) N-only liquid feed, same vermicompost. *From* K A Handreck *BioCycle* Oct: 58, 1986

(a)

(b)

Lignite (brown coal)

Hard grades of brown coal have been used in potting mixes, but use has decreased in recent years. The material is messy and unpleasant to handle. The fines tend to be quickly lost from pots in drainage water. Additions of more than 5–10% by volume can reduce air-filled porosity unacceptably. Some batches are saline, so check. The good things about brown coal are its high cation exchange capacity and its ability to give mixes a dark 'rich soil' colour. Lignite is a useful source of sulphur and provides some iron.

Sand

Many grades of sands are available. Those with mainly medium to very coarse particle sizes (0.25–2 mm) are generally preferred. Finer grades can be used to increase the water-holding capacity of mixes whose other components are coarser. Avoid sands containing more than a few percent silt and clay. Don't use calcareous sands. Sands with minerals other than quartz supply some nutrients. Sharp sands are preferred. Rounded particles can separate out during mixing or allow the mix to fall apart during repotting and transport. Sand provides ballast and also helps overcome re-wetting problems (p. 31).

Gravel

Gravel can be used instead of sand as ballast in the open mixes needed for orchids.

Perlite

Perlite is a porous (Fig. 13.6) siliceous material produced by rapidly heating a natural volcanic glass to 1200°C. It is sterile immediately after production and supplies no nutrients. Coarser grades are useful for improving the aeration of finer materials. Check each shipment, as rough handling in transport can crush coarse particles into a material that is so fine that it gives very poor aeration.

Figure 13.6
Above: Particles of perlite and
Below: Particles of exfoliated
vermiculite, showing the sizes of the
internal pores. Magnification: x2.5.
Photograph J Coppi

Vermiculite

Vermiculite is a flaky mineral that occurs naturally in many parts of the world. Supplies come from Africa and several Australian sources. The raw mineral is crushed and graded for size before it is heated very rapidly to between 700 and 1000°C. The particles expand (exfoliate) to many times their original volume. Exfoliated vermiculite (Fig. 13.6) has a low bulk density. In pots it has a lower air-filled porosity than perlite of similar size, but holds rather more water. When mixed wet, its physical properties deteriorate because the particles tend to collapse flat. Media containing vermiculite should be mixed dry. It supplies magnesium and some potassium. It is useful as a covering for germinating seeds, but pasteurize it first if there is any chance that it could have been contaminated after manufacture. Expense is a main drawback. It must not be included in mixes for gerberas and primulas: one piece in contact with a root tip can reduce flowering!

Plastic foams

Foamed polystyrene (styrofoam) is the most common form of plastic foam used. It is available in various pellet sizes. It behaves like large, light, non-wetting sand grains. The air trapped inside the pellet is not in contact with the other air in the mix. Styrofoam increases aeration and drainage through its large particle size. It contains no nutrients and has negligible cation exchange capacity. Lightness is a problem during mixing in windy conditions. Particles tend to float to the surface during irrigation. Its main use is in media for rooting cuttings.

Some polyurethane ester foams have been reported to contain toxins.

Figure 13.7
Excellent root growth on cuttings in an Oasis Rootcube and a Horticube. *Courtesy of Smithers Oasis, Elizabeth, South Australia*

Phenol formaldehyde foam, formed into wedges and cubes (Fig. 13.7) are increasingly being used for the rooting of cuttings. Two gradings, one with a very high air-filled porosity (AFP), are available. Watering frequency must vary accordingly. It is essential that the rootballs be kept wet by frequent watering for the first few days after transplanting or planting out.

Rockwool

Rockwool blocks are used extensively in Europe for growing some vegetable and flower crops. Growool blocks are used for the same purpose in Australia. Use of rockwool blocks for rooting cuttings has not been widely accepted. This appears to be mainly because the blocks have relatively low air-filled porosity and high water content, so watering frequency and amount must be carefully controlled. The depth of sticking of cuttings must be shallow. Both water-repellent and water-absorbing granulates are increasing in use in Europe as components of general potting media (Fig. 13.8). They appear set to increase in importance as pressures to reduce use of peat continue.

Scoria

Scoria is a hard, porous volcanic rock that can be crushed and screened to any desired particle size range. Sand-size particles (0.5–2 mm) behave like perlite, but have a higher bulk density. Its high and variable pH (7–10) means that each batch has to be tested and adjustments made to lime or dolomite additions. It is abrasive to mixing machinery. It is especially useful as the 'solids' phase of hydroponics media (Fig. 27.1).

Pumice

Pumice is a porous mineral foam of volcanic origin. Coarse grades improve aeration. It is expensive and not readily available in Australia.

Soil

Figure 13.8
Granulated rockwool is now a common component of growing media in northern Europe. It is available in water-repellent and water-absorbing forms. *Photograph K A Handreck*

Soil was once the basis of most potting mixes. It is still used in nurseries in the tropics as a means of increasing the water-holding capacity of media for large pots. Elsewhere, most media are now soil-less. A major problem with soil is maintaining access to a supply of consistent quality. Potting mixes with more than about 30 volume % soil usually have poor aeration in shallow pots. These mixes also have a high bulk density and can have a low level of readily available water if there is much clay in the soil. Clay soils can increase cation exchange capacity and do contribute microorganisms and nutrients, especially iron and other trace elements. Sandy loams will usually decrease the cation exchange capacity of a mix composed mainly of materials rich in humus. A small amount of some, but not all, clays can protect sensitive plants against P toxicity, but it is far better to have a low level of P present than to rely on an unknown clay. You should assume that any soil might contain pathogens that must be destroyed by air-steaming or with methyl bromide.

If soil is to be used, it should be a sandy loam or loamy sand (Chapter 3). Use the air-filled porosity of trial mixes to decide on the proportion of soil to use. Loams with more than about 20% clay and silt will be unsuitable for most mixes. Sandy loams amended with organic matter are very useful mixtures for use in large landscaping tubs and boxes. These need a mix that will not shrink much and that has a high capacity to hold water that is available over the suction range 10 to about 300 kPa.

Zeolites

Zeolites are silicate minerals with high cation exchange capacities. The main zeolite available at the time of writing had calcium as its main exchangeable cation, but it also had a moderate level of available potassium. Crushed zeolite included in a soil-less potting mix (about 20 g/L mix) reduces losses of ammonium ions by leaching and so can improve the efficiency of use of fertilizer nitrogen. Inclusion of 5% zeolite in mixes for bedding plants can ensure complete freedom from ammonium toxicity, even when Isobutylidene diurea (IBDU) is present at what would otherwise be a toxic rate. The inevitably high cost of zeolite will probably limit its use in the nursery industry to such special situations.

Hydrogels

Various manufactured materials that absorb large proportions of distilled water are being sold as additives for potting mixes. These materials, referred to variously as hydrogels or superabsorbent polymers, are sold for use in potting media and for incorporation into soils. The early starch-based materials appear to be much less effective than the more recent polyacrylamide materials such as

Table 13.3
Weight loss over six weeks of several types of hydrogel during incubation with soil humus (From M S Johnson Arab Gulf J. Sci. Res. 3: 745, 1985)

Polymer type	Weight loss (%)		
	Week 1	Week 3	Week 6
Starch-polyacrylonitrile	1.9	13.6	19.7
Urea-formaldehyde	1.4	3.9	9.5
Vinyl alcohol acrylic acid	0	2.4	4.9
Polyacrylamide	0	0	2.8

Alcosorb (= Broadleaf P4) (Table 13.3). There are many reports of benefits after incorporation into sandy soils.

Conflicting results of research make it difficult to come to a firm conclusion about their use in potting mixes. This research has shown that their absorbing capacity is reduced to less than a quarter by the normal level of nutrients in potting mixes, especially by iron and calcium, but this effect is much smaller with cross-linked polyacrylamide materials than with starch-based ones. If they are included in potting mixes, watering must be slow so that the gels have time to reabsorb water. Some species benefit from their presence; others growing under the same conditions do not. We conclude that anyone wanting to use hydrogels in potting media should do so only on the basis of positive results from trials under the same conditions as those of eventual use.

Attapulgite

Attapulgite is a clay mineral that occurs naturally in several parts of the world, including at Lake Nerramyne in Western Australia. As mined, it is a soft clay, but for use in containers it is heat-treated (calcined) to increase its hardness, then crushed and screened to give a range of size gradings. Calcined attapulgite has a high ability to absorb water, but the water inside the grains is held too tightly for plants to use. It therefore behaves in mixes as (expensive) sand of the same particle size, but with a higher buffer capacity. Attapulgite at 10% of a mix reduces P supply by about 30%.

Crushed slags and cinders and ash

These are a mixed bag of materials that can provide a cheap alternative to sand. The best are used with success, but the fines content of some limits their usefuless.

You *must* check the pH and salinity of any new materials and for the presence of toxins.

Coke breeze

Coke breeze is the 'fines' screened from coke produced for use in the steel-making industry. Its structure is similar to that of perlite, but the particles are less likely to be crushed. It is used with success in areas near sources of supply.

Shales

Shales are soft slate-like rocks formed by compression of layers of clay particles. They contain some organic matter. Crushed shale is used widely in the southern United States at about 20% of pine-bark/sand mixes. Shales have a high cation exchange capacity and supply some nutrients. They appear to have some of the advantages given by a small amount of soil, but without the problems caused by fine particles and pathogens in soils.

Mill mud

The 'mud' residue from the processing of sugar cane is used in media produced around sources of supply. As its name suggests, its average particle size is tiny, and so its use reduces the air-filled porosity of mixes. It has a high phosphorus concentration.

Miscellaneous

Many other wastes can be used in potting media. Such materials include straw, sunflower husks, cotton seed hulls, cocoa husks and coffee grounds, macadamia nut shells, tobacco wastes, brewery wastes and paper. Most can be used only after shredding, composting and/or other processing to reduce toxicity. Their use must always be based in the first instance on analysis and then on growing trials.

A product called Hortifibre is available in Europe. It is produced from pine wood. Chips are softened with steam and then passed between two plates rotating against each other. Hortifibre is fibrous and has a high porosity. It is commonly used at a rate of about 30% in mixtures with peat.

Solids separated from the washings from cattle feedlots can be used in mixes. An upper limit is about 40 volume %, with the rest being larger particles.

Shredded rubber tyres must not be used, as they contain toxic levels of zinc.

CHOOSING COMPONENTS AND FORMULATING A POTTING MIX

The simplest way of formulating a potting mix is to leave it to a specialist manufacturer whose products have a reputation of being excellent. An increasing proportion of nurseries have done just that in recent years.

But some nurseries choose to make their own mix, and in some areas that is the only option available. Here are some guidelines. We want to stress that materials of lowest initial cost may not necessarily produce quality plants for the lowest overall cost.

Assess the likely continuity of supply

It takes a lot of time and effort to work out a system for making and using a particular mix. Each mix needs its own watering and fertilizing schedule. A change in the quality of one component can upset the whole system and may cause serious losses of production. Especially difficult to detect are changes that cannot be seen with the unaided eye.

For example, a change in the level of phenols in pine bark—because of change in tree age or in time taken to detoxify the bark—can seriously reduce plant growth immediately after potting up. Incomplete composting can give considerable variation in the nitrogen drawdown potential of wood wastes, making it difficult to know how much fertilizer to use. Contamination with soil containing pathogens can be disastrous.

You need to have some assurance that the main components chosen will continue to be available, and of continuing acceptable quality.

Be sure of your goals

Ask yourself: 'What is my aim in growing plants in pots?' It might be one or more of:

- rapid growth and turnover, with quality of lesser importance;
- high quality, well-grown plants of excellent and uniform appearance;
- plants that have few problems when planted out into soils in minimum-care situations;
- plants that have a good 'shelf-life' in retail outlets;
- plants for hiring out in situations where watering more than once weekly is not possible;
- a need to keep weight to a minimum because of long-distance transport;
- freedom from diseases and soil because of the requirements of importing countries or local regulations;
- easy care in long-term display situations, etc.

Your answer will be a major guide to what you choose for your mix.

Cost

In a competitive industry, cost of materials used is important. But cost must not be allowed to override every other consideration. The materials you choose for your mix must allow you to reach your goals with the fewest hassles. Go for lowest cost, certainly, but try some other mixes too. Only then can you be sure that you are not economizing falsely.

Assess some important properties of the materials

Having decided on what you really want to achieve with your plants, and knowing the costs and availability of materials, the next step is to look in detail at the properties of those materials.

The first part of this chapter gave the properties of the main materials used. The differences and similarities between materials can be better seen by considering the properties under the groupings biological, chemical and physical.

BIOLOGICAL PROPERTIES

We consider two aspects:

- presence or absence of harmful microorganisms (pathogens);
- presence or absence of beneficial microorganisms. There is no such thing as a material that is completely free from pathogens. Perlite and vermiculite will be sterile immediately after being heated, but pathogens on dust particles in the air can easily contaminate them. In a well-balanced mix, other microorganisms that can feed on pathogens will normally keep them in check. But if the level of contamination is high and if conditions favour the pathogen and not its attackers, damage to plants in the mix can be severe.

You may choose to:

- Not use materials known to be grossly contaminated with pathogens.
- Disregard possible contamination, hoping that disease won't cause problems. Disaster might or might not be the result.
- Disregard contamination, but eliminate it by air-steaming, composting, or with

chemicals such as methyl bromide (if it continues to be available). Air-steaming is often standard practice for propagating media.

- Use materials known to have little contamination, and through good hygiene keep them that way.
- Disregard contamination, and when disease becomes a problem suppress it with chemicals. This is not a desirable course to take because usually the pathogens are not eliminated. Some are passed on to the customer.
- Encourage biological control by adding beneficial microorganisms to your mix (Chapter 26).

With good nursery hygiene and appropriate treatment of mixes before use, a low level of pathogens in materials being considered for potting mixes need not be a main reason for not choosing them. More detail on disease control and hygiene is given in Chapter 26.

CHEMICAL PROPERTIES

Check for presence of toxins

The most common causes of toxicity are damagingly high levels of salts, chemicals of natural origin, and added chemicals. Excessive salinity is caused in a variety of ways (Chapter 21). Leaching with sufficient fresh water eliminates the problem. Early detection is important.

Toxins of natural origin can usually be eliminated by composting or ageing, but note (p.116) that composts must be fully matured.

Added toxins might come from the use of sawdust from treated timber, MSW compost with a high level of boron, or contamination with, for example, herbicides or other chemicals. These problems are uncommon, but all have been reported.

Consider the effect of a component on plant nutrition

Nitrogen

The chemical property of overriding importance is the interaction of the material with nitrogen. Soluble nitrogen is consumed as wastes such as barks, sawdusts, coir and rice hulls are decomposed by microorganisms. This process, referred to as nitrogen drawdown, reduces nitrogen supply to plants growing in media containing these materials. The fertilizers used must provide enough nitrogen for nitrogen drawdown and plant growth. It is essential that you or your supplier use the nitrogen drawdown index (NDI) test (Chapter 33) as a guide to the need for fertilizer N (Chapter 16).

Other nutrients

Media components contain and supply nutrient elements. For example, composts have good supplies of all or most trace elements; grape marc and coir dust have very high K contents; pine barks supply K and manganese; and so on. Levels of particular elements that are too low for plant growth can easily be boosted with fertilizers. There is certainly no need to reject a component just because it lacks a particular nutrient.

A moderate concentration of a nutrient element calls for reduced addition in fertilizers. Very high concentrations of elements such as manganese and boron will limit the proportion of the component that can be used.

It is now very simple, through use of the extraction procedures given in the Australian Standard for potting mixes (AS 3743–1993), to adjust the levels of available plant nutrients in potting mixes before planting. Some details are given in Chapter 16.

Other chemical properties

Media components have a general effect on nutrition through their cation exchange and buffer capacities. These are increased as the proportion of fines, especially organic fines, in the medium increases (Table 11.13). Exchange sites take nutrients from solution when fertilizer is added and then slowly release them later. A high cation exchange capacity (CEC) evens out the supply of nutrient cations to plants. High buffer capacity will also reduce the possibility of large changes in pH. Losses of nutrients by leaching are reduced as CEC rises. High CEC is not as necessary when controlled-release fertilizers are used as when liquid feed is the main method of fertilization. Slow release from the fertilizer then takes the place of slow release from particle surfaces. High CEC is not essential, but it does help to even out nutrient supply. In other words, a proportion of humified organic matter in a mix is a *good thing*.

Physical properties

By 'physical properties' we mean mainly the proportions of air and water in a mix when drained and the ease with which plant roots can extract the water. Other important physical properties include bulk density, wettability following drying, and flowability.

These physical properties depend on the shape, size and density of individual particles, the relative proportions of different sizes present, whether or not the particles have internal pore space, their stability (both short-term and long-term), and the way the particles pack together.

You get only one chance at setting the physical properties of a potting mix, and that is before potting. Thereafter, it is usually all downhill as components decompose and roots fill pores. It is therefore critically important that a mix is formulated on the basis of measurements of air-filled porosity and water-holding capacity made on trial mixtures. But a word of caution is in order. There is no point in formulating a mix that has 'ideal' physical properties if it has faults such as a toxic level of a nutrient or a huge hunger for nitrogen. These other factors have to be kept in mind as you go through a formulation for excellent physical properties.

The basis of good physical properties

We saw in Chapter 10 that good growth of most plants is possible only when some of the pores in the medium around their roots contain air. Somewhere between about 10% and 50% of the volume of a medium in a container should be air immediately after drainage has stopped.

Mixes must also contain as high a proportion as is possible of readily available water—water that is released between container capacity and 10 kPa suctions—so that irrigation frequency is minimized.

Pores must contain either air or water. If many are to contain water, it is inevitable that few will contain air. An important aim in formulating a mix is to get a balance between air-filled porosity (at container capacity) and readily available water content. As we shall see below, these properties depend on the proportions of particles of different sizes in the mix and on the types of materials used.

Effect of particle size

We already know that:

- pores between large particles are larger than pores between small particles and, in a just-drained mix in a pot:
  - the smaller pores will be filled with water;
  - the largest pores will be filled with air;

- water in the largest of the smaller pores will be readily available to plants;
- water in the tiniest pores will be unavailable.

Therefore:

- the proportions of air and readily available water in a mix will depend on the proportions of pores of different sizes; and
- many large particles should give much air in the mix;
- many small particles should give a high ability to hold water.

But how large and small, and what are the proportions needed to give different proportions of air and water?

We give just a little more information for those who really want to fine-tune the physical properties of potting mixes. For most practical purposes it is not necessary to have any detail about the sizes of particles present in components and finished mix. Rather, you will make trial mixes, initially on the basis of feel, and then vary proportions of components on the basis of measurements of air-filled porosity.

Figure 13.9
Air-filled porosities and readily available water contents of separates of *Pinus radiata* bark of different particle size ranges. *From* K A Handreck *Comm. Soil Sci. Plant Analysis* 14: 209, 1983

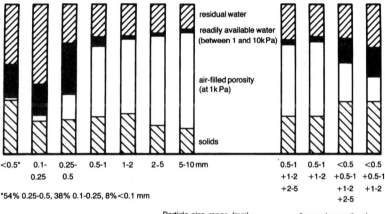

Detailed effects of particle size

Figure 13.9 shows that particles smaller than 0.5 mm have a dominating effect on the air-filled porosity and readily available water of *Pinus radiata* mixes. Including one-quarter to one-third of these particles in with larger particles halves air-filled porosity and increases readily available water content six-fold (the last two bars of Fig. 13.9).

Note that:

- Air-filled porosity is decreased more by particles smaller than 0.25 mm than by those in the range 0.25–0.5 mm.
- Readily available water content is increased more by particles in the range 0.1–0.25 mm than by either larger or smaller particles.
- Other materials behave in broadly similar ways to sand when mixed with coarse pine bark. For example, coarse grades of perlite increase air-filled porosity and decrease readily available water, whereas the opposite can be true for finer grades.
- The effect of very fine particles (<0.05 mm) is shown in Table 13.4. Increasing proportions reduces both air-filled porosity (markedly) and readily available water (a little). Mixes with high proportions of very fine particles still retain water that can be used by plants after that removed at a suction of 10 kPa has been used (Table 13.4, last two columns). Such mixes are used in large tubs and planter boxes and in somewhat smaller containers in hot climates. These mixes inevitably have a fairly low air-filled porosity, but time to wilting

Table 13.4
Effect of very fine particles of crushed quartz (<0.05 mm) on the properties of bark/sand (5:1) mix. (*From* K A Handreck *Comm. Soil Sci. Plant Analysis* 14: 209, 1983)

Fines in the mix (%)	Total porosity (volume %)	Air-filled porosity at 1 kPa suction (volume %)	Water released between: (volume (%)		
			1 & 10 kPa suctions	10 & 300 kPa suctions	1 & 300 kPa suctions
0	66	24	14	8	22
10	63	18	14	10	24
15	61	16	11	13	24
20	57	10	11	15	26
30	54	5	7	19	26

will be longer than for mixes with low proportions of fine particles. The internal pores of coir dust particles also hold considerable amounts of water that are available to plants at these higher suctions.

- If a very high (50 volume % or more) air-filled porosity is needed, most particles must be larger than 0.5 mm. No more than about 5% can be smaller than 0.5 mm.
- For mixes with air-filled porosities in the range 15–25 volume %—a desirable range for general nursery use—no more than about one-quarter of the particles should be in the range 0.1–0.5 mm. A few percent of finer particles is acceptable, but increasing proportions must be accompanied by more particles larger than 0.5 mm. The upper limit for particles smaller than 0.1 mm is about 10%.
- Mixes with air-filled porosities below 15 volume % will have more than about 40% of their particles smaller than 0.5 mm.
- The smaller the average size of the particles below 0.5 mm, the bigger the reduction in air-filled porosity for a given proportion in a mix.
- Particle shape has a variable effect that is difficult to predict.
- Mixes with a good balance between air-filled porosity and ability to supply readily available water will have about 20% of particles in the 0.1–0.25 mm range.

Sieves needed

Sieves are expensive. Only those with an ongoing need to monitor sands and other components will want to buy them. Those that have this need will be able to manage with three: 30 mesh retains everything larger than 0.5 mm; 60 mesh retains 0.25 mm particles; and 150 mesh retains 0.1 mm particles. Sieving is a hassle, and most people who produce potting mixes prefer to use direct measurements of AFP and water-holding capacity in formulating their mixes.

Other comments on physical properties

- The air-filled porosity of a mix increases as its height in a container increases. Larger plants remove water faster than do small plants, so they increase air space faster. Therefore, as container height and plant size increase, the mix used can have higher proportions of fine particles. Irrigation frequency will be reduced compared with that needed for more open mixes.
- Don't compact mixes into pots. Compaction reduces air-filled porosity (Table 13.5). Normal irrigation will soon give all the firming needed.

Figure 13.10
Counter-rotating blades of an
excellent Australian-made mixer.
*Courtesy of Chemical Plant and
Engineering, Broadmeadows, Victoria*

Table 13.5
**Effects of compression on the physical properties of some mixes (*From* B
Howard *Growers Chronical and Hort. Trade J.* Nov. 9: 27, 1979)**

Mix (50:50 by volume)	Air-filled porosity (volume %)		Water content (volume %)	
	Loose	Compressed	Loose	Compressed
Coarse sand/peat	11	5	33	36
Coarse sand/bark	11	5	23	27
Perlite/peat	28	17	29	38
Perlite/bark	34	25	20	25

- Drill holes for plants when potting; don't use a dibble that will compact the mix.
- Without information about particle sizes, it is impossible to tell whether particular proportions of materials will have acceptable or poor physical properties. For example a 1:1:2 sand/sawdust/bark mix could have anything from zero to perhaps 30% air-filled porosity in shallow pots, depending on particle sizes present.
- Mixing must be carefully controlled. The whole batch must be uniform otherwise the mix filled into different pots will have different physical and chemical properties. Batches of plants will be very uneven in quality. So mix thoroughly but with care. Long mixing times can reduce the particle size of materials such as peat, perlite, vermiculite, lignite and worm castings. Table 13.6 gives a typical example. Three minutes of paddle mixing reduced air-filled porosity by 32%.

At first sight, Table 13.6 suggests that a concrete mixer causes less damage than a paddle mixer. However, abrasion by the sharp sand did reduce the particle size of the peat, but this was masked by 'balling'. Barks and sawdusts are damaged less than peat.

Mixing by front-end loader is not good enough. Even mixing, with least damage, is achieved most easily with a belt mixer. Regulated amounts of each component are fed continuously from hoppers onto a conveyor belt. Almost complete mixing is achieved as the layered 'cake' of components falls from the end of the conveyor belt. A paddle mixer having double blades rotating in opposite directions (Fig. 13.10), can mix in as little as 15 seconds.

Always mix the light components first. Keep mixing time as short as possible after adding the heavier components. Mixing over-wet materials can cause them to form into tight balls.

- If you can't make a mix with the physical properties you would like, try to change your management to suit your mix. Amount and frequency of irrigation is the main thing to watch.
- Tests of physical properties are useful, but they don't go all the way. Let your plants be the final judge of new mixes you think you might use.

Table 13.6
Air-filled porosity of a 6:3:1 peat/sharp sand/soil mix after mixing for different times. The figures are volume % of air at container capacity in 125 mm pots

Mixing time (min)	Concrete mixer (volume % air)	Paddle mixer (volume % air)
0.5	—	10.7
1	12.6	9.4
2	10.2	7.9
3	12.8	7.3
5	11.2	6.2
10	12.9	5.7
15	13.3	3.9

FORMULATING A MIX

Table 13.7 lists the important properties of potting mixes. They must all be taken into account when formulating a mix. As discussed earlier, availability and cost must also be considered.

Mixtures of many materials in many different proportions can give satisfactory plant growth if all important chemical, physical and biological properties are met. Their formulations can range from straight, composted pine bark, through two-component mixtures such as 3 bark:1 sand and three-component mixtures such as 2 bark:1 sawdust:1 sand or 3 bark:1 peatmoss:1 sand to more complicated mixtures such as 4 peanut shells:1 cottonseed hulls:1 sawdust:1 sand:0.5 soil. Simple mixes are easiest to make and repeat consistently.

Table 13.7
Important properties of potting mixes

Property	Remarks
Chemical	
Nutrients	Balanced supply of all nutrient elements in amounts to give the desired level of growth
Cation exchange capacity	50–100 m.e./L
Buffer capacity	As high as possible
pH (water)	Depending on the plants being grown, 4.5–6.5, but mainly 5.5–6.0
Soluble salts (EC of a 1:1.5 volume)	Upper limit of 2 dS/m at potting; follow Table 21.13 during growth.
Toxins	Low enough levels so that growth is not affected to an unacceptable extent
Physical	
Air-filled porosity	7–50 volume %, depending on plant species and situation
Readily available water	As high as possible, preferably at least 20 volume %
Bulk density	In the range 0.3–0.6 g/mL gives reasonably low pot weight, plus resistance to tipping over
Particle stability	Materials used should be reasonably stable; if one is likely to decompose quickly (say, in 3–6 months) use a low proportion only
Wettability	Organic materials should be easy to wet with minimum agitation; if not, a wetting agent should be used
Flowability	Mixes need to be able to flow readily through pot-filling machines; sand helps
Infiltration rate	This will be satisfactory if air-filled porosity is more than about 15 volume %; it should be at least 25 mm per minute
Biological	Pathogens should be absent, but a wide range of beneficial microorganisms present.

A sequence

1. Find out what materials are available at an acceptable price, and with assured continuity of supply.
2. Reject any that are too salty or that are likely to contain pathogens or toxins, or be prepared to treat them.
3. Decide what properties are most important to you. For example, high bulk density may be needed for pot stability, low bulk density to lessen back injuries and lower transport costs, high water-holding capacity for maximum time between irrigations and maximum shelf life, high air-filled porosity for allowing maximum growth rate, etc.
4. Decide what level of nitrogen drawdown you can tolerate for the particular plants being grown. For example, a seedling producer will want all components to have a high nitrogen drawdown index (NDI), that is, components with little demand for soluble N. A manufacturer wanting to produce a mix that conforms with the provisions of the Australian Standard will probably find that it will not be possible to include composted eucalypt sawdust in Premium grade mixes and probably less than 10% in Regular grade mixes.

5. Form a short list of two or three organic and two or three mineral components.

6. Make up small (2–5 L) batches of mixes using these components in various proportions. You will try to maximize the proportion of the cheapest organic component, within the limits set by NDI, AFP and water-holding capacity. You may even try to make your medium from the one organic component, if it is available with the right particle size distribution. Usually, however, it is necessary to use at least two components to get the required properties.

7. Measure the AFP of each of these experimental mixes. On the basis of the figures obtained and the porosity range needed, either choose one of the mixtures or make more using different proportions of the components.

8. If no amount of juggling of proportions gives a mix with satisfactory AFP, search for another component or encourage a supplier to screen a component to provide you with a material with an acceptable particle size distribution.

9. Make sure that the mix has a bulk density within the desired range and that it flows as required in your potting machine.

10. Assess the need for any treatment to reduce the toxicity or to remove pathogens.

11. Measure the salinity of the mix. If it is too high, trace the source of the salts and take steps to reduce the hazard. Change to another component, get the supplier to wash the material, etc.

12. Measure the pH of the mix. If it is outside the desired range, set up a trial (Chapter 11) to determine how much liming materials or sulphur to add. In the first attempt you can leave out any fertilizers that you might eventually need to add to provide adequate pre-plant nutrition, but you must realize that adding such chemicals as ferrous sulphate will lower pH, so the final amount of liming materials to be added will be higher than initially measured.

13. Send to a laboratory some of the trial mix that is at the required pH. Ask for it to be extracted with water (1:1.5 ratio) and DTPA according to the provisions of the Australian Standard for Potting Mixes. Also ask the laboratory to indicate the amounts of fertilizers needed to overcome any deficiencies shown up by the analyses, or work it out yourself from the data in Chapter 16.

14. You can also ask the laboratory to determine the NDI of the mix, or you can measure it yourself (Chapter 33).

15. Add fertilizers to another experimental batch as indicated by the analysis results. Add liming materials at such a rate as to give about 0.5 kg more than had previously been found for mix without added fertilizers.

16. After 1–2 weeks, check the pH and EC of this mix, and make any minor adjustments needed to the amount of liming materials to be added to the larger batches.

17. On the basis of the NDI of the mix and the needs of the plants being grown (Chapter 16), choose a pre-plant addition rate for any controlled-release fertilizer that is to be used, whether the fertilizer is to be incorporated into the mix or dibbled at planting.

18. Make up a large enough batch of the mix so that you can grow in it a selection of the plants that you wish to grow. You may need to set up a series of trials (Chapter 33) to check your proposed fertilizer rate. You may need to keep a watch out for any undesirable slumping, and to check to make sure that the time-to-wilting of mature plants is long enough.

19. On the basis of your trials you may need to fine-tune by adjusting the proportions of the components or by replacing one with another.

Of course this all takes time, but when it is done thoroughly you will soon be reaping the benefits.

14 PLANT NUTRIENTS

We starve or feel ill if we eat too little or the wrong type of food. So do plants. They die, are stunted or look 'off-colour' if the supply of nutrients to them is poor or imbalanced.

Plants cannot hunt for nutrients. They can use only those in the air around their leaves or in the growing medium around their roots. The only hunting most are able to do is to grow longer root systems. It is important, therefore, that those who grow plants know how to supply enough of the right kinds of nutrients, and how to put them where plants can use them. These aspects of plant nutrition are dealt with in later chapters. Here we summarize information about the nutrients essential to plant growth.

THE NUTRIENTS

At least 16 elements are needed by all plants. Some plants seem also to need others for best growth. Of the 16, three (carbon, hydrogen and oxygen) come from the carbon dioxide in the air, and water and oxygen in the growing medium. Water supply is covered in Chapters 9, 22 and 23. Supply of oxygen to roots is dealt with in Chapter 10. Some comments on carbon dioxide are given on p.4.

All the rest come from the growing medium, entering plants through their roots. They are commonly divided into two groups, called major and micronutrient (or trace) elements, depending on whether they are found in plants in high or low concentrations. These elements, and some typical concentrations found in plant leaves, are listed in Fig. 14.1.

Miscellaneous elements

The other elements known to be essential are chlorine and nickel. Beneficial effects are also reported for aluminium, sodium and silicon. Aluminium may affect growth mainly by reducing phosphorus toxicity. The blue pigment of hydrangea flowers contains aluminium. Silicon enhances the growth and yields of such plants as rice and sugar cane. It does this mainly by helping the plants to cope with toxic levels of manganese and iron, and by allowing the leaves to be more erect, and so catch more light. Cobalt is essential to *Rhizobium* bacteria and vanadium to blue-green algae.

Many other elements are taken up by plants. A few—chromium, selenium, iodine—are essential to animals.

Where nutrient elements come from

Nutrients enter plant roots as ions that come from the water around their roots. As ions are removed from this water (Fig. 14.2), they may be replaced by others from:

- colloid surfaces;
- decomposition of organic matter;
- decomposition (weathering) of minerals;
- solid fertilizers;

Figure 14.1

Approximate concentration ranges of nutrient elements found in plant leaves. The ranges are % or ppm in the dried leaves. Note the linking between the two ranges, showing that the trace or minor elements are found in very much lower concentrations than are the major elements. (A concentration of 0.02% is equal to 200 ppm.) Plants whose leaves are found to have an elemental concentration that falls within the black part of a bar may be deficient in that element.

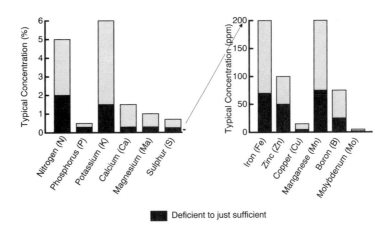

■ Deficient to just sufficient

- additions in liquid feeds;
- controlled-release fertilizers.

Ions from the last five sources can remain in the water in the medium or can exchange places with others on colloid surfaces. The needs of plants will be satisfied if reserves of nutrients on colloid surfaces are large and if decomposition of organic matter and minerals keeps pace with needs. Otherwise, more must be continuously or frequently supplied by solid fertilizers, in liquid feeds, or from controlled-release fertilizers.

Figure 14.2

Schematic diagram showing the exchange of cations between roots and colloid surfaces

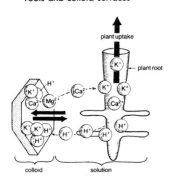

Availability of nutrients

If plants cannot get enough of a nutrient element from a growing medium, it may be either because:

- there is little of the nutrient there; or
- the nutrient is poorly available to the plant—this is poverty in the midst of apparent plenty.

Common examples of poor availability are:

- poor supply of nitrogen because the organic matter in a medium breaks down too slowly to release enough soluble nitrogen for rapidly growing plants;
- poor supply of nitrogen in organic potting media because microbes in them use much of any soluble nitrogen as they decompose the high-carbon materials in it;
- poor supply of phosphorus in soils because most of the phosphorus is tied-up ('fixed') in very insoluble minerals;
- poor availability of iron, especially, but other trace elements too, because of interference by other materials in the medium. Examples are interference with iron by bicarbonate and phosphate and the tightness with which peat holds copper.
- note that pH affects availability (Figs 11.1 and 11.2).

Availability might be improved by changing some property such as the pH of the growing medium. Otherwise, the nutrient element in short supply must be supplied in a more soluble (available) form in fertilizers.

Most analyses of growing media give estimates of the available amounts of nutrients present.

DEFICIENCIES AND TOXICITIES

Imagine a plant that has plenty of all but one necessity. It is said to be deficient in that necessity. The necessity might be a nutrient element, or water, or air in the growing medium, or light. Growth is not possible if that necessity is completely absent. Calcium cannot take the place of light, nor oxygen the place of zinc.

Now suppose we gradually increase the supply of that missing necessity. The plant will respond as shown in Fig. 14.3. First, growth will gradually increase as the deficiency is overcome. Then, increasing supplies of the necessity will give little extra growth, until 'luxury' supplies give none. Eventually, extra supplies are toxic, reducing growth.

Figure 14.3

General response of plants to the level of supply of a necessity (a nutrient, water, light, heat, etc.)

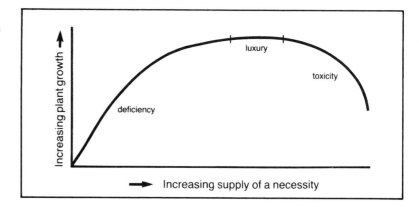

This is a general response of plants to the necessities of life. As far as nutrients are concerned, each nutrient is a separate necessity. One cannot substitute for another. Plant growth is limited by that nutrient in lowest supply (assuming all non-nutrient necessities are supplied). Increasing the supply of that nutrient will increase growth, as in Fig. 14.3, until it is again limited by the nutrient in second lowest supply, and so on (Fig. 14.4).

Maximum growth rate is possible only when all necessities are adequately supplied, and in balance with one another. Then the limit is set by the genetic makeup of the plant.

Deficiency symptoms

In the early stages of deficiency, or in mild deficiencies, often the only sign of the deficiency is somewhat retarded growth. This is difficult to pick up without a nearby well-fed plant for comparison. Analysis of leaves can sometimes pinpoint the deficiency.

More severe deficiencies announce themselves through:

- obvious stunting (Fig. 14.5);
- leaves that are 'off-colour', distorted, mottled, dead around the edges;
- leaves dying prematurely;
- twisted and distorted stems;
- poor root systems.

A general guide to deficiency symptoms is given below. Note that symptoms are first seen in the oldest leaves when the nutrient element can be easily moved about the plant. In deficiency, the small supply is shunted to areas of growth in an attempt by the plant to complete its life cycle. Symptoms are first seen in the youngest leaves when the element in poor supply is held firmly where it was first used.

Figure 14.4
General effect on plant growth of
overcoming one deficiency after
another, until a limit is set by the
genetic makeup of the plant

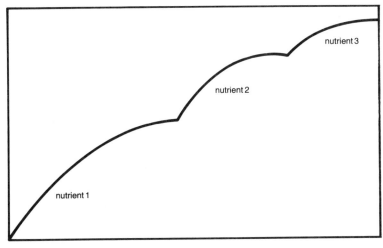

nutrient 3

nutrient 2

nutrient 1

Increasing supply ➡

Are they deficient?

Nutrient deficiencies are not the only causes of stunting and off-colours in plants.
The main other causes are:

- waterlogging;
- salinity;
- drought;
- diseases—root rots, insects, viruses;
- too much or too little light;
- wrong daylength;
- lack of carbon dioxide (in greenhouses);
- toxins in the medium;
- herbicides;
- unfavourable air or medium temperature;
- damage by wind (Fig. 14.6);
- effects of air pollution.

Look for clues to see whether any of these apply in a particular situation.

Figure 14.5
Effect of nutrient deficiencies on the
growth of tomato plants. C = control.
Photograph H Millen

Figure 14.6
Poor growth (centre and right) of
bean plants, caused by strong
winds, not nutrient deficiency. *From
J W Sturrock Physiological Aspects
of Dryland Farming ed U S Gupta;
courtesy of Oxford and IBH Publ.
Co., New Delhi, 1977*

A GUIDE TO NUTRIENT DEFICIENCY SYMPTOMS

Symptoms that appear first in the oldest leaves

Nitrogen: Leaves turning pale green, then yellow; in some species the leaves have red or purple tinting; oldest leaves dry to a light brown colour; leaves are small; stalks are stunted. The symptoms usually appear gradually.

　Phosphorus: General stunting; little branching, so that plants look spindly, 'thin' and 'lacklustre'; leaves take on blue-green and purple colours before gradually yellowing; grasses stand short and erect and are sparse.

　Potassium: Leaves may first become dull grey-green; leaf margins and tips and/or areas of leaf near the tips yellow in spots; the spots expand, with the parts first affected 'scorching' and dying; stalks are thin and shortened.

　Magnesium: Leaves look mottled, with patchy yellowing, sometimes accompanied by reddening, starting around the margins; tips and margins are cupped; sometimes brilliant colouring, especially around margins; tan dead spots appear in the yellow areas, expanding until leaves die.

　Molybdenum: Mottling over the whole leaf, with the leaves becoming paler; usually no other colours; leaf margins burn; in some species the leaves and/or stems are severely distorted.

Symptoms that appear first in either the oldest or the youngest leaves (depending on plant species)

Manganese: Mottled yellowing between the veins; veins pale green and with 'feathery' edges; in some species, water-soaked spots; dark brown, dead spots developing in the yellow areas; worst in dull weather.

Symptoms that appear first in the youngest leaves

Calcium: First, a slight paling of parts of leaf margins a little behind the branch tip; the margins cup upwards; successively younger leaves are affected; leaves may roll upwards and redden; finally, tips 'hook', blacken and die; affected leaves wilt even when there appears to be ample available water; root growth is severely reduced; roots die back from the tips, becoming stunted; root diseases proliferate; flowering and fruit formation are seriously reduced; spathe colour breakdown in *Anthurium andreanum*; blossom end rot in tomato.

Sulphur: General paleness, more noticeable in the youngest leaves; leaves become smaller, with the edges rolled down sometimes; affected leaves sometimes have reddish or other tints.

Iron: Interveinal areas in the youngest leaves become pale, then yellow to white, sometimes tinged pink; in the early stages the veins stand out sharply in green, later they may still be seen as faintly green. Worst in dull weather.

Copper: First, the leaves become blue-green or olive-green and may be twisted; often symptoms appear first in leaves halfway along stems; leaf margins begin to pale; young leaves become pale but with spots at the ends of veins often remaining green; young leaves are rolled inwards or curled; rows of spots of dying tissue sometimes appear; tip death may be followed by the formation of numerous weak shoots ('witch's broom'); stems become shortened, distorted and twisted, flowers become paler than normal, small and misshapen.

Zinc: Some mottling of older leaves; most spectacular symptoms are shown by younger leaves at growing tips; young leaves are much smaller than normal; leaf margins are often distorted; interveinal mottling in dull yellow green, bright yellow or ivory; severely shortened stems; formation of numerous short stems at the tip; sometimes purple tints in older leaves; fruit and seed production is greatly reduced.

Boron: Interveinal areas and minor veins crinkled, basal parts of leaf margins of young leaves often pale then dying, youngest leaves often blacken and shrivel when tiny; usually tips die, root tips blacken and die; cracks may develop across leaves and leaf petioles (stems); lower petals of flowers become brown, distorted and eventually dry.

A GUIDE TO TOXICITY SYMPTOMS

Any element can be toxic to plants if it is present in high enough concentrations in the growing medium, or if its concentration is out of balance with those of other elements. Toxicities of salts, sodium and chloride are covered in Chapter 21.

Nitrogen: Excessively high levels in media give lanky, succulent, weak plants that are susceptible to diseases, do not tolerate dry conditions and easily fall over. However, ammonium toxicity is the only true nitrogen toxicity. Ammonium toxicity kills the roots, so that they go greyish white to brown to black and slimy; tops quickly wilt; leaves show small dead spots and brown patches along

Table 14.1
Effect of various fertilizers, with and without Ca, on the incidence of marginal bract necrosis in *Poinsettia* 'Gutbier V-14 Glory'. (*From* B K Harbaugh and S S Waltz *Hortscience* 24: 465, 1989)

Fertilizer	Calcium addition	Necrotic lesions
Osmocote 19:2.6:10 (47% NO_3–N)	no	11
Liquid into medium (30% NO_3–N)	no	9
Liquid into medium (65% NO_3–N)	no	8
Liquid into medium (81% NO_3–N)	yes	3
Liquid onto foliage (81% NO_3–N)	yes	1

Figure 14.7
Relative growth of roots and shoots of wheat plants fed on nutrient solutions with ammonium, nitrate or nitrate plus ammonium forms of N. From S H Lips et al. in *Inorganic Nitrogen Metabolism* eds W R Ulrich et al. Springer Verlag, 1987, p 233

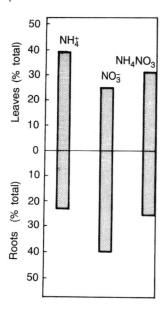

their margins, spreading from the tips, and yellowing between the veins; they soon drop off. The symptoms spread quickly, leading to stunting and early death when toxicity is severe. For some grasses, there is little burning; the plants wilt and become stunted, and are a very dark green colour. Seedlings are more easily damaged than are older plants. Sensitive species include *Acacia* species, *Thryptomene, Verbena,* alyssum, carnation, pansy, marigold, phlox, snapdragon, stock, *Impatiens, Salvia,* lettuce, *Pilea* and proteas.

Ammonium toxicity is most likely in dull, cold weather. This is partly because plants use more energy to assimilate ammonium than they need for nitrate, and so in dull weather they cannot produce enough extra photosynthate to deal with the amount of ammonium arriving in their roots (Fig. 14.7). The same concentration of ammonium will often not harm plants in a brighter and warmer environment.

Ammonium-fed plants have lower concentrations of calcium, magnesium and potassium compared with nitrate-fed plants. If severe enough, the reduction in calcium content can produce symptoms of deficiency, as in blossom end rot in tomato and bract necrosis in poinsettia (Table 14.1).

Phosphorus: In species that are very prone to phosphorus toxicity (p. 140) the first symptom is grey, rust or black discoloration of the margins of oldest leaves; the affected areas extend towards the centre of leaves, with those areas first affected 'burning' and dying; leaves eventually drop; when severe, the younger foliage yellows (through iron deficiency) and plants die. Other species do not show these severe symptoms; rather, they have inferior quality—a dull, 'off-colour' appearance—and/or reduced growth. High levels of phosphorus can markedly reduce iron availability.

Potassium: There is no such thing as potassium toxicity. However, repeated heavy use of fertilizers containing potassium can interfere with magnesium supply. Any symptoms produced are those of magnesium deficiency.

Magnesium: Rare. Use of well waters having magnesium as more than 60% of total cations can lead to calcium deficiency, especially if the water is used for misting. Using magnesite rather than dolomite and/or limestone to raise the pH of acid organic materials could have the same effect. High proportions of magnesium, relative to calcium, can interfere with trace element availability.

Iron: In species that are sensitive to moderate to high levels of available iron—*Salvia* (especially white and blue), geraniums, marigolds (especially Dwarf Crested and Bonita French), *Vinca, Gerbera,* lettuce, basil, alyssum, larkspur, *Chrysanthemum* 'Goblin', cabbage, tomato, *Phlox, Impatiens* and Elatior *Begonia*—first symptoms are interveinal stippling or chlorosis on mature and expanding leaves. The symptoms can include bronze spotting. The affected areas may die. High levels of iron in other plants can produce the symptoms of manganese deficiency.

Manganese: Straight toxicity gives marginal cupping of young leaves; leaf margins become white or yellow-green, with dark brown, black or purple spotting. More usually, high levels of manganese produce iron deficiency, with typical symptoms.

Copper: Toxic levels produce iron deficiency, with its typical symptoms, plus stunting; roots are stunted and dark.

Zinc: Stunting; general yellowing; areas of interveinal pale dead patches becoming larger with time. In some species the symptoms are those of iron deficiency.

Boron: The margins of the oldest leaves yellow, then scorch to a dark brown to black; spots may develop between veins.

Molybdenum: Rare. Leaves turn golden yellow, perhaps with a tinge of blue.

THE MAJOR ELEMENTS

Nitrogen

Nitrogen is present in many hundreds of compounds found in plants. Some of the most important ones are amino acids (the building blocks of proteins), enzymes, chlorophyll and the genes. Nitrogen is needed in highest concentrations in plant parts that are actively growing—young leaves and fruits (flowers) and root tips.

Causes of deficiency

- Removal of nitrogen from the medium in turf clippings; or
- Removal of soluble N by decomposition of organic materials with high C/N ratios; or
- Loss by leaching—especially of sandy soils and open potting mixes; or
- Loss of N by conversion to nitrogen gas under waterlogged conditions; coupled with
- Too little applied in fertilizers;
- Low levels of humus in soils;
- No legumes growing in the area (for information about the fixation of nitrogen by soil microorganisms, see Chapter 25).

Causes of toxicity

Toxicity symptoms can be produced in sensitive plants when the rate of production or release of ammonium in a medium is greater than its rate of conversion to nitrate, so that it accumulates to concentrations that the particular plants being grown cannot manage. Conversion of ammonium to nitrate is most rapid in the temperature range 20–30°C and at pH values near neutral (Fig. 14.8).

Plants can take up nitrogen in both nitrate and ammonium forms. In natural situations, ammonium ions are produced during the decomposition of organic materials. Some of these may be held on colloid surfaces or taken up by plants, but many are converted by bacteria to nitrate ions. This conversion is most rapid in warm, well-aerated media. Ammonium toxicity is unlikely in natural situations. However, toxicity can be a problem in several horticultural situations.

Toxicity is most likely in cool, dull weather that severely limits the ability to produce photosynthates, especially in media with low oxygen contents (low AFP), combined with:

- excessive use of fertilizers containing ammonium salts. Of course excessive use of soluble salts can damage plants through the high EC produced in the water around roots. But ammonium ions can damage some plants at ECs that are not damaging. This can happen when ammonium-based fertilizers also containing potassium chloride are applied to soils that have some salinity from sodium chloride. It is more likely in very sandy media than in clay soils. Toxicity is usually prevented by the use of fertilizers that contain no more than about 35% of their N in the ammonium form.

Note that urea and the magnesium ammonium phosphates, MagAmp and Enmag, are sources of ammonium. Limit their use in cool weather especially.

- As a result of steaming.

Pasteurizing to kill pathogens (Chapter 26) also kills the bacteria that convert ammonium into nitrate. Ammonium toxicity can result when:

- a high level of ammonium has been added to the mix;
- the mix contains readily decomposed organic materials such as hoof and horn, blood meal, cotton seed meal, etc.,—as little as 1 kg/m³ of them can lead to toxicity;
- the mix contains ureaformaldehyde (UF 38) or IBDU—steaming speeds their breakdown;

Figure 14.8

Influence of the rate of lime application on the conversion of ammonium to nitrate in a pinebark mix. From A X Niemiera and R D Wright *J. Amer. Soc. Hortic. Sci.* 111: 713, 1986

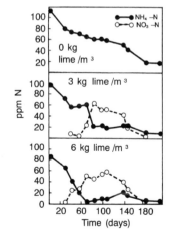

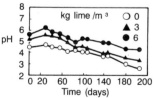

- steaming of mixes containing controlled-release fertilizers is excessively long or at too high a temperature.

Hot weather can have similar effects to steaming on mixes given high rates of organic fertilizers.

Mixes for bedding plants, seedlings and cuttings being propagated, which are usually pasteurized before use, should contain little or no easily decomposed, high-nitrogen organic materials.

Air-steaming at 60°C is less likely to cause toxicity than is steaming at 100°C. The organic fertilizers listed above can be safely used as surface applications to containers.

- During storage and use of potting mixes.

Including IBDU (as little as 0.5 kg/m³), ureaformaldehyde, other easily decomposed organics, or sulphur-coated urea in 'normal' concentrations in potting media being used in winter can lead to the production or release of toxic concentrations of ammonium. This can also happen during storage if the mix becomes anaerobic. Ammonium toxicity is usually more severe at low pH than at the preferred pH of about 6 in potting media. However, a rise in pH to above 7 may allow the production of the highly toxic ammonia gas.

- From using immature composted sawdust and pine bark.

During composting, the level of ammonia (and ammonium ions) in a heap first rises, then falls (Chapter 12). If the sawdust or bark is used while ammonium level is still high, plants can be severely damaged or killed.

- From the incorrect use of chemicals that stop the conversion of ammonium to nitrate (e.g. fungicides containing ethazol or metalaxyl).

Ammonium toxicity is avoided by keeping additions of sources of it low to sensitive plants in winter. Water extracts (1:1.5 volume) of media for sensitive seedlings should contain less than 50 mg/L ammonium-N. Zeolite incorporated at 2–5% by volume should completely eliminate any possibility of ammonium toxicity.

 Note that plants in the family Ericaceae, the cycads and the genera *Cactus, Kalanchoe* and *Sedum* that grow in arid areas prefer ammonium over nitrate.

Phosphorus

Phosphorus is essential to photosynthesis and the making of protein and new cells. It is therefore vital for rapid extension of shoots and roots. A deficiency stunts growth. There is a widely held myth that phosphorus stimulates root growth. This is bunkum: what really happens when phosphorus is applied to overcome a deficiency is that it produces more shoot growth, which in turn allows the production of a larger root system. Application of phosphorus in amounts above that needed to overcome deficiency *will not* grow more roots, or shoots. The extra P may well reduce growth and flower production.

Causes of deficiency

- Too little phosphorus in the medium—most Australian soils are naturally very deficient in phosphorus for plants other than natives.
- Too little available phosphorus—some soils have reasonable levels of total phosphorus, but most of it is unavailable to plants; mixing clay subsoils into topsoils usually reduces the availability of phosphorus in the topsoil.
- Additions in fertilizers that are insufficient for the species being grown.
- Leaching from soil-less media, combined with insufficient additions.

Causes of toxicity

- Applications to sandy soils and soil-less potting media of phosphogypsum containing several % P, and soluble phosphatic fertilizers, that are excessive for the plants being grown. Many heathland plants do not need any more P than that already in the soil.

- Runoff from urban streets onto heathlands of stormwater containing phosphorus dissolved from dog droppings.
- Toxicity becomes more severe as pH increases in the range 5 to 7.
- Phosphorus toxicity and iron deficiency are intimately connected in potting media. Increasing applications of P lead to proportionate reductions in the ability of plants to use iron, leading, in sensitive plants, to iron deficiency symptoms (new leaves) as well as to P toxicity symptoms (old leaves). Conversely, increasing applications of iron can reduce or eliminate P toxicity, but there is a limit to this protective effect. (For very sensitive species, a 1:1.5 volume 2 mM DTPA extract of a soil-less potting medium should contain less than 2 mg/L P and at least 30 mg/L iron, if iron has been supplied as ferrous sulphate or GU–49.)

A number of species in the genera *Acacia, Adenanthos, Brachysema, Banksia, Bauera, Beaufortia, Boronia, Bossiaea, Brachysema, Chorizema, Davesia, Dryandra, Eutaxia, Grevillea, Hakea, Hypocalymma, Isopogon, Jacksonia, Lechenaultia, Leucodendron, Leucospermum, Protea* and *Pultenea* show phosphorus toxicity symptoms when fed quite low amounts of phosphorus. Species normally having proteoid roots are particularly sensitive (Table 14.2). Different species of the same genus (Table 14.3), and different cultivars, have different sensitivities. Fertilizers for sensitive plants must contain only low concentrations of soluble phosphorus. Controlled-release fertilizers should contain no more than about 2% P (Fig. 16.4).

Many species of ornamental plants have inferior quality and/or reduced growth when grown with even moderately low levels of phosphorus (Table 14.4). Species known to be affected come from the genera *Rhododendron, Camellia, Magnolia, Elaeagnus, Skimmia, Erica, Calluna, Cytisus, Hydrangea, Senecio, Viburnum* and *Chamaecyparis*.

Table 14.2
Effect of superphosphate on the growth of several *Banksia* species (*From R K Ellyard and D K McIntyre Proc. Intern. Plant Propagators Soc. 28: 450, 1978*)

Application of phosphorus		Plant vigour[*] (and number of deaths out of 5 plants)			
In super-phosphate	In blood and bone meal	*B. baxteri*	*B. nutans*	*B. prionotes*	*B. verticillata*
108	60	1.2 (4)	2.2 (4)	1.0 (5)	2.8 (2)
0	60	4.8	4.0	5.0	5.0

[*]1 = dead; 5 = vigorous.

Table 14.3
Example of different responses to phosphorus by Australian native plants. The figures are growth in centimetres. (*From D Nichols Scientia Horticulturae 15: 301, 1981*)

Species	Osmocote (4.8% P)	Fertilizer IBDU (0% P)	Hoof and horn + K (1% P)
Acacia suaveolens	20.5	65.0	63.5
A. stricta	89.6	43.2	42.5

Table 14.4
Effect of extra phosphorus on the growth of several species of ornamental plants. The figures are g dry weight/plant. (Personal communication from M A Scott, Efford Experimental Horticulture Station, Lymington, England)

| | Fertilizers | | |
| | 3.0 kg/m³ Osmocote 18:4.7:8.8 plus superphosphate as follows in kg/m³: | | |
Species	0	0.75	1.5
Calluna vulgaris cv. Silver Queen	2.9	2.7	1.7
Erica carnea cv. Springwood White	4.6	5.3	2.9
E. ciliaris cv. Mrs C.H. Gill	4.2	3.7	3.3
Skimmia japonica formanii	8.3	9.0	6.0
Viburnum burkwoodii	6.1	4.3	dead

There has been increasing evidence in recent years that many plants show reduced growth and poorer quality in soil-less media if they receive as little as double the concentration needed to provide sufficiency. The high concentrations of P provided by so-called Blossom Booster fertilizers are completely unnecessary. Plants do not take up any more P as they go into flowering than during vegetative growth. Flowers typically have lower concentrations of P than do leaves.

Phosphorus is a vital nutrient for all plants. Applications, even to sensitive plants, must be enough for optimum growth, but not much more.

Potassium

Potassium is needed by plants to control water movements between cells, to aid all manner of essential chemical reactions and as a balancing cation for anions. It is needed if stems are to lengthen. It promotes thickening of cell walls, so helping to protect plants from disease.

Causes of deficiency

- Too little in the medium—this applies especially to quartz sands, to calcareous sands (palms are especially affected) and to potting mixes based on some peats that contain little potassium, combined with inadequate applications.
- Repeated removal of vegetation such as turf clippings from an area;

Coupled with:

- Leaching from deep sands, and sandy turf root zones, in areas of high rainfall and under excessive irrigation; coupled with:
- Too little applied in fertilizers.

Causes of toxicity

- Repeated, excessive application of fertilizers containing potassium, without balancing applications of magnesium—common on sandy soils after heavy application of poultry manure.

Calcium

Plants need calcium for normal cell division, as a component of cell walls, as part of the salts inside cells and as part of their genetic coding materials. It is also needed if *Rhizobium* bacteria are to form nodules on legume roots.

Figure 14.9
Calcium deficiency in petunias, caused by imbalance between calcium and potassium in the medium   *Photograph K A Handreck*

Causes of deficiency

- Very low pH; or
- Excessive applications of ammonium (Table 15.1) and/or potassium fertilizers, and;
- Rarely, high applications of potassium and magnesium, without applications of calcium (Fig. 14.9);
- An inadequate concentration in the medium (unamended coir dust is an example);
- High humidity can contribute, because it reduces uptake of calcium;
- High pH accompanied by high sodicity (Chapter 21).

Causes of toxicity

- There is no such thing as calcium toxicity. High pH caused by calcium carbonate in the medium may cause problems.

Magnesium

Every chlorophyll molecule has a magnesium atom at its centre. No magnesium, no green plants. Magnesium is therefore essential for photosynthesis.

Causes of deficiency

- Heavy application of fertilizers containing potassium.
- Use of limestone rather than dolomite or dolomitic limestone to raise the pH of potting mixes.
- Low pH in natural soils.
- Worst in soils that are too wet, too dry, or cold, and when root growth is limited.

Causes of toxicity

- See p. 136.

Balance between calcium, magnesium and potassium

It is clear from Table 14.5 that in natural soils the proportions of exchangeable calcium, magnesium and potassium soils mean that the total amounts of each nutrient held (cation exchange capacity x percentage of that cation) vary even more widely. For example, the soils listed in Table 14.5 have exchangeable calcium contents ranging from 2.8 to 25 m.e./100 g.

Plants grow on all these soils, so does it matter much what the levels are? Yes and no. Most plants seem to grow satisfactorily in soils and other growing

Table 14.5
Proportions of exchangeable cations in some Australian topsoils (0–10 cm) (*From* H C T Stace et al. *Handbook of Australian soils* Rellim, Adelaide, 1968)

Soil	Cation exchange capacity (m.e./100 g)	Percentage of cation exchange capacity occupied by					
		Ca^{2+}	Mg^{2+}	K^+	Na^+	H^+ or Al^{3+} (by diff.)	Soil pH
Acid peat (Tasmanian highlands)	74	8	4.4	2.0	1.8	84	4.8
Brown earth (Coffs Harbour, NSW)	37	30	20	0.8	5.1	45	5.3
Red earth (Nambour, Qld)	9	33	21	2.2	2.2	41	6.0
Black earth (Darling Downs, Qld)	41	61	27	4.1	2.7	5.4	6.8
Solonetz (Narrogin, WA)	6	47	32	3.3	8.3	10	6.9
Red clay (Oodnadatta, SA)	19	52	19	5.8	21	2.6	7.0
Desert loam (Oodnadatta, SA)	21	71	14	6.7	6.7	1.4	7.4
Desert loam (Whyalla, SA)	16	62	26	8.1	9	–	8.8

media with widely different exchangeable calcium, magnesium and potassium levels. Growth is affected only when there is gross imbalance between the three (assuming that all other nutrients are adequately supplied).

- For soils, the level of exchangeable magnesium should be between 15% and 50% of the level of calcium; 60% is too much for some plants. Potassium should make up between 2% and 5% of exchangeable cations. (These guidelines do not apply to soil-less potting media. The fertilizer recommendations given in Chapter 16, modified for some mixes with the help of analyses, will give the right balance.)
- Magnesium deficiency in Australian soils is restricted to the higher rainfall areas and more particularly to coarse-textured, acid soils near the coast. Those that have received large additions of potassium in poultry manure, fertilizers or wood ashes may have especially low levels of available Mg. Intensively farmed acid sandy soils often need applications of dolomite. But the need for dolomite is not widespread. Often a test for exchangeable cations will show that the usually much cheaper limestone is perfectly acceptable when raising soil pH.
- Generally, if the pH of a soil is above 5.5, there is a good chance that it will be able to supply enough calcium. Applying limestone to raise pH will supply extra calcium (and some magnesium).
- Soils will have a good balance between calcium, magnesium and potassium if their percentages of total exchangeable cations are about 60–80, 10–15 and 2–5, respectively.

Sulphur

All proteins contain some sulphur, because they all contain one or more of the amino acids that contain sulphur. The characteristic odours of cabbages, onions and brussels sprouts are mainly due to compounds containing sulphur.

Causes of deficiency

- Leached, sandy soils in areas of high rainfall often have poor supplies of available sulphur; potting mixes become depleted within weeks without a controlled-release source of S, or sufficient S in the water or liquid feed.
- Soils with low levels of humus.

Responses to superphosphate are sometimes responses to sulphur rather than to phosphorus.

Causes of toxicity

- Large applications of elemental sulphur or of rain containing sulphuric acid can damage plants through low soil pH.
- Sulphides produced in waterlogged soils are toxic to most plants.
- High concentrations of sulphur dioxide in the atmosphere.

THE TRACE ELEMENTS

Iron

Iron is essential if plants are to make chlorophyll and use nitrate. Growing plants must have a constant supply of iron because there is almost no movement of iron from old to new growth.

Causes of deficiency

- High bicarbonate level in the irrigation water.
- Alkaline media. ('A rhododendron set in lime, looks like a curate serving time!')
- Media whose pHs are higher than can be tolerated by the plants being grown; coupled with:

Figure 14.10

Manganese deficiency in oats due to omission of manganese from a peat-based potting mix. *Photograph K A Handreck*

- No or inadequate application of materials that supply soluble iron.
- Excessive applications of phosphorus, copper and zinc.
- Addition to bark-based potting media of insufficient iron to allow for inactivation by the bark.
- Wet soils, especially during tropical wet seasons.
- Lack of new root growth for whatever reason, be it waterlogging, low temperature, high temperature, root disease, calcium deficiency, etc. (iron is taken up at or close to the tips of young roots).
- Low soil temperatures.

Causes of toxicity

- See p. 136.
- Addition of more than about 100 mg/L of FeEDTA or as little as 200 mg/L FeEDDHA to soil-less potting mixes (especially bark-based) for bedding plants.

Manganese

Manganese is needed for photosynthesis and for the making of proteins. Its other roles appear to be many, but they are too complex to give here.

Causes of deficiency

- Interference with uptake by plants in soils of high pH.
- Inadequate additions to media based on sawdusts and peat (Fig. 14.10) or containing sewage sludge.
- High levels of iron, copper or zinc.
- Worst in cool, dull weather.

Causes of toxicity

- Acidification by fertilizers of soils and potting mixes containing moderate to high levels of manganese.
- Release of soluble manganese in soils during waterlogging.
- Steaming many media at 100°C.
- Air-steaming at excessively high temperatures (above 70°C) or for extended periods.
- Use of fly-ash containing toxic levels of manganese.
- Toxic amounts of soluble manganese released from some barks and sawdusts during composting—the only Australian materials likely to become toxic are eucalypt barks; pine barks and eucalypt sawdusts generally have total manganese levels well below 100 ppm, so toxicity is not a problem with them.
- Use in potting media of more than a few percent of soils that are rich in manganese minerals.
- Addition of trace element mixtures containing manganese when enough is already present, followed by a decline in medium pH.
- Use of more than perhaps 30% composted rice hulls in potting media, followed by a decline in medium pH to below 5.

Copper

Copper has an essential part in many chemical reactions taking place in plants.

Causes of deficiency

- Failure to add copper to soil-less media containing peat, sawdusts and pine barks.
- Low natural levels in some sandy soils.
- High levels of iron, manganese, zinc or phosphorus, without addition of copper.

Causes of toxicity

- Excessive and repeated use of copper-based fungicides and composts contaminated with copper, especially on acid media.

Zinc

Probably the most important role of zinc is in the production of the hormones that control extension growth such as stem and root elongation and leaf expansion. It is also needed if plants are to be able to use nitrogen.

Causes of deficiency

- Low natural concentrations, with effects most marked on alkaline soils; *and*
- Some coarse, sandy soils.
- Excessive use of phosphatic fertilizers.
- Liberal applications of nitrogen.

Causes of toxicity

- Toxicity always increases in severity as the pH of the medium drops, especially below 5.
- Some acid peats and some acid soils.
- Use of galvanized containers.
- Additions to media by water dripping from galvanized mesh canopies such as those used to exclude birds; galvanizing should be coated with plastic.
- Use of water from galvanized rainwater tanks, especially to irrigate acid media with low cation exchange capacities (the usual level of zinc in hydroponics solutions is 0.02 to 0.2 ppm; water in new tanks can have 7 to 8 ppm and can still have 2 ppm in 12-year-old tanks).
- Use of shredded tyres in growing media.

Boron

Boron is needed for the formation of new cells at growing points—root tips, the ends of stems and flower buds.

Causes of deficiency

- Acid, leached soils, especially coarse sands.
- Dry conditions can bring on boron deficiency if there is little boron in the medium.
- A drift up in the pH of potting media to 7 and above, notably with petunias.
- (Rarely) leaching from media in pots.
- High levels of calcium in the medium.

Causes of toxicity

- Use of irrigation waters containing excessive amounts of boron.
- Most common in arid areas and on soils formed from marine sediments.
- May be caused by applications of composted municipal wastes.
- Over-use of trace element mixtures in nurseries—commonly, this is the element that becomes toxic first.
- Use of by-products from wood treated with chemicals containing boron.

Molybdenum

Molybdenum is needed for the conversion of nitrogen gas from the air into soluble nitrogen compounds by nitrogen-fixing microorganisms. Legumes therefore have a special need for molybdenum. It is also essential if plants are to be able to use nitrate to make proteins. The colour of *Platycodon grandiflorum* (balloon flower) flowers changes from blue-violet to blue when extra molybdenum is supplied.

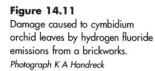
Figure 14.11
Damage caused to cymbidium orchid leaves by hydrogen fluoride emissions from a brickworks.
Photograph K A Handreck

Figure 14.12
As the concentration of fluoride ions in water in a vase is increased, the life of cut flowers standing in the water decreases. Here the flowers are roses. The measurements of quality were made 4 days after the flowers had been placed in water. For the quality index, 10 = excellent quality, 1 = very poor quality. *From W E Waters* Proc. Florida State Hort. Soc. *1968: 355, 1968*

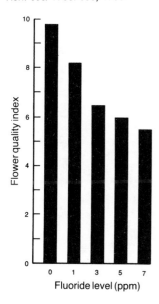

Flower quality index / Fluoride level (ppm)

Causes of deficiency

- Media that have become too acid.
- Leached acid soils.

Chlorine

The role of chlorine (or rather, chloride ions) in plants is not clear. Very small amounts are needed. All growing media other than those very specially purified, contain ample amounts. Excess chloride is the norm.

NON-NUTRIENT ELEMENTS

Fluoride

Hydrogen fluoride gas in the atmosphere is very toxic to some plants. The air around and downwind from aluminium smelters, brickworks and superphosphate works can contain the gas if mandatory scrubbers fail or are inadequate. Damage will show first in gladioli and cymbidium orchids (Fig. 14.11). In contrast, fluoride ions in irrigation waters are quickly made unavailable to plants on contact with soil minerals. Water containing 1 ppm fluoride can be used continuously.

However, fluoride can be toxic in two situations:

- A concentration of 1 ppm (common in tap waters) reduces the vase life of some cut flowers (Fig. 14.12); this effect can be overcome by using deionized water or by removing the fluoride in tap water by shaking it with a small amount of soil.
- Fluoride from superphosphate, perlite and some peats has been reported to produce toxicity symptoms on the leaves of some foliage plants in the genera *Chlorophytum, Cordyline, Dracaena, Maranta, Stromanthe, Yucca, Lilium* and *Gladiolus*. This happens only when they are grown in soil-less media. Superphosphate can contain 2% fluoride when made from Florida rock phosphate and about 1% when made from the rocks most often used in Australia. First symptoms are often small dead flecks at the leaf margin a little back from the tip. These grow to semi-circular dead areas at the margins. Eventually the whole tip dies. Often, oldest leaves are most affected, but in some plants all leaves are equally affected. Otherwise growth is affected little. The effect is mainly on appearance, but that of course is what counts in foliage plants.

Ways of avoiding fluoride toxicity are to:

- Leach perlite with about 2–3 volumes of water before using it for growing sensitive species.
- Prevent the pH of the medium from falling below about 6.5.
- Use nitrate instead of ammonium as a source of nitrogen—calcium nitrate is useful.
- Use triple superphosphate or soluble phosphates instead of superphosphate. It is only a minor problem in Australia.

Arsenic

Some soils contain high levels of arsenic from past applications of pesticides containing arsenic.

High levels of arsenic produce wilting of new leaves, stunting, sometimes burned reddish spots in older leaves, and death. Roots are more severely affected than tops.

For a given total concentration in a soil, toxicity is more likely in sandy than in clay soils. A limit before problems start is about 100 mg/kg for sands. If the concentration is not much more than this, normal growth can be promoted through annual applications of superphosphate.

Bromine

Fumigation with methyl bromide will leave some bromide ions in the medium. Most plants tolerate these bromide ions, but chrysanthemums, carnations and snapdragons do not. The symptoms of toxicity are similar to those of excess salts—marginal burning. For these plants, the bromide ions must be removed by leaching. Use about 400 mm of water for sands and other open media, and 600 mm for clay soils.

15 FERTILIZERS

A fertilizer is anything that can be used to supply nutrients to plants. There are two broad types—organic and inorganic. We will give details about them after a couple of general comments.

Complete or not?

Mixed fertilizers are often called 'complete' if they supply N, P and K. They may well be balanced sources of these three nutrient elements, but they deserve the title 'complete' only if they also supply all the other essential elements.

N–P–K or N–P$_2$O$_5$–K$_2$O?

The nitrogen, phosphorus and potassium contents of most fertilizers sold in Australia are given as percentages of the actual elements (N, P, K). For example, a 10–6.2–8.3 fertilizer has 10% N, 6.2% P and 8.3% K, by weight. The other 75.5% is oxygen, hydrogen and other elements (as shown in Table 15.3).

Some imported fertilizers, and many overseas publications, give the contents of phosphorus and potassium using the archaic system of percent 'phosphoric acid' (P$_2$O$_5$) and percent potash (K$_2$O). The fertilizer above would be given as 10–14–10 in this system.

If you are unsure about which system is being used, one clue is to look at the number for phosphorus. If it is larger than about 10, the chances are that it is for P$_2$O$_5$ If the numbers are something like 20–20–20 or 5–10–10, the N–P$_2$0$_5$–K$_2$0 system is probably being used. The numbers are not often as neat as this for the N–P–K system.

To convert: % P = 0.44 x % P$_2$O$_5$; % K = 0.83 x % K$_2$O. We use the N–P–K system throughout this book.

ORGANIC FERTILIZERS

For most of human history, most fertilizers have been organic. They have been plant residues and animal 'wastes', used as they were produced, or used after treatment by a variety of composting and ageing processes. Even now, in many forests, woodlands and grasslands, recycling organic residues are the only 'fertilizers' seen by the plants growing there. In farmlands, urban landscapes and gardens, nutrients released from decomposing residues are vital to continuing plant growth (and good soil structure), despite the use of large amounts of inorganic fertilizers.

We want to strongly emphasize the importance of organic matter to plants. In an age of ready availability of a wide range of manufactured fertilizers, it is easy to forget the vital contribution made to plant nutrition in many situations by recycling organic residues.

Not only are nutrients released from decomposing residues, but humus retains nutrients against leaching. They are slowly used by plants as required. Even in potting mixes containing sawdust or bark, where decomposition decreases soluble nitrogen supply, the organic materials are slow-release sources of calcium, magnesium, potassium and trace elements.

Wherever possible, organic residues should either be left where they fall or be recycled back to growing media after composting or other suitable treatment. They are far too valuable to be burnt or buried in land-fills.

Having said that, we must also say that organic fertilizers are of limited use in intensively managed plant-production systems. The main problems in using them are:

- Their composition is variable. Composts are enormously variable; animal manures vary according to diet and type of animal (Table 15.1). Treatment can make further changes.

Table 15.1
Nutrient contents of some natural organic fertilizers

Organic fertilizer	Nutrients supplied (approx. % of dry weight)			
	N	P	K	Others
Hoof and horn	11–13	0.3	–	–
Blood meal	10–13	0.3	–	–
Blood and bone	4.5–5	5	–	–
Sewage sludge (dried)	0.8–4.3	0.2–1.8	0.02–1.7	can have high levels of heavy metals
Poultry manure (dry)	4–8	1.1–2	0.8–1.6	full range of others
Poultry litter (dry)	1–1.7	0.25–0.8	0.8–1.2	full range of others
Cow manure (dry)	0.2–2.7	0.01–0.3	0.06–2.1	full range of others
Sheep manure	1–3	0.1–0.6	0.3–1.5	full range of others
Garden compost	1.4–3.5	0.3–1	0.4–2	full range of others

- Composted manures are more concentrated sources of most nutrients than the original manure. The exception is N, the concentration of which may be no more than half that in the original manure.
- With poultry manures, whether pelleted or not, one cannot be certain, without testing, what the level of soluble nutrients is. The high concentration of ammonium/ammonia in some freshly prepared products can harm plants. For many, high rates of application are needed if the rate of release of soluble nitrogen is to be sufficient for adequate plant growth.
- It is inadvisable to add poultry manures at more than 450 g/m^2. Higher rates may burn plants; even if they do not, they will probably not give any better growth.
- The fine mineral material in or added to manures can cause serious harm when added to sandy turf root zones.
- Hoof and horn, blood meal, and blood and bone have more definite compositions and can be very useful. However, there are not unlimited supplies of these materials and they are expensive. Hoof and horn continues to release nitrogen for about five months. These materials contain little or no potassium, so they must be supplemented.
- An attempt to supply all nutrient needs to plants in soil-less media via animal manures such as pelleted poultry manure can lead to ammonium toxicity and imbalances between nutrients.
- Composted materials have low concentrations of nutrients. They usually cannot supply nutrients fast enough for rapidly growing plants in nurseries. Composts will still contain weed seeds unless composting was done at a high enough temperature (Fig. 26.4). Note, however, that well-matured composts

are a balanced source of trace elements, and they can suppress pathogens (Chapter 26).

- Bulkiness means that it is too expensive to cart them far.
- Ammonium toxicity is often produced when mixes containing humified organic materials are steamed (Chapter 14).
- Unlike many soluble inorganic fertilizers, most of the nutrients in most organics are only slowly available to plants. This can be an advantage or a disadvantage, depending on how much nitrogen (mainly) is needed by the plants being grown.
- Some proprietary liquid organic plant foods supply very low levels of major nutrients. The levels of trace elements in most of them are very low. If better nutrition is the aim of using them, most other fertilizers are cheaper.

Manufactured organic fertilizers

Urea, ureaformaldehyde, isobutylidene diurea (IBDU) and crotonylidene diurea are all organic fertilizers that supply nitrogen.

Urea contains 46% nitrogen and is very soluble in water. In growing media it is quickly (less than two days generally) broken down into ammonium (and carbon dioxide) before it is used by plants. Surface applications must be watered in immediately after application, with about 25 mm of water, otherwise as much as 60% of the nitrogen can be lost (as ammonia). Urea is useful for supplying nitrogen in foliar sprays; it must contain less than 0.4% biuret if it is to be used in sprays and liquid feeds. (Biuret is a by-product of urea manufacture and is toxic to plants.)

The ureaformaldehydes (ureaform, UF 38, methylene ureas, Uramite, Nitroform, etc.) contain about 38% nitrogen. Release is by decomposition of the material by microorganisms. Release rate therefore increases with temperature but is slow in the depths of winter. At about 20–25°C, about 15–20% of the nitrogen becomes available to plants during the first four weeks. Thereafter release rate declines to perhaps 2% per week at 12 weeks, 1% at 18 weeks and about 1% per month after a year. In soils, after several years of annual or more frequent applications to turf, the amount applied can be reduced because of the trickle from previous applications. Release rate declines as pH rises.

IBDU contains 31% nitrogen. It is slightly soluble in water. Urea is released from the dissolved material. Temperature affects release so that at 4°C and 27°C about 50% and 75%, respectively, is released over three months. Fine particles dissolve faster than coarse particles. Mixed fertilizers such as Plantasan, Nitrophoska Slow Release, Floranid and Progress Duragreen have IBDU as a slow-release source of N.

Crotonylidene diurea (CDU) has not been used much in Australia, but it is widely used in Europe under the trade name 'Crotodur'. It contains 28% N, of which 90% is slow release and 10% is nitrate. N release is by microbial breakdown. There is little release until soil temperature rises above 10°C. Very little N is released in the first six weeks at a medium pH value of 6 or lower, and so this product, or fertilizers containing it, do not appear to have much use in potting media. However, slow, even release makes it useful for turf.

The sulphur-coated ureas contain 32% to 37% nitrogen, depending on brand. They are made by coating preheated granules or prills of urea with molten sulphur. An outer coating of sealants and conditioners prevents caking and helps to ensure slow release of urea. Release rate increases with temperature, is faster in dryish rather than wet media and is accelerated by roots. For a while, urea diffuses out through the sulphur, but when the sulphur layer is broken, all the remaining urea becomes available quickly. Typically, about 10–15% of the N is immediately released, with the rest becoming available at 1–2% per day. Sulphur-coated products reduce the pH of growing media at a greater rate than do many other fertilizers (Table 15.2). Note comments about ammonium toxicity in Chapter 14.

Table 15.2
Effect of various urea fertilizers on soil pH. The single rate of fertilizer addition was 7, 14 and 28 g N per tree for each of three years, respectively, or double these. (*From* R E Bir *Amer. Nurseryman* October 1: 83, 1990)

Treatment	pH after 3 years
Control	5.35
Urea	5.02
Urea x2	4.38
Sulphur-coated urea	4.46
Sulphur-coated urea x2	4.13

INORGANIC FERTILIZERS

Table 15.3 lists the main inorganic fertilizers. They can be bought as the separate chemicals or in a wide range of mixed fertilizers. Here are some notes about the varous compounds listed.

Ammonium nitrate (Nitram, nitrate of ammonia) is generally more useful in nurseries than is ammonium sulphate (sulphate of ammonia). It is less acidifying and less saline for the same amount of nitrogen supplied.

Calcium and magnesium carbonates, calcium hydroxide and dolomite are used to increase the pH of acid media. However, at the same time they provide calcium and/or magnesium.

Extra calcium can be supplied via calcium nitrate or gypsum. Pure gypsum from natural deposits lowers measured pH slightly if there is a low level of soluble salts in the medium. This gypsum is often less than 90% pure. The other 10% often includes limestone and soil minerals, so some natural gypsum may increase pH slightly. Phosphogypsum, a by-product of the manufacture of triple superphosphate, contains residual phosphoric acid and can be acid enough to lower the pH of sandy soils.

Calcium nitrate is useful in liquid feeds when the pH of the medium has to be raised or at least prevented from dropping as a result of the ammonium content of the fertilizer mixture. It is a useful source of N for plants that are sensitive to ammonium.

The several ammonium and potassium phosphates are useful mainly in liquid feeds. The ammonium salts acidify media, the potassium salts have the opposite effect. Their expense makes superphosphate the preferred source of phosphorus to use before planting.

Magnesium nitrate is not readily available. Magnesium sulphate is the preferred source of soluble magnesium. It is useful for quickly overcoming magnesium deficiency, especially for media whose pH is so high that dolomite cannot be used. Neither of these salts affects pH.

Potassium chloride (muriate of potash) is the cheapest source of potassium and is commonly used in NPK mixtures. It should not be used where irrigation waters and soils already contain some chloride, or where salinity could be a problem. The extra chloride increases salinity and the risk of chloride toxicity, but adds nothing to nutrition. It should not be used for plants in containers. The risks of high chloride levels developing in hot weather, when salt concentrations in media can increase rapidly, are too great. It must not be used on plants that are sensitive to salts and/or chloride. However, potassium chloride can be used for turf and in landscape situations in higher rainfall areas, and where ample good-quality water is available. Severe toxicity to plants can result

Table 15.3
Formulae, molecular masses and compositions of the commonly available fertilizers

Compound	Formula	Solubility in cold water (about 15°C)(g/L)	Molecular mass	Percent of elements
Sources of major nutrients				
Ammonium chloride	NH_4Cl	35	53.5	N, 26
Ammonium nitrate	NH_4NO_3	1183	80.0	N, 35
Ammonium sulphate	$(NH_4)_2SO_4$	706	132.1	N, 21.2; S, 24.3
Calcium carbonate (limestone, calcite)	$CaCO_3$	0.015	100.1	Ca, 40.0
Calcium chloride	$CaCl_2.6H_2O$	350	219.1	Ca, 18.3
Calcium hydroxide (slaked lime)	$Ca(OH)_2$	1.85	74.1	Ca, 54
Calcium nitrate	$Ca(NO_3)_2.4H_2O$	2660	236.1	Ca, 17.0; N, 11.9
Calcium sulphate (gypsum)	$CaSO_4.2H_2O$	2.41	172.2	Ca, 23.3; S, 18.6
Diammonium phosphate	$(NH_4)_2HPO_4$	575	132.0	N, 21.2; P, 23.5
Dicalcium phosphate	$CaHPO_4.2H_2O$	0.32	172.1	Ca, 23; P, 18
Di-potassium phosphate	K_2HPO_4	1670	174.2	K, 44.9; P, 17.8
Dolomite	$CaCO_3.MgCO_3$	0.01	184.4	Ca, 21.7; Mg, 13.2
Magnesium carbonate (magnesite)	$MgCO_3$	0.11	84.3	Mg, 28.8
Magnesium nitrate	$Mg(NO_3)_2.6H_2O$	1250	256.4	Mg, 9.5; N, 10.9
Magnesium sulphate (epsom salts)	$MgSO_4.7H_2O$	710	246.5	Mg, 9.9; S, 13.0
Monoammonium phosphate	$NH_4H_2PO_4$	227	119.0	N, 11.8; P, 26
Monocalcium phosphate	$Ca(H_2PO_4)_2.H_2O$	18	252.1	Ca, 16; P, 24.6
Phosphoric acid	H_3PO_4	5480	98	P, 31
Potassium chloride	KCl	238	74.6	K, 52.4
Potassium dihydrogen phosphate	KH_2PO_4	330	136.1	K, 28.7; P, 23.5
Potassium nitrate	KNO_3	133	101.1	K, 38.7; N, 13.8
Potassium sulphate	K_2SO_4	120	174.3	K, 44.9; S, 18.4
Sodium nitrate	$NaNO_3$	921	85.0	N, 16.5
Superphosphate: single	–	–	–	P, 9; S, 11; Ca, 21
triple	–	–	–	P, 20; Ca, 23.6
Tetra-potassium pyrophosphate	$K_4P_2O_7.3H_2O$	–	384.4	K, 40.7; P, 16.1
Urea	$CO(NH_2)_2$	1000	60.0	N, 46.7
Sources of trace elements				
Ammonium molybdate	$(NH_4)_6Mo_7O_{24}.4H_2O$	430	1236	Mo, 53
Boric acid	H_3BO_3	63.5	61.8	B, 17.5
Copper sulphate	$CuSO_4.5H_2O$	316	249.7	Cu, 25.4
Iron (ferrous) sulphate	$FeSO_4.7H_2O$	156	278.0	Fe, 20.1; S, 11.5
Manganese chloride	$MnCl_2.4H_2O$	1510	197.9	Mn, 27.7
Manganese sulphate	$MnSO_4.5H_2O$	1240	241.0	Mn, 22.8
Manganese sulphate	$MnSO_4.H_2O$	985	169.0	Mn, 32.4
Manganese sulphate	$MnSO_4.4H_2O$	1053	223.0	Mn, 24.6
Sodium borate (borax)	$Na_2B_4O_7.10H_2O$	20.1	381.4	B, 11.3
Sodium molybdate	Na_2MoO_4	443	205.9	Mo, 46.6
Sodium molybdate	$Na_2MoO_4.2H_2O$	562	24	Mo, 39.6
Zinc sulphate	$ZnSO_4.7H_2O$	965	287.5	Zn, 22.7
Some additional fertilizers				
Chelates of trace elements	see Chapter 16			
Controlled release formulations	see Chapter 16			
Potassium silicate	–	–	–	K, 16.5
Magnesium ammonium phosphates (MagAmp®, Enmag®)	see text			
Phosphate rock	mainly $Ca_3(PO_4)_2$	–	–	P, about 14

Many 'complete' formulations with a wide range of N–[P–K (plus) percentages.

from the use of potassium chloride and an ammonium fertilizer under saline conditions. Potassium chloride can increase the succulence of some plants and thereby increase their susceptibility to attack by mildews. Neither potassium chloride nor potassium sulphate alter the pH of a medium, except for the small decrease caused by soluble salts.

Potassium nitrate is particularly useful in liquid feeds, as it is all nutrient. It slightly increases pH.

Sodium nitrate is included for completeness. We want to discourage its use because of the damage sodium can do to media and plants.

Single superphosphate is a mixture of calcium phosphates of different solubilities, and gypsum. Part of the phosphorus is immediately available, with the remainder acting as a slow-release source. Some of the soluble phosphorus combines with clay minerals and so joins the ranks of the slow-release source. Note that this does not happen in soil-less media (p.139). In potting mixes, the sulphur of granulated superphosphate is released over 2–3 months. The larger the granules, the longer the release time.

Triple superphosphate does not supply sulphur. Most of its phosphorus is readily available, unless it combines with clay minerals.

Very dilute phosphoric acid is useful in liquid feeds.,

Potassium silicate frit is a useful slow-release source of potassium.

Magnesium ammonium phosphates (MagAmp, Enmag) come in a variety of formulations. The most commonly used is a mixture of magnesium ammonium and magnesium potassium phosphates. A typical analysis is 7–20–5(+9% Mg). The nutrients are supposed to be released slowly. In practice, these fertilizers are of limited use. The ammonium can be released quickly, causing toxicity; the potassium may not be particularly slow-release; the high phosphorus content can cause problems.

Phosphate rock varies widely in composition according to source. The phosphorus is only slowly available to plants. The so-called reactive rock phosphates are useful as a source of phosphorus for acid sandy soils in wet areas where part of the phosphorus from the more soluble superphosphate may be lost by leaching. It is not recommended for intensively managed turf and is of no use in nurseries. Its phosphorus is very poorly available in alkaline soils.

Details of controlled-release formulations are given in Chapter 16.

16 FERTILIZER PRACTICE IN NURSERIES

This chapter is devoted mainly to plants growing in containers, because the majority of plants produced by nurseries in Australia are grown that way. There are four main methods of applying fertilizer in nurseries:

1. Pre-plant additions of combinations of soluble and controlled-release fertilizers to the mix at the time it is being made.
2. Dibbling of controlled-release fertilizer at planting.
3. Liquid feeding in the irrigation water, or separately.
4. Additions of solid fertilizers to the surfaces of media after plants have been growing for some time.

Many nurseries use combinations of these methods, with pre-plant additions plus liquid feed being the most common.

The aim of any fertilizer application program is to provide a steady supply of nutrients in sufficient amounts to give the required level of growth.

DIFFERENT SPECIES (AND VARIETIES), DIFFERENT NEEDS

Many experiments have shown that different genera and species of plants and also different varieties of the one species have different fertilizer requirements. The differences are often small, but they can be quite large (Fig. 16.1). Examples include the dislike of even moderate rates of phosphorus by some Australian native plants and the need for more potassium by flowering plants than by foliage plants.

If a nursery is growing one species only, a fertilizer program must be found that best suits that species. But more often, a nursery will be producing dozens to hundreds of different plants. It is not possible to maintain each differently, so some compromise program must be worked out. At most, a nursery may have two or three different mix/pre-plant fertilizer combinations, with extra variation being provided by selective liquid feeding.

Normal practice

It is normal practice to add the following to all mixes at the point of manufacture:

- Sufficient lime/dolomite mixture to raise the pH into the required range and of a composition that provides balance between calcium and magnesium.
- Individual trace elements if the need for them has been shown by analysis or, less wisely, a shotgun mixture of trace elements.
- Superphosphate, except to mixes for plants of known sensitivity to phosphorus.
- A source of potassium as need has been shown by analysis.
- A low level of soluble nitrogen to help counteract nitrogen drawdown and to provide an early supply of soluble N.
- Gypsum as need for extra calcium and sulphate–sulphur is shown by analysis.
- Controlled/slow-release fertilizers in amounts and formulations shown by experience and a test of NDI to be optimum for the plants being grown.

Figure 16.1

Example of the differing response of different species to the same level of fertilizers: ▬▬▬ *Petunia* cv. Grant Prix; ▬▬▬ *Impatiens* cv. Minette; ▬ ▬ ▬ ▬ *Salvia* cv. Pixie; ▬▬ ▬▬ *Ageratum* cv. Wedgewood. *From* G A Boertje *Acta Horticulturae* 99: 17, 1980

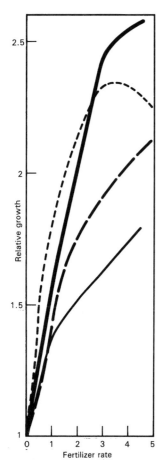

The next few sections contain detailed discussion about the various fertilizers that can be used.

Calculations

An ability to make some basic calculations is essential. These calculations are for choosing amounts and kinds of soluble fertilizers. Controlled-release materials are covered later. Every nursery should have two pieces of accurate weighing equipment, one to weigh up to 1 kg (to the nearest gram), the other up to 25 kg.

The basic calculations:

1. If n grams (g) of an element is required and the fertilizer chosen to supply it contains $y\%$ of that element, then the amount of that fertilizer needed is

$$\frac{n}{1000} \times \frac{100}{y} = \frac{n}{10y} \text{ kg.}$$

The y figure is obtained from Table 15.3. Example: If 200 g of N is needed and ammonium nitrate is to be used then the amount of ammonium nitrate needed is

$$\frac{200}{10 \times 35} = 0.57 \text{ kg.}$$

2. If you use w kg of a fertilizer and it contains $y\%$ of an element, then the amount of that element supplied is

$$w \times \frac{y}{100} \times 1000 = w \times y \times 10 \text{ g.}$$

Example: The amount of P supplied by 2 kg of a 10–4–6 fertilizer is 2 x 4 x 10 = 80 g P.

PRE-PLANT FERTILIZERS

This section lists and discusses the various fertilizer materials that can be added to potting mixes prior to planting.

Lime/dolomite

Lime and/or dolomite are used mainly to adjust pH into the required range. Use the technique given on p.92 to find out how much is needed. The following mixtures give calcium/magnesium (Ca/Mg) ratios of about 5 (or about 2). Mixtures with other ratios can be made by interpolation between these. The ratio is not highly critical, but where high levels of K are applied and the water used contains little Mg, the ratio could be nearer 2 than 5. Media in which plant growth is excellent tend to have extractable Ca/Mg ratios in the range 3–4 (Fig. 16.2).

- Dolomitic limestones with 30% Ca and 6% Mg (20,10).
- A 55:45 mixture of limestone and dolomite (10:90).
- A 4:1 mixture of limestone and magnesite (3:2).
- A 3:1:1 mixture of limestone, gypsum and magnesite (2:1:2).

Gypsum additions at rates up to 1 kg/m³ or superphosphate at up to 1.5 kg/m³ should not change the Ca/Mg ratio enough to require alteration to these mixtures.

Phosphorus

Single superphosphate is the cheapest and preferred source of phosphorus. It is about half calcium sulphate, and so it supplies calcium, phosphorus and sulphur.

Rates of superphosphate addition range from 0 to about 2 kg/m³ (0 to 180 g P/m³). For general nursery mixes, 1.5 kg/m³ (135 g P/m³) has been commonly used, but because much of the P added is likely to be lost in water draining

Figure 16.2

Example of the effect on root growth, here of chrysanthemums, of changing the ratio of exchangeable calcium to exchangeable magnesium. *From J L Paul and W H Thornhill J. Amer. Soc. Hort. Sci. 94: 280, 1969*

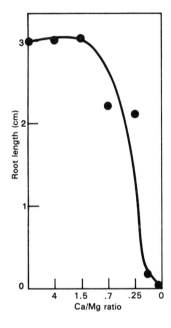

Figure 16.3

P concentrations in 2 mM DTPA extracts of peat, sawdust and pine bark media as affected by additions of P as single superphosphate. *From K A Handreck Commun. Soil Sci. Plant Analysis 22: 529, 1991*

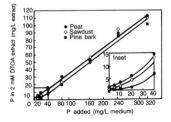

from pots during the first couple of weeks of normal irrigation, it is recommended that additions be no more than $0.6–0.7$ kg/m^3 to pine-bark mixes and $0.4–0.5$ kg/m^3 to peat- and sawdust-based mixes. DTPA extracts (Australian Standard method) of soil-less mixes so amended will have at least 7 and probably $10–15$ mg/L P (Fig. 16.3). Higher rates of superphosphate addition may be needed for mixes containing clay or lateritic (iron-rich) soils, attapulgite or shale.

There is no need to add superphosphate to peat-based media that are to contain at least 3 kg/m^3 of an Osmocote that has at least 4% P. An addition of $0.3–0.5$ kg/m^3 to bark-based media will overcome any early tendency to 'fix' some soluble P. The need for such an addition should be assessed by analysis. These remarks also apply to Nutricote Yellow, Nutricote Total (flowering grade), Macracote and Plantacote fertilizers.

The slow rate of release of P from other Nutricote products (see below) can be compensated for by inclusion of superphosphate at 0.75 kg/m^3. An alternative is to blend some Nutricote Yellow with the other Nutricote product being used. There is of course no reason why you should not use mixtures of different brands of controlled-release fertilizers if this will give you the pattern of release that you require.

The zero rate of superphosphate addition listed above is for soil-less media in which plants known to be very intolerant of even small amounts of phosphorus are to be grown (p. 139). Use of this zero rate of superphosphate does not mean that these plants do not need any P. They do, but usually in lower amounts than are needed by other plants. The proteoid roots of proteaceous species have a powerful ability to extract P from sources that are too insoluble for other plants to use. The seeds of P-sensitive species contain over 1% P. This provides their seedlings with an ample supply for a couple of months. It is really only after that that seedlings actually need an external source of P. DTPA extracts of soil-less mixes for the seedlings of very sensitive plants should not contain more than 2 mg/L P. The concentration can be up to 3 mg/L for somewhat less sensitive species and cultivars.

A zero rate of superphosphate may be inappropriate for mixes to be used for growing on of rooted cuttings and tubestock of sensitive species. Any addition should be based on analysis of the medium. The concentration of P in a DTPA extract should not be more than 3 mg/L.

All mixes in which P-sensitive plants are to be grown should have a high concentration of available iron. DTPA extracts should contain at least 35 mg/L iron.

Recommendations on the maximum concentration of P in controlled-release fertilizers that can be tolerated by P-sensitive plants vary with brand and formulation. These recommendations are based on the most recent information available at the time of writing. Readers should note that many controlled-release products are blends, and that manufacturers may change formulations from time to time. What is true in 1993 may not be quite as true in several years.

Hoof and horn can be used, but for most species there will come a time when some P should be added for optimum growth. Management will be simplest if one of the coated products is used as the main source of nutrients.

For Osmocote products, P should be added at a rate of no more than about 10 mg/L of mix per month. For example, if a $5–6$ month formulation is used at 3 kg/m^3, the maximum concentration of P in the Osmocote would be $10 \times 6 \times 100/3000 = 2\%$ (Fig. 16.4). A need to double the rate of N supply would mean that an Osmocote product of the same nominal longevity should have no more than 1% P. Temperatures well over the standard 21°C used as a basis for release times for Osmocote products will increase the rate of P release, perhaps with an increased risk of toxicity.

As far as P is concerned, Nutricote products come in two forms. The Nutricote formulation designated as Yellow and the Nutricote Total (for flowering plants) formulations have a high proportion of their P in water-soluble form; they

Figure 16.4

Growth response of (▲) *Protea* 'Pink Ice' and (●) *Leucodendron* 'Harvest' in relation to the % P in controlled-release fertilizer added at 3 g/L medium. *From G C Cresswell Proc. Int. Protea Assoc., 6th Biennial Conf.* 1991 p 303

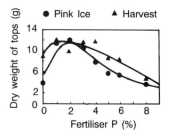

therefore release P in much the same way as do Osmocote products. In all other Nutricote formulations, much of the P is present in citrate-soluble form. The rate of release of this P is much slower than is that of water-soluble P, so formulations with P contents up to 6% have been found to be suitable for use with P-sensitive plants, but may not supply enough to others.

Use the guidelines given for Osmocote for the Macracote and Plantacote products. Note that some Plantacote formulations contain Plantasan, which has a high content of immediately soluble P.

Rock phosphates have been shown to release P rather too slowly for them to be used in potting mixes. Note that phosphogypsum can contain 2–3% P.

Sulphate–sulphur

Plants in containers obtain their sulphur requirements from components of the medium, from fertilizers added before planting, from controlled-release and soluble fertilizers, from the irrigation water and from the air around their leaves. In areas where polluted air contains much sulphur dioxide, plants can get all of their sulphur needs from the air. Very few places in Australia fit this description. Irrigation water containing at least 15 mg/L S can provide the total needs of the majority of plants growing in soil-less media devoid of other sources. Plants in the crucifer family (brassicas, *Matthiola*) need at least 25 mg/L S (Fig. 16.5). Many eastern Australian water supplies (and rainwater) contain rather less sulphate–sulphur than these concentrations, so a continuing supply from fertilizers is essential.

Figure 16.5

Effect of sulphate–S concentration in the liquid feed on growth of *Brassica oleracea* 'Lion Heart'. From L to R, 0 to 30 mg/L S. *From K A Handreck Scientia Horticulturae* 30: 1, 1986

An adequate starting supply of sulphate–sulphur will be provided by the ferrous sulphate usually added as a source of iron. Single superphosphate contains about 11% S, so it too will add to the initial supply. When it is not used, coarsely crushed rock gypsum (1–5 mm) added at a rate of about 2 kg/m³ will give enough sulphur for many months (Fig. 16.6). Crushed Gyprock plaster board of 2–7 mm particle size will provide sulphur for about the same length of time. The very much finer particles of phosphogypsum and mined gypsum dissolve more rapidly and so they usually last for no more than about six weeks. Apart from uptake by plants, the rate of loss of soluble sulphur increases in direct proportion to the amount of water lost as drainage from pots.

As a general guide, S supply should be something like one-eighth of the N supplied, but the ratio can widen to about one-twelfth in liquid feeds with N concentrations above 300 mg/L. All Osmocote NPK formulations on the market at the time of writing had sufficient S to balance their N contents, as did Macracote, Nutricote Total and Yellow and Plantacote. Other Nutricote products have 1–2% S and may need some supplementation with superphosphate or gypsum in areas where the water supply contains little S.

Sources of iron

Iron is the trace element needed in largest amounts in most mixes used in Australia. For many mixes it may be the only trace element not supplied in

Figure 16.6

Changes with time in the concentrations of S in water draining from a pinebark medium containing various sources of S. The gypsum sources had been added at 0.75 g/L and the superphosphate at 1.5 g/L. Gypsum lasts longer than is suggested because these data are lowered by the amounts of S taken up by the plants growing in the pots. *From K A Handreck Scientia Horticulturae 30: 19, 1986*

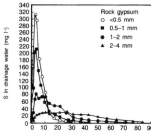

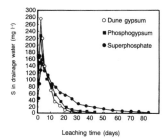

Table 16.1

Minimum concentration of iron that must be present in extracts (1:1.5 volume, 0.002 M DTPA) of soil-less media if plants are to receive adequate amounts of iron. Note the dramatic effect of pH on the need for iron, and the large differences between species. *From K A Handreck Comm. Soil Sci. Plant Analysis 20: 1297, 1989*

Plant	Medium pH				
	5.0	5.5	6.0	6.5	7.0
Eucalyptus macrorhyncha	22	25	29	40	> 70
Eucalyptus diversifolia	14	16	18	20	36
Melaleuca acuminata	8	15	15	20	> 40
Melaleuca styphelioides	< 4	4	6	13	24

sufficient amounts by mix components and as 'impurities' in fertilizers. When a DTPA analysis of the mix shows that iron is the only trace element needed, the choice of sources is as follows.

Iron (ferrous) sulphate ($FeSO_4.7H_2O$) is the cheapest source of iron and is very effective. Additions are best based on DTPA extraction (p. 165) but typically range from 200 to 400 g/m³ for peat-based mixes through 600 to 800 g/m³ for sawdust-based mixes to 600 to 1000 g/m³ for pine bark mixes (i.e. 40–200 g Fe/m³). The aim is to add enough ferrous sulphate so that a DTPA extract contains at least 25 mg/L Fe (Fig. 16.7 and Table 16.1), for the majority of plants, and at least 35 mg/L for plants that are sensitive to P or prone to iron deficiency. The rate of addition must be lower than these, and the pH of the medium must be in the range 5.8–6.3, for media in which species sensitive to iron toxicity are to be grown (p. 136).

Iron added as ferrous sulphate is firmly held by the organic components of the mix, and only tiny amounts are lost through leaching. A single pre-plant application will last for several years at least, so long as mix pH remains below 6.5, but preferably below 6.3.

A few plants may still show chlorosis at this pH. Lowering pH to 5.0–5.5 (and even lower) will allow most of these plants to get enough iron. The P supply in the medium must be at the low end of the adequate range if these measures are to be effective.

Dried ferrous sulphate ($FeSO_4.H_2O$) is more expensive than the undried form, and is no more effective, but it is used by potting mix manufacturers because it doesn't form lumps during mixing.

Resin-coated ferrous sulphate is six times the price of ferrous sulphate powder (Table 16.2) and is no more effective for the vast majority of plants. The very

Figure 16.7

Iron in 2 mM DTPA extracts of a pinebark medium of pH 5.5 following additions of ferrous sulphate. *From K A Handreck Commun. Soil Sci. Plant Analysis 20: 1297, 1989*

Table 16.2

Comparative costs of supplying iron in potting mixes (1993 prices)

Source	Rate (g/m³)	Cost ($/m³)
Ferrous sulphate	1000	0.71
GU-49	1000	2.00
Osmocote ferrous sulphate	600	4.24
Micro Mix	1000	1.63
Librel FeHi (FeEDDHA)	200	3.21
Micromax	1000	3.62

Note: The rates given are approximate highest amounts needed in pinebark-based mixes for plants fairly susceptible to iron deficiency. Micromax and Micro Mix as formulated at the time of writing (1993) may need to be supplemented with another source of iron for some plants.

low pH (less than 3) generated close to each granule has been shown to be lethal to the seedlings of at least some plants. A case might be made for its use with the more difficult of acid-loving plants, and where water of high total alkalinity is used, but in most situations ferrous sulphate powder is an entirely adequate source.

All fritted trace elements preparations tested in Australia have been shown to be incapable of supplying enough iron to plants in soil-less media based on wood wastes. An attempt to add them at a rate that might supply enough iron will produce boron toxicity.

Iron chelates are much more expensive than iron sulphate so they are not recommended for general pre-plant applications. Besides, the FeEDTA compound is toxic to some bedding plants even when added at well under 200 g/m^3. It decomposes in a few days at pH values above about 5.6, so it is of limited use either as a pre-plant application or in drenches. Fe lignosulphonate decomposes even more rapidly. The FeEDDHA compound is toxic to many of the seedlings listed on p. 136 when used at 200 g/m^3. The iron chelates are, however, useful as foliar sprays for curing chlorosis should it develop (Table 16.22). The pH of your mix is too high, you added too little ferrous sulphate or you are using too much P if you can get greening of chlorotic plants only by spraying with chelates.

Various iron minerals have been tried as sources of iron. The red minerals (hematite mainly) are of no use. Magnetites mined in Queensland are of no use. GU-49 (at 0.5–1.5 kg/m^3) was the only really effective mineral source of iron on the market in 1993. Rate for rate, it appears to be equal to ferrous sulphate. It can be useful if the salinity of iron sulphate cannot be tolerated.

Other trace elements

Proprietary mixtures (e.g. Micromax, Micro Mix, Librel BMX and Perk) supplying all trace elements are convenient to use, but we encourage you to save yourself some money by adding only those trace elements that have been shown by analysis to be needed in your mix. You will soon save the cost of the analysis, as you will almost certainly be able to supply all needed trace elements for much less than the cost of a proprietary mixture.

Another reason for basing trace element additions on analysis is that use of proprietary mixtures, even within the recommended range, can reduce the growth of some plants (Table 16.3). We urge you therefore to have your mix analysed, before and after trace elements have been added, so that you can base any additions on need.

Table 16.3
Effect of trace element additions on growth of some ornamental plants in a peat mix in containers. (Figures are g dry weight/plant.) (*From M A Scott, Efford Experimental Horticulture Station, Lymington, England, Annual Review* 1981)

| Species | Trace element source (kg/m^3) | | | | | |
	Nil	FTE 253A (0.3)	Librel BMX (0.1)	(0.3)	Micromax (0.6)	(0.9)
Abelia x grandiflora	3	17	15	20	17	16
Cotoneaster horizontalis	7	27	22	22	14	16
Elaeagnus pungens	6	5	7	5	7	7
Ilex aqui	10	18	10	12	10	6
Senecio greyii	21	18	21	19	22	19
Viburnum burkwoodii	6	11	6	13	9	7
Chamaecyparis lawsoniana	13	31	24	40	28	28

Table 16.4
A trace element mixture for potting mixes

Compound	Amount of compound* (g/m³)	Supplies (g element/m³)
A source of iron as given in the text above		
Manganese sulphate (MnSO₄.5H₂O)	18–36	Mn 4–8
Zinc sulphate (ZnSO₄.7H₂O)	0–9	Zn 0–2
Copper sulphate (CuSO₄.5H₂O)	10–30	Cu 2.5–7.5
Sodium borate (borax—Na₂B₄O₇.10H₂O)	2–3	B 0.2–0.3
Ammonium molybdate ((NH₄)₆Mo₇O₂₄.4H₂O)	0.08–0.2†	Mo 0.04–0.1

* Use the lower amount for seedlings and rooted cuttings and the higher amount for older plants.
† The same amount of sodium molybdate will give about the same amount of molybdenum.

Figure 16.8
Some controlled-release fertilizers that supply trace elements: (a) Macracote; (b) Nutricote Total; (c) Osmocote Plus; (d) Plantacote; (e) Plantacote Mix. *Photograph K A Handreck*

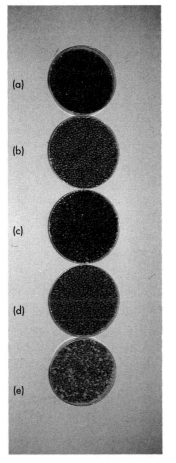

(a)

(b)

(c)

(d)

(e)

Here are some general guidelines.
- It is unlikely that you will need to add zinc over and above that already in commonly used components.
- Pine barks have enough manganese for at least a year of excellent plant growth. Manganese must be added to most peat- and sawdust-based media, if plants are to have sufficient manganese beyond six months of growth. Higher amounts of manganese than those listed in Table 16.4 may be needed by media containing sewage sludge; you must check by analysis.
- Some media require a small addition of boron, but none will be needed for media containing composts made from wastes. Adding boron to media containing composted municipal wastes will produce toxicity.
- In the absence of soundly-based guidelines for molybdenum, it is probably desirable to add a small amount, as given in Table 16.4. Seeds typically contain enough molybdenum for the full life cycle of an annual plant, but what happens with cuttings will depend on their nutritional history.
- All media based on peat, coir dust and wood wastes must receive copper, unless they also contain soil, sewage sludge, compost, vermicompost or MSW compost. Again, only analysis will show what is actually needed.
- If you choose not to have your medium analysed, you might find that the cheapest way of supplying trace elements is to add iron sulphate as discussed above, in combination with a low rate (0.3–0.4 kg/m³) of one of the proprietary mixtures.
- Uniform distribution through the mix is achieved most easily by first mixing the trace element mixture through a small amount of mix (say, 20 L) and then scattering that among the bulk mix in the mixing machine.
- Don't ever add twice as much trace element mix 'just in case'. That can produce toxicities, with boron toxicity likely to be the first to appear.

Controlled-release fertilizers containing trace elements

All brands of controlled-release fertilizers (Fig. 16.8) now offer products containing trace elements (and magnesium). These products cost about 25% more than the equivalent NPK fertilizers, so if they are used solely for their trace element content, those elements come at a very high price. For example, when added at 5 kg/m³, the extra cost for the trace elements (and magnesium) is about $4/m³. An adequate supply of trace elements added via ferrous sulphate and Micro Mix would cost less than $1/m³.

Research has shown that the trace elements of at least one coated product do not improve growth over a period of at least one year **if** adequate amounts of trace elements have been added to a mix. They should, however, prevent deficiencies of all elements except iron when used at recommended rates in media

Figure 16.9

Potassium concentrations in 2 mM DTPA extracts of a soil-less potting medium following the addition of various amounts of potassium. *From K A Handreck unpublished data*

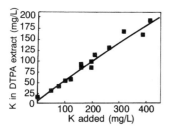

that have not been amended with trace elements. Their iron contents may be enough for plants in peat-based media, but will often be insufficient for plants in bark-based media, so it is probable that ferrous sulphate must be added anyway.

Production nurseries do not need to use controlled-release fertilizers as sources of trace elements. If all trace elements have already been added to the mix in sufficient quantities to bring concentrations in a DTPA extract into the ranges required by the Australian Standard for Potting Mixes, the mix will be able to supply enough for at least a year, and probably much longer.

Table 16.4 is included for those who want to make up their own trace element mixture. Leave out compounds supplying unwanted trace elements.

Potassium

Whether pre-plant soluble potassium is needed depends on the components in the mix and on the continuing fertilization program. Decide on the basis of the following information.

- Pine barks contain enough potassium to make it unnecessary to add more.
- Coir dust, fern fibre and most composts (not of sewage sludge) have high to very high concentrations of potassium, sometimes to the point of imbalance with calcium and magnesium.
- Much of any potassium added to sawdusts before composting will remain and make further additions unnecessary.
- No extra potassium is needed if a liquid feeding program is to be started immediately after potting.
- However, some peats (notably those from Russia) have extremely low concentrations of native potassium. Addition of potassium sulphate at 0.25 kg/m^3 is desirable, irrespective of any ongoing fertilizer program. Much of any higher additions will probably be lost in drainage waters.
- No pre-plant potassium is needed if a DTPA extract of the medium contains more than about 50 mg/L potassium (Fig. 16.9), assuming that a fertilizer program will start soon after potting.

Nitrogen

Nitrogen is the most important element in the nutrition of plants in containers. It is needed in the greatest amounts; it is used by microbes that are decomposing the organic components of the medium as well as by the plant. While most of the nitrogen needed will be supplied via the ongoing fertilizer program, it is often necessary to add some soluble nitrogen before planting, in addition to any controlled-release fertilizers added at the same time or later.

Transplanted seedlings, rooted cuttings and tubestock will start to grow soonest if their roots come into contact with soluble nitrogen at potting. They may not immediately get enough from controlled-release pellets scattered through the mix or in the bottom of the dibble hole.

Ammonium nitrate is the preferred source of N. The amount to add depends mainly on the types of organic components in the mix and the length of time that is likely to elapse between the addition of the ammonium nitrate and use of the mix. The greater the amount of drawdown of N, and the longer the time between addition and potting, the greater should be the addition of ammonium nitrate, up to a maximum of 1.5 kg/m^3. The data in Tables 16.5 and 16.6 give some examples of the rate at which soluble N is consumed by microorganisms in different potting mixes.

The ability of a potting mix to consume soluble N is indicated by its nitrogen drawdown index (NDI). The test method of determining the NDI of a mix is given in Chapter 33. This test measures the rate of disappearance of nitrate-nitrogen added to the mix from a solution containing either 75 or 150 ppm N. These two solutions give drawdown indexes designated as NDI$_{75}$ and NDI$_{150}$,

Table 16.5
Upper: Changes with time in the concentrations of nitrate and ammonium-N in 1:1.5 extracts of peat/sawdust mixtures after addition of ammonium nitrate at 1.0 g/L. Lower: NDI$_{75}$ values for the mixtures. (*From* K A Handreck *Commun. Soil Sci. Plant Analysis* 23: 201, 1992)

Incubation time (weeks)	% peat									
	100		75		50		25		0	
	NO_3^-	NH_4^+	NO_3^-	NH_4^+	NO_3^-	NH_4^+	NO_3^-	NH_4^+	NO_3^-	NH_4^+
0	58	61	90	90	97	97	90	108	90	112
1	94	68	87	68	108	54	119	54	115	90
2	64	76	58	7	39	4	14	4	0	0
3	90	76	87	7	32	0	0	0	-	-
5	97	79	90	0	0	0	-	-	-	-
7	122	36	72	0	-	-	-	-	-	-
9	130	0	86	0	-	-	-	-	-	-
10	104	0	83	0	-	-	-	-	-	-
0	0.95		0.67		0.25		0.12		0.00	
5	1.0		0.56		0.05		0.03		0.04	
10	1.0		0.98		0.1		0.12		0.00	

respectively. If all the added nitrogen remains after four days of incubation, the mix is said to have an NDI of 1. If there is no nitrogen left, the mix is said to have an NDI of 0. A measure of the degree of nitrogen drawdown of a mix having an NDI$_{75}$ of 0 can be obtained by retesting it with 150 mg/L N solution, to give an NDI$_{150}$ figure. NDI$_{75}$ and NDI$_{150}$ figures are related very approximately as shown in Fig. 16.10.

The data in Tables 16.5 and 16.6, linking NDI$_{75}$ with the rate of disappearance of soluble N in several organic media, can be used to suggest rates at which pre-plant ammonium nitrate might be added to different media (Table 16.7).

Inclusion of a controlled-release source of N will extend the time for which soluble N will remain in mixes. For example, including 1 kg/m^3 of a urea formaldehyde in the aged bark mix listed in Table 16.6 extended the time that an addition of 0.5 kg/m^3 of ammonium nitrate maintained soluble N in the mix from 2–3 weeks to 10 weeks.

- The need to have some soluble N in a mix at potting is greater for long-term controlled-release fertilizers than for short-term ones. But if a nominally long-term product has some shorter-term product in it, the need for soluble N is reduced. It is not possible to give any specific recommendations, other than to state again that potting media should contain some soluble N at potting.

Strategy for pre-plant additions of soluble fertilizers

1. First design your mix to have the required physical properties (Chapters 10 and 12).
2. Determine the amount of liming materials to be added to give the mix the chosen pH.
3. Have a sample of a trial batch analysed for all nutrients other than N by the DTPA extraction method of the Australian Standard for Potting Mixes. Table 16.8 gives guideline values. Its pH and EC should also be measured.
4. Make a further trial batch, this time adding all of the amendments shown by the analysis to be needed.

Figure 16.10
Approximate relationship between NDI$_{75}$ and NDI$_{150}$ indexes for pinebark/peat/sand media. *From* K A Handreck *Commun. Soil Sci. Plant Analysis* 24:2137, 1993, and sawdust media *From* K V Sharman *Commun. Soil Sci. Plant Analysis* 24:2171, 1993/4

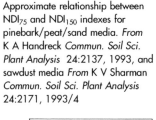
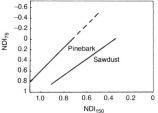

Table 16.6
Upper: Changes with time in the concentrations of nitrate and ammonium-N in 1:1.5 extracts of aged and composted pinebark following addition of various amounts of nitrogenous fertilizer. Lower: NDI data for the same materials. Next page: Shoot weights of cabbage seedlings grown in the materials starting at various times after fertilizer addition. (*From* K A Handreck *Commun. Soil Sci. Plant Analysis* 23: 217, 1992)

| Incubation time (weeks) | NH_4NO_3(g/L) added | | | | | | UF-38 (1g/L) + NH_4NO_3 (0.5 g/L) | |
| | 0.5 | | 1.0 | | 1.5 | | | |
	NO_3^-	NH_4^+	NO_3^-	NH_4^+	NO_3^-	NH_4^+	NO_3^-	NH_4^+
Aged pinebark								
0	29	25	75	58	105	86	25	25
1	36	14	83	43	105	68	47	25
2	43	4	90	32	104	58	25	18
3	18	11	65	36	83	68	36	29
5	0	4	46	21	100	47	14	29
6	0	0	56	0	110	0	38	0
7	–	–	41	0	68	0	–	–
8	–	–	25	0	54	0	29	0
9	–	–	22	0	59	0	11	0
10	–	–	19	0	36	0	14	0
11	–	–	17	0	38	0	13	0
12	–	–	11	0	34	0	7	0
13	–	–	5	0	27	0	1	0
Composted pinebark								
0	69	43	100	76	115	101	61	43
1	75	40	108	65	119	83	65	47
2	83	11	130	40	112	79	65	36
3	83	11	130	40	112	79	65	36
5	90	4	144	4	123	25	100	4
6	83	0	122	0	119	0	97	0
7	51	0	115	0	119	0	97	0
8	39	0	108	0	97	–	86	0
9	29	0	112	0	99	0	113	0
10	30	0	94	0	90	0	86	0
11	23	0	104	0	94	0	79	0
12	20	0	94	0	86	0	79	0
13	10	0	94	0	79	0	83	0

| Incubation time (weeks) | NH_4NO_3(g/L) added | | | UF-38 (1 g/L) + NH_4NO_3 (0.5 g/L) |
	0.5	1.0	1.5	
Aged pinebark				
0	0.70	0.95	>1	0.57
2	0.48	1.00	>1	0.85
3	0.37	–	>1	1.00
5	0.10	0.85	1	1.00
7	0.13	0.59	0.83	>1
10	0.08	0.46	0.61	0.39
Composted pinebark				
0	>1	>1	>1	0.85
2	>1	0.90	>1	>1
3	>1	–	>1	>1
5	1.00	>1	>1	>1
7	0.65	0.90	>1	>1
10	0.40	>1	>1	>1

Cabbage shoot weights after four weeks growth			
Incubation time before potting (weeks)	**NH_4NO_3(g/L) added**		**UF-38 (1 g/L) + NH_4NO_3 (0.5 g/L)**
	0.5	**1.0**	**1.5**	
Aged pinebark				
0	0.81	3.0	3.64	2.16
2	0.27	2.58	2.67	3.75
3	0.05	2.08	3.46	2.61
5	0.04	1.18	2.62	2.00
7	0.04	0.60	2.09	1.56
10	0.04	0.21	0.67	0.23
Composted pinebark				
0	3.80	3.82	3.91	3.48
2	3.04	3.29	3.73	3.50
3	1.97	2.20	2.76	2.51
5	1.39	2.04	2.33	2.22
7	0.56	2.19	2.22	2.15
10	0.21	1.92	1.58	1.82

*The aged and composted pinebarks had NDI_{75} values of 0.15 and 0.55.

5. Send a sample of the new batch to the laboratory, this time for a determination of NDI as well as a repeat of the earlier tests.
6. If necessary, adjust additions as recommended by the laboratory. Add soluble N according to the guidelines given above.
7. Add controlled-release fertilizer, chosen with the aid of the next section and experience. Use a rate based on manufacturers' recommendations, modified if necessary to allow for the NDI of your mix, as shown below.

Table 16.7
Approximate amounts of ammonium nitrate that should be added to media with different NDI_{75} values in order for there to be some soluble N remaining at potting time. (*Interpolated from* K A Handreck *Commun. Soil Sci. Plant Analysis* 23: 201; 217, 1992)

Medium	NDI_{75}	Ammonium nitrate addition (kg/m³)
Peat	1.0	0.2
Composted bark	0.6	0.5 for up to 10 weeks storage
Aged bark	0.2	0.5 for 2–3 weeks; 1.0 for up to 10 weeks; 1.5 for about 15 weeks
Sawdust	<0	1.0 for about 1 week; 1.5 for about 3 weeks

CONTROLLED-RELEASE (SLOW-RELEASE) FERTILIZERS

There are four main types of controlled-release fertilizers.

1. Most widely used are those in which granules or prills of fertilizer are coated with resin, plastic or wax. After water has entered through the coating, dissolved nutrients slowly diffuse out. The rate of release is governed by the properties of the coating. Three brands—Macracote, Osmocote and Nutricote (Ficote in Britain)—were widely available at the time of writing, each in a range of formulations and nominal release times. Plantacote products were being distributed for nursery trials at the time of going to press.

2. Also widely used are materials that release nutrients as they slowly dissolve or are broken down by microorganisms. IBDU and the ureaformaldehydes are sources of N. A number of mixed fertilizers contain one or other of these as a slow-release source of nitrogen. Potassium silicate frit is a source of potassium.

3. Also available are products in which granules or prills of fertilizer are coated with a mixture of elemental sulphur and various binding agents. Release is by diffusion out through the sulphur coating.

4. Composts, manures and animal by-products such as hoof and horn and blood and bone (Table 6.3) all release nutrients as they decompose. Note that some composts and manures contain high levels of soluble nutrients.

Table 16.8
Concentrations of nutrient required to be in potting mixes that conform to the Australian Standard. (*From* Standards Australia, AS3743-1993)

Nutrient	Concentration in extract (mg/L)
In 1:1.5 water extract	
NH_4-N	<100 (general)
	<50 (seedlings)
N	0 (regular)
	>50 (premium)
In 1:1.5 2 millimolar DTPA extract	
P	8–40 (soil-less)
	0.7–4 (soil mixes)
	< 3 (soil-less for P-sensitive plants)
	< 0.5 (soil mixes for P-sensitive plants)
K	> 50
S	> 40
Ca	> 80
Mg	> 15
Ca/Mg	2–10
K/Mg	1–7
Cl	< 200
Fe	> 25 (general)
	> 35 (P-sensitive and acid)
Cu	0.4–15
Zn	0.3–10
Mn	1–20
B	0.02–0.65

The Australian Standard

In various parts of this book we have referred to the Australian Standard for Potting Mixes, without giving much detail about it. This box gives this detail and also discusses its strengths and limitations.

The Standard (AS 3743) applies to potting mixes sold in retail packs. It specifies upper and lower limits for various properties. A mix that has its properties within these limits will have good drainage, will not harm plants and will have good baseline levels of nutrients. The Standard specifies minimum requirements for the physical properties of air-filled porosity, total water-holding capacity and wettability. The tests used for these properties are easy to carry out and are listed in detail in Chapter 33. They are routinely used by potting mix manufacturers.

The Standard lists a bioassay for determining whether or not the mix contains toxins that might restrict plant growth (see Chapter 33).

Some chemical properties are tested through extraction of the mix with deionized water, with a solid-to-water ratio of 1:1.5 by volume. The method is given in detail in Chapter 33. This extraction is used for pH, EC, nitrate and ammonium. These tests are also routinely used by manufacturers 'in house'.

The levels of other nutrients (except molybdenum) in the mix, and deemed to be available to plants, are determined by extracting the mix with 2 millimolar DTPA (diethylenetriamine pentaacetic acid—a chelating agent). This extraction is not described here because laboratory equipment is needed for it and for the determination of the nutrients in extracts. Research has shown that the concentrations of nutrients extracted by this reagent are fairly closely correlated with plant uptake. Some of the results are given in Figs 16.3, 16.7 and 16.9 and Tables 6.1, 13.2 and 16.8.

A critically important test for all media based on wood wastes and composts is that for nitrogen drawdown index (NDI). This test gives an estimate of the rate at which biological activity in the medium consumes soluble nitrogen. It is used as described in other parts of this chapter, as a guide to the amount of nitrogen that must be added via fertilizers if both microorganisms and plants are to be adequately fed. This test can be undertaken by manufacturers and nurseries. See Chapter 33.

All these tests are now offered by several laboratories across Australia. Their expense is small compared with the savings that can be had from minimized additions of nutrients and optimum growth rates.

While the Standard was primarily designed to ensure that all potting mixes sold in retail packs are of adequate quality, its tests are used as a basis for formulating mixes for use in nurseries. Such a use is entirely appropriate, but there are a few cautions that must be mentioned here.

- Some nurseries prefer to use mixes with lower air-filled porosities than those given in the Standard. With management of water that is more skilled than that of many home users, such a preference can give entirely satisfactory results and indeed may be necessary in some situations.

- For particular plants it may be desirable to use a mix with a lower pH than the minima specified in the Standard. Need for a pH that is higher than the upper limit of 6.3 will be rare, because of the severe reduction in iron availability at higher pH values.

- Some nurseries may find it acceptable to allow a higher EC and/or higher ammonium level than the upper limits specified. Note, however, that a high ammonium level inevitably leads to a fairly sharp drop in pH as the ammonium is converted to nitrate.

- A need to vary the concentrations of most other elements to outside the rather generous ranges allowed by the Standard will be rare. One exception might be higher concentrations of sodium and chloride for plants that are at least moderately tolerant of salinity.

- Growers of plants that show extreme sensitivity to phosphorus will want to specify a mix with a P level that is less than 2 mg/L, so that they have full scope for adding exactly what their plants need.

- Many nurseries prefer not to use a mix with the high NDI values specified in the Standard, e.g., most sawdust-based mixes will not pass the NDI provisions of the Standard, but they can still be successfully used in nurseries. We urge you, however, to determine the NDI of your mix as a basis for fertilizer applications, as listed in this chapter.

The methods listed in the Standard may also be used to test samples taken from pots during the growing season. We caution, however, that test results for major nutrients should be interpreted differently from the guidelines in the Standard. It is normal for the EC and levels of N, P and K to be quite low in extracts of mixes from pots, even when the plants are growing vigorously. Nutrients added via a regular liquid feeding program or being continuously released from controlled-release fertilizers will be quickly taken up by plants and so will not show up in extracts. The data of Table 21.13 should be used for interpreting EC figures. Some idea of the residual value of controlled-release fertilizers can be had if the mix is re-analysed after their granules have been crushed.

Facts and strategies for controlled-release fertilizers

We have had some difficulty in writing this section, partly because of the ever-increasing range of controlled-release fertilizers on the market. New products take time to evaluate. Research results from overseas never apply directly to Australian conditions. Some products are blends of two or more formulations with different nominal release times. And so on.

Nevertheless, there are some facts and these should be remembered when planning strategies for using these very important products. We first give these facts and then use some of them as a basis for suggesting rates of use of controlled-release products.

* All products release nutrients faster as temperature rises. Nominal release periods given by manufacturers apply at 21°C (Osmocote), and 25°C (Nutricote). Release rate increases with increase in temperature. Examples are given in Table 16.9. Note that the increase in release rate with increase in temperature was lower for the Nutricote than for the Osmocote product. Note also that the rate of release from the Nutricote product was lower at low temperatures than was the release from the Osmocote. These results agree with practical findings for various nominally similar formulations of these two brands. It is clear that in warm climates actual release times will be very much shorter than the nominal values.

* In view of the fact that temperatures on the sunny side of pots sitting in full sun will be higher than air temperatures (Chapter 28) it can be expected that controlled-release products will not last as long as their nominal release times when present in such pots during hot weather.

* The generally more rapid increase in release rate with temperature increase shown by Osmocote products than by Nutricote products can be used in choosing products for use under different climatic conditions and times of the year. Of course formulations of different longevities can be chosen for different times of the year.

* Fast release at high temperatures can give salinity levels high enough to injure or kill plants. For plants to be grown in hot weather, use a lower rate of addition and/or use one with a slower release rate. Make sure that media are kept watered to near container capacity, so that the likelihood of water in the mix reaching a damaging level of salinity is minimized. If possible, shade containers from direct sunlight so that the temperature of the medium remains as low as possible.

* Some research has shown that plants of equal quality can be grown with different brands or types of controlled-release fertilizers (Fig. 16.11). Other research (e.g. Table 16.10) has found that some are better than others under the conditions of the particular experiments. All of the products listed here have given good results when their longevities, nitrogen contents and known responses to temperature are allowed for. No doubt fault can be found with any of them if they are not used in recommended ways. Nurseries should

Table 16.9
Percent of the nutrients in two controlled-release fertilizers remaining after 19 weeks of shaking in water at different temperatures. (*From* G P Lamont et al. *Scientia Horticulturae* 32: 265, 1987)

Temperature °C	Osmocote 18:4.8:8.3 (8–9 month)	Nutricote 16:4.4:8.3 (8–9 month)
15	64	71
21	52	59
25	49	54
35	33	48
45	21	40

Figure 16.11
In this experiment, plant growth (here shown as the means of four species) was closely similar with four different fertilization schemes. Quality index: 10 = best. *From* G Smith and V Munday *Georgia Nursery Notes* May: 12, 1981

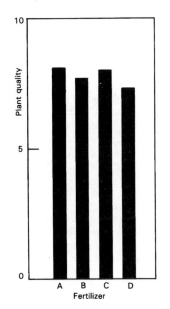

carry out comparative trials under their conditions as a guide to the most economical combinations of controlled-release fertilizers to use.

- Some controlled-release products do not contain 100% of the formulation with the longevity listed on the bag. Rather, they are blends of the formulation of that longevity with others with shorter release times. Check with the supplier before you blend a short-term product into one with longer-term release.
- Pasteurizing mixes containing controlled-release fertilizers at 60–65°C for 30 minutes does not release toxic levels of nutrient salts. However, steaming at 100°C reduces the usefulness of some controlled-release fertilizers from months to hours.
- Provided that the medium is at least damp, the rate of release from the coated materials is not affected by moisture content. This means that soluble nutrients are continuously released from coated fertilizers during storage of moist mixes. The salinity of the mix will increase, perhaps to a damaging level (Fig. 16.12), if the heap of mix heats during storage. Of course any massive release will seriously reduce the longevity of the fertilizer. Leaching, with its removal of nutrients, may be needed immediately after potting, but only if a test shows that salinity is high enough to cause problems. Whenever possible, use large heaps of mixes containing coated fertilizers within a couple of days of mixing.
- Damaging levels of salinity are, however, not likely when coated fertilizers are added at low rates (up to 3 kg/m³) to media to be packaged for retail sale. Such additions are necessary when media have to satisfy the requirements for a Premium Grade mix as defined by the Australian Standard for Potting Mixes.
- In cool weather, salinity can build up in pots under cover if there is little growth and no leaching, but probably not generally to a level that will do harm.
- Store all coated fertilizers in a cool, dry place. Even high air humidity will begin to release nutrients from them.

Table 16.10
Growth of *Rhododendron* 'Anna Rose Whitney' as affected by type of controlled-release fertilizer. (*From* C J French and J Alsbury *HortScience* 24: 91, 1989)

Growth parameter	Nutricote 16:4.3:8.3 (Types 180/40 3:1)	Osmocote 18:2.6:10 (9 month)
No. of shoots	23.5	22.2
Height (cm)	34.1	30.1
Width (cm)	51.7	48.0

Figure 16.12
Changes in the salinity of potting mixes during storage. The salts released from the Osmocote would have severely damaged many plants after 4 or 5 days of storage, if they had not been leached out. The drop in salinity after 30 days is due mainly to use of nitrate and ammonium by microorganisms.
From R L Self and O Washington
Southern Nurserymens Association Conf. 1977, p 15

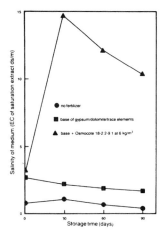

Table 16.11
Effect of irrigation method on response to topdressed Osmocote. Figures are g fresh weight of tops. (*From* R A Coleman et al. *Seed and Nursery Trader* Oct: 50, 1979)

Osmocote rate (kg/m³)	Irrigation method	
	Overhead	Drip
1.2	123	85
2.4	131	102

- Make sure that coated fertilizers are not damaged by mixing machinery.
- The rate of release of nutrients from top-dressed coated fertilizers can be higher than, lower than or similar to that of the same fertilizer mixed throughout the medium. It will be lower if the surface dries out, as when watering is by dripper (Table 16.11). It can be higher in hot weather, perhaps because the fertilizer pellets on the surface get hotter than those in the medium. Take care not to splash top-dressed controlled-release fertilizers from pots during watering. Sulphur-coated fertilizers are reported to give better results when incorporated than when top-dressed.
- Controlled-release fertilizers may also be applied into the bottom of the dibble hole during potting up. Reports suggest that some caution is needed. Results can be quite satisfactory in cool weather, but massive localized release in hot weather can damage plants. Damage by high salinity is likely to be greater for salt-sensitive plants than for salt-tolerant ones. Damage will be more likely when the pots are irrigated from below than from above. Do not dibble Osmocote formulations with nominal release times of less than five months. The rate of application used when dibbling can be about 1 kg/m³ lower than for incorporation. Dibbling appears to be most effective in media of low NDI, presumably because roots then have an increased chance of getting the soluble nitrogen before microbes do.
- The granules of some Osmocote products at the surface in packages tend to split if the packages are left open to the atmosphere. Either use Osmocote reasonably soon after packages are opened, or store it in tightly sealed metal, glass or thick-walled plastic containers. Nutricote is not similarly affected.
- Topdressing containers with coated fertilizers just before they go to a retail outlet will ensure that the plants do not starve while sitting there. Use about 1.0 g/L of mix. This will allow plants to hold condition without growing much.
- IBDU is a very useful product, but caution is to be exercised with it. The early rate of release of ammonium is quite high at typical nursery temperatures. This release of ammonium raises medium pH. The higher the application rate, the higher the concentration of ammonium and the higher the peak pH attained. The ammonium will gradually be converted to nitrate and the pH of the medium will fall to below what it was at mixing. An application should never exceed 2 kg/m³. Mixes for bedding plants being grown in winter may be harmed by the ammonium released from 0.5 kg/m³.
- The rate of release of nitrogen from ureaformaldehyde is quite slow after three months. This can be an advantage or a disadvantage. Growth can be limited to about that period by having ureaformaldehyde as the only source of nitrogen. However, topdressing or extra liquid feeding will be needed for longer growing periods. This also applies to mixed fertilizers having ureaformaldehyde as the only controlled-release source of nitrogen.
- Plantosan and Nitrophoska Slow Release fertilizers contain all plant nutrients. Part of the nitrogen is soluble, but most is present as 'urea compounds' or IBDU. The amount of soluble salts present limits additions to 3 kg/m³. The initial salinity is even too high for seedlings and plants sensitive to salinity when 2 kg/m³ is used. Extra nutrients are needed well before the end of a typical growing period for plants in pots, but these products can be very useful as a 'one-shot' application for bedding plants.
- Coated fertilizers are expensive. But if a single pre-plant addition eliminates later topdressing, their cost is worthwhile. Liquid feeding is cheaper if most of the liquid feed reaches the pots (as from drippers). It can be as expensive if a high proportion of the feed misses the pots (as during overhead irrigation of widely spaced pots). If such feeding pollutes water running from your property, your EPA might add to your expenses by shutting your nursery.
- It is cheaper to cope with heavy nitrogen drawdown through use of such N sources as IBDU, ureaformaldehyde and resin-coated urea and ammonium

nitrate, than via heavier applications of controlled-release NPK sources. Typical rates are 0.5–1 kg/m³.

- Use of these sources of N or of a faster-release formulation of a coated fertilizer is not necessary when the medium has an NDI near 1 (see below).
- Differing proportions of nitrate and ammonium-plus-urea in different controlled-release fertilizers mean that they differ in the amount of acidification they cause to potting media. The higher the proportion of ammonium and urea, the greater the acidification (Chapter 11). Nutricote products either have equal amounts of nitrate and ammonium or more nitrate than ammonium. Some Osmocote products have more nitrate than ammonium, and some have less. Macracote products have several times more ammonium plus urea than nitrate, and so are more acidifying (Table 16.12). Plantacote products have more ammonium than nitrate. It may be necessary in some situations to allow for this acidification by having the initial pH of the mix at the upper end of the acceptable range. Choose fertilizers with low nitrate concentrations when the mix must remain acid or become more so, and one with high concentrations when acidification is not wanted.
- Note that allowance must be made for the acidifying effect of the sulphur of sulphur-coated fertilizers. Note, too, the warning about ammonium toxicity in cool weather (p. 136).
- Rates of addition of all controlled-release fertilizers can be 10–20% lower for large containers than for small.
- There is less loss of nutrients (or none) from pots on capillary beds or mats than from pots irrigated from overhead. Rates of addition of controlled-release fertilizers can be reduced by about one-third. In fact, salinity may be too high at the 'normal' rate.

BEST P/N RATIO

The tissues of healthy plants have P contents that are mostly in the range 6 to 15% of their N contents. In other words, their P/N ratios are in the range 0.06 to 0.15 (Table 16.13). Of the plants grown in nurseries, only some ferns and some *Phalaenopsis* orchids seem to have higher P/N ratios. Flowers typically have P contents that are lower or equal to those of the rest of the plant (Table 16.14).

The P/N ratios of fertilizers do not need therefore to be higher than about 0.3. In fact a P/N ratio of no more than 0.15 will be entirely satisfactory for the majority of plants grown in nurseries. Yet quite a few fertilizers do have higher P/N contents.

High P content seems to be a hangover from the time when most potting media contained soil. It was also believed that the more of it that was added the better was root growth. The old 20:20:20 ($N:P_2O_5:K_2O$) of American literature has a P/N ratio of 0.44. This type of fertilizer has been displaced for foliage production by fertilizers with P/N ratios of 0.14. One experiment showed that *Poinsettia* 'Angelika Red' had reduced growth with a fertilizer having a P/N ratio of 0.45 compared with one having a ratio of 0.2.

Particularly interesting are research results showing reduced flower numbers in African violets with a fertilizer with a P/N ratio of 0.44 compared with numbers at a ratio of 0.14 (Table 16.15). The same research showed that high light intensity was the main factor ensuring high flowering rate in African violets. *Salvia greggii* grew best at a P/N ratio of 0.12. So much for the benefits of high-P fertilizers that are claimed to boost flowering! Be sure to provide your plants with enough P, but realise that their growth and quality will not be improved by applications of more than they need.

P added at higher rates than the ratios given above are not only of no use to plants but they can reduce growth as they accumulate in roots and shoots or in the growing medium. Furthermore, higher concentrations of K may be needed to overcome the adverse effects of excessively high P concentrations.

Table 16.12
Change in pH of two media during a three-month growing period with
***Lobelia* 'Blue Sapphire' fed with different controlled-release fertilizers.**
(*From* K A Handreck *Australian Hortic.* May, 23, 1992)

Fertilizer	Rate (g/L)	Sawdust/ bark	Peat/ bark
Osmocote 3–4 month	3	4.64	4.70
Osmocote 8–9 month	5	4.59	4.51
Nutricote Blue	3	4.82	5.10
Nutricote Black	5	4.80	4.96
Macracote 10	3	4.40	4.50
No fertilizer, no plants		5.55	5.51

Initial pH was 6.1.

Therefore, as a general rule, P concentrations should be such that the P/N (%/%) in the fertilizer combination chosen should never be over 0.3, and probably not over 0.15. Supplementing a coated NPK product with an N-only product will effectively lower the P/N ratio of the combination.

One benefit of using less P is that runoff waters from nurseries will contain less and therefore will be less likely to need cleaning up before release from the nursery.

Table 16.13
P/N ratios of the leaves of a range of ornamental plants that were deemed to be adequately supplied with all nutrients. (*From* D J Reuter and J B Robinson eds *Plant Analysis: An Interpretive Manual* Inkata Melbourne 1986)

Species	P/N ratio
Azalea	0.08–0.15
Boston fern	0.23–0.25
Carnation	0.07–0.11
Chrysanthemum	0.06–0.17
Cyclamen	0.06–0.08
Cymbidium orchid	0.08–0.10
Dieffenbachia	0.07–0.10
Grevillea	0.11
Phalaenopsis orchid	0.20–0.28
Protea	0.03–0.06
Schefflera	0.08–0.1

Table 16.14
N, P and K concentrations in the flowers and leaves of *Fuchsia* 'La Campanella' plants that were adequately supplied with all nutrients. (*From* K A Handreck unpublished data)

Plant part	N%	P%	K%
Leaves	3.2	0.83	5.3
Flowers	3.2	0.55	5.2

BEST K/N RATIO

The K/N ratio of plant tops is typically in the range 0.5 to 1.5, with a mean of about 1. However, as plants tend to continue to accumulate K as the external supply increases above the amount needed for optimum growth, quite often their leaves come to have K/N ratios above this range. This luxury accumulation may be beneficial to the plant if it limits extension growth during dull winter weather or helps protect it against disease. Several pieces of research have failed to find any protection against specific diseases from extra K above that giving maximum growth rate.

The coated fertilizers available in Australia have K/N ratios ranging from 0.37 to 0.83. When used in low NDI media, the effective K/N ratio will be higher than these values. This is because the microbes that are using N to decompose the organic part of the medium do not remove much K from circulation. Thus, if a quarter of the N applied is used by microbes, the K/N ratio of the fertilizer can be dropped by about one-quarter.

Excellent foliage plants can be grown with fertilizers with a K/N ratio of 0.55. The many fertilizers with K/N ratios of 0.83 will be suitable for flowering plants, but note the further information about K given on p. 178.

Table 16.15
Effect of fertilizer N:P:K ratios on the mean number of flowers on 12 cultivars of African violets. (*From R T Poole et al. Foliage Digest Sept: 5, 1990*)

Fertilizer		Flower number per plant
P/N	K/N	
0.14	0.52	4.0
0.44	0.83	2.8

INCLUDE MAGNESIUM?

Some controlled-release fertilizers contain magnesium. Here are some calculations that will help you decide whether your plants need any more magnesium than is supplied by the mix itself and irrigation water.

A 140-day (20-week) coated fertilizer containing 1.2% Mg will supply, for each gram added to a mix, 1.2 x 1000/(20 x 100) = 1.2 mg Mg for each of the 20 weeks. At a typical rate of addition of 4 g/L, the Mg supplied each week is 4.8 mg. If you apply irrigation water at a rate of 500 mL per litre of mix each week, that water must contain 4.8/0.5 = 9.6 mg/L Mg to supply the same amount of magnesium. This rate of irrigation is probably at the lower end of the normal range for nurseries. Weekly application of a litre of water per litre of mix will reduce the Mg concentration needed to 4.8 mg/L. Many Australian water supplies consistently contain at least 4.8 mg/L Mg (Table 21.1). Applications of extra Mg in other areas should be based on analysis of the water used, an assessment of reserves still in the mix and the relative cost of the several sources available.

RATES OF APPLICATION OF CONTROLLED-RELEASE FERTILIZERS

We could make this the shortest section in the book by telling you just to follow manufacturers' instructions, but we would like to provide a bit more guidance than that. The factors you need to consider when choosing controlled-release fertilizers are as follows:

- The NDI of the mix to be used.
- The temperature conditions that will prevail during the main part of the growing period.
- The length of time that you think it will take to produce the crop.
- Whether the plants to be grown respond much or little to an increase in the amount of N supplied.
- Whether vegetative growth (foliage, large frame) or flowers are the main feature of the plants to be grown.
- Likely losses of nutrients in water draining from pots, either from heavy rain or excessive irrigation.
- You can allow for the use of N by microbes as they chew their way through your mix if you know its NDI value. Research has shown that for each 0.1 of a unit drop in NDI_{75} below 1.0, the microbes will consume each week about 2.5 mg of N per litre of mix when the source of N is a controlled-release fertilizer. Therefore, for a mix with an NDI_{75} value of 0.2, you will need to provide an extra 8 x 2.5 = 20 mg of N per litre per week over and above that to be provided to the plant. For a fertilizer that contains 15% N, this works out at about 20 x 13/0.15 = 1.7 kg/m³ for a 3-month growth period using a 3-month product or 3.4 kg/m³ for 6 months with a 6-month product. While the 2.5 mg/L N figure is somewhat rubbery, use of it (and a test for NDI) should give your plants a better start than will a wild guess followed by emergency application of extra N.
- The amounts of N calculated above as being needed by microbes are based on experimentation in which the measured NDI of the mix increased during the growing period. This was presumably due to a drop in microbial activity as the more readily decomposed organic matter had been consumed. The calculated figures take this into account.
- Table 16.16 lists the amounts of N needed by plants showing a range of growth rates. These data are from experiments in which plants were grown in 125–140 mm pots, or 50 mm tubes (for the eucalypt). The amounts of N needed each week of the growing period were calculated from the total amount of N in plants of marketable size. These data can be used to calculate the amounts of fertilizer to use.

Table 16.16
Examples of shoot weights and total N contents of a range of plants growing in soil-less potting media. (*From* **K A Handreck unpublished data**)

Plant	N in shoots (%)	Shoot mass (g)	Total N in shoots (mg)	Total N in plant (mg)*	Growing period (weeks)	N used (mg/week)
Petunia	3.2	9	289	343	6	57
Philadelphus mexicanus, 21 weeks	3.0	22	660	792	15	53
P. mexicanus, 6 weeks	4.3	4.5	194	221	6	37
Pansy	4.1	4	164	188	10	19
Cuphea hyssopifolia	2.8	8	224	272	18	15
Eucalyptus obliqua	3.4	1.5	50	59	16	3.6

* Calculated from the shoot data by assuming that root mass was 0.4 of shoot mass and roots contained 1.5% N.

Example of calculation

You want to grow a leafy plant that is capable of growing relatively quickly. Assume that it will be ready for sale in 15 weeks. You guess that it will have a similar demand for N to that of the *Philadelphus* listed in Table 16.16. A fertilizer containing 15% N and with a nominal release time of 8–9 months (about 35 weeks) is used. The temperature conditions are such that it is likely to release totally in about 25 weeks. The pots hold 1.4 L of mix.

Total N needed is $53 \times 15 = 795$ mg N.
For a fertilizer use rate of 1 g/L (1 kg/m³), there will be

$$1.4 \times 15 \times \frac{1000}{100} = 210 \text{ mg N/pot.}$$

The total released in 15 weeks is $210 \times \frac{15}{25} = 126$ mg N.

Therefore, we need 795/126 = 6.3 g fertilizer per pot, just for the plant. This is 4.5 kg /m³.
To this amount must be added the amount of N that will be used by the mix itself and the amount likely to be lost in drainage water.

Fertilizers and cuttings

- Slow-release fertilizers can be used in propagation media (for cuttings), but the rate must be no more than 1 kg/m³ for coated products and about half that for products such as Nitrophoska and Plantosan. Use mini-sized grains of coated products so that each tube or cell gets some. An alternative is to use a base level of soluble nutrients plus liquid feeding as roots start to form. Excessive use of N may decrease rooting and total root growth.
- Roots form most readily on cuttings having high carbohydrate and low nitrogen levels. Stock plants can be most easily encouraged to provide this type of shoot when they are grown in containers with a carefully controlled low level of nitrogen application. Make sure that all other nutrients are well supplied. Then reserves in the cuttings will aid early growth. Select cuttings from the basal parts of shoots that have stopped growing rapidly.
- Fig. 16.13 gives an example of effect of N starvation of a stock plant on the rooting of cuttings taken from it, but note that for other plants rooting declines rapidly as N supply to the stock plant increases (Fig. 16.14).

Figure 16.13
Effect of weekly fertilization of stock plants of *Juniperus virginiana* on adventitious rooting of stem cuttings from them. *From* P H Henry et al. *J. Amer. Soc. Hortic. Sci.* 117: 568, 1992

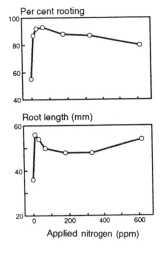

Figure 16.14
Effect of N fertilization of *Ilex crenata* 'Rotundifolia' stock plants on the percentage of stem cuttings that rooted. *From* W H Rein et al. *J. Environ. Hortic.* 9: 83, 1991

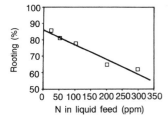

LIQUID FEEDING

Liquid feeding is the application of nutrients dissolved in water to a growing medium around plant roots. It is possible to make up a liquid feed containing all essential nutrients, and to use liquid feeding as the sole means of supplying nutrients. However, the most common use of liquid feeding is as a back-up to a pre-plant fertilization program that has supplied calcium, magnesium, phosphorus and trace elements, and often controlled-release N, P and K. The liquid feed need then supply only nitrogen and potassium (and sulphur if the water supply contains less than about 15 ppm S and the controlled-release fertilizer supplies none), although other nutrients can be included as required.

Liquid feeds are used in three ways: continuously, with all irrigation water being liquid feed; intermittently but regularly, perhaps once a week or fortnight; occasionally, as required.

Fertilizers to use

The simplest way to make up a liquid feed is to buy one containing the required nutrients in the required proportions. Choose one with P/N and K/N ratios near what you want (see below). Then dilute or dissolve it to give the required concentration of nitrogen, make up to volume, and inject. This is not the cheapest way, nor does it allow the ratio of nutrients to be varied. Greatest flexibility is allowed when the fertilizers listed in Table 16.17 are used as required.

For nitrogen and potassium, ammonium nitrate and potassium nitrate are the preferred fertilizers. Monopotassium phosphate and monoammonium phosphate are preferred sources of phosphorus. Use Table 16.17 to calculate the amounts of fertilizers needed to make up liquid feeds. Ammonium, potassium and magnesium sulphates are useful sources of S if it is needed, but note that ammonium sulphate will acidify the medium unless its acidity is balanced in some way (Chapter 11).

Calculation

Grams of fertilizer/litre of concentrate =

$$\frac{\text{ppm needed}}{100} \times \text{g fertilizer/L to give 100 ppm of element} \times \text{dilution factor}$$

Example: You want a liquid feed to supply 150 ppm N, 30 ppm P and 80 ppm K. A large batch is to be made for use without dilution.

1. Use monoammonium phosphate to supply P

   Amount to use is $\frac{30}{100} \times 0.38 \times 1 = 0.114$ g/L

2. Use potassium nitrate to supply the K.

   Amount to use is $\frac{80}{100} \times 0.26 \times 1 = 0.208$ g/L

3. Use ammonium nitrate to supply the extra N.

   (The monoammonium phosphate supplies $\frac{0.114}{0.85} \times 100 = 13$ ppm N

   The potassium nitrate supplies $\frac{0.208}{0.72} \times 100 = 29$ ppm N.)

   Amount to use $\frac{(150 - 13 - 29)}{1000} \times 0.29 = 0.313$ g/L.

A basic limitation

Salinity, from water and fertilizers, sets an upper limit to the concentration of nutrients that can be supplied in liquid feeds. An absolute upper limit is about

Table 16.17
Effects of various fertilizer salts on the EC (in dS/m) of liquid feeds

Fertilizer	ECs of solutions supplying 100 ppm of the element indicated (dS/m)*	Amount of fertilizer needed to give 100 ppm of the element (g/L)
N		
Ammonium nitrate[†]	0.51	0.29
Potassium nitrate	0.96	0.72
Monoammonium phosphate	0.72	0.85
Diammonium phosphate	0.76	0.47
Calcium nitrate	0.84	0.84
Ammonium sulphate	0.96	0.47
(Ammonium chloride)	(1.01)[‡]	(0.38)
Magnesium nitrate (6H$_2$O)	0.85	0.92
Urea	(0.315)[§]	0.21
P		
Monoammonium phosphate	0.33	0.38
Diammonium phosphate	0.69	0.43
Monopotassium phosphate	0.29	0.39
Dipotassium hydrogen phosphate	0.73	0.56
K		
Potassium nitrate	0.34	0.26
Potassium sulphate	0.34	0.22
(Potassium chloride)	(0.36)	(0.19)
Monopotassium phosphate	0.23	0.31
Dipotassium hydrogen phosphate	0.28	0.22
Mg		
Magnesium nitrate (6H$_2$O)	0.97	1.05
Magnesium sulphate (7H$_2$O)	0.84	1.01
Ca		
Calcium nitrate	0.59	0.59
S		
Ammonium sulphate	0.84	0.41
Potassium sulphate	0.83	0.54
Magnesium sulphate (7H$_2$O)	0.64	0.77

*Doubling the ppm in solution will double the EC; halving the ppm will halve the EC, etc.
† The brown material added to ammonium nitrate must be allowed to settle before the solution is injected.
‡The bracketed fertilizers are not recommended for use in liquid feeds.
§ Urea does not form ions in solution, so it does not affect EC. However, it still behaves towards plant roots as does any salt. If a liquid feed contains urea, increase the measured EC by 1.5 dS/m for each g of urea/L. Thus if the measured EC of a liquid feed is 0.65 dS/m and it contains 0.25 g urea/L, plants will 'see' the feed as having an EC of 0.65 + (0.25 × 1.5) = 1.03 dS/m.

3 dS/m (Table 21.2). Some leaching is needed for some plants at even lower salinities.

For many plants grown in nurseries an upper limit for continuous liquid feeding is 1.5 dS/m. Feeds applied intermittently can go up to 2 dS/m.

Example 1: In the example used under 'Calculation', the salinity (using Table 16.17) would be:

From the monoammonium phosphate $\dfrac{30}{100} \times 0.33 = 0.1$ dS/m

From the potassium nitrate $\frac{80}{100} \times 0.34 = 0.272$ dS/m

From the ammonium nitrate $\frac{108}{100} \times 0.51 = 0.551$ dS/m

Total salinity from fertilizers = 0.923 dS/m

Example 2: Is the salinity of a liquid feed supplying 250 ppm N and 200 ppm K too high for use on sensitive plants?

200 ppm K from potassium nitrate gives an EC of 0.64 dS/m.

This amount of potassium nitrate supplies $\frac{0.52}{0.72} \times 100 = 72$ ppm N, so the ammonium nitrate must supply 250 − 72 = 178 ppm N.

This gives $\frac{178}{100} \times 0.51 = 0.908$ dS/m.

Total EC = 1.548 dS/m

This is right at the limit for sensitive plants, if the water contains no salts. A water with an EC of 0.45 dS/m could push the feed to the upper limit for many nursery plants.

Concentrations to use

Apart from the upper limit set by salinity, the concentrations of nutrients to be used in liquid feeds depend mainly on:

- whether or not there is a controlled-release source in the medium;
- whether all irrigation water is to contain nutrients or whether the liquid feed is to be applied intermittently;
- the frequency of intermittent application;
- the time of the year;
- the rate of growth of the plants;
- the nitrogen drawdown potential (NDI) of the medium;
- losses in water draining from pots.

N is the key nutrient

As already discussed for controlled-release fertilizers, nitrogen is the key nutrient to be considered in any fertilizer application program. If all other nutrients are present in adequate amounts, plant growth is determined by the amount of N supplied. The first action is therefore to work out the concentration of N that the feed must contain to satisfy plants, microbes and the drains.

We discuss first the situation in which the liquid feed is the sole source of nutrients, other than the pre-plant additions to the medium.

- Allow for the N consumed by microbes by supplying 2.5 mg N/L mix for each 0.1 NDI unit that the mix is below an NDI_{75} of 1.0 (as discussed for controlled-release fertilizers, above).

So if a mix has an NDI_{75} of 0.7, the microbes in each litre will use about 3 × 2.5 = 7.5 mg of N each week. A liquid feed applied weekly at a rate of 200 mL per litre of mix will need to contain $\frac{7.5}{0.2} = 37.5$ ppm N just for the microbes. For a bark mix with an NDI_{150} of 0.5 (about an NDI_{75} of −0.4) (Fig. 16.10), the feed must contain 175 ppm N, just for the microbes.

- The concentration of N needed to feed the plants depends on the rate of growth needed and possible. We refer to the examples given in the section on controlled-release fertilizers. Again assuming a weekly addition of 200 mL per litre of mix, we can calculate that the feed has to contain 50 mg/L N for

Figure 16.15
Gear needed to measure the amount of drainage being produced during irrigation or rain *Photograph K A Handreck*

each 10 mg N/week needed. For example, a need for 25 mg N/week will require use of a feed containing $25 \times \dfrac{1000}{200} = 125$ mg/L N. To this must be added that used by microbes and that lost in drainage.

- These concentrations make no allowance for losses from the pots if irrigation between feeds causes drainage. Growers are urged to measure drainage amounts by suspending a few pots in each batch in styrofoam (cut from broccoli boxes) placed on the tops of buckets (Fig. 16.15). With this arrangement, all the water entering a bucket will have come through the mix in the pot. Measurement of the concentration of N in the drainage water may well encourage you to reduce the amount of irrigation water applied. It will also give you an idea of the proportion of the applied fertilizer your plants are not getting. One US study showed that placing saucers under pots allowed a 25% reduction in fertilizer use for similar growth.

Example: It is found that three irrigations between applications of liquid feed produce a total drainage of 250 mL (0.25 L) per 140 mm pot. Measurement with nitrate and ammonium dipsticks shows that the drainage water contains 100 ppm nitrate (100 × 0.226 = 22.6 ppm N) and 12 ppm ammonium (12 × 0.74 = 9 ppm N). The total amount of N lost per pot was 0.25 × 31.6 = 7.9 mg N. If the feed contains 300 ppm N and 300 mL is applied weekly to each pot, the total applied is 0.3 × 300 = 90 mg, so $\dfrac{7.9}{90}$ = about 9% of the N applied was lost.

Your response to this information may be to reduce drainage losses by reducing irrigation or to increase by 9% the concentration of N in your feed, if you can be sure that your plants will respond to the extra N.

The presence of actively-releasing controlled-release fertilizers in the mix calls for a reduction in the concentration of N in the liquid feed or a reduction in the frequency of its application. You have to be guided by a guesstimate of how much N is left in the coated fertilizer and by the condition of the plants. The first sign of N deficiency is yellowing of the oldest leaves. Measurement of the EC or N content of drainage water (Chapter 33) may aid decision making.

Examples of the concentrations of N needed in weekly liquid feeds are given in Table 16.18. A further example, for large plants, is given in Table 16.19.

Phosphorus

Adding P in liquid feeds is expensive. P is best added via pre-plant superphosphate. If present, coated NPK fertilizers will supply more. If P must be included, use the following levels:

- For soil-less mixes use a P/N ratio of 0.15 to 0.2.
- For mixes containing some soil, shale, attapulgite, etc., initially use a P/N ratio of 0.4, but later reduce it to about 0.2.

Example: A liquid feed is needed for plants being grown in a soil-less mix. The feed is to supply 250 ppm N, and the P/N ratio chosen is 0.15. Therefore the feed is to contain 37.5 ppm P.

The amount of monoammonium phosphate needed in a concentrate to be diluted 1:200 is 37.5 x 0.38 x 200/100 = 28.5 g/L.

Use only highest quality monoammonium phosphate, made with thermal process phosphoric acid, otherwise precipitates may form. Phosphoric acid may be used with hard waters.

Potassium

The discussion on K in the section on controlled-release fertilizers is equally applicable here. Higher K/N ratios than the commonly used 0.83 may be needed if it is necessary to improve flower stem quality in cold weather or to counteract

Table 16.18
Approximate concentrations of N needed in weekly liquid feeds for plants with a range of growth rates and in media with two contrasting rates of nitrogen drawdown

Growth rate required or possible	Weekly N needed per pot by:			N concentration in solution applied at 200 mL/pot (mg/L)
	Plant (mg)	Microbes (mg)	Total (mg)	
Maintenance	5	10	15	75
	5	40	45	225
Slow	10	10	20	100
	10	40	50	250
	20	10	30	150
	20	40	60	300
	30	10	40	200
	30	40	70	350
	40	10	50	250
	40	40	80	400
	50	10	60	300
	50	40	90	450
Very rapid	60	10	70	350
	60	40	100	500

the tendency of young plants to grow tall and spindly under low light conditions in winter. Under extreme conditions it might be necessary to go to an N–K ratio of 1:3 in the dead of a southern winter, but generally 1:2 should be sufficient to produce the hardening needed under these conditions. However, the most important action to be taken is to lower the concentration of N used in cold, dull weather. For example, if an N rate of 180 ppm is suitable in summer, perhaps 100 ppm is enough for winter.

Table 16.19
Contrasting response of two plants with different potential growth rates to the same fertilizer applications. (From P R Hicklenton J. Environ. Hortic. 8: 192, 1990)

N applied each week (mg/plant)	Shoot mass (g)	
	Cotoneaster dammeri 'Coral Beauty'	Juniperus horizontalis 'Plumosa Compacta'
70	46.4	14.9
140	67.7	21.0
280	79.4	18.6
420	82.9	17.4

Sulphate–sulphur

Unless the water used contains more than about 15 ppm S (Chapter 14), it is recommended that sulphate-S is included in the liquid feed. The main source will be potassium or magnesium sulphates. Aim for a concentration in the range 25–40 ppm for feeds to be applied weekly.

Calcium (Ca)

If calcium is needed over and above that supplied by the water used and by

Figure 16.16
This liquid feed formula contains all plant nutrients in the one pack.

pre-plant applications of gypsum, superphosphate and liming materials, it is best that it be supplied as calcium nitrate injected separately from a general liquid feed. One alternative is to topdress with gypsum (2–5 mm). Another alternative is to use the Grace–Sierra product Excel (Fig. 16.16). It contains all major nutrients, including Ca, and is completely soluble. Generally, if the pH remains in the recommended range (5–6.4), there should be enough exchangeable calcium held in the mix.

Magnesium

Magnesium is best supplied by pre-plant dolomite or magnesium sulphate. If more is needed, include magnesium sulphate in the feed at 20–30 ppm Mg.

Example: The amount of magnesium sulphate ($7H_2O$) needed (Table 16.17) to supply 20 ppm Mg in a liquid feed concentrate that is to be diluted 1:200 is: $20 \times 1.01 \times \dfrac{200}{100} = 40.4$ g/L.

Trace elements

If sufficient amounts of each of the trace elements have been added before planting, and pH is still in the range 5.0 to 6.4, there is no need for additional trace elements to be applied via the liquid feed for at least a year. Iron, copper and zinc are held tightly against loss in drainage water. There will be a small loss of manganese, but this will not lead to deficiency if the base level was high enough. Losses of boron will be somewhat greater, but as most water supplies contain some boron it is relatively rare for more to be needed.

If you *must* include trace elements in your feed, we suggest iron at 1 ppm (as chelate), manganese at 0.5 ppm, and copper and boron at 0.1 ppm.

Frequency of application

Every watering can be liquid feed, and it commonly is in bedding plant nurseries. For larger pots, applications are more commonly made weekly or fortnightly, although plants in some of the worst sawdust-based media need feeding each few days. Plant growth can be equally good with any of these frequencies, but of course the concentration of nutrients for fortnightly application must be double that for weekly application. Fortnightly feeding will not be successful if the salinity of the feed is too high for the plants.

An interval of a month between liquid feeds is too long to produce high-quality plants. If you do want to hold plants in a state of 'suspended animation'—that is, neither growing much nor going backwards—you should feed them weekly with a very dilute solution containing, say, 50 ppm N with balancing K. A somewhat higher concentration may be needed for plants in low NDI mixes (Table 16.18).

Feeding can be based on analysis of pour-through or other extracts of the medium in the pots (Chapter 21). Small trials in which a range of concentrations and frequencies of application are compared will be useful for fine-tuning a liquid feeding program.

Feeding with every irrigation is usually considered to be too wasteful of nutrients if irrigation is by overhead sprinklers. Trickle irrigation eliminates this waste. The frequency of intermittent liquid feeding needed depends on the amounts of nutrients being supplied from controlled-release fertilizers. Frequency should increase as the release rate from controlled-release sources decreases.

Liquid feeds can supply the total amounts of major nutrient elements needed. However, losses of nutrients are least and results are often best when liquid feeds supply 10–50% of total major nutrient needs. Choice within this range depends very much on personal preference and local experience. In hot areas, aiming for about 50% will keep pre-plant additions of controlled-release fertilizers low. This minimizes the risk of hot weather causing loss of plants through rapid release of salts from controlled-release fertilizers. But note that damage may be minimal if the mix is kept at a constantly high moisture content. It can be severe if the mix is allowed to dry down between irrigations.

Plants in open mixes will need more frequent liquid feeding than those in mixes that hold more water.

Losses of nutrients will be least if the mix is allowed to dry out somewhat before the feed is applied.

Using liquid feeds to modify mix pH

As with controlled-release fertilizers, the higher the proportion of the total N that is present as ammonium and urea, the greater will be the ability of the fertilizer to lower mix pH. Per unit of N, ammonium sulphate and monoammonium phosphate have about double the acidifying ability of urea and ammonium nitrate. Diammonium phosphate is halfway between these two groups.

Unlike controlled-release fertilizers, the proportion of the N in nitrate form in liquid feeds can be 100%. (High-nitrate mixtures liquefy, so they cannot be prilled and coated.) This means that any tendency for mixes to acidify during a growing period is easier to counteract with liquid feeds than with coated fertilizers.

With waters of very low total alkalinity, it may be necessary to use a nitrate-N to ammonium-N ratio of about 8:1 (Fig. 16.17). A more common ratio for pH stability is 2 or 4:1. The effects of alkaline water supplies (Fig. 11.6) can be countered by having more ammonium and urea than nitrate.

If further acidification is needed in areas where the water is highly alkaline, the water used must be acidified with concentrated acids (Chapter 11).

PREPARING AND APPLYING LIQUID FEEDS

Traps to avoid

It is all too easy to miscalculate when preparing liquid feeds. Always check the strength of the diluted feed with a salinity meter. The ideal is a meter in the line, hooked up to an alarm that goes off if the feed is outside a pre-set range.

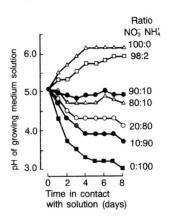

Figure 16.17
General effects on medium pH of fertilizers containing different proportions of their N as ammonium and nitrate. *From* S F Trelease and H M Trelease *Amer. J. Botany* 22: 520, 1935

- The fertilizers must be completely dissolved. Some dissolve very slowly in cold water, and so hot (65°C) water is commonly used. If some won't dissolve, or a precipitate is formed, allow the solids to settle before using the liquid. Try to find out which fertilizer is leaving the residue or causing the precipitate, and change brands or formulation.
- Borax (sodium borate) and boric acid used to supply boron must be dissolved in boiling water. Concentrate containing boron should be used quickly because the boron will slowly precipitate out again.
- Solid calcium sulphate will precipitate from concentrates if they contain sulphate ions and more than 500 ppm Ca. This will happen if calcium nitrate and a sulphate are both being used. If the liquid feed is to contain calcium, you must use a two-headed proportioner, so keeping the calcium and sulphate separate until both are diluted in the liquid feed. An alternative is to prepare the liquid feed at the strength at which it is to be used.
- A precipitate can form when phosphate is added to hard waters (Fig. 16.18). There may be a small amount formed immediately on dilution. It may cause problems with drippers, but not with sprinklers. After five or so days, more precipitate may be formed in diluted feeds. This can be prevented by including EDTA in the feed at 15 ppm.
- Newly forming roots on cuttings are easily damaged by salinity. Use a dilute liquid feed at first—say, 50 ppm N—and build up the concentration as the seedlings grow.

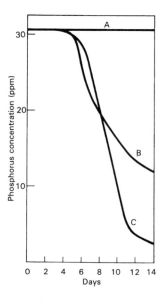

- Liquid feeding is not very useful to plants in containers out-of-doors in the season of highest rainfall. Topdressing with solid and controlled-release fertilizers is to be preferred then.
- Plants grown using liquid feeding alone can soon suffer from starvation in retail stores. A way around this is suggested on p. 168.
- The fertilizers for liquid feeds are no cheaper than those for dry topdressing. However, the cost of application may be 1 to 5, respectively. Besides, topdressed fertilizer is rarely spread evenly on the surface.

Preparing liquid feeds

Two methods of preparing liquid feeds are available.

1. *Bulk tank* The less commonly used method. Liquid feed of the strength that is to be applied to plants is made up in a large tank. The tank should hold enough feed for at least one full irrigation. A known volume of water is filled into the tank. If the fertilizers to be used are very soluble in water, the solids can be tipped straight into the tank. Stirring is easiest by cycling the feed through a pump. You must be sure that all solid fertilizer has dissolved. Use a salinity meter to check for complete mixing and to guard against errors.

   Example: A liquid feed is to contain 125 ppm N and 100 ppm K, using ammonium nitrate and potassium nitrate. What masses are needed for 50 000 L of feed?

   Amount of potassium nitrate = 0.26 g/L (from Table 16.17)

   $$\text{Total} = 50\ 000 \times \frac{0.26}{1000} = 13.0 \text{ kg}$$

   This will supply $\frac{0.26}{0.72} \times 100 = 36$ ppm N

   The ammonium nitrate is to supply 125 – 36 = 89 ppm N

   $$\text{Amount} = \frac{89 \times 0.29}{100} \times \frac{50000}{1000} \text{ kg} = 12.9 \text{ kg}$$

   Fertilizers that do not dissolve quickly (boric acid is an example) should be dissolved in hot water. The solution is then poured into the tank near the outflow from the pump, or pumped in.

2. *Injectors (proportioners)* The more usual method of preparing liquid feeds is to make up a stock solution that is injected into the irrigation water through a proportioner. Stock solution should be made up in such a way that any precipitate formed or remaining in it does not reach the injector. Figure 16.19 gives one method.

   Injectors are of several types (Figs 16.20 and 16.21). A commonly used dilution ratio is 1:200.

   When selecting an injector, work back from the anticipated amounts of liquid feed needed. Allow for expansion of the business.

   Water-supply authorities require a physical break—check valves or a tank—between the injector and the water supply.

   Concentrate solutions are highly corrosive. Use plastic and glass tanks, pipes and mixing vessels. Zinc toxicity can result from the use of galvanized materials. Stir with a wooden paddle.

Applying liquid feeds

Very careful consideration must be given to how liquid feeds are applied. Already there are in some areas restrictions on the levels of nutrients in water leaving nurseries or entering underground aquifers. These restrictions are likely to become more widespread and severe.

Concentrations of nutrients in runoff waters will be lowest if the liquid feed is applied to plants sitting on solid benches or in troughs, with the excess caught and recirculated back to the plants. Such systems are becoming the norm in

Figure 16.19
It is best to prepare stock solutions for liquid feeds in one tank, allow any solids to settle out and then to run the clear stock solution into the main tank. This need not be done if you are sure that no solids remain or are formed during mixing.

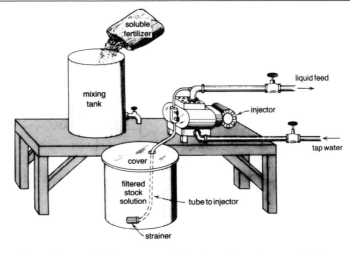

Europe, but will generally be too expensive in Australia, unless survival of a nursery depends on the reduction in nutrient runoff that these systems can provide.

Two alternatives offer minimal losses of nutrients: application through hand-held hoses, and application through drippers or spitters (hereafter called emitters). Hand-held hoses in reliable hands are ideal for small areas of plants. Emitter installations are best suited to large containers and crops that will remain in the one position for at least six months. The emitters must be reliable. Any blockage undetected for a couple of days in hot weather could mean the loss of a plant. There should be little variation between emitters in actual delivery, so pressure-compensated emitters are to be preferred. These systems are discussed further in Chapter 23.

Overhead sprinklers are still the preferred and cheapest way of applying irrigation water and liquid feeds to large areas of plants in small containers (smaller than 200 mm pots). Allowance must be made for feed that misses the containers (p. 307). When applying liquid feed, irrigate until you know from testing that the pots have received the required amount of feed. It is usually necessary to catch the runoff water and use it either to irrigate pasture or another crop or to recycle the water, after suitable treatment, back to the nursery.

Figure 16.20
A commonly used injection unit for liquid feeds. Several sizes are available.

FOLIAR SPRAYS

Foliar sprays provide a means of rapidly starting to overcome some nutrient deficiencies. They are not a substitute for feeding plants through roots. Spraying is costly in money and time. Uptake of nutrients through roots is more efficient than through leaves. Foliar sprays will not improve the growth of plants that are adequately supplied via the growing medium (Table 16.20).

Table 16.20
Data showing that application of foliar fertilizers did not increase fruit yield (kg) of muskmelons adequately fed through their roots. (From R R M Harun Proc. Intern. Soc. Soilless Culture p. 395, 1988)

| Fruit | Control | Foliar fertilizer | |
		Phostrogen 1 g/L	Nutrophos 3 g/L
1st	0.85	0.86	0.84
2nd	0.84	0.85	0.86
Total	1.69	1.71	1.70

Figure 16.21

Two devices for injecting fertilizer into irrigation water.

Photographs K A Handreck

Sprays are most often used for deficiencies of nitrogen, iron and zinc, but potassium and the other trace elements can be supplied in this way too. A surfactant (wetting agent) should be included in the spray when the leaves of the plants being treated are waxy. Sprays for other plants may not need a surfactant. Application equipment must be able to deliver very small droplets, so that all surfaces of the plant are covered and runoff is minimized.

Tables 16.21 and 16.22 give concentrations. Urea is the preferred source of nitrogen.

Table 16.21
Foliar sprays supplying nitrogen and potassium. (Either urea or potassium nitrate can be used alone, as needed.)

Plants being sprayed	Urea (g/L)	Potassium nitrate (g/L)	Wetting agent* (mL/L)
Those sensitive to salinity, or needing only a small boost in nutrition	5[†]	15[†]	1
General nursery plants	10	30	2.5
Those needing, and able to tolerate, a high concentration	15	45	5

*For Agral 600. The amount should be varied for others according to manufacturers' instructions.
[†]This may be too concentrated for some ornamental plants. Check by spraying a few plants first.

The urea and potassium nitrate combination of Table 16.21 is much cheaper than commercially prepared mixtures. In trials with vegetables in Victoria, commercial mixtures were five times the cost and gave only 50-60% as much response.

Magnesium may be applied as a solution of 2 kg magnesium sulphate/100 L water. Several sprayings may be needed.

Spraying is most effective when humidity is high—early in the morning, at night, or soon after irrigation or rain.

Young leaves may absorb half of the applied major nutrients in 24 hours under ideal conditions. Trace elements are absorbed more slowly. The rate of absorption of iron, zinc and manganese (from sulphates) can be increased by including urea in the spray at about 4 g/L.

Table 16.22
Foliar sprays supplying trace elements

Element	Fertilizer	Spray strength (g fertilizer/L)	Comments
Fe	Fe–EDTA	0.25–2 (usually 0.5)	More than one spraying may be needed; spots resembling fungal attack may be produced on the leaves of foliage plants
	Fe–lignosulphonate (e.g. CRG)	1–2	Effective and less likely to damage the leaves than other chelates or ferrous sulphate
	Ferrous sulphate (7H_2O)	3	Stains the leaves brown
Zn	Zinc sulphate	10	Dissolve the zinc sulphate in the water, then mix in 5 g of builder's lime per L; shake during use
Mn	Manganese sulphate (4H_2O)	2.3	More than one spraying may be needed
Cu	Copper oxychloride	1.0	–
Mo	Ammonium or sodium molybdate	0.25	Use at an early stage of growth

Seedlings in cells

A majority of vegetable transplants used in Australia are now grown in cells. Many bedding plants for retail sale are also produced in cell packs. We make some general comments before considering fertilizers for this growing system.

The very small volume of these cells (13–50 mL) means that control of watering and nutrition must be very precise indeed. Also critically important are light and temperature and the physical properties of the medium (Chapter 10). Mixes for plugs have a low AFP, so that water supply is maximized. What little AFP there is must not be reduced further by stacking plug trays on top of one another. Such stacking has been shown to reduce AFP in large cells from 4% to as little as 0.3% and in waffles from 0.3% to zero%.

Light intensity must be high enough to prevent etiolation of seedlings. Some height control can be had by dropping early morning temperature by about 6°C for two hours. Mechanical stress, as caused by wind and brushing, will also help.

Cell shape appears to have no effect on overall growth; cell size has a permanent effect on some seedlings and little effect on others. Reduced growth of marigolds and watermelons in small cells reduces later growth. With capsicum, plants produced in large cells give the largest early yields, but those from small cells eventually catch up.

Nutrition

The guidelines given earlier in this chapter on pre-plant nutrients apply to mixes for plugs too: add all trace elements; add liming materials to bring pH to about 6 and to supply calcium and magnesium; add single superphosphate at no more than 0.5 kg/m³ (0.25 kg/m³ is enough for many plants); add potassium nitrate and/or sulphate as need is shown by analysis, but typically potassium nitrate at about 0.4 kg/m³ or potassium sulphate at 0.25 kg/m³. Pre-plant N must be minimal for lettuce and the brassicas, otherwise you will get lanky growth.

Whether you include any slow-release fertilizer (mini forms of coated products or such materials as Nitrophoska Slow Release and Plantosan) depends on your production schedule and the needs of your customers. You have no control over growth when these products are used, so you must be assured that they will leave your care at the required time. Most growers find that scheduling is easiest when most or all feeding is with liquid.

There are two schools of thought on what liquid feeds should contain. Opinion in the USA is to use a feed containing all nutrients. Elsewhere, it has been found that excellent plugs can be grown with feeds containing only N and K (from ammonium and potassium nitrates). For a growing period of probably no more than six weeks, it is unlikely that the mix will run out of calcium and magnesium if the water used contains some of each. However, both might be needed when very pure (and acid) water is being used. Some sulphur should be included in the feed if your water contains less than 25 ppm S. This is essential if you are growing brassicas (cabbage, cauliflower, turnip, etc.).

As indicated earlier, including P in a liquid feed is expensive and a hassle. You should determine by trials whether you do or do not need extra P in the feed for the plants you are growing. We believe that very often some P should be included. The P/N ratio should be in the range 0.2–0.3 so that the seedlings have an ample supply when transplanted. The K/N ratio needed will vary with environmental conditions and the type of growth needed. K concentration should be at least that of N, and will be up to three times N during dull winter conditions, if lankiness is to be controlled. More typical K/N ratios will be 1–1.5.

The N concentration should be about 50 ppm early, rising to about 100 ppm later. Rapid, sturdy growth is obtained with 100 ppm N and 100–300 ppm K applied daily or 2–3 times a week. With 50 ppm N and 100 ppm K at each watering growth is slow and sturdy. These figures are for peat-based media.

Figure 16.22
Response of (▲) *Primula 'Peer Gynt'* and (●) *Pelargonium 'Ringo Scarlet'* growing in 13 mL cells to different N concentrations in the daily liquid feed. *Redrawn from E Meinken Acta Horticulturae 226: 703, 1988*

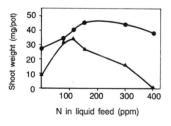

Higher concentrations of N will be needed when there is some N drawdown. Growers who produce large numbers of the one variety will want to fine-tune a fertilizer program specially suited to their situation (e.g. Fig. 16.22). Feeding of begonias and petunias must start at sowing. This early feeding cuts weeks off production time.

Plants can be held if they are fed weekly with 50 ppm N and 100 ppm K. Eliminating feeding altogether will give rapid deterioration in quality. Greening up is achieved with a feed containing 200 ppm N, 45 ppm P and about 100 ppm K.

Here is an example of a feed containing N, P, K and S at 100, 22, 170 and 25 ppm, respectively, when diluted 1:200.

Per 100 litres of stock: potassium nitrate, 4.2 kg; ammonium nitrate 4.2 kg; monopotassium phosphate, 1.6 kg and potassium sulphate, 2.8 kg.

It has been shown in England that seedlings in cells can be produced organically in a peat/zeolite (9:1) mix, amended with hoof and horn, blood and bone, poultry manure and calcified seaweed, plus 'fungal starter', whatever that is.

HINTS AND COMMENTS

The various 'recipes', amounts and proportions of nutrients given in this chapter must be taken only as general guidelines. Each nursery still has to fine-tune a fertilization program for each particular situation.

- Store fertilizers and herbicides in widely separated parts of the nursery. It is all too easy for herbicides to be spilt onto fertilizer bags, or for someone to use herbicide instead of fertilizer.
- Check the salinity and pH of containers every month or so, or as often as is necessary for you to be sure that your program is providing what your plants need. Use analytical services when setting up a program and as an occasional check on it.
- Use small trials to check the effects of changes in levels of nutrients (p. 413).
- Some plants grow more-or-less continuously. Others grow by producing a flush, then stopping, then producing another flush. These latter plants (holly is an example) grow fastest if they are fertilized about two weeks after a flush has finished.
- Plants are hardier if they are produced, or at least finished off, under conditions of slight stress. This stress can be given by keeping N applications to a minimum, by having the air-filled porosity of the mix a little less than that giving rapid growth or by restricting watering *slightly*. The lower growth rate during hardening off allows the accumulation of storage carbohydrates. The plants are thereby enabled to withstand stress better.
- Foliage plants need to be acclimatized before being taken indoors. Reduce fertilizing well before they are to leave the nursery so that there is only a little left in the mix when they do leave. Leach heavily, then reduce watering frequency to harden the plants. Increase shading to between 40% and 80%. No more than the equivalent of 2 kg Osmocote (34 month) per cubic metre should be in the mix when plants are moved indoors.

Nitrogen

- High nitrogen applications in winter will delay flowering (Table 16.23).
- The keeping quality of flowers is reduced by high levels of N during production. For annual crops, keeping quality is improved by reducing fertilizer applications in the four weeks before harvest.
- High nitrogen stimulates top growth and tends to depress root growth.
- Rhododendrons supplied with enough N to produce lush flush growth are much more susceptible to *Phytophthora* dieback than are plants fed at a lower, but adequate level.

Table 16.23
Effect of nitrogen supply and air-filled porosity on flowering of chrysanthemums. The figures are days to flowering. (*From* A C Bunt *Acta Horticulturae* 31: 163, 1973)

Medium	Air-filled porosity (volume %)	Low N* in medium		High N* in medium	
		Low N[†] in liquid feed	High N[†] in liquid feed	Low N in liquid feed	High N in liquid feed
75% peat/25% sand	7.3	97	99	99	106
50% peat/50% grit	16.8	87	99	93	112

*Low N in medium = 115 g N/m^3; high N in medium = 460 g N/m^3
[†]Low N in liquid feed = 100 ppm; high N in liquid feed = 300 ppm (both plus 150 ppm K).

- If all other nutrients are fully supplied, the level of nitrogen application can be used to control growth rate. A low application rate gives hardy plants that will transplant with minimal shock, and will stand up to the abuse of transport and retail store conditions.
- The proportion of ammonium that can be used without harming plants can be higher in mixes with a high cation exchange capacity than in those with a low cation exchange capacity.
- Heavy applications of ammonium salts cause leaching of calcium, magnesium and potassium from media and reduced concentrations in plants; pH is reduced.
- High nitrogen fertilization delays the onset of autumn colours in leaves.

17 FOUNDATIONS FOR GOOD TURF

If foundations for buildings are made from inferior materials, are inadequately reinforced or are too small, the buildings can crack, distort or even collapse. So it is with turf. If the foundations for turf—the soil in which it is growing—are composed of inferior materials, are inadequately drained or are too shallow, turf grows poorly, looks off-colour and may even die out altogether.

Great care is taken to design building foundations to suit each building and site. Such early care reduces later maintenance costs. In contrast, much turf is still established with little attention being given to its foundations. All too often the result is continuing costly maintenance.

This need not be. Enough information is available to provide excellent foundations for every type of turf. This chapter summarizes that information.

MATCH FOUNDATIONS TO USE

No self-respecting cricketer would play on a rough roadside verge, nor would a lawn bowls player use a football oval churned to a quagmire by winter play. On the other hand, Highways Departments cannot afford, nor do they need, to construct roadside verges as if they were to be used for playing bowls. Clearly, the care taken in preparing a foundation for turf must match intended use if users and those who pay are both to be satisfied.

The care taken and amount of money spent on design and construction are, or at least should be, determined by the likely intensity of use, and the financial and other consequences of not being able to use the turf in wet weather. Table 17.1 gives an approximate ranking according to intensity of use. No doubt readers will think of exceptions that would, for example, move some community sports fields right to the top of the list.

Effects of use on turf

Grass grows well on pasture soils. Why not grow all turf on similar soils? Much turf is, and all turf once was on pasture-type soils, but under intense use, the usually good structure of soils under grass breaks down.

- Turf grasses can be damaged by uprooting (as by golf clubs) or by being worn away by skidding, sliding and rapid turning movements of players.
- Skidding on wet, bare—or nearly bare—soils slicks the surface, giving poor conditions for grass growth and reducing the ability of water to soak into the soil.
- Repeated pounding of feet and movement of machinery compacts soils (Table 17.2), so that physical conditions for root growth deteriorate.
- Damaged soil grows poorer grass that is more easily damaged; cover becomes thinner and the soil more easily damaged, and so on.

This kind of vicious circle can only be broken by a vigorous renovation program (Chapter 19) or by remaking the area. With proper construction in the first place, it need never happen.

Table 17.1
Approximate ranking of areas of turf according to intensity of use

Intensity of use	Type of use
Most intense	Sports fields for games such as rugby that put extreme pressure on the turf
	Race tracks, polo grounds
	Cricket pitches, including bowlers' run-up area
	Lawn tennis courts; Golf tees; Golf greens
	Public parks near city centres
	Sports fields used almost daily all year round (many school and community fields fit in here)
	Athletics fields; More heavily trafficked areas of parks
	Bowling greens; Golf fairways; Large parklands; Domestic lawns
	Turf mainly 'for looking at'
Least intense	Roadside verges

IMPORTANT PROPERTIES OF TURF SOILS

Table 17.2
Infiltration rate and runoff from a loam soil as affected by pedestrian traffic (From J P Daniel and R P Freeburg *Turfgrass Managers' Handbook* p 143 Business Pubs. Div., Harvest Pub. Co., Cleveland 1979)

Traffic intensity	Infiltration rate (mm/hour)	Runoff (% of water applied)
None	38	0
Moderate	18	52
Heavy	8	76

Soils for turf have to satisfy the needs of both plants and users. Turf plants have the same general requirements as do other plants: enough water (but not too much), oxygen, low enough strength to allow easy root growth, a balanced supply of nutrients, and favourable biological conditions.

Users have widely differing needs, depending on how they are using the turf. Some require a hard even surface (as in a cricket pitch). Some require a firm surface with the grass cut very short. Where running, turning and dodging is involved, the soil–grass combination must provide traction, yet have some resilience to cushion falls. All users expect to be able to continue their use immediately after rain stops, if not before. They cannot be inconvenienced by the whims of plants or groundsmen.

Providing for both plants and users is possible, but not easy. Skilled management, based on a sound knowledge of soil properties and the growth patterns of turf plants, can achieve the near miracles sometimes needed. But management is so much easier and the results more certain if the soil foundation has been constructed to suit the use.

PREPARING FOR TURF

First, read this chapter and Chapter 19. Make sure that all members of your committee/planning team, etc., are familiar with the options available, as outlined here, and the maintenance requirements of these options. Thoroughly discuss these options; inspect other nearby facilities and assess their performance in relation to method of construction.

Then engage the services of one of the several turf design teams operating in Australia (see the appendix, 'Sources of Help'). They have wide-ranging experience and can save you from disaster or at least ensure that you get value for your money.

With the aid of the design team, sort out financial arrangements, decide on a design and prepare detailed plans and specifications. Arrange for testing of materials. Call tenders; make a contract and arrange for close supervision of all phases of site preparation and construction.

Except for those few situations in which the subgrade is to be compacted because it is not to be part of the root zone, it is **essential that the compaction be relieved by ripping, cultivation and the addition of gypsum and organic matter. This is critically important, as we shall see later in this chapter.**

CONSTRUCTION FOR TURF

Those who control purse-strings rarely seem able to understand that the cheapest way of providing turf is to construct the area properly in the first place. It must be a continuing aim of turf managers and groundsmen to impress this fact on management committees, engineers, clerks and accountants, who often appear unable to see further than the current budget, and who know little about turf. Many millions of dollars are wasted each year because of bad specifications and poor supervision of contractors. Insist on good specifications and supervise ruthlessly.

In the next few pages we give detail of proven methods of providing excellent foundations for turf. We start with those areas where only the best will do, working down through various compromises that may do, to alternatives that are often found suitable for lightly used areas. Many turf problems can be traced to the use of these alternatives when intensity or type of use requires better construction.

When only the best will do

One of several methods of construction can be used for turf that has to be excellent under intense use. The methods are:

- That originally developed by the United States Golf Association (USGA) for golf greens. It is often referred to simply as the USGA method or as the perched or suspended water table method of construction. This method of construction has stood the test of time and in fact is now better than ever because of continuing refinement of design criteria. By courtesy of the USGA, we are able to include in this edition the specifications that were to be published in early 1993.
- Various hybrid methods that use the essential features of the USGA method, but include modifications that take into account the climate and rainfall pattern of a local area.
- Several very expensive construction methods that are little used outside Europe, North America and the richer parts of the Middle East. They have names such as Purr-Wick, PAT and Cellsystem. We offer no further detail.

The merits of different methods of construction were the subject of much controversy in the early 1980s when we were preparing the first edition of this book. That controversy has continued and centres mainly on the relative merits of perched water table methods of construction versus pure sand placed onto the existing soil or subsoil. We expressed the opinion in 1984 that these methods were alternatives of equal merit, based on experience with pure sand constructions in California. While pure sand constructions can work in areas of low natural rainfall, the risk that they will become waterlogged when constructed in wetter areas, or that they need excessively frequent irrigation when constructed on permeable subsoils leads us to conclude that this method of construction is of little use in Australia.

USGA perched water table construction

The high cost of this method of construction means that it is used mainly for small areas such as golf and bowling greens and for football/cricket grounds that must perform well every week of the year. Features of the design are:

- a shaped subgrade;
- where necessary, a geotextile layer over the compacted subgrade;
- a gravel drainage layer that incorporates a plastic or clay pipe drainage system;
- an intermediate layer of coarse sand/fine gravel, except where the gravel used has a particle size distribution that makes it unnecessary, see p. 192 (geotextiles are specifically excluded from use);

Figure 17.1
The profile of a golf (or bowling) green as recommended by the US Golf Association. Note that the root zone depth must be based on the physical properties of the root zone mixture, as determined by testing

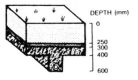

Figure 17.1
The profile of a golf (or bowling) green as recommended by the US Golf Association. Note that the root zone depth must be based on the physical properties of the root zone mixture, as determined by testing

- a root zone mixture having 90% by weight of sand particles of fine sand size or larger, together with soil and organic matter.

Construction of the subgrade and drainage system

The main functions of the subgrade are to provide a firm base for the layers above and to aid drainage.

Drainage down through the subgrade is likely to be adequate only in some deep sands, and then only through coarser sands. Drainage pipes are needed for all other situations. A decision not to install drainage pipes must be based on tests of the subgrade material.

Note that if the root zone is placed on top of the existing soil, without the installation of a gravel drainage layer, the benefit of increased water supply in the 300 mm root zone made possible by a perched water table construction (Table 9.5) is not provided.

As the turf will be 400 to 450 mm above the surface of the subgrade (Fig. 17.1), it is usually necessary to remove existing topsoil from the area. That means that most subgrades are formed from subsoil clays. Drainage lines will be needed. The elevation of the subgrade surface must allow outflow of water away from the site if it is not to become a stagnant pond.

We are all familiar with hollows in road surfaces caused by slumping of poorly compacted fill in excavations. The same can happen in turf unless the subgrade is thoroughly consolidated. Heavy vibrating rollers and/or sheepsfoot rollers are commonly used. Special care is needed to consolidate fill materials brought to the site. Each thinly-spread (about 10 cm) layer of material should be thoroughly compacted before more material is spread.

Materials such as quarry dust and soils with a low clay content are more stable if about 2% cement is mixed into them.

Make sure you know the origin of fill materials used. You don't want soil that is heavily contaminated with herbicides or industrial chemicals.

Shaping the subgrade

The whole construction area is to extend out to include collar areas around the green itself. The general slope of the subgrade must conform with that of the finished grade.

The subgrade is to be shaped so that it slopes towards any drainage pipes that are installed. Every slope should be in the range 1% to 2% (1 in 100, to 1 in 50); 1% is enough; at least 0.25% is essential. The shallower the slope, the greater must be the accuracy of construction. Slight humps will impede flow; hollows will allow pools of water to remain.

The actual design of the subgrade depends on the size of the area and the anticipated need for drainage (i.e. rainfall amount and intensity).

Typical designs for *golf greens* are given in Fig. 17.2; (a) and (b) are the simplest, and recommended, designs. When the surface slope of the green is close to the 5% maximum allowable, water will move through the root zone as shown by the arrows in (a). That design is then to be preferred over design (b), which is for flatter greens. The main drain should be placed along the line of maximum fall, with laterals placed at an angle to this. These laterals should extend to the perimeter of the collar.

In wet areas (1000 mm annual rainfall, intensity frequently more than 50 mm per hour), both designs should be supplemented with lateral pipes, as shown in Fig. 17.3 (b), connecting into the main pipe.

Calculations show that drainage pipes should not be more than 3.7 m apart if the system is to cope with rain falling at 50 mm/hour. To cope with that amount of rain, there will need to be one 100 mm main pipe for every 400 m² of surface. Laterals will be 50 mm diameter. These calculations assume that the infiltration rate of the root zone is at least 50 mm/hour.

Figure 17.2
The several ways of shaping the subgrade and installing drainage pipes under a golf green. It is essential that the construction extends out under the collar areas

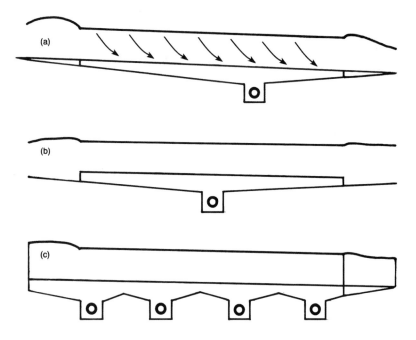

Figure 17.3
The subgrades of sports fields can be shaped in either of these ways

Spacing can be up to 5 m apart in areas where rainfall intensity is hardly ever anything like 50 mm/h. At the low end of the gradient, adjacent to the main line's exit from the green, drainage pipe should be placed along the perimeter of the green, extending to the ends of the first set of laterals. This modification to previous recommendations ensures that wet spots do not develop in this low area.

The main lines should extend a metre beyond the green at their upper ends, and into clean-out boxes.

An alternative for very wet climates is shown in Fig. 17.2(c), in which a number of short main pipes take the place of one plus laterals. This is an expensive and difficult method of construction and is rarely needed.

When larger areas are to be constructed by the perched water table method, the subgrade should be shaped to one of the configurations shown in Fig. 17.4.

For the subgrades of *bowling greens*, drain spacing should not exceed 7 m (Fig. 17.5), and the slope of the laterals should be at least 1:100. If the laterals run at an angle to the main slope of the base, then the base must have a slope of at least 1:50.

If drainage laterals are to be installed straight down each slope, the subgrade should be sloped towards them (Fig. 17.1(a)). Otherwise the laterals are run at acute angles across the slope (Fig. 17.3(b)).

Drainage system

Trenches for drainage lines are dug into the graded and compacted subgrade, with the excavated material being removed from the site. The trenches should be 150 mm wide and at least 200 mm deep. The bottoms of the trenches are to be smooth and clean and to have an even slope of 0.5–1.5% (5–15 mm/m length).

If the subgrade soil is a clay with shrink/swell activity, is very sandy or lacks stability, it is appropriate to install geotextile fabric immediately after trenches have been dug and the whole area cleaned up. This will prevent the gravel from settling into the subsoil. This is the only use of geotextile that is allowed in the USGA specifications.

Corrugated plastic drainage pipe is preferred. The USGA states that under no circumstances is geotextile fabric to cover the drain lines. It specifically does not recommend 'waffle drains or any tubing encased in geotextile sleeve'.

'Drainage' layer

The drainage layer consists of washed gravel, coarse sand or crushed rock. One advantage of crushed rock is that it is easier to lay, as it is more stable than rounded gravel. Movement of root zone sand tends to be greater into rounded gravel than into crushed rock. Any rock used must not be capable of rapid weathering, as discussed below. This layer speeds flow, to drainage lines, of water that has percolated from the root zone soil above. hence the adjective 'drainage'. But as pointed out in Chapter 9, this layer of coarse material allows material of finer texture above it to retain more water than if it were sitting straight on the subgrade. Up to a certain amount of rain or irrigation, the drainage layer behaves as an 'anti-drainage' layer by preventing percolation of water from the finer material above. Water will only drain into the drainage layer from soil having smaller pores after the soil immediately above becomes saturated.

The drainage layer therefore creates a water table that is perched, or suspended, immediately above it. Both the drainage and perched water table functions of a drainage layer are important in ensuring continued high quality of the turf under intense use. The drainage function ensures rapid removal of water from heavy rain or over-irrigation. The perched water table allows longer times between irrigations and gives turf a larger reserve of water on which to draw in hot weather.

The 1993 USGA recommendations allow for two gradings of gravel to be used. There is no need to use an intermediate (blinding) layer of coarse sand between the gravel and root zone *if* the gravel conforms with the specifications

Figure 17.4
The range of shapes that can be given to the subgrade surface so that drainage is facilitated

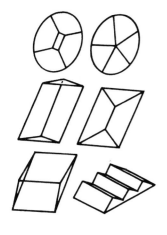

Figure 17.5
Shape of the subgrade under a bowling green

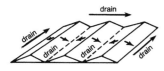

Table 17.3
USGA recommendations for drainage layer gravel that eliminates the need for an intermediate layer. (*From* USGA, Greens Section, New Jersey)

Performance factor	Recommendation
Bridging factor	D_{15} (gravel) $\leq 5 \times D_{85}$ (root zone)
Permeability factor	D_{15} (gravel) $\geq 5 \times D_{15}$ (root zone)
Uniformity factors	D_{90} (gravel)/D_{15} (gravel) ≤ 2.5
	No particles larger than 12 mm
	No more than 10% smaller than 2 mm
	No more than 5% smaller than 1 mm

listed in Table 17.3. Generally, the cost involved in obtaining gravel that meets these specifications will be much lower than the cost of spreading an intermediate layer, to say nothing of the hassle involved in its spreading.

But if the gravel available cannot meet these specifications, an intermediate layer is essential, with properties as specified in Table 17.4. The USGA states in the strongest possible terms that these specifications must be strictly adhered to, otherwise the green could fail.

Coarse sand can also be used for the drainage layer in areas where rainfall intensity is rarely high, or where the gravel available is likely to cement together as it weathers. (Some of the basalts of Victoria fit this description.) Table 17.5 gives the specifications devised by the Technical Services Unit of the ACT Parks and Conservation Service. The construction profile shown in Fig. 17.6 is now in successful use at a number of major Australian sports facilities.

Table 17.4
Particle size description of gravel and intermediate layer materials. (*From* USGA, Greens Section, New Jersey)

Material	Description
Gravel	Not more than 10% of the particles larger than 12 mm
(intermediate layer must be used)	At least 65% of the particles between 6 and 9 mm
	Not more than 10% of the particles smaller than 2 mm
Intermediate layer	At least 90% of the particles between 1 and 4 mm

Table 17.5
Specifications for coarse sands to be used for drainage layers, as prescribed by the Technical Services Unit of the ACT Parks and Conservation Service, Canberra

Fraction (mm)	% retained
>8	0
4–8	0–2
2.8–4	1–2
2–2.8	0–2
0.5–2	55–100
0.106–0.5	0–10
<0.106	0

Figure 17.6
Turf soil profile for high-quality turf, as specified by the Technical Services Unit of the ACT Parks and Conservation Service, Canberra

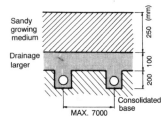

Soft limestones, sandstones or shales are not to be used. Tests for resistance to abrasion and for stability during construction (ASTM C-131), and weatherability (ASTM C-88, for long-term stability and to exclude materials that might cement together) should be commissioned. A loss of more than 12% in ASTM test C-88 makes the gravel unacceptable.

Place grade stakes at frequent intervals over the subgrade and mark them accurately for the surfaces of the gravel, intermediate layer (if needed) and final root zone surface. The gravel should then be spread evenly over the area and consolidated by rolling to give a depth of not less than 100 mm. The final surface grade is not to vary more than 25 mm. Consolidation is essential. The final contour of the gravel surface must closely match that of the root zone surface.

Intermediate layer

The intermediate layer sand is spread to a **uniform** thickness of 50–100 mm. Its surface is to conform to the contour of the root zone surface. Least penetration of the sand into the underlying gravel is had when it is slightly moist during laying. Intermediate layer sand is difficult to spread evenly. Bobcat type of machinery is useful, but large jobs may be speeded up through the use of a conveyor belt.

Geotextiles

We have already shown that the USGA is totally opposed to the use of geotextiles under turf root zones. This is on the basis of experience with dozens of failed greens in which geotextile blankets have become blocked by fine particles and/or by algal slimes. The British Sportsturf Research Institute has exactly the same attitude to these materials, for the same reasons. We have seen the same in Australia. By all means use these materials if you have a sharp crowbar. You will need it to punch holes through the geotextile when it clogs, as an intermediate step to complete remaking with gravel/coarse sand. There are plenty of areas of turf underlaid by gravel that have performed successfully for more than 20 years; there were areas based on geotextiles that had failed in less than five years. We strongly recommend that you never use geotextile blankets under turf, or indeed in tubs, planter beds and under other landscaped areas. Gravel and sand are still the best. Some further comment on geotextile-wrapped drains is given later in this chapter.

The root zone

If you want a mud bath, choose an 'ordinary' soil or non-specified sands for the root zone. If you don't, read on.

A main requirement for the root zone is that it allows rapid removal of rain or irrigation water from the surface, so that play is interrupted as little as possible. In other words, the infiltration rate of the root zone must still be high after it has been compacted through intense use.

Current (1993) USGA recommendations for the physical properties of root

Table 17.6
Required physical properties of root zone mixtures that meet USGA specifications. (*From* USGA, Greens Section, New Jersey)

Property*	Recommended range
Total porosity	35–55%
Air-filled porosity (at 40 cm tension)	20–30%
Capillary porosity (at 40 cm tension)	15–25%
Saturated conducitivty	
Normal range	15–30 cm/h
Accelerated range	30–60 cm/h
Organic matter content (by weight)	1–5% (ideally 2–4%)

* These properties must be tested for by specific USGA methods.

zone mixtures are given in Table 17.6. Note that the emphasis is totally on the porosity of the mixture, and in particular on the rate at which water is able to flow through it. This flow rate is described by the term 'saturated conductivity', which is directly related to the steady infiltration rate of a growing medium. The 'accelerated range' for saturated conductivity is to be preferred in situations where rainfall can be intense and where water quality is poor. Values at the lower end of the normal range should give satisfactory results in the drier areas of Australia.

Continuing high infiltration rates /saturated conductivities under the compacting conditions that are the norm for sports turf can be achieved only through the use of root zone mixtures with sand contents of at least 90%. Even when compacted, the sand grains form a 'skeleton' that still has plenty of pores through which water and air can quickly move. But even with these sands water flow will decrease under use because the pores become clogged by grass roots. So even the best root zones need some cultivation (Chapter 19).

Sands and root zone mixtures are assessed both by the properties listed in Table 17.6 and by sieve analysis. Tables 17.7 and 17.8 give USGA and Australian Turfgrass Research Institute recommendations. Note that in the new USGA specifications the boundary between very fine sand and fine sand has been put at 0.15 mm (100 mesh sieve), not 0.1 mm. This change, coupled with an increase in the amount of fine sand allowed, means that some sands previously rejected can now be used for USGA greens. The specifications are, however, still for a predominance of sand particles of medium–coarse size.

Final selection must be made on the basis of laboratory tests for the properties listed in Table 17.6. These tests are made on compacted mixtures of the available sands with any other materials that are to be mixed with the sand. The testing

Table 17.7
Particle size distribution specified by the USGA

Name	Particle diameter (mm)	Recommendation (by weight)
Fine gravel	2.0–3.4	Not more than 10% of the total, including a
Very coarse sand	1.0–2.0	maximum of 3% fine gravel (preferably none)
Coarse sand	0.5–1.0	Minimum 60% must be in this range
Medium sand	0.25–0.5	
Fine sand	0.15–0.25	Not more than 20%
Silt	0.002–0.5	Not more than 5% Total shall not
Clay	<0.002	Not more than 3% exceed 10%

Table 17.8
Specifications for sands for root zones for perched water table construction, as used by the Australian Turfgrass Research Institute

Name of fraction	Particle size (mm)	Sieve range (mesh)	Golf (%)	Bowling (%)
Gravel	> 2.0	+7	0	0–10
Very coarse sand	1.0–2.0	+16, –7	Max 10	0–10
Coarse sand	0.5–1.0	+30,–16	}	20–40
Medium sand	0.25–0.5	+60,–30	} Min 65	40–60
Fine sand	0.1–0.25	+150, –60	Max 25	10–20
Very fine sand	0.05–0.1	+300, –150	1	1–5
Clay and silt	< 0.05	–300	Max 8	0–5

also leads to a recommendation on the ideal depth of root zone. A root zone that is too deep for the physical properties of the mixture will stress the turf through poor water supply. The 300 mm specified by the USGA can be taken only as a rough guide to the actual depth that must be used.

Uniform, rounded sands and extremely angular sands are to be avoided. Quartz sands are the best, but a sprinkling of other minerals is useful as a source of plant nutrients. It is impossible to know how a sand or sandy mixture will perform simply by feeling it or looking at it. Only laboratory testing can ensure success.

Soil

USGA recommendations have always been uncompromising in their insistence on there being some soil (really some clay and silt) in the sandy root zone mixture. The 1993 specifications have, however, recognised a reduced use of soil in root zones in recent years, perhaps as a result of increasing difficulty in getting soils of adequate quality, or because of the difficulty of mixing small amounts of soil into sands, or because of the need for high drainage rates under the extreme compaction pressure of intense use of facilities. Nevertheless, the official USGA policy is still strongly in favour of including some clay and silt in root zone mixes.

Any soil included must have a minimum sand content of 60% and a clay content between 5% and 20%. The % silt to % clay ratio must be less than 2.5 and preferably a little less than 2. In other words, the soils used will be of loamy sand, sandy loam, light sandy clay loam or loam texture. Soil additions must be on the basis of testing of its mixtures with the main sand to be used.

Those who advocate the inclusion of a small amount of soil in root zones emphasise that it makes management easier, because it increases cation exchange capacity and water-holding capacity and reduces the incidence of take-all disease. They state that soil buffers against wild shifts in pH and reduces the amount of fertilizer needed because it reduces losses in drainage waters. Inclusion of soil can improve the rate of cover after seeding (Fig. 17.7).

Organic amendment

The USGA specifications state a preference for fibrous sphagnum peat as an organic amendment, with that peat being at least 85% organic matter by weight. Fine sedge and reed peats are usually unsuitable, because even a small addition of silt can fill pores (Fig. 17.8) and sharply reduce hydraulic conductivity. But as can only be shown by laboratory testing, a very low addition of such peats might be used as a replacement for soil plus another organic amendment.

Extreme caution is stressed when organic amendments are being considered.

Figure 17.7
Example of the effect of including soil (10%) in the root zone mixture (sand/peat (70/30 or 70/20 + soil) on the rate of cover of Pencross creeping bentgrass. *From A R Mazur and C B White* Agron. J. 75: 977, 1983

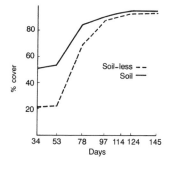

Figure 17.8
A relatively small amount of fine particles will clog the large pores between larger sand grains

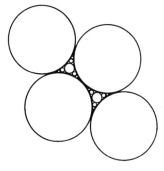

Composts must have gone through a thermophilic stage and must be aged for at least a year. They must be proven to be non-toxic to the roots of grass seedlings or sprigs of the species/cultivar to be used. As composts, including those made from sewage sludge, can vary with source and between batches from the same source, it is essential that the whole amount to be used should be thoroughly mixed together before blending with the sand and soil. Composted sewage sludges added at about 10% by volume have given excellent results.

It is absolutely essential that the effect of any organic amendment (including pelleted poultry manure) be tested by a laboratory before it is used. It is also absolutely essential that a choice be made only on the basis of laboratory tests that specify a proportion of organic matter that will not harm infiltration rate.

A number of turf authorities advise, sometimes strongly, against the addition of any organic amendment to root zone media. They point to many instances where the organic material has degraded and separated out into a layer that has impeded drainage. Such a layer can become anaerobic and can then be a toxic barrier to root growth—the dreaded black layer of turf root zones. They also point to the fact that the turf itself soon produces much (even too much) organic matter, and this will give all the benefits of an expensive and potentially dangerous addition of organic matter. This generation of organic matter within the root zone itself has been shown to give performance that is at least equal to that of root zones to which outside organic matter has been added.

We have noted that research in the UK has shown that including peat in the sand of sand carpet constructions reduced hardness and ball rebound resilience compared with sand alone, but after four months the organic matter produced in the sand by the turf gave the two root zones similar properties. A peat application rate of 5%, and only into the top 50 mm of sand, was enough to give maximum response. The peat reduced the water infiltration rate. It was noted that the soil underlying the sand carpet may have helped reduce the need for peat.

We leave readers with the suggestion that organic matter should be incorporated into the top 50–100 mm of a root zone constructed with washed sand that contains no silt or clay, but not into other materials. Organic matter must *never* be included in the root zone materials below this uppermost layer. Such an action can lead to severe problems as decomposition of the organic matter produces anaerobic conditions in the perched water table zone.

The sometimes poorer seed germination and early rate of cover that has been reported to result from not using organic matter can be avoided by establishing the turf with washed sod (p. 209). Where seed must be used, frequent light irrigation is essential, as is frequent application of fertilizer and the use of slow-release N, P and K.

For areas other than greens, hydro-sprigging or hydro-seeding (Chapter 31) will be useful techniques. In the former, 75–125 mm stolons, each with at least three nodes, are blasted onto the area through a water cannon. They are then incorporated into the surface by light rotary hoeing. Irrigation must be frequent for the first three weeks.

Other amendments

The USGA recommends against the use of other amendments. In the discussion that accompanies the 1993 specifications, materials such as vermiculite, perlite, pumice and calcined diatomites are ruled out altogether. Calcined clay is stated to have been found to degrade.

Clinoptilolite zeolite is stated to have potential but is not recommended until questions of particle stability and its weathering have been settled. A 1992 US thesis report showed successful use of a grade with particles in the 0.25–0.5 mm range, added at 5–10%. At the time of writing (early 1993), trials with local zeolite had been established in Australia, but there were no published results. Australian zeolite is likely to perform better than many other zeolites because its extreme hardness makes it resistant to weathering.

Polyacrylamide gels improve waterholding capacity, but only for a couple of years. Presumably they are totally decomposed by about that time (Table 13.3). They have been found to cause puddling and heaving of green surfaces, and to reduce the rate of grass cover from seeding, and so they are not recommended for fine turf.

Reinforcement materials such as Netlon were considered not to be of benefit in golf greens, but see p. 204 for a discussion of their use in root zones for other types of turf.

Testing

As we have repeatedly emphasised, it is essential that expensive turf must be based on root zone materials selected on the basis of laboratory testing. Laboratories that do this testing are listed in the appendix 'Sources of Help'. Ask them what they need for testing. Typically, it will be about 10 L of each of the sands being considered for use and 5 L for soils. The laboratory will advise on the proportions in which they should be mixed and the depth of root zone required to optimise water relations in it.

Mixing the root zone materials

Any requirement to use more than one material to produce a root zone mixture calls for very careful mixing. First, the laboratory recommendations, often given on a dry weight basis, need to be translated into a volume basis. The moisture content of the materials must enter into these calculations, as must the compaction condition of the material when its volume is being measured (see p. 56) for a discussion of the pitfalls).

All mixing must be done off-site. This is absolutely essential. It has been repeatedly found that on-site mixing gives non-uniformity across the construction. This gives droughty and wet patches. Layers are likely to be created.

Pre-mixing can be done by a front-end loader dumping the materials in a heap which is then turned a few times. The materials must be moist, otherwise there will be considerable separation of sand particles of different sizes. Final mixing for sand/soil/organic mixtures should be via a shredder–mixer. A quality control program must be in place to check that the final mixture is indeed the same as that specified. This obviously delays the whole operation, but it is essential. Supervision must be constant. Close attention to all details of mixing and installation is essential if problems are to be prevented.

When calculating the amount of material needed, be aware that the volume of the compacted root zone may be 30% less than the volume when loose. The volume of mixtures is always less than the sum of the volumes of the components, so allow for that too. Also allow an extra 3 m³/100m² that can be stockpiled for use in filling any hollows and for use as a topdressing.

It is essential that the root zone mixture, whether an actual mixture or just sand, is maintained moist during all handling operations, otherwise separation of particles of different sizes will create layers and areas of drought or over-wetness. The moist condition will also minimise the movement of fines into the gravel or intermediate layer. But problems also arise if the root zone mixture is allowed to become too wet.

Spreading the root zone

Spread the root zone starting at one corner or one edge (Fig. 17.9). The drainage layer must not be disturbed during spreading. Remember that the mix will sink

Figure 17.9
Root zone materials are to be
spread from one corner of the area
or from one side. Equipment is to
travel only over the root zone
materials, not the drainage layer or
subgrade

during the first few months of use. The depth spread must allow for this so that the final compacted depth is as required.

The root zone mix is to be spread in layers, with the first one being 150 mm thick. This reduces the risk of disturbing the interface that would result from use of a shallower layer. The rest of the root zone material should be added in 50 mm layers. If organic matter is to be included in the top layer, it is important that the lower layers are compacted and graded to become parallel to the final surface. This ensures that the top layer has a uniform depth across the whole construction.

Addition in layers will reduce later problems due to settling. Each layer should be scarified before the next layer is spread so that they blend into a uniform profile. A light roller is useful for consolidation. Heavy machinery is not to be allowed on the mix. Small 'caterpillar' tractors or mini-tractors with turf tyres are useful.

The final level is determined with the help of a surveyor or a dumpy level. The surface is further consolidated by watering and light rolling. Hollows must be filled, ridges planed-off. Soft, puffy patches must be consolidated. Turf must not be established until the surface is firm and evenly contoured as required.

The irrigation system is to be installed in two steps. The pipes are laid in the base before the drainage layer is spread. Stand pipes for sprinkler heads are closed off to prevent entry of sand. Then, after the area has been consolidated to its final level, the sprinkler heads are installed. The system should be operating before the laying of turf (Fig. 17.11).

Depth of the root zone

The depth of the root zone is usually in the range 230–400 mm after final consolidation. The preferred depth is 250–300 mm. This depth gives a reasonable height above the perched water table at the bottom of the root zone, and a reasonable amount of available water held. However, depth must match the properties of the mix (Fig. 17.10, Table 17.9). Mixes of fine texture must be deeper than those of coarse texture. The ideal depth for a particular mix can only be determined by laboratory tests.

Figure 17.10
The amount of water held in the top
90 mm of a sand root zone
underlain by gravel is greatest for
fine sands and when the root zone
is shallow. *From* D V Waddington
Golf Superintendent Aug: 21, 1977

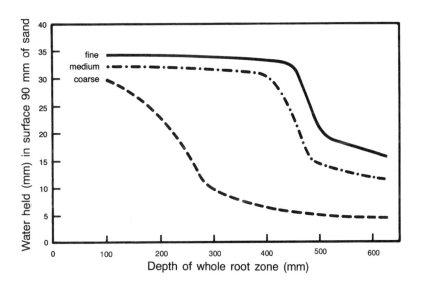

Figure 17.11
Turfing with washed sod. *Photograph P Semos and Strath Ayr Instant Lawn Pty Ltd, Seymour*

Notes on sands

Readers will be aware from the remarks above (and earlier in this chapter) that only specially selected sands are suitable for the best root zones. Best results will be obtained when selection is guided by laboratory tests.

Many turf experts prefer sands whose grains have rounded edges. Others are less fussy. For a given particle size distribution, sharp sands will tend to hold more water than rounded sands. Their infiltration rate will usually be less. Actual properties depend very much on the distribution of particle sizes present. The pores in sands with a narrow particle size range will be uniform in size. They will hold little reserve water once the water that is easily taken up by plants has been used. These sands do not bind together well. On the other hand, a very wide particle size range will allow interpacking during compaction, and a low infiltration rate. A spread right across the 0.1 to 0.5 or 0.6 mm range is best. The finest 10% of particles controls the properties of sands (Fig. 17.12).

The turf for contact sports must provide good traction for players. Best traction is provided by a dense turf whose roots bind the root zone together firmly. However, the root zone solids also contribute; the greater the traction provided by the sand itself, the less will be the strain on the root system, and the lower the risk of losing grass. Traction is best for particles of very fine to fine sand size (0.05–0.25 mm), followed by medium sand (0.25–0.5 mm). Very little traction is provided by particles larger than 0.7 mm. Clay causes slipping in wet conditions. For best traction most particles should be in the 0.1–0.6 mm range. This means that the USGA specification is too coarse for use under turf for contact sports.

Figure 17.12
A small amount of silt drastically decreases the rate of infiltration of water into a medium-fine sand. *From P Boekel et al. Report 7–80 Inst. Bodemvruchtbaarheid, Haren (Gr.) Netherlands, 1980*

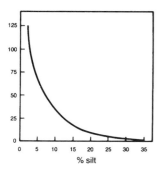

% silt

Table 17.9
Water retained in 100 mm sections of cylinders, starting at the top, containing compacted coarse, medium and fine sands, after saturation and being allowed to drain for 12 hours. (*From* C S Throsell and W H Daniel *Golf Course Manag.* 58: 48, 1991)

| Sand fraction | Water retention by 100 mm sections (% of total mass) | | | |
	0–100	100–200	200–300	300–400
Coarse	2	3	10	16
Medium	4	9	13	18
Fine	20	21	23	23

Figure 17.13
Turf profiles used in Germany.
(A) Construction when the natural soil has good permeability.
(B) Construction when the natural soil is slightly permeable. *From German Standard DIN 18035, part 4, July, 1991*

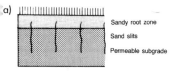

Figure 17.14
Sand carpet construction equipped with drains, as used in the UK. *From S W Baker in Science and Football E and F Spon Publ, London, 1987*

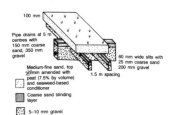

Readers are referred to Chapter 20 for information about fertilizers for turf being established on sandy root zones.

Turf establishment is fastest if you simply lay washed sod of the chosen grass cultivar (Fig. 17.11). Establishment with seed calls for very frequent light waterings (about 12 per day) until the seedlings have rooted down into the sand.

During the first year or so, the playing surface of pure sand root zones will be faster and less resilient than will that of a root zone that includes soil and organic matter. Resilience will gradually increase as the organic matter content of the sand increases.

OTHER METHODS OF HIGH-QUALITY CONSTRUCTION

The method of construction described so far is artificial, in the sense that it makes no or little use of the soil underlying the sandy root zone. The subsoil is usually deliberately compacted to the extent that water does not percolate through it. The grass grows in the sandy root zone materials.

There are those who shun universal adoption of this artificial approach. They favour using the natural soil of the area as much as is possible. This is sound from an environmental point of view but it also makes economic sense: the less of the turf profile that has to be bought, the cheaper will be the construction. These construction methods mostly require the spreading of a sand carpet over the existing soil. Sand carpets are widely used for intensively used football pitches in Europe, but they are also used for golf greens.

We now describe sand carpet construction methods and assess their applicability to a range of Australian conditions.

Sand carpet constructions come in a range of profile forms. In Germany, the preferred profiles (Fig. 17.13) are:

A Sandy root zone material spread 80–100 mm deep over the existing permeable soil.

B Sand mixed with the existing soil and then topped with a sandy root zone material.

Construction method A is used where the underlying soil is permeable, with a saturated conductivity of more than 18 mm/hr. The root zone sand must be less than 100 mm deep, otherwise the roots of cool-season grasses may not penetrate into the underlying soil. The drainage slits allow rapid movement of water into the subsoil.

Construction method B is used when the subsoil is naturally of poor permeability, but can be improved through ripping and the application of gypsum. This is now the 'standard construction' in Germany. It is used wherever the subsoil is stable but insufficiently permeable by itself for use of method A. The sand slits allow rapid removal of surface water into the subsoil, for later use by the turf. Excess water is removed through the drainage pipes. Such a method of construction is most suited to areas where rainfall intensity is rarely high and where the subsoil has a permeability of several mm/h. (Where the subsoil is even less permeable (less than 1 mm/h), the requirement in Germany is for a USGA type of construction.)

The Prunty Mulqueen (PM) method of construction (Fig. 17.14) which originated in Ireland and is widely and successfully used for football pitches in the UK, is similar to the German designs. The earliest pitches constructed by this method are now nearly 30 years old and are still giving excellent service.

With all of these types of construction, it is essential that the soil of the area, whether topsoil or subsoil, be treated as a growing medium, not as a civil engineering material. In other words, it must not be compacted, and any compaction that is produced during its shaping must be relieved by ripping and harrowing. Only then will roots grow into it and only then will its permeability be high enough for it to do its work. The subsoil in these sorts of construction is at least as important as the root zone!

Figure 17.15
Patterns of slopes that can be given
to the surfaces of playing fields

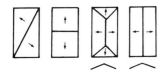

Table 17.10
**Specifications for root zone
sandy loam for general
sports fields, as devised by
the Technical Services Unit of
the ACT Parks and
Conservation Service,
Canberra**

Fraction (mm)	%
>2.0	0
1.0–2.0	0–10
0.106–1.0	55–70
<0.106	30–45
clay	2–15

Sand carpet constructions clearly work well in northern Europe, but under the high evapotranspiration conditions of much of Australia they will be less than satisfactory if the subgrade is impermeable and does not support root growth (see next section). When constructed on a subgrade of low permeability, too much rainwater from storms will be lost to the turf via the drainage system. Sand carpet types of construction will be useful in Australia only where the subsoil is permeable and can be guaranteed to form part of the root zone and probably then mainly in the cooler parts of the country. In most other parts, consideration should be given to constructing fields for contact sports using one of the methods now to be described.

An Australian innovation in sand carpets

One of the cheapest ways of providing good turf for community facilities is that devised by the Technical Services Unit of the ACT Parks and Conservation Department. It is solidly based on the facts of soil physics, as applied to Australian soil and climatic conditions. It arose out of a need to provide good sports fields in the Canberra area. In this area some subsoils have saturated conductivities of less than 1 mm/h; grass roots have difficulty in growing in them. A 100 mm deep layer of sand over these subsoils will not hold enough water for a day of summer heat.

The essentials of the method are a shaped subgrade with slope of 1 in 70 (minimum 1 in 70; maximum 1 in 60) and maximum length of any slope of 70 metres, overlain with 230 mm of sandy soil. Here is some detail:

- The subgrade must be treated with gypsum to ensure that its permeability is as high as it can be made. Its saturated conductivity should be at least 2 mm/h. With that conductivity, slow percolation of water into the subsoil will cope with most rainfall events in those parts of Australia not subject to repeated tropical/subtropical downpours.
- The subgrade must be given one of the shapes illustrated in Fig. 17.15.
- The subgrade should be graded and levelled only when the soil is so dry that it crumbles. The smearing and moulding that takes place when many soils are worked when wet could produce a totally impermeable subgrade.
- After shaping and before addition of the root zone material, the surface of the subgrade must be ripped and harrowed so as to allow good keying-in of the root zone material.
- The root zone material is to have a composition as listed in Table 17.10. Its saturated conductivity should be more than 5 mm/h when moderately compacted, and its water-holding capacity should be at least 14% at field capacity (10 kPa suction).
- A root zone material depth of 230 mm maximises the amount of water that is available for turf growth, yet is deep enough to quickly absorb most rainfall without 'overflowing'. Such a root zone will hold about 30 mm of available water—sufficient for at least five days of summer evapotranspiration (ET) losses in much of the coastal strip of Australia.
- Root zones as shallow as 150 mm are permitted only when the underlying soil itself has a permeability of several mm/h.
- The surface of the root zone is to accurately follow the contour of the subgrade. That is the main reason for limiting the slope of the subgrade to 1 in 60: players will feel that they are running up and down hill all the time on more steeply sloped grounds. The limit to no shallower than 1 in 70 is to ensure rapid removal of surface water that arrives at a greater rate than the infiltration rate of the root zone.

Another option for producing excellent sports fields

If the thick sandy soil carpet construction just described is still too expensive for you, construction with the natural soil of the area, amended with sand slits, might be the way to go. We describe the method in Chapter 24, but state here that if you do decide to use sand slits as part of a new field, you should be aware that you must be prepared to maintain the surfaces of the slits through a sand topdressing program. Having thought about that, you might reconsider the more-or-less once-off nature of sandy soil carpet construction.

UPGRADING EXISTING TURF

Several options are available for upgrading an existing area that is not performing as well as is needed. Whatever is finally done, it is essential to first find reasons for poor performance. These may be only skin deep and easily corrected.

- Problems caused by a layer of coarse material at shallow depth require that you insert holes through that material. See Chapter 19 for the range of methods on offer.
- A groundwater table at shallow depth calls for the installation of drainage pipe (Chapter 24).
- Poor grass growth due to the soil being too acid calls for the application of lime.
- Poor growth due to starvation calls for the application of fertilizer.
- Quagmire conditions in winter may have several causes. Lack of surface slope would require reconstruction for correction. A low infiltration rate or impermeable subsoil at shallow depth might best be dealt with by the installation of sand slits (Chapter 24), or perhaps through the use of a Verti-Drain machine (Chapter 19).
- You might be tempted to remake the area by mixing sand into the existing soil. The information given below discusses the pitfalls of this action and how they might be avoided.

Amending topsoil with sand

This method of construction or reconstruction is successful only if enough sand is used.

The aim is to mix sand and organic matter with the existing topsoil to produce a root zone of modified soil. The thickness of modified soil needed will vary with the permeability of the underlying soil. A thickness of 100–150 mm will probably be enough if the underlying soil has a saturated hydraulic conductivity of more than 10 mm/h, as it will then form part of the root zone.

Subsoils of very poor permeability call for root zone layers of a thickness approaching that used for the sandy soil carpet method of construction, described above. What you will in effect be doing is making such a construction on-site.

The existing topsoil is intensively ripped to break up compaction layers and thoroughly cultivated to break up clods and clumps of sod. It is left rough, but approximately with the required final contour. Amending materials are then spread uniformly over the area. Equipment should travel only over the newly spread fill, and not over the soil, so as not to compact the soil again. The amendment is thoroughly mixed with the top 50–70 mm of original soil using disc harrows or a rotary tiller. Gypsum and phosphatic fertilizer are best applied before mixing. The area is then graded, rolled, watered heavily, left to settle and then re-graded until it has consolidated and has the desired contour.

Crowning to give a 1 in 70 slope in two or four directions from the centre is essential. Giving the outer 20% of the field a 1 in 65 slope will speed removal of excess surface water.

Nothing is gained by adding 10% sand to a heavy clay loam. In fact the final result will be far worse than before. Figure 17.16 shows that a small amount of amendment is 'lost' in the larger volume of original soil, just as a few marbles are lost in porridge. As the proportion of sand increases, the physical properties of the mixture *worsen* because the pores between large particles are filled with smaller particles, just as the spaces between tennis balls can be filled with peas.

Figure 17.16
Stages of amending a soil with sand . (a), (b) Small amounts of sand 'float' in the soil filling much of the pore space. (c) As more sand is added, a network of sand grains is formed, with the pores almost completely filled with soil. (d) Eventually there is not enough soil to fill the pores between sand grains; the infiltration rate increases

a b c d

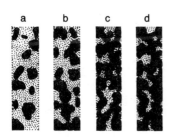

Only after a certain critical amount of sand is in the mixture do the properties of the mixture begin to improve on those of the original soil. Only laboratory tests can give the best proportion of sand, but the final mixture should have a composition that meets the specifications listed in Table 17.10. It will therefore have a sand content of at least 70%, a necessary amount if it is still to have reasonable permeability under use (Fig. 17.17). You will create a huge expensive mess if you do not use laboratory tests as a basis for amending soils with sands.

Figure 17.17
After compaction, mixtures of soil and sand containing low proportions of sand have infiltration rates that are too low for use under turf. *From J B Elliot J. Sports Turf Res. Inst. 47: 66, 1977*

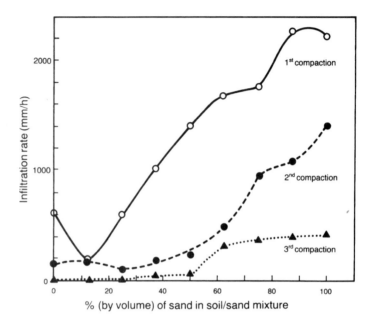

Using the existing soil

This is the cheapest method of construction there is. At its simplest, a field is set aside for a park or oval with nothing else being done than that the necessary lines are marked on the grass and goal posts or nets installed. Under infrequent, light use, such a field can give quite adequate playing conditions for players who are not very fussy.

A slightly more complicated preparation is to add extra topsoil—perhaps from roads being constructed nearby—to that already there. The two topsoil layers should be mixed by cultivation and shaped to a contour that allows surface water to drain to the edges.

If a sloping site is to be levelled, it is essential that the topsoil be removed, stockpiled, and then spread over the levelled subsoil. *Never* use topsoil as fill, *Never* bury the topsoil and attempt to grow good turf in subsoil. You won't.

Wet weather performance will be improved if the surface is crowned to a 1 in 70 slope.

This method of 'construction' is usually more successful with light, sandy and loamy topsoils than with clays. Soils that set hard on drying will give the worst results.

The aim must be to keep damage to existing soil structure to an absolute minimum. Work and form the soil only when it is moderately dry, never when it is wet. Keep vehicular traffic to a minimum.

Good structure can be maintained by encouraging earthworms, restricting use in very wet weather, and relieving compaction as needed. Install sand slits if the surface remains too wet for more than a few hours after rain.

Use of filled sites

Lack of open space in and near larger cities has forced local councils to use filled sites—old quarries, tidal swamps, flood plains, etc.—for playing fields. The results are usually very poor indeed, but with better construction methods they can be a lot better than they often are.

A serious problem that cannot be overcome is that deeply filled areas containing such objects as buried car bodies sink irregularly as the objects collapse, creating depressions in the surface. These must be filled in if a usable playing surface is to be maintained.

Another almost insoluble problem is toxic gases escaping from buried rubbish, and seepage of toxic liquids.

More commonly, the main problems are caused by the properties of the fill materials being very variable across a site. Even when the site is carefully graded, there is usually wide variation in permeability. It can be zero through large chunks of concrete or boulders to nearly zero through heavy clay subsoil materials to high through sandier materials.

Usually the root zone material spread to hide this mess is of little better quality. Even if it is of reasonable quality, the depth spread is rarely enough to give good conditions for play and grass growth.

Drains are difficult to install because of the rocky nature of the underlying fill and the irregular sinking.

Where it is known that a fill site is to become a playing area, it is important that careful attention be given to the top metre or so of fill. Material that looks anything like topsoil should be stockpiled until the site is ready to receive its final coat. The levelled 'undercoat' should be ripped to relieve compaction. Superphosphate and gypsum should be added to the stockpiled 'topsoil' as shown by tests, the whole lot thoroughly mixed and spread evenly over the 'undercoat'. Traffic should now be restricted as outlined for other methods. If possible, sand should be mixed with the 'topsoil' as in the method above, 'Amending topsoil with sand'.

Only when the fill in these sites has been reasonably uniform in quality (as mine dumps can be), and has been consolidated during dumping and spreading, is it possible to construct a top-class area for turf. The deeper the fill, the less its uniformity, and the less the care taken during construction, the poorer will be the results.

Some precautions needed when establishing turf on mine dump materials are given in Chapter 31.

SPECIAL SITUATIONS

Turf in wet, low-lying areas

Some extra precautions are needed when turf is to be established in low-lying areas. A drainage system must be installed to lower the groundwater table (Chapter 24).

When the water table cannot be lowered below 40 cm, some special management practices must be followed. The high water table will keep the surface soft and liable to damage. Its bulk density must be kept in the range 1.5–1.6 g/cc. This is achieved by limiting its organic matter content to 2–3% with regular topdressing, and by rolling before use. To judge whether rolling is needed, use the heel test given in Chapter 33.

Slope and landscape turf

The slope given to the soil for general landscape turf should wherever possible allow mowing by large mowers. For large areas, that means gang mowers. Steep humps and sharp changes in slope will mean costly hand mowing.

Figure 17.18
Traction is better with medium–fine sands than with medium-coarse sand. 'Nm' stands for Newton–metre, which is a measure of the amount of work that must be done in dragging a simulated football boot through the turf. The larger this number, the greater the amount of traction experienced by a player. From S W Baker *Soil Use Land Manag.* 5: 116, 1989

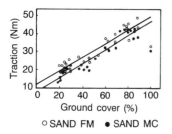

Figure 17.19
Example of the effect of inclusion of soil in a sand on the retention of ground cover under simulated football play. From S W Baker *J. Sports Turf Res. Inst.* 67: 83, 1991

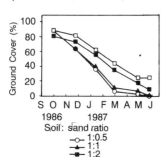

Some special aspects of root zones for contact sports

Much of what has been written already in this chapter has relevance to root zones for contact sports, but we thought it would be useful to readers if we highlighted here the most important findings from research carried out mainly in Europe. Unlike golf, lawn bowls and cricket, contact sports require that the turf provide excellent traction.

- A dense root mass is the most important factor in providing excellent traction. Grasses whose roots have large diameters give the greatest traction.
- The other main factor influencing traction is the size grading of the sand. Traction is greater for medium-fine than medium-coarse sands (Fig. 17.18). Most of the particles in the root zone should have diameters in the range 0.125–0.5 mm.
- Ball bounce is also greater on soccer fields constructed with medium-fine than with medium-coarse sand.
- Acceptable ball bounce resilience is possible only when the root zone contains at least 90% sand.
- The greater compaction and other damage caused by play to natural soils or soil mixtures than to sand root zones causes them to lose cover at a greater rate as the playing season progresses (Fig. 17.19). This loss of cover greatly reduces traction.
- In the UK, research has shown that natural-soil football pitches could not sustain more than two hours of play weekly. Perched water table sand profiles could withstand 9.5–10 hours of play weekly, but *only* if the grass cover is maintained. Failure to maintain the grass cover soon leads to erosion of the sand surface. A practical upper limit to use of such grounds might well be 8 hours of adult play per week. The need for a very high level of maintenance is repeatedly stressed by turf advisers. Don't even start to think about constructing with sand if you are not prepared to pay for the cost of this maintenance program.
- There is some research evidence that inclusion of Netlon (randomly-oriented polypropylene mesh elements, Fig. 17.20) in sand root zones for contact sports helps to maintain ground cover and speeds up the healing of injuries to the turf. The claim is that the intensity of use can be doubled. Certainly Netlon included at 6 kg/m³ into the root zones of racecourses has been successful. Watch the Outer of the Melbourne Cricket Ground for an idea of its performance in another situation. It was installed there in late 1992.
- Research by the Sportsturf Research Institute in England has found that a seaweed product called Alginure considerably improves the rate of ground cover development when included in the root zone at about 100 g/m². No explanation for this effect has been given.
- Note the reference to polyacrylamide gels on p. 196, but if you do choose to use them in sandy root zones for contact sports, add them at no more than 0.1% (w/w) and do not incorporate them into the top 25 mm. Traction will be reduced (Fig. 17.21).

Construction of cricket pitches

Cricketers are very fussy about cricket pitches. Bowlers like the surface of the pitch to be such that their method of delivery, not some irregularity in the surface, determines where the ball goes. Batsmen don't like pitches from which one ball might bounce dangerously into their faces and the next grub along the ground. The way a ball bounces depends greatly on the way the pitch has been prepared for a match. It also depends on the type of soil used.

The following is a summary of what is known about soils for cricket pitches.

- All pitches for tests and interstate matches have a root zone of clay soil underlain by a loamy sand or sandy loam. This in turn is underlain either

Figure 17.20

Netlon. *Photograph K A Handreck*

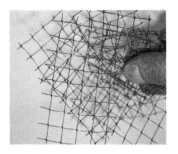

Figure 17.21

Increasing amounts of the polyacrylamide gel Alcosorb in a turf root zone reduced traction. See Fig. 17.18 for an explanation of Nm. *From S W Baker J. Sports Turf Res. Inst. 67: 66, 1991*

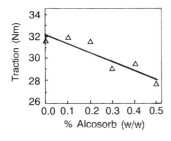

Table 17.11

Approximate relationship between the clay content of a cricket pitch root zone and the potential pace it can be given by rolling (*From V I Stewart and W A Adams Soil Factors Affecting the Control of Pace on Cricket Pitches University College of Wales, Aberystwyth*)

Pace	Clay content at least (%)	Bounce[†] (cm) at least
Very fast	43	76
Fast	33	64
Moderately fast	23	51
Easy paced	15	38
Slow	5	25

[†]The bounce test is described on p.418.

by coarse sand or gravel. A typical profile is shown in Fig. 17.22. Much more complicated profiles are used both in Australia and in England, but they do not seem to give any better results. In Australia, the main root zone soils used have a clay content of at least 50% and up to 82%. Clearly, all Australian pitches should be able to be prepared to give a very fast wicket (Table 17.11). This potential pace can be achieved only if the rolling during preparation of a wicket squeezes the surface of the root zone soil into a solid mass (Chapter 19). Pace will be slower than the potential if the soil is not sufficiently compacted and dried.

- The required characteristics of soils suitable for use for cricket pitches in Australia are summarized in Table 17.12. Several practical tests that can be used as a first assessment of a potential soil are described in Chapter 33.

Table 17.12

The main characteristics required of soils for cricket pitches. (*From Technical Services Unit of the ACT Parks and Conservation Service, Canberra*)

Characteristics	Requirement
Weeds	Totally free; fumigate with methyl bromide
Clay type	Smectite to be at least 50% of total clay
	Linear Shrinkage Ratio 0.08–0.15 (ideal 0.10)
pH	6–7
Total dissolved salts	below 200 ppm
Calcium carbonate	below 5%
Exchangeable sodium	below 5% of exchangeable cations
Exchangeable Mg/Ca	below 1.0
Organic matter	below 5%
Hydraulic conductivity at 5 hours	> 2 mm/h
Particle size distribution	
Larger than 1.0 mm	0
0.25–1.0 mm	0, but maximum of 10%
< 0.002 mm	50–60%
Cohesion on air drying	0.6–1.2 MPa

- The clay mineral smectite in these soils gives them an ability to shrink on drying and swell on becoming wet. Cracks produced during drying, as during a match, will allow rapid re-wetting of the soil for quick recovery of the grass. The high clay content will allow the surface to be moulded and compressed into a solid mass during preparation for a match.
- Some soils used contain mainly kaolinitic clay minerals. These soils shrink little on drying, so they do not crack.
- It is to be noted that the soils used in England have lower clay and smectite contents than those specified in Table 17.12. Maximum pace possible there is generally therefore slower than is possible in Australia.
- A generally similar situation applies in New Zealand, where there is in fact a preference for non or limited swelling soils for most grounds. It has been found that consistently good wickets can be more easily produced on these soils for club competition than is possible with shrink–swell soils. *But*, it is necessary to mechanically relieve compaction after a match, so that water can penetrate the profile. Subirrigation has been useful in rewetting these soils.
- The soil should not contain any gypsum. When present, it will not allow the soil to be compacted into a solid mass during preparation for a match. The wicket may crumble during play. Superphosphate (half gypsum) must not be applied to pitches.

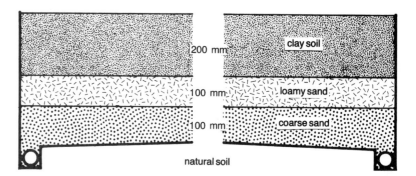

- An exception to these comments on gypsum is made for sodic soils (Chapter 21). Their high content of sodium in relation to calcium and magnesium calls for the application of gypsum as a means of pushing some of the sodium from them. This has been done with some success in Perth.
- Nodules of limestone in the soil appear to do little harm, but finely divided limestone can cause crumbling.
- Clay soils with high proportions of very fine clay (particles <0.2 μm) make wickets that crack excessively during four- and five-day matches and are difficult to manage. These very 'strong' soils need large amounts of water (> 40% of dry weight) to make them soft enough for moulding into a wicket.
- The soil layer for first-class matches should be at least 150 mm thick, and preferably 200 mm thick if football is to be played on the oval.
- But note that there are successful pitches with soil layers as shallow as 130 mm.
- The usefulness of a coarse sand or gravel drainage layer has been questioned in recent years. In England, wicket performance was the same with and without such a layer. One Adelaide pitch square performs well without a drainage layer, but it is slightly elevated above the surrounding area.
- Trials in New Zealand have shown that the clay root zone soil dries out faster if it is relatively thin (70 mm) and is underlain with sand. Such profiles might be most useful in areas where the climate frequently makes drying of thicker root zones too slow for optimum preparation of the pitch for a match.
- The soil must be carefully prepared for use in construction or topdressing. Clods must be broken and the soil passed through a 4 mm screen. An old wire mattress makes a fair substitute for this. Clods are broken by passing the soil through a hammer mill or by spreading it on concrete and running over it with a roller or a flail mower. Self-mulching soils will automatically break into small aggregates on drying.
- Why is it that the root zone does not remain permanently waterlogged? After all, it has a coarser layer underneath. Actually, it hasn't. The grass growing in the clay forms aggregates in the lower root zone that are of the same size or larger than the sand grains in the loamy sand beneath. This means that at least some of the pores in the lower part of the root zone will be larger than those in the loamy sand. Water can therefore drain down. There might be a perched water table at the loamy sand/coarse sand interface but it will not adversely affect the upper root zone.
- The grass is a vital part of a cricket pitch. It stabilises the root zone against break-up into small pieces when dry. It gives a deep even drying of the root zone that is essential before a wicket can be used for a match.
- Warm-season grasses (mainly common couch) are the main grasses grown on pitches in Australia. In areas where they are dormant until at least mid spring, they do not dry the root zone enough to allow a stable wicket to be prepared at the beginning of the season. Heating cables are installed at about 150 mm depth in some pitches in Melbourne and Canberra to allow earlier growth of

the warm-season grass. Couch cultivars with short dormancy periods give improved spring growth, but it is often necessary to use oversown ryegrass to aid drying of the soil for wicket preparation.

- The method of preparing a wicket for a match is given from p. 234.
- The salinity of the soil should be kept below about 2 dS/m (saturation extract). Increasingly higher amounts of salts cause the soil to self-mulch into a crumbling surface.

Bunkers (sand traps)

Bunkers must be designed so that surface water does not flow into them. That means that careful attention must be given to the direction of slope of surrounding areas. Where necessary, drains need to be installed to catch surface runoff water (Fig. 24.1).

Water must not lie in the trap itself, so, except where the underlying soil is very permeable or rainfall in the area light and infrequent, it too must be provided with a drainage system.

The faces of a new bunker or of one being remade must be cut to the exact contours required for the finished bunker. Cut them to the required shape; do not over-excavate and then fill loose soil back. High faces will hold sand better if they are stepped. Careful attention must be paid to the edges of bunkers; they must be kept grassed and not be given the opportunity to erode into the sand. One method of stabilising new edges is by laying sod vertically over them, including over sand-filled hessian bags installed as an edge. The sod is pegged in place.

The sand has to be carefully chosen if players are to be satisfied. A crust must not form on it, wind must not blow it easily and balls must not sink out of sight in it. Another requirement is that sand sprayed by players onto the green will not interfere with play nor damage mowers.

Experiment has shown that the sand should have less than 3% clay plus silt; no more than 25% of particles smaller than 0.25 mm; no more than 10% (preferably none) larger than 1 mm; and none larger than 2 mm. The sand grains should be somewhat angular ('sharp'), rather than rounded, so that they hold up on the side of the bunker. A simple test for deciding if the clay plus silt content is below 3% is given in Chapter 33.

Some prefer the sharp contrast to green offered by white sand, but the glare from it on sunny days generally encourages the use of sands with light tan coloration.

The sand is filled into the bottom of the bunker to a depth of 200–250 mm and then packed up the sides as needed. Soft new sand can be settled in with a concrete float after liquid wetting agent has been added at the recommended rate.

The sand of small bunkers is normally rejuvenated by hand raking. Where machine rakes are used, they must be operated in such a way that the sand is not spread from the bunker along the exit path. Sand has to be repacked onto the sides every five to six weeks. Clippings and coring plugs must not be allowed to contaminate bunker sands. Tired, dirty bunker sand can be recycled after washing.

Golf tees

Tees might be considered as the orphans of golf courses, yet they are critically important.

- They must be level.
- They must be large. Provide 9 m² of useable space per 1000 rounds of golf annually for par-4 and par-5 holes, and double that for par-3 holes.
- The grass must be kept growing vigorously on them.
- They must not be heavily shaded.

- They must receive ample amounts of fertilizer.
- They must be included in the mechanical maintenance program, including topdressing.
- Weeds that cannot withstand wear or slight drought should be eliminated with selective herbicides.
- A divot mixture of soil/sand/seed should be provided so that players help staff in maintaining the tee.

Domestic and landscape lawns

Most domestic lawns do not have to take intensive use. They are commonly constructed from the soil of the area, or from that soil with added sand. Best results will be obtained if a 50 mm (or more) layer of sandy loam of low silt content is spread over the soil of the area.

Many domestic and landscape lawns are constructed on disturbed sites. Builder's rubble must first be cleared away. Compaction caused by heavy vehicles *must* be relieved by ripping. If coarse sandy fill has been spread to combat wet conditions during construction, it *must* be thoroughly mixed with the underlying soil, and with any other soil spread over it, so that there are no layers.

The more intense the likely use, the greater the care that must be taken during construction if turf quality is to continue to be acceptable.

Coping with heavy traffic

Repeated movement of vehicles across turf, especially in wet weather, will severely damage the turf and the soil beneath. One way of coping with vehicles is to lay a paved road. Another is to try to have the best of both worlds with paver blocks and cells. Generally, they don't work very well.

A more useful alternative is to incorporate hard clinker ash or scoria into the root zone of heavily trafficked turf. Use about 30–40% by volume. This allows a 'skeleton' of hard particles to be formed that protects the soil itself against compaction. Water is held in the holes (vesicles) in the ash or scoria particles, yet at the same time air can easily penetrate the root zone.

Figure 17.23
Machine used to wash soil from turf.
Photograph P Semos and Strath Ayr
Instant Lawn Pty Limited, Seymour

Figure 17.24

Levelawn being used to prepare an even bed for instant turf. *Photograph K A Handreck*

TURFING

Turfing, or sod laying, is the formation of an 'instant lawn' by laying rolls of thinly cut sod or turf on a prepared base. The turf rolls are cut with special machines from areas of turf that are grown for that purpose.

For success, observe the following:

- The turf is often grown in a fairly heavy soil, because this is more readily retained by the turf roots after cutting than is a sandy soil. A two-layer profile is formed when the turf is placed on the soil base. Water movement into the lower layer will be satisfactory if its texture is similar to or heavier than that of the turf. However, there will be problems if the lower soil is of lighter texture than the turf soil; the turf will remain saturated after drainage has stopped. The best solution to this problem is to use turf from which all the soil has been washed by a special machine (Fig. 17.23).
- Washed turf is the ideal way of quickly establishing grass on golf and bowling greens and other areas that must come into use within as short a time as possible.
- Apply soluble nitrogen at a rate of about 10 g/m^2 (N).
- Irrigate well, then allow to drain before laying the turf.
- Use a Levelawn (Fig. 17.24) to give an even bed for the turf.
- Stagger the joints in the same way that bricks are laid. All edges must fit tightly together.
- Work from boards placed on the newly laid turf.
- Tamp the area lightly to ensure a firm bond between turf and soil. A light roller may be used, but it can cause the turf to creep, opening some joints.
- Keep the turf moist-to-wet while it is awaiting laying.
- Irrigate as soon as possible after laying and certainly within an hour. Irrigate hourly for a week, or until you are sure that roots are growing into the subgrade throughout the whole area.

18 TURF PLANTS

Turf plants are abused more than almost any other group of plants. They are repeatedly trodden on, crushed and skidded over. As soon as they hold their heads high, a mower comes along and cuts them down to size again. After all this they must still look green and have the characteristics needed by users. To achieve this, turf managers chop them with vertical mowers, cut them with coring machines, run spikes through them, drench them with pesticides and supposedly selective herbicides and deluge them with water and fertilizers.

It takes a lot of skill if these operations are not to do more harm than good. Skill is based on sound knowledge of the way turf grasses grow. The information given in this chapter provides a basis for the chapters on turf management that follow.

TURF GRASSES

Annual plants grow from seed to seed production within one year and then they die. Perennial plants go through annual cycles of growth but continue to live for many years. Most turf grasses are perennials. Exceptions include *Poa annua* (annual bluegrass; wintergrass; annual meadowgrass), that common component of much turf, and *Lolium rigidum* (annual ryegrass), used to oversow warm-season grasses for winter green in cool areas.

Turf grasses are of two main types—cool-season and warm-season. Cool-season grasses come from temperate to cold areas where rain falls mainly in the winter and spring. Warm-season grasses come from subtropical and tropical areas where rain falls all year or mainly in the warmest part of the year. Table 18.1 gives a list of the main species to which grasses used for turf belong, together with some of their characteristics.

There are many cultivars available for each of the different genera of turf grasses. Some are selections from within the one species; others are interspecific hybrids.

Turf grass structure

Figure 18.1 combines in one plant the several types of turf grass structure. Grasses with a creeping habit spread by sending out stolons and/or rhizomes. All the warm-season turf grasses are like this. Most cool-season grasses spread shorter distances mainly by producing more tillers around the first shoot that comes from the seed.

What happens inside

In Chapter 1 we learnt that the raw materials for plant growth come from the growing medium and air. In green plant parts, carbon dioxide from the air is converted into sugars, using sunlight as energy. An understanding of what happens to these sugars is a good basis for sound management of turf.

Sugars are the simplest members of a group of organic compounds called carbohydrates. The name comes from the fact that they all contain carbon,

Figure 18.1
The main parts of turf grass plants

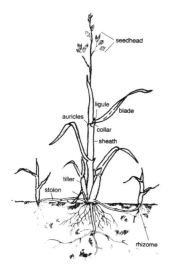

hydrogen and oxygen. The carbohydrates of plants are of three types. The simple sugars (glucose, fructose, sucrose) dissolve readily in water (think of the sucrose you put in your coffee). They move easily from one part of a plant to another; they are used as a source of energy or they are converted into one of the other types of carbohydrates.

Some sugars are used to make the cellulose and hemicellulose of cell walls. These are the structural carbohydrates. Once formed, they cannot be converted back into sugars for use elsewhere in the plant.

When there is more than enough sugar for current needs, some is converted into carbohydrates called starches and fructosans. These are often called storage, or reserve, carbohydrates. They can quickly be broken down into sugars again when more are needed.

Reserve carbohydrates are stored mainly in roots, stem bases, rhizomes and stolons. A moderate level of reserve carbohydrate is essential if turf grasses are to be able to meet any unexpected need.

Reserves rise and fall throughout the year, and from day to day. They are built up at times when photosynthesis produces more carbohydrates than are needed for current growth. Reserves build up most rapidly in cool-season grasses when days are mild (12–15°C) and nights cool (7–10°C). Temperatures a little higher than this produce growth, rather than storage. Even higher temperatures stress cool-season grasses; reserves fall. Corresponding temperatures for warm-season grasses are about 5°C higher than those for cool-season grasses.

Reserves are built up naturally in the weeks before grasses go into dormancy because of falling temperatures. If grass is to remain healthy, this natural tendency must be allowed to proceed unhindered. Don't stimulate growth or reduce leaf area during this time.

Usually, current photosynthesis provides most of the carbohydrates needed for current growth. Reserves are important as a back-up for the times when, for one reason or another, photosynthesis is temporarily inadequate.

CARBOHYDRATES AND MANAGEMENT

The importance of carbohydrate reserves to management practices may be seen from the following examples.

- Mowing removes part of the ability of grass to make sugars. Reserves will be drawn on for a couple of days. If there are no reserves, the grass will be weakened.
- Removal of a high proportion of top-growth at one mowing will severely drain reserves, leaving little for any other emergency such as a burst of hot weather. If cutting height is to be reduced, it must be done gradually. Never remove more than one-third of total green growth at one mowing.
- Grass repeatedly cut very close must be managed carefully as reserves cannot be high. Short tops tend to have sparse root systems, especially in cool-season grasses (Fig. 18.2).
- Encouraging rapid top-growth by applying large amounts of nitrogen will severely drain carbohydrate reserves. Again, the plants may not cope well with any extra demands such as high or very low temperatures.
- Carbohydrate reserves are generally low in heavily shaded turf. It should be cut high to give it more leaf area that can catch a little more light.
- Renovation operations such as intense scarifying and coring place heavy demands on reserves. These operations should be carried out only at times of the year when new growth will use products of current photosynthesis rather than reserves.
- Encourage reserves to build before turf is to be subjected to severe wear. Such wear includes cricket matches of several days' duration, lawn tennis tournaments, etc.

Figure 18.2
Close mowing greatly reduces the depth of rooting of, and the total amount of roots on, cool-season grasses. The mowing heights are in inches. *Courtesy E P Roberts, University of Rhode Island*

- Hot weather by itself lowers carbohydrate reserves. Cutting high will aid survival, as will eliminating nitrogen applications.

Cool-season and warm-season grasses

There is a fundamental difference between cool-season and warm-season grasses. It has to do with the way carbon dioxide is converted into sugars in them. Without going into detail, the important end result is that warm-season grasses are about twice as efficient at using sunlight to make growth as are cool-season grasses.

Accompanying this difference are big differences in water use and drought tolerance (Table 18.1). These differences are important when water for irrigation is in short supply (p. 294).

Table 18.1
The main turf grasses and some of their requirements (*From J B Beard* **Turfgrass: Science and Culture** **Prentice-Hall 1973)**

Grass	Drought tolerance	Tolerance to salinity	Heat tolerance
Warm-season grasses:			
Cynodon dactylon and hybrids (couch grass; green couch; Bermuda grass)	excellent	very good	very good
Pennisetum clandestinum (kikuyu)	excellent	very good	very good
Digitaria didactyla (blue couch)	excellent	very good	very good
Paspalum distichum (salt water paspalum)	excellent	excellent	excellent
Stenotaphrum secundatum (buffalo; St Augustine grass in the USA)	fair	very good	very good
Axonopus affinis and *A. compressus* (carpet grass, narrow and broad leaf)	poor	poor	good
Zoysia japonica, Z. matrella, Z. tenuifolia (zoysia grasses; respectively Japanese lawn grass, manila grass, mascarene grass)	good	good	excellent
Cool-season grasses:			
Poa pratensis (Kentucky bluegrass)	medium	poor	medium
Festuca arundinacea (tall fescue)	good	medium	good
F. rubra cv. *commutata* (chewings fescue)	good	poor	poor
Lolium perenne (perennial ryegrass)	fair	medium	poor
Agrostis tenuis (colonial bent; browntop; highland bent)	poor	poor	poor
A. palustris (creeping bent; seaside bent)	poor	medium	medium

- The growth cycle of cool-season grasses:
  The roots of cool-season grasses grow most rapidly at soil temperatures between 10 and 19°C. That means that they grow most rapidly in autumn and spring, with some growth in winter and not much in summer (Fig. 18.3). In areas with very cold winters, growth may be slight or nil during winter. There will be a flush of new root and shoot growth in spring.

  Growth of roots declines at soil temperatures over 19°C, finally stopping altogether at about 23°C. Any root growth in summer will take place only in deeper, cooler parts of the soil profile. Cool-season grasses tend to go dormant in summer. If growth is forced, the plants will have little ability to cope with stress.
- The growth cycle of warm-season grasses:
  The roots of warm season grasses grow most rapidly at soil temperatures between 23 and 32°C. There is still some growth at 35°C. These grasses are therefore able to grow right through the summer, provided that they are irrigated. As soils cool in autumn, growth slows and, for many grasses, stops altogether in areas with cold winters.

  Shoot growth starts again in early spring, in response to rising temperature and day-length increasing to 13 hours. There is no point in trying to get earlier growth by applying fertilizer, because these grasses simply cannot respond until day-length and temperature allow them to.

  For the first couple of weeks the new growth is produced at the expense of carbohydrate reserves. No extra stress should be imposed until this drawdown has stopped. The call on reserves is less severe or does not occur in warmer areas.

  Establishment of warm-season grasses in the cooler parts of their growing range should start as early in the growing season as is possible, so that maximum cover is attained before the next dormancy.

Effects of defoliation

Mowing and other activities that reduce the leaf area of turf grasses have the following effects:

- there is a temporarily decreased sugar production;
- there is a temporary drain on carbohydrate reserves.
  These effects last longer as the frequency and severity of defoliation increase.
- Removal of 40% of the tops of cool-season grasses in one mowing stops root growth. At higher rates of removal, fewer and fewer roots resume growing.
- Root growth of grasses with a creeping, horizontal habit of growth is much less affected. Mowing removes the upper leaves, allowing lower leaves that had been shaded to take over.
- Mowing usually increases tillering and the branching of stolons and rhizomes. This is especially so if the ends of stems are removed.
  Mowing newly established turf encourages it to thicken up.

CULTIVARS

Large numbers of cultivars of the most commonly grown turf grasses have become available in recent years, so much so that it is difficult to keep up with them all. Local trials are needed to select the most suitable cultivar for each of the very wide range of climatic, microclimate and soil conditions in Australia.

COUCH

As couch in its many forms is the most widely grown grass, we offer here some comments on its cultivars. National trials with the different cultivars had not long started at the time of writing, so these comments are based mainly on general observations rather than hard data.

Figure 18.3

Contrasting patterns of root and shoot growth in cool-season and warm-season grasses (Southern Hemisphere). *From Landscape Management February, 1991*

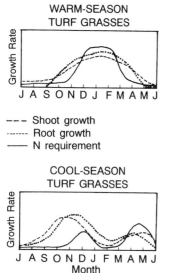

WARM-SEASON TURF GRASSES

Growth Rate

J A S O N D J F M A M J

--- Shoot growth
...... Root growth
—— N requirement

COOL-SEASON TURF GRASSES

Growth Rate

J A S O N D J F M A M J
Month

Seeded common couch doesn't make particularly good turf. Its leaves are coarse. It lacks competitiveness, thins out under wear and is readily invaded by weeds.

In contrast, hybrids such as Tifdwarf, Tifgreen, Tifway and Santa Ana are vigorous to very vigorous—as long as they are given heavy applications of nitrogen.

Santa Ana requires less fertilizer than the others for similar performance. It shows good winter survival. It has a more erect habit of growth than the others, so it uses water faster than do other hybrids of lower growth habit. (One measurement showed that it uses 40% more water than does the cultivar Windsor Green, which has a very low, compact growth habit.) However, it is very tolerant to drought. It is easily scalped with rotary mowers. It should be mown with reel mowers, and frequently in summer if its appearance is to remain good. The fairly heavy mat produced by Santa Ana gives it high wear tolerance. Its greater vigour than other hybrids allows it to recover quickly from wear injury.

Tifdwarf, as its name implies, hugs the ground and tends to grow fairly slowly. It seems ideally suited to humid areas where low growth rate is desirable, so it is widely used on bowling greens in Queensland.

Tifway and Tifgreen produce fine, very dense swards if fertilized adequately. They show spindly growth and poor colour if they do not get plenty of nitrogen. However, vigorous growth gives much thatch; swards of these grasses therefore demand high maintenance in terms of scarifying, topdressing and heavy dethatching. Such actions are especially necessary in hot dry climates, where natural decomposition of the thatch is less than in moister areas.

There are now many cultivars that are selections made from common couch. Those most widely grown are Wintergreen (also sold as Casablanca), Greenlees Park and National Park, but there are at least a couple of dozen others, often with limited localized use. New ones showing promise at the time of writing included Windsor Green and ATRI 29. Windsor Green is a mutant of Wintergreen. It is slow-growing: full establishment takes about twice as long as for Wintergreen, but once established it has about double the density of Wintergreen. It is really tough, because it has a 30% higher fibre content, so it is very hard wearing. Mowers must be sharp. It has a rich emerald green colour. National Park is popular in Perth, but elsewhere it seems to have performed less well than Greenlees Park and Wintergreen. Greenlees Park goes into dormancy earlier in autumn than do the others. Of all the currently available cultivars, Wintergreen appears to be the least affected by frost. It has performed well on football grounds and greens alike in the warmer parts of the country (Sydney and north). However, it grows more slowly than Santa Ana in more southerly areas.

Tolerance to salinity is not known for all of these cultivars, but it is greater for the hybrids, notably Santa Ana, than it is for common couch.

CLOVERS FOR TURF

Clovers have no place in the fine turf of bowling and putting greens. Their poor ability to withstand wear means that they are of limited usefulness in turf for contact sports.

However, clovers are useful in many other areas of turf. Their ability to fix atmospheric nitrogen can greatly reduce the amount of fertilizer nitrogen needed. They are green in winter when warm-season grasses are dormant. *Trifolium fragiferum* (strawberry clover) is reasonably tolerant of dry conditions. The other clover in common use—*T. repens* (white clover)—is suited mainly to cool, moist areas.

19 MANAGING TURF SOILS

Figure 19.1
A very serviceable core sampler can be made from the shaft of a golf club. Oil the sampler before storing it so that rusting is minimized. *Photograph J Coppi*

The aim of any turf management program is to ensure that the turf being managed continues to serve the needs of users. A basic rule is to work along with the natural character of the turf grass as far as is possible. For example, if it wants to go dormant, let it go dormant. Don't try to keep it going with massive amounts of nitrogen. The end result is weak or dead turf.

A sound management program will aim to keep the grass healthy. If this happens to mean that the grass is pale green rather than bright or dark green, so be it. Sport is played on grass, not green.

The carrying out of every management operation must be an answer to a question about what is really needed. If the turf looks wilted, the answer to the question 'What is wrong?' is to irrigate. If water lies on the surface of the soil for many hours after rain, one answer to the same question would be to core the soil. Don't blindly follow a routine. Seek causes to problems, then find solutions and apply them. Be aware that a change in one part of a program will usually make it necessary to change other parts too.

This chapter is about turf soils. However, turf soils and turf plants come intertwined. Whatever affects one will have some effect on the other too. We therefore discuss all turf management operations, but concentrate on those that directly affect turf soils.

A knowledge of what is happening in the root zone is basic to any management program. The main way of finding out is to regularly look by using a probe (Figs 19.1 and 32.1) or cutter (Fig. 19.2). Every turf manager should have one and use it.

Diagnosis

- Look at site conditions—exposure, slope, drainage pattern, extent of interference by tree roots and shade, traffic distribution.
- Look at the grass to see what species it is, and maybe cultivar.
- Look more closely—colour, presence of chlorosis, patterns of affected areas, weeds, general vigour and density, level of thatching.
- Look at the pattern of damage—circular (disease?), ring with undamaged grass on both sides (fairy ring), straight lines (damage by fertilizers or pesticides), follows drainage pattern (pythium?).
- Look at the leaves for signs of disease.
- Look at the roots—dark, discoloured (poor drainage), severed (cockchafer grubs).
- Look at the soil and thatch—depth of soil, black layer, sweet or bad smell, dry patch, excessive thatch, layers, poor root development, clogging of pores, compaction.
- Look at the mowing program—height of cut, frequency, sharpness of blades, adjustment of mower.
- Look at the fertilizers and pesticides used—types, rates, overuse, underuse, imbalance.

Figure 19.2
Soil profile sampler, showing marked layering due to topdressing with different soils. *Photograph J Horner, Better Methods, Sydney*

- Look at any soil and clippings test data.

Put it all together and take action.

Types of management operations

The main routine management operations are mowing and irrigation. From time to time it will be necessary to apply fertilizers and pesticides. The other common operations—usually grouped under the terms 'renovation' or 'cultivation'—are coring (hollow tining), slitting, spiking, 'Verti-Draining', 'HydroJecting', grooving, rolling, scarifying, brushing and raking. These may be used in an ongoing maintenance program that does not disrupt use, or in a major renovation to upgrade an area. Occasionally, a whole area has to be rebuilt.

The frequency of carrying out these operations and the number of them used varies with the intensity of use of the turf. A roadside verge will be lucky to get one mowing a year. A golf green is mown daily and regularly irrigated, topdressed, de-thatched, cored, brushed, sprayed, fertilized, etc. We cannot give 'recipe'-type management programs for every situation. Rather, we encourage you to become skilled in assessing your own situation. Then apply one or more of the management operations discussed here, as required.

We look first at operations that are used to relieve compaction and clogging, the most widespread problems of turf soils.

COMPACTION AND CLOGGING

Compaction is the pressing together of soil particles and crumbs so that the pores between and within them become smaller. Compaction reduces infiltration rate and can adversely alter the balance in the supply of oxygen and water to roots; it increases soil strength. Readers are referred to Chapter 8 for a discussion of compaction and its main effects.

We use the term 'clogging' to describe the tendency for vigorous root growth to block pores in soils and sandy root zones alike. In fact, with sands, there is evidence that it is this clogging, rather than compaction, that is responsible for greatly reduced infiltration of water. Movement of fine particles may also contribute to clogging.

In turf, compaction and clogging lead to other problems.

- Lowered infiltration rate allows the surface to remain wet longer. Use is then more likely to cause more collapse of soil crumbs, puddling, and tearing and burial of the grass.
- An extremely low infiltration rate can cause ponding of water in surface depressions. Grass can die from waterlogging and, in hot weather, from scalding.
- Turf can also be damaged by high salinity, because salts are difficult to leach from the medium.
- Lack of deep water penetration reduces rooting depth. The turf becomes less tolerant of drought or infrequent irrigation.
- Prolonged compaction under continuously moist conditions encourages roots and stolons to grow above the surface of the medium, adding to the formation of thatch, and making the grass prone to drought in hot weather.
- These combined effects of compaction weaken turfgrasses (Fig. 19.3) and reduce root growth, especially when nitrogen applications are high (Table 19.1), so that they are more susceptible to a number of diseases.
- One indicator of compaction and poor drainage is a high proportion of *Poa annua*, which is a shallow-rooted plant (Fig. 19.4).

Prevention by special construction

Prevention is always better than cure. With sports turf, prevention means that the area must be constructed with materials that drain rapidly even when fully

Figure 19.3

As a turf becomes more compact, root growth is increasingly restricted; the tops thin out. Here the compacting pressures are given in pounds per square inch (PSI) and the depths in inches. *From F A Pokorny Georgia Agric. Res. 11(1): 5, 1969; Courtesy of the University of Georgia*

Table 19.1

Root growth is greatly reduced by soil compaction and excessive use of nitrogen, as shown in this example for perennial ryegrass. Figures are root growth in mg/100 cm². (*From M J Sills and R N Carrow Agron. J. 75: 488, 1983).

Soil depth (mm)	N application kg/100 m²			
	0.5		1.0	
	Compaction level			
	None	Compact	None	Compact
0–50	259	256	238	165
50—150	245	227	268	108
150—250	183	127	181	53

Figure 19.4

A New Zealand study of racetracks found that the *Poa annua* content of the turf increased as compaction increased. *From T Field and J Murphy New Zealand Turf Manag. J. May: 16, 1991*

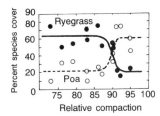

compacted. Details of these materials and construction methods have been given in Chapter 17.

Note, however that on even the best root zones there is still a need for various maintenance operations to increase infiltration rate into the soil and improve gas exchange. Such operations are needed because pores become clogged with roots and the organic matter produced by their decomposition (Table 19.2). Inevitably, a vigorous sward of grass adds to the effects of machinery and human feet.

Partial prevention by special care

The effects of compaction can be kept to a minimum as follows:

- forbidding use for some time after rain or irrigation. Such an action should be taken if walking on the area squeezes free water from the turf. A few hours of such restriction must be accepted by users if the long-term health of the turf is to be maintained.

More acceptable action includes:

- restricting traffic to pathways placed so as to anticipate short-cuts; or

Table 19.2
Differences in the properties of racetrack soils of different ages since installation. (*From* T Field and J Murphy *New Zealand Turfgrass Culture* May 1991: 9)

Age of turf (years)	Organic matter (%)	Bulk density (g/cm³)	Total porosity (% volume)	Macro-porosity (% volume)	Water-holding capacity (% volume)
1–5	4.35	1.56	40.4	22.8	20.4
6–15	11.7	1.16	54.6	14.1	42.9

Figure 19.5
The 'Better Methods' golf cup cutter.
Photograph C J P Smith

Table 19.3
Example of the effect of killing earthworms (with arsenic) on the infiltration of water into a turf soil (From J J Jensen and A J Turgeon *Agronomy J.* 69: 67, 1977)

Treatment	Infiltration rate (mm/h)
Worms in soil	360
No worms	100

- encouraging traffic to spread over a whole area so that compaction is 'diluted';
- separating irrigation and use by as much time as possible;
- using light machinery only, or using wide (balloon) tyres that reduce pressure on the soil;
- on golf greens, frequently changing the cup position (Fig. 19.5);
- on golf tees, having a large tee in the first place and then spreading wear by moving the markers frequently.
- as much as possible, using machinery only when the soil has dried after rain or irrigation;
- varying patterns of mowing so that compaction by wheels is spread over the whole area;
- not using chemicals (such as some fungicides and preparations containing lead and arsenic) that destroy soil life (Table 19.3);
- using rollers only as needed, and no heavier than needed to do the job;
- banning the use of spiked shoes on golf courses;
- where users find it acceptable, allowing some thatch as a cushion between user and soil.

Improving a compacted/clogged soil

If, in spite of your best efforts to prevent it, a soil becomes compacted or clogs enough to give poor growth, the next step must be to relieve that condition. Compaction by foot traffic affects mainly the top 30–40 mm of soil (Fig. 19.6). Compaction by heavy vehicles and horses goes deeper, but rarely deeper than 150 mm. Whatever the depth, treatment must go beyond that depth.

Digging will relieve compaction in garden soils. Cultivation will break compaction in farm soils. Both operations severely disturb the surface, so they cannot be used for turf. Instead, special machines that remove cores of soil, make slits or grooves, or spike or blow holes into it have been developed.

The aim of all these operations is to make large pores down through the compacted/clogged soil. At one time it was thought that the main benefit was to allow air into the soil and waste gases to escape. As a result, it has become common to say that these operations aerate or 'aerify' (USA) the soil.

However, the main effect of these operations is to allow more rapid penetration of water into the root zone or to allow deeper drainage of water that does enter it. In other words, the main effect of punching holes in a turf root zone is to reduce its wetness. Hence, it has been common in recent years to use the word 'drainage' to describe these various operations. Of course the act of providing channels for drainage also allows increased entry of oxygen into the soil and escape of carbon dioxide and other waste gases.

Another main effect is a reduction in the strength of parts of the soil so that roots can proliferate there. As these other effects are at least as important as improving the entry of air into the root zone, we prefer to use terms such as 'core', 'spike', etc., which describe what is being done. We also use the word

Figure 19.6
Foot traffic compacts soils to a depth of no more than about 4 cm. *From O R Lunt Southern Californian Turfgrass Culture* 6(3): 1, 1956

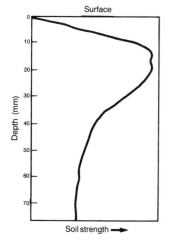

Figure 19.7
Lines of equal bulk density in the soil around a hollow-tine hole. Note that the soil is most heavily compacted at the bottom of the hole. *From A M Petrovic PhD Thesis, Michigan State University, 1979*

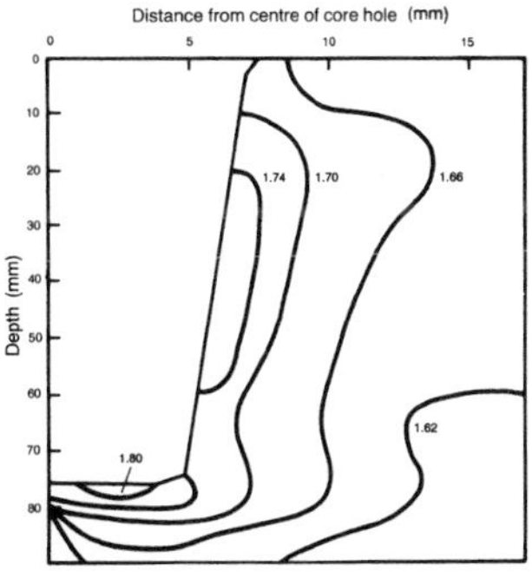

'cultivation' in the general sense in which it is used in the US turf industry, to cover all actions that penetrate/disturb the root zone.

Another point must be made clear from the beginning. While slitting, grooving and spiking do improve infiltration of water into the root zone, these effects typically last no longer than a few weeks. The sides of the slits, grooves and spike holes collapse into the hole, so the layer through which they penetrated returns to its original state. The effects of hollow-tine coring last somewhat longer.

However, all of these machines inevitably compact the soil just below their depth of penetration (Fig. 19.7). The long-term result of frequent cultivation to the same depth is the formation of a compacted layer at and below that depth. This compaction must eventually be relieved. The advent of the Verti-Drain and HydroJect machines has made deep cultivation possible and easy, as is discussed later in this chapter.

Coring

The main decisions that need to be made about coring are:

- Size of machine: Size ranges from large units for fairways (Fig. 19.9) through smaller machines for greens (Fig. 19.8) to hand-held corers (Fig. 19.10). Width must match the area needing treatment. Heavier machines are to be preferred for soils that quickly become hard on drying. The extra weight helps penetration of the tines.
- Spacing of holes: The range is from 25 to 150 mm between core centres, with 80–100 mm spacing being generally adequate. Closer spacing may be useful when changing to a frequent sand topdressing program. Tufts of greener, more vigorous growth above holes indicate the need for more intensive coring, a switch to sand topdressing, or renovation.
- Diameter of holes: The range is from 6 to about 20 mm, with 10–12 mm diameter being common. Anything much larger than 12 mm may give a pockmarked surface even after backfilling and one topdressing.
- Depth of coring: The compacted layer or any zone of layered materials of different texture must be fully penetrated. Take core samples to see just how deeply the tines should go.
- Remove extracted soil? The extracted soil can be removed, or it can be worked back into the holes and turf surface, with brushes or steel mats, after breaking up the plugs with a vertical mower if necessary. The turf then receives the added benefits of topdressing. Removal is recommended if the soil is of heavy texture; it can then be replaced by sand or sandy loam that still has an adequate infiltration rate when fully compacted. Whether removed or not, some extra topdressing is usually needed a week or two after coring to fill in depressions left by slumping of soil into core holes. More detail on topdressing materials is given later in this chapter.
- Time of year: Low infiltration rate and declining turf quality will be the main indicators of when to core. However, times when weed seeds usually germinate are to be avoided. Their germination is often stimulated by coring. Usually the best times to core are when the most active turf growth is to be expected. Coring dormant grass or grass that is just coming out of dormancy (e.g. couch in early spring) is asking for trouble. Don't core in hot weather—extra evaporation through the core holes causes severe wilting and death of turf around the holes (Fig. 19.11). This can happen even in cool dry weather. Be prepared to irrigate more frequently for a few weeks after coring.
- Frequency: 'As often as the turf needs it' is the short answer, but the range is from never to every two to three weeks. Turf growing well on soils that have a high infiltration rate and excellent drainage need never be cored. This would apply to soils of excellent structure that are lightly trafficked and to turf on special root zone sands that have good physical properties even when

Figure 19.8
A commonly available coring
machine for greens. *Courtesy
S J Banks & Son Pty Ltd*

Figure 19.9
Australian-made Coremaster 12
coring machine. *Courtesy Greencare
Industries, Sydney*

fully compacted (Chapter 17). The best USGA and pure sand root zones typically get two corings a year, provided thatch is controlled by careful management, including frequent light scarifying and topdressing, and the pores are not yet clogged with roots. Coring frequencies of twice to six times a year are usually tolerable, provided the expense is justified by use. If turf can be maintained only by coring every two to four weeks, then complete remaking of the area or starting an all-sand topdressing program (p. 223) should be considered as alternatives that will be cheaper in the long term. Such frequent coring implies very poor soil structure and texture and/or use that is excessive for that soil.

- Soil moisture content: For successful coring the soil should be at about field capacity, or just a little drier. This means waiting for a while after irrigation or rain. Sands drain to field capacity in hours. Heavier soils may take a day or two. Coring soil that is wetter than this enhances the formation of a cultivation pan.
- Finally, coring tines must be cleaned thoroughly after use. Oil them to prevent rusting. If this is not done, they may clog and become like the feet on a sheeps-foot roller.
- Coring does not seem to disrupt the usefulness of previously applied pre-emergent herbicides.

Spiking

With spiking, solid tines of about 6 mm diameter are pushed into the soil to make holes. As they are pushed in, the soil is pushed aside and compacted further. The sides of the holes in wet soil may be slicked over. The holes do increase infiltration rate (Table 9.1) but the effect is usually temporary. Spiking does not relieve compaction; all it does is temporarily overcome one of the effects of compaction and clogging.

The advantages of spiking over coring are that it can be done quickly and therefore frequently, that it causes little disruption to the surface and that there are no cores to remove. Many football pitches in northern Europe are spiked twice a week to every two weeks during the football season. The results of one such program are shown in Fig. 19.12.

The spiking of non-compacted soils will inevitably reduce their macro-poros-

Figure 19.10
A hand corer for small areas of turf.
Photograph J Coppi

ity, so you should be sure that you actually have a problem before spiking. Whenever possible, spiking—and coring—should be done when the soil is somewhat dry. Of course the tines must be able to be pushed into the root zone, but the least damage to existing structure is produced when these cultivation operations are undertaken on dryish soil.

The inevitable cultivation pan produced by spiking has led to the conclusion for golf greens that coring is to be preferred. On golf courses, spiking might be best restricted to dry areas of fairways with low infiltration rates. The cultivation pans of European football pitches are mainly relieved through the use of Verti-Drain cultivation.

'Verti-Draining'

Verti-Drain machines (Fig. 19.13) have been likened to giant forks. These machines insert long solid or hollow tines vertically into the soil and then rapidly move the tines backwards in the soil, with the pivot point being at the surface (Fig. 19.14) in much the same way as a pitchfork is used. This pivoting action lifts and shatters the soil, so creating long-lasting fissures and disruption of layers. Tine lengths range from 300 to 400 mm, but penetration depths can be from 50 to 400 mm. The best tine diameter is 19–25 mm if sand is to readily penetrate the holes. The Verti-Drain machine has virtually replaced the Vibra-mole plough, which severely disrupts the surface and does little to improve drainage.

As with all machines, there are some limitations and precautions to observe.

Figure 19.11
Plenty of water must be applied to turf after slitting (or coring) it in hot dry weather, otherwise the soil around the slits will dry out and grass will die, as shown here

- There is no point in using a Verti-Drain if there is no subsurface compaction or layering to overcome; look before calling the contractor.
- There are cheaper means of relieving shallow compaction.
- There is no point in attempting to use a Verti-Drain machine to improve drainage if the root zone is underlain by deep subsoil of very low permeability that is controlling water movement from the root zone. Increasing the thickness of the root zone (p. 201) or installing a drainage system are more useful actions then.
- The soil must be a little drier than field capacity for maximum benefit.
- The tines must not be allowed to penetrate to the intermediate or gravel layers of USGA profiles (unless you deliberately want to shatter a gravel layer that has become cemented together).
- Nor must they be used where they could shatter irrigation pipes.
- Shallow-rooted turf can be severely damaged.
- Surface disruption is least on bowling greens with 12 mm tines. The machine must be very carefully adjusted if surface disruption is to not be too large. If you do decide to Verti-Drain a bowling green, you should apply topdressing sand first, rail and lightly roll afterwards and be prepared to add more topdressing as needed to even up the surface. Water frequently.
- Make sure before calling in a Verti-Drain contractor that the roots of your turf are strong enough to take the inevitable pounding they will get. Of course one reason for using a Verti-Drain machine is to improve root growth. That all leads to the conclusion that the best time is just before the period of maximum root growth, so optimum times are early spring and mid-autumn for cool-season grasses and mid- to late spring, or even later, for warm-season grasses.
- The longevity of benefits to be had from using a Verti-Drain depend on soil texture. The fissures in fine-textured soils will inevitably close unless topdressing sand has penetrated them to depth. Shattering of layers may be permanent with one or two treatments. The need for further treatment can only be judged by performance.

'HydroJecting'

The Toro HydroJect machine (Fig. 19.15) uses pulsed jets of water under very high pressure (34 MPa (megapascals) = 5000 PSI) to punch holes into the turf root zone. It markedly increases the soil's water infiltration rate (Fig. 19.16). Its capabilities and limitations are:

- There is little disruption of the surface, because the holes produced have a diameter of 4–5 mm and very little soil material is brought to the surface.
- This machine is therefore ideal for cultivation when there must be no disruption to use of the area.
- The area of affected medium increases as the water jet disperses deep within the root zone (Fig. 19.17).
- Depth of penetration can be varied in the range 100–200 mm, although penetration to 500 mm can be achieved with multiple shots into the same hole.
- No cultivation pan is produced.
- Wetting agents can be injected via the water.
- It is essential that the water used be very clean. A 5 μm filter has been found to be needed.
- Successful HydroJect treatment of the root zone requires that you first mechanically remove any accumulation of thatch.
- Some caution is needed with areas of turf that have a sandy surface overlying finer materials. There may be some mixing of these underlying materials up into the sand.

Figure 19.12
Very frequent spiking (52 passes) was able to increase the infiltration rate of a football pitch. *From P M Canaway et al. J. Sports Turf Res. Inst. 62: 67, 1986*

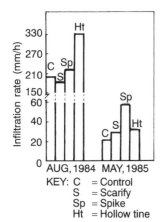

KEY: C = Control
S = Scarify
Sp = Spike
Ht = Hollow tine

Figure 19.13
Verti-Drain machine. *Photograph T Siviour, Turspec Pty Ltd, Sydney*

Figure 19.14
The action of Verti-Drain tines in the soil

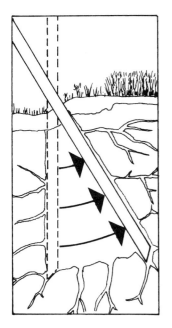

Grooving

A grooving machine makes deep (down to 100 mm) vertical cuts in turf, bringing the soil from the cut to the surface. The soil should be fairly dry. This is a more severe treatment than coring, but it can be useful if thatch has to be removed as well. Chunks of turf can be torn out if the root system is shallow. It will be particularly useful in re-establishing contact between the surface and sand slits.

Slicing/slotting

The knives of a slicing machine make vertical cuts in the turf. Soil is not removed. As with spiking, any improvement in soil physical properties is of short duration as the cuts soon close over. This alternative to spiking may be useful if the slicing of grass rhizomes and stolons increases turf density, but intensive slicing may damage some turf. If clay soils are sliced when wet, slicking of the sides of the cuts can make barriers to sideways movement of water, air and roots. Spiking is preferred to slicing when the root zone contains reinforcement materials such as Netlon.

TOPDRESSING

Topdressing is the practice of applying a thin layer of growing medium to turf. It is an important management operation, especially for heavily used turf.

Topdressing of the greens has long been practised at the Royal and Ancient at St Andrews in Scotland. A composted mixture of two-thirds beach sand and one-third leaf mould has been used. After going through all manner of different mixtures of materials, those currently recommended, based on scientific experiments, are similar to materials used 300 or more years ago.

Benefits of topdressing

The most important benefits to be had from topdressing are:

- a smooth level surface—hollows are filled in;
- biological control of thatch (p. 228);
- improved infiltration rate, through improved texture of the top of the root zone;
- therefore, less disease and fewer insect problems.

Other benefits include:

- better establishment—topdressing newly planted turf (sprigs or seed) every two weeks will hasten the development of a dense sward;
- fewer weeds—many seeds need light for germination; *Poa annua* (winter grass, annual bluegrass, annual meadowgrass) and the crabgrasses *(Digitaria sanguinalis* and *D. ischaemum)* are two common turf weeds that do; burying them may prevent germination;
- a tighter turf of finer texture;
- a firmer surface to football pitches in wet weather, with increased ball rebound;
- a 'live' surface on golf greens;
- reduction in erratic ball roll on golf greens caused by grass stem stubble;
- the topdressing is a useful carrier for fertilizers, herbicides and pesticides.

Materials to use for topdressing

Whatever material is used, there is one rule that must be obeyed: *Always use the same material on the same area of turf.* This means: *Never use materials of different texture on different occasions.* And: *Never, ever, topdress with materials that contain more fines (clay and silt) than there is in the root zone already.*

Before you start topdressing you must have an assured source of supply of material of closely similar texture and grading. Layering of materials of different

Figure 19.15
HydroJect machine in action on a bowling green. *Photograph K A Handreck*

Figure 19.16
Example of the effect of using a HydroJect machine on a couch turf. *From* J A Murphy and P E Rieke *Golf Course Manag.* 59(7): 6, 1991

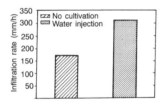

textures gives perched water tables, poor drainage and low infiltration rates if the pores in the upper layer are smaller than those in the lower layer. Poor turf quality will soon broadcast your incompetence if you do create layers.

All materials used should be free of weed seeds, stolons and rhizomes, and disease-causing organisms. Fumigation will achieve this.

Because topdressing materials must be of sandier texture than the underlying soil, most will be sandy loams, loamy sands or pure sands. They may be natural soils or specially prepared mixtures.

- *Natural soils:* Unamended natural soils are useful only for topdressing turf that gets little use. Even then, the only suitable soils will be light loams, sandy loams and loamy sands. Clay loams, clayey sands, silty soils and clays are all unsuitable. Using them on heavily used turf will produce or worsen all the problems listed on p. 216. Check the texture (Chapter 3) of any soil you think you might use for topdressing.

- *Pure sand and high-sand mixtures:* The best topdressing materials are pure sands and high-sand mixtures. The sand used should meet the specifications given in Tables 17.7–17.9. A basic requirement is that the topdressing has a high permeability to water when fully compacted. This is most likely when the particles are in the range 0.1–0.75 mm diameter, with most in the range 0.1–0.6 mm. No more than 5% of the particles are to be larger than 0.75 mm, and none larger than 1 mm. Larger particles damage mowers and players.

The main difference between pure sands and high-sand mixtures is in the proportion of particles smaller than 0.1 mm present. The proportion must be no higher than is in the root zone already. That means that only pure sand topdressings are to be used on pure sand root zones. Pure sands should also be used at dusty sites where particles of clay and silt size will accumulate on turf. They are preferred at sites where earthworms bring clay and silt to the surface. Pure sands can be used at other sites but high-sand mixtures that contain some fine particles are also used.

Fine particles (clay and silt) provide some nutrients and some cation exchange capacity. They increase the water-holding capacity of a sand. In one North American study, the appearance of a bentgrass turf was better with sand/soil than with pure sand topdressing. However, root growth was better in the sand, and much more thatch accumulated with sand/soil (12 mm) than with pure sand (2 mm). The benefits of clay and silt must be weighed against possible problems from decreased infiltration rate. Sometimes fines move down from topdressings to form a thin impermeable layer.

Clay plus silt should not exceed 4% of the mixture, and clay plus silt plus very fine sand no more than 8%. Don't guess; send a sample to a laboratory or, at the very least, measure the fines content as outlined in Chapter 33. Use the example in Chapter 3 and Fig. 3.4 as a guide to deciding on the approximate proportion of a soil to add to a sand.

A final decision is whether or not to include organic matter in the topdressing. Opinions differ and there are different practices. It is difficult to get composts completely free of weed seeds. Fine peats often contain much silt.

Compost does provide some nutrients. However, this is a small benefit if at the same time thatch production is encouraged by a clogged surface to the root zone. The best way to increase the rate of thatch decomposition is to provide good conditions for the existing population of microorganisms (p. 231).

There is no point in including organic matter in topdressings applied to control thatch. Decomposition of the thatch will provide all the humus needed. The thatch cost money to produce. Why not use it? Do not include organic matter if the turf is already soft. Include up to 10% organic matter (by volume) if the surface being treated is hard and you want to give it a little more resilience.

All things considered, topdressing is generally safest, and results are best, with pure sand.

Figure 19.17
The effect of the jet of water from a HydroJect machine is mainly well down the profile. *Photographs Toro and K A Handreck*

Figure 19.18
Boards being used to drag topdressing sand into the tine holes produced by a Verti-Drain machine

Frequency and amount of topdressing

Topdress only if one or more of the benefits listed above is needed. There is little to be gained if the current management program is giving the required quality of turf. For most turf, a couple of topdressings during establishment, plus an occasional partial topdressing to fill hollows, is all that is needed or affordable.

More frequent topdressing is desirable, even essential, for intensively used turf. But even there the benefits must match the cost involved. The benefits can be considerable, and topdressing is often the cheapest method of maintaining excellent turf on golf and bowling greens. For these areas, topdressing frequency is determined by the rate of production of thatch.

Two situations warrant a frequent topdressing program:

- When the root zone has less than ideal properties, frequent topdressing with a material of better texture will soon build up a root zone with better properties. This is less disruptive than complete rebuilding or a major renovation. The method of beginning this type of topdressing program is given on p. 226. Three examples are given.
- The British Sports Turf Research Institute has recommended that soil-based football pitches equipped with slit drains should be topdressed with pure sand at an annual rate of at least 16 kg/m^2 for at least two seasons. This would give a 20 mm layer of sand. Thereafter, the annual application could be in the range 4–10 kg/m^2. Rates of 8–16 kg/m^2 are added via two applications, while lower amounts are added as a single application in summer.
- It has been recommended that 8 kg/m^2 be applied before using a Verti-Drain. Boards (Fig. 19.18) or a rail are needed to work such a heavy application into the Verti-Drain holes.
- A golf fairway constructed on a heavy soil that is often wet can be improved over several years through a sand topdressing program. One recipe is to apply 6 mm of sand each three to five weeks during the growing season, for a total of about 40 mm for each of four years. Sounds expensive, but it is a lot cheaper than total reconstruction.
- Frequent light topdressing is a powerful way of coping with thatch. But first modify other management practices if these are the cause of excessive thatching. If thatching is still a problem, regular topdressing with pure sand can be cheaper and is less disruptive to play than are other management operations. For this type of program, the frequency of topdressing will depend on turf growth and on the type of surface required by players. The more frequent the applications, the greater the speed of a golf green, because there will be less thatch, with its cushioning effect. Every two to three weeks at the height of the growing season is common for high-speed golf greens. The amount of sand to apply each time will be no more than 900 g/m^2—usually 500–600 g/m^2. This light dusting just covers surface stolons.

Switching to a frequent topdressing program

As already stated, a frequent topdressing program is warranted when thatch is a continuing problem or as a means of upgrading the root zone. In either case, it is not good enough just to start applying topdressing.

Any thick layer of thatch should be removed by vertical mowing. (Applying sand straight onto it could cause the thatch to become a barrier to drainage.) Then double core the root zone. Remove the core material if the root zone has a heavy texture. Otherwise break the plugs with a vertical mower. Apply enough sand to fill the holes and give a 2 mm thickness over the whole area. Each of the first five or six topdressings should be accompanied by double coring. This will provide a transition zone without layers.

Applications to give a modified root zone can each continue to be of about 2 mm depth until perhaps 20 mm has been applied. Otherwise, topdressings for thatch control should be of about 0.8–1.6 mm. Apply as little as possible so as

Figure 19.19
Examples of machines used for applying topdressing sands to turf.

Upper: *Courtesy of OMC, Lincoln, Nebraska, USA;*
Lower: *Photograph J Westwick, Courtesy of B and R Industrial Maintenance and Engineering Services, Sydney*

Figure 19.20
Small fertilizer/topdressing spreaders are suitable for topdressing many areas of turf.
Photograph J Fakes

to keep the cost down. Some turf managers find that a light scarifying before topdressing improves results (see below).

Spreading

The shallow depth (0.8–2 mm) of topdressing materials required by the programs suggested here are best spread by drop or broadcast spreaders. A machine such as that shown in Fig. 19.19(a) is needed for golf greens. Larger units (Fig 19.19(b)) are needed for fairways and ovals and hand-operated spreaders for bowling greens. The aim is even spreading.

Example: How much sand is needed to apply 1 mm to an area of 500 m²? Each application will need (500 x 0.001) = 0.5 m³. At a bulk density of about 1.4 g/mL for loose sand, this will weigh about 700 kg.

The sand is worked into the turf with some form of matting. Flexible steel mesh, upside-down synthetic turf and coir matting are commonly used. Patterns of dragging are shown in Fig. 19.21.

Figure 19.21
Topdressing sand may be worked
into turf by dragging matting over it
in patterns such as these

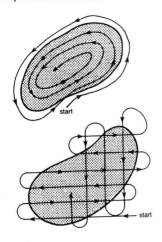

Figure 19.21
Topdressing sand may be worked
into turf by dragging matting over it
in patterns such as these

Figure 19.22
Thatch and mat on the surface of a
turf soil

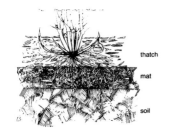

General comments

Plan ahead. Have plenty of sand and other topdressing materials on hand. Fungicides, some herbicides, fertilizer, lime and seed can all be applied with the sand. When mixing a small amount of material into the sand, first mix it thoroughly with a portion of the sand and then mix that through the rest of the sand. Use a concrete mixer.

Topdressing is just one of the ongoing actions necessary for maintaining excellent turf subjected to intensive use, but it is a very important one. It forms a very powerful partner with frequent, light scarifying as a means of maintaining excellent fine turf.

THATCH

Roofs covered with a thatch of straw, reeds, rushes or palm leaves have kept people dry for thousands of years. Some people are said to have a thatch of hair on their heads. Thatch in turf is defined as a layer of dead and living shoots, stems and roots that develops on the surface of a root zone below the green tops. Decomposing thatch that becomes intermingled with soil particles is called 'mat' (Fig. 19.22).

A small amount of mat and thatch, up to 6–8 mm (Fig. 19.23), is usually considered beneficial in many types of turf because it:

- gives turf some resilience;
- increases wear tolerance;
- cushions the underlying soil against compaction;
- acts as a mulch in reducing evaporation of water from the soil and smoothing temperature fluctuations in the soil;
- reduces the possibility of weed seeds germinating.
  Moderate to heavy thatching is definitely not beneficial to turf because:
- thatch can reduce infiltration rate either by becoming water repellent or by being squashed into a dense layer; dry patches can develop;
- heavy thatch reduces the tolerance of turf grasses to heat damage and cold;
- scalping is all too easy;
- thatch can harbour pathogens and insects, leading to greater disease problems; dollar spot (caused by *Sclerotinia homoeocarpa*), *Pythium* and *Fusarium* blights and *Helminthosporium* leaf spot are diseases often associated with heavy thatch;
- overseeding is difficult;
- a smooth, even, fast surface is impossible;
- on warm sunny days, phytotoxic substances can be produced as some thatches decompose;
- thatch and mat layers can inactivate pesticides, decreasing their effectiveness.

Note that different types of turf can tolerate, even require, more thatch than others. For example, the turf of racecourses needs to have a good cushion so as to minimize injury to horses' legs. Home lawns are another example. Rarely are they subjected to intensive use that requires a fast surface; rarely do they need coring or other cultivation treatments.

Causes of thatch accumulation

Rapid accumulation of thatch is a sign of bad management. Thatch accumulates when the rate of decomposition of dead turf parts on the soil surface is less than the rate of production of dead turf. Factors leading to high rates of production are:

- use of very vigorous species and varieties of turf grasses;
- heavy fertilization, especially with nitrogen;
- irrigation so that maximum growth rates are maintained;

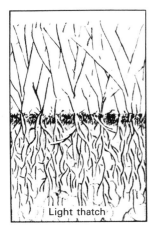
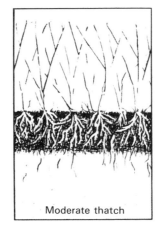
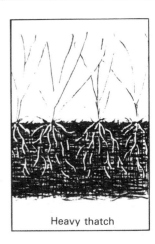

Figure 19.23
In heavily thatched turf, many roots grow only in the thatch itself and not in the soil below. The turf is then very susceptible to drought

- environmental conditions favourable to rapid growth;
- return of clippings (sometimes).

Factors leading to reduced rates of decomposition are:

- acid soil conditions (pH below about 5), which reduce the activity of decomposer fungi;
- alkaline conditions (pH above about 7);
- soil compaction (Fig. 19.24) and poor drainage, which encourage root and stolon growth on or above the soil surface rather than in the soil;
- in dry climates, allowing the thatch to become dry between irrigations—so reducing the activity of decomposers;
- frequent applications of pesticides which destroy earthworms and other decomposer macro- and microorganisms (Fig. 19.25);
- infrequent or excessively high mowing (Fig. 19.26);
- tough residues—many wear-tolerant grasses have high lignin contents that reduce decomposition rates.

Management for minimal thatch

Thatch is managed by reducing production and/or increasing the rate of decomposition. Production of thatch can be reduced by:

- switching to less vigorous cultivars or species of grasses, if this is possible;
- keeping nitrogen applications to vigorous turf species to the minimum needed for acceptable growth and appearance;
- keeping water supply as low as is possible for the appearance needed;
- lowering mowing height;
- removing clippings, if they are adding to the thatch.

Natural biological decomposition by earthworms is encouraged by:

- increasing soil pH to at least 5.5 and preferably 6;
- not using chemicals that kill earthworms (Table 19.4);
- introducing earthworms if there are none there already (Fig. 25.1).

Figure 19.24
In this experiment, thatch thickness was greatest on the most compact soils. *From K A Hurto et al.* Agronomy J. 72: 165, 1980

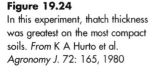
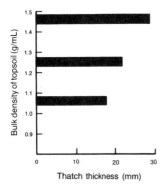

Many turf managers consider earthworms to be a menace in turf, mainly because of the castings that some species leave on the surface. These are easily brushed into the turf if they would otherwise interfere with play. But where they do not interfere with play, we encourage you to look after the worms in your turf. They will silently do a fair amount of work for you as they munch their way through mat and thatch. They are very cheap coring and dethatching 'machines' (Table 19.5).

Natural microbiological decomposition of thatch is encouraged by:

Figure 19.25
Profiles of areas of turf to which no fungicide had been applied (upper left) or that had been treated with fungicides for 3 seasons. Note the build-up of thatch in some profiles. *From* R W Smiley *Plant Disease* 65: 17, 1981; *Courtesy of American Phytopathological Soc.*

Figure 19.26
Thatch tends to accumulate faster as cutting height increases. *From* J H Dunn et al. *Agronomy J.* 73: 949, 1981

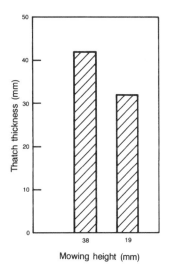

- Increasing soil pH (Table 19.6). This is an essential, cheap first step in minimizing thatch (Table 19.7).
- Using urea and other organic forms of N (Table 19.8).
- Applying fungicides only as needed. Applying them often, in the hope of preventing fungal attack, can do more harm than good. Some increase thatchiness (Fig. 19.25).
- Relieving compaction and improving drainage.
- Undertaking a regular program of sand topdressing (as given earlier in this chapter). This is probably the best way of keeping thatch under control with almost no interruption to use. The topdressing mingles with the thatch, keeping it moist and so giving better conditions for decomposer microbes.
- Undertaking frequent, light scarifying (Fig. 19.27). 'Frequent' means weekly to fortnightly, accompanied by light topdressing as discussed above. The scarifying is shallow: the blades just make contact with the blades of grass— they are set at 1.5–3 mm below the bed knife.
- Coring, with brushing of the core material into the turf. This is especially useful for golf fairways, for which frequent topdressing is too expensive. The more soil that is brought up the better.
- Using lightweight mowers, rather than gang mowers, on golf fairways.
- Not using proprietary de-thatching preparations and 'enzymes'. Don't waste your money on these 'magic cures'. All tested so far by people other than manufacturers or their agents have been found to have no effect on thatch thickness or the infiltration of water into soils. Research in New Zealand showed much higher levels of enzymes were already in the thatch and soil than were present in a product tested. Use the decomposers already in the area, as suggested above.

Table 19.4
Chemicals known to be toxic to earthworms (*From* K E Lee *Earthworms: Their Ecological Relationships with Soils* Academic Press, Sydney, 1985)**

Very toxic	Moderately toxic
Herbicides	
Calcium arsenate	
Lead arsenate	
Insecticides	
Chlordane	Endrin
Heptachlor	Isobenzan
Toxaphene	Azinphosmethyl
Ethoprop	Dyfonate
Phorate	Fensulphothion
Aldicarb	Karathion
Bufencarb	Parathion
Carbaryl	Zinophos
Carbofuran	Dithiocarbamate
Methomyl	
Oxamyl	
Propoxur	
Tirpate	
Fungicides	
Benomyl	
Carbendazim	
Copper oxychloride (with long use)	
Thiabendazole	
Thiophanate-methyl	
Compounds containing mercury	
Fumigants	
Chloropicrin	
Methyl bromide	
Metham sodium	
D-D	

Table 19.5
Example of the effect of earthworms on thatch (*From* A J Turgeon *Agronomy J.* 67: 563, 1975)**

Earthworm count (number/m^2)	Thatch (kg/m^2)
0	1.7–2.4
47–65	0

De-thatching/vertical mowing/scarifying

When all else fails, a scarifier (Fig. 19.28) or vertical mower must be used to penetrate more deeply into the thatch than is done during frequent, light scarifying. Two levels of severity may be used.

In de-thatching, blades spaced 5–15 mm apart penetrate several millimetres into the thatch. The turf surface is playable soon after de-thatching and cleaning up.

In heavy scarifying the blades are allowed to penetrate deeply through the thatch and into the mat layer, sometimes as far as the true soil surface. Heavily matted turf must be scarified in two directions, in a diamond pattern. Sometimes the removed thatch must be swept up before a second pass is made. Don't be frightened by the large amount of material removed. You are doing much more good than harm.

Heavy de-thatching/scarifying might be necessary every year or two if a frequent light scarifying/topdressing is not in place. It is best carried out when the grass is capable of rapid recovery, which means early autumn or early spring for cool-season grasses and mid-summer for warm-season grasses. Avoid times of peak germination for weed seeds.

Encourage rapid recovery by topdressing immediately after scarifying and by light fertilization (e.g. 2 g/m^2 N and 2 g/m^2 K). A small amount of nitrogen (2 g/m^2 N) applied two weeks before scarifying will help too. When all else fails for cricket pitches, it is necessary to remove the top organic-rich layer and replace it with new soil. Organic-rich soil at the surface of a cricket pitch gives poor bounce and slow pace. No amount of rolling can give it enough compaction to produce a fast wicket. Such action may need to be taken every 20 years.

Putting it all together for a couch golf green

Here is a maintenance program for couch golf greens that must always be of very high quality. It is assumed that the root zone is sand with the best of compositions, that the cultivar is suited to the area and that the turf is not shaded.

- Topdress lightly each two to four weeks during the growing season, depending on growth.
- Apply N at 5 g/m^2 monthly, and use a fertilizer with as much K as N.
- All watering is to be deep and relatively infrequent.
- Scarify lightly each two to three weeks.
- If necessary, undertake a deeper de-thatching in mid-summer.
- Cultivate twice a year, by coring or use of a HydroJect machine.
- Mow daily. Use walk-behind mowers, and double cut if extra speed is needed. Groomer attachments can also be used on mowers to increase speed.
- Speed of greens is measured with a Stimpmeter (Fig. 19.29). Table 19.9 gives guidelines for interpretation of its readings.
- Very high speed can be achieved by very close mowing (less than 3 mm), regular light topdressing, use of starvation levels of nitrogen (5 g/m^2 N annually), frequent grooming and allowing the surface of the root zone to dry out. Sustained use of extremely low cut and low N inevitably weakens the turf. It will thin out and be prone to disease.
- Note that excessive speed kills [grass].

MOWING

Mowing height

The aim of mowing is to keep turf suitable for use. Height of cut is mainly decided by type of use. It can range from a couple of millimetres for a bowling

Table 19.6
Example of the effect of a decrease in soil pH on the numbers of fungi present capable of decomposing cellulose (From J I Williams et al. J. Sports Turf Res. Inst. 48: 36, 1972)

Soil pH (mean)	Relative numbers of fungal species
5.7	1
6.3	4.2

Table 19.7
Low pH of the thatch layer accelerates the accumulation of thatch. (From J B Sartain Agron. J. 77: 33, 1985)

Fertilizer	pH of 0–50 mm layer	Relative amount of thatch
Ammonium sulphate	4.0	2.4
Ammonium sulphate + lime	4.5	1.0
IBDU	5.8	1.2
IBDU + ammonium sulphate	4.8	1.9

Table 19.8
Thatch thickness in a Kentucky bluegrass turf as affected by organic sources of N. (From L Berndt et al. Golf Course Management 60(8): 8, 1992)

N application rate (g/m² annually)	Fertilizer	
	Urea	Natural organic
	Thatch thickness (mm)	
0	30	30
10	21	17
20	16	17
40	15	21

Table 19.9
Guide to interpreting and using Stimpmeter readings. (From D A Oatis USGA Greens Section Record Nov/Dec 1990: 1)

Subjective assessment	Stimpmeter measurement (m)
Championship play	
Fast	3.2
Medium fast	2.9
Medium	2.6
Medium slow	2.3
Slow	2.0
Club membership play	
Fast	2.6
Medium fast	2.3
Medium	2.0
Medium slow	1.7
Slow	1.4

green, to 80 mm or more for roadside verges. Mowing height affects every other aspect of turf growth.

In particular, as mowing height decreases:

- Tillering can be stimulated. For those species that respond in this way, turf density increases, provided the height does not go below a critical minimum that varies with species.
- Ground cover is reduced if mowing height goes below the minimum. Weeds are more likely to invade.
- The total mass of roots per plant tends to decrease. This effect is most pronounced with cool-season grasses (Chapter 18); it seems to be slight with warm-season grasses.

Figure 19.27
The blades of a vertical mower

Figure 19.28
Australian-made renovator with scarifying, de-thatching and other options. *Courtesy of Turf Irrigation Services Pty Ltd*

- Turf will have less ability to withstand stress. It must be more carefully managed, especially during times of extra stress, if it is not to be destroyed.
- The volume of soil contacted by roots decreases. Therefore:
- Irrigation must be more frequent.
- Fertilizers must be applied more frequently, but in smaller doses. Application of nitrogen must be kept to a minimum.
- Iron deficiency becomes commoner in some species.
- Disease problems tend to increase if the plants are weakened.
- Mowing must be more frequent. Never remove more than 40% of the green leaf area at any one mowing, and preferably no more than one-third. Greens are typically mown 5–7 times a week.

Conversely, as mowing height is increased:

- Depth of root penetration increases, so ability to withstand drought increases somewhat.
- Water use will increase (Table 19.10). Note that the increase for cool-season grasses is about 25%, but is much less for warm-season grasses.
- Overall plant vigour increases, and with it resistance to diseases.
- Cutting height should always be higher in shaded areas than in nearby areas in full sun.

Bowling greens must be mown short. Golf greens need not be as short, but for them the limit is 4–5 mm. Going down to 3 mm is asking for trouble. Most other turf will be, should be, cut much higher than this. Far too often in Australia, lawns, sports fields and other amenity turf are cut too short. No wonder the turf thins out and is invaded by weeds. Follow the rule that mowing height should be as high as use permits. Cutting height for golf fairways will be about 15–20 mm.

Table 19.10
Example of the effect of cutting height on water losses from turf. The figures are losses from 6 cm high turf as percentages of losses from 3 cm high turf (*From I Biran, et al. Agronomy J. 73: 85, 1981*)

Species	% loss
Warm-season grasses	
Couch	112
Paspalum distichum	103
Buffalo grass	108
Cool-season grasses	
Tall fescue	129
Ryegrass	125

Figure 19.29
Stimpmeter being used to assess the speed of a golf green. *Photograph KA Handreck*

Other hints on mowing

Mowing height is all-important, but other aspects of mowing also affect the management of turf soils.

- Mowing increases the rate of water loss for a while. Either don't mow on very hot days, or irrigate immediately after mowing.
- When changing the height of cut, do it in small steps, especially when reducing height. A sudden change does not give the plants' roots time to adjust.
- Vary mowing patterns so as to spread compaction and the imprinting of wheels on turf. For bowling greens, mow at 45° to the line of play.
- Mowing when the soil is very wet can cause puddling or excessive compaction. Don't!
- Sharp mower blades will cut leaves cleanly. Invasion by disease is less likely through cleanly cut leaves than through battered, jagged stumps.
- Mowers that have their blades ahead of the wheels do not leave the turf marked as do those with wheels ahead of the blades.

Should clippings be removed?

Our answer is 'wherever possible, no'. Clippings contain large amounts of nutrients (Table 20.1). If they are left, these nutrients soon become available to the plants. Much potassium is immediately available; nitrogen becomes available within 14 days. Nutrients lost in removed clippings must be replaced either from reserves in the soil or in fertilizers. Less fertilizer need be used if clippings are left.

The organic matter of clippings provides humus and food for earthworms. These improve soil structure, infiltration rate and drainage. Research has shown that leaving clippings can give a better looking turf (Table 19.11).

Clippings must be removed when:

- they interfere with use, as on bowling and golf greens;
- they damage the turf—this can happen when large amounts of succulent clippings are being produced at the peak of the growing season;
- their presence on the surface gives an unacceptable appearance;
- they add to thatch.

We agree with the first two reasons, and offer thoughts on the other two.

Appearance is very much a matter of personal taste. If a small amount of dry clippings on turf is unacceptable to you, you have three alternatives. You can continue to find it unacceptable and continue to remove clippings. You can change your attitude and find that you can put up with the clippings, knowing that they are good for soil and turf. You can get a mulching mower—this will chop clippings finely, allowing them to fall out of sight between the turf plants. One study in Florida found that couch turf quality was better when it was mown with a mulching mower than with a reel mower. However, mowing is slower with a mulching mower than with reel mowers, so overall costs are higher.

Clippings are mainly leaf blades. These contain only a few percent lignin and therefore decompose quickly (Table 5.1)—usually in a couple of weeks. They usually contribute little to thatch (Tables 19.11 and 19.12). However, the turf is a little softer and the underlying soil not as firm as when clippings are removed. That will not always be acceptable.

We are aware that there has been a tendency in recent years in the USA to remove clippings from golf fairways. Weed problems are lessened with clippings removal. When left, they are said to contribute to disease by increasing humidity within the surface of the turf. That may be so for cool-season grasses under high-humidity summer conditions, but such a combination is rare in Australia. We cannot see any reason to follow this practice in Australia, other than when removal significantly reduces a weed problem that cannot be overcome by other means.

If you have been removing clippings because everyone else does, try leaving them. You may like the results: you don't have to dispose of the clippings either. However, you will need to mow a little more frequently so that the clippings are smaller and fall into the turf more easily. If you find that in your area they do contribute to thatch, you will have to go back to removing them. Many find that turf quality is best with frequent mowing, leaving the clippings, and applying nitrogen at a low rate (10–15 g/m² N annually). Clippings that are mainly older, lignified tissues must not be left.

Table 19.11
In one experiment, turf on which clippings were left was of higher quality than turf from which clippings were removed, provided the soil was cored regularly and the pH was maintained near 7. The measurements were taken four years after treatments started; quality was measured during a heat wave. (From J J Murray and F V Juska Agronomy J. 69: 365, 1977)

Treatment	Thatch weight (kg/m²)		Quality*
	Control	Soil cored	
Clippings left	5.9	5.1	6.7
Clippings removed	5.1	4.9	5.6

*1= poor; 10 = excellent

Cricket pitches: maintenance and preparation for matches

Cricket pitches are unique in the sports turf world. Their soils are chosen for their high clay content; for matches, their bulk density is deliberately increased by heavy rolling to be as close to maximum as is possible; yet both before and after matches they must support a vigorous sward of grass. And all this must often happen on grounds that are used for winter sports as well as cricket. Here is how these miracles can be achieved.

Pre-season

- Start before use for football has finished. Take soil samples and have them analysed as a guide to fertilizer use.
- At the earliest opportunity, repair the surface of the whole pitch square. Remove dead grass and any sandy soil that has encroached onto the square. An industrial vacuum cleaner is useful. Mow and scarify. This is essential if the topdressing soil (screened to 4–5 mm) is to key into the existing soil surface. Use a Levelawn pulled along steel tubing, both across and along the square, to produce a level surface. The soil addition should be no more than 2–3 mm. Reseed or sprig into bare soil.

Table 19.12
Effect of clippings removal and type of mower on thatch under a tall fescue turf (From G L Horst et al. Texas Turfgrass Res. 1979–80. Texas A & M University, College Station)

Treatment	Thatch* (mm)
Standard rotary mower, clippings returned	15
Standard rotary mower, clippings removed	13
Mulching mower	14

* These figures are not significantly different from one another.

- Apply fertilizer and water as needed to produce a vigorous sward of grass, or rather, a grass that has a vigorous root system to at least 100 mm into the soil. Therefore, encourage root growth by using the lowest amount of nitrogen that will give full cover. Roots are also an essential cement in binding the soil mass together.
- Start to prepare the entire pitch square as early as possible in the season, and certainly no later than about three weeks before a match.
- Delay the start of rolling until the surface soil has dried a little.
- Early rollings can be weekly, with two to four passes. Rotate direction through along, across and diagonal to the pitches.
- Actual preparations for a match are started three weeks before a first-class game and about 10 days before club games. The stages of preparation are the same for each, but for club games the whole process is shortened. We give the schedule for first-class games.
- The soil must be evenly wet to at least 100 mm. Irrigate with low-precipitation heads (about 1 mm water per hour) if the soil is not wet enough. This irrigation may take two days. Don't guess: use a soil sampler to check for wetness.
- The first rollings are done with a light (250 kg) roller for 20–30 minutes in the morning and again in the afternoon. Stop rolling as soon as you see water coming to the surface.
- Continue this process for about a week.
- During this time it is essential to irrigate lightly if the surface shows any sign of drying. An alternative or addition to irrigation is to use covers to trap water vapour coming from down the profile and to drop the condensate on the surface.
- Mow as needed during this first week to maintain a height of 12–15 mm. Do not remove the clippings.
- Increase the weight of the roller when the existing weight no longer depresses the soil. Note that for rollers of equal weight but different diameter, the larger the diameter the greater the pressure (weight per unit of contact area) on the soil.
- One week before play begins, irrigate with just enough water to wet the whole profile to 100 mm. The subsoil must not be sticky-wet, otherwise the surface layer may separate from this lower layer.
- Lower the mowing height to 2–4 mm, but don't scalp the surface. Leave the clippings so that they can be bound into the surface of the soil. Sprinkle clippings over any bare patches.
- Roll and cross-roll for up to two hours morning and afternoon.
- Irrigate the surface only as is needed to keep it moist enough for rolling. The aim is to get the grass to slowly and steadily dry the soil to at least 75 mm depth. Slow drying is essential if the soil particles are to bind together into a wicket with the high strength needed to provide a stable, long-lasting wicket.
- The main rollings are designed to compact the soil to some depth into a hard non-crumbling mass that will give the required amount of bounce to the ball. Soil crumbs are destroyed by pressing them together. Great care is needed so that rolling is done when soil moisture is just right. The surface must be dry enough not to flow, yet the weight of the roller must still be able to squeeze water from deeper soil into the drier surface soil. Moisture content is about right when a thumb pressed on the surface makes a slight indentation.
- Final preparation one day before a match is done using rollers weighing 1.5–2 tonnes (Fig. 19.30) in short bursts. Use of such heavy rollers should be delayed until the last stages of preparation, so that the soil surface is not smeared. Each burst is continued until moisture moves to the surface. Don't over-use a heavy roller when the soil is too dry. There is a danger of crumbling the surface.
- The aim is to press the aggregates in the top several centimetres of root zone

into a solid block of soil. The more nearly this soil is moulded into a solid mass, the faster the pace of the pitch.

- The very last rollings are designed to give a glazed surface. A 500 kg roller is used and water is sprinkled on the surface so that it is slightly 'pugged'. More clippings may be applied to help bind bare patches.
- On the first morning of a match, double cut the grass to a final height of 2 mm. Roll with a 500 kg roller to press the remaining grass into the soil so as to give the pitch a glazed, shiny finish.
- Progress towards preparing a pitch that will give good bounce may be gauged with the bounce test described in Chapter 33 or, more accurately, through the use of a Clegg Hammer (Fig. 19.31). Rebound height is closely correlated with Clegg impact value (Fig. 19.32).
- Fast and very fast pace can be produced only if the soil is compacted to more than 80% of its maximum possible dry bulk density. That is why heavy rollers must be used during final preparation.
- It is not possible to produce more than an 'easy' pitch if the critical bulk density is not attained. An example is given in Fig. 19.33.
- Moisture content is critically important to the attainment of high bulk density and therefore fast pace. Fast pitches require that the moisture content of the soil is within a very narrow range. Fig. 19.34 shows that for two New Zealand soils, the optimum moisture content was greater for a strong soil than for one of intermediate strength.
- It is impossible to produce a fast pitch on low-strength soils, including soils that would normally have high strength but now contain much organic matter that has reduced the strength.
- Pace is a combination of ball bounce and friction between the ball and the pitch surface. The higher the bounce, the faster the pitch; the lower the friction, the greater the pace.

The solid block of soil formed by rolling will slowly shrink as it dries. Cracks formed in some root zone soils will be many centimetres apart and will not interfere with ball bounce, provided they are less than 20 mm wide. Many fine cracks can form in less suitable soils, so that under heavy use they can crumble.

Figure 19.30
Self-propelled roller of the type used for preparing cricket wickets.
Courtesy Metray Steel-Fab Constructions

Figure 19.31
Using a Clegg hammer to measure the hardness of a cricket pitch.
Photograph A Lawson and New Zealand and Turf Culture Institute

Figure 19.32
The relationship between ball rebound height and Clegg hammer impact value (0.5 kg hammer) on cricket pitches, using very old and new balls. *From* W M Lush, *J.Sports Turf Res. Inst.* 61: 71, 1985

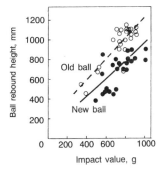

The usual causes of this 'self-mulching' character are the presence of free finely divided lime and/or gypsum, high salinity, a high level of exchangeable sodium or (perhaps) too little exchangeable magnesium in relation to exchangeable calcium. It is better in the long run to correct these causes, but in the meantime, rolling will need to be more prolonged and severe if suitable pitches are to be formed from these soils.

After the match is over

Cricket wickets need much loving care immediately after a match has finished. The grass must be given every chance to grow again.

- Remove any loose debris.
- Scarify as needed.
- Irrigate to wet the full depth of the root zone. The cracking soils normally used in Australia will usually have enough cracks by the end of a match to allow rapid entry of water. Other soils may need coring or spiking to increase infiltration rate.
- Use low-precipitation sprinkler heads so that irrigation rate is low enough to match infiltration rate.
- Topdress as needed to fill worn areas and core holes.
- Boost grass growth with small applications of nitrogen as needed.
- There will usually be no need to re-sow couch if there was a full cover before the match. Otherwise, seed should be sown on any bare patches, or for non-seeding cultivars, plugs of turf from the nursery area should be inserted.
- The whole square may need uniform application of these treatments at the end of a season.

Use of rollers for other turf

Rolling is used to consolidate soil materials during the construction of new areas of turf. Rolling is necessary to help restore the trueness of surfaces damaged by vigorous use, as in contact sports. Light rollers are also used to flatten grass so as to provide the surface required for sports such as lawn bowls. The mowers commonly used for mowing bowling greens also act as rollers.

Rolling can be useful for consolidating loose surfaces of fields for contact sports. In wet weather, biological activity in some soils decreases their bulk density to the point where traction is poor. Play can cause severe damage. Even consolidation by rolling will improve traction and help reduce damage. The 'heel test' given in Chapter 33 will show whether rolling will help.

These are some of the situations in which rolling is a useful management operation. Rolling should always be done for a specific purpose and to give proven benefits. It should not be used just 'because others roll' or 'because we have always done it'. The machinery now used for many management operations means that rolling is needed less than in the past. Generally, rolling should be kept to the minimum needed to get proven results, otherwise the soil can be severely compacted and growth reduced (Fig. 19.35). The outfield of a cricket oval might respond like the soil in Fig. 19.35 if the heavy roller used for wicket preparation is repeatedly run along the same path.

Never roll a soil when it is so wet that mud is squeezed through the turf. It is a waste of time trying to 'roll out' large undulations in turf. Either topdress or, when height has to be changed by more than 20 mm, cut the sod away, add fill or remove soil and replace the sod.

SOME OTHER ASPECTS OF MANAGEMENT

Management for minimum disease

Turf becomes diseased only if disease-causing organisms are present, if the grass

Figure 19.33

Fast pace is possible on a cricket pitch only if the soil is heavily compacted and has on optimum moisture content. *From J W Murphy and T R O Field New Zealand Turf Manag. J.* Nov: 15, 1991

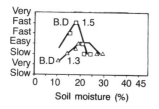

Figure 19.34

The weaker a cricket pitch soil, the more must it be dried before it can be compacted into a very fast wicket. *From J W Murphy and T R O Field New Zealand Turf Manag. J.* Nov: 15, 1991

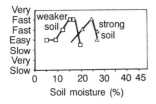

is susceptible, and if conditions for infection are right. Good management will minimize the chances of infection. Attack of turf by pathogens is discouraged by:

- Using a well-balanced fertilization program that takes account of seasonal conditions.
- Encouraging good drainage.
- Watering early in the morning. Watering in the evening or at night will leave the turf wet all night. This gives pathogens maximum opportunity to infect. Some diseases are aggravated by dry conditions; some are worst when the root zone is continuously wet. Learn how to manage watering for minimal disease in your situation. For couch, this will mean infrequent heavy irrigation. The incidence of spring dead spot has increased enormously in couch lawns in Perth following the widespread use of automatic watering systems that are programmed to irrigate every day!
- Not mowing too low.
- Keeping thatch to a minimum.
- Not covering the leaves when topdressing.
- Trying thoroughly matured, weed-free composts (not gassed) as a source of biological control microbes. There is some evidence that such composts can be helpful, but note the cautions in Chapter 17 against clogging the root zone.
- Using wetting agents (Fig. 19.36). We discuss in Chapter 6 the use of wetting agents for controlling dry patch. But wetting agents also help suppress some soil fungi (e.g. *Pythium*) through effects on their outer membranes and those of their spores.
- Using fungicides only to control outbreaks. Applying them 'just-in-case' can increase disease problems by harming microorganisms that keep pathogens in check. Rates of use should be lower for turf on sands than for those on heavier soils.
- Using slow-release fertilizers rather than soluble sources on diseased grass.
- Supplying potassium as needed, especially during the months before a grass goes dormant.
- Using herbicides sparingly and with care. Most herbicides have some effect on non-target grasses. Pre-emergent herbicides do considerable harm when they are applied at the time when desirable turf plants are producing many new roots.
- Not allowing shade to fall on turf that is to be of top quality. Shade increases the susceptibility of turf to diseases. The turf remains wet longer after rain, irrigation or dew. Carbohydrate reserves may be too low to cope with the stress of disease.

Here are some non-chemical measures that will help in disease control.

- Fusarium patch: increase air flow, improve drainage, use more than 10 g/m^2 of N annually, use at least 15 g/m^2 K annually on turf on sand.
- Red thread: ensure that there are no deficiencies of N, P and K.
- Take-all: eliminate compaction, improve drainage, don't use methyl bromide, keep pH low for cool-season grasses, apply K.
- Anthracnose in *Poa annua*: eliminate stresses such as drought, heat and poor nutrition.
- Brown patch: reduce N inputs and boost K, increase air flow, allow the turf to dry between irrigations.
- Dollar spot: fertilize, irrigate, remove excessive thatch.
- Fairy ring (not a disease): fertilize, core, apply wetting agent, try applying sugar to help bacteria control the fungus.

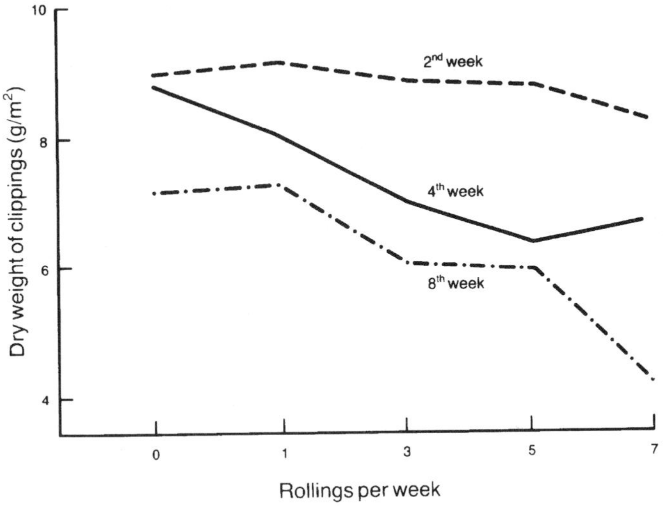

Figure 19.35
Turf growth is drastically reduced through the compaction caused when turf growing on natural soils is repeatedly rolled. *From D E Aldous and J Diamond* Australian Parks and Recreation *Nov: 36, 1975*

2nd week

4th week

8th week

Dry weight of clippings (g/m^2)

Rollings per week

Figure 19.36
Applying wetting agent to a golf green. *Courtesy of Wetta Chem Products, Bunbury, Western Australia*

Herbicides and pesticides

As this book is mainly about growing media, we will not say much about chemicals that are mainly for the above-ground parts of turf. In several places we have discouraged their over-use because of their effects on soil organisms. We do not want to imply that they must never be used. Turf management would be difficult without modern chemicals. But use them sparingly. Repeated appearance of the same disease is a sign that the soil or management needs improving, or that another grass should be grown. Your turf will be healthier if control of diseases is encouraged by sound management.

Poa annua (winter grass, annual meadowgrass, annual bluegrass) is considered by some to be a serious weed of fine turf, to be eradicated at all costs. Others have chosen to learn to live with it and even to enjoy it. For those who wish to eradicate it, observe the following:

- Keep applications of phosphorus to a minimum.
- Allow the root zone to dry out between irrigations. A controlled drought when winter grass is young may enable you to eliminate it for that season.
- Do not renovate at times when the seeds of this species are likely to germinate—late summer to early autumn and late winter.
- Keep nitrogen applications to the minimum needed by the main turf grasses present.
- Use pre-emergent herbicides at appropriate times of the year.
- Keep abreast of the latest findings on the use of selective herbicides or other chemicals for the control of this plant. Rubigan, Embark and Progras can be useful.
- If you can knock *Poa annua* in autumn, you will have better couch growth. It will remain green for longer into late autumn/early winter and should also start to green up earlier in late winter.
- Topdress regularly.
For those who wish to maintain *Poa annua*, observe the following:
- Irrigate lightly and frequently so that this shallow-rooted plant can survive.
- Ensure good drainage.
- Control diseases through the use of systemic fungicides.
- Keep the thatch layer to a minimum thickness so that the roots of *Poa annua* can reach the soil.
- Use fertilizers with NPK ratios in the region of 3–1–3 to 4–1–4.

- Try to find strains with biennial or perennial rather than annual growth patterns.

Moss growth means that the root zone is remaining too wet for too long. A main contributing factor is poor turf cover, typically caused by excessively low mowing height and starvation (of N). By all means temporarily kill the moss with an application of 20 g/m² of iron sulphate combined with 5 g/m² of ammonium sulphate, but it will return unless you improve drainage and increase sward density.

The harmful effects of spills or errors during herbicide use can be overcome with activated charcoal. If testing (Chapter 33) shows that charcoal will be helpful, apply about 35 g/m² in 250 mL of water. Loosen the top 20 mm of soil first. After the charcoal has dried, rake it into the loosened soil. Chemicals that can be detoxified with charcoal include 2,4-D, amitrole, chlorthal, dicamba, endothal, mecoprop, oxadiazon, picloram and propyzamide.

Overseeding

Warm-season grasses go dormant and pale-green or brown in winter in cool areas. They are often overseeded with annual cool-season grasses for winter green.

Prepare the seedbed for overseeding by regular light scarifying during the previous couple of months. Allow mowing height to rise a little just before seeding so that the seed is held in place. Spread the seed evenly by making several passes from different directions. Topdress lightly, then irrigate as needed to keep the seed moist, but not saturated. Keep mowing height a little higher than usual until the new grass is well established. Delay overseeding until the warm-season grass is becoming dormant. Earlier overseeding could weaken the warm-season grass through competition.

The rate of seed application to be used depends on the effect required and on the species being used. For ryegrass, the range is 50–250 g/m², and for bents 20–100 g/m². The lower rates are for a visual effect only; the higher rates are for putting greens.

FINAL COMMENTS

The best way of managing turf is to have an ongoing renovation program based on the present and likely future needs of the turf. Light, frequent renovation operations, as described in this chapter, can take the place of a major renovation that temporarily removes an area from use. Anticipate its needs, so that it never starts to decline. Get to know your turf in all its different moods; act on what you see.

20 FERTILIZING TURF

You will be disappointed if you are looking in this chapter for a recipe that will, when exactly followed, always give you perfect turf with no extra effort on your part. That is impossible; growing turf is not like baking biscuits. Climate, soils, grass species and cultivar, and user requirements, vary much from place to place. Each area of turf must be fertilized according to local conditions and needs.

What this chapter does do is set down some principles. The effects fertilizers have on turf are fairly predictable. Known effects are listed and discussed. Knowledge of these effects will allow turf managers to use fertilizers to give the type of turf they want.

Many factors affect the need to apply fertilizer. The most important are:

- past applications;
- type of turf growth needed;
- soil type;
- grass species and cultivars present;
- presence or absence of clovers;
- whether or not clippings are removed;
- climate;
- time of the year;
- irrigation water quality and amount applied.

These factors won't be discussed in turn, but many references to them will be made in the different sections that follow.

STRATEGY

The simplest way of managing turf nutrition is to supply the turf with adequate levels of all nutrients except nitrogen. Growth is then controlled by application of nitrogen at appropriate times and in appropriate amounts. Potassium supply must match the amount of nitrogen applied (p. 256). Occasionally—from each year to every few years—nutrients other than nitrogen and potassium may be needed.

There are three aids available for deciding whether or not to apply fertilizer. They are:

- looking at the turf, and at its rate of growth;
- trial applications of fertilizers;
- laboratory testing of samples of soil and/or clippings.

Looking

Reduced growth and paleness will be the two main symptoms of poor nutrition. Growth reduction will be seen as longer intervals between when mowings are necessary, or by decreasing amounts of clippings caught in a regular mowing program. The turf will look sparse and weak when deficiencies are severe. Paleness is most likely to come from deficiencies of nitrogen, sulphur or iron. Simple tests that show the cause of paleness are given below. Other deficiencies will either never be seen or they will only rarely produce easily recognizable symptoms.

Check your conclusions by making trial applications of fertilizers, but also look for other causes of poor growth and off-colours. Look for:

- poor soil physical conditions—compaction, waterlogging, excessive thatch;
- lack of water—dry patch, insufficient irrigation;
- disease—root rotting, fungal attack of tops, nematode attack;
- insect attack—mites, root cutters, etc.;
- injury from excessive wear;
- effects of toxic chemicals—over-use of herbicides;
- bruised and brown tips caused by blunt mowers;
- effects of high salinity—white crusts on the soil surface, 'burnt' leaf tips.

Trial applications

A simple way of checking to see whether off-colours or poor growth in turf are caused by nutrient deficiencies is to apply fertilizers and see what happens. Apply the fertilizers in strips across the area. For added interest, make a large template cutout of the chemical symbol of the element suspected of being deficient. Apply the fertilizer around and within the template (Fig. 20.1).

Figure 20.1
The template test. *Photograph J Coppi*

Useful tests are as follows:

- Plants deficient in nitrogen or sulphur are pale green to yellow. Although nitrogen deficiency mainly shows up first in the oldest leaves and sulphur in the youngest, the two deficiencies are easily confused in turf. To check, apply urea and ammonium sulphate separately to adjoining squares or strips of turf. Apply 8.6 g/m^2 urea or 18.9 g/m^2 ammonium sulphate to add 4.0 g/m^2 N. The only difference then is the sulphur applied in the ammonium sulphate. If both green up equally, the paleness was due to nitrogen deficiency. If the area treated with ammonium sulphate greens up in a day or so and the other doesn't, the grass was deficient in sulphur. If neither greens up, or they look even worse, the paleness has some other cause. Deficiencies of magnesium, molybdenum, manganese, boron and iron all give pale grass. The paleness can become worse if nitrogen is applied. Other causes of off colours are listed above.

- Symptoms of iron deficiency (Chapter 14) are fairly easy to recognize. If you are unsure, spray a strip of turf with a solution containing 3 g/L ferrous sulphate. You have your answer if the grass greens up overnight. If it doesn't green up, search for another cause.
- One spraying with a solution of 5 g/L manganese sulphate will give rapid greening if paleness is due to manganese deficiency. This deficiency is likely only on alkaline soils.
- Liming of acid soils may correct molybdenum deficiency but the effect may take months to show up. Spraying pale turf growing in acid soil with a solution of 1 g/L sodium molybdate or ammonium molybdate will give greening over a few days if the paleness was due to molybdenum deficiency.
- Turf growing in heavily irrigated sands composed mainly of quartz can become deficient in boron, especially if pH rises. Spraying with a solution containing 1 g/L boric acid will give rapid greening if turf is deficient in boron.

Laboratory testing

The most useful soil tests are for pH and salinity (Chapter 33). Calcium and magnesium supply will usually be satisfactory if the pH is above 5.5. The other useful tests are for available phosphorus and potassium, followed by calcium and magnesium. Tests of soils for other elements are difficult to interpret for turf and not worth their expense.

Analysis of clippings can give useful information. In the example given in Table 20.1, a check of pH would probably have led just as well to a conclusion to add liming materials, but it would not have shown the need for both calcium and magnesium. Interpretation of analytical results will be easiest if it is possible to analyse clippings from nearby areas of good and poor growth.

Chapter 32 gives methods of sampling soils and clippings.

Table 20.1
Example of the successful diagnosis of combined calcium and magnesium deficiency through analysis of grass clippings. (From *Turf Craft Australia* August: 5, 1992)

Nutrient	Acceptable range (%)	Southport's 12th green (%)
N	2.5–4.0	3.5
P	0.3–0.6	0.44
K	1.5–2.5	2.26
Ca	0.2–1.0	0.05
Mg	0.2–0.5	0.05
S	0.25–0.4	0.42

SUPPLYING NUTRIENTS

In many places in the remaining pages of this chapter, figures in g/m^2 (grams per square metre) are given for the amounts of nutrient elements to be applied to turf. For worked examples showing how to calculate the amounts of different fertilizers needed to supply these amounts of elements, see Chapter 16.

- Fertilizers must be applied uniformly, otherwise growth and colour will be uneven. Use a two-way spreading pattern (Fig. 20.2), applying half the total fertilizer in each direction. Drop spreaders are preferred for small areas. They

Figure 20.2
Pattern to be used when spreading fertilizer with a hand spreader

spread more evenly, but more slowly, than do rotary spreaders. Large areas of turf are most quickly fertilized with rotary spreaders.

- Thoroughly wet the root zone. Then allow the turf leaves to dry before spreading starts. Irrigate immediately after spreading to dissolve the fertilizer and wash it into the root zone. Apply at least 10 mm of water. This water will eliminate losses of ammonia from applied urea. Such losses can be as much as 60% of the application if the urea is not quickly watered into the soil.

Phosphorus

Surveys some years ago of golf greens in Victoria and New South Wales showed that more than 90% had levels of phosphorus well above the optimum. The cause had been repeated application of mixed fertilizers containing more phosphorus than is needed. No doubt there are still many areas of turf that contain unnecessarily high amounts of available phosphorus, but the use in recent years of fertilizers that have P/N ratios more like the approx. 0.11–0.15 found in turf shoots should have stabilized phosphorus levels or allowed them to decline by now.

High levels of phosphorus waste money. More importantly, they may cause or aggravate iron deficiency and encourage the growth of weeds such as *Poa annua* (winter grass). Research has shown that the proportion of *P. annua* in turf increases as the phosphorus level increases. If you do want to maintain a *P. annua* stand you should add annually about 2.2 g/m² P, unless of course there is plenty of P in the root zone already.

The fescues dislike even quite small amounts of phosphorus; they die out quickly as the phosphorus level increases. As a general guide, fine-leaved grasses require less phosphorus than do those with broader leaves.

Phosphorus should be applied as need is shown by soil testing. (Ask for an 'Olsen bicarbonate-P' test or a 'Colwell-P' test. For the Olsen test, the minimum test value for good turf is about 8 parts per million (ppm); 12 ppm and above will certainly be adequate for grasses, especially the warm-season grasses. Anything over about 20 ppm will mean that further applications will not be necessary for many years. The optimum range for the Colwell test is 30–50 ppm. A level of 15–20 ppm in an Olsen test will be needed if clovers are to be part of the sward. Analytical laboratories often interpret test figures as if turf was an agricultural crop. It is not; the lower figures for an adequate level given here should be used for turf.)

An early test of root zone materials will allow the right amount of phosphatic fertilizer to be mixed in before sowing or planting. Seedlings need a higher concentration of P than will be needed during later growth. Further applications should be made every 6–12 months until tests show that there is an adequate level of available phosphorus in the soil. This leaves the soil with a 'bank' of phosphorus that can be drawn on by plants. The 'bank' can be topped-up with small amounts applied once a year or less frequently.

The only loss of phosphorus from most natural turf soils is in clippings. Losses through leaching are usually very small. However, this is not the case for many acid, sandy, root zone soils. In one test in Western Australia, more than 70% of the phosphorus added (as superphosphate) to an acid sand over a period of 20 years was lost by leaching. Such losses from turf sands must be made good by more frequent applications of superphosphate or, preferably, by use of less soluble fertilizers. The choice is between lime-reverted superphosphate (a mixture of lime and superphosphate), reactive rock phosphate and bone meal. The first is useful if pH has to be raised too. Bone meal is rather expensive. Reactive rock phosphate can be used when the sand is slightly acid (about pH 6). First applications to new sandy root zones can be equal parts of superphosphate and rock phosphate, the first to supply the new grass, the second to begin a 'bank' for later. For pure sand root zones, applications of rock phosphate (at about 100 g/m²) could continue annually until the 'bank' is big enough. Leaching of phosphorus from alkaline sands is usually slight, so superphosphate is the preferred fertilizer for them.

We stress that applications should be based on soil tests. However, as approximate guidelines we give the following figures.

For many Australian soils that have never had phosphorus applied, pre-plant applications will need to be in the range 40–130 g/m² superphosphate (400–1300 kg/ha). For clay soils that 'fix' phosphorus (make it less available), this amount may need to be applied annually for several years before the 'bank' of available phosphorus is big enough. Little or no phosphorus will be needed when resowing old turf soils, but check!

The essentially nil P content of sands and the fact that soluble P is easily leached from them, combined with the fact that grass seedlings need more P than do more mature plants, suggests that P applications to sandy root zones should be fairly high. A reasonable pre-plant application might be about 20 g/m² superphosphate and 60 g/m² rock phosphate. The grass may also benefit from inclusion of P in early soluble fertilizer applications.

Clippings annually remove phosphorus equivalent to about 40 g/m² super-phosphate (about 4.5 g/m² P) from very vigorous turf. Losses from most turf will be rather less than this, so annual applications need never exceed this. Where clippings are returned and the 'bank' is large, phosphatic fertilizer will not need to be applied for many years. But where clippings are removed from sandy root zones, the turf might benefit from more frequent applications of P than annual ones. In fact, much P can be lost in drainage water if an application is much over about 2 g/m² P at any one time. Testing will tell when it is needed.

Use general garden fertilizers only as a need for their high P contents has been shown by analysis. Otherwise, use an N–K mixture or an N–P–K mixture with a low level of P (Fig. 20.3). Such mixtures are now widely available, so it is generally not necessary to specially make up your own. But if you do, it is advisable to use it within a few days, otherwise it might set solid.

The N–P–K ratio of clippings is about 8:1:5. When a 'complete' fertilizer is used, its N–P–K ratio should be about that.

In summary, we suggest a rapid setting up of a 'bank' of phosphorus, followed by annual or less frequent additions, as need is shown by soil testing. More is needed where clippings are removed than where they are returned. Where possible, additions should be made after coring, so that some of the fertilizer quickly gets into the root zone.

Calcium

Calcium deficiency is only possible if the soil has become very acid. Where the pH is maintained at 5.5 or above, and where superphosphate and/or gypsum are applied, a deficiency of calcium is impossible.

Magnesium

Most natural soils have an adequate level of magnesium. If their pH is maintained with limestone containing 1–2% magnesium, the level should remain adequate. The level in those that are alkaline or that are irrigated with hard water should also remain adequate.

Magnesium deficiency is most likely on acid sandy soils and when potassium is applied often. Testing these soils for levels of exchangeable cations will soon show up any imbalance between potassium and magnesium. Finely ground dolomite is the best source of magnesium if soil pH has also to be raised. If pH is not to change, magnesium sulphate is the best source. Amounts to use depend on soil test results. A typical application of magnesium sulphate would be 45

Figure 20.3
Some of the fertilizers formulated
specially for turf.   *Photograph J Coppi*

g/m^2. (The magnesium level will be adequate if the ratio of calcium to magnesium, in ppm in an extract, is less than 20.)

Acute magnesium deficiency is most quickly overcome by spraying the turf four or five times with a solution containing 10 g/L magnesium sulphate, at two-week intervals. This is not a substitute for long-term correction of imbalance in the soil, as given above.

Trace elements

Except for iron, deficiencies of trace elements are not common in turf. Many natural soils contain minerals that give adequate supplies. More arrive as impurities in fertilizers and dust. When a soil is known to be deficient in a trace element—perhaps through agricultural experience in the area—the element is most easily applied mixed with superphosphate. Molybdenum deficiency has been reported in turf on acid, sandy root zones.

For zinc, copper and molybdenum, one application every seven years or so should prevent deficiencies. Rates are commonly 0.7–1.4 g/m^2 of zinc and copper sulphates and 0.035 g/m^2 of sodium molybdate. One application of sewage sludge at 200 g (dry)/m^2 would provide about the same amounts of these trace elements. Just make sure that any high level of soluble salts is washed out before it is used.

Manganese is likely to be in short supply only in the most alkaline soils. Lowering soil pH will increase supply. If you can't lower soil pH and trial strips show a need for manganese, you may have to spray affected turf with manganese sulphate solution (2.3 g/L) or a manganese chelate as required. Soil applications may not be successful. A more useful long-term solution is to grow grasses that are adapted to alkaline soils. These include buffalo grass, common couch grass and *Paspalum distichum*.

Boron deficiency is fairly common on sand greens, but is rare in turf growing on natural soils. It is most likely in couch grasses growing on very acid, heavily-leached sands or in some sandy soils if their pH rises to neutrality and higher. It is most simply corrected through applications of borax (sodium borate) at about 1.2 g/m². There is only a small margin between deficiency and toxicity, so don't add more than this at any one time.

Fertilizers containing small amounts of all trace elements are on the market. The amounts of trace elements added in some are too small to have much effect on any serious deficiency. Repeated use can produce toxicities of manganese and perhaps zinc and copper if the root zone becomes very acid.

Iron

Iron is the trace element most commonly in short supply in turf soils. Deficiencies are associated with high soil pH, excessive applications of phosphorus, manganese, copper and zinc, waterlogging and excessive thatch. High concentrations of copper and zinc from long-term applications of fungicides containing them are a common contributor to iron deficiency in sandy root zones. Iron deficiency is common in turf during tropical wet seasons. But grass on acid root zones can also show improvement from applications of iron sulphate, perhaps due more to the sulphur than to the iron. Long-term improvement, but perhaps not elimination of the problem, is achieved by lowering soil pH, improving drainage and removing thatch.

The deficiency is best and most rapidly overcome by spraying with a solution containing 3 g/L ferrous sulphate, applied so as to provide about 1 g/m² (about 0.2 g/m² Fe). Use the solution as soon as it is made. Sprayed paths, etc. will be stained brown. If the water is alkaline, add 0.5 mL sulphuric acid per litre. Otherwise the iron will precipitate as a brown 'rusty' compound that is less effective. Do not irrigate until the next day, so the leaves have had a chance to absorb some of the iron.

The application rate suggested should maintain turf colour for several weeks. Don't be tempted to use very high rates in the belief that you can reduce frequency. As little as 1.8 g/m² Fe can cause severe blackening to some grasses, including Kentucky bluegrass. Many fertilizers formulated for turf contain iron as well as major elements. There is some evidence that overcoming Fe deficiency can reduce the amount of N needed by turf by perhaps 30%.

Low soil temperatures restrict iron uptake by plants. In cool areas, spraying with iron several times during winter to early spring can give better winter colour and earlier spring growth.

All types of iron chelates can be used instead of ferrous sulphate, but they are more expensive and research has shown that they are no more effective as foliar sprays than is ferrous sulphate.

Potassium

Apart from being an essential nutrient, potassium is particularly valuable for turf for the following reasons:

- It encourages thickening of cell walls in turf leaves. This toughens them, so that they are more wear resistant. Toughening is especially useful for grasses such as the bents that are easily injured.
- Thickening of cell walls also increases the resistance of turf grasses to diseases.
- It promotes the storage of carbohydrates. Extra potassium applied when turf is going into dormancy will help it survive and enhance its ability to grow away quickly after dormancy.
- Optimum levels of potassium ensure maximum root growth.
- It has an essential role in controlling the opening and shutting of stomata, and hence in the regulation of water use (Fig. 20.4).

Clippings contain large amounts of potassium (Table 20.2). If they are not removed from turf, this potassium quickly (in a matter of days) becomes available for re-use by the turf plants. Provided that the soil contains good reserves of available potassium, there will be little or no need for additions in fertilizers. A soil test for exchangeable cations will show whether reserves are good or not.

Figure 20.4
Increasing applications of potassium decreased the tendency of Kentucky bluegrass to wilt. Upper curve: 40 g/m² N annually; Lower curve: 10 g/m² N annually. *From* R N Carrow, R C Shearman and J R Watson *Agronomy Monograph* No 30 eds B A Stewart and D R Nielsen *Amer. Soc. Agronomy* p 889, 1990

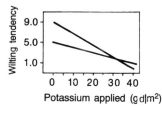

Table 20.2
Example of the amount of nutrients removed annually in clippings from vigorous turf (*From* Bulletin 2, Turf Service Bureau, Milwaukee Sewerage Commission, 1959)

Nutrient element	Annual loss in clippings (g/m^2)
Nitrogen	24
Phosphorus	3
Potassium	13

In general, soils in dry climates (< 500 mm annual rainfall), soils with moderate clay contents (> 10%) and soils with clay minerals of the smectite group usually have good reserves of potassium.

Sandy soils, particularly nearly pure sands with quartz as the main mineral, have repeatedly been shown in surveys to have exchangeable potassium levels below the minimum considered desirable for healthy turf. A sandy soil with an adequate level of potassium for turf will have at least 145 ppm exchangeable K (= 0.37 m.e./100 g soil). On the other hand, about 90 ppm K (= 0.23 m.e./100 g soil) is enough in heavier soils (loams). The ratio of ppm exchangeable K to ppm exchangeable Mg should be less than 5.

However, clippings are removed from much turf. The potassium removed in the clippings must be replaced. Additions are absolutely essential to turf growing in sands.

Water percolating through soils takes some potassium with it. Heavy rain or excessively heavy irrigation can, in time, leach much potassium from soils. However, losses in removed clippings are usually greater than losses by leaching. Sooner or later these losses from turf soils will reduce reserves to deficient levels. Fertilizer potassium must be applied. The amounts of potassium needed depend on:

- level already in the soil;
- whether clippings are removed or left;
- the amount of nitrogen being applied;
- time of year;
- use being made of the turf.

Detail is given later in this chapter.

Potassium is usually supplied by the chloride, sulphate or nitrate salts. Where irrigation waters contain little chloride and where leaching by rain prevents salt build-up, potassium chloride—the cheapest salt—is the preferred source. The sulphate or nitrate should be used when waters and soils are moderately saline. Whether or not potassium nitrate is used will depend on its cost relative to potassium sulphate plus another source of nitrogen. Sufficient potassium is to be supplied to balance the nitrogen being applied, as is discussed later in this chapter.

Nitrogen

If turf is well supplied with all other nutrients, its growth can be regulated by the amount of nitrogen applied. Within limits, more nitrogen gives more shoot growth and a greener, lusher turf; less nitrogen gives reduced shoot growth, sparse coverage and pale turf. Root growth is nearly the opposite of these effects on shoot growth.

The aim of growing turf is *not* to get maximum growth, but to provide a surface and appearance that is acceptable to users. Trying to get maximum growth is silly. It is costly, wastes resources, makes unnecessary work and can ruin turf. Fertilize with nitrogen only to get the results needed by users. The amount of nitrogen needed per month of growing season ranges from perhaps 1 to (rarely) 6 g/m^2. Establishment on sands calls for applications at the upper end of the range for the first year.

One general rule is that no one application of a soluble fertilizer should supply more than 5 g/m^2 of nitrogen. Another is that turf quality is usually best when nitrogen is applied on the basis of 'a little, often'. Remember that slightly hungry grass is tough grass. Growth forced by large amounts of nitrogen is not healthy growth. N applied to slightly hungry grass is very rapidly taken up (Fig. 20.5), so little or none will be lost in drainage water.

Losses in drainage waters of N from soluble fertilizers decrease as the frequency of application increases (for the same total application) (Fig. 20.6). Losses of N are always great if excessive irrigation leads to much drainage of water from the root zone, whatever the method of application.

Figure 20.5
An application of 5 g/m² N to slightly starved Kentucky bluegrass was all taken up by the grass in 48 hours. *From D C Bowman et al. J. Amer. Soc. Hortic. Sci.* 114: 229, 1989

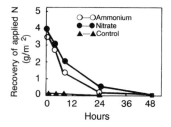

Figure 20.7 shows some typical responses of turf to several different programs for applying nitrogen. In each case there is a rapid increase in turf growth soon after application, followed by a slow decline as the nitrogen is removed in clippings or lost in other ways.

Curve (a) shows what happens when applications are infrequent and large. Most of the time there is little growth; the turf is prone to invasion by weeds. The occasional bursts of intense growth may eventually weaken the turf.

Curve (b) shows the response to more frequent applications. Growth rate is generally greater than for less frequent applications, but there are still quite large bursts of growth.

Curve (c) shows the response to very frequent, small applications. Growth rate is maintained with only small fluctuations.

The very flat curve (d) shows the growth that can be produced by slow-release sources of nitrogen.

Note that the amount of growth produced by fertilization programs (b), (c) and (d) can be raised or lowered, depending on the amount of N applied. Less N, giving less growth, would be shown by curves drawn closer to the base line.

The top curve (e) represents the situation where excessively high levels of nitrogen are applied very frequently. The time may come when some of the weakened turf is destroyed by disease or excessive salinity.

DECIDING HOW MUCH NITROGEN IS NEEDED

No nitrogen

Many mixed pastures containing both grasses and legumes grow well year after year without fertilizer nitrogen. The grasses get nitrogen mainly from that fixed by the legumes. Even in the year of establishment, the grass will get several g/m² of nitrogen from the legumes. These pastures often produce more growth with extra nitrogen. However, the point we want to make is that where very rapid growth is not needed, and where nitrogen is recycled, a mixture of grasses and legumes can survive without fertilizer nitrogen. Some turf is like this. Fertilizer nitrogen is usually never applied where:

- all that is needed is rough ground cover, as for erosion control or among trees in larger parks;
- maintenance cannot be more than several slashings a year;
- natural rain is all the water the turf ever sees;
- more than minimal growth is a nuisance;
- invasion by weeds does not matter;
- turf quality is not important.

At the most, this type of turf may get a complete fertilizer before sowing to aid establishment. Growth is maintained at a low level, but similar to that shown

Figure 20.6
Losses of soluble N in water leaching from a turf root zone were much greater from infrequent, large applications (upper curve) than from frequent, small applications (lower curve). *From G H Snyder et al. Proc. 3rd Intern. Turfgrass Res. Conf. p. 185, 1980*

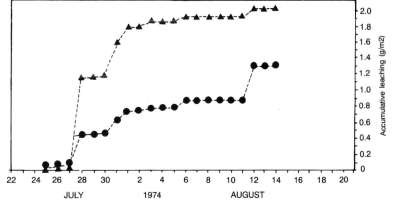

Figure 20.7
Effects on turf growth of different frequencies and rates of application of nitrogen. (a) infrequent, (b) more frequent, (c) frequent small applications, (d) from slow-release fertilizer, (e) excessively large amounts

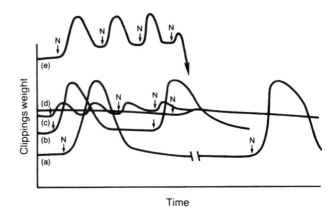

Table 20.3
Approximate ranking of turf grasses according to their need for nitrogen when used in general-purpose turf such as home lawns. The actual amounts needed vary with turf use and environmental conditions, as described in the text. (*From J B Beard Turfgrass Science and Culture* Prentice-Hall, 1973)

Turfgrass	Nitrogen requirement per month of growing season (g/m²)
Carpet grass Centipede grass Chewings fescue	0.75–1.5
Zoysia Perennial ryegrass *Poa annua* Colonial bent grass Tall fescue Buffalo	1.3–1.9
Kentucky bluegrass *Paspalum distichum* Blue couch Creeping bent grass Kikuyu Couch	1.5–2.5

by a lowered curve (d) of Fig. 20.7, through decomposition of organic matter, including clippings.

Nitrogen should not be applied when:

- the turf cannot be irrigated within an hour or so—soluble fertilizers damage turf if not washed from leaves and diluted;
- the grass is dormant;
- the weather is very hot;
- water is in limited supply.

Some nitrogen needed

All turf that has to take people-traffic must be fertilized to maintain acceptable appearance and cover. The amount of nitrogen to be applied will vary with the season and the species of grass being grown. However, it is the grass itself that should guide nitrogen use. It can be damaged by excessive use of nitrogen (see below), and it will thin out and be invaded by weeds if it is not given enough. Be guided more by turf density, amount of ground cover and root growth than by colour.

The aim should be to use as little nitrogen as is needed to give acceptable appearance, complete cover and the type of surface needed. That means that the amount of N applied will vary according to turf use, and the species being grown (Table 20.3). Note that extra N does not compensate for reduced root growth due to soil compaction (Table 19.1).

Golf greens

The turf of golf greens is mown frequently and the clippings removed. Root zones are very sandy and so hold little fertilizer against leaching. Soluble nitrogen must be applied regularly or slow-release fertilizers applied as needed (see below).

The actual amount of nitrogen needed depends on length of growing season, grass species (Table 20.3), losses by leaching, and appearance needed. It will probably be in the range 15–30 g/m²/year, with a maximum of about 3 g/m² per month of growing season. Everything else being equal, the lower the amount of N applied, the greater will be the Stimpmeter speed of the green (Fig. 20.8).

US recommendations are for 12.5–15 g/m² N annually when a green experiences less than 25 000 rounds per year, through 15–20 g/m² N at 25 000, to 20–25 g/m² N for more intense use.

Frequent, small applications are needed to maintain quality, unless slow-release fertilizers are being used. Soluble fertilizers are commonly applied in small amounts every two to three weeks. Use the amount of clippings being removed

Figure 20.8

Increasing applications of N to a golf green reduces its speed. *From* T Colclough *J. Sports Turf Res. Inst.* 65: 64, 1989

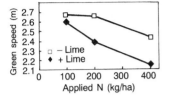

as another guide to when to apply more nitrogen. Less frequent applications give coarse turf.

Bowling greens

The ideal turf for lawn bowls is even, very short and very firm. Lush growth or thatch will not give this. Nitrogen is needed only to produce and then maintain cover. The turf is maintained in a 'just-growing' condition during use. The leaves will be pale green because the turf will be just deficient in nitrogen. Small applications of fertilizer can be made as need is shown by clippings volume and appearance. A popular method of application is as a liquid feed through a boom spray or through hand-held hoses. Once every six weeks is often enough. However, if your equipment is able to quickly deliver very small amounts of N, more frequent application is to be preferred.

Extra nitrogen is normally applied during renovation to ensure rapid surface cover.

The total amount of nitrogen applied will be in the range 10–20 g/m²/year. Increasing applications of nitrogen will give increasing growth, lusher turf and slower playing conditions.

Turf for contact sports

It is very important that groundcover be maintained for turf to be used for contact sports. A strong, dense turf will give good traction to players of vigorous sports (Table 20.4), will cushion the soil against compaction, will withstand even severe wear and will lessen invasion by weeds. Weak turf will soon show bare patches that are difficult to repair.

Figure 20.9

Effect of N applications on the extent of perennial ryegrass ground cover on soil and sand root zones, after one month of wear. *From* P M Canaway *J. Sports Turf Res. Inst.* 60: 8, 1984

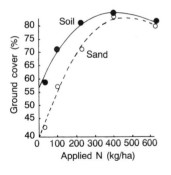

Table 20.4

Example of the effect of nitrogen application rate on some characteristics of turf, in this case a Kentucky bluegrass sod. Note: Only the general trend is relevant to other turf. The application rates must not be taken as applying directly to other species and other situations. (*From* K R English MS Thesis, Michigan State University, 1971)

Nitrogen application rate (g/m²/month)	Annual clippings dry (g/m²)	Relative strength of the turf	Rhizome dry weight (g/m²)
0	52	78	10.8
1.7	202	100	9.7
3.4	286	69	13.1
6.7	636	51	4.7
13.4	947	36	1.5

Research on football pitches in the UK has provided us with a beautifully comprehensive understanding of the effects of N on all aspects of turf for football. Some of the results are summarized in Figs 20.9 to 20.15. What a pity we do not have similar data for a range of Australian conditions.

The figures show that for perennial ryegrass, as N application increased from zero, there was a rapid increase in ground cover, up to a maximum at about 40 g/m² (Fig. 20.9). On sand, this increase was accompanied above a certain point by a decrease in root growth (Fig. 20.10), so that root to shoot ratio declined as N applications increased (Fig. 20.11). Traction first increased with increasing N (Fig. 20.12) and then declined. Note that traction peaked at a much lower N application rate (a little over 20 g/m²) than did ground cover (Fig. 20.9). Increasing N increased the moisture content of the grass shoots (Fig. 20.13), leading to poorer wear tolerance (Fig. 20.14).

Figure 20.10

Root weights of perennial ryegrass as affected by N application. *From P M Canaway J. Sports Turf Res. Inst. 60: 19, 1984*

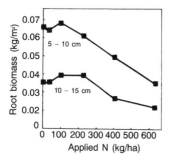

Figure 20.11

The proportion of perennial ryegrass plants that are roots declines markedly as N applications increase. *From P M Canaway J. Sports Turf Res. Inst. 60: 19, 1984*

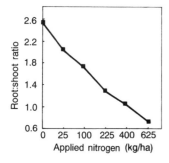

Another interesting finding was that the infiltration rate of the sand root zone decreased sharply as N application rate increased (Fig. 20.15), as a result of roots clogging pores and increasing thatch thickness. Such clogging must be relieved by spiking (Chapter 19) and topdressing.

The general trends shown by these figures are universally applicable, but the optimum amount of N needed for different grasses and different climatic and soil situations will often be different. Thus annual rates of N suggested for south east Queensland are in the range 16 g/m^2 N for low-maintenance grounds to 40 g/m^2 N for high-maintenance grounds. The total application is split into four applications, in September, October, January and April.

Monthly applications of nitrogen needed to maintain turf quality will probably be in the range 2–3 g/m^2. The lower the cut, the less the amount of nitrogen needed. On the other hand, overfertilized, lush turf will be more easily damaged than turf hardened by lower applications. Aim for a full cover of 'hardened', tough turf with a carefully controlled minimum N application program. Let the turf be your guide to nitrogen use. It is always a better guide than the Grounds Committee, if you read it correctly. Sometimes, you may have to argue on its behalf.

Clippings are normally not removed, so the monthly (growing season) amounts of nitrogen needed will probably be in the range 1–3 g/m^2. The amount will be towards the upper end during the first couple of years after establishment, dropping back to the middle or lower end for older swards. Some turf in the tropics may need as much as 35 g/m^2 N annually.

Home lawns

Often all that is required of home lawns is that they look good. That usually means that they should be green and reasonably uniform. They usually get fertilized infrequently, after the style of curve (a) of Fig. 20.7. Feasts, often to the point of burning by high salinity, are followed by long periods of famine.

Where clippings are removed, most all-grass lawns will have an acceptable appearance with annual applications of nitrogen at the rate of 6–20 g/m^2, with 12–20 g/m^2 being most commonly needed. This should be spread over 5–7 applications. Less nitrogen need be applied to lawns containing clover, but when clippings are removed, the saving may be no more than 4 g/m^2 of nitrogen per year.

But clippings need not be removed. When left, the amount of nitrogen applied can be reduced. A lawn with clover uniformly throughout it may not need any at all. However, most lawns still benefit from some extra nitrogen to replace that lost by leaching or conversion to nitrogen gas. Let the lawn be your guide, but the annual amount of nitrogen needed may be no more than 5 g/m^2. Most such home lawns can be maintained in excellent condition through an annual application of slow-release N plus a little P and K.

General turf

By general turf we mean golf fairways, playgrounds, parks and other large areas of turf, often under the care of local authorities. Use varies from heavy to relatively light. A turf quality that is lower than that of the areas discussed so far is usually acceptable.

Often, however, quality is very bad because of the incompetence of those who control finance for the maintenance of these areas. Typically, so little money is set aside for a regular fertilization program that the much more expensive operations of partial or complete returfing become necessary. The cheapest course of action in the long term is to apply fertilizer as needed to maintain cover and quality. That usually means more than a once-a-year application given almost as an afterthought. Rather, it involves a careful matching of fertilizer applications

Figure 20.12
Traction of perennial ryegrass turf as affected by N applications. See Figure 17.18 for an explanation of Nm. *From P M Canaway J. Sports Turf Res. Inst.* 61: 104, 1985

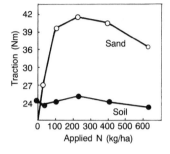

to each area of turf, taking into account type and intensity of use, the species being grown, climate, etc.

It could well be that some areas need no fertilizer at all. However, most are best maintained with an annual application of a slow-release fertilizer. The amount of N needed can be minimized by returning clippings and by growing a legume as part of the sward. The annual rate of application will probably approach that given for home lawns.

During establishment

Rapid cover of the ground after seeding or sprigging can be achieved only through careful attention to nutrition. Before planting, apply a phosphatic fertilizer according to the guidelines on p. 244. Apply about 2 g/m² N and 1 g/m² K (10 g ammonium sulphate plus 2.2 g potassium sulphate per square metre) and water it in thoroughly. Sow the seed or sprigs. Once the seed has germinated or the sprigs have started to grow, apply more N and K every two weeks at about the rate given above. Vary the rate and frequency to give the rate of growth needed.

Greens on pure or high-sand root zones must be fertilized frequently for rapid establishment. Apply 5 g/m² N weekly for at least six weeks. P and K may be needed in these feeds. There is some evidence that incorporation of poultry manure into the surface of the seedbed can enhance germination and speed cover. This could happen because the organic matter allows the seed to remain moist during germination, because of the nutrients supplied or because of improved retention of some nutrients against leaching. Some caution is needed in the use of poultry manure because of the possibility of it reducing the infiltration rate.

SUPPLYING BALANCED AMOUNTS OF NITROGEN

Fertilizers supplying nitrogen

Figure 20.13
The succulence of perennial ryegrass turf increases with increases in N applications. *From P M Canaway J. Sports Turf Res. Inst.* 61: 100, 1985

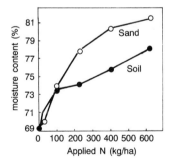

Table 15.3 lists the main soluble fertilizers supplying nitrogen. Ammonium sulphate is the cheapest source and the one most commonly used on turf. It is the most common nitrogen carrier in 'complete' turf fertilizers, although urea, ammonium nitrate and potassium nitrate may be used in some formulations. Most of these fertilizers increase soil acidity; lime application may eventually be necessary. They are all very soluble in water, and so they increase soil salinity. They must be diluted with irrigation water soon after application if turf is not to be damaged. Turf leaves should be dry before dry fertilizers are applied, otherwise they will be 'burnt' by high concentrations of fertilizers dissolving in droplets of water on them.

'Complete' fertilizers should be granulated or prilled. If they are not, spreading (especially through spinners) will separate the different fertilizer compounds. Different growth rates across the direction of spreading can give turf a streaky appearance. Separation will be less through drop spreaders.

Greens and other areas of intensively managed turf are often fertilized with liquid fertilizers applied through proportioners and hand-held hoses or boom sprays (Fig. 20.16). With a little care, coverage can be very uniform. Use a commercial feed or mix your own using the figures in Table 16.17. A typical feed containing 400 ppm N and 300 ppm K, applied at a rate of 5 L/m² would provide 2 g N and 1.5 g K per square metre. Application through automatic watering systems is less satisfactory because the application rate varies with the distance from sprinkler heads and the amount of overlap.

Slow-release and organic sources of nitrogen

Synthetic slow-release sources of nitrogen have increased in importance in recent years. The main ones used are various methylene ureas (e.g. Azolon, Nitroform,

Figure 20.14

Effect of N applications on the extent of perennial ryegrass ground cover on soil and sand root zones, after six months of wear. *From P M Canaway J. Sports Turf Res. Inst.* 60: 8, 1984

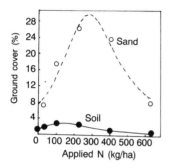

Figure 20.15

Clogging of pores in this sand root zone was nearly complete when perennial ryegrass was heavily fertilized. *From P M Canaway and R A Bennett J. Sports Turf Res. Inst.* 62: 204, 1986

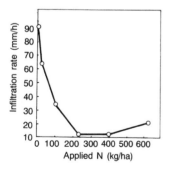

Nutralene and liquid formulations), crotonylideneurea and IBDU. There are a number of NPK formulations based on these products. Brand names include Floranid, Nitrophoska, Triabon, Oz Gro 4 and N-Duragreen. Only the latter has both N and K in slow-release form. Also available are coated products such as sulphur-coated urea and resin-coated products such as Once.

While they are more expensive than soluble fertilizers, they offer several advantages over them.

- They are cheaper to spead because they are typically applied only once or twice a year.
- They allow heavy applications of N without the risk of burning the grass.
- Losses of N via drainage waters are much lower than when soluble fertilizers are used.
- Thatching tends to be less with some of them than with soluble fertilizers applied at the same rate of N.
- Turf quality can be better than is produced by infrequent soluble fertilizer use, because of the even release of N over time.
- Reduction in soil pH is less with them than from equivalent applications of ammonium sulphate.
- In areas where the climate is relatively even for some months at a time, slow-release and soluble fertilizers can give turf of equal quality.

The main disadvantages are:

- Whether lower spreading costs outweigh their three- to five-fold higher cost per unit of N is for users to work out for local conditions. NPK mixtures are even more expensive than the equivalent soluble fertilizers.
- Coated products, especially those with large granules, cannot be used on closely cut turf because they are chopped up during mowing or scarifying. Those with brittle coatings are easily ruptured by normal traffic.
- Results with them have been disappointing in cool weather, because the rate of release of nitrogen is often too slow for optimum growth.
- Coated products especially–but this applies to some extent to them all, release N too rapidly in hot weather. If there is much in a soil when hot weather arrives, turf can be overstimulated. Forced growth in a warm autumn is prone to serious damage by frosts.
- They must be spread very evenly.
- Sulphur-coated products acidify the soil and this reduces the decomposition rate of thatch.
- The slow-release N sources need to be used in mixtures, or K (and P) need to be mixed with them before they are applied.

Research is continuing into the best ways of using these products. Here are some results gleaned from local and overseas reports.

- In trials in Melbourne, resin-coated products released too rapidly in hot weather. Maintenance of turf was good with N-Duragreen, Rennomix, sulphur-coated urea, IBDU and Azolon. Nitrophoska and MagAmp might have performed better if they had been added at higher rates. (In the same trial, fowl manure performed poorly.)
- Australian Turfgrass Research Institute personnel have found that it is often necessary to use a combination of slow-release and soluble fertilizers for best results. Ratios and rates will vary with cultivar and climate.
- For grasses that require plenty of N in summer (the warm-season grasses), a single spring application can give as good turf quality as several applications of soluble N.
- IBDU has several times been reported to give superior growth in winter to that provided by urea formaldehyde. However, the results might have been different if urea formaldehydes (= methylene ureas) of different formulation had been used.

Figure 20.16
Liquid-feeding a bowling green via a hand-held hose and simple venturi dilution device.   *Photograph J Coppi*

Figure 20.17
The establishment of a creeping bentgrass on a sand root zone was faster when it was fertilized with IBDU than with eight applications of urea giving the same amount of N.
From A R Mazur and C B White Agron. J. 75: 977, 1983

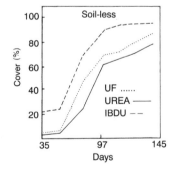

- IBDU and urea formaldehyde have been reported as giving equally good results in summer.
- Two applications, in October and May, might be best for cool-season grasses (according to information from France, transposed to the southern hemisphere).
- IBDU mixed into the top of the root zone at 29 g/m² N gave more rapid grass cover during establishment than did eight applications of urea (Fig. 20.17).
- In UK football pitches, two applications of IBDU (in November and March—southern hemisphere) gave better traction than did four to six dressings of ammonium sulphate. Total N application was 22.5 g/m².
- IBDU applied at the end of summer in the UK gave better turf growth the following spring
- In Ireland, crotonylideneurea gave more even growth than other materials. IBDU was reported to be slow and urea formaldehyde inferior. All were applied at 16.3 g/m² N.
- There is general agreement that two applications a year give more even growth than one.

Other slow-release souces of nutrients

Soil organic matter continues to be important. Composted plant 'wastes', including lawn clippings, are a valuable addition to soil organic matter. Many golf clubs recycle clippings through composts. Make sure that composts are weed-free before they are applied to turf. Fumigate them with methyl bromide if necessary.

Many blood-and-bone formulations are available. They supply N and P in slow-release forms, but no K unless it has been deliberately added. They are useful in seedbeds, but the imbalance between the nutrients means that they should not be used regularly on turf.

Organic fertilizers can be useful when applied at renovation time. More frequent use is unwise. Over-use can increase the amount of disease, may seal the soil surface, increase thatch formation and give soft, easily damaged turf.

Times to apply nitrogen

Soluble N is to be applied when extra turf growth is needed—if seasonal conditions allow that growth.

For warm-season grasses, fertilizer nitrogen is applied from soon after the break of dormancy in spring to late summer in southern areas. An attempt to stimulate early growth with large applications of N may damage the turf. Early spring green-up is best achieved through a light application of N in late autumn. Use a fertilizer with an N:K ratio of 1–2 applied at about 2.5 g/m² N. Soluble fertilizer is preferred, but some of the N can be supplied via IBDU, as there will still be some release of soluble N from it in cool soil. Timing is important. The application should be no later than 30 days before the first frost is likely. That makes it April–May in southern Australia. Applying the fertilizer too early will stimulate shoot growth at the expense of root growth, and can give lush growth that is prone to damage by frost.

For warm-season grasses that are to be oversown with cool-season grasses for winter colour, the N application should be not later than 30 days before seeding.

The longer the growing season, the earlier the start of fertilization and the later the finish. But even in the tropics, any tendency for turf to become dormant for a while must be respected.

In colder southern areas, warm-season grasses become dormant in the coldest two to four months. Applying nitrogen then may green them up a little, but it will often do more harm than good. Any top growth will be at the expense of food reserves in the roots. Winter applications of N appear to be more harmful in areas of winter rainfall than in those areas where winters are relatively dry.

Reduce the amount applied during the hottest month or two. In fact, anything higher than moderate applications in summer tends to produce lanky growth that must be cut very frequently if scalping is to be prevented. This tendency is particularly noticable in *Paspalum distichum*.

In areas where warm-season grasses are overseeded with cool-season grasses for winter green, some nitrogen is usually needed in winter to feed the cool-season grass. Keep applications to 1–2 g/m² N each month. Much more nitrogen than that will give excessive growth in early spring, which will tend to shade out the warm-season grass.

Cool-season grasses grow most rapidly in autumn and spring and slow down in winter. In summer in cooler areas they will continue to grow with irrigation, but in hotter areas they tend to become dormant. Little or no nitrogen should be applied in the hottest weather. The large flush of growth commonly produced in early spring should not be further stimulated.

A typical program for bentgrass turf is: start in mid spring with 2.5–3.5 g/m² N (less than 25% slow-release); decrease the rate in late spring; don't apply any in early summer; add an organic source in mid-summer at 1 g/m² N; apply 1–1.5 g/m² N in late summer, as needed; autumn–winter applications will total 5–10 g/m².

As already discussed, regular (e.g. each two to three weeks) applications during the growing season give the most even growth, if soluble sources are being used. The frequency, as well as the rate, can be reduced when clippings are left. If rapid coverage is required—as during establishment or when injured turf is being repaired—application should be more frequent (e.g. fortnightly) and the total amount higher than for maintenance. Providing a constantly high plane of nutrition is essential in the first six to twelve months of a new area of turf.

Nitrogen–potassium balance

Turf grasses take up nitrogen and potassium approximately in the ratio 3:2 (Table 20.2). When clippings are left and when the soil has a large reserve of potassium, fertilizer potassium may not be needed, even when small amounts of nitrogen are being applied.

Potassium will be most needed when clippings are removed from turf on sandy root zones. It is essential that all nitrogen applied to such turf is accompanied by potassium at a ratio of at least 3:2. For turf on sandy root zones, especially pure sands, the ratio should be 1:1. A high sodium concentration in the irrigation water also calls for an N–K ratio close to 1:1. There is little need for most of the year to add more K than these ratios give - most of the extra will be lost in drainage waters. Such losses of K will increase as the pH of the root zone decreases. That is another good reason for maintaining root zone pH above 5.5.

However, late-autumn fertilizer applications should have N–K ratios of about 1:2.

Less fertilizer potassium will be needed by turf growing on less sandy soils. Some will still be needed if clippings are being removed. The best guides to needs are soil tests and the 'toughness', or lack of it, of the turf. Otherwise, a fertilizer with an N–K ratio of about 3:1 could be used for most of the year.

Effects of excessive fertilizer use

Turf overfed with nitrogen is like overfed people; both have large tops and are unhealthy. If you follow the strategy outlined in this chapter and apply fertilizer to just maintain turf density, you will not be applying excessive amounts. But if you repeatedly apply nitrogen to always have bright green turf, you may soon run into problems.

Table 20.5
The turf grass diseases listed below are often associated with nitrogen applications as shown

Excessive nitrogen	Low nitrogen
Brown patch	Dollar spot
Damping off (*Pythium*)	Red thread
Fusarium patch	Rusts

Figure 20.18
Increasing the rate of ammonium nitrate application to turf increases the acidity of both soil and thatch. *From D A Potter et al. Agron. J. 77: 367, 1985*

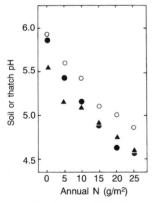

○ = Lower soil (2 – 4 cm)

● = Upper soil (0 – 2 cm)

▲ = Thatch

The fescues evolved in areas of acid soils of low fertility. If fertilized excessively, they are weakened and invaded by unwanted plants (= weeds), including ryegrasses and *Poa annua*. In mixed swards, it is possible to shift the proportions of species back and forth through changes in fertility.

Excessive use of nitrogen causes or contributes to the following problems:

- injury through high salinity; this can happen even when lower applications are not watered in quickly;
- excessive leaching of calcium, magnesium and potassium caused by repeated use of ammonium salts;
- rapid decrease in soil pH (Figs 11.10 and 20.18), perhaps leading to manganese toxicity and death of earthworms;
- increased lushness (Fig. 20.13);
- thatch build-up;
- more fungal diseases (Table 20.5);
- poorer root systems (Table 20.4);
- reduced ability to withstand drought and heat stress (after heavy applications in spring);
- decreased turf strength (Table 20.4);
- decreased heat tolerance;
- losses of nitrogen through leaching; groundwaters are polluted.

Of course excessive use of fertilizer nitrogen rapidly empties bank accounts and uses fossil fuels unnecessarily. If you have been applying fertilizer nitrogen at high rates, try gradually reducing the rate. Be guided by what happens. Greener is not always better!

CALCULATIONS

1. How much ammonium sulphate is needed to apply 5 g/m² N to an area of 500 m²?

Total N needed = 500 × 5 = 2500 g.
Ammonium sulphate contains 21.2% N (Table 15.3).

Therefore, amount of ammonium sulphate $= 2500 \times \dfrac{100}{21.2}$
$$= 11\ 792\ g = 11.8\ kg.$$

(Otherwise, use Table 20.6).

2. How much potassium chloride is needed to supply the turf in Calculation 1 with N and K in the ratio 3:2?

Total K needed = 2500 × ⅔ g = 1667 g.
Potassium chloride contains 52.4% K (Table 15.3)

Therefore, amount of potassium chloride $= 1667 \times \dfrac{100}{52.4}$ g
$$= 3181\ g = 3.2\ kg$$

2. How much complete fertilizer of composition 18–2–12 is needed to apply 4 g/m² N to an area of 800 m²? What amounts of P and K will it supply?

Total N needed = 800 × 4 = 3200 g.

Fertilizer needed $= 3200 \times \dfrac{100}{18} = 17\ 778$ g
$$= 17.8\ kg.$$

It will supply $\dfrac{2 \times 4}{18} = 0.44$ g/m² P

and $\dfrac{12 \times 4}{18} = 2.67$ g/m² K.

3. It has been decided to use potassium nitrate as a pre-dormancy liquid feed for a couch golf green. The area is 480 m² and the required application of K is 3 g/m². How much potassium nitrate is needed?

Table 20.6
Amounts of nitrogenous fertilizers needed to supply different amounts of nitrogen to turf

Nitrogen carrier	Amount of carrier needed to supply N at the following rates (g/m²)							
	1	2	3	4	5	10	20	30
Ammonium sulphate	4.7	9.4	14	19	24	47	94	141
Ammonium nitrate	2.9	5.7	8.5	11	14	29	57	86
Urea	2.1	4.3	6.4	8.6	10.7	21	43	64
UF-38	2.6	5.3	7.9	10.5	13	26	53	79
IBDU	3.2	6.5	9.7	13	16	32	65	97
SCU (36% N)	2.8	5.6	8.3	11	14	28	56	83
Mixed fertilizer, 5% N	20	40	60	80	100	200	400	600
10% N	10	20	30	40	50	100	200	300
15% N	6.7	13	20	27	33	67	133	200
20% N	5	10	15	20	25	50	100	150

Total K needed = 3×480 = 1440 g.

Potassium nitrate contains 38.7% K.

Therefore, amount of potassium nitrate = $1440 \times \dfrac{100}{38.7}$ g = 3721 g.

A typical liquid feed strength is 400 ppm K. How many litres must the 3721 g potassium nitrate be dissolved in? From Table 16.17, 0.26 g/L potassium nitrate gives 100 ppm K.

Therefore number of litres = $\dfrac{3721}{0.26 \times 4}$ = 3578 L.

For a proportioner set at 100: l, the 3.72 kg of potassium nitrate would need to be dissolved in about 36 L of water.

4. A fertilizer company brochure states that their product having an analysis of 15.5–0.2–6.0 should be used at the rate of 50 g/m² each 6–8 weeks. Does this rate give excessive amounts of nitrogen?

Each application applies $50 \times \dfrac{15.5}{100}$ g/m² N = 7.75 g/m² N

This is too much in one application.

If the growing season is of 8 months (34 weeks), the total applied per year would be about $\dfrac{34}{7} \times 7.75 = 37.6$ g/m² N.

This is excessive for all but the most intensively managed turf.

SUMMARY

- Correct deficiencies of P and trace elements.
- Adjust pH.
- Apply the minimum amounts of nitrogen needed to achieve the desired groundcover and appearance.
- Accompany nitrogen applications with potassium, varying the proportion with season, soil, and clippings' fate.
- Remember that soil physical conditions are at least as important as nutrition.

21 SALINITY: A GROWING PROBLEM

All waters (except very pure distilled water) have some salts dissolved in them. They could all be said to be saline.

However, the word saline is used mainly for waters that have concentrations of salts that can harm plants. Seawater is highly saline. Many well and bore waters are moderately saline and therefore undrinkable; they are then said to be brackish. Some creeks and rivers are moderately or slightly saline if they are fed by saline groundwaters. Most domestic water supplies have low concentrations of salt and so are not considered to be saline.

Waters in growing media also contain salts. They come from the medium itself, from irrigation water and from fertilizers. A low level of salinity from plant nutrients is essential to plant growth. But as salinity rises, plant growth suffers. As we shall see, plants differ in their tolerance to salinity, and to different types of salts.

TYPES OF SALTS IN WATER

Before going any further it is worth remembering that salts are combinations of electrically charged ions (Chapter 4). These ions separate from one another when a salt dissolves in water. Thus water in which sodium chloride and potassium nitrate are dissolved will contain sodium, potassium, chloride and nitrate ions. The simplest way of describing the salinity of a water is to list the ions in it.

Natural waters

The ions present in greatest concentrations in natural water are:

Cations	Anions
sodium (Na^+)	chloride (Cl^-)
calcium (Ca^{2+})	carbonate (CO_3^{2-})
magnesium (Mg^{2+})	bicarbonate (HCO_3^-)
	sulphate (SO_4^{2-})

Different waters can have very different proportions of these ions. Some typical analyses are given in Table 21.1. If there is no carbonate in the water,

Table 21.1
Ionic composition of some water supplies (The concentrations are in mg/L.)

Water supply	Na^+	Ca^{2+}	Mg^{2+}	Cl^-	HCO_3^-	SO_4^{2-}	Total alkalinity (as $CaCO_3$)	EC dS/m
Melbourne	4	3	1	6	—	1	—	0.04
Sydney	10–39	2–12	2–7	16–27	—	2–14	—	0.1–0.3
Brisbane	21–46	43–78	39–88	32–111	72–101	1–85	51–72	0.3–0.6
Adelaide	78–106	23–36	14–27	142–195	70–164	8–40	50–117	0.5–0.8
Perth	36–140	3–30	4–12	57–240	10–140	8–70	7–100	0.2–0.9

its total alkalinity is approximately 0.71 × (concentration of bicarbonate).

Natural waters also contain low concentrations of many other elements. For most, the amounts are too low to be either harmful to plants or particularly beneficial, if they are nutrients. The main exception is boron (p. 266).

Comments on the effects of different proportions of ions on the quality of water used for irrigation are given on p. 265.

Water in growing media

In addition to the ions listed in the previous section, water in growing media also contains ions from fertilizer salts and soil particles. The main extra ions are potassium, ammonium, nitrate and phosphate. The concentrations of these will depend on the amounts contributed by media components, plus the amounts added in fertilizers, minus amounts taken out by plants, held by colloid surfaces, or lost by leaching.

UNITS OF MEASUREMENT

The salinity of water is given either by the amount of salts dissolved in it (total soluble salts, or *total dissolved solids* (TDS)) or by its ability to conduct electricity—its *electrical conductivity* (EC). Increasing total dissolved solids gives increasing electrical conductivity.

The units used for salinity are:

- For TDS
  — parts per million (ppm)
  — milligrams per litre (mg/L)
  (1 ppm = 1 mg/L)
- For EC
  — deciSiemens per metre (dS/m)
  — milliSiemens per cm (mS/cm)
  — microSiemens per cm (µS/cm)
  (1 dS/m = 1 mS/cm = 1000 µS/cm)
  (1 µS/cm = 0.001 dS/m)

Older books used the units millimho/cm (often incorrectly shortened to 'millimho') and micromho/cm. The metric term for 'mho' is 'Siemens', with 1 Siemens = 1 mho. Also, for a while the unit milliSiemens/cm was used to describe the salinity of growing media and the term microSiemens/cm for waters. Another unit in common use is the 'CF' (standing for conductivity factor). A solution with a CF of 10 will have an EC of 1 dS/m.

The standard term now being used internationally is dS/m, the numbers for which are the same as for the older mS/cm. Because of this wide usage, we have chosen to use dS/m throughout this book.

The EC of a solution can be converted to TDS as follows:

$$EC \text{ (in dS/m)} \times 640 = TDS \text{ (in ppm)}$$

This conversion is only approximate; the actual formula depends on the types of salts present.

Salinity is now usually given by EC, measured as described in Chapter 33.

WHERE DO THE SALTS COME FROM?

Consider the water cycle:
The sun evaporates water from sea, lakes, soil and plants.

- Each water molecule is separate, pure, uncontaminated.
High in the sky, water molecules join together into droplets around tiny dust particles.
- First salts, dissolved from the dust. EC 0.005 dS/m
Falling rain. Drops of water pick up more dust.
- More salts, some from sea spray blown inland, some from pollution. EC 0.04 dS/m.

Rain hits plant leaves.
- More salts, dissolved from the leaf surfaces. EC 0.130 dS/m.

Rain hits soil, runs across its surface.
- Some salts removed by soil particles; others dissolved from soil particles. EC 0.2 dS/m.

Rain soaks into soil, becomes soil water.
- Some salts removed by soil particles; others dissolved from soil particles. EC 0.39 dS/m.

Soil water flows slowly through the soil, then seeps out as mineral spring water.
- More salts from minerals in the soil. EC 0.9 dS/m.

Spring water flows into stream, then river, then storage dam.
- Salts diluted by rain. EC 0.42 dS/m.

Some water evaporates from the dam.
- Concentration of salts in the remaining water increases. EC 0.5 dS/m.

Dam water becomes tap water.
- Concentration of salts in the remaining water increases during 'purification'. EC 0.52 dS/m.

Tap water becomes base for liquid feed in a nursery.
- Fertilizer salts are dissolved in the water. EC 1.7 dS/m.

Plants standing in pots on a sealed surface are watered with the liquid feed.
- Some salts are removed from the water by plant roots, some water is transpired. Concentration of salts in the remaining water increases. EC 5.0 dS/m.

Next watering. Pot leaching time. Leachate runs to the waste water system, mingling with sewage.
- More salts from water softeners, urine, cooking, industry. EC 2.25 dS/m.

Back to the sea again, as sewage effluent.
- Evaporation leaves the salts behind. The sea gets saltier. EC 54 dS/m.

The numbers are 'fair average' for a dry climate; many would be lower in a wetter climate.

Salts, therefore, enter waters naturally from a variety of sources, with soils being the main source. People provide other salts in fertilizers and waste products.

ASSESSING WATER QUALITY

The first step in assessing water quality is to determine its EC. The method is given in Chapter 33. Then compare the measured figure with the data in the first line of Table 21.2.

Table 21.2
Generalized irrigation water quality guidelines (*From 'Water Quality'* Leaflet 2995 Division of Agricultural Sciences, University of California, 1979)

Measurement	No problem	Increasing problems	Unsuitable
Effect on plant growth:			
EC (dS/m)	< 0.75	0.75–3	> 3
Sodium (evaluated by the SAR*)	< 3	3–9	> 9
Chloride (ppm)	140	140–350	> 350
Boron (ppm)	< 0.5	0.5–2	> 2
For overhead sprinklers:			
Sodium (ppm)	< 70	> 70	
Chloride (ppm)	< 100	> 100	
Bicarbonate (ppm)	< 90	90–520	> 520
Effect on soil permeability	See Table 21.3		

*SAR = sodium adsorption ratio (see Specific ion effects, below, and Chapter 33).

Table 21.3
Guidelines for assessing the effect of water on soil permeability (*From* R S Ayers and K K Tanji *Proc. Conf. Water Forum '81* Amer. Soc. Civil Eng., 1981)

SAR*	EC (dS/m)	
	Severe problem	No problem
0–3	< 0.2	> 0.9
3–6	< 0.25	> 1.3
6–12	< 0.35	> 2
12–20	< 0.9	> 3.1
> 20	< 1.8	> 5.6

moderate to slight problem

SAR = sodium adsorption ratio (see Chapter 33)

- If it is in the 'no problem' range, no further tests are needed. The only precaution is that if water with a very low EC is to be applied to a sodic soil, gypsum should also be applied.
- If it is in the lower part of the 'increasing problems' range, the water should still be quite suitable for many plants. Some extra leaching (p. 272) will be needed. It will become unsuitable for use in making liquid feeds somewhere in the range 1–1.5 dS/m.
- As the EC moves towards the upper end of the 'increasing problems' range, it will become unsuitable for plants that do not tolerate salinity.
- Having the water analysed for sodium, calcium, magnesium, chloride and bicarbonate will become increasingly important as EC increases through this range. The results will help you decide on the need for extra calcium and on the type of irrigation system needed. Sometimes they will show the water to be totally unsuitable for a particular use (Table 21.3).
- Note that the information just given refers to the effects of salts arriving at a plant's roots through the soil. The level of damage is much greater if water of the same salinity falls and remains on the plant's leaves. Damage via leaves increases with the time of contact, so it is greater for hairy-leaved plants than for those with smooth leaves that shed most water. Research indicates that the plant is affected as if its roots were receiving water of five to ten times the actual salinity.

ASSESSING THE SALINITY OF GROWING MEDIA

Knowing the salinity of a growing medium is also important. After all, roots 'see' only the salts in the medium around them. Saline irrigation water will tend to increase the salinity of a medium. However, management practices, fertilizer type and amount, and amount of water applied, have a big effect too.

The salinity of a growing medium is assessed through the EC of a water extract of it. Several methods are used (Chapter 33). Each gives a different EC that must be interpreted with the standards for that method. For soils, the methods most commonly used in Australia are the 1:5 (soil–water) extract and the saturation extract methods. We recommend the 1:1.5 volume extract method for potting media, but the saturation extract method can also be used for them.

Interpretation guidelines are given in Tables 21.4 to 21.6.

EFFECTS OF SALINITY ON PLANTS

Plants affected by salinity are stunted and grow more slowly than those not affected. Some examples of the response of different plants to salinity are given

Table 21.4
Approximate maximum allowable EC values for saturation extracts of growing media if growth reductions are to be kept to the levels indicated (*Based on* R S Ayers *J. Irrigation and Drainage Division, Amer. Soc. Civil Eng.* 103: 135, 1977)

Rating of the ability of the plant to cope with salinity*	Reduction in growth rate (%)			
	0	10	25	50
	Maximum allowable EC (dS/m)			
Very sensitive	1	1.4	1.8	2.5
Sensitive	1.4	2.0	3.0	4.6
Moderately tolerant	2.5	3.4	4.8	7
Tolerant	4.5	5.8	8	12
Very tolerant	8	10	13	18

*See the appendix 'Tolerance to Salinity' for lists of plants.

Table 21.5
Guidelines for interpreting the ECs of 1:5 (weight/volume) soil extracts. The figures are in dS/m and are the maximum safe values if growth reductions are to remain small.

	Level of tolerance of plants to salinity				
Texture	Very sensitive	Sensitive	Moderately tolerant	Tolerant	Very tolerant
Sand, loamy sand	0.2	0.5	0.8	1.0	> 1.0
Loams	0.3	0.6	0.9	1.2	> 1.2
Clays	0.5	1.4	2.2	2.7	> 2.7

To obtain approximately equivalent saturation extract data, multiply the numbers in the first line by 11, those in the second line by 10 and those in the third line by 9 (light clays) to 6 (heavy clays).

Table 21.6
Data for interpreting EC values for 1:1.5 volume extracts of growing media for plants that are moderately tolerant of salinity. For general nursery conditions it is unwise to exceed about 1.8 dS/m.

Salinity hazard	EC (dS/m)
Nil	< 0.7
Low	0.7–1.2
Moderate	1.3–1.8
Fairly high	1.9–2.7
High	2.8–3.6
Very high	> 3.6

in Fig. 21.1. The tolerance to salinity of different species is given on pp 428–432.

Leaves are smaller and often thicker, more succulent and darker green. Growth rate is progressively reduced, and stunting more severe, as salinity increases.

For woody plants (trees, vines, shrubs), leaf margins often turn yellow (chlorotic), then brown or black as they die. Oldest leaves are often affected first. Some leaves take on a 'bronzed' appearance. Eventually, affected leaves drop from the plant. These 'burning' symptoms are mostly a result of the accumulation of chloride and sodium ions in leaf margins. If the salinity is due to salts other than sodium chloride, and water supply is maintained at a high level, 'burning' symptoms are usually not produced (Fig. 21.2).

Mild, but probably economically important, effects are not easy to detect without nearby unaffected plants for comparison, or reliable EC measurements.

Plants are damaged in two main ways:

- So-called specific ion effects. The plant is damaged by too much of one or more ions.
- A general effect, caused by the total concentration of salts in the water around plant roots being too high. This general effect may come about in two ways.

A gradual increase in salinity

As plants remove water from a growing medium, the EC of the remaining water increases. This is normal. The plants gradually adjust internally to keep pace with these changes outside. Above a certain point the adjustment has a penalty. Growth is reduced in proportion to the adjustment needed.

If the EC is still moderately low, the growth reduction will be small and acceptable. But if the level of fertilizer use is high, the water used is moderately saline and/or the growing medium has not been leached recently, the EC could climb so high that growth is seriously reduced. The plant has to divert energy from growth to maintain its water supply.

The concentration of the solution inside root cells is usually much higher

Place a dried sultana in 100 mL of tap water. Within a few hours it will have absorbed enough water to swell to near its size when first picked. Water has moved into the cells of the sultana because the concentration of soluble materials in them (sugar in this case) is greater than the concentration in the water. The grape will continue to take up water until it bursts. If, before that happens, you dissolve two tablespoons of salt in the water, you will find that the grape will begin to shrink again. The higher concentration of dissolved materials in the water around it has caused water to move out of the grape again. This movement of water from a less concentrated to a more concentrated solution is called osmosis.

Figure 21.1

Plants differ widely in their response to increasingly saline irrigation water. ━•━• Azalea 'Mrs Fred Saunders', very sensitive to salinity; ━━━ Magnolia grandiflora, sensitive; •••• Acacia saligna, tolerant; ━━ Russian olive, very tolerant. From H C Lunt et al. J. Amer. Soc. Hort. Sci. 69: 543, 1957; B Shaybang and A Kashirad J. Amer. Soc. Hort. Sci. 104: 823, 1978; L E Francois J. Amer. Soc. Hort. Sci. 107: 66, 1982

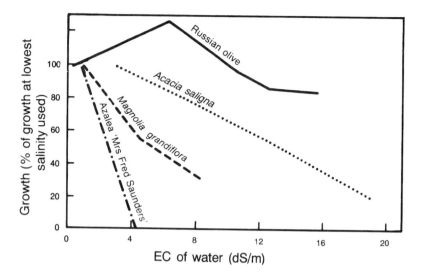

than the concentration of salts in water in growing media. Water will normally move into them until the rigidity of their walls stops it. However, as the concentration of materials dissolved in the water around roots increases, their ability to take up water decreases. The plant stores soluble materials in cells in an attempt to maintain their water content. Energy is diverted from growth.

Growth stops when the salinity of the external solution prevents water from entering the plant. The plant cannot use the water in the medium. It wilts and begins to die. Salinity, therefore, reduces the proportion of the water in a medium that is available to plants.

The actual amount of growth reduction will depend on how high the EC has gone (Fig. 21.2) and the species being grown. Somewhere along the way, one or more ions may start to poison the plant, reducing growth even further.

Figure 21.2

Response of marigolds to increasing salinity of the liquid feed used. From D West Australian Horticulture June: 7, 1981; Courtesy of Ramsay Ware Stockland Pty Ltd

A sudden slug of salinity

Suppose that you are growing plants in containers in a nursery. You have a base level of controlled-release fertilizer in the mix, but you need to supplement this with extra nitrogen to replace that removed by decomposing sawdust. You ask an employee to make up a liquid feed and apply it. There is a misunderstanding and the liquid feed is ten times as strong as is needed.

Within an hour of so, many plants will be severely affected. They will be wilted. If the day is hot, young leaves may be so badly affected that they are beyond help. Young seedlings may have totally collapsed.

As soon as you see what has happened and have stopped yelling and tearing your hair out, you start watering the plants with large quantities of tap water. Your aim is to wash the fertilizer from the plant leaves and the mix. Over the next few days many plants recover, although they have obviously had a severe setback. Some, especially the young, those with broad leaves, and many indoor plants, never recover. Their roots will be much more likely to be invaded by pathogens as a result of their brief exposure to high salinity (Fig. 26.1).

Similar damage is often done when fertilizing turf. The fertilizer is applied dry.

- If it remains on the leaves, it will damage them directly.
- If it is washed into the soil with too little water, the turf plants will be damaged in the same way as the plants in the story above.

Damage can only be avoided by diluting the fertilizer in ample amounts of water.

Don't be caught with the question 'What happened to it?', and have to reply 'I fertilized it'. But if you are caught, you will be in good company. Everyone we know has been caught at one time or another.

Specific ion effects

The ions that do most damage are chloride, sodium, bicarbonate, ammonium and borate (boron). (Effects due to the ions fluoride, ammonium and phosphate are not usually classed under this heading, so are dealt with in Chapter 14.)

Chloride: Chloride is often the most common anion in water. Often it is the first ion to affect plants and to produce recognizable symptoms. The first sign of excess chloride is a yellowing of the margins or tips of leaves. As the yellow areas extend, those first affected die, turning brown or black. Sodium ions give similar symptoms, but they usually begin to have an effect later than does chloride, because roots have some ability to stop them from getting to plant tops.

This death of leaf margins reduces leaf area and hence the ability of the plant to catch sunlight and photosynthesis. Growth is inevitably affected. Even if the supply of chloride to the roots is stopped, affected parts of the plant cannot recover. The chloride cannot be removed from the plant.

When present at similar concentrations, chloride is much more toxic to plants that is sulphate or nitrate (Table 21.7).

Chloride in waters and liquid feeds will increase the succulence of plants. Their leaves are then more easily attacked by various fungal diseases. Do not use fertilizers containing chloride salts (potassium chloride is the one most likely to be used) in nurseries.

Sodium: The damage done by sodium depends very much on the levels of calcium and magnesium in the water.

Most roots have some ability to stop sodium from being taken into the plant. But when there is little calcium and magnesium in the water, the sodium soon overcomes this ability. It can damage root cells: it accumulates in leaf margins where it adds to any damage done by chloride.

Damage to leaves by sodium and chloride eventually becomes so severe that

Table 21.7
Differing effects of different anions in waters on the growth of roses. The roses were irrigated with the different waters for 45 days (*From* B Yaron et al. *J. Amer. Soc. Hort. Sci* 94: 481, 1969)

Main anion	EC of saturation extract (dS/m)		
	4.1	5.4	7.5
	Weight per plant (g)		
Chloride	97	34	0
Nitrate	110	—	24

the leaves are shed. That gets rid of that salt from the plant, but of course then it has that much less leaf area. Continued losses eventually lead to the death of the plant.

The ability of the sodium in water to cause damage is given by the sodium adsorption ratio—SAR for short. Chapter 33 shows how to calculate the SAR of a water. Here it is sufficient to know that increasing SAR causes problems.

Chloride and sodium: Appearance is all-important for most ornamental plants. Even relatively mild dieback of leaf margins can be unacceptable. Levels of chloride and sodium around the roots and tops of ornamentals must be kept as low as possible. It is especially important to prevent waters containing these ions from falling onto the leaves of sensitive plants.

For some plants, the chloride level of the irrigation water limits its use before total salinity does. Low chloride and sodium are especially important when foliage plants are being acclimatised before being taken indoors.

Boron: Boron is an essential trace element. However, excessive amounts are toxic to plants. The only Australian surface waters that contain toxic levels of boron are some effluent waters from sewerage treatment works.

Hazards arise in five main situations.

- Some bore waters contain toxic levels of boron. Before using bore water, have it analysed for EC and for all ions likely to be toxic.
- Composted municipal wastes can have high levels of soluble boron. It comes from glues used in packages.
- The boron in effluent waters comes mainly from laundry detergents, some of which contain as much as 1.2% boron. Effluent waters commonly contain around 1 ppm boron, making them unsuitable for some plants. If laundry effluents are to be used on gardens, the detergents used should not contain boron (or sodium).
- The subsoils in parts of inland southern Australia contain very high levels of boron. This certainly damages cereal crops in dry years. The extent of damage to other plants is not known.

Bicarbonate and carbonate: Bicarbonate and carbonate decrease the availability of some nutrients, notably iron. These ions combine with calcium and magnesium ions in growing media, forming their carbonates. The end result is that the proportion of exchangeable sodium in the medium increases, making it more sodic. This effect of bicarbonate and carbonate ions is allowed for when calculating the SAR of a water (Chapter 33). Repeated application of bicarbonate and carbonate will raise the pH of acid to slightly alkaline media.

Other effects of salinity on plants

- If salinity damages soil structure, plant growth will be reduced through poor aeration, increased soil strength or reduced water supply.
- Saline water falling on plant leaves is often much more damaging that is the same water falling only on the soil. An example of this is given in Table 21.8. If saline water has to be used for irrigation, it must not touch leaves. Use low-throw sprinklers, flooding or trickle irrigation.
- The effects of salinity continue even after the outside source of salts is removed. For example, cut chrysanthemums had shorter vase lives after the plants from which they were being cut had been exposed to high salinity (Table 21.8).
- Plants growing in a medium with a very low EC, and suddenly subjected to saline water containing much sodium and little calcium plus magnesium, can become deficient in calcium and/or magnesium.
- Salinity often makes plants more suscepible to attack by diseases (Fig. 26.1). The attack is often more damaging than if salinity had been less.
- The effects of phytotoxins are often made more severe by salinity.

Table 21.8
Effect of salinity on growth and vase life of chrysanthemums (*From* R B Rutland *HortScience* 7: 57, 1972)

EC dS/m (saturation extract)	Watering method	Stem length (cm)	Vase life (days)
1.8	capillary mat	44	12
3.6	capillary mat	47	9
3.6	overhead	39	5
4.0	capillary mat	40	7

EFFECTS OF SALINE WATERS ON GROWING MEDIA

Saline waters have three main effects on growing media: accumulation of salts; increased pH; increased sodicity.

Accumulation of salts

Examples of the amounts of salts that can be added to soils by irrigation waters are given in Table 21.9. It is clear that very high levels can quickly build up if there is no leaching.

Several things can happen to salts added to growing media.

- They can be taken up by plants. Some or all of the ions of nutrient elements are eventually removed by plants.
- However, only small proportions of added sodium and chloride are taken up.

Table 21.9
Examples of the amounts of salts added to soils by irrigation water, and the effects on the salinity of the soil. The calculations are for an application of 500 mm water per year

EC of water (dS/m)	Salts added (tonnes/ha)		EC of saturation extract if no salts leached (dS/m)	
	1 year	5 years	1 year	5 years
0.15	0.5	2.5	0.2	1
0.8	2.5	12.5	1	4*
1.6	5	25	2	8*
3.1	10	50	3*	16*

*The growth of many plants is reduced at these EC values (Table 21.4).

Most remain in the medium. As water is removed by evaporation or transpiration, the EC of the remaining water increases. High EC will give a crust of solid salts on the surface where water evaporates.
- If the medium is to remain usable, accumulated salts must be removed by leaching with extra water.

Increased pH

Repeated use of alkaline irrigation water will eventually increase the pH of growing media. The increase may be beneficial if the medium was too acid, but often the pH rises to a level at which plant growth is reduced. Acidification will then be necessary (Chapter 11).

Sodicity

The term 'sodicity' applies much more often to soils than to other growing media, so this section is mainly about soils.

Irrigation waters damage soils more through the sodium they contain than by any other means. Sodium ions in the water exchange places with other ions on colloid surfaces in the soil. The proportion of (exchangeable) sodium on these surfaces increases. Structure, especially of clay soils, eventually deteriorates.

When the proportion of exchangeable sodium is high enough to impair its physical properties, a soil is said to be *sodic* (Table 21.10). Soils with increasing proportions of exchangeable sodium are said to increase in sodicity. Another term used is *exchangeable sodium percentage* (ESP), it being the percentage of the cation exchange capacity that is taken up by sodium. Increasing sodicity means increasing ESP.

Sodic soils are difficult to manage. When wet, they are sticky and slippery. Infiltration of water is slow. In a sodic soil the individual particles disperse away from one another when the soil becomes wet through application of water of low salinity (e.g. rain). Structure is poor. On drying, the mess of individual

Table 21.10
Criteria for classifying sodic soils

Type of sodicity	ESP (%)	EC of saturation extract dS/m	pH (saturated paste)
Saline-sodic	> 6*	> 4	8.2–8.5
Sodic	> 6*	< 4	> 8.5

*This has been found to be the most suitable figure for Australian soils. To see whether a soil is or is not sodic, use the simple test in Chapter 33.

particles at the surface forms a crust that seedlings break through with difficulty. The rest of the soil forms large, hard clods. Making a decent seedbed is impossible. Sodic soils on slopes erode easily; subsurface tunnels form, then huge gullies. Sodic subsoils are a common cause of poor drainage in many areas of inland Australia.

Saline-sodic soils behave differently from sodic soils. The high level of salts allow the individual particles to clump together. (A simple example of this effect can be seen in earth dams. If the water in a dam remains muddy for weeks on end, it is certain that the level of salts in the water is low. Clear water means that there never were any soil particles in the water, or that they have been precipitated out by salts in the water. Adding a solution of any salt to muddy water will cause the water to clear. Try it with sodium chloride and gypsum.) The structure of a saline-sodic soil can be quite good—provided the salts remain in the soil. But as soon as the salts are washed out—or down a bit—all the problems of a sodic soil appear. This is exactly what happens when rain falls on a saline-sodic soil, or when it is irrigated with non-saline water.

Causes of sodicity

Soils become sodic when the water soaking through them contains much sodium (and lower amounts of calcium and magnesium).

An hour of contact with seawater will send any soil sodic. Many soils of inland Australia are sodic (Fig. 21.3) because they have formed on old marine deposits. Irrigation waters can do the same thing, although more slowly.

The ability of a water to do this is measured by its sodium adsorption ratio (SAR) (see Chapter 33). Here all we want to say is that the higher the proportion of sodium in a water in relation to the proportions of calcium and magnesium,

Figure 21.3
The soils of much of Australia are either saline or sodic, or both. There are increasing areas of salinity in places other than those shown. *From K H Northcote and J K M Skene CSIRO Division of Soils Soil Publ. No. 27, 1972*

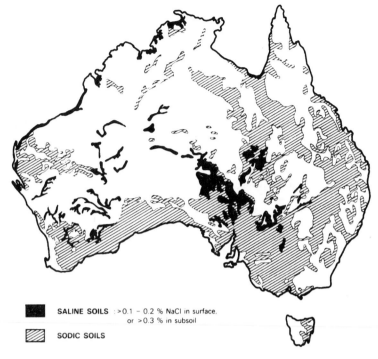

SALINE SOILS : >0.1 – 0.2 % NaCl in surface. or >0.3 % in subsoil

SODIC SOILS

the higher the SAR of that water, and the more damage will it do to a soil. Guidelines for the use of SAR are given in Table 21.2. It is virtually impossible to grow plants successfully on poorly drained soils using water with a high SAR.

Increasing SAR means that sodium increasingly replaces other ions on colloid surfaces. The soil becomes increasingly sodic. Three types of waters have especially high SARs:

• Laundry detergent powders contain very high levels of sodium, present in compounds such as sodium sulphate and sodium carbonate. Laundry effluent waters containing these can only be safely run onto soils if soluble calcium is also applied. Detergent powders contain about 25% sodium. The SAR of laundry effluents can be raised to above 11 by this sodium. That is a very damaging water indeed. These waters are also highly alkaline (pH >9 often) so effects of that will have to be corrected too. Liquid detergents are much less hazardous.

• Water softeners contain resins that remove calcium and magnesium from water, replacing them with sodium. The SAR of water from softeners is very high. It can only be safely used to water plants if soluble calcium is also supplied.

• Swimming pool waters contain high concentrations of sodium and chloride ions from chlorinating chemicals and acid added to lower pH.

Never use these waters to irrigate plants.

COPING WITH SALINITY AND SODICITY

The effects of salinity and sodicity on plants are minimized by reducing evaporation, growing salt-tolerant plants, using fertilizers wisely, applying gypsum, acidifying a soil, and careful irrigation.

Reducing evaporation

Any loss of water from a medium will increase the EC of the water remaining in it. Therefore the more evaporation from the surface of the medium is reduced, the less the rise in EC. Mulching (Table 21.11) is an important tool to use in coping with salinity.

The message is clear: mulching reduces water use, salt stress on plants, and the need for extra leaching water.

Table 21.11
Example of the ability of a mulch to reduce salinity problems. (Assume that the irrigation water contains 600 ppm TDS (total dissolved solids), that the depth of watering is 30 cm and that the soil holds 90 L water/m^2/30 cm depth at field capacity.)

Item	Bare soil	Heavily mulched
20-week transpiration (mm)	270	270
20-week evaporation from the soil (mm)	330	96
Therefore, water needed to keep soil at field capacity (mm)	600	366
This works out at (L/m^2)	600	366
Hence salts added (mg/m^2)	360 000	219 600
Therefore, concentration of salts in the soil water (ppm)	4 000*	2 440
The EC of the saturation extract would be approximately (dS/m)	3.1	1.9

*Actually, with massive surface evaporation, the salts would become concentrated in the top few centimetres of soil. The concentration there could be more than twice the figure given. That would be lethal to most plants.

Table 21.12
Table 21.12
The Salt Index—a measure of the effect of fertilizers on the salinity of soils*. These figures give the ability of the same weights of each fertilizer to increase the salinity of a soil, relative to sodium nitrate being given an index of 100. (*From* L F Rader et al. *Soil Sci.* 55: 201, 1943)

Fertilizer	Salt Index
[Sodium chloride]†	154
Potassium chloride	114
Ammonium nitrate	105
Sodium nitrate	100
Urea	75
Potassium nitrate	74
Ammonium sulphate	69
Calcium nitrate	53
Potassium sulphate	46
Magnesium sulphate	44
Diammonium phosphate	34
Monoammonium phosphate	30
Superphosphate, triple	10
Monopotassium phosphate	8
Calcium sulphate	8
Superphosphate, single	8
Calcium carbonate	5
Dolomite	1

*These figures do not apply to situations where soil is not present. Thus, they do not apply to liquid feeds, hydroponics solutions, and to soil-less potting mixes. For them, the data of Table 16.17 are to be used.
†Sodium chloride is included to show just how damaging it is.

Growing salt-tolerant plants

In many situations it is not possible to remove salts from soils. Drainage is too expensive or there is not enough water of suitable quality available. In other situations, the only available water is saline.

The only alternative then is to grow plants that are salt tolerant. There are many from which to choose (see the appendix 'Tolerance to Salinity').

Using fertilizers wisely

All fertilizers increase the salinity of a medium to which they are applied. The amount of increase depends on:

- the amount of fertilizer applied;
- the solubility of the fertilizer;
- whether or not the fertilizer interacts with the medium so that ions are removed from solution.

Table 21.12 lists the relative salinities to be expected from different fertilizers. Note that this list applies only to soils. For several reasons, the salinity produced by a given amount of almost all fertilizers is less in a soil than in water alone. Use the data of Table 16.17 when checking the salinity hazard of liquid feeds.

Extra care is needed when applying fertilizers from the top part of the list in Table 21.12.

- Make sure that at least the top 100 mm of soil is moistened to field capacity before applying them.
- Allow plant leaves to dry before applying the fertilizer.
- Apply fertilizer at no more than the recommended rate.
- Irrigate with at least 5 mm of water immediately after fertilizing.
- Apply less than the recommended rate if these precautions are not possible.

All this might suggest that fertilizers should not be used if soils and irrigation waters are saline. Not so. Well-fed plants are better able to tolerate salinity than are poorly fed plants. Just don't apply too much fertilizer at the one time. When water containing a high concentration of chloride ions must be used, it is essential to maintain about 140 ppm N (as nitrate) in the soil solution.

Ammonium-based fertilizers can seriously harm plants growing in soils that contain a high concentration of chloride. The combination of ammonium sulphate and potassium chloride—the cheapest of all fertilizers supplying N and K—can be very damaging indeed to plants if the soil and irrigation water already have much chloride.

Salinity from fertilizers in nurseries is discussed on p. 274.

Preventing and overcoming sodicity

The physical properties of a sodic soil may be improved by making the soil acid, by increasing the level of soluble salts in it, or by applying a source of soluble calcium.

Acidification increases the proportion of exchangeable aluminium ions in the soil (p. 85), so allowing the formation of crumbs. The expense of acid (normally sulphuric acid or iron sulphate) limits its use in Australia to tiny areas.

Gypsum is the material most commonly used to improve sodic soils. It is slightly soluble in water (2.41 g/L) so it increases the level of soluble salts in the soil as well as supplying calcium. The first effect of application is that dissolved gypsum causes the particles of clay in the soil to clump together into crumbs. This effect disappears as soon as there is no more gypsum dissolved in the soil water.

However, gypsum also has a more permanent effect. Calcium ions from it exchange places with sodium ions on colloid surfaces. The calcium ions are more tightly held than are sodium ions. One result of this is that colloid particles are able to move closer together to form crumbs.

Note that the response to a poorly soluble source of calcium (limestone—Fig. 21.4) is much slower than is the response to gypsum.

Gypsum is used as follows:

- Gypsum can be dissolved in irrigation waters to lower their SARs. The gypsum–water mixture must be agitated to dissolve some of the gypsum. The

Figure 21.4
Flow of water through columns of a sodic soil (control) or the same soil treated with gypsum or limestone at 22.5 tonnes/ha. *From* G R Saini *Plant and Soil* 34: 159, 1971

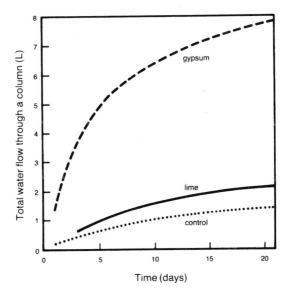

rest has to be allowed to settle out. Special equipment is needed.

- Usually, the cheaper alternative of spreading solid gypsum on the soil, or mixing it in, is preferred. Leaving the gypsum on the surface gives greater improvement in infiltration rate and erosion control than does mixing in.
- When gypsum is to be used to prevent the development of sodicity, apply 500–750 g/m² (5–7.5 tonnes/ha). Do this whenever the water used has an SAR of 4.5 or more. It is especially necessary when using effluent waters.
- Use this same rate when a dispersion test on the soil (Chapter 33) shows that a response is likely. This rate will be enough for soils with ESPs below 20. If structure and infiltration rate remain poor after six months, apply a further 500–750 g/m². Use 1000 g/m² if the ESP is between 20 and 30. Repeat the application as needed.
- Seek professional help when soils with very high ESPs (>30) are to be reclaimed. Special techniques are needed.

Removing salts

The only way to remove salts is to wash (leach) them out with plenty of fresh water. Leaching is possible only if water can move fairly quickly down through the soil and out of reach of plant roots. In practice that means:

- Doing whatever is necessary to improve the structure of the soil and to remove barriers to drainage (Chapter 24). Deep ripping can break such barriers.
- Where deep drainage away from roots is not possible, install a drainage system. Gypsum slotting has been shown to be an effective way of getting water into sodic soils. Make closely-spaced (0.6–1.2 m intervals), narrow (100–150 mm), 400 mm deep slots, backfilled with the soil amended with gypsum at a rate of 3.5 kg/m² of slot surface.
- Where sodicity gives poor structure and slow drainage, apply a soluble source of calcium.

How much leaching water?

We have said that the only way to overcome salinity problems is to leach the salts from the soil. But how much water is needed, and how often must it be applied? The answer depends on what you consider to be an acceptable growth reduction.

The rate of growth of most plants is gradually reduced as salinity increases (Fig. 21.1). This means that the longer the time between leachings, the greater the reduction in growth. If you cannot accept any reduction in growth, then you must leach frequently. The actual frequency will depend on the EC of the water used and plant tolerance.

The amount of extra water to apply can be calculated as follows:

1. First look up the appendix 'Tolerance to Salinity', or guess the tolerance of your plants to salinity.
2. Decide on the amount of growth reduction caused by salinity that is tolerable.
3. Find in Table 21.4 the maximum allowable salinity of the medium.
4. Calculate the leaching requirement (LR)

$$LR = \frac{EC \text{ of the water being used}}{(5 \times \text{maximum EC allowed in saturation extract}) - EC \text{ of the water}}$$

5. Calculate the amount of water to be applied

$$\text{Amount of water} = \frac{\text{evapotranspiration loss}}{1.00 - LR}$$

Example: Dahlias are being grown. They are very sensitive to salinity. No more than 10% reduction in growth is allowable, so the maximum EC of the saturation extract will be 1.4 dS/m.

The water being used has an EC = 1.0 dS/m.

$$LR = \frac{1.0}{(5 \times 1.4) - 1.0} = \frac{1.0}{7.00 - 1.0} = 0.17$$

If evapotranspiration losses have been 25 mm since the last watering, then:

$$\text{Amount of water} = \frac{25}{1.0 - 0.17} = 30.1 \text{ mm}$$

Notes:

- These calculations have not allowed for rainfall. As the EC of rain is very low, it will be much better at leaching salts than will irrigation water (provided that the soil is not sodic). Occasional rain during an irrigation season will reduce the need to apply extra water for leaching.
- These calculations assume that the plants are kept well supplied with water by frequent irrigation. They then take most of the water they need from the top part of the root zone, where the water is less saline than that further down the profile.

If water is not applied frequently, the plant will be forced to draw on the more saline water. The only way of getting away with less frequent irrigation is to leach more heavily.

Method of irrigation

- Light, frequent sprinkling is useful. The salts accumulate in high concentration in the surface few centimetres of soil, soon reaching toxic levels there. Irrigate infrequently, but deeply.
- Low-throw sprinklers keep wetting of leaves—and salt uptake by them—to a minimum.
- Low-throw sprinklers also allow less evaporation of water from sprinkler droplets as they travel through the air. A 50% loss (common on hot windy days) doubles the salt content of the remaining water.
- Drippers reduce evaporation even further. Salts are distributed around each outlet as shown in Fig. 21.5. This pattern needs to be kept in mind in any replanting of an area, or when taking soil samples. Keep drippers running during summer rain. This prevents salts from moving back from the edge of the wetted zone into the root zone.

Plants preferentially take water from the least saline part of a growing medium. For example, having two-thirds of a plant's root zone at the salinity of seawater will cause little harm, provided the other third is kept constantly moist with water of low salinity. When there is a limited amount of fresh water available for plants in a saline soil, always applying it to the same part of the root zone will give plants maximum benefit from it. Drippers are useful for this.

With turf, it is critically important when using saline water to look after the top 50 mm of the root zone. That is the zone of greatest root concentration. Maintaining the lowest possible salt concentration in this zone will maximize grass growth for the particular conditions. This upper 50 mm must never be allowed to dry out. So, contrary to general practice with non-saline water, it is necessary to irrigate frequently with salty water, but not shallowly. Make sure that the salt is frequently leached from that top 50 mm.

Figure 21.5
The patterns of salinity in soils watered by overhead sprinklers and by drippers

Sprinkling

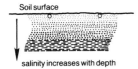

salinity increases with depth

Trickling

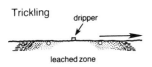

salinity increases with distance from dripper

SALTS IN LANDSCAPES

High levels of salts in soils cause problems in many parts of Australia. So-called dryland salinity is becoming an increasing problem in non-irrigated areas. Its main cause is shown in Fig. 21.6. Clearing of deep-rooted trees and their replacement with shallow-rooted pasture and cereal plants has reduced annual removal of water by evaporation and transpiration. Groundwater levels have risen, bringing salts from deep in the subsoil to the surface in lower parts of the

Figure 21.6
The water balance in a landscape is drastically changed when trees are replaced by annual crops. After clearing, the water table rises, bringing salts with it. Streams become saline. *From A J Peck CSIRO Information Leaflet* No. 1–32, 1980

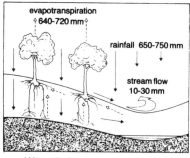
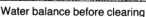
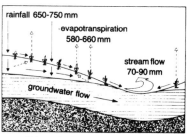

Water balance before clearing   Water balance after clearing

Figure 21.7
The end result of clearing the native forest in the south-west of Western Australia.   *Photograph B van Aken*

landscape. Stream waters have become more saline. The results are not pretty (Fig. 21.7).

The most important means of combating dryland salinity is to re-establish deep-rooted trees on the upper parts of the landscape. Lower areas should be planted to salt-tolerant species to reduce erosion.

Groundwaters have risen or are rising in irrigated areas too. Many such areas rely on drainage schemes to keep them viable.

Outflow of saline groundwaters into streams makes them more saline. Most water supplies are becoming more saline. Not every reader of this book can do anything about this. Those that can are urged to do whatever is in their power, especially by planting trees and encouraging others to do the same.

SALINITY IN NURSERIES

Judging by the comments from extension officers serving the nursery industry, problems related to salinity are common in nurseries. The salts come from fertilizers, water and some solid components of mixes.

Mix components

- Always check the salinity of any new material being considered for use in a mix. Sands and gypsum can be quite saline.
- Make sure that materials supplied as 'washed' have been washed.
- Composts and poultry manure are usually quite salty. They must be checked, and no more used than will keep the salinity of the mix within the acceptable range.

Fertilizers

- Adjust fertilizer additions to suite the tolerance of the plants being grown.
- Always measure the EC of liquid feeds as a check on accuracy of making up.
- In automatic systems, an in-line conductivity meter attached to an alarm will prevent mishaps from too high an EC or blocking of the concentrate bleed-in line.
- If potting mix containing controlled-release fertilizers has to be stored in a large heap for more than a day or two, check its EC and if necessary leach immediately after potting up.
- Don't air-steam at higher than 65°C, nor for longer than 30 minutes. That amount of pasteurization will not normally release harmful amounts of salts from controlled-release fertilizers.
- The rate of release of salts from controlled-release fertilizers increases as temperature increases. This means that rates of application should be reduced

during the hottest part of the year, or formulations with long release times used.

- Note the point made in Chapter 16 about the effects on controlled-release fertilizers of heating in a heap of mix containing them.
- The water content of pots containing controlled-release fertilizers must be maintained at a high level in very hot weather. If this is not done, the salts then being released at a high rate will cause a very high salinity indeed in the little remaining water in a dried mix. Plants will be damaged or killed. This action is especially necessary when Osmocote fertilizers are being used because of the very steep increase in release rate as temperature rises (Table 16.9).
- Germinating seeds are especially sensitive to salinity, closely followed by seedlings and cuttings in the early stages of root formation. Fertilizer use in propagating media must be kept low
- Select fertilizers carefully. Sodium is out; so is chloride. There is no room for sulphate in *excess* of requirements. Use such fertilizers as potassium and ammonium nitrates.
- Guidelines for liquid feeds are given in Chapter 16.
- The EC of the water in a medium can be used as a guide to the amount of nutrient available to plants growing in that medium. But note that any sodium chloride from irrigation water will contribute to the salinity of the water in media. Guidelines for nutrient application based on EC alone could seriously underestimate nutrient need if most of the nutrients in the container have been used, so that the water contains mainly useless salt. The guidelines given here can be used without modification in areas where the water is of very low salinity. In other areas, either make some mental allowance for the effect of saline water or also check the nitrate level in the medium (Chapter 33).
- The two extraction methods described in Chapter 33—the saturated media extract and the 1:1.5 volume methods—give equally reliable results which are interpreted according to Table 21.13.
- The simplest method of measurement is the pour-through (PT) technique, in which water is poured onto the surface of the medium and leachate collected out the bottom for analysis (Chapter 33). This method is widely used as a quick indicator of nutritional supply. It is claimed to be as accurate as methods that involve extraction of samples of medium removed from pots. In our experience, it gives somewhat more erratic results than do the extraction methods. Nevertheless, it is useful for a quick assessment of nutrient status or salinity hazard.

PT extracts have EC values that are about 1.5 times those for saturation extracts of the same media. For liquid-fed plants, pour-through EC values for optimum growth are typically in the range 0.5–2 dS/m, although poinsettia has been reported to need 2.5–3.2 dS/m.

EC values for plants fertilized with controlled-release fertilizers are lower, with foliage plants needing an average of about 0.8 dS/m under conditions capable of giving vigorous growth, and woody perennials growing optimally in media giving PT extracts of 0.3–0.6 dS/m. Some species (*Codiaeum variegatum* is one) need higher nutrient levels than these ranges. These general conclusions about the optimum EC for plants fertilized with coated fertilizers apply equally well when other extraction methods are used. Claims that optimum growth of plants is possible in media testing at a very low to almost zero EC when coated fertilizers are used are not supported by the research data listed above. Such a low EC may be acceptable so long as some nutrients are being released and if you do not want the plants to grow fast.

The ECs of 1:1.5 and saturation extracts must be less than 0.8 and 1.6 dS/m respectively for many foliage plants being acclimatised. In a medium with an EC of 3 dS/m, there can be a severe leaf drop on taking a plant into a low light situation.

Table 21.13
Guidelines for using the EC of a potting mix to decide when to fertilize woody plants of moderate tolerance to salinity*

EC (saturation extract) (dS/m)	EC (1:1.5 volume extract) (dS/m)	Action
< 1	< 0.35	Fertilizer needed, except when slow-release fertilizers are still releasing nutrients
1–1.5	0.35–0.7	Acceptable when feeding is by slow-release fertilizer; otherwise fertilizer can be applied
1.5–2	0.7–1.3	Acceptable; do not fertilize above 1.7 dS/m (saturation extract)
2–3.5	1.3–1.8	Do not fertilize; do not allow the mix to become dry
> 3.5	> 1.8	May be too high; leach

*Halving these figures would give a fair guide for plants that are sensitive to salinity. Note that when a mix contains functioning slow-release fertilizer, a low EC does not necessarily mean that fertilizer is needed, but a high EC does show a need for leaching.

Figure 21.8
Change with time of the EC of 1:1.5 extracts of medium from the upper, middle and lower parts of a pot irrigated from below with nutrient solution of EC 1.6 dS/m. *From* C de Kreij and N Staver. *Acta Horticulturae* 221: 245, 1988

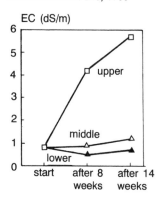

- Amounts of fertilizer that are ideal under conditions allowing rapid growth will be excessive if growth is less. For example, plants maintained indoors may need as little as 10% of the feeding that they need when grown outside.
- These last two points apply especially to plants being moved to retail stores or indoors. Nurserymen can help by planning fertilization so that when their plants are moved to these places of often poorer care, the level of fertilizer in the mix is low. Leach the pots thoroughly near dispatch time.
- Lime or dolomite used to raise the pH of many mix materials will provide a steady supply of calcium ions that will help plants cope with water with a moderate SAR.
- Those who irrigate plants via capillary or via ebb and flood systems need to be aware that salts accumulate in the upper part of the root ball (Fig. 21.8). They do no harm so long as they remain there. If it is necessary to remove the salts by leaching, the amount of water applied must be sufficient to dilute them and carry them away through drainage holes.
- Water for misting systems should have a low salinity. An EC of 1.0 dS/m is about the limit for sensitive plants, although below 0.5 dS/m is preferred (Table 21.14). The EC can be up to 3.0 dS/m for plants tolerant of salinity, but check carefully before using such saline water. Fog (p. 318) will be less damaging than mist when saline water must be used.

Management

- The salinity of potting mixes must be kept lower than the limits given in Table 21.13. Higher salinities mean that pots must be leached. But how much extra water should be used? Soluble nutrients will be lost in leaching water. The aim is to leach as little as is necessary to reduce EC. The best guide is to leach according to EC measurements. Otherwise, a fair average is to allow between 10% and 20% of applied water to flow out of the bottom of the pots.
- Water percolates quickly through very open mixes (those with air-filled porosities above about 28 volume %). The water doesn't stop long enough for salts to diffuse into it from small pores. Leaching is very inefficient: large volumes of water are needed under continuous flooding. Efficiency is greater if the flooding is intermittent.

Table 21.14
Effect of the salinity of the misting water and IBA concentration on rooting of Japanese Boxwood after 13 weeks. (*From* Yin-Tung Wang, *Acta Horticulturae* **246: 191, 1989**)

Water EC (dS/m)	IBA concentration (mg/L)	Rooting %	Root length (cm)
1–1.5	0	12	0.1
	1250	56	0.3
	2500	68	0.4
0.02	0	68	2.6
	1250	88	4.9
	2500	88	5.0

- The greater the water-holding ability of a mix, the greater the protection it offers plants against a damaging rise in salinity as plants use water. Ways of maximizing the proportion of water held in potting media are given in Chapter 13.
- Salinity problems are likely to be most serious in hot, dry weather. Evapotranspiration rates are high then, so the concentration of salts in the water remaining in the medium rises quickly.
- Earthenware pots need to be leached before re-use as continued evaporation of water from their outer surfaces gives them very high salt contents.

22 WATERING: WHEN AND HOW MUCH

Water suitable for irrigating plants is everywhere increasing in price. In some places, demand exceeds supply and rationing is normal. The trend for the future will be to higher prices and larger areas of scarcity. Increasingly, those who want to grow plants must get the most out of both the bought and the free (rain) water they use.

The information given here builds on that already given in Chapter 9. Our aim is to help you decide when to irrigate and how much water to use to get the amount of plant growth needed. A broad theme is to encourage conservation through wise use.

Before growing plants, you must decide on answers to three basic questions:

- First, is the level of growth allowed by rain alone enough? If the answer is 'yes', all that is needed is action to get maximum benefit from that rain. If the answer is 'no', a second question must be answered:
- Do I want maximum potential growth rate, or will something less than that be suitable?
- A third question is: Can I afford the equipment and water needed to get the chosen level of growth? The answer to that may modify the answer to the second question.

HOW MUCH WATER DO PLANTS USE?

**Table 22.1
Shading and lowering air temperature greatly reduces the rate of evaporation of water**

Air temperature (°C)	Full sun (mm/h)	Shade (mm/h)
30–44	0.81	0.32
4–17	0.09	0.02

Fill equal amounts of water into two identical shallow dishes. Place one in full sunshine and the other in heavy shade nearby. Record how long it takes for all the water to evaporate from each dish. Do this on a hot day and also on a cooler day. Your results will be something like those of Table 22.1. Similar results would be obtained if plants of similar size in containers were used instead of dishes of water.

Research has shown that losses of water from groups of *continuously well-watered* plants follow similar patterns to losses from large areas of open water. Evaporation from lakes and swimming pools could, therefore, be used as a guide to water use by plants.

Lakes are few and far between, and swimming pools are expensive, so it is common to use pans of water—called evaporimeters—for measuring the ability of sun and air to evaporate water in an area. The type of evaporimeter most commonly used is the Class A pan (Fig. 22.1). Experiments have shown that the rate of evaporation from a lake or swimming pool is about 80% of that from a Class A pan.

Some other conclusions from research are:

- Water loss from a medium in which plants are growing is partly by evaporation from the surface of the medium and partly by transpiration from the leaves of the plants. These two are often grouped together as evapotranspiration (ET).
- ET increases with increasing air temperature, sunshine intensity and wind speed, and decreasing air humidity.

Figure 22.1
Refilling a Class A pan evaporimeter. The wire cage prevents birds and animals from bathing in or drinking the water

Table 22.2
Increasing the amount of water available to plants (here sun-flowers*) increases the amount they lose by transpiration

Water stress level	Transpiration (mL/container for 1 week)
Control	231
Low stress	173
Moderate stress	103
High stress	23

*These figures were obtained with the plants shown in Fig. 22.2.

In other words, losses of water from well-watered plants are greatest on hot, cloudless, windy days of low humidity. They are least under a thick, chilly, still fog.

- Transpiration from a vigorously growing group of continuously well-watered plants whose canopy fully covers the ground surface is about 70–90% of Class A pan evaporation. Thus an area of vigorous bluegrass turf watered daily or more frequently will lose water at about the same rate as a nearby swimming pool.

However, loss of water from a group of plants is usually less than this because:

- In warm to hot weather, water is unable to travel fast enough from roots to leaves to keep up with the ability of the air to take water. This happens even when the growing medium has ample water in it.
- After a while the plants begin to protect themselves by beginning to shut their stomata. They try to keep the rate of water loss at the same level as the rate of arrival from below. The ability of plants to do this ranges from excellent to poor. We describe those with an excellent ability as being drought tolerant.
- As plants continue to remove water from a medium, the rate of flow of water to roots decreases, further limiting the amount of water available for transpiration (Table 22.2). This is usually the main reason for loss of water from a group of plants being less than losses from a similar area of open water.
- Some plants transpire less water than others even when they are well-watered (see Table 22.11). This is due partly to differences in internal control of transpiration, but mainly to differences in the openness of the canopy. For two plants of the same size, one with an open canopy will transpire water faster than will another with compact growth (Table 22.3).
- With turf, ET increases as the rate of vertical elongation increases, and decreases as shoot density increases (Table 22.4). Some growth regulators can reduce vertical elongation and so reduce ET by perhaps 30% for several months.
- Water loss from scattered plants separated by areas of bare soil, mulched soil,

Table 22.3
For marigold plants of approximately equal mass, the more open the shoot canopy, the greater is the transpiration rate. (From K A Handreck Australian Hortic., Oct: 28, 1993)

Openness index*	Transpiration per pot (g water/h)
103	21
130	26
162	30
205	43
248	45

* Total area of silhouettes of the plants looking from a side and from above.

bitumen or concrete will usually be greater than loss from an area of water equal to that of the ground area covered by the plant's canopy. This is because of extra heat flowing into the plant's canopy from the surrounding bare areas.

• The total amount of water transpired by a plant is somewhere between 250 and 1000 g per g of dry matter produced. It is towards the lower end of the range for plants such as the cacti and tropical (warm-season) grasses. A poorly fed or diseased plant uses water less efficiently than does a healthy, adequately fed plant of the same species growing nearby.

• In summary, plants use water supply according to climatic conditions, their size, compactness, state of health and supply in the growing medium. When supply is restricted, transpiration is much less than evaporation from open water. As supply increases transpiration losses increase to about the level of evaporation from open water.

Insight into rain and irrigation

Rainfall is measured in millimetres (mm). Irrigation water can also be measured in mm.

Ten mm of rain falling into a swimming pool will raise the height of the water in it by exactly 10 mm.

One litre of water spread evenly over 1 m² of waterproof surface will give a depth of water of exactly 1 mm. (A bowling green has an area of approximately 1370 m². A storm delivering 20 mm of rain will dump 20 × 1370 = 27 400 L (= 27.4 tonnes) of water on the green.)

One mm of rain or irrigation water falling on dry soil will soak in more than 1 mm. The actual depth of wetting could range from 20 mm for a very coarse sand to about 2 mm for a clay. The depth for loams will be about 3–4 mm/mm water.

Thus, 25 mm of irrigation water falling on a dry loam could bring the top 75 mm or so to field capacity.

A light sprinkling by hand-held hose, delivering 5 mm, will soak in about 15 mm—hardly enough to keep thirsty plants going for long!

If you want to soak a fine sandy loam to a depth of 30 cm, you will need to apply about (30 × 10)/4 = 75 mm of water. A sprinkler delivering 15 mm/hour would need to be left on for 75/15 = 5 hours.

These are the figures for bone-dry soil. There will always be some water in a soil, so the amount to apply will be less than that calculated above. For example, if the soil was a little moister than wilting point it might have contained 1.2 mm of water per centimetre depth (Fig. 9.6). This works out at 30 × 1.2 = 36 mm for a 30 cm depth of soil. The water needed to bring 30 cm of the soil to field capacity is 75 – 36 = 39 mm. The sprinkler would need to be run for 39/15 = 2.6 hours.

Table 22.4
The rate of water loss from Kentucky bluegrass cultivars was greatest for those cultivars that had a tall, open structure and was least for dense low-growing forms. (From R C Schearman HortScience 21: 455, 1986)

Cultivar	ET (mm/day)	Vertical elongation rate (mm/week)	Shoot density (number/m²)
Adelphi	7.35	10	3.79
Touchdown	7.92	12	3.00
Sydsport	8.17	15	2.57
Park	10.36	19	2.39
South Dakota	10.43	19	2.03

PLANT GROWTH AND WATER SUPPLY

Plants in media that are close to field or container capacity are able to grow as fast as nutrients, light and other environmental factors allow. But as media dry out, plants must divert energy from growth to extracting some of the remaining water. They use sugars to increase the concentration of materials dissolved in water inside the roots to aid water uptake. That sugar is then not available for growth.

Another effect of poor water supply is that stomata in the leaves begin to shut—ranging from a little if the stress is small, to completely when it is great. This restricts or completely shuts off the exit of water through the stomata so as to bring losses more in line with the ability of the plant to extract water from the medium. But shutting stomata is like a shopkeeper preventing shoplifting by shutting everyone out of the shop. Carbon dioxide is unable to move into the plant. Photosynthesis decreases, and with it growth (Fig. 22.2).

Thus a general effect of reduced supply of water in a growing medium is reduced rate of plant growth. Elongation of stems is affected before weight gain. Those who want rapid production of tall or wide plants must ensure that their plants are never short of water.

With continued imbalance between water supply and losses, plants may protect themselves by shedding leaves (Fig. 22.3).

The proportion of the available water reservoir (p. 69) that is used before a plant becomes stressed decreases as evaporative demand increases. Rapid use of water quickly leads to a situation where the rate of movement of water to roots is too low to keep pace with transpiration.

A small amount of water stress can have beneficial effects on some of the plants we want to grow. For example, in nurseries, plants grown with an abundance of all their requirements will be soft, perhaps rangy, and will lack an ability to withstand sudden environmental stress. Hardier plants can be produced if water and nutrients are carefully limited to a little below the amounts needed to produce lush growth.

Figure 22.2
The amount of water supplied to each pot decreased from left to right.   *Photograph J Coppi*

Figure 22.3

Ficus benjamina plants respond to drought stress by shedding leaves. The greater the stress, the greater the proportion of leaves shed. *From J C Peterson, et al.* Florists' Review *Jan 1: 11, 1981*

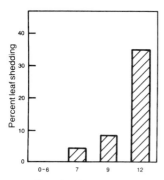

Critical times

As well as general growth reduction caused by water stress at any stage of plant growth, there are some critical stages of growth at which water stress has especially severe effects.

For plants that are capable of producing a number of stems per plant (e.g. the grasses and cereals), stress at the time the young stems are forming reduces the total number of stems formed. Bud initiation time is a critical time for flowering plants. Plants such as carnations that flower continuously must be continuously well watered.

For most annual plants, flowering time is also critical. One reason is that at flowering, root growth is reduced so that there are fewer new roots to contact more water.

For foliage plants, water stress at any time reduces leaf size and number, and therefore quality.

Some benefits of water stress

- The lower rate of water use by moderately stressed plants (p. 292) is an effective way of keeping water use by turf and landscape plantings to a minimum. This statement assumes that the lower growth rate of the stressed plants is acceptable.
- Reduced growth rate in established ornamentals means reduced need for thinning and cutting back.
- The disease problems often found in over-wet turf and landscape are much reduced at a lower level of watering. (On the other hand, severely stressed plants have a reduced ability to withstand some diseases and attack by insects.)
- Plants organize their lives in the most energy-efficient ways possible. Hence they take water first from those parts of the growing medium from which it can be extracted with least effort. As these parts are dried, other parts are exploited. If the top part of the soil profile is always the wettest part—because of frequent shallow watering—it is the part from which the plant will get most of its water. That will also be the part in which most of its roots will be concentrated.

If, on the other hand, water is applied deeply but infrequently, the roots will be forced to grow into and extract water from deeper in the profile (Fig. 22.4). The end result of the moderate stress imposed by this strategy is more efficient use of the soil and its stores of water and nutrients.

- Brief water stress can be beneficial if it encourages a plant to produce more of a part that we want. For example, many fruit trees need a short period of stress to enable them to produce flower buds. But continued water stress once the buds start developing will reduce yields.

DECIDING WHEN TO WATER

- The main methods of deciding when to water are:
- overkill;
- waste-not, want-not;
- careful observation;
- using the water budget procedure;
- using instruments.

We now go through these methods so that you have a good understanding of the interactions between plants, water, soils and environmental conditions. We show how you can use careful observation and some fairly simple measurements to enable you to apply water when it is required and in appropriate amounts. But in the end, we encourage those who want to really get the most out of the water available to them to use one of the several methods that use soil moisture

Figure 22.4

Buffalo grass that had been previously exposed to water stress had more roots than did grass that had been watered frequently. The greater amount of roots deep in the soil is especially noticeable. *From J M Dipoala MS Thesis Texas A&M University, College Station, 1977*

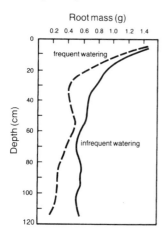

sensors to minimize their water use. The technology is here right now and will pay for itself in a very short time.

Overkill

When ample water is available and cost is of little concern, plants are often irrigated very frequently so as to make sure that they never run short. This is normal practice in many nurseries. Owners of automatic irrigation systems tend to apply water in this way. The plants certainly do not suffer from lack of water. When maximum growth rate is essential and the drawbacks listed below are avoided or are of no concern, this is an acceptable method of irrigation. The drawbacks are:

- Losses of nutrients can be large, especially from sandy turf root zones and nursery pots when feeding is mainly via soluble fertilizers, but also from some short-term, coated controlled-release fertilizers in the first few weeks after application. These losses reduce the effectiveness of the fertilizers. Concentrations of nutrients in effluent waters above permitted levels may encourage anti-pollution inspectors to require reductions.
- The growing medium will remain very wet if its permeability is low; attack by root-rotting fungi can be severe; turf soils will be more likely to be damaged during use.
- Water is wasted.

Waste-not, want-not

This is the opposite of 'overkill'. Plants are watered only when they are obviously suffering from lack of water. Where a high growth rate, excellent appearance or full ground cover are not needed, this method of watering is acceptable. It may be the only method possible if water is in extremely short supply. Infrequent, deep irrigations followed by long periods when the plants just survive may be the only way of getting them through a drought.

However, this method becomes false economy if the attempt to save money on water gives:

- unsaleable plants;
- losses by dehydration;
- poor fruit set in fruit trees;
- poor quality in vegetables;
- thin turf that is severely damaged by normal use.

Careful observation

Both the 'overkill' and 'waste-not, want-not' methods are much improved if they are modified by careful observation of the plants being cared for. Those who develop this 'green-fingers' approach keep plants growing as needed and water use low by:

- Learning to recognize subtle changes in plant colour and appearance that are early warnings of unacceptable stress. Leaves on stressed and unstressed plants usually project at different angles.
- Using the wilting of a particularly sensitive 'indicator' plant as the trigger sign to irrigate.
- Having an appreciation of the effects of different weather conditions on water loss.
- Knowing how much different plants can be stressed before their growth is unacceptably affected.
- Taking core samples to check the water content of a soil.
- Experimenting with irrigation frequency and the amount of water applied until suitable combinations are found.

Most who care for plants and care about them learn some 'green-fingers' skills in time. Learning can be speeded up and skill greatly increased by using the method of calculation that follows, or by using instruments.

USING THE WATER BUDGET PROCEDURE

With the water budget procedure, water is applied to a growing medium when calculation (or shrewd guessing) shows that ET has removed the maximum allowable amount of water from the medium. The information needed to work out a budget is the size of the reservoir in the medium and daily ET. We outline the method here and encourage you to work through it at least once for your situation, so that you gain a better understanding of the interactions between plants, soils, water and weather.

We are aware that it is a real hassle to use the water budget method for deciding when to water. We therefore point out the existence of commercial services that use computerized versions of the water budget method (based on local measurements of air humidity, wind speed, solar radiation heat flux, and so on) that can automatically control your whole watering system. These systems have been shown to be more reliable guides to ET than are pan evaporimeters. But in the same paragraph we must also point out that several systems that use sensors buried in the soil of the area are even better. They give much more precise control of watering at the actual site. Several sensor systems are discussed below.

Reservoir size

A growing medium can be thought of as a reservoir for water. When it is dry, the reservoir is empty. When it is at field capacity or container capacity, the reservoir is full. When it is saturated, water will be flowing over the spillway.

But all growing media are leaking reservoirs. Some water is lost through deep drainage down the profile or out the bottom of a pot. Some water is lost by evaporation from their surfaces.

For soils, the maximum usable size of the reservoir is between field capacity and the permanent wilting point. For media in containers, the size is between container capacity and about 5 kPa suction for rapid growth and up to perhaps 12 kPa for acceptable growth.

The actual usable size of the reservoir is usually less than the maximum. Its size depends on:

- Properties of the medium. For soils, texture has a big effect. Loams and well-structured clays have the biggest reservoirs of available water (Fig. 9.6). Improving structure increases the size of the reservoir. The generally better structure of the top few centimetres of a soil profile (due to its organic matter content) means that it will hold more water per centimetre of depth than will a soil of the same texture but with poorer structure. Application of an amount of water calculated without taking into account the extra water-holding capacity of the surface soil will give shallow water penetration. The root systems of plants in the area will be shallower than they could be with deeper watering, so irrigation will have to be more frequent than it could be.

  It takes effort and skill to work through the calculations needed to determine reservoir size for root zones in soils whose texture varies with depth. Such effort is easily avoided. Apply a known depth of water to your soil. Allow it to soak in for 24 hours. Dig several holes throughout the area to find the depth of water penetration. Reduce or increase the amount of water applied to vary the depth of penetration and hence the size of the soil reservoir.

- Salinity. As salinity increases, the availability of water to plants decreases (p. 73).

- Levels of plant growth needed. Allowing depletion of the reservoir to the permanent wilting point (soils), or to beyond about 12 kPa (potting media) will give a greatly reduced rate of growth. When plants must continue to grow rapidly, the reservoir must be refilled well before the permanent wilting point (soils) or before about 8 kPa (potting media).

- Depth of rooting. In soils, the size of the reservoir increases as the depth of root penetration increases. Further information on this is given in the next section. In containers, the size of the container sets an absolute limit to the size of the reservoir. It will be smaller if waterlogging limits root growth to the top part of the mix.
- Presence of a coarse layer under the root zone. Such a coarse layer (an 'anti-drainage' layer (p. 65) can increase the amount of water held in the root zone.

Calculations

To find the size of the reservoir in a container:

$$\frac{\text{Volume of mix (mL/pot)}}{100} \times \text{readily available water content (volume \%)}$$

$$= \text{reservoir size (mL/pot)}$$

This formula can be used only if you know the readily available water-holding capacity of the medium. Laboratory apparatus is needed to find this figure. You can get a rough idea of reservoir size by weighing a potted plant at container capacity (i.e. soon after irrigation) and at the first sign of wilting. The difference between these two weights, multiplied by 0.8, gives the approximate maximum reservoir size for continuing excellent growth.

To find the size of the reservoir in a soil:

1. First measure or guess the effective depth of the root zone. The greatest proportion of the roots of any plant will be in the top 30–40 cm of soil (Fig. 22.4). Many plants will have at least some roots below this. If the top 40 cm is kept close to field capacity, plants will extract most of the water they need from that top 40 cm. The effective rooting depth can then be assumed to be 40 cm. However, when water use is being reduced to a minimum by allowing the soil to become very dry, the effective depth of the reservoir will be something like the depth of root penetration.

   Table 22.5 gives some depths for turf grasses. Mowing height affects the depth of root growth of some species. Provided the ground is fully covered with green leaves, cutting height has little effect on the rooting depth of warm-season grasses. This is not the case for grasses with an erect habit of growth. For them, lowering cutting height decreases rooting depth. Thus, after a couple of months of very close cutting, the roots of bent grasses in bowling greens might penetrate no deeper than 1 cm. The water content of the soil and the style in which water is applied will affect root distribution (Fig. 22.5).

   The roots of many ornamental trees and shrubs extend to a depth of at least 1 metre and often 2 m. Some send roots deeper than 25 m if there is water available to that depth. How then does one decide on the depth of the root zone?

   - In turf, look by taking core samples. Then either always water to that depth, or when the roots go very deep, choose some depth such as 500 mm and water to that depth.
   - For other plants, look at the depth of root penetration or choose some figure such as 300 or 400 mm.

2. Decide on the vigour of growth needed.

   - If you are growing plants for sale; or plants that give saleable produce, you will want vigorous growth.
   - If water is expensive, a lower growth will have to be accepted. You then have to decide just how much lower is acceptable to you.

Table 22.5
Approximate maximum depth to which the roots of turf grasses penetrate well-structured soils

Species	Rooting depth (cm)
Warm-season grasses:	
Couch, hybrid	150–240
Kikuyu	150–240
Paspalum distichum	120–150
Digitaria didactyla	100–150 (?)
Couch, common	100–150
Buffalo	80–100
Zoysia grasses	60–100
Carpet grass	30
*Cool-season grasses:**	
Tall fescue	60–120
Kentucky bluegrass	20–40
Bent grasses	5–35
Poa annua	3–15

*Close mowing can greatly reduce the depth of rooting of cool-season grasses.

3. Determine the texture of the soil (Chapter 3). Then read from Table 22.6 the amount of water than can be extracted from the soil before the growth rate becomes unacceptable. The lower the growth rate that can be accepted the greater can be the draw-down on the available water in the soil.
4. Multiply the figure found in Table 22.6 by the depth of the root zone to get the size of the reservoir of water that can be used.

Table 22.6
Approximate amounts of water that can be removed from soils, starting at field capacity, if plants are to be maintained as shown. (Figures are mm of water/cm depth of soil.)

Soil texture	Level of growth/appearance				
	Vigorous, lush	Strong, less lush	Moderate, acceptable	Low, just acceptable	Minimum
Sand	0.3	0.4	0.5	0.6	0.6
Loamy sand	0.4	0.6	0.7	0.8	0.9
Sandy loam	0.6	1.0	1.1	1.2	1.3
Loam	0.9	1.5	1.7	1.8	2.0
Clay poor structure	0.5	0.8	1.0	1.1	1.3
Clay good structure	0.7	1.1	1.3	1.6	1.9

Example 1: Core samples from a golf green show that roots penetrate to 35 cm. The grass is to kept growing strongly, but it does not need to be very lush. The soil is a loamy sand. From Table 22.6 the reservoir of water will be about 0.6 mm/cm depth.

Figure 22.5
Patterns of root growth of turf grasses as affected by soil water supply: (a) Constantly adequate supply of water and ample oxygen. (b) High water table giving waterlogged soil. (c) Soil that has been allowed to dry out after initially having an adequate water content to some depth. Lack of water has caused the death of many roots. New roots are formed only in the deeper, moister parts of the profile (d) The effect of light, shallow watering of turf that had once been adequately supplied

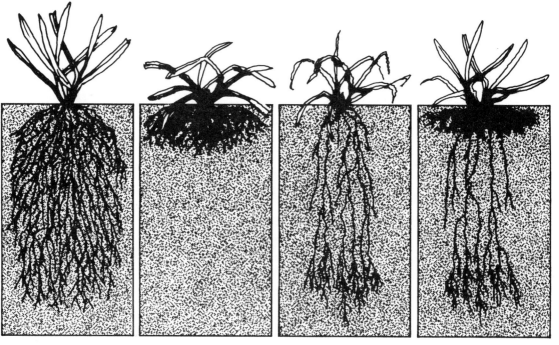

a   b   c   d

Total reservoir size = 35 × 0.6 = 21 mm

Example 2: A mixed group of ornamentals is to be maintained at a low rate of growth. You decide that you are going to irrigate until the soil is wet to 50 cm. Any water the plants get from below that is a bonus for them. The soil is a loam to 20 cm, then a clay of fair structure.

Total reservoir size = 20 × 1.8 + 30 × 1.3
= 36 + 39
= 75 mm.

'Guestimating' ET

ET = pan evaporation × a factor.

Pan evaporation can be measured on-site (Fig. 22.1) or (less accurately) can be read from Table 22.7. The factor has to be guessed from Table 22.8.

A set of figures for your area can be obtained from the nearest office of the Bureau of Meteorology. These figures will be different from the ones you would get from an on-site evaporimeter. The figures are averages and of course no day, week or month ever has 'average' weather.

Small differences between the microclimate of your area and that of the meteorological station affect evaporation. For example, windbreak trees a hundred metres upwind can reduce evaporation by more than 20%. Carparks, buildings or open dry paddocks can increase evaporation by a similar amount. Evaporation will be lower in cool hills areas and higher in open plains country.

Measuring evaporation

Evaporation is measured with an evaporimeter. It should be a Class A pan, but a cheaper alternative is to make one from an old drum (Fig. 22.6). Experiments

Table 22.7
Evaporation rates for some localities around Australia (*Courtesy of Australian Bureau of Meteorology*)

Place	Evaporation rate (open Class A pan figures)* (mm per day)												Total annual evaporation (mm)
	Jan	Feb	Mar	Apr	May	Jun	Jul	Aug	Sep	Oct	Nov	Dec	
Coastal													
Sydney	7.5	6.7	5.5	4.5	3.2	3.0	3.2	4.0	5.1	5.8	7.1	8.7	1961
Melbourne	7.6	7.0	5.1	3.4	2.0	1.4	1.6	2.3	3.2	4.4	5.5	7.0	1534
Adelaide	8.9	8.2	6.2	4.2	2.7	2.0	2.0	2.7	3.9	5.6	6.9	8.4	1876
Brisbane	6.3	5.3	4.9	4.1	2.9	2.4	2.6	3.6	4.6	5.3	6.3	7.0	1679
Perth	9.3	8.5	6.9	4.3	3.1	2.3	2.4	2.8	4.0	5.6	7.1	8.7	1977
Hobart	5.2	4.5	3.6	2.3	1.2	0.9	1.0	1.4	2.3	3.3	3.8	4.6	1030
Darwin	7.4	6.9	6.6	8.0	7.9	7.7	8.2	8.8	9.5	9.7	9.1	8.2	2964
Townsville	8.8	7.7	7.2	7.1	6.3	5.6	6.1	7.1	9.0	10.2	10.7	10.2	2916
Inland													
Canberra	8.8	7.6	5.7	3.8	2.5	1.8	1.8	2.7	4.0	5.5	6.8	9.2	1828
Alice Springs	13.4	12.1	10.3	7.7	4.9	4.0	4.2	5.7	7.7	10.2	11.7	13.0	3187
Griffith	9.8	9.1	6.7	4.2	2.4	1.6	1.8	2.7	3.9	5.8	8.1	10.2	2016
Tatura	7.9	7.0	5.3	3.1	1.6	1.2	1.2	1.8	2.8	4.2	6.1	7.8	1518
Mildura	11.7	10.9	8.0	5.0	2.8	1.9	2.2	3.4	4.8	6.7	9.2	11.6	2366
Oodnadatta	17.8	16.2	13.3	9.2	5.8	4.3	4.9	6.4	9.2	12.6	15.1	17.7	4026
Moree	10.9	9.6	8.2	5.9	3.8	2.7	2.8	3.7	5.5	7.8	10.2	11.2	2500
Merredin	13.5	12.3	10.2	6.2	3.6	2.3	2.4	2.8	4.3	7.1	9.9	12.9	2655

*These figures were obtained by multiplying figures from pans having bird guards by 1.081.

Table 22.8
Factors to be used to obtain evapotranspiration losses from evaporimeter figures

Type of growth and appearance needed	Factor*
Turf:	
Cool-season grasses:	
Vigorous, lush	0.8–0.85
Strong growth, acceptable appearance	0.7–0.75
Moderate growth, just acceptable	0.65–0.7
Warm-season grasses:	
Vigorous, lush	0.55–0.7
Strong growth, acceptable appearance	0.45–0.55
Moderate growth, just acceptable	0.25–0.4
Ornamentals:	
Vigorous growth, during establishment, broad-leaved species	0.7–0.85
Strong growth	0.6–0.7
Moderate growth, some drought tolerance	0.4
Low growth rate acceptable, moderate drought tolerance needed	0.2–0.4
Minimum, for desert plants	0.05–0.2
Vegetables, fruit trees	0.7–0.85

*These factors apply when at least 70% of the soil surface is shaded by the plants. When the shaded surface is less than this the factors can be reduced by 0.1 to 0.3. For example, if widely spaced trees separated by dry bare soil shade 50% of the soil, and a low growth rate is acceptable, the factor could be 0.3 – 0.2 = 0.1

in Victoria and Western Australia have shown that figures obtained from simple evaporimeters agree well with those obtained with Class A pans.

We now describe how to construct and use a simple evaporimeter. There is a fair amount of hassle in using an evaporimeter, but if maximum benefit must be obtained from a limited water supply, that hassle will be time well spent. However, we again point out that commercially available services can eliminate the hassle, for a fee.

Figure 22.6
Example of a simple, but effective evaporimeter. This one was a black-plastic drum, cut down and with aluminium foil wrapped around the outside. The wire netting cover was removed for the photograph.
Photograph J Coppi

Use any round, straight-sided container with a diameter of 30 cm or more. Steel drums of 60–200 L capacity, cut down to about 30 cm high, rustproofed, and painted with bituminous aluminium paint are suitable, as are straight-sided, light-coloured plastic containers of similar size.

Stick a plastic ruler to the inside wall, with the zero at the rim. Sit the evaporimeter on the ground *in the open* close to or in the area that will need irrigating. Fill it to the 50 mm mark in spring or towards the end of the rainy season. Thereafter read the water level every 1 to 7 days, depending on the weather. Record the readings. A cover of 2 cm mesh wire netting stops birds and animals from using the evaporimeter as a bath or trough.

Clean the evaporimeter occasionally and kill algal growth with small amounts of swimming pool chlorine or liquid bleach (e.g. White King).

Rain that does not overflow the evaporimeter is automatically allowed for (Table 22.9). (Actually, the allowance is over-generous. If 20 mm of rain falls, the plants receive that amount of water, but the evaporimeter figures assume that it has received only 20 × 0.7 = 14 mm. You can make some allowance for this by applying less water. However, as rain is generally infrequent during the irrigation season in Australia, the small amount of extra water can be a bonus to help leach salts from the root zone.)

Table 22.9
Example of a record sheet from a simple evaporimeter. Allowable total loss from the evaporimeter between irrigations was 30 mm.

Day	Pan reading (mm)	Pan evaporation (mm)	Total pan evaporation
0	50	0	0
2	65	15	15
4	75	10	25
5	80	5	30
	50	(irrigate 21 mm)	
7	62	12	12
		(rain 5 mm)	
9	64	2	14
		(rain 20 mm)	
10	45	−19	−5
13	70	25	20
15	82	12	32
	50	(irrigate 21 mm)	

You will have to make some allowance on the rare occasion when heavy rain causes the evaporimeter to overflow.

The simplest way of allowing for irrigation water that gets into the evaporimeter is to take a reading before irrigation starts and remove added water back to that reading immediately afterwards. Taking out 1–2 mm extra will allow for evaporation during irrigation.

When starting to use a water budget as a basis for irrigating, choose a factor that seems right. After some weeks assess plant response. Raise or lower the factor until you are using the least water to give your plants the required appearance and growth rate.

The amount of water you actually apply must allow for losses during watering and include an extra amount for leaching salts from the root zone.

Using a water budget

The amount of water needed = evaporation losses + losses during application + leaching water − rainfall since last watering.

Example 1: We continue with Example 1 from (p. 286). The turf is to grow strongly, so choose a factor of 0.7 from Table 22.6. Therefore, total pan evaporation can be 21/0.7 = 30 mm before water must be applied.

Table 22.9 shows the trends in readings of a nearby simple pan evaporimeter. No rain fell in the first 5 days, so water was applied as soon as the evaporimeter had lost 30 mm. During the second period 5 mm of rain fell on day 8 and 20 mm on days 9–10. This rain stretched to 10 days the time till the next watering.

Example 2: We continue with Example 2 from (p. 287). The ornamentals are to be maintained at a low rate of growth. Choose a factor of 0.3. Evapotranspiration can go to 75 mm before water must be applied. Therefore, water when an evaporimeter has lost 75/0.3 = 250 mm. If the average daily pan evaporation is 6 mm (from Table 22.7), 75 mm of water is to be applied every 250/6 = 42 days.

Example 3: A hybrid couch lawn in a garden is growing in a deep loam to clay loam soil. It is to be maintained at a just acceptable level of growth. Assume that the main root zone extends to 150 cm.

Acceptable water loss (Table 22.6) will be about 150 × 1.6 = 240 mm. From Table 22.6, the factor is about 0.3.

Therefore, total evaporimeter losses will be 240/0.3 = 800 mm.

If daily pan evaporation is 9 mm, the lawn need not be watered for 800/9 = 89 days.

Example 4: A group of plants is in containers, each holding 10 litres of mix. The canopy of tops is continuous, with each plant covering an area with a diameter of about 30 cm. The mix has a readily available water content of 17 volume %. How often must water be applied when pan evaporation is 7 mm/day?

$$\text{Reservoir size} = 10\ 000 \text{ mL} \times \frac{17}{100} = 1700 \text{ mL}$$

$$\begin{aligned}\text{Area of ground cover} = \pi r^2 &= 3.14 \times (0.15)^2 \text{ m}^2 \\ &= 0.07 \text{ m}^2\end{aligned}$$

Assume a factor (Table 22.8) of 1.0 to allow a reasonable safety margin.

Therefore, ET = 7 mm/day.

$$\begin{aligned}\text{ET per plant} &= 0.07 \times 7 \text{ L/day} \\ &= 0.49 \text{ L/day} \\ &= 490 \text{ mL/day}.\end{aligned}$$

Therefore, apply water every third day if growth must continue to be rapid.

Example 5: Fruit trees are being watered via drippers. It has been decided to run the drippers every day. There are four drippers per tree, each rated at 5 L/hr. For how long each day should the drippers be run?

The area covered by the canopy of each tree is about 28 m². Daily pan evaporation averages 6 mm. Therefore, the daily loss of water by each tree is about 0.8 × 6 × 28 = 134 litres.

Therefore, the drippers should be on daily for $\dfrac{134}{4 \times 5}$ = 6.7 hours

Notes on the water budget method

- This method is best suited to large areas planted to one or similar species (turf, plantations). For small areas, poaching of unknown amounts of water from the area by plants outside it makes it almost impossible to use.
- The growing medium must be at container capacity, or field capacity to the depth of the root zone, before you start using the water budget method.
- This method automatically takes care of the different frequencies of watering needed by soils of different textures.

Figure 22.7
Examples of probe moisture meters.
If a probe is inserted into pure
distilled water it will read 'dry'. A
small amount of salt added to the
water will allow it to read 'wet'.
Salts affect the reading in growing
media too. For example, a wet,
leached potting mix may be shown
to be 'moderately dry'. A dryish mix
that has just been fertilized may
read 'wet'. Enough said? *Photograph
J Coppi*

Figure 22.8
Typical installation of the Watermatic
soil moisture sensor in turf. *Courtesy
of Cuming & Associates, Melbourne*

- With a little experimentation, you can soon find the best factor (Table 22.8) for your situation.

USING INSTRUMENTS

Not so long ago the only instruments available for monitoring soil water status and helping with timing of applications were toys (Fig. 22.7), gypsum blocks (monitoring only), neutron moisture meters (monitoring only) and tensiometers (monitoring and controlling). Now the choice is all of these plus four excellent Australian-made sensor-controlled systems. Two have been around for long enough for independent research reports to show just how effective they really are. They owe much of their effectiveness to advances in microelectronics. We offer comments on these systems.

In all systems, sensors are installed into the root zone of the area to be irrigated. In the first two described, the sensors are permanently buried in intimate contact with the soil. The electrical signals they send back to a monitor change as the moisture content of the soil immediately around them changes. When the signal reaches a pre-determined point it triggers changes in the monitor, which then instructs solenoid valves to open and irrigation to start. The monitor is programmed so that watering is permitted only at times of the day when you want it to happen.

With both of these systems, it is necessary to set and fine-tune the trigger conditions on the basis of trials at the site, as outlined in the instructions that come with them. This tuning allows you to minimise water applications that still give acceptable plant growth/quality. For turf, you will typically be looking for water application rates that are about 50–60% of pan evaporation.

The third system to be described is replacing neutron probes as a monitor in irrigated orchards. In the not too distant future it will be produced in forms that will enable it to control solenoid valves.

Readers will sense our excitement over these instruments. We know that they work and that they can take much of the guesswork out of irrigation. But we also know that they do not replace a sound knowledge of the basics of the interactions between water, plants, soils and environmental conditions. Don't be lulled into a false sense of security by hi-tech instruments. Their effective use rests on a sound knowledge of basics.

Cuming Watermatic Irrigation Management System

The Watermatic system uses ceramic block sensors (Fig. 22.8) that are buried at a depth of one-third to one-half of the effective root depth. That typically means burying them at 100 to 150 mm below the soil surface. The electrical properties of these sensors respond to the water content of the soil around them. Irrigation is triggered when the electrical properties reach a certain critical, pre-set level and is switched off when the water percolating through the soil re-wets the sensor. Variation in the salinity of the soil does not impair operation.

Independent assessments in the USA and Australia have shown that plants whose watering is controlled by Watermatic sensors can be maintained at equal quality with 35% to 70% of the water that is applied according to 'guessing' or the use of computerised water budget methods. Typical savings in water are about 50%, so the system can pay for itself in one irrigation season.

DRW MicroLink system

The sensors in this system are stainless steel cylinders 90 mm long, which are buried in the soil at any depth, but typically at about 120 mm (Fig. 22.9). Sensors apply pulses of heat to the soil and measure the response, which varies with the

Figure 22.9
The MicroLink system for controlling irrigation. *Courtesy of DRW Engineering, Tanunda, South Australia*

Figure 22.10
Typical EnviroSCAN probe, in this case with four sensors, showing how the probe is sealed into a PVC pipe inserted into the soil. *Courtesy of Sentek Pty Ltd, Adelaide*

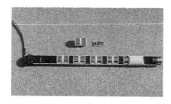

Figure 22.10a
Sensor of the Dataflow Systems (Perth, WA) irrigation control system which was under advanced testing prior to commercial release in late 1993. *Photograph G Smith*

wetness of the soil. One MicroLink control unit can control up to eight sensors. Each sensor can be independently calibrated so that the area it controls can be watered at any amount of drawdown of soil water right to permanent wilting point.

An installation in an oval at Gawler, South Australia, resulted in better turf and a saving of 40% in the amount of water applied compared with control by timeclock. For this oval it was a saving of $4000 in one year. The excellent control of soil water also allowed the grass roots to grow more deeply into the soil. The larger soil reservoir so created allowed watering to be less frequent.

EnviroSCAN Soil Water Monitoring System

This system uses probes that measure the dielectric constant of the soil. Each probe is installed in a PVC access tube sunk into the soil (Fig. 22.10). Probes are run from batteries or solar panels. Data on soil moisture status is recorded at intervals of 10–60 minutes and the data stored for later downloading to a laptop computer. The EnviroSCAN does what a neutron moisture meter does—it measures the water content of the soil—but it does it better and much more cheaply. It is rapidly replacing neutron meters in irrigated agriculture and horticulture.

The EnviroSCAN system is precise and flexible. We await with interest its further development.

Table 22.10

In one experiment, water use by couch (*Cynodon dactylon*) was greatly reduced when irrigation was guided by tensiometers. The grass was grown in a sandy loam soil. (*From* V B Youngner et al. *Proc. 4th Intern. Turfgrass Conf.* p. 251, 1980)

	Annual water use		
Treatment	(mm)	% of 'normal'	Quality rating*
Irrigation when tensiometer reached 15 kPa	830	62	8.8
Irrigation when tensiometer reached 40 kPa	670	50	8.2
Irrigation when tensiometer reached 65 kPa	590	44	7.8
Irrigation at 76% of pan evaporation	1010	76	8.5
'Normal' greenkeeper practice	1330	100	7.5
(Pan evaporation)	(1330)	(100)	

*10 = best, 1 = poorest. There was no significant difference in turf quality between the treatments except that the 'normally' watered turf contained more *Poa annua*.

Tensiometers

Earlier editions of this book devoted much space to tensiometers and their use for controlling the irrigation of turf and horticultural crops. The giant leaps in technology represented by the systems just described have almost, but not totally, eliminated tensiometers from serious consideration for most situations of interest to readers of this book. They no longer merit consideration for turf and commercial field plantings, but they may see increasing use in nurseries.

Tensiometers (Fig. 22.11) measure the tightness (tension) with which water is held in growing media. The greater the tension with which the water is held, the greater is the suction needed to remove it (see Chapter 9).

A tensiometer consists of a hollow plastic tube tipped with a porous ceramic cup and connected at the other end to some form of pressure-measuring device such as a vacuum gauge (Fig. 22.11) or pressure transducer. The instrument is

Figure 22.11

Examples of tensiometers.

Photograph J Coppi

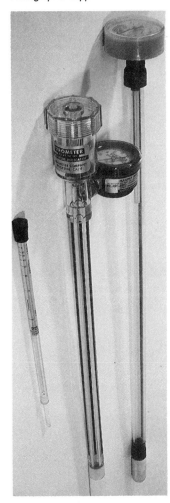

filled with water and installed permanently in the growing medium with the ceramic cup in the middle of the root zone. As plants remove water from around the cup, they also remove some water from the tensiometer. This loss registers as a negative pressure on the tensiometer gauge. Irrigation water is applied when the tensiometer reading reaches 3–5 kPa (for plants that must always grow rapidly) to about 50–70 kPa (for plants that need not grow as rapidly).

When set up properly and managed skilfully, tensiometers allow precise control of watering and reduced use of water (Table 22.10), but so do the other methods described above, and with fewer hassles.

A main problem with tensiometers is that the column of water that is their working 'part' is easily broken if the soil is allowed to become too dry between irrigations. This limits their usefulness to water suctions from zero (saturated soil) to about 80 kPa. They cannot be used in situations where water must be conserved through allowing the soil to become drier than this.

Small solid-state tensiometers have recently been shown to be useful for controlling the irrigation of plants in containers, via drippers or sub-irrigation.

USING WATER WISELY

Water is used wisely when the amount applied matches the needs of the plants being grown. If vigorous growth is needed, large amounts of water are needed; if growth can be minimal, little water need be applied. Precious water is wasted when more is applied than is needed to achieve the required growth rate.

On the other hand, we defeat our aims if the amount of water applied is less than that needed to give the desired growth. This section is a collection of guidelines for using water wisely.

General comments

- Match water applications to the level of growth needed.
- Water infrequently and deeply, unless your water is very saline, when you will have to water frequently enough to maintain the salinity of the main root zone low enough to keep growth rate adequate (Chapter 21).
- Avoid using sprinklers in the heat of the day. Losses by evaporation are high then. Also avoid watering in the evening in areas of high humidity. Allowing the leaves to remain wet overnight encourages attack by fungi. Rather, whenever possible, water early in the morning.
- Reduce evaporation by mulching wherever possible.
- Remember that extra water is needed for leaching when the water used is saline (Chapter 21). Never apply saline water by sprinkler on a hot windy day. The increased salinity of the water that does reach plant leaves can kill them.
- This is for those who want maximum plant growth from minimum amounts of water. Plants receiving a balanced supply of nutrients produce more growth per unit of water applied than those that are less well fed. They may also use a little more water, but for each litre of water used they may produce as much as twice as much growth. For example, in one experiment, fertilizer increased the yield of wheat from 2 to 3 tonnes per hectare, increased water use from 428 to 453 mm and so increased the efficiency of use from 470 to 660 kg of wheat per 100 mm of water.

There is a limit. If extra fertilizer does not increase growth, it will not increase the efficiency of water use.

There is little point in irrigating plants that are supposed to grow fast if they lack nutrients. The plants will not be able to make much use of the water and most will be wasted.

- On the other hand, fertilizing plants that do not need to grow much will only increase the amount of water they use. They will become less tolerant of dry conditions.

Turf

Between a third and half of the water used in urban areas is applied to turf. A small improvement in the efficiency with which it is applied will save much water.

- The most powerful way of reducing water consumption by turf is to grow warm-season grasses. At any level of water application they use less than do cool-season grasses (Table 22.11).

At any level of water application, the warm-season grasses are much more efficient at using the water to make growth (Table 22.12). Note in the table that couch grass is more than twice as efficient as perennial ryegrass at using water.

Whenever the climate permits it, the main turf grasses used should be warm-season grasses. The amount of water needed to maintain an acceptable

Table 22.11
Water losses by evapotranspiration from two warm-season and two cool-season grasses (From V B Youngner et al. _Proc. 4th Intern. Turfgrass Conf._ p. 251, 1980)

Water applied	Couch grass	Buffalo grass	Tall fescue	Kentucky bluegrass
	Evapotranspiration as % of pan evaporation			
Tensiometer = 15 kPa	62	55	90	86
Tensiometer = 40 kPa or 35 kPa*	51	45	81	76
Tensiometer = 65 kPa or 55 kPa*	44	44	75	70[†]
Seventy-six % of pan evaporation	76	76	84	83

* The first figure in each case applies to the warm-season grasses, the second to the cool-season grasses. Allowing the soil under the cool-season grasses to dry as much as that under the warm-season grasses gave very poor turf.
†All grasses in all treatments had excellent quality except for this driest bluegrass plot, which was of poorer quality.

Table 22.12
Example of the very much higher efficiency with which warm-season grasses use water, compared with cool-season grasses (From I Biran et al. _Agronomy J._ 73: 85, 1981)

Species	Water use over 12 weeks (litres)	Transpiration ratio (g water/g dry matter)
Warm-season grasses:		
Couch grass (cv. Santa Ana)	33.6	308
Paspalum distichum	36.1	343
Kikuyu	40.1	346
Buffalo	37.3	365
Zoysia sp.	33.7	420
Cool-season grasses:		
Tall fescue	55.9	586
Perennial ryegrass	49.6	671

turf of warm-season grasses is about half that needed for cool-season grasses. The only snag is that in cooler parts of Australia warm-season grasses may need to be oversown with annual cool-season grasses for winter green.

- A main reason why tall fescues are more drought tolerant than other cool-season grasses is that they have much deeper root systems (Table 22.5). Unfortunately, they also use huge amounts of water compared to warm-season grasses (Table 22.11), so even they cannot be recommended for warm areas where water is expensive or in short supply.
- Anything that reduces the total leaf area of a turf reduces total water consumption. Of course mowing is the main way in which leaf area is reduced. However, the effect on warm-season grasses is much smaller than the effect on cool-season grasses (Table 22.13). Most warm-season grasses have small leaves and a horizontal habit of growth. Leaves deep inside the sward are shaded by the leaves above, so they contribute little to total transpiration. Lowering the cutting height does not reduce the total effective leaf area by much.

Table 22.13
Effect of increased height of cut on water consumption by infrequently watered turf grasses (*From* I Biran et al. *Agronomy J.* 73: 85, 1981)

Species	$\dfrac{\text{Water loss of grass 60 mm high}}{\text{Water loss of grass 30 mm high}} \times 100\%$
Warm-season grasses:	
Couch (cv. Suwannee)	115 ⎫
Couch (cv. Santa Ana)	109 ⎪
Paspalum distichum	103 ⎬ 108
Kikuyu	110 ⎪
Buffalo	108 ⎭
Zoysia sp.	104
Cool-season grasses:	
Tall fescue	129 ⎫ 127
Perennial ryegrass	125 ⎭

On the other hand, the leaves of most cool-season grasses have a vertical habit of growth. High cutting greatly increases the total area of leaf surface that is transpiring.

This information suggests that close mowing will reduce the amount of water that must be applied to turf. Actually, it usually doesn't. Close mowing, especially of cool-season grasses, reduces total root production and depth of rooting. The reservoir of water available to the turf decreases. It will have to be watered more frequently, so losses during sprinkling are increased. Survival in dry weather is best when mowing leaves the sward as high as can be tolerated by users.

For cool-season grasses, keep mowing height moderately high during spring, raise it during summer and gradually lower it during autumn. For warm-season grasses, mowing height can be high during spring, gradually lowered during summer and then raised again during autumn to promote winter hardiness.

- After choosing a warm-season grass, the next most important way of reducing water consumption by turf is to water infrequently and deeply. We strongly urge turf managers to prepare water budgets for the different parts of their area or to invest in a sensor-controlled system, as outlined earlier.

Otherwise, second best is to water only when the turf wilts. Look for bluish-grey coloration and 'footprinting' when you walk on it. Another alternative

Table 22.14
Effect of mowing frequency on evapotranspiration by Penncross bent grass (*From R C Shearman and J B Beard Crop Sci.* 13: 424, 1973)

Mowings per week	Relative water loss
0.5	0.8
1	1.0
6	1.15

Figure 22.12
The roots of these *Juniperus chinensis* 'Torulosa', 'Sylvestris', 'Pfitzeriana' and 'Hetzii' had grown well beyond their drip circles by 12 months after planting out. *From* F F Gilman *J. Environ. Hortic.* 7: 88, 1989

for turf on sandy root zones is to take a core sample. Water if the core falls apart through dryness.

Frequent light watering encourages shallow rooting. The turf then needs frequent watering. The more frequently you water, the more often you will have to water. Frequent watering of heavily used turf allows greater soil compaction, with all its damaging side-effects (Chapter 19). Frequent watering also encourages *Poa annua*. It has relatively shallow roots (Table 22.3) so infrequent watering weakens it.

- One exception to the infrequent watering rule is during establishment. Newly sown seed must be lightly watered many times a day until the seeds have germinated and a root system has been established. Especially on sandy root zones, watering will need to be carefully managed and should be relatively frequent for the first dry season.
- Mowing slightly increases the transpiration rate of grasses for a short time (Table 22.14) because of losses through the cut stubs of leaves. Another effect of mowing is that root growth slows down for a few days. It is therefore often useful to water soon after mowing. Wait for a few hours, until the cut ends have become sealed against pathogens.

Try to avoid mowing on days when the temperature is likely to exceed 35°C. Blunt mower blades mutilate grass leaves, increasing losses of water and the risk of disease. Keep mower blades sharp.

- Apply nitrogen sparingly. Excessive use of nitrogen gives a large leaf area and reduced root growth (Fig. 20.11). One increases water use, the other decreases the ability of the plant to get water. However, some fertilizer nitrogen must be applied. Starved grass might lose 1000 g of water for each gram of growth. Grass fertilized as suggested in Chapter 20 will use much less water for each gram of growth. Therefore, a sparingly, but adequately fertilized turf will be using water efficiently.
- Prepare for severe water restrictions by reducing the use of nitrogen, supplying more potassium, making sure that the turf is adequately supplied with iron and by decreasing the frequency of watering. Reserve the water that is available for the most important turf. The grass in other areas will go dormant. It will not be permanently harmed if a drought-tolerant (warm-season) grass has been chosen. When the shortage is upon you, do not apply any more fertilizers.
- On hot afternoons, some closely cut cool-season grasses wilt badly. Their leaves are in danger of becoming over-heated and desiccated. One or two light sprinklings of water (syringing) will cool them and overcome the wilting. If this happens often, you probably should be growing a tougher grass.
- Seriously consider redesigning your irrigation system if the present one wastes water. It could be wasting it because areas with different needs are on the same line. Uneven application often means that the sprinklers must be left on until those areas receiving the least have been given enough. Use cans to check the system (Chapter 23).
- Turf shaded by buildings will need less water than unshaded turf nearby. However, if the shading is by trees that have roots throughout the turf soil, water will often be needed at a higher rate to satisfy both turf and trees. Roots of trees often extend far beyond the drip circle (Fig. 22.12). Their extent can be limited only by repeated ripping.

Landscape plantings

- First and foremost, follow the guidelines given earlier in this chapter so that you match water application to the growth rate needed.
- Try gradually increasing the length of time between waterings. The more a soil is allowed to dry out, the lower will be losses of water by evapotrans-

Figure 22.13
Like a mulch, hairs on the underneath surfaces of leaves of *Grevillea rosmarinifolia* help the plant conserve water. Magnification: x200. *Photograph R C Foster*

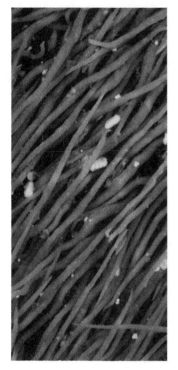

piration. You may find that you can apply much less water than you have been using, while still keeping growth and appearance the way you like it.

- Group plants of similar water requirements. For example, a corner of drought-tolerant native and exotic plants may never need irrigating once established. A mixture of plants with different abilities to cope with drought will need to be irrigated to keep the most sensitive alive; the others may then grow excessively fast, have shortened lives and be more likely to be attacked by root-rotting fungi.
- Make extensive use of mulches.
- Weeds use water too: remove them.
- Water well ahead of forecast hot weather. The plants are then better able to cope with the heat.
- When water is in very limited supply, or very expensive, grow mainly drought-tolerant plants. These have ways of surviving with little water including:

  - deep and extensive root systems;
  - storage of water in enlarged roots and stems (e.g. cacti);
  - low transpiration rate through having sunken stomata;
  - waxy coatings and hairs on leaves (Fig. 22.13) that act as 'mulches' that slow water loss;
  - small and vertically oriented leaves;
  - few leaves (leaf shedding under stress reduces the number further);
  - an ability to close stomata early in the onset of water stress;
  - an ability to shut down internally without damage until water is again available;
  - stomata that open only at night—cacti and many succulents have this ability.

- Even when water is reasonably abundant, it still makes good sense to mainly grow plants that grow well in your area without vast amounts of extra water.
- Diseased plants use water very inefficiently. Those with root diseases may not be able to use much of the water in a soil. Get rid of them.
- Mounds add interest to landscapes. However, they shed water more quickly than ground with a gentler slope. Sprinkler water must be applied to them slowly. If watering is prolonged to ensure deep wetting of mounds, surrounding areas receive too much water. Either don't use mounds, or contour them (Fig. 22.14) so that runoff from them is reduced; flatten existing mounds.

Figure 22.14
Roughening or contouring mounds in a landscape will reduce runoff from them

- When watering an isolated plant in a landscape, keep the application within its drip line. Much of the water will be wasted if you spread it thinly over the whole area.
- Many drought-tolerant plants survive without irrigation water, provided that the soil reservoir under them is full at the start of the dry season. When necessary, fill the reservoir, even if this means that there will be little water left for later.
- When you have almost no water, and the soil reservoir is not filled at the beginning of the dry season, shrubs may survive better if they are heavily thinned to reduce transpiration. You can also selectively remove plants from crowded groups to aid the survival of those remaining.
- Under natural conditions, regeneration of shrubs and trees takes place mainly in wet years. In landscapes you must be prepared to copy this by providing extra water for the first year and possibly the first two years.

Nurseries

The limited size of the reservoir of water in a pot means that water must be applied frequently in nurseries. Applying too little water will reduce growth rate.

However, watering too frequently can keep the mix too wet. This can reduce growth rate (Fig. 10.5) by reducing oxygen supply to the roots. Diseases are usually more of a problem when mixes are constantly wet.

Nursery people must walk the narrow path between applying too much or too little.

- Choose your mix carefully so that its air-filled porosity and readily available water content are suited to your plants and environment.
- Note very carefully that the reservoir size given by a measurement of readily available water content is the *maximum* size. It is best to keep water loss to no more than two-thirds of this amount. Allowing more drying increases the chance that plants will be damaged by high salinity. At the first hint of water repellency you must apply a wetting agent (Chapter 6).
- Work out some likely watering frequencies based on: the readily available water content of the mix;

  - pot size;
  - canopy width and type;
  - a range of evaporation rates.

An example is given on (p. 72 and p. 290).

- Large plants remove water from pots more rapidly that do small plants. That's obvious, but there are also differences between different plants of about the same size but of different species. Generally, losses will be less from plants with small, narrow and sparse leaves than from those with large, broad and numerous leaves. The difference could be as much as three-fold.
- The simplest way of finding out whether water is needed is to knock a few plants from their pots and look at their rootballs.
- Tensiometers have been used successfully as an aid in watering plants in pots. However, they do break down from time to time, especially in open mixes.
- Apply only enough water to fill the reservoir and to give a small amount of leaching. The amount of leaching water will usually be 5–10% of total water applied, but could be a little more if the water used has a high EC. Check by measuring the EC of the mix (Chapter 33).
- Group plants according to their water requirements. In other words, don't have plants and pots of different sizes in the one group.
- When watering by hand, use a water breaker so that mix is not splashed out of the pot. Direct the water onto the mix, not over the foliage.
- Losses of water by evaporation from the mix itself vary considerably from mix to mix (Fig. 22.15). Water can be saved by mulching peat-based mixes with chips or bark.
- Weeds can be eliminated and evaporation reduced by placing geotextile mats treated with trifluralin herbicide on the mix surface.
- Even one weed in a pot will significantly reduce the growth of the plant being grown (Table 22.15).
- When planning a watering system and its use, be aware that the rate of water use is reduced by shading, increased air humidity and decreased wind speed.
- Plants out in fierce sunshine on hot days will not take up water fast enough to keep up with transpiration. Light sprinkling (syringing) several times during the day will often be beneficial, but only if the water has a very low salt content. A better long-term solution is to provide shade and windbreaks.
- Check automatic watering systems frequently. Adjust them to suit changes in weather and plant needs.
- Irrigating via capillary beds, drippers or by hand onto each pot is very much less wasteful of water than is overhead sprinkling. Losses of nutrients from soluble fertilizer applied in the irrigation water will be very much less (Table 22.16)

MULCHES

A mulch is a layer of material on the surface of a growing medium. Mulches

Figure 22.15
Evaporation of water from pine bark in a pot is slower than evaporation from peatmoss. The bark 'self-mulches' whereas peatmoss continues to act as a wick until its water content is very low. *From D V Beardsell et al. Scientia Horticulturae 11: 9, 1979*

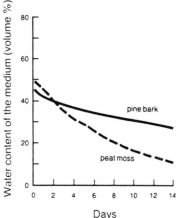

Table 22.15
Just one weed in a pot can reduce the growth of the plant being grown. (From K L Walker and D J Williams HortScience 25: 650, 1990)

Number of weeds per container	Juniper growth (cm)
0	34.2
1	30.1
2	30.6
3	30.2
4	27.2

Figure 22.16
A nearly complete cover of black plastic greatly reduces evaporation of water from a soil. *From* W O Willis et al. *Soil Sci. Soc. Amer. Proc.* 27: 577, 1963

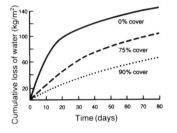

have three main uses: to reduce evaporation, to alter soil temperature, and to reduce the number of weeds.

Table 22.16
Example showing differences in nutrient losses from nurseries due to fertilizer type and irrigation method. (*From* T M Rathier and C R Fink *Amer. Nurseryman* Sept. 1: 99, 1989)

Nitrogen source	Nitrate–N(kg/ha)		
	Leachate	Runoff	Total
Trickle irrigation:			
Controlled-release	10–27	4–6	14–33
Soluble	163	6	169
Overhead irrigation:			
Controlled-release	17–28	6–7	23–35
Soluble	163	157	320

Materials

The soils of all natural plant communities have mulches of litter—fallen leaves, twigs and branches—on their surfaces. The mulches used in many man-made landscapes copy these litter mulches, but often other materials are used:

- organic materials that decompose readily—straw, hay, compost, leaves, animal manures, seaweed;
- organic materials that decompose more slowly—pine bark, wood chips, shredded corn cobs, and walnut, almond and cocoa bean shells;
- mineral materials—pebbles, gravel, sand, crushed bricks, finely cultivated soil;
- synthetic materials—woven and solid black plastic sheeting, reinforced aluminium foil, plastic/paper laminates.

Reduced evaporation

Mulches reduce evaporation partly by shading the soil and partly by slowing the movement of water vapour and liquid from the soil to the atmosphere. Evaporation from the bare surface of a medium draws water from below, as through a wick, if the columns of water in the medium are unbroken. A main effect of a mulch is to break the 'wick'.

Table 22.17
Effects of several organic mulches, applied 75 mm deep, on evaporation of water from a soil (*From* R C Shearman et al. *J. Amer. Soc. Hort. Sci.* 104: 461, 1979)

Mulch material	Water evaporated in 2 days (g/m²)
Lucerne hay	4.9*
Oat straw	4.9
Lawn clippings (dried)	5.2
Bare soil	27.9

*This is an 82% reduction in evaporation compared with bare soil.

- Table 22.17 shows the effect of 75 mm depths of several organic materials. A straw layer 40 mm thick reduces evaporation by about 70%. Thicker mulches are undesirable as they hold a lot of water, so reducing the proportion of rain or irrigation water reaching roots. Turf clippings must be dried before being used as mulch. Wet clippings will pack into a mat that allows little water through to the soil.
- Black plastic film is very effective at reducing evaporation (Fig. 22.16) but its effect on soil temperature (Fig. 22.17), oxygen supply and water entry make it an undesirable mulching material.
- Aluminium foil can reduce evaporation even more than black plastic because it keeps the soil cooler.
- When other materials cannot be used, a surface layer of finely tilled soil is a very effective mulch (Fig. 22.18). For continued effectiveness, the soil must be lightly cultivated 1–2 days after rain or irrigation; this breaks up the 'wick' made by any surface crusting. Thus maintained, soil mulches are very effective in reducing evaporation. However, finely tilled soil is more likely to be eroded

Figure 22.17
Soil temperature, 30 mm below the surface, as affected by various mulching materials. The soil was at field capacity at the start of the measuring period. This allowed evaporative cooling of the bare soil. Dry, bare soil nearby reached a temperature of 51°C at the same depth

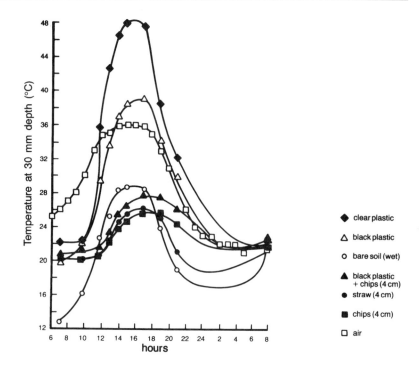

◆ clear plastic

△ black plastic

○ bare soil (wet)

▲ black plastic
  + chips (4 cm)

● straw (4 cm)

■ chips (4 cm)

□ air

by wind or rain than is soil protected by vegetable or organic mulches. For this reason, organic mulches are to be preferred wherever possible.

Altered temperature

As Fig. 22.17 shows, soil temperatures under organic mulches are lower than under bare soil, while black plastic increases soil temperature. Organic mulches shade and insulate the soil while plastic acts as a mini greenhouse. The consequences of this are:

- Organic materials make ideal summer mulches: roots grow right up into the moist, cool, surface layer of soil.
- Plants mulched with organic materials grow more slowly in late winter and early spring than do unmulched plants or those mulched with black plastic, because of lower soil temperatures. Frost damage may be increased too.
- Mulches of black plastic can increase growth rates in early spring. This is especially useful for clay soils, whose high water content means that a lot of heat is needed to warm them.
- However, in warmer weather, the high temperatures under black plastic first lead to excessive transpiration, and then kill the roots unless the plastic is shaded by plant leaves or an organic mulch. Death is especially likely if the plastic has allowed the soil to remain too wet in the cooler months. The roots then tend to grow mainly on or near the soil surface so that they can get some oxygen.

We strongly discourage the use of black plastic as a mulch.

Figure 22.18
Finely tilled soil is a very effective mulch. *From* J W Holmes et al. *Proc. 7th Intern. Congress Soil Sci.* 1: 188, 1960

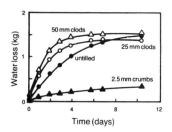

Fewer weeds

Most mulches reduce the numbers of weeds growing in an area (Table 22.18). Many seeds do not germinate under a mulch, or if they do the seedlings die before reaching the light. Those that do struggle through are weakened and easy to remove.

Table 22.18
Example of the effects of mulches on weed growth (*From J B Gartner, Amer. Nurseryman May 15: 9, 1978*)

Mulch material	Numbers of weeds/m²	
	50 mm mulch	100 mm mulch
Bare soil	260	260
Sawdust	8	1
Pine bark	4	0
Chips	1	0

These statements are not always true, because:

- Organic mulches that contain many weed seeds will increase the number of weeds in an area.
- Nutgrass, whose emerging shoots can pierce through many mulches, including black plastic, continues to thrive in mulched areas. It can only be eliminated through fumigation or repeated use of herbicides.
- Other vigorous grasses—couch, kikuyu, etc.—are best killed with herbicides before laying a mulch.

A combination of weed control mat plus 50–100 mm of chunky bark provides better control of weeds than does a thick mulch of finer materials, with or without mat. But note that weed control mat can be clogged if it is overlain with fine organic materials.

Other effects of mulches

- Mulches must have 'breather holes' that allow oxygen to reach the soil. These holes also allow rain or irrigation water to reach the soil. That means that sheet plastic must not be used as a mulch.
- Don't use organic materials that will pack down into a water-shedding layer. Turf clippings can do this if used before drying or if more chunky materials are not mixed with very fine clippings.
- Chunky mulches that have large holes between particles can be applied more thickly than can mulches of finer texture. Optimum thickness for fine composts is about 30 mm, for coarse composts about 40 mm, for chipped tree trimmings about 60 mm, and for bark nuggets about 80 mm.
- Pine bark is more durable than most other organic materials.
- Fertilizer nitrogen is easily washed to the soil below through mulches of chips and bark.
- Plants can be harmed by mulches applied to the lower parts of sloping ground. These areas are normally wetter than those higher up the slope. A mulch will allow them to remain excessively wet, even waterlogged. Plants growing in such areas often die from root-rotting diseases.
- Mulches absorb the energy of drops of rain and sprinkler water. This reduces crusting of the soil, allows increased infiltration and greatly reduces erosion. Mud is prevented from being splashed onto plants.
- Don't mulch with organic materials from plants that have been recently sprayed with herbicides.
- One special mulching situation is when a thin layer of vermiculite is used to cover and keep seeds moist in seedling flats.
- There is more nitrogen fixed by free-living nitrogen-fixing microorganisms in a soil under mulch than there is in the same soil when unmulched.
- Young plants to be mulched with woody organic materials often benefit from applications of extra nitrogen (about 5 g N/m²) to make up for that used as the mulch decomposes. Mature plants usually do not need any extra nitrogen, as a reduction in growth rate will hardly be noticeable.
- Mulches of more succulent organic materials—turf clippings, animal manures, compost, hay—supply considerable amounts of nutrients as they decompose.
- Specially prepared mulches containing binding agents and seeds are often used to establish plants on sloping ground (Fig. 31.9).
- In landscaping projects, mulches should be of a colour that blends in with rather than clashes with buildings. When chosen wisely, mulches greatly enhance the aesthetic appeal of a landscape.
- In cold weather, a temporary mulch of clear plastic film over seeds will hasten germination. In hot weather, a similar mulch will cook them, and any pathogens in the topsoil (p. 382).
- Always thoroughly wet a soil before applying a mulch. Regularly check underneath it to decide when to irrigate.

- Paper makes a poor mulch. It does reduce evaporation, but holes made in it for water to reach the soil will soon allow it to become a tatty mess.
- Consider having a living mulch of ground cover plants. They may not save any water, but they will keep the roots of other plants cool and can suppress weeds.
- Some fresh organic materials such as young bark from pine trees contain natural chemicals that can inhibit the growth of plants. These materials should not be spread around young plants. They should be moistened and stacked in a heap for a couple of weeks to allow the toxins to be decomposed.

USING EFFLUENT WATER

Shortages and the increasing price of existing water supplies mean that effluent waters will increasingly be used for irrigation. The nutrients in these waters can completely or partly replace the need for other fertilizers. Only a test of each source will tell how much extra fertilizer is needed. Other comments are:

- The salinity of effluent water is always higher, sometimes several times higher, than that of the domestic supply of the area. Extra leaching will be needed. The water will not be suitable for some plants.
- Sodium levels can be high, so precautions that prevent soils from becoming sodic should be taken.
- Some effluents will contain high enough concentrations of boron to make them toxic to sensitive plants.
- Some effluents will supply excessive amounts of phosphorus.
- During sprinkling, more than 50% of the nitrogen in effluents can be lost into the air as ammonia.
- Because effluent water is cheap, there is a tendency to irrigate heavily. The lush, green growth produced is prone to disease. It will have little ability to withstand a sudden drought.
- Don't use effluent immediately after it has been chlorinated. Wait until the chlorine has reacted or dispersed into the air.

23 IRRIGATION OVERVIEW

This chapter is not a design manual for irrigation systems. (The best design manual is the expert advice of a company that is able to design a system for your particular needs.) Rather, this chapter gives an overview of the several types of systems available, their capabilities and their effects on growing media and plants. We do not cover control systems or 'plumbing'.

Other aspects of the interactions between water, growing media and plants are discussed in Chapters 9 and 22. Take particular note of the guidelines in Chapter 22 for deciding when to water and how much to apply.

Types of irrigation systems

- For turf: sprinkler.
- For landscapes: sprinkler, trickle.
- For open-ground production: sprinkler, trickle, furrow.
- For nurseries: sprinkler, trickle, capillary beds and mats, misting.

Choice is made mainly on the basis of the balance needed between capital cost and running costs, water quality and quantity and the level of plant growth needed.

SPRINKLER IRRIGATION

In sprinkler irrigation, water under pressure (200–1000 kPa) is allowed to flow through a nozzle or series of nozzles. As it passes through the nozzles and the air, the stream of water breaks up into droplets of varying sizes. By various means the sprinkler distributes the droplets over the area around itself. A good sprinkler system will come close to duplicating the even wetting that rain gives an area. A poor system will give very uneven wetting.

Sprinklers are either fixed or movable. Those that are fixed are either pop-up or permanently at the same height. Movable sprinklers are either moved by hand or are self-propelled. Sprinkler heads come in a multiplicity of styles and sizes (Fig. 23.1).

Sprinkler spacing

Turf and standing grounds in nurseries: The distance between sprinklers must be chosen carefully if you want something better than the effect shown in Fig. 23.2. Only expert design for your particular situation will show what you need. But as a rough guide, the distance between sprinklers will be 40% to 60% of the diameter of the wetting circle of each. This allows the area of low application rate of one sprinkler to match the area of high application rate of another (Fig. 23.3).

The sprinklers will be closest together in windy situations and for sandy root zones. Allow for drift from the direction of the prevailing winds when siting sprinklers at the edge of an area (Fig. 23.4). It is usually false economy to accept the lowest quote for a pop-up sprinkler system. Too often the low price is achieved by using too few sprinklers.

Figure 23.1
Sprinklers with anti-backsplash arms are useful in preventing water from going onto roads and walls. Examples of sprinklers. *Photograph J Fakes*

It is best not to mix half-circle and full circle sprinklers on the same line, but if you must, use half-circle sprinklers that deliver at half the rate of the full-circle sprinklers. The sprinklers for the centre of a football/cricket field should be on their own line so that this area can be watered separately if necessary.

Landscape plantings: Spacing is a little less critical for ornamentals where turf is not also being grown. Their roots will soon find and proliferate in those parts of the soil that receive most water. Provided that at least half of the area under each plant receives water, growth should still be acceptable.

Figure 23.2
Patchy growth in turf caused by insufficient overlap of sprinklers. *Courtesy P Jones, Rain Bird (Australia)*

Figure 23.3

Some typical patterns of wetting depths around sprinklers

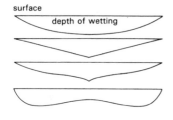

Droplet size

The size of the droplets of water produced is an important characteristic of any sprinkler system. The size range is that of raindrops (Table 23.1).

Table 23.1

Some properties of water droplets of different sizes (*From 'Compaction of Agricultural Soils' Amer. Soc. Agric. Eng. p. 108, 1971*)

	Intensity (mm/h)	Droplet diameter (median, mm)	Energy (relative to light rain = 1)
Fog	0.1	0.01	–
Mist	0.05	0.1	0.0001
Drizzle	0.25	1.0	0.2
Light rain	1.0	1.2	1
Moderate rain	3.8	1.6	5
Heavy rain	15	2	29
Cloud burst	100	3–6	270–380

Figure 23.4

You can allow for the effects of wind by appropriate adjustment to the arcs covered by sprinklers on the edges of areas being watered

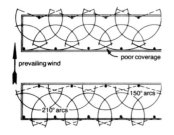

Table 23.2

Approximate proportion of water lost by evaporation during sprinkling

Weather	Proportion lost
Extremely hot and very windy	0.4
Hot, windy	0.3
Moderately hot, light wind	0.2
Cool to mild, calm	0.1
Night-early morning, cool, calm	0.0

Big drops make big splashes (Fig. 23.5) when they hit bare soil. They shatter soil crumbs, leading to the formation of crusts. They compact the soil. On slopes, they greatly increase the erosive power of thin sheets of running water. As shown in the last column of Table 23.1, the force with which droplets hit a soil increases very rapidly as they increase in size. If a sprinkler produces mainly large drops, it can cause considerable damage to unprotected soils. Mulches and ground cover plants, including turf that fully covers the ground, prevent this damage.

On the other hand, small droplets are more easily blown away from the area being watered. Much of their volume can be lost by evaporation as they fly through the air. As much as 90% of the water from a sprinkler producing small droplets can be lost on a hot windy day. Losses double for each doubling of wind speed. An approximate guide to likely losses from droplets of average (light to moderate rain) size is given in Table 23.2.

Choose sprinklers that give droplets of a size that suits the situation.
- when there is much bare soil, the droplets should be small (about 1 mm diameter).
- For most situations, most of the droplets should be in the 1 to 1.5 mm range.

Note that the smallest droplets fall close to the sprinkler; the larger fly to the edge of the wetted area (Fig. 23.6).

The average size of the droplets produced by a sprinkler decreases as nozzle size decreases and water pressure increases. One consequence of this is that for every 70 kPa increase in water pressure, losses through evaporation and drift of mist increase by about 25%. Reduce the pressure or increase nozzle size if you are getting too much misting.

A simple method for measuring drop/droplet size is given in Chapter 33.

Measuring water delivery rate

Any fool can turn a sprinkler on. It takes more skill to know when to turn it off. A major part of that skill is a knowledge of the rate at which your sprinklers are delivering water. Here are three simple methods of measuring delivery rate.

Use the water meter

Read the meter, run the sprinkler(s) at the desired setting for an hour, and re-read the meter. Divide the number of litres used by the area watered in square metres to get the millimetres of water delivered to the area. (One litre of water spreads over 1 m² of surface to give a depth of 1 mm.)

Figure 23.5
Raindrops damage bare soils

Example:
Meter readings: 4263.725 and 4264.150.
Difference: 0.425 kL = 425 litres
Radius of watered area (r): 3 m.
Therefore, area watered (πr^2): 3.14 × 3 × 3 = 28.3 m².

Average amount of water delivered: $\frac{425}{28.3} = 15$ mm.

Make sure that no other water is used during the test!

Use the 'can test'
A 'can test' must be used where a water meter cannot be used. Divide an area between two rows of sprinklers into equal squares on a grid pattern and place a can in the centre of each square (Fig. 23.7). Any fruit, soup or pet food can will do. Run the system for an hour or so, and measure the depth of water in each can with a steel tape measure. Average the readings to get the average depth of water delivered.

Calculate the coefficient of uniformity of the system as follows:

Figure 23.6
Average droplet size is smallest near a sprinkler head and greatest at the edge of the wetted area. Droplet size decreases as water pressure increases, here in the range 210 kPa ——, 280 kPa — — and 415 kPa - - - -. *From* K R Frost and H C Schwalen *Agric. Eng.* Aug: 256, 1955

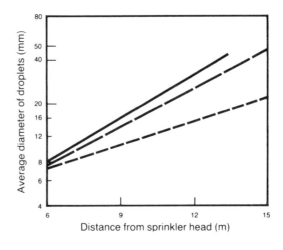

Figure 23.7

Typical patterns for placing cans around sprinklers in a 'can test'. Top: fixed system; Bottom: movable sprinkler. (For a movable sprinkler, a line of cans from the sprinkler to the edge of the wetted area is just as good.)

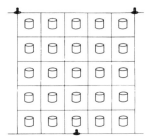

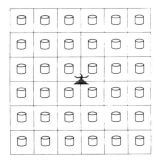

1. Calculate the average depth of water delivered (A).
2. Calculate the difference between A and each of the readings. Add together all of these differences to get a total (T).
3. The coefficient of uniformity $= (1 - \dfrac{T}{A \times \text{numbers of cans}}) \times 100$

If the coefficient of uniformity is less than 85%, you should seriously consider improving the system by using other sprinklers or by changing spacing. If you don't, applying enough water to satisfy plants in the driest patches will mean that other parts of the area get too much water. You will be wasting a lot of money in paying for the extra water or extra pumping costs. Irrigation system designers also calculate the distribution uniformity (DU) and scheduling coefficient (SC) for systems.

An alternative to the grid pattern suggested above is to place a line of cans at equal intervals from one sprinkler to the next.

The can test measures the amount of water falling onto the area. This will usually be a little less than the amount of water flowing from the sprinkler (Table 23.2). Do the test at night if you want to know the total amount of water (delivered + evaporation + drift) being used.

Hand-held hose

This is for a sprinkler on a hand-held hose. Turn the hose on the required amount. Run it for a measured time into a bucket or drum. Measure the volume of water. Calculate the time needed to apply the required amount of water to the area.

Example: Nitrogen is to be applied to a bowling green via a liquid feed. The rate of application is to be 2 g N/m². The total area is 1400 m². The stock solution contains 80 g N/L and is to be diluted 1:200. If the rate of water flow is 30 litres/minute, how long must you take to cover each 100 m² of green?

Total amount of N needed per 100 m² = 200 g.

Concentration of N in the liquid feed $= \dfrac{800}{200} = 0.4$ g/L (= 400 ppm N).

Rate of supply of N $= 30 \times 0.4 = 12$ g/min.

Therefore, the time needed to feed 100 m² $= \dfrac{200}{12} = 16.7$ min.

This is 1 min 40 s per 10 m², and 3 h 53 min for the whole area.

Sprinkling containers

Typically, less than a third of the water applied by sprinklers to groups of containers actually reaches the medium in them (Table 23.3). Calculations must take this into account. Each situation is different, so only local measurements will show what the efficiency of application is. On solid surfaces, measure runoff volume. Otherwise, guess from the amounts caught in cans placed between containers. (This last method does not measure all of the water lost by runoff from plant foliage.)

Table 23.3
Example of the savings in water use possible when drippers are used instead of sprinklers to irrigate plants in containers (*From* D M Weatherspoon and C C Harrell, *Hort. Science* 15: 488, 1980)

Irrigation system	Water applied (L)	Water runoff and drainage (L)	Water in containers (L)	Water in containers (%)
Dripper	91	23	68	75
Sprinkler	350	259	91	26

Figure 23.8
Toro 680 low pressure/low precipitation sprinklers in action. *Courtesy Hunter Australia*

Figure 23.9
Hunter low pressure/low precipitation sprinkler heads in action. *Courtesy Hunter Australia*

Figure 23.10
Rainbird 1800 series low pressure/low precipitation sprinkler heads. *Courtesy Rainbird Australia*

Example: You want to apply 400 mL of water to each pot in a large standing ground. Each pot has a surface area of 160 cm². Past measurement has shown that 35% of water delivered reaches the pots. The rate of delivery is 20 mm/hour. The amount of water reaching the pots is $\frac{35}{100} \times 20 = 7$ mm/hour.

The area of each is 160 cm² = 0.016 m².
Therefore, 7mm/hour delivers $7 \times 0.016 \times 1000$ mL/hour to each pot (1 litre/m² = 1 mm depth) = 112 mL/hour.
Therefore, leave the sprinklers on for $\frac{400}{112}$ = 3.6 h = 3h 34 min.

Application rate and infiltration rate

If the infiltration rate of a soil is less than the rate of application of water, some will either pond on the surface or be wasted as runoff. You can reduce this loss of water in two ways.

- You can reduce the rate of application. Provided coverage is still even, reducing pressure or using smaller nozzles will achieve this. The other method is to cycle the application (e.g. 15 minutes on 15 minutes off, etc.) until the required amount of water has been applied. This latter method is easy with automatic systems. The period 'on' should only be until water starts to pond on the surface.
- You can increase the infiltration rate of the soil.

Example: You want to apply 35 mm of water. The application rate of your sprinkler system is 15 mm/hour, but the infiltration rate of your soil is only 10 mm/hour. How many 15 minute bursts do you need to finish the irrigation?

Each 15 minutes the system will deliver $15 \times \frac{15}{60} = 3.75$ mm.

Therefore, total number of 15 minute bursts will be $\frac{35}{3.75}$ = 9 (approx.).

How long should the 'off' period be?
Of the 3.75 mm delivered each 15 minutes, 2.5 mm is able to sink into the soil.

That leaves 1.25 mm. This will need $\frac{1.25}{10} \times 60 = 7.5$ minutes to soak in.

For safety, have 'off' periods of 10 minutes each.
Infiltration is rapid into some soils that crack deeply. However, much of the water can run straight through the root zone via the cracks. The rate of application of water to such soils should be low enough to allow wetting of the soil between the cracks.
Several brands of low-pressure/low-precipitation sprinkler heads (Figs 23.8 to 23.10) have become available in recent years. They operate effectively at pressures of 200–300 kPa (compared with 400–500 kPa for conventional heads) and have application rates in the 3–6 mm/hr range, even when installed at 21-metre spacings. Clearly these heads can deliver large savings in pumping costs. More important for turf is that they apply water at sufficiently low rates to allow complete infiltration into even the tightest turf soils, without the complications of on/off scheduling of controllers.

Advantages and disadvantages of sprinkler systems

No irrigation system is as good as rain. However, a well-designed sprinkler system is about the nearest substitute we have for rain for large areas of turf and landscape.

Apart from cost, the main advantages are:

- Losses by evaporation (Table 23.2). These can be minimized by watering at night, by choosing sprinklers that produce mainly fairly large drops, and by keeping the drops in the air for as short a time as possible. Whenever possible, don't use sprinklers that throw the water high in the air.

- Increased damage by saline water, compared with application direct to the medium (Chapter 21).
- Very greatly increased loss of nutrients in runoff waters if containers in nurseries are irrigated via sprinklers with water containing nutrients, compared with losses when irrigation is via drippers (Table 22.16).

Notes on sprinkler systems

- Employ an irrigation expert to design a new or remodelled irrigation system. These experts use computer software such as SPACE (Sprinkler Pattern and Coverage Evaluation) to produce the most efficient combination of spacings, sprinkler heads and pipe diameters for an area. On large jobs, they can easily save you tens of thousands of dollars in hardware costs, and untold thousands in annual operating costs. One US report showed that the cost of totally replacing the irrigation system with low-pressure sprinklers allowed the pumping station to be reduced in size. Annual operating costs were reduced by about 70% and the payback time for the revamping was four years. Every extra 7 kPa pressure that you must use adds 1% to operating costs!
- It is desirable to filter surface water before it goes into the sprinkler system. This will reduce the wear and jamming of solenoid valves, sprinkler mechanisms and sprinkler nozzles caused by grit. Filtration is essential before water is treated to kill pathogens (Chapter 26). Sand/gravel filters are generally not suitable for turf as they give unnecessarily fine filtration and therefore clog easily. For turf, there is no need to filter finer than 200–400 μm, so disc and screen mesh filters are preferred.
- When letting a contract for the installation of a sprinkler system, insist on carefully detailed written specifications. Insist on close supervision of work. Require a plan of the installation as it was finally installed. Standards of performance of the finished system should be agreed on before a contract is signed, and the system checked for compliance when finished.
- With fixed systems, have the sprinklers that water slopes and those that water flat areas on separate lines. This will allow the different requirements of these two types of areas to be satisfied.
- Use anti-drain heads. These prevent the formation of wet spots around the sprinklers in the lowest parts of lines.
- In parks and large landscaped areas, use blocks of sprinklers on the one line. This can work well in flat areas, but in hilly terrain it is necessary to use valve-in-head sprinklers so that water in the lines does not all flow out of the lowest sprinklers and make the area around them very wet.
- Coverage of an area becomes less uniform the further the water pressure deviates from the correct one for a sprinkler.
- Choose low-throw sprinklers for windy areas. Knocker-type sprinklers for these areas should have only one nozzle. Sprinklers with two nozzles give best coverage in calm conditions.
- Microsprays are a useful and cheap means of applying water in domestic gardens and other 'vandal-free' situations.
- The greater the number of interruptions given to the water stream by a knocker, the greater is the proportion of the water falling near the sprinkler.
- Design the system so that different sections can be cut off separately.

TRICKLE IRRIGATION

In trickle (or drip) irrigation, water is applied slowly and frequently to a limited part of a plant's root zone through devices called drippers or emitters (Fig. 23.11). The aim is to ensure that the plants are never short of water, so they are able to grow as rapidly as other factors allow.

Figure 23.11
Trickle irrigation of a plant on a rockwool block

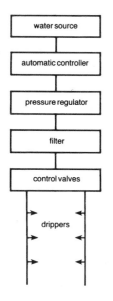

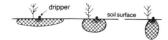

Trickle irrigation is used most extensively in orchards and for vegetable crops such as tomatoes and cucumbers. Its use in nurseries is increasing. There is some use in landscapes.

Most of this section applies to trickle irrigation of soils and for plants grown for sale or the production of saleable produce. Additional information about trickle irrigation in nurseries and landscapes is given under separate headings.

Trickle systems

Every trickle irrigation system will contain the components shown in Fig. 23.12. Some will also have an injector for putting fertilizers and pesticides into the water.

The best method of operation is to water daily. The rate of application will be in the range 2–10 litres per hour. Running times are usually in the range 1–10 hours.

Rate of application depends mainly on soil type. The rate will be lowest for soils with low infiltration rates. Rapid application to such soils gives surface ponding and shallow wetting (Fig. 23.13). For any soil, lowering the rate of application gives deeper penetration of water (Fig. 23.14).

Running time is decided on the basis of the amount of water needed. A method of calculation is given in Chapter 22.

A slight excess of water is needed when the water is saline. This will keep the salt out at the edge of the wetted zone.

There should be little variation in water pressure from one dripper to another. Pressure-compensating drippers must be used if there is much variation. An alternative when using microtubing (spaghetti tubing) is to decrease the length of tube used as pressure decreases along a line.

Forget about trickle if you are not prepared to put in an automatic controller. The system must usually be run every day. Forgetting to turn it on or off can be disastrous. You should include an alarm in the system to warn you of a failure to go on or turn off. In critical situations, you should have some backup ability to supply water.

Advantages of trickle irrigation

Compared with sprinkler or furrow irrigation, trickle irrigation has the following advantages:

- It is cheaper than a fixed sprinkler system.
- Plant growth rates can be high because the plants need never be short of water.
- It is possible to use more saline water than can be safely applied through sprinklers.
- If properly operated, less water is used.
- Weed growth is less of a problem because only a small part of the soil surface is made wet.
- Fertilizer is easily included in the water.
- Careful application to field-grown nursery stock can limit root growth to a small volume of soil. Harvesting will be easier and less disruptive to the roots.
- For plants that have to be kept growing at top speed, total water use can be less with trickle than with other methods. There are no savings when maximum growth is not needed (Chapter 22).
- Work can continue in the area during watering.
- Wind does not alter the distribution of water.

Disadvantages of trickle irrigation

- Clogging of drippers is usually the biggest problem. A filter must be used to remove particles. Blockages caused by the growth of microorganisms can be

Figure 23.14

Increasing the rate of application of water from a dripper (here from 4 to 20 litres per hour) increases the width of the area watered in a given time (here about 50 minutes). The drippers were located at the 'o' points. *From* 'Drip irrigation management' Division of Agric. Services, University of California, Leaflet No. 21259, 1981

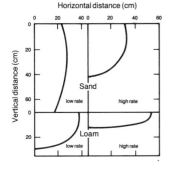

Horizontal distance (cm)

Vertical distance (cm)

Sand

low rate   high rate

Loam

low rate   high rate

Figure 23.15

(a) Pattern of water movement through a pot watered with a dripper. (b) in very open mixes, the water tends to move down through the mix below the dripper. Salts move to the outer parts of the mix

(a)   (b)

overcome through the use of chemicals. One successful method of clearing lines is to fill the system with water containing 500 ppm chlorine. Leave the solution there for 16–24 hours, then flush thoroughly. Calculate the amount of sodium hypochlorite solution as follows:

$$\text{Litres of hypochlorite} = \frac{\text{volume of system} \times 500}{\text{\% chlorine in the hypochlorite} \times 10\,000}$$

Another successful formula that can be used when the water is pumped from a tank is to add about 9 L of an algaecide such as Path Free and 4.5 kg of calcium hypochlorite per 1000 L of water. Run each line for long enough to fill it with the solution, then leave it to sit overnight.

If problems recur, fill the system after each irrigation with water containing chlorine. Avoid this wherever possible because the extra chloride added to soils will need a small amount of extra water to leach it from the root zone. Inject the chlorine downstream of any metal parts. Use black plastic pipes. Algae grow easily in light-coloured PVC pipes. Clogging by chemical precipitates is most easily overcome by flushing with acid water of pH 1 to 2. Use nitric or phosphoric acid.

- Salt accumulates at the edge of the wetted zone (Fig. 23.10). This must be leached away by rain or by occasionally applying extra water through sprinklers. Place drippers near stems or trunks so that salt does not accumulate there.
- Root development is most vigorous in the wetted zone. In the driest part of the year, the plants rely almost totally on this zone for water. It is essential that water supply is not interrupted for more than a day or two.
- In windy areas of low rainfall, the relatively limited root system sometimes means that trees are easily blown over.
- Trickle irrigation systems must be set up with care. Setting up and early adjustment of the system can be quite time-consuming.

Trickle irrigation of pots

High cost and the inflexibility of the installation limits the use of trickle irrigation in nurseries. It is best suited for watering large, widely-spaced pots that can remain in place for many months. Trickle irrigation is essential when the tops (flowers, foliage) will be damaged by overhead watering. Compared with sprinkler irrigation, the savings in water use are large (Table 23.3).

The drippers used must all be closely similar in delivery rate. Note that even a small slope in a line can cause a 50% change in the amount of water delivered by drippers that are not of the pressure-compensating type.

Run the system until the required amount of leaching water drains from the pots. The actual amount of water to apply will be close to evaporation from an evaporation pan (Chapter 22).

The water should be allowed to drip near the centre of the surface of the pot. Application on one side may allow an excessive build-up of salt on the other side (Fig. 23.15).

Water trickled onto very open mixes (above about 25% air-filled porosity) tends to move straight down through the mix below the dripper. There is little sideways movement. Either have the mix less open than this, use several drippers per pot, or use a 'spitter', an emitter that sprays water over the surface of the mix in the pot.

Full coverage of baskets calls for several drippers or spitters, a ring dripper or a device such as the Wingfield Octa-emitter.

Thoroughly wet the medium before starting to trickle. If this is not done, most of the water can channel down through dry medium that does not contain wetting agent.

Regularly check the salinity of the medium, especially at the edges of the pots.

When necessary, leach by applying water from overhead, or by running the drippers for a little longer.

Trickle in landscapes

Many have tried trickle in landscapes, and failed. The many public plantings that contain the remnants of systems are silent witnesses to that. Several difficulties must be overcome before trickle can be used in landscapes.

- For public areas, the system must be vandal-proof. That means burying the supply lines and emitters. Maintenance is difficult, but must be allowed for by, for example, providing capped access tubes hidden under mulch. Multiwall tubing (e.g. Biwall, T-Tape) or tubing with in-line drippers (e.g. Driplex, Drip-in) may be more useful.
- The different needs of plants of different size are best dealt with by varying the number of drippers per plant.
- A reliable person must be made responsible for maintaining the system.

If your main aim in installing trickle in a landscape is to save water, forget it. Because only a small proportion of the root zone receives water, it must be kept constantly wet. The plant therefore uses water at the maximum rate allowed by weather conditions. The savings made possible by allowing the root zone to dry out somewhat (Chapter 22) cannot be realised.

On the other hand, much water can be saved where scattered trees must be watered in an area that otherwise does not need to be watered. Trickle is also a useful aid to establishing trees in dry areas.

In gardens, watering through drippers gives excellent results with fruit trees. The watering of narrow beds and borders is easier by trickle than by sprinklers. Bi-wall tubing is useful for watering rows of plants, and 'Leaky Pipe®' is useful for sub-irrigation.

CAPILLARY BEDS AND MATS

Capillary beds and mats offer a precise method of irrigating containers in nurseries. The principle is the same for each. The containers stand on either a bed of sand or a special mat about 5 mm thick. The sand or mat is kept constantly wet by means of drippers, soaker hoses or by sub-irrigation. Water is drawn up into the medium in the containers by capillary action. Of course for this to happen the medium must be in direct contact with the bed or mat through the drainage holes in the containers.

Sand beds are mainly used outdoors and mats in greenhouses, but both can be used in both situations.

A number of other systems, generally referred to as 'ebb and flood', have increased in popularity in Europe and the USA in recent years as a result of a need to reduce or eliminate nutrient runoff from nurseries. One system uses narrow channels to accommodate the pots. Another uses wide benches or troughs into which water or nutrient solution is flooded from time to time. The potting medium used when irrigation is by ebb and flood must have an air-filled porosity of at least 12% as measured by the Australian Standard method (about 17% at 10 kPa suction).

Advantages

Compared with other methods, watering by capillarity has many advantages:

- Once set up, irrigation by this method is simple, essentially automatic and needs very little labour.
- The plants are never short of water. Therefore, they can grow at the maximum rate allowed by other factors. Uniform watering gives uniform batches of plants.

- All plants get the water they need, irrespective of their size, pot size and shape, or spacing.
- Indoors, the plants' foliage is rarely wet. The incidence of fungal diseases is reduced.
- The system can be fully automatic.
- Losses of nutrients by leaching are nil or small. Those leached from containers into sand beds by rain are mostly returned later. Some experiments have shown that rates of fertilizer use can be halved by comparison with those for containers watered by sprinklers. A more usual figure is a reduction of one-third.
- The water pressure needed is very much less than that needed to operate sprinklers. Variations in water pressure have no effect.
- Total water use is very much less than when irrigation is by sprinklers.
- Work in the area is not interrupted during irrigation.
- The top part of the medium in the pots remains drier than when watering is from above. Weeds are much less of a problem.
- The medium is not splashed onto plant leaves.

Disadvantages and limitations

- Salts accumulate in the containers. They must be leached out from time to time. For short-term crops in areas where the water supply is of high quality, leaching may never be needed. The saltier the water, the more frequent must the leaching be, so the less will be the advantage of using capillary beds or mats. The upper practical limit appears to be water with a salinity of about 0.6 dS/m, and that for plants of moderate tolerance to salinity.
- The initial cost is high, but not all that much higher than some alternatives.
- The ground must be dead level for sand beds fed from a header tank. Levelness is a little less critical for beds fed by drippers or 'soaker' hoses.
- Algae can grow profusely, eventually breaking capillarity. This disadvantage can be relatively easily overcome by treating beds with an algaecide such as Algo, Panacide or Kendocide. If these amounts do not control algae, the bed is too wet; lower the water level. Algal growth in mats is overcome by covering them with woven mesh (Fig. 23.16) or slotted black polythene sheet. These covers also reduce water loss by evaporation from the mat and cut root penetration into the mat. The algae do not release chemicals that are toxic to plants.
- Plastic liners under sand beds leak in time. Remaking may be necessary every 4–5 years.
- It takes a little effort to re-establish capillarity if it is broken.
- Roots can grow into the sand or mat. One application of an algaecide containing dichlorophen (eg. Algo, Panacide, Kendocide) to the sand or mat surface will prevent this growth, without harming the plants.
- The rapid growth allowed by constant capillary watering produces soft plants. The hardier growth produced when the growing medium is allowed to dry down somewhat between irrigations tends to give better growth after planting out (Fig. 23.17).
- One report has shown that the pH of the medium in the lower parts of pots irrigated from below can fall to below 4. This may have been a result of inappropriate fertilizer composition, but it suggests that the pH of medium in sub-irrigated pots should be monitored.
- In all recirculating and non-leaching systems there is the possibility that pesticides and metals such as zinc and copper can build up to toxic levels. Inputs must be minimized and solutions must be monitored.
- Root rots can be a problem if capillary mat is kept continuously saturated. The simplest way of avoiding this problem is to allow the mat to dry out

Figure 23.16
Capillary mat incorporating a seep hose for application of water and a woven cover to reduce growth of algae

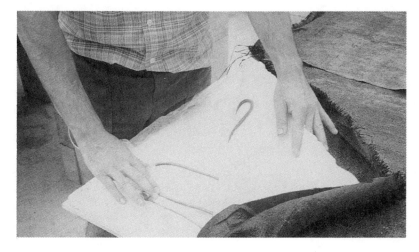

Figure 23.17
Petunia plants grown under constantly wet conditions grew poorly after planting out compared with plants that had been hardened by allowing the potting mix to dry somewhat between irrigations. *From M Th Zande Acta Horticulturae 272: 191, 1990*

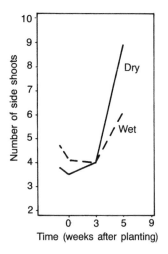

between floodings. Time the floodings to ensure only moderate drying out of the mix. The flooding soon re-establishes capillarity.

With this precaution, and *provided that hygiene is excellent*, it is general experience that disease is rarely a problem with plants on capillary matting indoors.

Because the water table is a few centimetres below the surface in sand beds, the pots are always better drained than if they were standing on a bench. Outdoors in wet areas, sand beds give better results than do mats.

However, capillary irrigation may not be suited to areas where there is a high risk of infection by *Phytophthora cinnamomi*. The 'water bridge' through the bed or mat between pots can give very rapid spread from a source of infection.

- The pots used must have holes in their bases, so that contact can be made with the bed or mat. Both plastic pots and polybags are suitable.
- Compared with plants watered from overhead, plants on capillary beds and mats tend to be more lush, and to flower later.

Sand bed construction

On the ground
1. Decide on bed size. Ease of use is the main basis. A width of about 1.7 m is the limit for easy access to pots at the centre of the bed from either side. Beds wider than this work (Fig. 23.18), but concrete slabs must be laid on them as stepping stones. The limit to length is set mainly by the need to have the site level. About 50 m is a practical maximum. It is often easier to have terraced beds of about half this length. Disease spreads rapidly once a pot on a bed is infected. Losses will be fewer when there are several small beds rather than one large one.
2. Level the site. Spread a thin (1–2 cm) layer of sand over the site for final levelling of the subgrade.
3. Install the boards (or concrete blocks, etc.) that will act as the retaining walls of the bed (Fig. 23.18).
4. Re-level the sand subgrade.
5. Where needed, form a channel in the sand where the water supply/drainage pipe is to sit.
6. Drape the plastic liner over the subgrade. Fix it to one side.
7. Add sand so that the plastic is settled to its final position down one side of the bed.
8. Install the water supply/drainage pipe. Make a hole in the plastic liner and

Figure 23.18
Cross-sections of two types of sand
capillary beds. In both constructions
(a) is sand used to level the site
before the plastic liner is installed,
(b) are retaining walls of timber (75
× 25 mm, treated with preservatives)
or concrete blocks, (c) is
polyethylene sheeting, black,
50–100 mm thick, (d) is sand, 50
mm minimum depth, (e) is slotted
drainage pipe, 50 mm diameter,
wrapped in filter fabric or with a
piece of fabric (e.g. TerraFirma 140)
300 mm wide over it, (f) are paved
pathways, and (g) are 'soaker'
hoses or similar.
Top: The level of water is controlled
by the level of the outlet from the
drainage pipe (e). This level can be
varied by movement of an elbow on
the end of the outlet. Bottom: The
level of water is controlled by the
height at which the plastic liner (c) is
attached to the retaining boards (b).
*From M A Scott, Efford Experimental
Horticulture Station, England, Report
No 78/30/a, 1978*

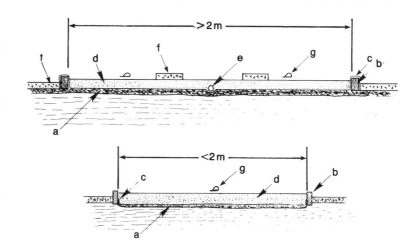

push the pipe through. Draw 5 cm or so of liner out along the pipe and
tape it in place to give a watertight seal.

9. Complete the sand infilling. Secure the plastic to the boards on all sides.
10. Settle the sand by tamping with the edge of a board. Flood the sand to
complete the settling. Form the final level.

A simpler version for narrow (<2 m) beds is given in the lower bed of Fig.
23.18. In this bed, excess water simply leaks out over the top of the polyethylene
liner. This is stapled to the boards about one-third of the way up.

On benches: Figure 23.19 gives a profile of a capillary bed suitable for
installation on benches. The fibro-cement base can be placed straight onto the
bench framework. The bench must be dead level. Watering is by header tank in
the set-up shown in Fig. 23.20, or by 'soaker' hoses.

The sand: Sand should be chosen on the basis of the results of two simple
tests described in Chapter 33. As a rough guide, a suitable sand will have a
particle size range within the limits given in Table 23.4.

Figure 23.19
One method of constructing a sand
bed on a bench. *From D A Wells
and R J Soffe Agric. Eng. Res. 7:
42, 1962*

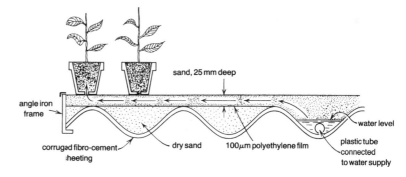

Table 23.4
**Sands that are suitable for
use as capillary beds will
have a spread of particle
sizes within the range given
here**

Particle size (mm)	Volume %
< 0.05	0
0.05–0.25	10–20
0.25–0.5	50–60
0.5–2	20–40

Methods of applying water

Two methods of supplying water are used. In one, a constant level of water is
maintained 2–4 cm below the surface of the bed by means of a float valve in a
header tank (Fig. 23.20). Watering with this system is fully automatic. Rainwater
is removed through the water supply pipe and out through an outlet in the
header tank. For this system to work, the bed surface and the top of the subgrade
must be dead level.

In the other method, water is applied through 'soaker' hoses running the full
length of the bed midway between the drainage pipe and the edge boards, or

Figure 23.20

Typical header-tank arrangement

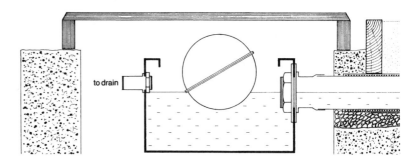

straight down the middle (Fig. 23.18). With this method, excess water either flows over the edge of the plastic liner, or it flows out through the drainage pipe. The level of the water table when drainage pipe is installed can be altered by rotation of an elbow on the end of the outlet. With this method the bed can have a slope of up to 1 in 100. The 'soaker' hoses can be hooked to a time clock.

Capillary mat benches

Set up the surface of the bench so that it is without hollows or bumps. Slope it either from one end to the other, from one side to the other or from the centre to two sides. A slope of 10 mm per metre is enough. Lay a black plastic membrane (50 μm), the capillary matting; cover with weed mat, other woven material or slotted black plastic sheeting to minimize algal growth. Install a dripper line along the highest part of the bench.

Starting up on sand beds

Just before setting pots out:

- Apply an algaecide such as Algo, Kendocide or Panacide.
- Rake the surface lightly to ensure good contact between the pot and sand.
- Water heavily from overhead to establish capillarity.
- Resettle pots whose plants are not getting enough water because of poor contact between sand and medium.

Other comments

- Sand beds and mats can be disinfected by flooding them with 1–2% formalin. Wash the formalin out before re-using. Masks must be worn.
- The medium in tall pots (more than 20 cm high) may not be kept wet enough on sand beds for maximum growth rates to be achieved. Using a medium with a rather low air-filled porosity (try 10 volume %) could allow tall pots to be used.
- There is not enough capillary rise in very open mixes for them to be watered from capillary beds.
- Salinity problems are less with 'soaker' hoses or drippers than with sub-irrigation. This is especially so if a small excess of water is applied to constantly remove salts. However, root rotting diseases are more of a problem if watering with soaker hoses allows free water to stand around the pots.

WATER DURING PROPAGATION

The act of taking a cutting severs it from its source of water. It will soon dehydrate and die unless another source of water is provided or losses are stopped. Putting the base of the cutting in water or moist propagating mix will allow it to take up some water for a day or two. However, uptake is soon stopped because the base becomes sealed with callus tissue.

It is therefore essential that loss of water from leaves is reduced to a low level. This can be done by raising the humidity of the air around the leaves to close to 100%. However, this then prevents the cooling that transpiration normally gives. For successful propagation, cuttings must have 'warm feet and cool tops'.

The main ways of allowing cuttings to have their water and their cooling are through intermittent misting, fogging and the use of enclosures.

Readers are referred to p. 81 for additional information about water relations during propagation.

Intermittent misting

Figure 23.21
Typical misting sprinkler. *Photograph J Fakes*

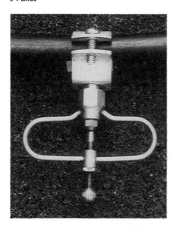

The aim of propagation under mist is to keep water on the leaves but still to maintain evaporative cooling. The mist is produced by forcing water under high pressure 300–700 kPa) through special misting sprinklers (Fig. 23.21).

Some of the water on the leaves enters them to keep them turgid. The rest cools as it evaporates. Cooling is possible only if there is evaporation, and evaporation is possible only if the air is less than fully saturated. It is essential, therefore, that the misting be frequent enough to keep a film of water on all leaf surfaces, but infrequent enough to allow evaporation.

Misting frequency is controlled by a time clock, 'artificial leaf' (Fig. 23.22), or a temperature/light intensity integrator. These must be set carefully because over-frequent misting will reduce evaporative cooling and leach the leaves. A propagating mix with a low air-filled porosity could be kept too wet.

Heavy shading helps by reducing heat input. (Misting does, however, allow the use of a higher light intensity than if no mist had been used. The extra light speeds root production.)

The effectiveness of misting can be greatly improved when the benches are 'tented' with plastic film (Fig. 23.23).

Start misting immediately after sticking the cuttings.

The water used for misting must be of low salinity, otherwise the cuttings will be damaged. Don't include nutrients in the mist. Doing so will give much algal growth on the cuttings and surface of the propagating mix. Feed the cuttings via a controlled-release fertiliser included in the mix at a low rate (1 g/L) or via liquid feeds applied from about the time roots start to emerge.

Suspending the mist lines overhead gives the most flexible system. Drainage of water from the lines after misting has stopped can be prevented by using misting nozzles fitted with ball valves.

Figure 23.22
Commonly used 'artificial leaf' for controlling misting of propagation benches. *Photograph K A Handreck*

Figure 23.23
Polyethylene enclosures over propagation benches improve rooting percentages by helping to ensure that cuttings remain fully moist

Propagation in fog

With this now widely used system, cutting turgidity is maintained by increasing the humidity of the propagation house to close to 100% with fog. Droplets of fog size (0.01–0.03 mm diameter—see Table 23.1) are generated by one of several means. In one system—the pressurized air/water system—air at about 450 kPa and water at about 35 kPa are fed separately into a nozzle. The air sets up a sonic wave in the nozzle which breaks up the water into fog-sized droplets. Another system forces water under pressure of about 6200 kPa through nozzles with very fine holes. Another increasingly popular system uses high frequency vibration of a crystal—the piezoelectric effect—to generate fog. Fogging is controlled by an electronic humidity sensor.

Advantages of air/water systems over high pressure water systems include:

- Droplets are somewhat larger, so the fog is somewhat 'drier' and leaves are not made wet.
- Less blocking of nozzles, because their holes are larger.
- Their lower pressure is less dangerous than the very high pressures of water systems.
- Lower maintenance costs.

Whichever system is used, the water must be of low salinity and must be filtered. Inclusion of a bromine-based biocide in the water decreases problems due to algal growth. Gentle stirring of the air in the propagation house is recommended as it ensures that all parts of the house are maintained at the desired humidity level (Fig. 10.11). Little water reaches the propagation mix so occasional watering is needed, especially when the bench is heated. Rooting percentages are typically better in fog than under mist, and disease problems fewer.

Enclosures

Most propagation was done in enclosures before the technology of misting was developed. It is difficult to get the right balance between high humidity and ventilation for cooling in enclosures.

However, enclosures can be used successfully if some simple precautions are taken.

- Success is greatest in the coolest part of the year.
- Shade must be provided at a level that maintains the temperature in the enclosure below 35°C. That usually means very heavy shading. Apart from allowing high temperatures, light shade allows a 'solar still' effect. Water is evaporated from wet surfaces in the enclosure and condenses on the walls.
- The enclosure must be small so that excess heat can be quickly removed through the walls. Best success has been had when the polyethylene enclosure is draped over the cuttings. Water condensing on the polyethylene then runs back onto the leaves, keeping them wet.
- Success is least with plants with large leaves. They need mist.
- Enclosures in which mist is also applied (Fig. 23.23) are usually very effective.

FURROW AND FLOOD IRRIGATION

In furrow irrigation, water is run from a pipe or channel into a furrow made beside a row of plants or between rows. The furrows slope from one end to the other so the water eventually flows right along. Water must be applied at a high enough rate so that it is not all absorbed into the soil at the top end of the furrow.

A furrow irrigation system is cheap to set up, but it is very wasteful of water. It is still used in production horticulture, but it has little place in the type of enterprises covered in this book.

In flood irrigation, water is allowed to flow freely over the ground, usually in 'bays' between low walls of soil. Leaching at the start of a bay and general uneven watering are serious drawbacks to this method.

SHOULD FERTILIZER BE APPLIED IN THE IRRIGATION WATER?

The answer to the question in the heading above is 'yes' for some irrigation methods and 'no' for others.

It is 'yes' and 'no' for sprinklers. Liquid feeding via sprinklers is a not uncommon practice in nurseries. For success, coverage of the pots must be as even as possible. Note that much fertilizer is wasted because it does not reach the pots (p. 307).

For 'fertigation' of turf to be successful, the irrigation system must have a high coefficient of uniformity. Otherwise some parts of the area will be more lush than others or the turf will have a patchy appearance.

An exception is when application is via a hand-held hose or a boom spray from an injector.

The answer is a definite 'yes' for trickle systems. Just make sure that there are no parts that can be corroded by the fertilizers. Flush through with water immediately after fertilizer so that drippers are not blocked by deposits of salt. All drippers must be closely similar in output if growth is to be even throughout the installation.

Plants in pots on capillary beds and mats are usually fed by controlled-release fertilizers in the mix. Including fertilizer in the water can quickly lead to high salinities in the pots.

Inclusion of nutrients in mists leads to excessive algal growth in propagation beds.

24 DRAINAGE

Gentle rain falling on an area of almost level soil will be seen to soak into (infiltrate) the soil. All will soak in if the rain continues to be gentle. Only if rainfall intensity exceeds the infiltration rate of the wet soil will water begin to run across the surface. Water on the surface may erode the soil or it can interfere with use.

After infiltration, the water percolates down through the soil. Some flows into small pores and stops; some continues to percolate down through the larger pores. Eventually, if rain falls for long enough, some water will drain into an underground band of soil or rock called an aquifer. In areas with dry climates, water may only rarely percolate beyond 1–2 metres.

Water in an aquifer can either flow slowly downslope and eventually drain into a deeper aquifer, or it can appear as a spring. The top of an aquifer, called the water table, rises to the surface if the water drains into it faster than it can drain away. In many natural situations, water tables rise during the wettest part of the year and fall in the driest as water continues to drain away or is used by plants.

Water moves from high parts of landscapes to lower parts. It moves by surface runoff and by percolation through soils. Some water becomes springs, creeks, streams and rivers. Other water causes swamps, bogs and other wetlands.

In urban landscapes, excessive amounts of water must be removed before they harm buildings, roads and playing fields. Removal is usually via drains. Some drains are designed to remove water from soil surfaces. Others prevent groundwater from rising too close to the surface. Some drains do both.

Note that this chapter is not a drainage system design manual. All we hope to do is give you an overview of some of the principles of drainage, so that when you have a problem with water you have some idea of what sort of things to look for as you attempt to find a cause. You will be looking for sources of water entering the area, the presence of coarse layers in the soil, impermeable layers, rising water table, inadequate infiltration rate, barriers to lateral movement of water, blocked drains, and so on. Diagnosis of the cause of a problem is the first and essential step to finding a solution. Solutions should be sought from skilled professionals who have expertise in the design of drainage systems.

REMOVING EXCESS SURFACE WATER

Excess surface water can be dealt with in several ways.

Interceptor drains: The simplest way of stopping water flowing into an area from uphill is to install interceptor drains. These are especially important in protecting high-quality sports turf from stormwater. Sand slits will protect golf bunkers from limited flows of surface water (Fig. 24.1(a)), but larger flows from more extensive upslope areas call for surface drains (Fig. 24.1(b)). Stormwaters must not be allowed to flow onto turf racing tracks either from the surrounds or from central areas. The surface drains must have slopes of about 1 in 50, and the distance to floodways or sumps is to be less than 50 metres (Fig. 24.2).

Increased infiltration rate: The faster water soaks into a soil, the less there

Figure 24.1
Examples of interceptor drains

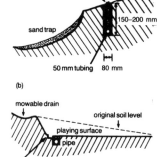

Figure 24.2
Examples of methods of preventing stormwater from flowing onto turf

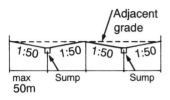

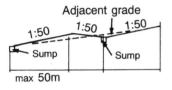

Figure 24.3
Examples of plastic drainage pipe. Corrugated pipe is stronger than the smooth-walled pipe and easier to install. *Photograph E. Lawton*

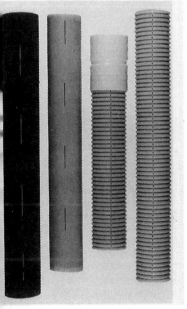

will be on the surface. Infiltration rate is greatest when the soil contains many large pores. Soils with sandy texture and good structure are like that. Methods of improving soil structure are given in Chapter 8.

Maintaining an adequate infiltration rate into turf soils is a major problem for turf managers. Infiltration rate will be greatest when the sands used as the turf root zone have been chosen for high permeability on the basis of laboratory testing, as outlined in Chapter 17. But even these sands experience reduced infiltration rates through the compaction caused by intense use and through the clogging caused by grass roots. Techniques for re-introducing large pores are discussed in Chapter 19. A further technique for speeding the removal of surface water from more-or-less natural soils being used for sports turf involves the installation of sand slits. This technique is discussed later in this chapter.

In dry areas, when water is expensive, and when salinity is a problem, increasing the infiltration rate is the preferred method of coping with excess surface water. In dry saline areas, the low salinity of rainwater is especially precious.

Increased slope: The steeper a slope, the faster the flow of water over it. Think of the difference between a waterfall and a river in flat country. The surfaces of sports fields must be given a slope of 1 in 70 (usually) to 1 in 60 (in high rainfall areas) from the centre in two or four directions (Fig. 17.15). Giving all surfaces in children's playgrounds slopes of 2–4% will eliminate low spots that could become bogs under intense use. There must be adequate catch basins at the bottom of each slope.

There is a limit to slope. Some playing areas (bowling greens, croquet lawns) must be dead flat. For most other areas, a slope of more than 1 in 60 is too much for best play. In any case, steep slopes will allow too much water to run off before it has a chance to soak in. Erosion hazard increases as slope increases, especially for soils unprotected by plants. A disadvantage of steep slopes in man-made landscapes is discussed on p. 203.

Surface drains

Creeks and streams are natural surface drains. They should be used whenever possible in landscaped sites. In some situations the lower parts of a landscape can be graded to provide artificial creeks and streams. The soil of their banks must be stabilized with plantings of soil-binding trees and other plants.

An alternative is to grade broad channels to take occasional flows of excess water. These channels should be kept grassed. The contours should allow for mowing with gang-mowers.

Another alternative for low volumes of water is shallow drains of channel pipe or brick.

French drains

French (or rubble) drains are trenches, often 300 mm or more wide, filled with rubble, which are sometimes installed to take surplus water from an area. They can be sited so as to intercept surface or subsurface flow. More often they are used as an alternative to large pipes for taking outflow from a drainage system. As they are really no cheaper and they tend to become clogged fairly quickly, trenches with pipes are generally to be preferred.

However, in some situations, wide French drains, topped with water-worn boulders and gravel, can be an interesting feature of a landscaped area. If constructed on an impermeable base, they can also act as reservoirs of water that can be tapped by trees planted along their edges. They are then similar to the meandering watercourses of inland Australia.

BURIED DRAINS

Figure 24.4
Agricultural pipes being installed in
an orchard to lower the water table
and remove drainage water.
Photograph R Seccombe

Much sports turf and many low-lying landscaped areas are equipped with pipe drains buried in or under the root zone. We described in Chapter 17 how these are used to carry away excess water that percolates through USGA root zones. In other situations pipe drains may be used to lower the groundwater table under low-lying areas. Drainage pipe is also used in the bottoms of sand slits installed in sports turf to rapidly remove surface water. Before we describe these drainage systems, it is essential that we provide a very clear understanding of how buried drains work.

How buried drains work

Drainage pipe is really just a large permanent hole running through the soil. It and the coarse sand or gravel that surrounds it provide large pores in the part of the soil into which they are installed. The pores in the surrounding soil are much smaller than those of the gravel and pipe, and so the pipe behaves as a coarse layer in the soil.

We showed in Chapter 9 that water can enter a coarse layer from soil of finer texture only if it is given a 'push'. That push is usually the weight of extra water arriving from above. Therefore, water will flow into drainage pipe only when the soil surrounding it becomes saturated with water to a little above the level of the pipe. A perched water table will remain above the drainage pipe when drainage into it has stopped. Drainage pipe does not—cannot—pull water from a soil. All it does is allow removal of (most of the) water that percolates down to it. It is the rate of flow of water through the soil above it that determines the rate at which water can be removed by drainage pipe.

Types of drainage pipe

Figure 24.4
Agricultural pipes being installed in
an orchard to lower the water table
and remove drainage water.
Photograph R Seccombe

Figure 24.5
Core drain must be completely
surrounded by drainage sand

Figures 24.3 and 24.4 show some of the types of drainage pipe available. Also available are strips of moulded plastic encased in a geotextile sleeve (Fig. 24.5). These strips are more expensive than some plastic pipe and are difficult to join. In most situations only the very bottom of the strip will be used for water flow. They *must* be surrounded with coarse sand if the geotextile is to remain porous. We have noted that the USGA recommends against the use of geotextile materials in turf, but we also note that strip drains have not clogged during four years of use when surrounded by fine gravel or sand.

Plastic drainage pipe is available in diameters ranging from 35 to 200 mm. Those of smallest diameter are used in sand slitting. Laterals in USGA and sand constructions typically have diameters of 50–100 mm. The closer the pipe spacing, the smaller can be the diameter of each pipe. Main pipes taking drainage water from an area are solid and typically 100–200 mm diameter.

Corrugated pipe has about 75% of the flow capacity of smooth bore pipes of the same internal diameter.

Take care when laying plastic pipe in hot weather. The pipe softens and can stretch. It may collapse under the weight of the backfill if it is not allowed to cool before backfilling.

Trenches

Trenches should be just a little wider than the pipes being used (Fig. 24.6). They are usually dug with a continuous-bucket ditch digger. The best have an elevator that can discharge the soil removed directly into a bin towed alongside (Fig. 24.7).

The trench bottoms should slope towards the point or points where water is to be discharged from the area. The slope should be 0.5–1.5% and certainly not less than 0.33% (1 in 300). The faster water flow given by the steeper slopes carries more silt away, so reducing the possibility of clogging.

Figure 24.6
Correct positioning of a drainage pipe to remove surface water and that standing on top of an impermeable subsoil clay

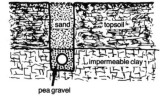

Figure 24.7
Digging a drainage slit with a special ditch digger that does not allow the spoil to fall onto the turf.
Courtesy of Ramsomes Pty Ltd

Figure 24.8
The shape of the surface of the water table above drainage pipes

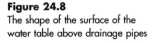

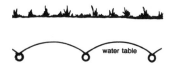

Always start at the lowest point—the point of water discharge—and work back. Firms specializing in turf drainage use laser graders to establish levels.

The backfill

Just dumping the soil removed during trench-making back onto the pipe will soon allow it to clog. It must be surrounded with a permeable material that will reduce or eliminate movement of soil particles into it. The permeable material is usually coarse sand or fine (pea-sized or smaller) gravel. Coarse quartz sand is often preferred and must be used in areas where the only gravel available is known to weather into a solid mass during several years in the ground. Some basalts behave like this. Coarse sand must also be used for pipe in silty soils, as the silt can move to clog gravel. A general rule is that the particle size of the filter should be no more than 10 times that of the soil it is to keep out.

Gravel or coarse sand is the only backfill material used in USGA types of construction. The sand of the root zone will be used for sand carpet types of construction. Finer sand will be used right to the surface in sand slits. The removed soil is normally used when the pipes are for lowering the water table (Fig. 24.4).

LOWERING THE WATER TABLE

In wet weather, the water table in some low-lying soils can rise close to the surface. The uppermost part of the soil may remain relatively dry, but the saturated soil not far beneath the surface will kill roots and will give the soil a sponginess that can easily lead to quagmire conditions in sports fields. The only way of improving such an area is to install drains to lower the water table.

For sports turf in non-saline areas, the drains should be installed at 800–900 mm below the surface (Fig. 24.8). Distance apart will probably be in the range 1–4.5 m for heavy soils and 6–9 for sandy soils. When groundwaters are saline, the depth should be about 1.5 m. These figures are provided to give you an idea of the spacings that might be used. It is essential that anyone who wants to

Figure 24.9

Use this diagram to calculate pipe spacings for water table lowering, if you know the saturated hydraulic conductivity of the subsoil. d = height of pipe above an impermeable base, D is half the distance between neighbouring pipes, H_m is the height of the water table, q is the steady-state rainfall rate and K is the hydraulic conductivity. When $d = 0$ (the pipes are sitting on the impermeable base) $q/K = (H_m/D)^2$. *From E G Youngs J. Agric. Eng. Res. 31: 321, 1985*

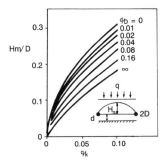

Figure 24.10

Slit drainage system for a football field. *Courtesy of Turspec Pty Ltd, Sydney*

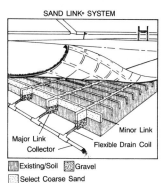

lower a water table should seek the help of someone with professional skills in soil physics and sports turf drainage. Pipe spacing must be based on measurements of the hydraulic conductivity of the soil. If you already know the hydraulic conductivity of a soil, you can use Fig. 24.9 to calculate pipe spacing.

It is essential that readers understand that these installations only lower the water table. They do not speed the removal of surface water; they do not increase the rate at which water infiltrates the soil. All they do is remove water from saturated subsoils. This has been demonstrated time and time again in natural soil sports turf equipped with widely spaced drainage lines as used in agriculture. The surface quickly becomes a quagmire if used soon after rain, because soil compacted by play has no hope of allowing quick percolation of water to the drainage lines.

Even if the trench is backfilled right to the surface with sand, the large distances between the drainage lines will do almost nothing to the rate of removal of surface water. Besides, the trenches are usually wide and will be seen as lines of drought-affected grass in summer. Effective removal of surface water calls for more intensive installations, as given below.

REMOVING EXCESS SURFACE WATER FROM TURF

We have already stressed the need for turf root zone soils to have a water infiltration rate that will allow entry of rainfall of most anticipated intensities. That is possible where most rain comes as drizzle or light showers. It is not possible in areas of high rainfall intensity.

It is also not possible when the root zone is rather shallow (say, 100–150 mm) and is underlain by a subgrade or subsoil that has a very low permeability. Once rain or irrigation has filled the root zone pores, the infiltration rate will equal the permeability of the subgrade. If that is only a few millimetres per hour, any rain heavier than a drizzle will cause ponding of water on the surface. A deeper root zone, as specified on p. 197, will allow a greater total amount of rain to enter the soil before the subsoil essentially stops infiltration.

After infiltration rate and root zone depth, a next line of defence against excess surface water is a sloped surface. The surfaces of most sports fields (of course, not bowling and croquet greens) should have a slope of 1 in 70, so that water arriving at a greater rate than the infiltration rate of the soil is reasonably quickly removed.

Sand slitting is another very effective technique for dealing with surface water. Water flowing across turf equipped with sand slits very quickly reaches and falls down a slit. It then flows downhill through the sand. If the surrounding soil is drier than field capacity, much of the water will soak into it from the sand. In other words, the sand slits have allowed an enormous increase in the infiltration rate of the soil, and at the same time have retained the water within the soil for later use by the turf.

Continuing rain will cause flow from the smaller sand slits into larger slits and then into drainage pipes installed in them (Fig. 24.10). Design details vary, but in one system used in Australia sand-filled grooves at 200–300 mm centres, 12–30 mm wide and 100–200 mm deep are installed at right angles to major slits at 0.5–2 m centres, 50–75 mm wide and 300–350 mm deep (Fig. 24.10). As with other drainage systems, the pipe is usually surrounded with coarse sand, but sometimes the backfilling sand is continued to the bottom of the trench to surround the pipe. The pipe is then fitted with a sock to screen out the smaller sand particles. Some of the machinery used in sand slitting is illustrated in Figs 24.11 and 24.12.

The sand used to fill the slits will meet the specifications for sand carpet construction (Table 17.8) and will typically have most of its particles in the

0.1–0.6 mm range. Trenches must be over-filled (Fig. 24.13) to allow for settling over the first few weeks.

Research in the UK has compared the performance of football pitches constructed on natural soil equipped either with pipe drains (as described above for lowering a water table) or sand slits, with sand carpet and perched water table constructions. The conclusions were:

- Sand-slit natural soil performed very well and was the most cost-effective method of construction. The number of games per winter playing season had to be restricted to fewer than 125.
- Sand carpet constructions gave the best overall performance and were recommended when a pitch had to withstand more than 125 games per season.
- Perched water table constructions worked very well, but their expense could not be justified for most situations.
- Pipe drains were useless. The surface soil was quickly churned into a quagmire; it deteriorated if subjected to more than two hours of play per week.

Sand slits remain effective only if the sand column is continuous to the surface of the field. The best way of maintaining the slit surfaces is through a regular sand topdressing program, at least until there is a 25 mm layer of sand on the surface (Fig. 24.14).

Outflow detail

Water flows out from the lowest point of a drainage system. The simplest way of disposing of the water is to run it into a stream, dam, the street water table, an open surface drain or the municipal stormwater drainage system (if that is legal). If it is not too saline, drainage water can be stored for re-use. It probably contains plant nutrients that would otherwise be lost.

In some situations, the outlet of a drainage system must unavoidably end below the level of any disposal system. There are two methods of coping with this. One is to lead the water to a soakage area such as a deep well feeding into an aquifer or large holes loosely filled with stones. In some areas these work quite well for a while, but usually they eventually become clogged with silt or

Figure 24.12
Machine for injecting sand into
narrow slits cut into turf. *Courtesy of
Turspec Pty Ltd, Sydney*

Figure 24.13
Leave a slight mound of sand over
drainage lines to allow for settling

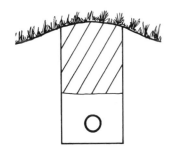

Figure 24.14

Sand slits must remain connected to the surface if they are to continue to be able to remove surface water

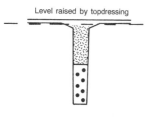

Level raised by topdressing

Figure 24.15

Sump for collecting drainage water at sites where the drainage pipes cannot discharge in any other way

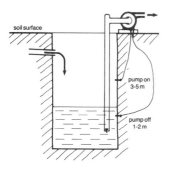

soil surface

pump on 3-5 m

pump off 1-2 m

Figure 24.16

Masonry walls must be protected by providing weep holes through them and by installing drainage pipes behind them. The fill above the pipe can be gravel, crushed brick or other rubble. Its thickness should be at least half the thickness of the wall.

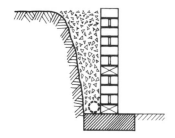

algal growth.

A better alternative is a sump that can be automatically pumped out (Fig. 24.15).

PROTECTING MASONRY WALLS

Masonry walls holding soil back on terraced slopes soon collapse unless the pressure of water accumulating behind them is relieved. Minimum protection is given by seep holes. Better protection is given when drainage pipe is also installed behind the wall (Fig. 24.16).

DRAINAGE IN NURSERIES

The drainage of nurseries must be carefully planned.

- Splashing onto plants and containers of water from pools in pathways and roadways greatly increases disease problems. Any mud splashed onto plants and containers must be cleaned off before sale.
- Therefore, pathways and roadways should be crowned or cambered and preferably sealed. Otherwise they must be constructed of rubble or coarse sand. Water running from them is to be collected in drains.
- Stabilize the ground beneath gravel roadways and paths. Use lime or cement as specified by an engineering test.
- Where possible, give the whole standing ground a slope of 3%. Where this is not possible, slope individual areas to collection drains.
- The best standing grounds have a layer of at least 70 mm of gravel on which the pots stand. Such a method of construction is required by accreditation schemes operating in several states.
- We strongly discourage the use of black polypropylene mesh or sheet plastic as a substitute for gravel. Disease in one pot is too easily spread to other pots. Also, disease is encouraged to develop in pots that happen to be sitting in puddles that accumulate in low spots.
- Increasingly, local authorities will require that all water leaving nurseries is of a quality that will not pollute the stream or area into which it flows.
- Water running from standing ground beds must be able to quickly reach underground drainage pipes.
- In many nurseries shortage of water means that all water draining from the site must be caught for re-use. Shape the site to make this possible.

25 LIFE IN GROWING MEDIA

Table 25.1
Approximate mass of living organisms in a fertile soil (*From* E J Russell *The World of the Soil* Readers Union/Collins, 1959)

Organisms	Mass in top 15 cm of soil (g/m²)
Earthworms	400
Millipedes, ants, etc.	80
Nematodes	5
Protozoa, etc.	40
Microorganisms	2000

Plants are rarely seen unaccompanied. Being alone is possible only for a plant growing by itself, from a tissue culture, in filtered air and sterilized medium. All other plants are surrounded by myriads of other organisms, both micro and not-so-micro.

Most of these organisms are good neighbours to plants. Many keep their distance. Others are always helpful. A few even move in by special invitation. Only a few throw poison, creep in stealthily at night or batter the walls down.

This chapter is about the main living things found in growing media. In order of decreasing size, the life in growing media can be:

- rabbits, snakes, wombats, mice, etc.;
- earthworms, slugs, snails;
- millipedes, centipedes, grubs, etc.;
- ants, termites, spiders, beetles, etc.;
- springtails, mites, aphids, etc.;
- nematodes;
- protozoa, algae, etc.;
- fungi, actinomycetes, bacteria;
- bacteriophages, viruses, mycoplasms, if considered to be living.

Ignoring the first group, the mass of life in a fertile soil can be as shown in Table 25.1. Many soils will have much less than this. Growing media in nurseries may have similar levels of microorganisms, but usually not much of the others.

INTERACTIONS BETWEEN ORGANISMS

Plants are the primary source of food for all life in growing media. Parts shed from plants are eaten by small animals. They may then be eaten by birds or other small animals. Microorganisms help in the decomposition of dead plant material, excreta from small animals, and so on. Other microorganisms use these first microbes as food and they in turn may be food for others.

Some animals and microbes also feed on living plants. Some climb the tops to graze there. Others bite off pieces of root or invade and slowly suck the life from the plant.

Growing media are seething cauldrons of activity in which every organism has its own weapons for destroying and digesting some of its neighbours. The greater the amount of fresh organic matter reaching the medium, the greater the activity and the larger the populations.

The whole environment of a growing medium—temperature, wetness, types of organic matter reaching it, types of minerals, oxygen supply, pH, nutrients, etc.—affects the types of organisms present. If all remain constant, the balance between organisms will remain the same. But any change in the environment will aid one part of the population at the expense of another part.

For example, adding large amounts of green organic matter to a soil will increase the population of organisms that are able to use it as food. Those that use them as food will then increase in numbers. Amidst this activity, it is likely that those that feed on living plants may also be used as food. An example is the reduction in the level of the fungus *Phytophthora cinnamomi* in soils receiving large amounts of organic matter. Trees in avocado orchards so treated show little or no signs of attack by this fungus, which is so destructive in other avocado orchards.

Other examples include the successions of microorganisms in a compost heap, the explosion of activity when a dry soil becomes wet, and the changes that take place when a medium is drenched with a fungicide.

If we know something of the likes and dislikes of the inhabitants of growing media, we are often able to use management practices which favour those that can benefit our plants.

EARTHWORMS

If you are sick of digging your soil or of coring turf, why not let earthworms do it for you? They have been doing it for rather longer than humans have and are quite good at it.

Earthworms improve soils and help plants by:

- leaving channels that increase the rate of infiltration of water into the soil (Table 25.2); these channels also improve soil aeration;
- increasing the rate of decomposition of organic materials;
- gradually turning the whole topsoil over, if they leave casts on the surface;
- increasing the availability of nutrients in soils to plants;
- increasing the amount of water held in a soil by improving soil structure (Table 25.2).

Table 25.2
Effect of earthworms on the steady infiltration rate and available water content of a New Zealand pasture soil (From S M J Stockdill *Proc. New Zealand Ecol. Soc.* 13: 68, 1966)

Treatment	Steady infiltration rate (mm/h)	Available water (mm/cm soil)
No earthworms	14	1.8
With earthworms	26	3.1

The combined effects of ample food and continuously moist soil have been dramatically shown in peach orchards at Tatura, Victoria. After three years of heavy mulching with straw and sheep manure, accompanied by annual applications of 1500 kg/ha of ammonium nitrate, 150 kg/ha of superphosphate and 100 kg/ha of lime, the number of earthworms rose from 151 to 2000/m², the air-filled porosity from 5 to 19 volume % (at 4 kPa suction) and the infiltration rate from 63 to 3000 mm/hour.

Be kind to your earthworms and they will repay that kindness many times over.

Encouraging earthworms

Soil management practices will either encourage earthworms or discourage them. If your aim is to encourage them you must:

- Feed them well. More than 70% of an earthworm's dry mass is protein. They grow and reproduce rapidly only when there is an ample supply of high protein food available. That means that green cover crops, lawn clippings, compost and animal manures will all encourage worms. Adding sawdust, straw or bark without high protein food can reduce earthworm numbers.
- Keep them cool. Many of the earthworms of urban and farmed southern and

subtropical Australia are from Europe. They do not like temperatures much over 25°C. To avoid getting roasted they move deep underground in hot weather. In winter rainfall areas they are most active in late autumn to spring. They remain active for longer in gardens and other irrigated areas than in open fields. Organic mulches and shading by plants prolong the period of activity. These remarks apply also to the native worms that may still be found in the fields and gardens of moister areas. Some earthworms of tropical areas can survive for extended periods at temperatures up to 30°C.

- Keep them moist. Earthworms must always have a layer of moisture on their outer surfaces. They soon become dehydrated in dry soils. The combined effects of drought and high soil temperatures has limited the spread of European earthworms in Australia, and has limited their period of activity where they have become established. Those most commonly found keep below the surface. Only in the coolest, wettest southern areas are surface-casters found in any numbers.
- Adjust soil pH. Most species of earthworms tolerate soil pH values within the range 4.5 to 8, with the greatest number of species being present in soils with pH values in the range 5–7.4.

Discouraging earthworms

The following management practices will usually reduce earthworm populations.

- Soil fumigants, most fungicides and many insecticides (Table 19.4) kill earthworms.
- The acidification caused by repeated application of ammonium sulphate will reduce earthworm numbers. Applications accompanied by lime will not, unless the high salinity of an application is left undiluted.
- Frequent cultivation will reduce earthworm populations.
- Increasing soil temperature, decreasing its moisture content, removing organic matter or supplying organic matter of low protein content, will all discourage earthworms.
- The normal maintenance operations used on bowling greens seem to discourage earthworms.

Other remarks about earthworms

With 1½ exceptions, we encourage all who grow plants in soils to look after their earthworms, for the benefits already listed. The main exception is golf and bowling greens in areas where surface-casters damage the playing surface. Leave the earthworms if they do not interfere with play. Avoid management practices that damage them.

The other exception is in those rare areas where large numbers of surface-feeders eat young seedlings. This is occasionally a problem in Europe, but so far as we know, not in Australia.

The only way to find out whether a soil contains earthworms is to dig into it during the time of the year when earthworms come near the surface. Finding none in hot, dry soil tells you nothing.

Earthworms are best introduced into a soil by leaving a dozen or so in each of many holes dug at 1 metre intervals throughout the area. Leave a supply of food in each hole. Moistened poultry food is useful. Otherwise, it is essential to increase the organic matter content of the soil. Don't expect earthworms added to a dry soil low in organic matter to do much more than die out. Don't use worms bought from fishing bait shops. They are usually of a species that thrives only in wet soils rich in organic matter. Rather, collect earthworms from a nearby garden. They will be adapted to the area.

Earthworms can be introduced into turf by placing on it, upside down, 10–20 cm cubes of soil from other turf having earthworms. The earthworms migrate down from the cubes over several days (Fig. 25.1).

Figure 25.1
Earthworms may be introduced into turf by placing cubes of turf containing worms upside down on it for a couple of days

Figure 25.2
Just a few of the many thousands of small animals living in or on soil.
(a) Adult scarabaeid beetle and
(b) larvae—some eat living roots and are pests, others are dung-eating beetles;
(c) termite soldier, *Nasutitermes exitiosus*—feeds on wood;
(d) an enicocephalid bug—eats other insects;
(e) millipede *Ommatoiulus moreletii*—feeds mainly on decomposing plant material;
(f) wood-louse (slater) *Porcellio levis*—feeds on dead organic matter;
(g) mite—feeds on dead organic matter and microorganisms. *From* 'Soils: an Australian viewpoint' CSIRO, 1983; drawn by L. Howard

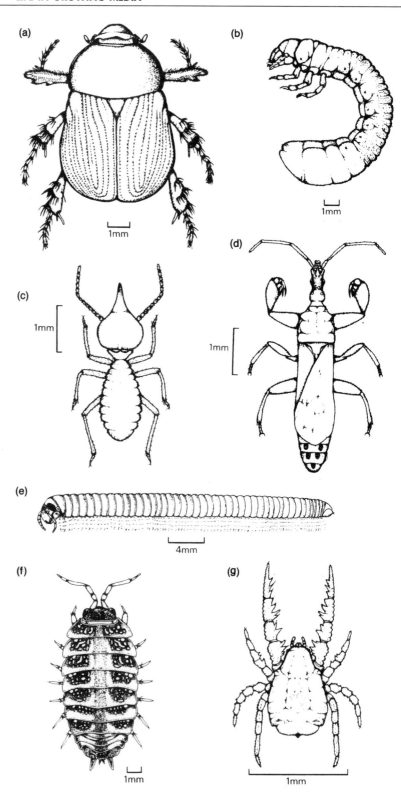

OTHER SMALL ANIMALS

Most soils are home to large numbers of small animals. Many feed on dead organic materials; they are therefore the first link in the chain of decomposition and recycling. Some feed on other animals and their larvae. A small proportion of the total eat the roots, stems or leaves of living plants. They can do enormous damage unless checked by natural enemies or with pesticides. The numbers of small soil animals wax and wane with food supply.

There are dozens of groups of animals and thousands of species. We can give no more than a brief introduction here. More detail is given in the books listed in the appendix 'Further Reading'.

The most common groups are woodlice, landhoppers, millipedes, centipedes, pauropods, symphilids, spiders, ants, termites, mites, flies, bugs, grasshoppers, cockroaches, earwigs, beetles, springtails, proturans, bristletails, slugs and diplurans. Some are illustrated in Fig. 25.2.

Ants and termites are often the dominant small animals in many arid and semi-arid ecosystems. They store large amounts of organic matter in their burrows and mounds. Most termites live on dead wood, but some tropical species destroy living trees.

NEMATODES (EELWORMS)

Nematodes are small roundworms, mainly 0.5–1.5 mm long, living in soils in large numbers. Most are found within a few centimetres of the surface. There are often 200–400 in each gram of topsoil. The free-living group live on fungi, bacteria, algae, actinomycetes, protozoa, rotifers, other nematodes, etc. They do not eat dead organic matter or living plants. They live in the water in pores and around particles, changing to a resting stage as the soil dries.

Figure 25.3
Parasitic nematodes use juices they suck from plant roots as their food. Illustrated is the nematode *Trichodorus similis* feeding on a root hair of a tobacco plant.
Magnification: x1400. *Courtesy of U. Wyss, University of Hanover*

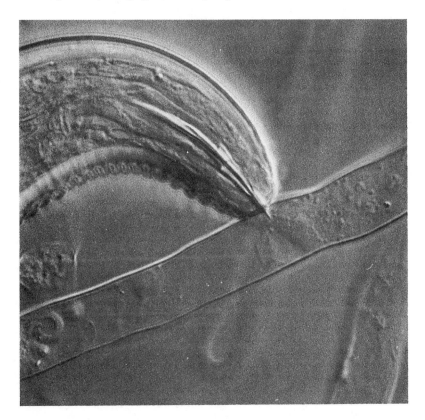

Figure 25.4
Protozoa come in many weird shapes and forms

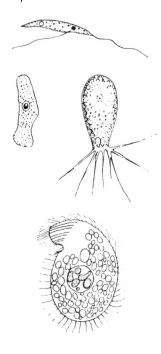

The other group—the parasitic nematodes—spend the active part of their lives with their heads attached to plant roots (Fig. 25.3). They feed on juices extracted from the roots. The females produce cysts containing eggs and it is in this form that these nematodes survive until more roots of host plants are available.

Parasitic nematodes prefer light, well-aerated soils so they tend to damage plants more severely in sandy than in clay soils. Each species of nematode attacks a fairly limited range of plants. One way of reducing their numbers in a soil is not to grow those plants in the soil for a couple of years. Otherwise they are killed by aerated steam, fumigants, solarization (p. 382) and nematicides.

MICROORGANISMS

The mass of microorganisms in a soil usually far exceeds that of all other inhabitants combined (Table 25.1), despite their individual smallness. It's their enormous numbers that makes the difference. A gram of fertile topsoil may contain 1000–4000 million bacteria and up to 100 metres of fungal mycelium (Fig. 25.5). With such numbers, it is not surprising that they have a large effect on the rest of the growing medium and on plants growing in it.

Microorganisms are found in greatest numbers where food supply is most abundant—in the top 5 cm or so of soils, around plant roots, and in and around dead organic matter. There will be many more in a potting mix composed largely of organic materials than in one composed mainly of sand, perlite and soil.

The important effects of the several groups of microorganisms are given below. Together, they have been essential to the development of soils as we know them. Their secretions dissolve nutrients from rocks, so speeding the weathering process; their activity is important in giving soils structures that aid plant growth. We do not see them unless they are in large groups (mouldy bread) or we use a microscope. But their effects can be seen wherever we look. We call some effects harmful because our plants are damaged or killed.

For too long, the attitude 'if it moves, shoot it; if it doesn't, ringbark it', or its more recent version 'if it lives, it must be harmful, so spray it' has ruled our thinking. Remember that most microorganisms are of benefit to our plants, and to us.

The rhizosphere

Figure 25.5
Strands of mycelium from mycorrhizal fungi weaving their way amongst and through soil aggregates and earthworm castings magnification × 30.
Photograph R C Foster and S McClure

The rhizosphere—that part of a growing medium closely surrounding a root—is a very special place. It is through the rhizosphere that all water and nutrients taken up by a plant must pass. It is through the rhizosphere that any microorganisms which will affect plant roots must act.

The concentration of microorganisms in the rhizosphere is many times that in the rest of the growing medium. Food supply makes the difference. Roots are a source of considerable amounts of organic materials—fragments of cell walls, exudates, leaking cell contents and eventually dead cells and completely dead roots. The total amount of organic matter transferred annually into a growing medium by a living plant is in the range 30% to 60% of the annual production of tops. As shown in this chapter, many of the microorganisms attracted by these organic materials are beneficial to the plant. Ways of altering the populations of microorganisms in the rhizosphere, mainly to biologically control root diseases, continue to be the subject of much research.

PROTOZOA

Protozoa are small single-celled animals (Fig. 25.4). They range in size from several mm down to 0.003 mm. Many are able to swim through water in media in search of food. Bacteria are their main food but the larger also eat algae, fungi, other protozoa and eelworms. Soils typically contain 10 000–100 000 /g.

(a)

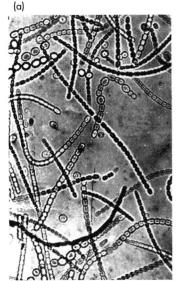

(b)

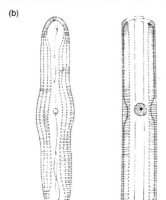

ALGAE

Algae are tiny plants. Most contain chlorophyll. They are often seen as a green, slimy coating on the surface of wet soils, and wet potting mixes. This is usually a sign that the medium is remaining too wet for best plant growth. Growth on capillary matting may reduce its efficiency. Their growth on rockwool blocks does not appear to be harmful in any way.

Some algae occur as single cells, but many form long strings of cells (Fig. 25.6). The blue-green algae (Fig. 25.6) fix atmospheric nitrogen, and so they are beneficial in soils. But they are definitely not beneficial in waterways and lakes whose pH values are over 7 and which receive additions of phosphorus. The algal blooms that can grow in warm water containing this phosphorus release toxins that make the water unfit for consumption by humans and animals. The group known as diatoms have an outer 'skeleton' of silica (Fig. 25.6). Deposits of diatomaceous earth are the remains of countless millions of marine diatoms.

BACTERIA

Bacteria are tiny, single-celled organisms. Most are about 0.0005 mm in diameter and 0.001–0.003 mm long. Some have a 'tail' that enables them to move through films of water around particles in growing media. Most, but not all, need oxygen. Most, but not all, are beneficial to plants.

Most bacteria live on organic matter, both dead and alive. About 10% of bacteria live on carbon dioxide, with their energy coming mainly from sulphur compounds, iron compounds, ammonium ions or sunlight.

Bacteria reproduce by splitting in two. With plenty of food, they can do this each 20 minutes, although every few hours is a more common time. This means that they can quickly exploit any new food supply, but of course they quickly use it up. Many bacteria are protected by an outer coating, or capsule. Some species survive heat and dryness by forming spores.

Bacteria generally prefer rather more moist conditions and a higher pH than do fungi. As a medium dries or becomes more acid, fungi make up an increasing proportion of total microbial life.

Bacteria beneficial to plants

Bacteria benefit plants in the following ways:

- Many species live on dead organic matter. In using it as food they eventually release nutrient elements from it for re-use by plants. The bacteria satisfy themselves first, so the lower the concentration of an element in the organic matter, the longer the time until some is released to plants. An example is the 'draw-down' of soluble nitrogen when organic materials rich in carbon (high C/N ratio) are being decomposed. It may be months before any nitrogen is freed for use by plants. The effect of this on plants being grown in potting mixes based on wood wastes is discussed in Chapter 16. Nutrients are quickly released from fresh green plant materials.
- Some bacteria are able to use pesticides and herbicides as food, thus preventing their build-up in soils to levels that are permanently lethal to plants. An example is given in Fig. 25.7.
- Many bacteria use other soil life, especially fungi, as food. Some release chemicals (antibiotics) that kill their prey. All produce enzymes that dissolve holes in the outer walls of their prey (Fig. 25.8), so releasing the cell contents. This is especially important to plants when the attack is on parasitic fungi. Any management practice that encourages a build-up of bacteria able to attack parasitic fungi is a means of improving biological control.
- Bacteria that decompose organic matter release its nitrogen as ammonium ions (ammonification). Other bacteria convert this ammonium into nitrate

Figure 25.7

Linuron is broken down more rapidly in soils to which it has previously been applied (○) than in previously untreated soil (▲). *From A Walker et al. Hortic. Res. Intern., UK, Ann. Rept, 1990/91, p 34*

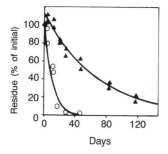

Figure 25.8

Hyphae of a fungus being destroyed by bacteria. Note the small holes where the bacteria have dissolved part of the hyphal wall. Magnification: x1750. *From A D Rovira and R Campbell Microbial Ecol. 2: 177, 1975. Courtesy of Springer-Verlag, New York*

(nitrification). If these latter bacteria are absent from a medium, ammonium ions can build up to toxic levels.

- *Thiobacillus* bacteria convert organic sulphur compounds—sulphides, sulphur, etc.—to sulphate, which is the form plants can use.
- A few species are able to fix nitrogen from the atmosphere into forms that can be used by plants.

Nitrogen fixation

Seventy-eight percent of the air is nitrogen, but plants cannot use it until it is converted into ammonium or nitrate. This is done in factories, where large amounts of fossil fuels are used to make ammonia, then ammonium sulphate, ammonium nitrate, urea. When nitrogen gas is converted into these compounds, it is said to be 'fixed'. It takes the energy of about 2000 L of liquid fuel to fix 1 tonne of nitrogen. This works out at about 420 L of fuel per tonne of ammonium sulphate or 930 L per tonne of urea. No wonder these fertilizers are expensive!

The original nitrogen-fixing 'factories' were, and still are, lightning flashes and soil microorganisms. The main soil microorganisms fixing nitrogen biologically are:

- *Rhizobium* bacteria that live in nodules on the roots of legumes (Fig. 25.9).
- Actinomycetes that live in association with the roots of species of several genera, including *Alnus* and *Casuarina* (Figs. 25.10, 25.11).
- Blue-green algae that live on or near the surface of moist soils, in pockets in the leaves of the *Azolla* fern that provides so much nitrogen to tropical rice crops, and in association with the roots of cycads.
- Free-living microorganisms found in most soils. The most common genera are *Clostridium*, *Azotobacter*, *Chromatium* and *Methanobacillus*.

The energy needed by microorganisms in these 'factories' comes from the sun via the sugars produced during photosynthesis.

Biological nitrogen fixation is very important in all natural plant communities and sown pastures. In revegetating disturbed soils, legumes should always be included amongst the plants grown. 'Natural' gardens containing some leguminous shrubs and trees need no extra fertilizer nitrogen once established.

Commonly grown Australian native legumes include species of the genera *Acacia* (Fig. 25.12), *Albizia, Bossiaea, Brachysema, Burtonia, Cassia, Chorizema, Daviesia, Dillwynia, Eutaxia, Gomphelobium, Gastrolobium, Hardenbergia, Hovea, Indigofera, Jacksonia, Kennedia, Mirbelia, Pultenaea, Swainsonia, Templetonia, Viminaria* and *Zornia*.

Nitrogen fixed by *Rhizobium* bacteria goes direct to their host plants. Other plants will eventually get some of this nitrogen when parts of the legumes decompose in the soil. Legumes are often among the first plants to colonize disturbed areas.

Seeds of crops such as beans and clovers can have *Rhizobium* bacteria mixed with them before sowing (inoculation). Most ornamental legumes have to rely on whatever bacteria are in the soil. Alternatively, they can be inoculated from mature plants of the same species. Remove about 20 nodules from a mature plant, grind them in 50 mL of water and tip the mixture around the base of the new seedling. The nodules used must be pink inside, and plump, not white or green and small. Native plant nurseries have found that growth of acacias is much better if the seed is inoculated with an effective strain of *Rhizobium* bacteria.

Bacteria harmful to plants

A couple of hundred types of soil bacteria, out of many thousands, are able to attack plants, causing various rots, wilts, blights and galls. Examples are halo

Figure 25.9
Rhizobium nodules on the roots of an *Acacia* seedling

Figure 25.10
Casuarina cunninghamiana.
Left: no nitrogen or actinomycetes added;
Middle: nitrogen added;
Right: actinomycetes added.
Photograph P W Reddell

Figure 25.11
Nodule formed by actinomycetes on the roots of *Casuarina obesa*. The protrusions extend to the surface. They provide oxygen to the nodule and the roots. *Photograph P W Reddell*

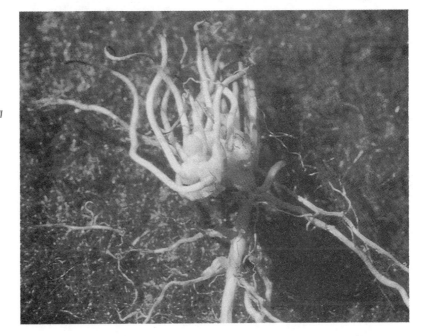

blight of beans, caused by *Pseudomonas phaseolicola*, crown gall of peaches, caused by *Agrobacterium tumefaciens* and bacterial wilts of many plants, caused by *Pseudomonas solanacearum*.

Figure 25.12
Seedlings of *Acacia holosericea*.
Left: nitrogen added;
Middle: Rhizobium bacteria added
(and nodules formed);
Right: no nitrogen, no bacteria.
*Courtesy of P L Langkamp and Shell
Development Co*

ACTINOMYCETES

Actinomycetes are between bacteria and fungi in appearance, perhaps looking most like branched bacteria (Fig. 25.13). Soils may contain between 0.1 and 36 million per gram. Most need oxygen, and many grow best at temperatures between 45 and 65°C. They are especially good at decomposing the more 'difficult' parts of organic matter such as the hemicelluloses. Some are very active in hot compost heaps, where they show their presence as a grey-white coating on the decaying vegetation.

Many soil actinomycetes produce chemicals that kill other nearby organisms. We know these chemicals by such names as Streptomycin and Aureomycin. High populations of some actinomycetes reduce the numbers of parasitic fungi, including *Pythium* and *Fusarium*. Recent research has found high populations of actinomycetes in potting media that are suppressive to pathogens.

Several actinomycetes, notably of the genus *Frankia*, form nitrogen-fixing nodules on the roots of plant genera such as *Casuarina* and *Alnus* (Figs 25.10, 25.11). An inoculant can be prepared by blending nodules with water, sieving the mash and spraying the water onto a seedbed or over young plants. The roots of transplants can also be dipped into it.

A number of actinomycetes cause diseases. Scabs of potatoes and sugar beet are the most common in plants. (Others include tuberculosis and leprosy in animals.)

FUNGI

There may be only 20 000–1 million fungal units per gram of soil, but because individually they are much larger than bacteria, their total mass is often larger. Most fungi live on dead organic matter; they are very efficient at decomposing woody litter A few live only on living plants. Some use both living and dead materials as food. Those that attack plants are called parasitic fungi. Those most important in nurseries are listed in Table 26.3. Some fungi attack amoeba, nematodes (Fig. 25.14) and other small animals. One group—the mycorrhizal fungi—invade roots, then live in harmony with the plant.

Fungi improve soil structure by producing humus and because their hyphae stick soil particles together (Fig. 25.5).

Most fungi thrive over a wide pH range—from 2 to above 9, for many. They prefer moist conditions but many survive semi-arid conditions better than do bacteria. Most do not tolerate waterlogged conditions. *Pythium* is an exception. Few survive a moist 60°C for more than a few minutes.

Figure 25.13
Examples of actinomycetes, highly
magnified

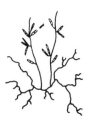

Table 25.3
Effect of inoculation with mycorrhizal fungi on growth and phosphorus uptake by *Pinus radiata* seedlings in a sand highly deficient in phosphorus (*From G D Bowen et al. Aust. Forest-Tree Nutrition Conf. p.68, 1971*)

Treatment	Dry mass (g/seedling)		Phosphorus uptake (mg/seedling)	
	No P added	Rock phosphate	No P added	Rock phosphate
Control	1.65	3.65	0.58	1.50
Inoculated	2.65	4.42	1.10	1.77

Figure 25.14
Any nematode that tries to pass through a loop in a nematode-trapping fungus is strangled and then eaten. Magnification: x240. *Courtesy of B. Nordbring-Hertz and C. von Meklenburg, University of Lund, Sweden*

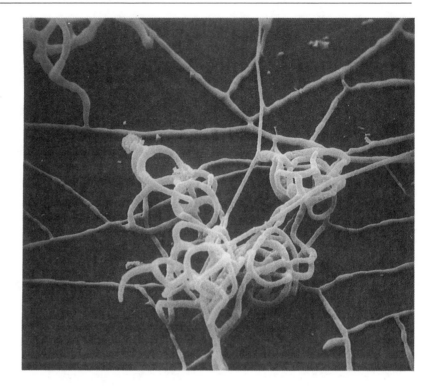

Mycorrhizal fungi

A mycorrhiza is formed when a mycorrhizal fungus infects a young plant root, changing its pattern of growth and appearance. The word literally means 'fungus root'. The association of fungus and plant is a kind of symbiotic relationship from which both partners gain. However, unlike the relationship with *Rhizobium* bacteria, that with mycorrhizal fungi is a kind of controlled disease. In fact, some of the fungi (*Rhizoctonia solani* is an example) that form orchid mycorrhizas are pathogens to other plants. Under some conditions they can in fact destroy their host orchid.

There are four main types of mycorrhizal infection.

- Ectotrophic mycorrhizas (ectomycorrhizas) are found on the roots of most tree species, including conifers, pines and eucalypts. Infection occurs when hyphae from a germinating spore penetrate between the outer cells of short lateral roots just a little back from the tip. An infected root becomes shorter and thicker than an uninfected root and is often branched (Fig. 25.15). The outer surface of the root is thickly covered with hyphae that also penetrate far out into the growing medium. At certain times of the year, the fungi send up fruiting bodies to the surface. We see them as the mushrooms and toadstools of coniferous forests.
- Vascular–arbuscular mycorrhizas (endogone) are formed on the roots of most other plants. Plants on whose roots mycorrhizas are not formed are found in the families Cruciferae, Chenopodiaceae and Resedaceae. Included are the brassicas (cabbage, turnip, etc.), wallflower, candy tuft, stocks, horseradish and the saltbushes. Hyphae move between the outer cells of roots and then penetrate other cells in which they coil around to form vesicles and arbuscules (Fig. 25.16). A sparse network of hyphae penetrates the soil around the root.
- The roots of plants in the families Epacridaceae (*Epacris* and other heathland plants) and Ericaceae (e.g. *Rhododendron, Calluna, Vaccinium, Kalmia, Erica,*

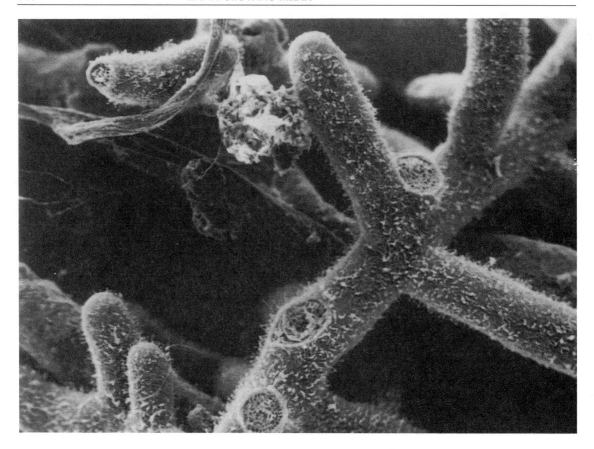

Figure 25.15
White ectomycorrhizas on the roots of *Eucalyptus marginata* (jarrah). These mycorrhizas are particularly abundant in decomposing litter. The many small projections from the surface (cystidia) enormously increase the area of contact with soil particles. Cystidia on the mycorrhizas take the place of hyphae found on other mycorrhizas formed by other species of fungi. Magnification: x60. *From* N Malajcuk and F Hingston *Australian J. Botany* 29: 453, 1981. *Courtesy of CSIRO*

Arbutus) form two somewhat different sorts of mycorrhizas, referred to as ericoid and arbutoid mycorrhizas. Infection is confined to the finer hair roots. It is presumably these mycorrhizas that enable these plants to so successfully grow on soils and in climates that are quite hostile to plants of other families.

- Orchid seeds do not germinate in the wild unless they are invaded by the hyphae of certain mycorrhizal fungi. Even with the best tricks of modern biochemistry, some still need their natural helpers, or grow better with them than without. The mycorrhizal strands that grow from the infection are in many orchid species the sole source of nutrients for the plant in its first months to years of development.

Benefits from mycorrhizal infection

Mycorrhizal fungi and plants both benefit from their association. The fungus receives carbohydrates (energy) from its host. The benefits to plants come mainly from the fact that the network of fungal hyphae increases by several hundred-fold the volume of medium accessible to the roots.

- This greatly increases uptake of nutrient elements that are poorly supplied and that move only slowly towards roots. The most important is phosphorus (Table 25.3), but the supply of some trace elements, including zinc, can be greatly improved. Without mycorrhizas or phosphatic fertilizers, many trees grow very slowly in soils deficient in phosphorus. Mycorrhizal infection allows the use of less fertilizer for the same amount of growth.
- Mycorrhizal plants often have improved resistance to drought and will tolerate higher soil temperatures than those not infected (Table 25.4).

Table 25.4
Effect of mycorrhizas on the death rate and growth of *Pinus taeda*
seedlings held with their roots in medium at a temperature of 40°C for 5
weeks (*From* D H Marx and W C Bryan *Forest Sci.* 17: 37, 1971)

| Treatment | Death of plants (%) | Changes during 5 weeks at 40°C | |
		Height (cm)	Leaf mass (mg)
No mycorrhizas	55	−3.0	−62
Mycorrhizas	30	+2.4	+36

Table 25.5
**Mycorrhizas protect roots against attack by *Phytophthora cinnamomi*. In
this example the plants were *Pinus echinata* (*From* J A Dangerfield *Proc.
Intern. Plant Propagators Soc.* 25: 105, 1975)**

Treatment		Plant dry weight (mg)
No mycorrhizas	} no *Phytophthora cinnamomi*	233
With mycorrhizas		316
No mycorrhizas	} with *P. cinnamionia*	167
With mycorrhizas		337

Table 25.6
**Some mycorrhizal fungi enhance root formation on cuttings during
propagation. This example is for *Arctostaphylos iva-ursi* (cv. Oregon
hybrid). (*From* R G Linderman and C A Call *J. Amer. Soc. Hort. Sci.* 102:
629, 1977)**

Treatment	Cuttings with roots (%)	Root ball rating*
No mycorrhizal fungi (but with hormone treatment)	15	0.15
Eleven different mycorrhizal fungi	45–95	0.55–1.40

*Root ball rating: 0 = no roots; 1 = 25 mm root ball; 1.5 = 25–40 mm

Table 25.7
**Growth of mycorrhizal and non-mycorrhizal *Rhododendron simsi* plants 4
months after planting out into a soil from containers. Thirty percent of
non-mycorrhizal plants died; the rest grew as shown. (*From* C R Johnson
and C E Crews *Amer. Nurseryman* July 1: 15, 1979)**

Treatment	Height (cm)	Tops fresh weight (g)	Roots fresh weight (g)
No mycorrhizas	22	142	82
With mycorrhizas	34	326	291

Figure 25.16

Spores (S) of endomycorrhizal fungi germinate on the surface of roots. Hyphae (H) extend into the growing medium. Another strand penetrates root cells to form vesicles (V) and arbuscules (A), through which nutrients are exchanged. *From F E Sanders et al. (eds) Endomycorrhizas, 1975. Courtesy of Academic Press, London*

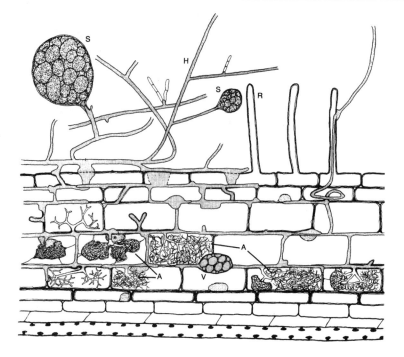

- Mycorrhizas protect roots against attack by some pathogenic fungi (Table 25.5).
- The presence of spores of mycorrhizal fungi around cuttings during propagation somehow improves root formation on at least some plants (Table 25.6).
- Mycorrhizal plants have a better chance of survival after transplanting than those not infected (Table 25.7).
- Plants infected with mycorrhizal fungi are better able to cope with toxic levels of arsenic in soils than are those not infected.
- Orchid seeds are unable to germinate unless the right strain of mycorrhizal fungus is in the medium around them.
- Some mycorrhizal plants recover from drought much faster than do non-mycorrhizal plants.
- A batch of mycorrhizal plants in containers has often been found to be more even in appearance than is a batch of non-mycorrhizal plants, even when these have ample nutrients.
- Tolerance to herbicides is greater amongst mycorrhizal plants than amongst non-mycorrhizal plants.
- In one experiment, plants having VA mycorrhizas and fertilized with 1 g Ficote controlled-release fertilizer per cubic metre of medium grew better than non-mycorrhizal plants fertilized with 4 g Ficote/m^3.
- It is easier to produce plants in nurseries without the hassle of trying to inoculate them with mycorrhizal fungi, but early and long-term vigour after field planting is often greatest with mycorrhizal plants.

Practical use of mycorrhizal fungi

To gain the most from mycorrhizal fungi, note the following:

- They are killed by steaming, even at 60°C for 30 minutes.
- Fumigants (such as methyl bromide, formaldehyde and methyl isocyanate) decimate mycorrhizal fungi at standard rates of application.
- The systemic fungicides Benomyl, Botran, Basamid Dazomet and Thiabenda-

zole reduce the numbers of mycorrhizas formed and the number of viable spores in a medium. The effect usually increases with increasing application rates. The fungicides Terrazole, Captan, Maneb, Ridomil, Aliette and Thiophanate have little effect on endomycorrhizal fungi.

- Mycorrhizal fungi need oxygen, so media in which they are able to be established on roots must drain readily.
- Shading reduces the effectiveness of mycorrhizas.
- Each plant species of those that form ectomycorrhizas respond best to a few fungi, sometimes to one only. Plants that form endomycorrhizas can be infected by a much wider range of fungi.
- Formation of mycorrhizas is inhibited or stopped by quite low levels of phosphorus in the water around roots. The normal levels added to soil-less potting mixes prevent infection and hyphal growth.
- The levels of nitrogen applied to plants in containers may slightly reduce the infection rate.
- High potassium does not interfere with infection.
- An upper limit for controlled-release fertilizer is the equivalent of 4.5 kg/m^3 of an 8–9 month Osmocote with a 21:3:11.6 NPK formulation.

Commercial use of ectomycorrhizal fungi

For many years now the seeds of conifers, including *Pinus* species, have been inoculated as follows so that seedlings are quickly infected.

1. Wash any fungicide from the seeds to be treated.
2. Surface sterilize fruiting bodies (mushrooms) of the chosen mycorrhizal fungus with absolute alcohol. Shake 5 mm pieces in 10 mL of sterile distilled water for 15 minutes.
3. Immerse the seed in the suspension for 15 minutes. Drain.
4. Sow immediately or dry and sow within a month.

This technique may still be useful, but it is now possible to buy 'Mycobead' ectomycorrhizal inoculants (Biosynthetica, East Perth, Western Australia) containing fungal mycelium of the most appropriate ectomycorrhizal fungi for particular tree species. Their use has produced very large increases in eucalypt growth in plantations established, for example, on rehabilitated mine sites in Western Australia.

Commercial use of VA mycorrhizal fungi

Inoculants of VA mycorrhizal fungi are now commercially available. They can only be produced on living roots. One commonly used technique is to grow plants aeroponically (Chapter 27), with the roots being infected using pure cultures. The root mass is then blended in a food processor. The inoculum can be stored for up to six months if it is air-dried and stored at −10°C.

The main benefits likely from using VA mycorrhizas in nurseries are:

- improved rate of survival of young rooted cuttings;
- faster growth;
- better survival after planting out, especially in 'droughty' conditions.

The latter benefit is of particular interest when mine dumps are being revegetated, and when horticultural crops are being planted into fumigated soils.

Inoculated plants should be given less than one-quarter of the level of phosphorus normally given to plants in nurseries and perhaps 30–40% less of other nutrients.

Microbes in composts and potting mixes

1. Microbes that might harm users

All composts, organic mulches, leaf moulds and organic potting mixes contain huge numbers of microbes. Most of them are completely harmless to humans. However, some parts of this population can harm us, given large enough numbers and the right conditions. For example, the clouds of grey spores sent up from dryish compost heaps can be irritating to some people after inhalation. Most of these materials contain populations of various *Legionella* bacteria, many of which are not associated with disease in humans. But populations of *Legionella longbeachae* have been found in many potting mixes based on composted wood wastes. The occurrence of pneumonia-like disease in some people has been thought to be related to use of such mixes. At the time of writing, a causal link had not been established, but since 1992 potting mix manufacturers have placed labels on all packages of potting mix, suggesting that users avoid breathing the dust from bags of potting mix and to wash their hands after gardening.

There are some millions of cubic metres of potting mix, composts and mulches used each year, and only a tiny handful of people develop pneumonia caused by *L. longbeachae*. The chance of contracting this disease during gardening or working in nurseries is very, very much less than that of being injured or killed by motor vehicles.

2. Unsightly microbes

Users of composts and potting mixes comment unfavourably about the occasional presence in them or on their surfaces in pots of white, grey or yellowish mould. Almost always, these moulds are a sign of normal, healthy biological activity in the mix. Such activity is essential if pathogens are to be kept in check. Only a few wood-rotting fungi produce in the medium massive growth of mycelium that can cause water repellence. Their fruiting bodies (mushrooms) can produce clouds of unsightly spores. These fungi tend to grow only on materials that have not been matured properly after composting.

26 SOIL-BORNE DISEASES IN NURSERIES

Three things are necessary before disease can develop in plants:

- The plant must be susceptible. Some species are much more resistant to a particular pathogen than are other species. Even within species, different cultivars can have very different susceptibilities.
- Pathogens must be present.
- The environment must be favourable for attack. A plant can be surrounded by pathogens, yet remain free from attack until a critical part of its environment changes (Fig. 26.1). This change may stimulate the pathogen to greater activity or it might weaken the plant's resistance to attack.

Disease is prevented or reduced by:

- selecting resistant strains of plants;
- in mixes, using components that are free of pathogens;
- eliminating pathogens from growing media;
- encouraging biological control by encouraging large populations of micro-organisms that are antagonists to pathogens in growing media;
- keeping plants free from stress;
- having the growing environment unsuitable for pathogen growth.

Prevention is easier and better than control.

NURSERY HYGIENE

It is usually attention to little things that makes the difference between diseased and disease-free plants in nurseries. Certainly start with clean medium and planting materials, but they are useless if sloppy hygiene soon contaminates them with pathogens.

Figure 26.1

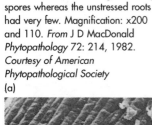

Chrysanthemum roots, (a) unstressed and (b) subjected to a solution with a salinity of about 5.5 dS/m for 24 hours. Thirty minutes after being inoculated with *Phytophthora cryptogea* spores, the salt-stressed roots were covered with germinating spores whereas the unstressed roots had very few. Magnification: x200 and 110. *From J D MacDonald Phytopathology 72: 214, 1982. Courtesy of American Phytopathological Society*

(a)

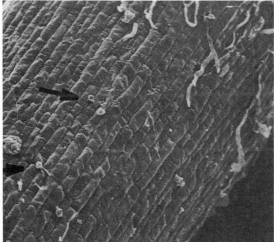

(b)

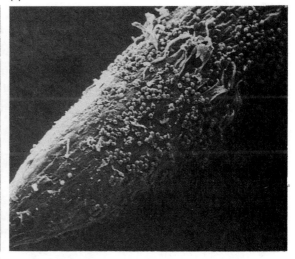

Observe the following and losses of plants through disease should be very small.

Propagation area

- Keep propagation facilities clean: each day remove all unused plant materials; never leave mix, plant materials, tools, etc., just lying around the place.
- The propagation area must have a concrete floor, and benches made of materials that are easy to clean. The floor should slope to drainage outlets.
- The whole propagation area should be regularly treated with a disinfectant such as 0.5% sodium hypochlorite (40 mL 12.5% sodium hypochlorite to 1 L), 0.7–2% formalin (19–55 mL industrial formaldehyde (37%) diluted to 1 L), 1% Biogram (10 mL concentrate in 1 L) or Leonard XL277 (1:400 dilution). The chemicals are swabbed or sprayed onto surfaces. Formalin is dangerous; full protective clothing, including a respirator, must be worn. Close the area for 24 hours, then ventilate it until no smell of formalin remains. XL277 is effective, less toxic and the least offensive to staff of the chemicals listed above.
- Areas that can be closed can be fumigated by adding potassium permanganate (110 g) to formalin (500 mL) in 10 L containers. Allow one container for each 100 m^3 of space. The reaction is violent. A quick exit or a respirator is needed. Leave for 24 hours, then ventilate.
- Dip cutting instruments frequently into disinfectant (methylated spirits or XL277 at 1:400).
- Tools can be sterilized by soaking in 70% methylated spirits or XL277 (1:400).
- Disinfect benches between batches of cuttings.
- Exclude as much dust as possible from the propagation area. Dust is a main source of *Rhizoctonia* infection. Maintain plant cover on all soils in the area; have paths and driveways of concrete or bitumen.
- All materials brought into the propagation area must have been disinfected.
- Restrict access to the propagation area to those who need to be there.
- All people in the propagation area must have clean hands and must be aware at all times of the basic rules of good hygiene as set out here. Reminder signs are useful (e.g. 'Have you washed your hands?')
- Place baths or pads of XL277 in entranceways to propagation areas whether or not there is infestation elsewhere in the property.
- Take special care when applying hormones to cuttings. One infected cutting can contaminate all others dipped into the hormone!
- Keep dogs, cats, rats, mice and birds from propagation areas.
- Footwear must never be placed on benches, especially in propagation areas.
- Undipped cuttings must be kept away from dipped cuttings. Hands must be washed between handling undipped and dipped cuttings.
- Benches are highly recommended for holding containers in propagation areas.
- Cuttings that die should be removed as soon as they are noticed because they will infect others if they are diseased.

Beyond the propagation area

- Control weeds along fence lines, etc. Weeds can carry diseases.
- A basic aid to good hygiene is to have the nursery set out so that there is flow from mix treatment and propagation through growing areas to dispatch/selling.
- Runoff from one section of the nursery must not flow onto other sections. Get the water into drains as quickly as possible.
- Containers must never sit on bare soil. Place them on benches that allow free drainage or on standing grounds as described on (p. 326).

- Never allow hose nozzles to touch, drag across or lie on the ground. Pathogens can be spread to many plants when the hose is next used.
- Cover containers of medium when they are not being used. The cover must be clean.
- Keep away from the nursery (especially the propagation area) all diseased plant materials or other materials that might carry pathogens.
- Inspect plants frequently and ruthlessly cull all those that are diseased. One advantage of hand watering is that it encourages this frequent inspection.
- Destroy all diseased plants by burning, fumigation or removal from the property.
- Any containers that must be re-used must be disinfected. Clean them by brushing, then soak them for 5 minutes in 0.5% sodium hypochlorite solution, or treat them with aerated steam (below).
- As much as possible, make sure that soil cannot be splashed onto leaves or into pots. Have excellent drainage in nurseries.
- Keep new containers in their cartons or wrapping until needed. Store those supplied loose in a dust-free, clean room.
- Always remember that preventing disease is cheaper and more effective than trying to cure it later.

TREATING GROWING MEDIA

Is it or is it not necessary to treat potting media to eliminate pathogens or to at least reduce their numbers? We offer some guidelines before giving some detail of the several treatment methods available.

- Soil-less potting media based on composted wood wastes do not need to be treated in any way before use. Many of them contain microorganisms that are capable of suppressing potential plant pathogens. The level of suppressiveness tends to increase with the length of composting and maturation period, from little at five weeks to much at 12 and more weeks.
- All natural soils must be assumed to be contaminated with plant pathogens. They must be treated before addition to the other components. The preferred method is with methyl bromide. Spread the soil out on a concrete apron or hold it in approximately 300 mm layers in stackable bins with numerous small openings in their sides and bottoms. Soil is difficult to treat effectively with aerated steam.

  Formalin can be used, and will have to be if methyl bromide is banned. Apply a solution containing 0.5 L of 38% concentrate and 2.5 L water to each square metre of soil stacked in a pile 500 mm deep. Treatment is effective even when the soil is close to 0°C. The formalin is decomposed over a period of seven to ten days at a soil temperature of 25°C, ranging up to about six weeks near 0°C.
- Earlier printings of this book carried the suggestion that all media for bedding plants should be treated to kill pathogens, preferably by aerated steaming. That may still be sound advice for media that carry a heavy load of damping-off pathogens, but in recent years the trend has been away from steaming to the use of media that carry high populations of suppressive microbes. Composted pine bark has some suppressive activity against pathogens that cause damping-off diseases in seedlings. Its ready availability in suitably fine grading has led to its widespread and successful use in bedding plant nurseries without further treatment.
- It is desirable that all propagation media be treated. However, media containing only materials known to be free of pathogens do not need to be treated. Such materials include perlite, vermiculite and styrofoam. Materials composted at high enough temperatures should be free from pathogens. Peats cannot be assumed to be free from pathogens.

Figure 26.2

Both drought and waterlogging markedly increased the susceptibility of *Rhododendron* 'Caroline' to attack by *Phytophthora cinnamomi*. *From* N S Blaker and J D MacDonald *Phytopathol* 71: 831, 1981

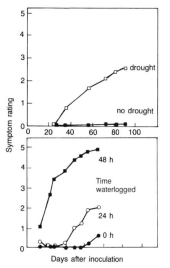

Figure 26.3

Suppressiveness to *Rhizoctonia solani* of: □ peat; ● composted hardwood bark that had been heated at 60°C for 5 days; ○ composted hardwood bark. *From* E B Nelson and H A J Hoitink *Phytopathology* 73: 274, 1983

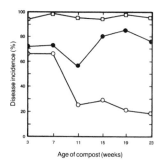

Reasons

There are several reasons for a low incidence of disease when soil-less media are used:

- Most mixes now used have a high air-filled porosity. This openness allows rapid drainage. Conditions are relatively unfavourable for attack by many pathogens.
- Careful management of watering and nutrition enables plants to grow rapidly without periods of stress. They are therefore able to resist attack by pathogens that might be present (p. 343).
- Note that wilting or waterlogging for 24 hours can greatly increase the susceptibility of plants to attack by pathogens (Fig. 26.2). Excessively frequent watering of the low-porosity media used in the production of bedding plants is a common cause of disease in them. Reduce watering frequency if nitrite is found in pour-through leachate from the containers. (Nitrite is detected through purple coloration of the uppermost patch on Merck-o-Quant nitrate test strips.)
- Balanced nutrition. (Excessive use of fertilizers and a low calcium level are two major contributors to root diseases.)
- Pathogens are killed during the composing of sawdust and barks.
- Research has shown that many composted materials contain chemicals that have a mild inhibitory effect on at least some pathogens.
- In addition, matured composts (Fig. 26.3) prepared from a range of materials, including eucalypt, pine and *Acacia* barks, eucalypt sawdust (sometimes), municipal and animal wastes, are often suppressive to pathogens. This suppressiveness is directly related to the level of biological activity in them. In other words, they are suppressive because of continuing decomposition. Suppressiveness can be transmitted to a potting mix even when it contains as little as 10% of a suppressive compost. The suppressiveness can last for as long as three years in some eucalypt barks, but in pine barks the period is more like two months. Suppressiveness lasts longest with materials that undergo long, steady decomposition. The only peats that are suppressive are the lightest-coloured, least-decomposed ones, and then only for a few weeks.

It is especially important to use suppressive media of high (25%) air-filled porosity for ericaceous plants (see Fig. 10.10), as these plants are particularly susceptible to *Phytophthora* root rots.

There is currently no quick test that nurserymen can use to assess the degree of suppressiveness of a mix. Including a proportion of well-matured compost seems to be good insurance, but its presence must not be taken as meaning that attention to general hygiene can be relaxed.

There are now on the market at least two microbial inoculants that are claimed to suppress pathogens when added to potting media. In some media under some conditions they certainly do that, but the complexities of the microbial world are such that sometimes inoculants do not do what they are supposed to do. Those containing a range of microorganisms have a much better chance of being effective than do those containing only one microbe. We recommend their trial use as environmentally friendly alternatives to chemicals.

- Don't let hygiene become sloppy because you think that your mix is suppressive.
- Prefer barks that have had some readily decomposed organic materials added to them before composting or ageing.
- Prefer organic components that have been aged for at least several months before use.
- Don't allow such aged materials to begin composting again. Heating them to 60°C for a few days will destroy most of the suppressiveness (Fig. 26.3). Aerated steaming at 60°C for 30 minutes does not.

Figure 26.4
Chart showing the temperatures at which various organisms and seeds are killed in 30 minutes of moist incubation. *From* K F Baker, 'The U.C. system for producing healthy container-grown plants' *Manual 23*, University of California Agric. Exp. Service, 1953

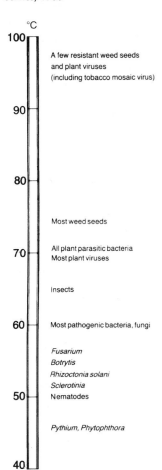

°C

100 — A few resistant weed seeds and plant viruses (including tobacco mosaic virus)

90

80 — Most weed seeds

70 — All plant parasitic bacteria
Most plant viruses

Insects

60 — Most pathogenic bacteria, fungi

Fusarium
Botrytis
Rhizoctonia solani
Sclerotinia
Nematodes

50 —

Pythium, Phytophthora

40

If treatment is necessary, the choice is between:

- pasteurization with aerated steam;
- solarization;
- steam at 100°C or higher;
- fumigation;
- less satisfactory methods.

Pasteurization with aerated steam

In aerated steaming, a mixture of steam and air is blown through the medium, so that its temperature is raised to between 60 and 80°C and held there for 30 minutes. The actual temperature reached is controlled by the proportion of air mixed into the steam (Table 26.1).

Table 26.1
Properties of air–steam mixtures

Temperature °C	Steam–air ratio (kg steam/m³ air)	Air–steam ratio m³ air/kg steam	Heat available kJ/m³ air–steam
50	0.09	11.1	250
55	0.13	7.7	360
60	0.18	5.6	480
65	0.24	4.2	650
70	0.34	2.9	900
75	0.46	2.2	1240

Aerated steaming at temperatures in this range kills most plant pathogens (Fig. 26.4), but it also kills many microbes that are beneficial to plants. Thus, *Rhizobium* bacteria and mycorrhizal fungi are all killed. Even at 60°C, the populations of many of the fungi that are capable of suppressing the activity of pathogens are severely depleted. The medium can be described as having been pasteurized. It is certainly not free of microorganisms, so it is not sterile. The term 'sterilization' must not be used to describe aerated steaming.

Note in Fig. 26.4 that most weed seeds are killed only if they are held for 30 minutes at temperatures over 70°C. When weed seeds are not present, pasteurization is usually carried out at 60–65°C for 30 minutes.

Note also the hazard in pasteurizing fresh *Pinus radiata* bark (p.34).

Equipment: Figure 26.5 shows that the main equipment needed is a steam generator, an air blower and a chamber in which to hold the medium. Another typical type of steaming chamber is shown in Fig. 26.6. In the best systems, a pre-set temperature sensor in the aerated steam line near its point of entry into the steaming chamber automatically regulates the proportions of steam and air. Another sensor in the medium near the outlet from the chamber can automatically cut back the air–steam flow rate as soon as all the medium has reached the required temperature. It can also be connected to a time clock that will automatically cut off steam flow after 30 minutes, leaving the air flow to cool the medium.

Concrete mixer bowls are useful if large quantities of mix are to be pasteurized, but considerable care is needed in setting them up and operating them. Worn blades on secondhand bowls must be replaced. The drive mechanism must allow variable and fairly slow rotation (perhaps 6 to 7 revolutions per minute). The temperature sensor must be covered with mix at all times. The bowl should be no more than half full. Sufficient steam should be blown in to heat the medium in about 15 minutes. Steaming at peak temperature is continued for a further 45 minutes. A hopper of sufficient size to hold one bowlful is desirable.

Preparation for aerated steaming: The components are thoroughly mixed at

Figure 26.5
Typical trailer used for aerated steaming of potting mixes.
Photograph J Fakes

Figure 26.6
Chamber for treating medium in flats or pots with aerated steam.
Photograph J Coppi

the moisture content that is a little drier than that used for potting. For many mixes this will be about 25–40 volume % water. Moisture beyond this decreases efficiency by using more steam and by decreasing the use of penetration of steam through the medium. Leaving the medium moist for at least four hours before air-steaming will enable seeds and spores to take up water. Seeds and spores are less resistant to heat when moist than when dry. Clods or large lumps of medium must be broken up. Pathogens near their centres will probably not get hot enough for long enough to be killed.

The medium is filled loosely and evenly into the chamber. Any compacted medium may be by-passed by the steam and so remain unheated. Depth should be less than 600 mm.

Medium in which cuttings are to be propagated or seeds germinated is normally filled into containers—flats, trays, etc.—before heat treatment. This allows the containers to be pasteurized at the same time. Handling after pasteurizing, and hence the risk of re-contamination, is reduced. The containers should be separated by at least 1 cm in all directions to allow steam to penetrate freely. No container should hold more than about 12 L.

Applying aerated steam: Aerated steam can be applied to medium in trailer-type bins from above or below. Most trailers used in Australia are equipped for steam entry below the medium (Fig. 26.5). Some find that top entry gives more even heating because 'blow-outs' are avoided. When entry is at the top, a centrifugal trap must be inserted in the steam line to remove water droplets. Medium immediately below the inlet will become saturated if droplets are not removed.

For vaults (Fig. 26.6) pure steam can be used for initial heating. The steam becomes aerated as it hits the air in the vault. The blower can be automatically turned on when the temperature reaches 15°C below that needed.

Heating-up time should not be longer than 30 minutes. The 30-minute treatment time is counted from when medium at the furthest point from the steam inlet—near a top or bottom corner of a bin or about two-thirds down a container near the top or bottom of a vault—reaches the chosen temperature. The steam is cut off at the end of the 30 minutes and air alone blown in until the temperature drops to about 35°C. It should not be lowered below 30°C. It is wise to cover the air intake to the blower with an oiled filter (of fibreglass or matting such as Terrafirma®) to catch dust, at least during cooling. The medium is ready for use as soon as it has cooled to 30–35°C.

Aerated steaming is an effective method of treating perlite for recycling.

Solarization

Potting mixes as well as soils (Chapter 31) can be disinfected via solarization. The moist medium is spread 150 mm deep on a clean surface in full sun and covered with clear plastic sheeting, sealed down at the edges to prevent loss of heat and moisture. Treatment takes about one month in high summer. Solarization appears to favour a build-up of microbes that are beneficial to plants.

Steaming at 100°C

This method involves blowing high-pressure, 'dry' steam through the medium, so that its temperature reaches 100°C. It is held at that temperature for up to 30 minutes. Essentially all microorganisms are killed, so the medium becomes sterile.

Compared with aerated steam, 100°C steam has the following disadvantages:

- More steam is used (perhaps twice as much), so the cost is higher.
- Microorganisms that are beneficial to plants through their ability to attack pathogens are killed. Any pathogens that contaminate the medium after steaming find a 'biological vacuum'. They grow unchecked and can cause the death of many plants.
- Toxic levels of ammonium ions can accumulate in the medium because microorganisms that convert them to nitrate have been killed.
- Toxic levels of soluble manganese can be released (Fig. 26.7).
- Delay between steaming and using the medium is greater, because of the higher temperature.
- Plastic containers cannot be used.
- Slow-release fertilizers mixed into the medium before steaming will release large amounts of salts during steaming. This either gives salinity problems or large losses of nutrients by leaching after potting.

However, 100°C steam is needed if all weed seeds and pathogens such as cucumber mosaic virus and *Fusarium oxysporum* must be killed.

Fumigation

A number of chemicals can be used to kill a wide range of pathogens and weed seeds in media.

Methyl bromide and chloropicrin are liquids that boil at 3.6 and 112°C, respectively. They both kill most fungi, insects, nematodes and weed seeds, but because methyl bromide does not kill *Verticillium albo-atrum* wilt fungus, and chloropicrin does not kill all nematodes, commercial preparations usually contain both chemicals. Methyl bromide is colourless and odourless, so it should always contain at least a few percent chloropicrin as a warning of leaks. Preparations come in pressurized cans (Fig. 26.8) and larger cylinders. The chemicals are led to the centre of the medium being fumigated. The temperature of the medium should be at least 15°C. Use about 500 g/m³. At the time of writing (1993) it seemed likely that methyl bromide would be banned. Carbonyl sulphide was a promising replacement.

The medium to be fumigated is covered with plastic sheeting, the outer edges of which are covered or buried and the soil made wet to give a gas-tight seal. The cover is left on for 2–4 days and the medium ventilated for 4–10 days before it is used.

Chloropicrin is not used by itself to treat potting media, but it is used sometimes to treat ground beds.

A number of chemicals (Metham sodium, Vapam, Dazomet, Sistan, Basamid, etc.) break down in media to give methyl isothiocyanate, which is toxic to many fungi, insects and nematodes. It is also very toxic to plants. Allow all traces of it to dissipate by turning the medium several times during a period of several weeks before planting.

Raised beds of very freely draining materials can be sterilised with 1–2% formalin solution. You must removal all traces of formalin before planting.

Figure 26.7
Increasing amounts of soluble manganese are released in growing media as the temperature of air-steaming increases. *From J W White, J. Amer. Soc. Hort. Sci.* 96: 134, 1971

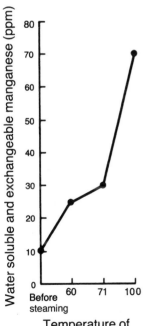

Figure 26.8
Fumigating a heap of mix for orchids with a methyl bromide/chloropicrin mixture.
Photograph J Coppi

The disadvantages of these chemicals are:

- They are all toxic to humans and must be handled with great care. A licence is needed before methyl bromide can be used.
- You must wait for several days to several weeks before the treated medium can be used.
- Beneficial microorganisms are killed, creating a biological vacuum. It is easier then for pathogens to proliferate in the medium (Table 26.2).
- Bromide ions left in media fumigated with methyl bromide are toxic to some plants, especially carnation and snapdragon. They must be leached out.
- They are expensive.

The advantages of these chemicals are:

- Methyl isocyanate releasers are useful for treating small areas of outdoor beds and small amounts of other growing media.
- When used correctly, methyl bromide is a very effective sterilant. It is the preferred treatment when tobacco mosaic virus must be eliminated—as when orchids are being grown.

Less satisfactory methods of treating media

Three methods of treatment are summarized here

1. Dozens of other chemicals are available for coping with pathogenic fungi, bacteria and nematodes in growing media. None of them totally kills pathogens. Rather, they inhibit their activity for shorter or longer periods. They are useful for controlling mild outbreaks of disease. However, they are no substitute for the chemicals listed in the previous section, treatment with steam, or excellent hygiene.

    Pathogens soon develop resistance to most of these chemicals. New chemicals are continually being invented to take the place of the old ones. Because of the ever-changing range of chemicals available, we do not list any of them here. Consult your local advisory service for current recommendations. It is most unwise to routinely use fungicides 'just in case'. Excessive use is expensive, builds up populations that are resistant to the chemical and, in the end, is self-defeating. Use them only as needed.

2. Flame pasteurization was at one time used in a few places. Heating was with a flame burning amongst the medium in a revolving drum. The difficulty of controlling temperature was one reason for the demise of the method.

3. Microwave energy can quickly heat a potting mix to 70–80°C. The heated mix can then be pasteurized by storing it in such a way that its temperature

Figure 26.9
Poor-man's way of treating seed with hot water, using a sink and slowly-running hot water tap

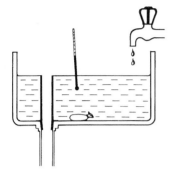

remains above 60°C for at least 30 minutes. Commercialization has been hampered by high capital cost.

Table 26.2
Example of a biological vacuum effect. *Pinus radiata* seedlings were grown in soil pasteurized with aerated steam or sterilised with methyl bromide. Natural antagonists left in the pasteurized soil gave some protection to the plants after the soil had been reinfected. Note that 30 minutes of aerated steaming is enough to give this result. (*From* C Theodorou *Australian Forestry* 31: 303, 1967)

Soil treatment	Emergence of seedlings (%)	Seedling survival (%)
Aerated steam 60°C for 1½ hours	93	100
Aerated steam plus non-sterile soil	40	70
Methyl bromide 500 g/m^3	75	91
Methyl bromide plus non-sterile soil	19	48

REMOVING PATHOGENS FROM SEEDS

Many seeds carry pathogens on their surfaces, under their outer coats or within their tissues. These must be killed if losses of seedlings are to be avoided. Three methods can be used. We recommend one, mainly.

Chemicals seed dressings are widely and successfully used on seeds to be sown into field soils. However, they have some limitations in nurseries. Treatment with chemicals is never 100% effective. Chemicals such as thiram, maneb, captan, chloranil and dichlone protect the germinating seed from attack by pathogens in a medium, but do not kill all pathogens in or on the seed. Others such as thiabendazole, benomyl and benzene hexachloride may not penetrate to kill all pathogens. Chemicals suppress rather than eliminate pathogens. Besides, pathogens have a habit of developing immunity to chemicals. Many are toxic to humans; staff handling seed treated with them often suffer from respiratory irritation. Particularly for bedding plants, one of the other methods is usually found to give better control of soil-borne diseases.

Hot water treatment, whereby seeds are soaked in water at 49–53°C for 30 minutes, is second-best after aerated steaming. Use an immersion heater equipped with a stirrer and thermostat, or trickle hot water into a sink (Fig. 26.9). The seed is held in thin cotton bags. Cool them by plunging into sterile, cold water. Your hands must be clean. The seeds are severely leached. Germination percentage can be greatly reduced; sow them as soon as possible after treatment.

Aerated steaming is now a well-proven method for pasteurizing seeds. The principles are the same as those for pasteurizing medium, but temperature must be very accurately controlled. The seeds to be treated are spread on standard sieves of the largest possible mesh size. Small quantities can be held in smaller containers having mesh bases and placed on larger sieves. The sieves are placed in an insulated chamber over an inlet connected to an aerated steam unit (Fig. 26.10). The steam should be dried before it enters the chamber. Heating should be for 30 minutes, followed by 15 minutes of cooling and drying.

The temperature used is in the range 49–60°C, usually about 50–54°C. A temperature of 54°C for 30 minutes is commonly found to be very effective.

Another useful method of killing pythium on seed surfaces is to soak them for 10 minutes in 0.5% hypochlorite solution.

All treated seed not used immediately must be dried and stored in sterilized containers. New plastic bags are suitable without further treatment.

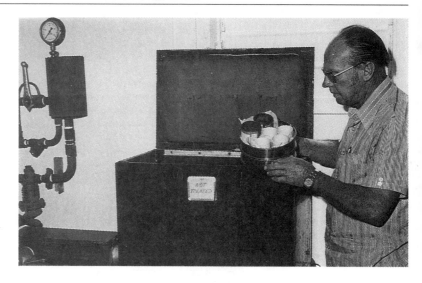

Figure 26.10
A cabinet for air-steaming seeds. It has given 30 years of excellent service at a bedding-plant nursery.
Photograph J Coppi

BULBS AND CORMS

Gladiolus cormels may be treated with hot water (58°C for 30 minutes), rhizomes of lilies at 50°C for 60 minutes, and begonia tubers at 44°C for 30 minutes.

CUTTINGS

A first rule with cuttings is to select material from obviously healthy, vigorous plants that are not watered by overhead sprinklers. The cuttings then have the least possible chance of carrying pathogens. Vigorous plants are less likely to be attacked by pathogens than are plants stressed by poor nutrition or under- or overwatering.

When possible, cuttings should be from stock known to be free of viruses. Virus-free ('Indexed') plants of some species are kept by Departments of Agriculture. Plants propagated by tissue culture will usually be free of pathogens. Viruses in living tissues cannot be eliminated by chemicals.

Other rules are:

- Mother plants are best grown in large containers, where they can be looked after carefully and protected by regular spraying. Ensure excellent drainage around and beneath the containers. Maintain the area so that soil or water does not splash onto the plants.
- Otherwise, take cuttings from as high up a plant as possible. Avoid wherever possible taking cuttings from parts contaminated by soil splashed up by rain. That usually means taking them from at least 300 mm above the ground.
- Use clean secateurs or knives. Dip them into 70% methylated spirits or Leonard XL277 every few cuts.
- Make sure your hands are clean.
- Obviously, don't drop the cuttings on the ground or put them on surfaces that might be contaminated.
- Transport them in new plastic bags. Don't cook the cuttings by leaving the bags in the sun. Bags to be re-used are soaked in 30 ppm chlorinated water (0.5 mL sodium hypochlorite containing 12.5% active chlorine to 2 L) before use. Chlorine bleach available at retail stores has no more than about 3% active chlorine by the time it is sold.
- Hypochlorite solutions are not much use in reducing pathogen populations on cuttings. Vegetative forms of pathogens can be killed with 1% (w/v) solution applied for 20 minutes. At least 4 hours of treatment is needed to kill spores, and even then may not be totally effective. Pool chlorine is the

cheapest source of hypochlorite. It has a nominal 10% (w/v) available chlorine content so mix 100 mL of it with 900 mL of water to make a 1% solution. Hypochlorite of this strength, applied for these times, is effective but can damage the cuttings themselves. Starting with clean stock plants is still the best defence against pathogens.

It is not necessary to soak cuttings in fungicidal solutions, as this action can spread pathogens.

STERILIZING WATER

Water supplied by water supply authorities is usually chlorinated so pathogens should not be present. Water from deep aquifers and from groundwaters from several metres down will usually be pathogen free. Water pumped from streams and dams, and runoff water being re-used, must all be assumed to be contaminated unless testing has shown and continues to show that pathogens will not be a problem. We list the methods that can be used to treat contaminated waters and indicate the state of their development in early 1993.

Slow sand filtration (Fig. 26.11) appears to be the most cost-effective method of removing pathogens from recirculating waters and solutions. The hourly rate of flow is 100-300 L/m^2 of sand surface. Cleaning is by scraping off the top few centimetres of sand every few weeks or months. Sand grain size is critically important, with 10% to be smaller than about 0.22 mm and the uniformity coefficient (d_{10}/d_{60}) being lower than 5 and preferably lower than 3 (d_{10} is the upper diameter of the smallest 10% of grains).

Another potentially cost-effective method of treating water is via *settling tanks*. It has been found that many of the pathogens in drainage and stream waters settle out when the water is held in a tank. Two tanks are used. The first one receives the runoff water. A syphon on the other side of the tank takes water to a second tank from which the irrigation water is pumped. The intake is suspended under a floating platform so that water is taken from about 300 mm below the surface but not from near the bottom of the tank. Overnight settling is apparently enough, so long as the water is still. It is important to note that this cleansing is unlikely to occur in outdoor water storages subject to the stirring that wind will produce. Some caution is needed in the use of this method. What we have written is based on limited experimentation only.

Chlorination has long been used and is highly effective. Chlorine gas (extreme caution needed in its use) and solutions and solids (pool chlorine) that contain hypochlorite can be used. Water must be filtered to reduce its organic matter content before treatment. For waters known to be no more than lightly contaminated, add enough chlorine to allow a residual level of 2 ppm active chlorine to be maintained for 15 minutes. Added concentrations need to be at least 3 ppm active chlorine and in the range 5–10 ppm for surface waters. Even higher dose rates may be needed in summer and in hot climates. Increase the chlorine addition by 2 ppm for each ppm of hydrogen sulphide in the water and by 0.6 ppm for each ppm of ferrous iron. Concern about the production of chlorinated hydrocarbons during chlorination has encouraged a search for alternatives. *Chlorine dioxide* is an alternative to chlorine that appears to be more effective against *Phytophthora*.

Kill of pathogens with hypobromous acid is faster than it is with hypochlorite, so *bromination* has the potential of being a relatively safe and highly effective method of disinfecting water. Disinfection can be accomplished with lower concentrations than with chlorine, especially with waters with pH values in the 7–8 range.

Microfiltration through membranes whose largest pores are 0.1 µm will not eliminate *Phytophthora*.

In *ultrafiltration*, the water is passed through a special membrane with pore sizes no larger than 0.001 µm, so they can completely disinfect the water. Some

Figure 26.11
Sand filter for destroying pathogens in recirculating water, as used in Germany.

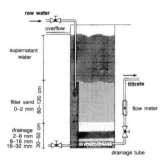

raw water

overflow

supernatant water

filtrate

filter sand
0–2 mm

flow meter

80–120 cm

drainage
2–8 mm
8–16 mm
16–32 mm

30–50 cm

drainage tube

20–30% of the water is lost in backflushing to overcome clogging. Commercial units are in use in the Netherlands but they may prove to be too expensive for use in Australia.

Disinfection by *heat* treatment is very effective, and Dutch machines are available. The water is heated to 95°C for 30 sec or 97°C for 10 sec.

Treatment with *ultraviolet (UV) light* is relatively inexpensive and has the potential of being highly effective. Some units tested overseas have been found to perform poorly, apparently because some water can pass the lamps without being exposed to the full intensity of the UV light. This method is undergoing further development. Organic contaminants must be removed by filtration before the water moves past the UV light sources.

Treatment with *ozone* is used in Europe and is considered to be an effective method of disinfection. It has good anti-viral ability. The water must be filtered before it enters the unit. Excess ozone must be removed by charcoal before the water leaves the treatment system. This method appears to be fairly expensive.

Table 26.3
The main soil-borne pathogens of nurseries

Fungi	Common names	Symptoms	Attack favoured by
Fusarium spp.	basal rot fusarium wilt fusarium yellows	Attack is through the roots or the stem where it enters the growing medium. In young plants, wilting, toppling over and death. In older plants, wilting, yellowing of the leaves, often more on one side than the other. Plants become lopsided. Stems and roots can be seen to be coloured orange-red to brown when cut.	Temperatures in the medium of 15–30°C (but active at 5–35°C). Low–moderate moisture (drier than container capacity). Water-logging and poor aeration suppress *Fusarium* growth and attack. Plants stressed by high temperatures are susceptible to attack. High nitrogen, especially high nitrate.
Pythium spp.	water mould root rot collar rot black leg	Young seedlings mainly attacked, first at the point of emergence from the seed or at the root tip. Pre-emergence damping off is caused by total infection of the seedling before emergence. Soft, wet rot (hence the term water mould) of roots and/or stem; they turn tan to mid-brown or black. In seed boxes, attack can occur in the wetter patches of medium.	Moderate to high moisture content. Poor drainage; poor aeration. Temperatures below 20°C favour attack by many species. High CO_2 level in the medium. Poor seedling vigour.
Phytophthora spp.	dieback collar rot root rots	Plants of all ages attacked. Roots attacked, often at points of injury. Soft wet rot through to dark dry lesions. Plants are stunted, leaves pale-green to yellow or reddish. They wilt and slowly die back from the tips or they die suddenly. The leaves remain attached. Roots can be seen to be rotted long before this.	Moderate to high moisture. Optimum temperature is 20–32°C but active at 10–34°C. Poor plant vigour. Small numbers of antagonists. High levels of wetting agent.
Rhizoctonia spp.	wire stem damping off collar rot	Mainly seedlings but also mature plants. Infection normally at or slightly above ground level, eventually girdling the stem and causing collapse. Under a hand lens, black mycelium threads can be seen in the girdled area. Lesions drier than those caused by Pythium. Roots show rotting around the outside. Then the roots rot through completely, leaving brown 'spear' tips.	Medium dryish to damp, not wet. The effect of temperature varies with species.

Sclerotinia spp.	sclerotinia blight blackrot	Patches of soft rot on stems and leaves. Affected tissues covered with white cottony growth. Plants may suddenly wilt and die.	Cool, showery weather, misting, irrigation.
Verticillium spp.	wilt	Leaves wilt, sometimes generally, sometimes only the lower leaves and sometimes one or a few branches only. Leaves turn pale and eventually brown but sections of stem are seen to have brown or green-brown discoloration.	Worst in cool weather.
Sclerotium spp.	stem rot	Attack is on the stem where it enters the medium. Water-soaked areas appear which soon blacken and become covered with white thread-like growth. Plants wilt and die rapidly.	High temperatures (25–35°C), fluctuating moisture content in the medium, an abundance of undecomposed organic matter, acid pH (3.5–5.0) and good aeration.

Nematodes	Common names	Symptoms	Attack favoured by
Meloidogyne spp. *Pratylenchus* spp. etc.	root knot root lesion	Plants of all ages attacked. Plants are stunted, appear to suffer from poor nutrition; leaves are often pale. Roots that have been invaded develop galls (knots), areas of dead tissue (lesions), cracks, splits, blackened areas, etc. Some nematodes cause multiple branching of roots immediately behind the point of attack.	Soil texture, water content and the seasonal patterns of change in water content greatly influence nematode populations. Temperature, pH, aeration, organic matter content and other properties of the growing medium all affect nematodes. The effects vary greatly from species to species.

Bacteria	Common names	Symptoms	Attack favoured by
Agrobacterium tumefaciens	crown gall	*Prunus* family (almonds, peaches etc.). Roots of seedlings invaded. Trees grow poorly. Large galls are formed on the roots near the trunk. The trees eventually die.	The organism enters through wounds. Routine use of the biological control agent 'Strain 84' has all but eliminated this disease.
Erwinia spp.	soft rot bacterial stem rot	Soft slimy rot. Often first at the base of the stem. Unthriftiness and wilting; often death.	Infection is mainly through an injury. Hot, humid weather.

27 NUTRIENT SOLUTION AS A MEDIUM: HYDROPONICS

There are many techniques for growing plants in a solution of nutrients in water. They are popularly called 'hydroponics', from the Greek words for water and labour. In many techniques the plants' roots grow in gravel, sand, scoria, expanded clay balls, vermiculite, perlite or rockwool, kept wet with nutrient solution. In the Nutrient Film Technique (NFT) there is no solid medium, just nutrient solution.

The principles behind these techniques and the growing of plants in other media are the same. A main difference is that other media have a much greater ability to hold and supply cations and to buffer against changes in pH.

This chapter gives a brief account of general principles. For detailed information, readers are referred to specialist books and to the suppliers of commercial systems.

TECHNIQUES THAT USE SOLIDS

In these techniques the solids are contained in troughs or pots from 80–200 mm deep. The solids anchor the plants and also retain solution between irrigations. Sand, perlite and vermiculite retain more solution than does gravel, so irrigation frequency can be less with them than with gravel. Aeration may be unsatisfactory if more than about 30% of the particles are smaller than 0.5 mm. A suitable mixture is given in Table 27.1.

Sands must be mainly quartz or other relatively inert minerals. Calcareous sands (containing lime and/or dolomite) are unsuitable. Scoria and some other crushed rocks may be alkaline and/or contain salts. They should be leached before use. The pH of the nutrient solution will need frequent adjustment for a while. Figures 27.1–27.3 illustrate two common commercial systems. A useful system for pot plants is shown in Fig. 27.4.

TECHNIQUES THAT USE NO SOLIDS

Scientists have long grown plants in nutrient solutions without any solid medium. Roots are supplied with oxygen from air bubbled vigorously through the solution. This technique has been used commercially but it has usually been found more expensive and difficult to control than techniques in which a solid is used. All this has been changed since the development of the Nutrient Film Technique (NFT). In NFT, the plants are supported with their roots in special channels set on an incline of about 1 in 50. A film of nutrient solution less than 2 mm deep runs continuously down the channel to a sump, from which it is pumped again to the upper ends of the channels (Fig. 27.5). An advantage of NFT in cool climates is that heating the nutrient solution to 18–30°C allows optimum growth at lower air temperatures than would otherwise be needed.

NFT has been used for lettuce and cucumbers, but results have been less than satisfactory with flower crops. There appears to have been a tendency in Europe to favour rockwool slabs and grow-bags rather than NFT. The huge difficulties

Table 27.1
Particle size range of crushed scoria found to be excellent for hydroponics beds 90 mm deep

Particle size (mm)	Percent by volume
>2	50
0.5–2	22
0.25–0.5	10
0.1–0.25	10
0.05–0.1	5
<0.05	3 max.

Figure 27.1
Carnations being grown in polystyrene foam trays containing crushed scoria. Water and nutrient solution are applied through drippers. *Courtesy of W R D Bliss, Hydroponics Industries*

Figure 27.2
Tomatoes being grown in rockwool blocks. Nutrient solution is applied through drippers

and cost of waste disposal with rockwool are being overcome through the re-melting of the slabs after several seasons of use.

There is a trend to wider use of aeroponics. In this system, the plants' roots, hanging in air inside an enclosure, are sprayed every few minutes with a fine mist of nutrient solution. Waste production is minimal, and growth rates can be very high indeed.

THE NUTRIENT SOLUTION

Any fertilizer that is suitable for use in liquid feeds (Table 16.17) will be suitable for hydroponics solutions. Many recipes are in use. They usually contain concentrations of nutrients in the ranges given in Table 27.2. Those who want to grow large areas of one crop should use a recipe found by research to be best for that crop. Otherwise, there are several commercial preparations available; just follow the instructions on the label.

Note in Table 27.2 that hydroponics solutions contain little or no ammonium–nitrogen. The solids of hydroponics media hold few cations, so ammonium toxicity is a greater risk in them than in other media. Ammonium toxicity is aggravated if the water used is saline (from sodium chloride), so with such waters it is best to use an all-nitrate solution.

Concentrations of phosphorus and boron in peat bags have been reported to increase over time, even when tomatoes are fed with solution containing 42 ppm P (P/N ratio 0.26) and 0.33 ppm B. P/N ratios in the range 0.16–0.22 seem appropriate for most plants (Table 27.2). A selection of nutrient solution concentrations used in rockwool culture in Holland is given in Table 27.2. Note that FeEDDHA is preferred over FeEDTA because the latter compound breaks down quite quickly at solution pH values over about 5.5 The polyflavenoid compound of Fe is even less stable.

Water quality

The allowable upper salinity of the water used for nutrient solutions depends on the sensitivity of the plants being grown and whether the solution is to be recycled or not.

The concentration of unwanted ions such as Na^+ and Cl^- will build up in recycled solution. The higher their concentrations in the water, the more frequently must the solution be replaced. An EC of 0.5 dS/m is about the upper

Figure 27.3

Close-up of root growth of tomatoes grown in rockwool blocks

Table 27.2

Optimum EC (dS/m) and concentrations (mg/L) of the nutrient solution used to fertilize various crops being grown in rockwool in the Netherlands. (*From* C Sonneveld and N Straver, Naaldwijk Research Station for Crops under Glass, Publication No. 8, 1990)

EC or nutrient	Cucumber	Tomato	Lettuce	Carnation	Rose	Gerbera	Chrysanthemum
EC (dS/m)	2.0	2.3	2.3	1.7	1.5	1.5	1.4
NO_3–N	224	193	266	182	154	158	147
NH_4–N	18	18	18	14	18	21	14
P	38	38	62	38	38	38	31
K	313	342	430	244	196	215	196
S	44	32	36	40	40	40	32
Ca	160	180	180	150	140	120	110
Mg	33	49	24	24	18	24	24
Fe*	0.8	0.8	2.2	1.4	1.4	2.0	3.4
Mn	0.5	0.5	0.3	0.5	0.3	0.3	1.1
Zn	0.3	0.3	0.3	0.3	0.2	0.3	0.2
B	0.3	0.3	0.3	0.3	0.2	0.3	0.2
Cu	0.05	0.05	0.05	0.05	0.05	0.05	0.03
Mo	0.05	0.05	0.05	0.05	0.05	0.05	0.05

*As FeDTPA chelated iron

limit for water for recycled solutions. The limit for the water for non-recycled solutions is about 1.5 dS/m. ?. See next pg.

You should know the analysis of the water you use. Ask your water supply authority or have it analysed (see the appendix 'Sources of Help'). Acid must be added to alkaline waters to bring their pH into the range 5.5–6.5. When waters contain high concentrations of calcium and magnesium, the amounts of these elements in the stock solutions should be reduced.

Example: Analysis shows that a water supply contains 60 ppm Ca and 10 ppm Mg. If nitric acid is used to reduce pH, it will provide nitrate ions to balance the calcium and magnesium in the water. The concentrations of Ca and Mg in the water are about one-third to one-half of the total requirements (Table 27.2). Reduce the concentrations of these two nutrients in the stock solution(s) by about these amounts.

> Concentrated nitric acid is corrosive and burns skin and clothing. Splashes in eyes can blind. Wear protective clothing and goggles when handling it.

Some people use phosphoric acid to control pH. It is safer than nitric acid, but other sources of P must be reduced if it is used. Potassium phosphate could be replaced with potassium sulphate.

Figure 27.4

Hydroponics system for indoor plants. The solid medium illustrated is expanded clay pellets but other materials can be used. Note the simple water-level indicator

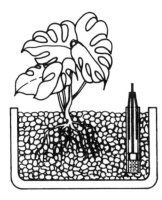

Recirculated solution

Nutrients removed by plants from recirculating solutions must be replaced. Stock solutions are added to bring the EC of the solution back to its original value. Water used by the plants must also be replaced. An increasing proportion of the EC of the solution will be made up by salts from the water. This has to be

Figure 27.5
Diagram showing the main parts of an NFT installation

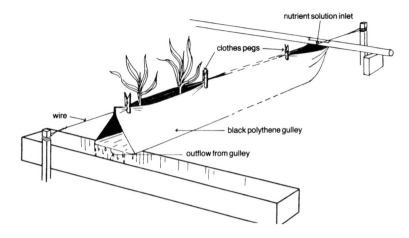

Figure 27.6
In rockwool installations, the drainage holes must be positioned between the drippers and at both sides of the rockwool block. The lines drawn on the blocks show the progress of the wetting fronts through the rockwool. *From* M van Noordwijk and P A C Raats *Report 9.81 Inst. Bodemvruchtbaarheid,* Haren (Gr.) Netherlands, 1981

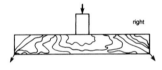

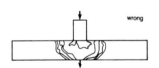

allowed for by bringing the solution to a slightly higher EC each time stock solutions are added.

Example: There is 1000 L of nutrient solution, and 100 L of water is used each day. Suppose that the EC of the water is 0.5 dS/m and half of it is due to non-absorbed, non-nutrient ions. Each day the EC of the solution will increase by $\dfrac{100 \times 0.25}{1000} = 0.025$ dS/m because of these ions.

Discard the solution when the EC reaches a pre-determined upper limit. This limit will be in the range 2–3 dS/m, depending on the plants being grown. Adjustment of EC is done continuously and automatically in larger installations and every one to several days in smaller units.

Solution pH must also be adjusted. Use a 1:1 mixture of 5% phosphoric acid and 5% nitric acid to lower pH and 10% potassium hydroxide to raise pH. Concentrated nitric acid is a 70% solution, so mix 70 mL with 930 mL water to make a 5% solution. Use only food grade phosphoric acid (p. 176). Including some ammonium may stop an upward pH drift in the solution.

Non-recirculated solution

Management is easier when solution is not recirculated, but losses of nutrients are higher. Nutrient solution is trickled onto the solids near each plant stem. The frequency varies from several times a week to several times a day. Frequency depends on the rate of water loss in relation to the amount of solution held by the solids. For daily application, the solids must hold twice daily losses. That's about 10 L of rockwool for a tomato plant.

The system is controlled so that the EC of the run-off solution is in the range 2.0–2.4 dS/m. Monitor at least daily and adjust applications as needed. Study the trends and gradually make small adjustments. A typical summer feed will have an EC of 1.3 dS/m. Always apply nutrient solution rather than alternate solution and water.

HINTS AND COMMENTS

- The main advantage of hydroponics is that plants are never short of water and nutrients.
- The main disadvantages are that capital cost is usually higher, the fertilizers may be more expensive and a whole new set of skills has to be learnt. These techniques are not suitable for producing plants that are to be planted out into soils.
- Disease can be devastating when nutrient solution is recycled. Planting stock must be free of pathogens and hygiene must be constantly excellent. Contain-

ers and solids are either discarded after one crop or thoroughly disinfected with formalin, hypochlorite or steam. Rockwool may be used for 3–4 years if steamed before re-use.

- Nevertheless, if hygiene is excellent, hydroponics systems of all types are remarkably free of disease problems. Dutch experience is that chemicals are rarely needed to control root diseases. If fungicides are needed there, the rate of application is only about one-tenth of the rate used on soils.
- Tipburn on lettuce is reduced if the solution circulated at night is either calcium nitrate (100 ppm Ca) or water, rather than full nutrient solution.
- One way of adjusting stock solutions to increase the K/N ratio is given in Table 27.3. Increased K/N ratio in winter tends to increase plant hardiness. It seems also to aid flower production.
- A K/N ratio of 2:1 seems to be high enough for most situations. It is often useful to lower the N concentration as well as to boost K.
- The nitrogen level should be dropped to around 110 ppm when prolific flowering is needed in African violets and hibiscus. Species such as begonias and pachystachys require a nitrogen concentration of more than 200 ppm for best flowering.
- In summer, when the transpiration rate is high, the nutrient solution can be more dilute than at other times of the year.
- The level of nitrogen should be reduced if, when crops are setting fruit, the roots show signs of poor growth or damage.
- The tops of beds that remain wet for long periods after irrigation will grow algae that can seal the surface, giving poor aeration. A layer 2–5 cm thick of some coarser or water repellent material (gravel, expanded clay balls, styrofoam) on the surface will help reduce algal growth.
- Leaves may become soft when humidity is high. They can be hardened by increasing the EC of the nutrient solution, to slightly stress the plants.
- Make sure that outlets under rockwool blocks are remote from drippers so that the whole block can be used and excess salts leached out (Fig. 27.6).

28 TEMPERATURE

Plants do not grow when the medium around their roots is frozen. They die if the soil temperature stays at 60°C for more than a few minutes. Growth is greatest over a narrow range of temperatures between these extremes.

This short chapter summarizes information about the effects on plants of changes in the temperature of the medium around their roots. These effects are separate from, although often related to, the effects of change in air temperature. Little will be said about air temperature.

EFFECTS OF LOW AND HIGH TEMPERATURES

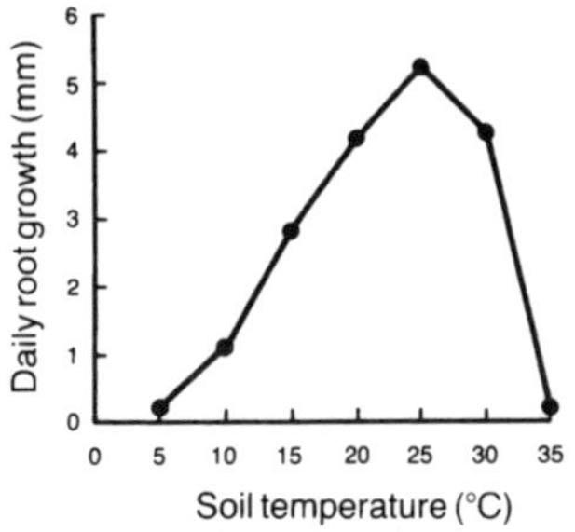

For many plants from temperate areas, root growth is almost non-existent at soil temperatures below 7°C. Plants from tropical lowlands need at least 12–16°C before there is much growth.

At the other end of the scale, a temperature of 60°C for more than a few minutes will kill the roots of all plants. A four-hour burst at 50–55°C will kill the roots of many plants. Those of a few species will regenerate after cooling. Four-hour bursts at 40–45°C will kill the root tips of many plants, but they will regenerate. Longer periods above 40°C will be more likely to kill beyond repair. The growth of most species is reduced at root temperatures of 40°C, and of many at 35°C (Fig. 28.1). Roots killed or damaged by high temperatures are easily invaded by pathogens if there are any in the medium. Young plants suffer more damage at a given temperature than do older plants of the same species. They are often damaged at lower temperatures than the lowest that reduce the growth of older plants.

TEMPERATURE RANGE FOR BEST GROWTH

Growth of roots and tops is usually most rapid when the temperature of the medium is in the range 15–30°C (Table 28.1). Precise temperatures for best growth cannot be given because they vary with plant species and variety, the wetness of the medium, air temperature, light intensity and nutrient supply. Generally, plants that evolved in cool areas tend to be towards the lower end of the range; for some, growth rate is already decreasing at 20°C. Plants from tropical areas vary in their requirements depending on the altitude at which they or their parents evolved. Those from tropical lowlands grow best at root temperatures of about 30°C. A few of them (e.g. couch grass) show increasing growth rate up to about 37°C. Plants from tropical highlands have optimum temperature requirements in the range of 20–30°C. For example, fuchsias, bred from parents found at elevations of 2000 m and higher, are intolerant of rootball temperatures above 25°C.

Propagation from cuttings

It is common to aid the formation of roots on cuttings by warming the medium into which they have been stuck.

The formation of roots takes place in two stages. First is the formation of

Figure 28.1
Example of the effect of soil temperature on plant roots, here the roots of seedlings of *Pinus taeda* (loblolly pine). *From* C W Barney *Plant Physiology* 26: 146, 1951

Figure 28.2

Roots grow more rapidly on cuttings of many species if the temperature of the propagation medium is around 30°C until roots form and is then dropped to around 20°C. From B Dykeman *Proc. Intern. Plant Propag. Soc.* 26: 201, 1976

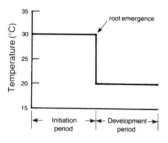

Table 28.1

Effects of temperature* on the growth and carbohydrate content of the tops of warm and cool-season grasses. The significance of carbohydrate content is discussed in Chapter 18. (*From* C M McKell et al. *Crop Sci.* 9: 534, 1969)

Temperature (°C) Day-Night	Couch grass (warm-season grass)		Kentucky bluegrass (cool-season grass)	
	Top growth (g/pot)	Carbohydrate (%)	Top growth (g/pot)	Carbohydrate (%)
13–7	37	8.0	70	6.5
18–13	95	5.8	110	3.6
30–18	140	3.0	56	1.2
30–24	195	4.8	40	0.6

*The plants were in containers in a growth cabinet so both tops and roots were kept at the temperatures shown.

Figure 28.3

Influence of temperature of the medium on rooting of *Hibiscus rosa-sinensis* 'Jim Hendry' cuttings. From W J Carpenter *J. Environ. Hortic.* 7: 143, 1989

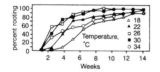

callus and the initiation of roots, then root development. The first stage occurs most rapidly for many temperate species when the medium is held at 27–30°C. The optimum temperature for root development is in the range 17–25°C (Fig. 28.2). The roots will be soft and easily damaged, or can be scorched, if the higher temperature is maintained during root development.

This two-stage system is usually too difficult to provide in practice so most propagation benches are maintained at 20–25°C, mainly 20–22°C. The range for tropical foliage plants is 24–27°C (Fig. 28.3).

Insulating the sides and bottoms of propagation benches can reduce heating costs by as much as 50%—25–50 mm of polystyrene is enough. Make sure that the propagation bench can be made hot enough to ensure any required temperature in the propagation medium. Heat is conserved, and heating of the propagation mix most efficient, when as much as possible of the propagation bench is covered with containers.

The high humidity of a fogged propagation house allows cuttings to remain turgid even at temperatures well above 40°C. This observation has encouraged some propagators to allow air temperature (and therefore root zone temperature) inside their house to reach and remain above 40°C for extended periods. We strongly recommend against this for the following reasons.

The rate of photosynthesis of a plant rises with temperature up to an optimum that is different for species from different climatic zones. Up to this point the plant's respiration rate (its rate of use of food reserves to keep it going) also slowly increases. But as temperature rises above the optimum, photosynthetic rate declines and respiration increases dramatically. In other words, the plant starts using its food reserves faster than it can make them. It begins to starve. Starvation arrives faster under heavy shade than in brighter conditions.

In a heavily shaded, fogged propagation house, it is unlikely that the rate and extent of rooting will be improved by allowing temperature to rise above 30°C for temperate species and about 35°C for tropical and subtropical species. At temperatures above the optimum, plants tend to give off ammonia and various smelly organic compounds. Drop the temperature of your house if it smells 'off'.

Germination of seeds

The dry seeds of many species can be frozen or kept near 90°C for weeks or months without ill effects. It's a different story when they are wet and beginning to germinate.

Figure 28.4

Typical daily changes in the temperature of bare soil at three depths. *From E S West Australian J. Sci. Res. A5: 303, 1952*

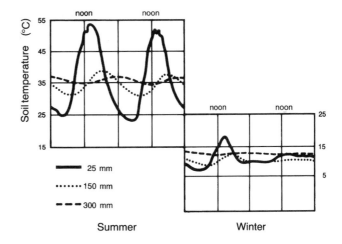

Figure 28.5

Temperature sequence needed for early flowering of *Hyacinthus orientalis* cv. L'Innocence. *From I Luyten et al. Verhandel. Koninkl. Ned. Akad. Wetenschap. Afdel. Natuurk. Sect. 1129: 1, 1932*

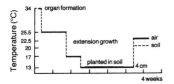

Seeds do not germinate at 0°C and most are killed if the temperature reaches 50°C. Between these extremes, there is a minimum temperature for each species below which its seeds do not germinate. The minimum may be as low as 1°C (*Convolvulus arvensis*), is often between 3 and 10°C, and is over 20°C for many tropical species. As the temperature rises above this minimum, germination rate increases to a maximum and then falls off. Optimum temperatures are in the range 15–40°C, mostly 20–30°C.

The seeds of some species (those whose native habitat is freezing in winter) do not germinate until they have spent some time fully moistened at a very low temperature. This is a protective mechanism that stops them from germinating in autumn in cold climates. If they did germinate, the seedlings would be killed during the winter. Nurserymen must 'stratify' the seeds of these species—that is, allow them to take up water and then store them moist in a refrigerator (1–10°C, usually 5°C) for one to four months, mostly two. Examples include species in the genera *Abies, Acer, Betula, Crataegus, Cupressus, Elaeagnus, Liquidambar, Picea, Rosa* and *Vitis*.

The seeds of some temperate species, particularly those of grasslands and other open areas, germinate best when night temperatures are lower than day temperatures. Presumably this is because they have evolved with the pattern of temperature change shown in Fig. 28.4. Seeds of plants from forests and tropical areas do not show this effect.

Figure 28.6

Temperature variation in different parts of medium in containers during a mild, partly cloudy day (southern hemisphere). *From K Young and K R W Hammett Agric. Meteorology 21: 165, 1980*

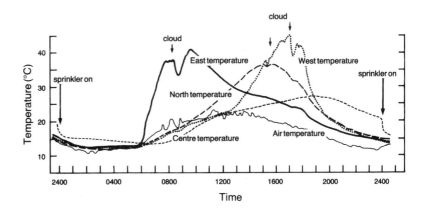

Figure 28.7
Temperatures 25 mm in from the sides and 70 mm from the bottoms of 4.5 litre containers in a group. There were no plants in the containers. Southern hemisphere. *From* T A Fetz *HortScience* 6: 400, 1971

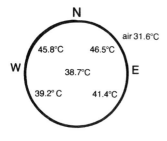

Figure 28.8
Winter sun provides some heat to the slope facing it (a), but almost none to the other side of the hill (b). Both slopes receive sunshine in the summer (c, d).

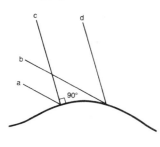

Table 28.3
Temperatures of medium inside plastic and clay containers (*From* A C Bunt and Z J Kilwiec *Plant and Soil* 32: 65, 1970)

Container		Temperature (°C)
Plastic, black		43.5
	terracotta	43.0
	white	39.8
Clay		38.9

Bulbs

Bulbs have special temperature requirements if they are to produce flowers. Fig. 28.5 shows the sequence needed to give early flowering of *Hyacinthus orientalis*. The sequences for other species are quite different. Freesias can be picked about four weeks earlier if the medium is cooled from about 22 to about 18°C. Consult specialist publications for more details.

SOME PRACTICAL CONSEQUENCES

If we want plants to grow rapidly, we must keep the temperature of the medium around their roots within the optimum range for these species. A common problem in Australia is that the temperature goes above this range. This happens especially to plants in containers.

Containers

Even on a cool summer day (max. 23°C) the temperature of the outer centimetre of mix in containers exposed to full sun can reach a lethal level (Fig. 28.6). On hotter days the temperature of the medium can exceed 50°C for hours—hot enough to cook roots. Little wonder that roots are absent from the sides of containers exposed to the sun.

Whether elevated temperatures do or do not damage plants depends on the maximum temperature attained and for how long, and on the sensitivity of a species to high root temperature. Heat stress in sensitive species will reduce growth and can increase their susceptibility to root-rotting disease. Under the same conditions some species may suffer no more damage than a slight check in growth.

Containers on the northern and western sides of groups of containers (southern hemisphere) reach higher temperatures than those in other positions (Fig. 28.7). The temperature is higher inside black pots than inside white pots (Table 28.2), or others of light colour.

Giving the standing ground a white or reflective surface raises the maximum temperature reached in containers (Table 28.2). This can be an advantage in cold areas and a disadvantage elsewhere.

Table 28.2
Effect of pot and background colour on temperature in potting mixes (80 mm below surface and 50 mm from western side of the pot at 3.30 p.m.) (*From* C E Whitcomb *Seed and Nursery Trader* Aug: 9, 1980)

	Temperature (°C)	
Pot colour	Black background	White background
Black polybag	38	43
White polybag	35	35
Difference	3	8

The following will help keep temperatures in containers within the optimum range in summer.

- Use shade cloth, especially to protect them from the afternoon sun.
- Use light-coloured, opaque containers. An example is poly bags having an outer white layer and an inner black layer. A problem is that some light-coloured plastics become brittle after a few months' exposure to sunlight (p. 373).
- Place the containers close together.
- Protect the outer row of containers from direct sunshine.

- Irrigate with cool water, if possible, or mist frequently.
- Allow as much air movement as possible through the area.
- If high temperatures are a serious problem, it could be useful to use clay rather than plastic containers. Evaporation from their outer surfaces keeps the medium in them a little cooler (Table 28.3).

In winter, some protection against freezing temperatures is given by using square containers jammed hard against one another.

Root systems damaged by high or freezing temperatures must be looked after carefully if new roots are to be produced quickly. Make sure that the mix is kept moist, but avoid overwatering. Fertilize as for seedlings or rooted cuttings for a while.

Transpiration

Transpiration rate increases as the temperature of the medium increases, even when air temperature is constant (Table 28.4). This means that plants given bottom heat will need to be watered more frequently than those not given bottom heat.

Plants are often seen to wilt in the afternoons of sunny days in early spring, even though the medium around their roots is wet. The reason is that the medium is cold. Cold roots are less 'leaky' than warm roots; cold water is more viscous than warm water. Water cannot enter the roots fast enough to replace that lost by transpiration. The wilting soon disappears in the evening. Growth is not reduced much. The only way of overcoming this temporary wilting is to cool the air or warm the medium. The latter soon happens as the season advances.

Landscape soils

Slope and direction of slope in relation to the sun (aspect) have a big effect on the temperature of soils. A soil is heated most when the sun shines on it at an angle of 90°. Heating will be less at other angles (Fig. 28.8). This means that:

- The soils of slopes that face north are warmer in winter than those of slopes that face south (southern hemisphere).
- The soils of slopes that face west tend to be a little warmer than those of slopes that face east.
- In winter, the soils of slopes that face the sun will be warmer than the soils of flat areas.
- In cool areas, in the coolest months, budburst and seed germination will be earliest and growth greatest on slopes in the order northern > western > eastern > southern (Fig. 28.9). The steeper the slope, the bigger the effect.
- In hot areas, the damaging effects of high soil temperatures will be least on southern slopes.

A separate effect of slope is that hollows or low areas in a landscape are usually colder than nearby areas further up slopes. Cold air drains into them. Frost damage is worst in such hollows.

Soil temperature is also greatly influenced by its colour, the thickness and type of mulch present and shading by vegetation.

Temperatures a few centimetres under a light-coloured surface can be about 5°C less than under a dark surface. This means that in cool areas, plantings in dark soils will start growing earlier than those on light-coloured soils. On the other hand, a light surface colour can benefit plants in hot areas.

The effects of mulches on soil temperature are dealt with in Chapter 22. One of the reasons for the decline and early death of isolated trees in landscapes is that litter is removed by grazing animals or unnecessarily tidy people. Soil temperatures the trees had become adapted to are then too often exceeded. Organic mulches are vital to the survival of plants in landscapes, especially un-irrigated ones.

Table 28.4
Transpiration rate of *Antirrhinum majus* as affected by the temperature of the medium (gravel/peat/vermiculite). Air temperature was 25°C. (*From* R R Rutland and J E Pallas *J. Amer. Soc. Hort. Sci.* 97: 34, 1972)

Temperature of the medium (°C)	Relative transpiration rate
10	1.0
25	1.5

Figure 28.9
In a cold climate, germination of seeds is more rapid in soils on northern (N) and western (W) slopes (southern hemisphere) than on southern (S) and eastern (E) slopes or on flat ground (H). On the northern aspect, germination rate increases as slope increases. *From* J W Ludwig et al. *J. Ecology* 45: 205, 1957

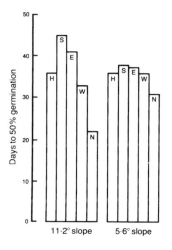

29 SOILS AND LANDSCAPES

As we travel around we notice that:

- Land may be flat, gently sloping, hilly or mountainous.
- Surface soils have many different colours and textures.
- In road cuttings, erosion gullies and excavations, the soils often have many layers that look and feel different from one another.
- In areas of natural vegetation, soils of different appearance support different types of plants.

It is obvious that landscapes, and the soils on which they are founded, come in an enormous range of forms. This chapter gives a very brief overview of the processes that have shaped landscapes and formed soils.

IN THE BEGINNING

According to geologists, in the beginning there were gases that condensed to form a hot blob of liquid. Eventually a solid crust (the earth's crust) formed on this liquid. Uplifting formed mountains; collapsing formed deep depressions. Tumbling rocks pulverized one another to sand and dust which mingled with volcanic ash—the first erosion and 'soil' formation. Much later, cooling allowed rain and lakes, accompanied by much more erosion.

Thick layers of sediments began to be formed, to be eventually squashed into rocks, uplifted into mountains, pushed sideways by earthquakes, tilted by movement of continents, and eroded again. Glaciers crunched all before them, in retreat leaving enormous areas of pulverized rock. Materials dissolved from rocks and sediments reacted to form new minerals, to be deposited in the sediments or as slimes on ocean floors.

Life, when is appeared, accelerated the chemical changes taking place and altered them, so that soils as we know them, with their distinctive profiles, began to be formed.

SOIL FORMATION

The soil profile

The profiles of people and soils have much in common. Both must be viewed from the side; both come in an almost infinite variety of shapes or forms; both are fascinating. The diverse shapes of nose and chin in one are replaced in the other by a multitude of colours, textures, structures, mineral types and depths. Under every square kilometre of landscape there will usually be several soils with different profiles (Fig. 29.1).

The processes that have formed soil profiles are complex but they are now reasonably well understood by soil scientists. Only a brief summary needs to be given here.

Figure 29.1
Every landscape is founded on soils having a variety of profile forms. Profiles are described as shown. The A horizon is the topsoil which is often seen to be darker in its uppermost part (A_1) due to the presence of organic matter. The A horizon goes abruptly or gradually into the B horizon—the subsoil. Below that again is the C horizon of decomposing rock or unchanged sediments

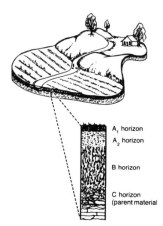

A₁ horizon
A₂ horizon

B horizon

C horizon
(parent material

Weathering processes

Soils are formed from rocks and sediments (parent materials) by physical chemical and biological processes. These are generally grouped together under the term 'weathering'.

- Physical weathering processes include the breaking up of rocks by thermal expansion and contraction and grinding by wind- and water-borne solids.
- Chemical weathering requires water and oxygen. Minerals are dissolved; others are formed from the dissolved materials. Chemical weathering is most rapid in warm, moist, well aerated materials, such as the topsoils of the tropics.
- Living organisms change the rate and direction of chemical weathering processes.

Weathering processes can be grouped under four headings:

Additions

- of organic matter and its nutrients to soil surfaces;
- of sediments carried by wind and water.

Removals

- of soluble salts in leaching waters;
- of organic matter by fire;
- of particles by erosion.

Transfers

- of plant nutrients from deep in soils to the surface;
- of soil to the surface in earthworm casts;
- of materials dissolved or suspended in leaching water from topsoil to subsoil;
- of solids down a slope.

Transformations

- of one mineral to another, by elements being dissolved from the first; examples include mica to vermiculite, feldspar to clay minerals, silicate minerals to hydrated oxides of iron and aluminium;
- of dead plant materials to humus.

All these processes take place in every soil, but at different rates and in different proportions to one another. The proportions and rates for a particular area depend on:

- rainfall;
- time of the year when the rain falls (hottest or coldest);
- depth of materials above a layer that is impermeable to water;
- whether the soil is or is not free-draining;
- oxygen supply in the soil;
- temperature;
- type of parent material;
- type of plant cover;
- topography;
- length of time during which weathering has been taking place; this is usually thousands to millions of years.

Little wonder that there is almost an infinite variety of soils to be seen.

Examples

Desert loams, such as those of the region where the state borders of South Australia, Queensland and New South Wales meet, have been formed from alluvium and sedimentary rocks, often from ancient seabeds, over perhaps hundreds of thousands of years. The climate has been one of short wet periods separated by long droughts. Materials dissolved from the topsoil have been

Figure 29.2
Diagrams summarizing the main features of the soil types described in the text. Numbers are depths below the surface in cm. *From* H C T Stace et al. *Handbook of Australian Soils* Rellim, Adelaide, 1968

Desert loams

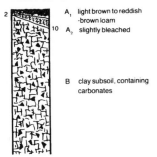

Red-brown earths

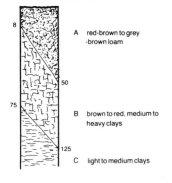

Black earths

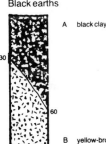

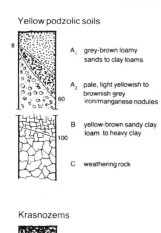

Yellow podzolic soils

A₁ grey-brown loamy
    sands to clay loams

A₂ pale, light yellowish to
    brownish grey
    iron/manganese nodules

B   yellow-brown sandy clay
    loam to heavy clay

C   weathering rock

Krasnozems

A₁ dark reddish-brown
    clay loam

A₂ red clay

B   dark red, medium to
    heavy clay

C   weathering rock

transferred to the subsoil where they have formed deposits of calcium and magnesium carbonates and gypsum. Subsoils are also saline because there is not enough rain for deep leaching. Limited amounts of organic matter, with their nutrients, are added to the soil surface. High levels of exchangeable calcium and magnesium, together with limited leaching, mean that topsoils and subsoils are at least of neutral pH and mostly alkaline.

Red-brown earths are the main soils of much of the New South Wales wheat country. They have been formed from loose sediments. Moderate rainfall (<500 mm annually) has leached salts and some calcium and magnesium from the A horizon into the subsoil. Some clay has been carried down too. Topsoils are neutral to slightly acid. Subsoils contain deposits of calcium and magnesium carbonates. They are alkaline medium to heavy clays that crack into blocks on drying. Topsoils are sandy loams and loams. They are often sodic and hard-setting.

Black earths are found covering extensive areas in northern New South Wales and the Darling Downs of Queensland. They are also found bordering many creeks and streams throughout the wetter parts of the country. Most have formed from alluvium. The very high clay contents (50–80%) have allowed little leaching, so the soils are neutral to slightly alkaline. Smectite is the main clay mineral, so as these soils dry they crack strongly. The drying soil breaks into small clods (self-mulches). Most of the soils used for cricket wickets are black earths.

Yellow podzolic soils have been formed from a variety of rocks under high rainfall conditions and strong weathering. Salts, much of the calcium and magnesium and some silica have been leached from the A horizon. The topsoils are therefore acid, with kaolin as a main clay mineral. Subsoils have magnesium as a main exchangeable cation. The yellow colour of the subsoils indicates that the soils are moist for long periods and sometimes waterlogged to the top of the B horizon. Two other effects of this waterlogging are that subsoils are usually mottled yellow-brown and there is usually a layer of iron/manganese nodules at the interface between A and B horizons.

In contrast, the krasnozems of eastern Australia (north-west Tasmania, northern New South Wales, coastal Queensland) have been formed mainly from volcanic rocks on well-drained sites. Heavy leaching has removed much of the silica from these soils, transforming the original minerals into kaolinite and hydrated iron and aluminium oxides. Removal of calcium and magnesium has left them acidic. Many topsoils have high contents of organic matter left over from the time when they grew forests.

A CONTINUING PROCESS

The processes that have formed soils and landscapes from rocks and sediments continue today. In every soil, plant nutrients are being released, as minerals slowly dissolve and as organic matter slowly decomposes. Roots grow and die. The changing seasons bring changes in the populations of living organisms. Cycles of wetting and drying break and reform crumbs and other structural units of soils. Leaching continues to remove nutrients from topsoils and plant uptake, followed by litter fall, continues to bring them back to the surface.

Each year, perhaps 0.02 mm, often less, of soil is formed from parent materials. At that rate, a layer of soil 15 cm deep will take at least 7500 years to form.

Compare that with the fact that a heavy storm lasting 20 minutes can strip 10 cm of topsoil from a cultivated paddock on a hillside. We doubt that any farmer who allows this to happen will be thanked by his and our descendants who might need to grow food on that land. All who use soils must be aware of the great responsibility they have to future generations. Soil is not like many other things that are bought and sold. There is a limited amount of it. When lost, it will be a very long time before it will be replaced. We hold our soils on trust to be used, certainly, but to be preserved and improved for future generations.

Look after your soil as you look after your most valued possession.

SOIL MAPPING

Those who have stopped to look at the multitude of soils around them have usually been fascinated by what they have seen. Many have pondered the reasons for soils being as they are. Some, the soil scientists, have devoted their lives to finding answers. Some soil scientists have spent much time making maps showing the position of different soils in the landscapes studied. They have described soils and compared them with soils found by others in other places.

This comparison is easier if soils with similar-looking profiles and similar properties are given a name. Other soils can be given other names. In this way a classification system for the soils of a region or country is built up. If you know what the names mean, you can quickly understand what a soil will be like and how it will behave if another person describes it by that name. The classification thus becomes a kind of language.

But one trouble is that there are many classification systems. Some, such as the Soil Taxonomy system, contain many thousands of soil names. The whole matter is too complicated to deal with here. Those who want to know more should consult the books listed in the appendix 'Further Reading'.

Much more important than a classification is a knowledge of how to read and use soil maps. These maps are invaluable to anyone who must use soil, be it for growing crops, making sports fields or building roads. The summaries of soil properties accompanying soil maps allow rapid assessment of the limitations a particular soil may put on any planned use of the soil.

Any reader about to use an area of soil would be wise to first consult a soil map of the area if one has been produced. Soil scientists in Departments of Agriculture and Primary Industries, Soil Conservation offices, CSIRO and private consulting firms are often able to help.

30 CONTAINERS

The rate at which plants grow in nurseries, and the way they perform after planting out, are strongly influenced by the containers in which they are grown.

SHAPE AND SIZE

Container shape and size have a marked effect on root form and plant growth rate.

Depth

Figure 30.1
Early root growth from plants raised in tall containers tends to be more vertical than lateral

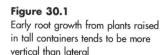

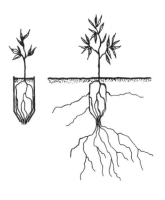

As described in Chapter 9, as the depth of mix in a pot decreases, air-filled porosity also decreases. This may not harm plants if the mix is very open. But if the mix has a fine texture, lack of oxygen around plant roots can reduce growth rates, especially if watering frequency is excessive (Fig. 10.5). Soil-borne diseases often become more troublesome.

For best aeration and drainage, choose containers that are as deep as is practically possible for the particular situation. However, there seems to be no benefit to be gained from going deeper than about 22 cm. Oxygen supply to the centres of very deep pots can be poor.

A possible disadvantage of deep, narrow containers (such as tubes) is that after planting out, the roots that have been trained downwards tend not to grow laterally (Fig. 30.1). Resistance to being blown over is not very high. However, lateral roots soon grow.

Width

Wide containers are less likely to tip over than are narrow containers. However, the need for stability must be balanced against the need to use space efficiently. As a general rule, pots should be deeper than they are wide.

Shape

Most containers are round in horizontal cross section. This is the cheapest shape to manufacture and the easiest to stack. However, a major disadvantage is that roundness without internal checks allows roots to circle. Before planting out, the circling roots must either be cut through (Fig. 30.2), removed or teased out.

Circling can be reduced or prevented as follows:

- Coat the inside walls of pots with paint containing copper. Use a flat, white, acrylic exterior house paint containing copper carbonate, copper hydroxide or Kocide at 100 g/L paint. The tip of any root hitting the copper is killed and so prevented from circling. The plant is not harmed (Table 30.1).
- Roots tend to be directed downwards when they hit a corner in a square pot. Root systems are often much better in milk cartons without bottoms than in round pots.
- Wedge-shaped containers train roots towards the one hole in the base

Figure 30.2
Circling of roots continues after planting out (L), unless the roots are cut at the time of planting (R). In this case the roots were cut by drawing a knife deeply down the full length of two sides of the rootball. *From P Persson Proc Symp. on Root Form of Plant Trees Victoria B C, Canada, 1978*

Figure 30.3
Wedge-shaped containers are ideal for training the roots of plants that are to be transplanted. *Courtesy of D. Trimboli, Arthur Yates & Sons*

Figure 30.4
Tapering the bottom of the container (R) prevents the circling of roots usually found in flat-bottomed containers (L)

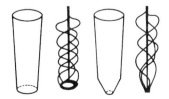

(Fig. 30.3). Containers whose sides curve gently into the base (Fig. 30.4) do the same.

- Root systems of plants in polybags tend to have less circling than do those in round containers with rigid walls. Fold in polybags tend to deflect circling roots downwards. Root systems tend to be more branched and fibrous in polybags than in rigid containers.
- One report has shown that weirdly-shaped pyramid-type pots, containing holes in their sides, were no better than other pots in preventing circling.
- One research finding of somewhat limited practicality was that a liner made from shadecloth prevents circling.
- Vertical ribs moulded as part of the inside surfaces of pots reduce circling a little.

Figure 30.5
Change in height of *Magnolia grandiflora* 'St Mary' over time when grown in 10, 27 and 57 L containers. *From* C A Martin et al. *J. Amer. Soc. Hortic. Sci.* 116: 439, 1991

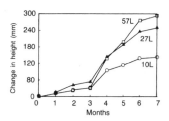

Figure 30.6
Effect of fertilizer rate and pot size on the growth of *Rhododendron* 'Pink Supreme'. *From* G J Keever and G S Cobb *HortScience* 22: 891, 1987

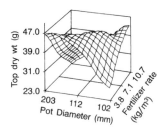

Figure 30.7
Contrasting effects of increasing pot size on plants that are capable and less capable of growing rapidly. *From* D Nichols *Australian Hortic.* Dec: 20, 1992

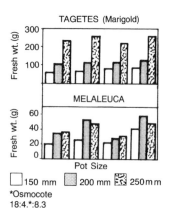

Table 30.1

Effect on root quality and plant height of painting the inside of pots with paint containing copper hydroxide. (*From* M A Arnold *J. Environ. Hortic.* 10: 114, 1992)

Copper hydroxide in paint (g/L),	Root rating*	Height (cm)
0	0.0	77
25	1.0	81
50	1.9	78
100	2.5	83

* Root rating: 0 = no control of root deformation; 3 = complete control

Volume

Pot volume must match plant size. A large plant in a small pot will grow more slowly than a similar plant in a large pot (Table 30.2). If you want rapid growth, you must have seedlings and rooted cuttings in as large a container as possible as soon as possible.

Overall growth rate is most rapid when seeds are sown and cuttings stuck into the pots in which they are to be sold. Otherwise, potting up should be done as early as possible. Fewer deformed roots is an added benefit of early potting up (Fig. 31.21).

Other effects of container volume are as follows:

- The root restriction and repeated water deficits that can be suffered by plants in small pots restrict their shoot growth too. Their leaves may be thinner and they have a lower ability to transport calcium to shoots.
- In situations in which the rootball is likely to get hot during the day, the larger the total volume of the pot, the cooler will be the centre of the rootball. This relative coolness can aid the survival of plants whose roots do not tolerate high temperatures. Figure 30.5 gives an example.
- The rate of application of controlled-release fertilizers should be lower for mix going into large pots than for that going into smaller pots. How much lower depends on the plants being grown but could be about 25%. An even greater lowering is necessary for salt-sensitive plants, otherwise they can be damaged by excessive salinity in the larger pots (Figs. 30.6 and 30.7).

Several research studies have shown that the containers used for growing advanced deciduous trees should be of low profile, that is of 'squat' design rather than 'standard'. For example, a study with *Pyrus calleryana* (pear) and *Cryptomeria japonica* showed that root systems were more fibrous in squat than in standard pots. This led to faster establishment after planting.

OTHER FACTORS

Drainage holes

Drainage holes must be of a number and size that allow rapid removal of excess water from the pot. Ideally, they should straddle the bottom corner so that they are partly in the side and partly in the base. The holes must be cleanly formed: no slivers of plastic left during moulding must obstruct them.

Pots that are to stand on capillary beds and mats must have holes in their bases (Fig. 30.8).

Materials and colour

Most containers used in Australia are now made from plastic, mainly polyeth-

Figure 30.8

Holes such as these in the base of a pot are essential if watering is to be from below *Photograph K A Handreck*

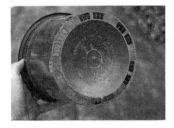

Table 30.2
Effect of container size on the growth and quality of *Brassaia* (*Schefflera actinophylla*) (*From R T Poole and C A Conover Proc. Soil and Crop Sci. Soc. Florida* 38: 12, 1978)

Container size		Plant	
Area of top (cm²)	Volume (mL)	Height (cm)	Grade*
175	1990	61	2.7
315	3860	77	3.6
490	9140	89	4.1
615	14330	99	4.6

*! = unsaleable; 3 = good, saleable; 5 = excellent.

Figure 30.9
Lännen multicell trays with various cell sizes *Photograph K A Handreck*

ylene. A few terracotta pots can still be bought, but their greater weight, lower strength and higher cost preclude their use in nurseries. Pots of compressed peat are really pot-less medium.

All plastics become brittle during prolonged exposure to the sun. The length of time before this happens depends on the formulation of the plastic. The inclusion of carbon black and of organic compounds that absorb ultraviolet (UV) light prolongs the life of the plastic. Carbon black is especially effective: black pots last many years. Grey pots, containing some carbon black and some UV absorbers, are also long-lived. White and other light-coloured pots have much shorter lives. However, they can all be formulated to last at least one growing season. Plastic pots can be made in almost any colour needed to suit any promotion of plants by a nurseryman. One disadvantage of black pots is the high temperatures found in them in summer (Chapter 28).

There are at least three reasons for light-coloured pots being used less often than are black pots. One is the usually higher cost of light-coloured pots. Another is their shorter life. Yet another is that most light-coloured plastics are translucent. Light penetrating through them restricts root growth in the outer part of the rootball. When judged by the amount of visible root growth, the quality of plants growing in translucent pots seems to be poor. However, research has shown that the rate of growth of the tops is either unaffected or only slightly reduced. Watering has to be more carefully controlled to allow for the smaller mass of roots.

Practical aspects of design

Several practical aspects of design should be considered:

- Containers should stack together, but must be able to be separated easily from one another.
- Containers to be handled through a potting machine must be compatible with the machine.
- They should be stable enough to stand up by themselves.
- Multicell trays that allow easy pulling of seedlings are the norm for seedling production (Fig. 30.9).
- Polybags are cheaper than rigid pots, but one difficulty with them is that filling is more difficult to mechanize.
- Pots with several raised rings around the inside just below the top are easier to grip when wet than those without these rings.

31 FROM NURSERY TO LANDSCAPE

The soil of a garden or some other landscaped area is the destination of many of the plants grown in nurseries. The move can be a traumatic experience for some plants: the environment of a landscape is often harsher than that of the nursery.

A plant's survival and long-term health depend on:

- how well the soil has been prepared;
- skilled planting;
- suitable aftercare;

but also on:

- the condition of the plant as it leaves the nursery;
- the treatment it gets at the retail centre, and afterwards, before planting.

This chapter outlines techniques to be used to improve the survival and growth of plants after they leave nurseries.

PREPARING FOR LEAVING

Whenever possible, plants intended for planting outdoors should be hardened before they leave a nursery.

- Move them to a less shaded area.
- Reduce the level of nutrition, especially of nitrogen.
- Leach heavily if mix salinity is moderate to high, then:
- Slightly increase the time between waterings so that they become slightly stressed.
- Apply wetting agent at a low rate (0.1 mL concentrate per litre of mix) if the mix is difficult to re-wet after drying. Also apply controlled-release fertilizer at 1–1.5 g/L if the sources of nutrients in the pots have been exhausted. This should ensure that your plants maintain condition even if they have to remain in the retail nursery for a month or two.
- Tell the retailer that the plants from you have enough fertilizer for several months.
- Put some of your plants in a situation that is similar to that of a retail store so that you can see how they perform. If needed, modify your methods of production to ensure better performance.

SITE PREPARATION FOR LANDSCAPING

A garden or park can (perhaps) be made by throwing a few seedlings into quickly dug holes scattered through an area, but a more pleasing effect is usually obtained with more care and planning. We cannot give any detail on landscape design here, but we do give a method of approach that starts at the base—the soil. This section applies to any area being landscaped—parks, gardens, roadside verges, mine dumps being revegetated, etc.

Figure 31.1

The only way of finding out what is happening to roots in a container is to look. *Photograph J Coppi*

Care at the retail store

There are two main causes of many of the problems that retail garden centre staff have with plants in containers. One is the different levels of fertilizers in mixes from different wholesale nurseries. Unless the staff have been told, how do you know how much fertilizer to apply to maintain stock? Applications to pots already fertilized may give a damaging level of salinity. Plants may yellow if no fertilizer is applied to mixes containing few reserves. Plants in retail stores can be maintained with slow-release fertilizers or a liquid feed of about 75 ppm each of N and K.

The other cause of problems is the wide variation in the water holding capacities of the different media used by different nurseries. A plant in a 15 cm pot holding 20 volume % readily available water may need watering every second or third day. A plant of similar size in a 15 cm pot holding 5 volume % readily available water could need watering twice a day. The first mix might remain over-wet if watered at the same frequency as the second mix. Wherever possible retailers should group plants needing similar frequencies of watering.

Get into the habit of inspecting roots by knocking plants (carefully) from containers (Fig. 31.1). If the lower half of the mix is still wet, there is no need to water.

Take care not to allow mixes to dry out too much. Re-wetting may be difficult with some mixes, to which you may have to add wetting agent to keep them in saleable condition. Make allowance for any 'umbrella' effect of foliage that reduces the amount of water reaching the mix in surrounding pots.

Protect your plants from heat, wind and diseases. Containers must never be placed directly on the ground.

Plan ahead

There is a right time and many wrong times for most landscaping jobs:

- Soil is damaged if it is pushed around when very wet.
- Plants are most likely to survive if planted out when rain will water them.
- Weed control is easiest before seedlings have been planted out or seeds of required species sown.
- Soils must be analysed and the necessary fertilizers bought and spread if mixing with the soil is needed.
- Where necessary, drainage systems are easiest to install before an area is planted.
- Any cultivation needed is easiest before planting.

Look at the area, assess what is needed, and then set up a schedule for doing it.

Look at the area

- Look at the shape of the area—its topography and the topography of the surrounding area that can affect it.
- Look at the surface drainage pattern. A natural, undisturbed area will have a long-established system of streams and channels for collecting runoff water. Any site works should blend in with this pattern. A new system of surface drainways may have to be made in severely disturbed areas such as large construction sites and mine dumps.
- Look for wet areas. These could be in hollows, at the bottom of large paved areas, low-lying flat areas, or as soakages at the bottom of hills. Soakages are often saline, but check. Decide whether you need to drain these areas or whether they can be used to advantage as they are. Soakages can eventually be dried up by trees planted up-slope.

- Erosion gullies will need special treatment to stop them from becoming larger. Consult your state soil conservation group.
- Try to see in your mind's eye how the area will look after plantings have grown. Will they blend in with the topography? How should plantings be varied to make best possible use of the topography?
- Are there parts of the area that need to be re-shaped so that the topography is better suited to the intended use? If so, what is involved and what might be the cost?

Assess the soil(s)

- Determine the texture of the topsoil. This will give clues to its ability to hold water and its behaviour on becoming wet.
- Assess the structure of the topsoil. Is it friable or is it cloddy? What happens when it becomes wet? Dispersion and stickiness suggest sodicity. Check with a test (Chapter 33).
- If the structure is poor, infiltration of water may be slow. Action to increase the infiltration rate may be needed (Chapter 9).
- For larger areas, have the topsoil analysed for pH, available phosphorus and exchangeable cations. The results will show the need or otherwise for fertilizers.
- Check the salinity of the topsoil, and the subsoil at several depths. The results can be used as a guide to the species to be planted and/or the need for improved drainage.
- Dig holes into the subsoil to at least 500 mm. Look for natural heavy clay layers or compacted layers that signal a need for a drainage system. Look for buried layers of lighter texture that may have to be mixed with the soil above. Look for compaction and colour changes that tell of waterlogging.
- While making these assessments, look for variations in the soil across the site that might mean different treatments for different parts of it.
- Look for evidence of past cut-and-fill (Fig. 31.2).

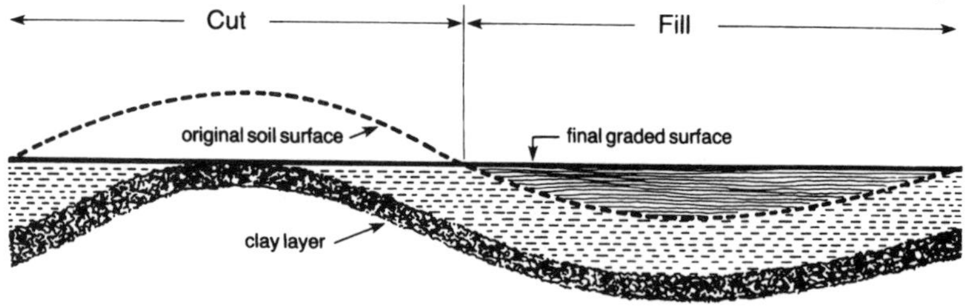

Figure 31.2
When a cut and fill job has been done like this, plant growth will be poor on the 'cut' areas

- For mine-spoil dumps, special tests may be needed to check for the presence of toxins such as sulphides and heavy metals as well as for the usual hazards of high salinity, unacceptable pH and low levels of nutrients.
- Are there rocks lying around that must be removed before the soil can be worked, or can they be left as part of the new landscape?

Site works

- First, remove all builders' debris. Take special care to remove soil that is heavily contaminated with mortar residues. Remove any rocks that will interfere with landscaping.
- Wherever possible, retain vegetation as a protection against erosion. Otherwise:
- If vegetation must be cleared, the plants plus the top centimetre or so of topsoil can be scraped off and composted. Weed seeds can be killed by fumigation. The compost can be spread over the area just before planting.

Figure 31.3
Severe erosion at a development site. The soil had been left without a protective cover of plants or mulch.
Courtesy of Soil Conservation Service of NSW

- A basic rule in any landscaping is to establish plants on disturbed areas as quickly as possible. Only then can the serious damage shown in Fig. 31.3 be avoided. At the very least, spread a mulch that will break the impact of raindrops.

For areas not requiring extensive earthworks

- Relieve any compaction with a chisel plough (large areas) or with a long-handled shovel (smaller areas). Break up large clods with disc harrows or spring tine cultivators (large areas) or with a fork (smaller areas). Use harrows or

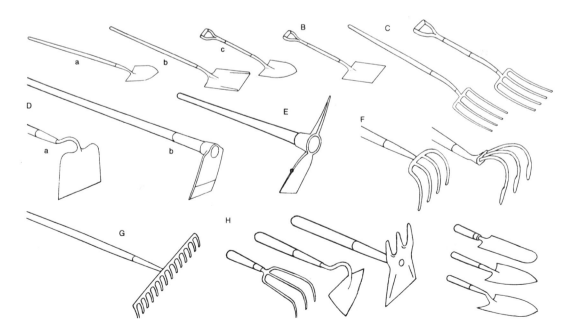

Figure 31.4

The main types of hand tools used when working with soils. (A) shovels: (a) Long-handled, round-point for general digging, digging planting holes, clearing surface drains and irrigation ditches; (b) Long-handled, square-point for shovelling soil, sand and gravel and for levelling; (c) Short-handled, both round and square-pointed, for moving soil, picking up litter etc. (B) Spade, for digging trenches, transplanting trees and shrubs, and edging. (C) Long and short-handled forks, for digging hard soils, loosening soils, shifting compost, lifting clumps of perennials and tubers, breaking surface crusts and mixing fertilisers into soils. (D) Hoes: (a) Various sizes, used mainly for weed control and for breaking surface crusts. Use a smooth, almost horizontal, swinging movement rather than a chopping movement; (b) Heavy style used for smashing through hard root-filled soil and for cutting tough weeds. (E) Pick mattock. The sharp pick is used to break hard and rocky soil and asphalt. The wide mattock is used for loosening soil when digging trenches, etc. (F) Cultivators come in several styles. They are used for breaking surface crusts and to kill weed seedlings. (G) Rakes are used to level the surface of a seedbed and to remove clods, sticks and stones. (H) There are many styles of hand cultivators and hoes. (I) Trowels also come in a variety of shapes and sizes. They are used to remove weeds, for loosening and digging small areas of soil and when planting bulbs and seedlings

a rake to give a fine seedbed for turf. Figures 31.4 and 31.5 show some of the implements that can be used.

- Note that rotary hoes can seriously damage soil structure. They tend to create a hardpan at the bottom of the cultivated soil. The alternative implements listed above are to be preferred.
- Shallow cultivation encourages shallow root growth in trees. When planting trees at windy sites, survival is often best when the soil is ripped deeply with winged ripper blades. This encourages deep root penetration and good anchorage. Ripping is most effective when the soil is dry.

Improving a degraded area

An area of soil can become degraded through excessively frequent and vigorous cultivation, excessive traffic, overgrazing, erosion, inadequate fertilization and invasion by weeds. Such a soil must be improved before it is suitable for horticultural use.

Erosion gullies must be filled in, but what topsoil there is must be reserved for a coating over the whole area. Compaction must be relieved by cultivation; plough pans must be broken through by deep ripping. Cultivation must, however, be kept to the minimum needed to produce a reasonable tilth. The soil will be formed into beds or mounds as required by the proposed planting.

During cultivation, any imbalance in fertility must be corrected on the basis of tests. Soil pH should be adjusted as required and, for clay soils, gypsum applied if needed.

Most importantly, the organic matter content of the soil must be increased, either by importing organic materials or via a green manure crop, or both.

Only through careful attention to these steps will it be possible to ensure good growth of horticultural crops. Many of the general remarks on this and the next several pages apply here too.

When extensive earthworks are needed

- Always consult your state soil conservation service before you start. Soil conservation officers will give advice about the soils of the area and ways of avoiding problems.
- Never bulldoze straight into an area, mixing subsoil and topsoil together.
- Rather, when extensive reshaping is needed, first remove topsoil and stockpile it for spreading back later over exposed subsoil. Topsoil, with its higher organic matter and nutrient content, and usually better structure, is the most valuable part of the soil profile. Look after it with great care. Use it as soon as possible. Stockpiling leads to a depletion of the populations of mycorrhizal fungi and *Rhizobium* bacteria. The longer the storage, the greater the depletion. Eventually the populations left may not be able to infect seedlings that are establishing in the soil. The time taken for this to happen varies from site to site. Six months will usually cause few problems. Increasing storage times over 12 months often gives rapidly decreasing ability to infect plants. Seeds of native shrubs and trees may lose their viability if the topsoil is stored for 12 months.
- In sandy areas, the extra organic matter in the 'topsoil' allows it to supply more nutrients and hold more water than the sands deeper down the profile. It may be valuable because of the seeds of native plants it contains if it is from a once natural area. Even the poorest topsoil is usually better than pure subsoil at the surface. As little as 50 mm of topsoil has been known to dramatically improve plant growth.
- The quality of bought topsoil can be judged by comparing it with the recommendations of Australian Standard 2223 (which, in 1993, was in the early stages of being upgraded).
- If the subsoil is toxic to plants (pH less than 4; high salinity, high level of

Figure 31.5

Some of the machine-drawn implements used for cultivating soils. (a) Chisel plough. This is used to loosen and shatter the subsoil with minimal disturbance to the surface. (b) Mouldboard plough. This inverts a slice of soil, with a relatively small amount of shattering. Mouldboard ploughs are often used in the preparation of horticultural land. They are especially useful for fine-textured soils. Make sure that the soil is a little drier than field capacity before starting. (c) Disc plough. This does much the same job as a mouldboard plough. (d) Disc harrows. This implement is used to break up large clods, for breaking surface crusts, for weed control and for levelling roughly cultivated ground. Not illustrated are ripper blades, sometimes used to break up clay subsoils (often only temporarily); spring-tine cultivators—wide-span alternatives to disc harrows; rotary hoes, used for rapid seedbed preparation of small areas (they tend to severely damage soil structure); solid-tine harrows, used for final smoothing of seedbeds. Note that excessive cultivation with any implement tends to destroy soil structure. A layer of severely compacted soil (a plough pan) is often formed just beneath the depth of penetration of the implement with repeated use. *Photographs J Fakes and N Black*

(a)

(b)

(c)

(d)

Figure 31.6
This is one way of aiding the stabilization of steep banks

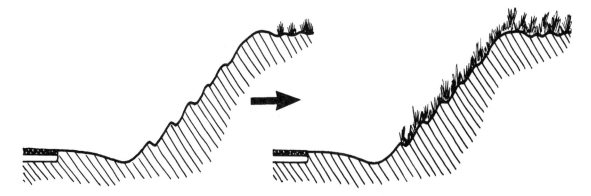

Figure 31.7
The several types of shapes that can be given to surfaces in landscapes

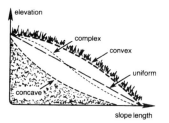

arsenic, etc.) it is essential that a layer of some other soil be spread over it to a depth of 15 cm or more. Otherwise plant establishment and growth may be very poor.

- Give the area its required shape and drainage system before spreading the topsoil back.
- On slopes, the shaped subsoil should be furrowed on the contour so that topsoil is held more firmly in place (Fig. 31.6). This will also allow more water to be held on the slope.
- New contours should be mainly of concave shape (Fig. 31.7) in areas of high rainfall intensity. Natural hills of these areas have been eroded to this shape. It is the most efficient shape for rapid shedding of runoff water with minimum damage. Straight, flat slopes are much more likely to erode. Slopes should usually be less than 10° from the horizontal. Any slope over about 14° may need special stabilisation. Sometimes retaining walls must be built so that the slope of the soil above can be reduced.
- Pay particular attention to the physical properties of the top of the subsoil. Any severe compaction must be relieved by chisel ploughing or discing. Any 'slicked' areas and crusts must be broken up by cultivation before the topsoil is spread. Failure to do this is likely to severely limit taproot growth in trees (Fig. 31.8) and so make them prone to being blown over. No amount of fertilizer can overcome the effects of poor physical properties. However, the materials of some spoil dumps are very loose; they retain little water, so are 'droughty'. Some compaction of these materials can be beneficial.
- Don't leave hollows that will later cause problems by remaining wet during use of the area.
- Where the topsoil material is of poor quality or when there is only enough for a thin layer, amend the top of the subsoil with gypsum, lime and fertilizer as the need is shown by tests.
- Site works are least damaging to soil structure if carried out when the soil is 'dryish'. The soil will be a little drier than field capacity.
- The topsoil is spread evenly over the subsoil as soon as possible after the subsoil has been prepared. Delay may allow a crust and erosion gullies to form. That means more work to break them or fill them in.
- 'Blur' the interface between newly spread topsoil and subsoil wherever possible by ripping or cultivating down into the subsoil without turning the soil over. This will help key the two layers together and will usually aid infiltration, drainage and root growth.

Figure 31.8
Growth of the tap root of *Ailanthus altissima* (Tree-of-Heaven) is dramatically reduced by soil compaction but that of lateral roots is little affected. *From E Pan and N Bassuk J. Environ. Hortic.* 3: 158, 1985

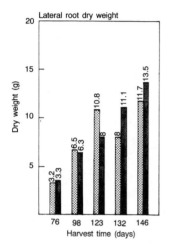

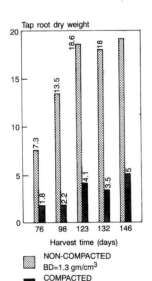

NON-COMPACTED
BD=1.3 gm/cm^3
COMPACTED
BD=1.64 gm/cm^3

- Any general amendments (lime, gypsum, organic matter) should be mixed into the topsoil before plants are established.
- If grasses are to be sown, fertilizer will usually be spread before seeding.
- Work the returned topsoil until it has a tilth suited to the planned method of planting. It will need to be finest when grass seeds are to be sown. A cloddy uneven surface may be quite acceptable if tree seedlings are to be planted.
- Sow seed before a crust has formed on the surface.
- Paths are to be constructed in such a way that they do not cause erosion.

Stabilizing steep slopes

So far this discussion has applied mainly to flat or gently sloping land. Many of the remarks apply also to steeper slopes, but for them other techniques must often be used to stabilize the soil. Steep slopes are often man-made, as in road cuttings, but they can be any steep hillsides that need revegetation to reduce erosion.

- Roadside cuttings can be stepped (Fig. 31.6) so that any topsoil spread on the slope is more likely to be retained.
- In areas not usually subject to frequently heavy rain, contour banks can be a useful method of retaining extra rainwater on the slopes.
- Contour banks in areas of heavy rain—the tropics mainly—can accelerate erosion, because the soil upslope from the bank will be even steeper than it was before. Any banks constructed in these areas are best made by moving soil up the hill, not down. But usually these areas are best stabilized by disturbing and uncovering the soil as little as possible. Erosion gullies can be treated, but the important thing is to establish vigorous plants as quickly as possible.
- Hydromulching is the cheapest method of quickly establishing grasses and other plants on steep slopes accessible to heavy vehicles. A wet mulch of chopped straw or paper pulp plus fertilizer, binding agents, seed and colour is sprayed from machines onto the slope being stabilized (Fig. 31.9). The binding agents help stick the mulch to the underlying soil. Roots from the germinating seeds soon penetrate into the soil. Of course hydromulching is more successful when it is quickly followed by gentle rains that allow rapid germination of seeds and growth of seedlings. Fertilizers used should be mainly slow-release, otherwise dry conditions could cause salinity problems. Details of the method are available from contractors who have the necessary machinery. Drying winds or very heavy rain soon after mulching can damage the mulch.
- Other methods must sometimes be used for small areas beyond the access of machinery. A mulch is spread by hand and then held in place by wire or plastic netting (Fig. 31.10). Obviously, laying is expensive, but it may be the only way of stabilizing some areas.

CONTROLLING PATHOGENS IN FIELD SOILS

Before growing vegetables or flower crops it may sometimes be necessary to kill pathogens that would otherwise greatly reduce yields.

Fumigation

Field soils can be fumigated with methyl bromide (if it is still available), chloropicrin, or methyl isocyanate releasers. Methyl bromide, containing 2% chloropicrin as a warning agent or 33% to widen the range of pathogens killed, is applied under plastic sheeting at the rate of 500–1000 g/10m^2. Leave the soil covered for two days, then aerate it for three days before planting. The soil should be a little drier than field capacity. Severe compaction should be relieved,

Figure 31.9
Applying hydromulch. *Photograph Barry Murray and Associates, courtesy, of Spraygrass Services*

Figure 31.10
Polymesh may need to be used to help stabilize stream banks and the sides of new water channels

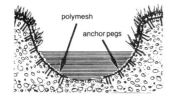

but methyl bromide diffuses so rapidly that most soils need no treatment before fumigation. Delay to planting is less with methyl bromide than with all other fumigants.

Chloropicrin is applied through a hand injector. Depth of placement and spacing vary with soil structure and depth to be treated. Read manufacturer's instructions carefully. Cover treated areas for three days, either with plastic or by light, frequent watering to give a water seal to the surface. Wait at least two weeks before planting.

Methyl isocyanate releasers (Metham sodium, Vapam, Dazomet, Sistan, Basamid, etc.) are applied as recommended by manufacturers. Covering is not necessary. The soil must be aerated by cultivation for a couple of weeks before planting.

Note that fumigation also kills most beneficial soil microorganisms. Some crops will suffer from nutrient deficiencies unless extra fertilizer is applied to make up for the temporary absence of mycorrhizal fungi and *Rhizobium* bacteria.

Solarization

Solarization is a beautifully simple method of killing most of the pathogens and many weed seeds in small areas of soil. Clear plastic sheeting is stretched tightly and closely over moist soil. The soil is heated by the sun through a 'greenhouse effect'. The detail is as follows:

1. Cultivate the soil to normal spade or cultivator depth.
2. Carefully level and smooth the surface. It is important that all clods on the surface are broken up or removed. Use the back of a rake or a board to get a smooth surface. Ensure that the soil is consolidated, but not compacted. Any hollows produced by slumping will not be fully treated.
3. Apply water for long enough to wet at least the cultivated layer to field capacity.
4. As soon after watering as possible stretch clear plastic film over the prepared soil. Highest temperatures are attained under the thinnest film. Preferably use 0.05 mm (50 micrometres) linear low-density polyethylene (e.g. Union Carbide's Ag-tuff® mulching film), but 0.1 mm (100 micrometres) normal polyethylene film will be satisfactory. The 'linear' film is not as easily torn as the 'normal' film. Hold the edges down with soil. Use enough soil to ensure that wind cannot get under the plastic. The plastic must be stretched tight and must not be able to flap up and down.
5. In sunny weather, the temperature in the top 4–5 cm will soon reach 50–60°C. Leave the plastic on for 4 weeks in mid-summer and up to six weeks in less sunny and cooler weather. Seeds of a few weed species, and nut grass, are not killed. Fungi and nematodes vary in the degree of control from excellent to moderately good.
6. The soil is ready for planting immediately after the plastic has been removed.

Solarization is cheaper than using fumigants such as methyl bromide and often cheaper than repeated drenching with fungicides. Trials have shown that solarization is often more effective in controlling disease than are chemicals.

Alternative strategies include:

- Rotating crops so that pathogens hopefully do not build up to damaging levels. Marigolds (*Tagetes minuta* and *T. patula* especially) greatly reduce nematode populations.
- Applying large amounts of organic manures, including green mulch cover crops, so that biological control of pathogens is encouraged. The example of avocado orchards (p. 328) is an excellent model to follow.

TYPES OF PLANTS TO USE

We all have our favourites amongst the thousands of species of plants available for growing. Our choice for a particular area must, however, be guided by practicality.

The choice will be widest where constant care and attention can be lavished on the young plants. Some may need to be watered every day for months, shaded or protected from frost or strong winds. In other situations, choice must be in keeping with soil and climatic conditions.

- Generally, it is a waste of time trying to grow large trees where only low shrubs grow naturally. Exceptions are where the main cause of poor growth is in the soil and that cause can be overcome. Thus where rainfall is sufficient, trees may be established if nutrient deficiencies are overcome, drainage provided, hardpans broken through, etc.
- Grasses are the first choice when soils on slopes must be quickly protected against erosion. They soon develop extensive root systems that bind the soil together. It takes much longer for trees and shrubs to give this protection. 'Grasses' includes cereals. Wherever possible, legumes should be grown along with the grasses.
- Seedlings of trees and shrubs can be planted out once a sloping site has been stabilized. Ideally, the grasses should be killed to a radius of about 50 cm around each seedling for the first year or two.
- On more-or-less flat ground, where the erosion hazard is slight, and where

trees are to be planted, there is little point in sowing grass or cereals. These so-called 'nurse' crops may protect seedlings from strong winds, but they compete for water and nitrogen and often do more harm than good (Fig. 31.11). Grasses are considered particularly harmful where trees are to be established by direct seeding.

- Where turf and trees are to be established together, the growth of each will be lowered by the other. The grass should not be allowed to grow within about 30 cm of young trees (Fig. 31.11). The surrounding grass should receive extra fertilizer and water to make up for that used by the tree.

- Direct seeding is faster and cheaper than planting seedlings, and it can be successful. However, losses of seed and seedlings can be high. Weather conditions soon after sowing affect the outcome. Only local trials can tell whether direct seeding will be successful in a particular area. The dormancy of seeds to be used for direct seeding should be broken by hot water treatment, scarifying or stratification before sowing. For success, weeds must be killed before seeding. A herbicide containing Amitrole and Atrazine (e.g. Vorox AA) works well.

- The soils of highly disturbed sites such as mine spoil dumps have been 'bulked up'. Like the 'fluffy' soils mentioned on p. 35, they hold less water than they would have in their natural state. This means that the trees planted in them should usually be rather more tolerant of drought than those native to the area.

- First plantings in extensive areas of revegetation must include legumes. The nitrogen they fix will allow them to grow more rapidly than non-legumes in soils of low nitrogen status. Their litter will quickly build up soil organic matter. On breaking down, some of the nitrogen in the litter will be released to non-leguminous trees. Acacias are widely used, but other legumes can be used, as can casuarinas. These species are often the first to 'pioneer' disturbed areas during natural revegetation.

- The species planted must suit the soil as it is, not as it was before disturbance. For example, spoil dumps containing sulphide minerals will become acid, so species tolerant of acid soil must be grown.

- Obviously, choose the time of planting carefully. The success rate is improved when the soil is moist and more rain is likely, when temperatures are mild and when frosts are unlikely.

- Plants that grow into large trees must be kept well away from buildings. A usual distance from a building is at least the height of the mature tree. This is absolutely essential for buildings set on 'reactive' soils—that is, those that

Figure 31.11

The growth of young trees is greatly reduced if turf is allowed to grow close to them. Growth reduction is due partly to toxins released by grass roots and partly to competition for nutrients and water. *From* S L Fales and R C Wakefield *Agronomy J.* 73: 605, 1981

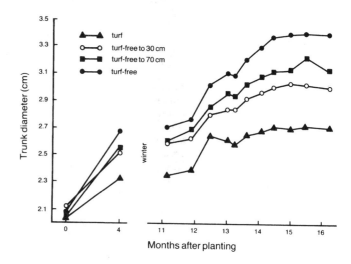

shrink and crack on becoming dry and then expand again on becoming wet. Shrinkage caused by a tree drying the soil under one part of a building can cause serious cracking of its walls (Fig. 31.12).

Figure 31.12
The tree has removed water from the clay soil beneath the wall, causing the soil to shrink and part of the wall to crack and slump.

Considerable interest is being shown in revegetation by direct seeding techniques (Fig. 31.13). As with other planting into landscapes, weed control is essential to success. Existing weeds should be killed with knockdown herbicides such as glyphosate, diquat and paraquat. Residual herbicides such as oryzalin, oxyfluorfen, propazamide, propazine and simazine may need to be applied before seeding. Scrape the treated soil aside from the narrow rows where tree seed is to be spread. Detailed information is contained in the book 'Growing trees for farms, parks and roadsides' (see p. 428).

PLANTING OUT FROM CONTAINERS

The first week after planting out into soil is usually a most difficult time for any container-grown plant. Up till then it has been watered frequently, sheltered and been given a steady stream of nutrients. Suddenly, watering is less frequent, the shelter has gone, and it may be given too much fertilizer. As well, some of its roots will have been damaged during transplanting. Little wonder that there are deaths of plants in the first few weeks after planting out. In this section we offer some guidelines that will help reduce the early death rate, and later problems.

Preparing plants for planting

- It is essential that the plants have been hardened. Decrease shade gradually to zero for those that are to be planted out into full sunshine. Don't store them in the shade once they have been hardened in full sun.
- Reduce the level of nutrition, but not to zero. It is essential that the plant is making some growth. It will then be able to quickly grow roots out into the surrounding soil. So, if necessary, lightly fertilize the hardened plant about a week before it is to be planted.
- Reduce the frequency of watering a little to prepare the plants for what is to come.
- Even though the plants in containers are to be in full sun, the containers themselves should be shaded to prevent roots from being killed by high temperatures.
- Whenever possible, don't use staked plants. Staking (and close spacing) does

Figure 31.13

Machine designed and built by the Woods and Forests Dept. of South Australia for rapid direct sowing of seeds of native trees and shrubs.

Photograph G Dalton

give more rapid vertical growth in nurseries. However, staking prevents the movement necessary for trunks to become strong. Movement causes cell walls in the trunk to thicken. Plants that have been staked in the nursery usually need continued staking if they are to remain erect (Fig. 31.14). If top-heavy advanced plants must be used, tie them loosely to stakes until their roots have grown into the soil. Then remove the stakes and let the wind strengthen them. If plants need to be made visible or protected from mowers, place the stakes a little way from them. Do not tie.

- The slightest indication that the rootball will become difficult to re-wet if it dries out is a warning that you *must* apply wetting agent, using one of the methods described in Chapter 6. Without such action, you could condemn the plant to death if the rootball dries out before roots are exploring the surrounding soil.
- A final point. Flushes of shoot growth are followed by flushes of root growth. Therefore, establishment may be best if plants are planted out at the end of a period of shoot growth.

The planting hole

When preparing to plant a new garden border or large bed, the whole area should be prepared before the individual planting holes for shrubs and trees are dug. Apply pre-emergent herbicide if weeds are likely to be a problem.

- Dig an oversize hole. Loosen the soil around and beneath the hole with a fork. This is most necessary when planting into turf. Some well-decomposed organic matter such as compost can be mixed with the loosened soil.
- Do not dig into *impermeable* subsoil. All you will be doing is sitting the plant in its own pond (Fig. 31.15). However, if the permeability of the subsoil can be increased by the addition of gypsum (Chapter 21), this restriction need no longer apply.
- Score and roughen the sides of the planting hole. If they are slicked over (glazed), it will be difficult for the roots of at least some species to penetrate them (Table 31.1). This is especially necessary when holes have been dug with an auger in heavy clay and for plants intolerant of waterlogging.
- The depth of the hole should be such that the top of the root ball is just level with the final surface of the soil (Fig. 31.15). Allow for a few centimetres of setting in the first few months. Also allow for a dish-shaped bay to be made around the plant to hold water for deep soaking.
- There are now many reports of improved survival rates and early growth when cross-linked polyacrylamide hydrogels are incorporated into the soil backfilled around a rootball in a planting hole. These effects will be greater in sandy than in heavier soils. Use about 1 g of dry gel per litre of backfill material.
- In-ground growers on sandy soils may find benefit from incorporation of a polyacrylamide hydrogel into the planting soil before planting. Use a rate of 15–50 kg/ha within the planting rows.
- Damage to the roots of bare-rooted trees during transport and storage for sale, and survival and growth after planting, has been reported to be improved if their roots are dipped into a hydrogel slurry immediately after digging.

Planting

- Thoroughly soak the rootball and then allow it to drain before removing the container.
- Wet the soil around the hole by adding water and allowing it to drain.
- Trim off roots growing through the drainage holes.
- Remove plants from plastic pots by placing a hand over the top of the mix, with the stem between the fingers of one hand. Turn the pot upsidedown, and hold its base with the other hand. Move the pot and plant rapidly through

Table 31.1

Loosening the sides of a planting hole allows more roots from some transplants to penetrate into the soil (*From R T Nicolosi and T A Fretz HortScience 15: 642, 1980*)

Treatment	Number of roots per core in the soil
Loosened soil	3.3
Glazed (slicked) sides	1.2

Figure 31.14
Staking does not allow the movement that is necessary if tree trunks are to become self-supporting. *From A T Leiser et al. J. Amer. Soc. Hort. Sci. 97: 498, 1972. Courtesy of Amer. Soc. Hort. Sci.*

Figure 31.15
Right and wrong ways of planting out into shallow topsoils underlain by heavy clay subsoils. In wet weather water will fill the hole in the subsoil, killing many roots

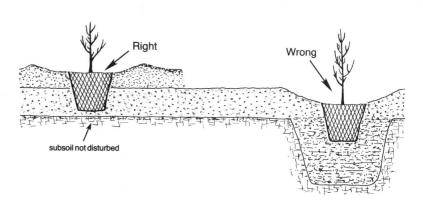

a short distance. Stop the hand holding the pot but allow the hand holding the plant to continue to move. This action usually jerks the rootball from the pot. If this doesn't work, sharply tap an edge on some solid object. The rootball should easily fall out of the pot onto the hand.

- Remove plants from tubes by running a sharp knife down the side. Don't penetrate the mix deeply with the knife.
- Remove any circling root mass that has accumulated at the bottom of the rootball. Cut any circling roots around the outside of the rootball by making shallow (5 mm) vertical slices in the sides of the rootball. This sounds drastic, and it does damage the plant, but it is definitely in its best long-term interests. Circling roots left intact will thicken (Fig. 31.16) until they severely restrict the plant's growth. The root/trunk joining area cannot develop naturally. It becomes an area of weakness (Fig. 31.17). Eventually trees snap off in this weak area, or restricted root growth allows them to be easily blown out of the ground. The effects of circling or girdling roots tend to show up only after several years of growth. If the trunk of a young tree goes straight into the ground like a post, or if it is hollowed on one side at the soil surface, suspect that just below the surface its growth is being restricted by a girdling root. The plant might be saved if the girdling root is cut through.

  As always, prevention is better than cure. Taking just a few seconds to prepare the root system is time well spent. New roots will soon be pushing out into the soil from the cut ends.

- The 'instant forest' effect of using plants 2 m high for landscaping may be very pleasing, but it may also be short-lived. Small plants of many native species soon catch up with those planted as more advanced plants (Fig. 31.18). If super-advanced plants must be used, rootball volume must match top size and watering must be very frequent for the first few weeks. There is evidence that planting stock of some exotic species survives better if 'advanced' (200 mm pots) rather than tubestock size plants are used (Fig. 31.18).
- Some further information about the effects of container and plant size is given in Fig. 31.19. Early planting out gives trees stouter trunks than they have if confined in the nursery for longer.
- Use the following technique if you suspect that there is circling inside the rootball. Firmly grasp the plant and the top of the rootball and turn it upside down. Cut straight down through the rootball as far as you are able to go without splitting the trunk. Use a knife, pair of secateurs or an axe. When planting, spread out the two halves of the rootball like a butterfly. This may

Figure 31.16
Examples of circling roots of plants that had been growing poorly.
Photographs R Hotchkiss and R Ellyard

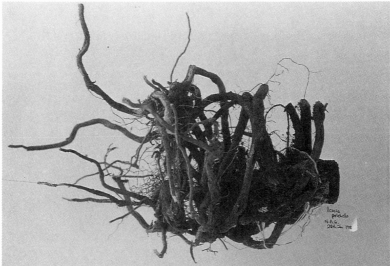

sound very severe, but it will be much less damaging to the tree in the long run than allowing girdling to run its full course.

- Any roots protruding from the rootball that are not removed should be carefully straightened out during planting.

- Place the rootball at the required place in the hole, push soil gently around it and lightly firm it down. Good contact between rootball and soil is essential, and may be achieved by jiggling the rootball about in the hole after partly filling with soil and adding a small amount of water. Make sure that the stem is vertical. Bring the soil up to the level of the top of the rootball, and no higher. If the rootball is covered, water may not be able to enter it. Potting mixes are usually of a coarser texture than most soils. Water cannot enter such a mix until all of the surrounding soil is completely saturated. Figure 31.20 shows what happens. Leaving the top of the rootball uncovered will allow water to flow through it and out into the surrounding soil.

Figure 31.17
Sequence of events that leads from root circling to the formation of a weak mass of woody tissue just below ground level. Trees often snap off at this point

- The last point must be qualified for potting mixes containing mainly peat. Leaving them open to the air will allow rapid loss of water through the 'wick effect' of the peat (Fig. 22.15). Rather than bury such mixes and run the risk of them not getting wet, it is better to mulch the top of the mix with pine bark, bagasse, wood chips, etc.
- The newly planted-out plant must be thoroughly watered as soon as possible, certainly on the same day, unless rain is doing it for you. Form a dish of soil around the plant, or on the down-slope side if the ground slopes. A typical dish will be about 300 mm across and 50–80 mm deep. Some have suggested that dishes are not necessary, and may even be detrimental in their effects. They could be detrimental if drainage is very poor. The extra water held in the dish could then cause extended waterlogging of the soil around the plant. Let local conditions be your guide. Form a dish if extra water must be allowed to soak in around the young plant. Don't make a dish, or break through an existing dish, on poorly drained soils during rainy weather.
- Fill the dish several times if rain has not fallen for a day or two. The aim is to bring as large a volume of soil around the rootball as possible to field capacity, and to make sure that the rootball itself is wet.
- If you are planting during the rainy season, and the weather is kind to you, this initial watering will be all that is needed, provided that you mulch the area and keep it weed free.
- Any weather conditions that are less than this ideal may call for you to apply some water. The first few days is the critical time. The need for extra water will be greatest for plants that were grown in the most open mixes.
- These instructions on watering apply mainly when planting at the wrong time of the year (soil too dry, rain not expected, rapid root growth not possible) or with plants not suited to the area (not drought-tolerant). Recent experience with native plants in southern Australia shows that many can be successfully (better than 90% survival) planted into any type of soil without any watering so long as it is done at the right time of the year and weed control is total. Best times range from October in areas of 1000 mm annual rain through August–mid September for 600 mm areas to May–early June for 300 mm areas. Spring planting in wet areas allows weed seed germination to be complete and so allows a complete kill with one application of herbicide. The soil must of course be wet from recent rain.
- If it will not be possible to water plants frequently after planting out, choose plants which have small tops in relation to rootball size—tiny plants in tubes or smallish plants in larger pots. When possible, choose plants grown in a mix which has an air-filled porosity of 7–12% (p. 80). Plant out during rainy weather.
- Planting will be successful at any time of the year if plenty of water can be applied. Otherwise, deciduous plants should be planted in the winter and evergreens early in the rainy season.
- One American report has shown better root growth into the soil as the bulk density of the rootball increases, but Australian experience in New South Wales (Worrall, R. J. *Aust. Horticulture* Oct 1985 p. 54) and in South Australia (G. S. Dalton, personal communication) has shown that establishment of a range of Australian species is unaffected by the bulk density of the rootball.
- When planting into harsh environments with hardy, drought tolerant species, one watering may be all that is needed. In sands, even that watering may be unnecessary if the sand is moist. Do not mulch with plastic. Total weed control to a radius of at least 0.5 m is *the* most effective aid to survival. Apply a light organic mulch in situations where high soil temperature from direct sun could harm roots (p. 300) or where excessive evaporation will exacerbate salinity (p. 270). Thick organic mulches may impair growth by intercepting all but the heaviest rains.

Figure 31.18
Data showing that after planting out, tube stock of some, but not all species, quickly catch up with more advanced plants. In this experiment, conducted near Sydney, the slower-growing species tended to take longer to catch up. *From J Clemens and S P J Radford* Environ. Manag. *21: 263, 1985*

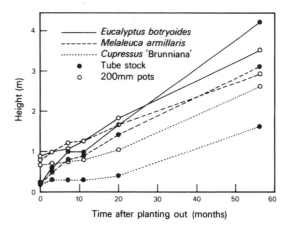

Figure 31.19
Effect of pot size in the nursery on the growth two years after planting out of *Melaleuca armillaris, Callistemon citrinus, Eucalyptus citriodora and Acacia pravissima. From A Whitham et al.* Australian Hortic. *October: 75, 1986*

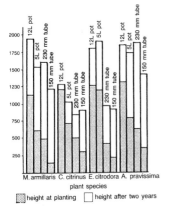

Fertilizers

- Don't place any soluble fertilizer into the hole, or mix any into the backfill soil.
- However, with the poor supply of phosphorus in many Australian soils, it is often useful to put some superphosphate in the hole. Dig the hole a couple of centimetres deeper than is needed. Place about 20 g of superphosphate in the bottom and cover with soil to the required planting depth. The plant's roots will soon find the phosphorus. Concentrating the phosphorus in one place is the preferred technique for soils that have a great ability to 'fix' phosphorus. Little of the phosphorus of a more general application would be available to the plant.
- Phosphatic fertilizer must not be applied if plants sensitive to phosphorus are to be grown. The need for fertilizers for the establishment of native trees and shrubs will depend on the species being grown and on the soil. Local trials are usually needed for mine-spoil dumps as each has its own special requirements.
- Slow-release fertilizer tablets (e.g. Agriform®, IBDU briquettes) inserted into the backfill soil near the rootball (Fig. 31.22) are the easiest way of providing nutrients. They may not give better growth than conventional fertilizers applied to the surface, but they are safer and do not encourage rampant weed growth as can surface applications.

Transplanting in nurseries

A plant growing from seed in its natural environment will quickly send its roots in all directions through the soil surrounding it. Under favourable conditions, roots can extend tens of centimetres each day. Each species of plant will grow its own particular type of root system.

By comparison, root systems developed on plants in pots are restricted in depth and width. Unless care is taken, the effects of this restriction can have a big effect on plant growth and survival after planting out.

Any kinks put in roots during pricking out can become points of weakness later. They also restrict the movement of carbohydrates. Avoid this by pricking out young plants as soon as possible after roots have been formed. Apart from giving poor root systems, delayed transplanting gives a lowered growth rate (Table 31.2). Pinch or cut off the lower half of excessively long roots that would otherwise have to be bent or curled to fit into a planting hole. Choose wedge-shaped containers for seedlings and cuttings that are to be potted up; the wedge shape prevents circling, and makes transplanting easy. Delayed potting up from other pots can give severely distorted root systems (Fig. 31.21). The distortion will be hidden from view—until its presence is seen in poor growth or even death several years after planting out. The rootball must not be buried in the new pot. The correct depth of insertion is for the top of the rootball to be level with the top of the mix in the new pot.

The problems caused by transplanting are eliminated when seeds and cuttings go directly into the containers in which they are to be sold. Many nurserymen now find that the extra space needed is cheaper than the extra handling of transplanting. A sound rule is to transplant as infrequently as possible. Growth rate will be more rapid if your plants start off and remain in as large a container as is practicable.

Table 31.2
Delaying transplanting of *Eucalyptus sideroxylon* seedlings greatly reduced their later growth rate (*From* R T Harris et al. *J. Amer. Soc. Hort. Sci.* 96:109, 1971)

Treatment before transplanting into 4 L pots	Height after 6 months in 4 L pots (cm)	
	Roots pruned at each move	**Roots not pruned at each move**
35 days in seed tray + 21 days in peat pot	176	162
46 days in seed tray + 84 days in peat pot	134	128

Figure 31.20
Cores of sand of coarse texture inserted into a clay loam soil, being used to show what happens when a rootball is completely buried. Water cannot enter the rootball until all of the soil surrounding it is saturated.
Photograph J Coppi

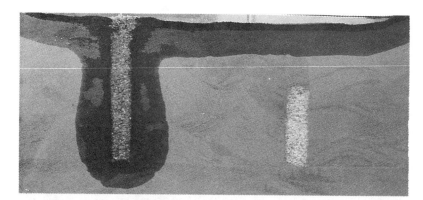

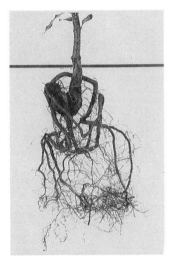

Figure 31.22
Typical placement of a slow-release fertilizer pellet in a planting hole

CARE OF ESTABLISHED TREES AND SHRUBS

The amount of care given to established trees and shrubs will range from near zero in extensive areas of bushland to much for prized garden plants. 'Near zero' might include fencing to exclude animals, and protection from fire.

Prized trees and shrubs will be healthiest when their environment is suited to them. If it is not naturally suitable, we must provide the missing parts—drainage or extra water, shade or full sun, fertilizer or none, best soil pH, modified soil structure, etc.

Established trees and shrubs remain healthiest when litter is left where it falls. The structure of the topsoil is improved; the roots are shaded and kept moister than if they were not protected by the litter.

After the first couple of years, applications of fertilizers to environmental plants can usually be light. Native shrubs and trees will usually not need any fertilizer at all. Exotic species will usually need some when they are in lawns. Apply fertilizer with an elemental ratio of about 10:4:6 at the rate of about 500 g per 50 mm trunk diameter each year or as needed. Place the fertilizer in holes augered to about 200 mm deep at intervals around the drip circle of the tree (i.e. under the outer part of the canopy). The need for fertilizers is least when the plant's roots have access to nutrients released from decomposing litter. The smaller the area of litter under a tree or shrub, the greater will be the need for regular fertilizer applications. Trees in paved areas commonly need extra potassium and nitrogen. Read the signs in the leaves (Chapter 14) and let local trials be your guide to amounts of fertilizers to apply.

Excessive fertilization usually gives excessive growth that must be hacked back. For some species, the more rapid growth shortens their lifespan.

Severe lime-induced iron chlorosis (Chapter 14) may call for replanting with species that are more tolerant of the high pH of the soil. Milder chlorosis might be overcome through one of these techniques.

- Make 8–10 holes of spade width square into the root zone and to a depth of about 30 cm. Fill each hole with mixtures of ferrous sulphate (1–2 parts) and compost, animal manure or peat (10 parts). Use fewer and smaller holes for shrubs. This method is very effective.
- Dig two holes of about 350 mm diameter and 800 mm deep approximately 1 m from the trunk. Mix 10 L of sulphuric acid (extreme caution) and 250 g ferrous sulphate with the soil removed from a hole and return it to the hole.
- Ferrous sulphate and the iron chelates FeEDTA and Fe lignosulphonate are of no use as soil drenches in overcoming chlorosis. FeEDDHA may give relief for a month or two, but if the chlorosis is due to manganese deficiency, the FeEDDHA will make it worse.

A plant is only as healthy as its roots. Declining health of tree tops can often be traced to poor conditions for, or damage to, roots. If the crown of a tree begins to thin, or if the leaves are smaller than normal, the stems shortened and branches dying back, suspect that something might have happened to the tree's roots. Decline can be sudden, but more often it takes several years before you are aware that something is seriously wrong. It may then be too late (Fig. 31.23), but try the following:

- Look for possible causes—lack of air entry through paving, waterlogging, drought, poor nutrition, gas leaks, damage by construction activity.
- Provide extra soil surface area (Fig. 31.24) to allow more oxygen into the soil, gas to escape and extra water to enter the soil. Supply extra water if necessary.
- Remove dead branches and trim back those that are dying.

Prevention is easier than cure, so take special care around trees and shrubs during construction operations.

- Don't scrape away any of the soil from under them.

Figure 31.23

This *Jacaranda mimosifolia* lingered on for two years after the major part of its root system had been sealed over, in the interests of 'tidiness'.

Photograph K A Handreck

- Don't run heavy machines about under trees, especially when the soil is wet. The soil will be compacted; the trees' roots may get too little oxygen and too little water.
- If the level of the surrounding area must be raised, protect the roots of the tree as shown in Fig. 31.25.
- Keep trenches as far away as possible from the trunks of trees.
- Protect roots near the surface by spreading a thick layer of sand or chips over the area. Remove them carefully later.
- Don't ever spread heavy clay over roots.
- Note that many of the roots of large trees are growing in soil that is well outside their drip circles (Fig. 22.12).

Look after their roots and trees will continue to provide shade, attract birds, cool their surroundings and look beautiful.

PLANTER BOXES AND TUBS

Many plants in interior and exterior landscapes are now grown in large containers. Several things must be observed if plants are to prosper:

- An outlet for surplus water must be provided.
- A drainage layer should be installed in the bottom of the container, in much the same way as under turf (p. 191).
- The growing medium should have physical properties to suit the depth of the container. In practice, the medium for most containers can be a sandy loam amended with organic materials to the extent of perhaps 15–20%. Such mixtures will have adequate aeration in deep containers (0.5 m or so), yet will hold enough water to minimize watering frequency for large plants. Such a medium may have an air-filled porosity of 5–7% as measured by the standard method (Chapter 33).
- Amending with perlite and even styrofoam may be necessary where weight must be kept to a minimum.

TRANSPLANTING LARGE TREES

The requirement for 'instant landscapes' around large urban developments has made it common to transplant large trees. These trees come from open-ground

Figure 31.24

An excellent way of providing a footpath and an ample area for water and oxygen to reach the roots of street trees

Figure 31.25
This is the sort of action needed if established trees are to survive a rise in soil level

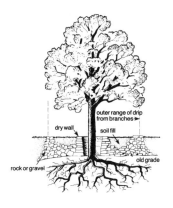

Figure 31.26
Two ways of producing excellent root systems on advanced trees (a) Root Control Bag (b) SpringRing container. *Courtesy of Ronneby Trees, Victoria*
(a)

(b)

nurseries, construction sites and nurseries specialising in super-advanced trees in containers. The one feature common to trees from all sources is that the size of the rootball is very small in relation to the tops. This dictates all post-planting management operations.

Trees being transplanted from open-ground nurseries or from other sites have to be carefully prepared for the move. It is normal in nurseries to periodically rip the soil between rows of trees so as to encourage proliferation of fibrous roots close to the trunk. Established trees from other situations should have their roots pruned back gradually by trenching, preferably over a period of a year or two. The rootball is wrapped in hessian (burlapped) to hold the remaining soil and to prevent desiccation of the roots. As little as 5% of the root system of these trees comes with them to their new site. It is best, however, not to trim the foliage back, other than light thinning of weak limbs; the tree will lose some leaves but experience suggests that survival is better without rather than with trimming. Note (Table 31.3) that it can take many years for the root system to attain its original size. Also note that relatively small trees (100 mm trunk diameter) regenerated their root systems much faster than very large specimens.

Trees in open-ground nurseries are increasingly being grown in bags that restrict root growth (Fig. 31.26). These bags have solid bases but the sides are made of a synthetic material that allows passage of small, fibrous roots but not larger ones. The bags are installed in holes in the ground and filled with the soil of the area or some other medium, typically sandy loam amended with organic matter or potting mix with a low AFP. There is a free movement of water between soil and medium and many fine roots grow into the surrounding soil. Unlike a solid-walled container, roots cannot circle within the bag. The many root endings left on the outside of the rootball after removal of the bag prior to planting ensure rapid growth into the new soil. Never transfer trees grown in bags of soil into containers with impermeable sides. The low air-filled porosity of the soil of the rootball can allow waterlogging, leading to death of roots and tree.

Large trees are heavy and often top heavy. They must be protected from falling or being blown over. Trunks and limbs must be wrapped as protection against injury to the bark during handling. Of course, the whole of the rootball must be kept moist at all times. Spraying the leaves with an antitranspirant may improve the chances of early survival (Table 31.4). Winter is the preferred time for transplanting. Do it before the buds start to swell but wait until the tree has gone dormant, if it does in your area. Autumn or spring transplanting can be successful if the rootball has plenty of fibrous roots. Palms should be transplanted during their growing season.

The large rootballs of big trees will extend into the subsoil of the new site. All may be well if the subsoil allows rapid percolation of water, but if it drains slowly, the rootball will be sitting in a pool of stagnant water most of the time (Fig. 31.27). Death is inevitable. You must check for excellent drainage well before the arrival of your expensive tree. Pour a known depth of water into the planting hole and note the infiltration rate (Chapter 9). You can do two things if the infiltration rate is too low. You can raise the level of the whole area, so raising the level of the base of the rootball, or you can provide a drainage system in the base of the hole (Fig. 31.27) provided of course that there is somewhere lower for the water to run to. Never use a layer of geotextile (p. 192): there are many reports of rapid clogging of geotextiles, and they will restrict root growth.

The best backfill is the soil of the site. It is essential that the backfill is uniform in texture. Any layering will cause problems (p. 66). For every sandy soils the water-holding capacity of the top 300 mm of backfill should be increased by amending it with such organic materials as cow manure, peat and composts (Fig. 31.27). Amending all of the backfill is not necessary. Applying a wetting agent to the rootballs and rooting hormone to the roots can be beneficial.

The most important actions you can take to ensure the survival of a large tree is to prepare it thoroughly for its move and to frequently, but not excessively,

Figure 31.27
Diagrammatic representation of the planting hole when drainage through the existing soil is inadequate

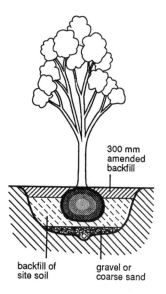

300 mm amended backfill

backfill of site soil

gravel or coarse sand

water the rootball itself (Fig. 31.20) for at least many months, but probably for several years (Table 31.3).

Table 31.3
North American data on the rate of regeneration of roots from trees after transplanting (From *Ground Maintenance* April 1987, p 124).

Small tree (10 cm dia.)		Large tree (25 cm dia.)	
Years after transplanting	% original root system	Years after transplanting	% original root system
–	Original	–	Original
1	9	1	5
2	23	2	8
3	41	3	12
4	68	4	17
5	103	5	23
7	192	7	34
10	390	10	71
13	674	13	109

Table 31.4
Effect of watering frequency and other treatments on survival of *Quercus virginiana* following transplanting. The trees had 100 mm diameter trunks (*From* D L Ingram and W Burgage, *American Nurseryman* August 1, 1986 p. 81)

Treatment	Percent survival
Irrigation:	
Daily	65
Weekly	55
Antitranspirant:	
None	67
Wilt-Pruf	80
Cloud Cover	38
Hydrogel:	
Terra-Sorb	54

32

COLLECTING SAMPLES FOR ANALYSIS

Those who grow plants sometimes run into problems that can be solved only with outside help. Analysis of the growing medium or of plant tops is one type of outside help available.

The quality of this help depends very much on how well the sample sent to a laboratory represents the whole amount of growing medium or the plants being grown. Taking a representative sample is a most important part of testing.

Skilled testing laboratories have instructions on how they would like samples taken to fit their methods. Follow these instructions. Otherwise, follow the guidelines given here.

Remember: plan well ahead. The absolute minimum time needed by most laboratories to record the sample, dry it, grind it or otherwise prepare it for analysis, analyse it, interpret the results and have them typed and posted is one week.

SAMPLING GROWING MEDIA

Sampling tools

Figure 32.1
Taking a core sample of a turf soil

Turf soils are best sampled with a thin-walled tube about 10–20 mm in diameter. These can be bought (Fig. 32.1) or you can make one from strong, thin tube such as that used for the shafts of golf clubs (Fig. 19.1). Other soils can also be sampled with a tube, but when they are dry or stony an auger of 50–100 mm diameter (Fig. 32.2) is more useful. A spade or trowel can also be used: a hole is dug and a sample 10 mm thick is sliced from its side (Fig. 32.3).

The easiest way of sampling media from containers is to first knock the rootball from the pot. Then remove a vertical wedge of mix, as shown in Fig. 32.4. Sample on the side opposite that of watering, if this is always on one side, and between the plant and the side of the container.

Long sampling tubes are useful for sampling heaps of soil, sand or potting mix. Never sample heaps by grabbing a handful or two from around the edge. Sample deeply into the heap from many different directions. When buying for turf construction or renovation, make sure that the supplier can supply enough material of the same quality.

Sampling depth

Turf is usually sampled to 7–10 cm. Other soils can be sampled to this depth, or up to 15 cm if the topsoil is that deep. Don't mix topsoil and subsoil in the one sample. If deeper sampling is needed, keep different soil layers separate from one another.

The full depth of medium in containers is to be sampled. Sometimes the top couple of centimetres should be separated from the rest. Do this if the top is likely to contain large amounts of fertilizer from surface applications or a high level of salts left behind by evaporating water.

Figure 32.2
An auger is easier to use than a core sampler when soils are stony or dry. *Photograph J Coppi*

Figure 32.3
A spade can be used to take samples when neither a core sampler nor an auger is available

Figure 32.4
Collecting a sample from a container. *Photograph J Coppi*

Number of samples

A composite sample representing an area of turf, a part of a landscape, a pile of potting mix or a batch of containers should contain at least 15 separate samples and preferably 20. Between 20 and 30 separate cores should be taken from areas of several or more hectares.

Don't mix samples from a golf green and nearby rough if you want to know what fertilizer to apply to each of them. Each must be represented by its own set of 15+ cores. Don't skimp on the number. After all, a hectare of soil contains about 1300 tonnes per 10 cm depth. Your sample might be only one-thousand-millionth of that!

Soils often vary greatly across a landscape: those at the top of a hill are usually very different from those down the slope or at the bottom of a valley. In sampling, the first thing to do is to divide the area up so that each section is likely to be reasonably uniform. Position on a slope, type of vegetation, vigour of vegetation, or soil colour or texture—these are usually the main means of dividing an area into sections.

The samples must be taken at random across the area or throughout a heap or batch of containers (Fig. 32.5).

Special care is needed when sampling an area irrigated by drippers. Salts will be concentrated at the edges of wetting zones. Sample midway between a plant and the edge of the zone around it, unless you need information about the salinity at different points.

Two alternatives

- Sometimes it is useful to know how variable a patch of soil is in a particular characteristic, say pH. Then, instead of mixing all the cores together, each is analysed separately. Of course this is expensive if tests have to be paid for, so it is not recommended for general use. This alternative can be particularly helpful in gardens or other areas where different parts may have had very different histories—different imported soils, different fertilizers at different rates, different plants growing there, etc.
- More insight into the causes of poor plant growth can be gained by taking two samples, one from an area of poor growth, and one from a nearby area of good or better growth. Each sample should contain at least 15 cores, unless one area is small enough for fewer to be enough. Five is a minimum; one is never enough. A comparison of the analytical figures for the two areas will often suggest a cause of the poor growth, if nutrient imbalance is involved.

General comments on sample-taking

- Each core in a composite sample should be of the same diameter and should penetrate the soil to the same depth.
- Make sure that the composite sample is large enough for the tests to be done. Usually 500 g dry soil is enough. Potting mix volume needed can vary from 0.5 to several litres depending on the tests needed. Check with your laboratory.
- Push aside, or carefully remove, plants or plant litter on the surface of the soil at each sampling point. Do not remove any of the soil itself as the top centimetre or so often contains the highest concentration of plant nutrients. Living turf grass and any coarse thatch should be removed, but partly decomposed thatch immediately on top of the soil should be included in the sample.
- Between sampling different areas, batches or series of pots, clean all augers, spades and other tools used by washing or at least wiping. All containers into which samples are put must also be uncontaminated. *Never* use bags or buckets that have previously contained fertilizers or pesticides.

Figure 32.5
Different parts of a landscape
should be sampled separately

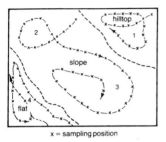

x = sampling position

- Don't drop cigarette ash onto samples, allow dust to blow onto them, or allow dogs or cats to use them as toilets. Don't laugh, it has happened!
- Extra precautions are necessary when handling samples for microbiological analysis. Check with the laboratory that is to do the testing.
- Delay sampling until at least a day after irrigation.
- Carefully remove any fertilizer applied as a topdressing to media in containers, or elsewhere.
- Remove all granules of coated fertilizers before sending a sample to a laboratory. If they are ground up during sample preparation, they give falsely high readings. At the very least, warn the laboratory of their presence.
- Don't sample in small areas of soil that are obviously very different from the general area being sampled.

Sample preparation before dispatch

Without drying:

When results are needed quickly and the tests can be simply done on the spot, it is not necessary to dry the composite sample. Tests for pH and salinity are of this sort. Potting media must not be dried before dispatch to a laboratory.

Spread the sample out on a clean plastic sheet. Remove any obvious pieces of gravel and lumps of fresh plant materials. Break up any clods with the fingers.

Mix the sample by rolling it about on the plastic sheet as follows:

Opposite corners of the plastic sheet are grasped and one is pulled diagonally across the sample slowly so that it *rolls* over towards the opposite corner. Then that opposite corner is pulled back over the sample to roll it back. The process is repeated using the other two corners. Roll in each direction at least five times and up to ten. (An alternative for smallish, light materials is to mix the samples by shaking them in a large plastic bag that has been 'ballooned up' before the end is held shut.)

Using a small trowel or flat spatula, form the sample into a cone in the middle of the sheet. Flatten (not spread) the cone and divide into quarters. Take one quarter for use in the testing, or, if this is still too big, repeat the rolling and coning with it only until a small enough sample is obtained.

With drying:

If the testing is to be done elsewhere or has to be delayed for more than a day or two, it is usually best to dry a soil. Drying is done at temperatures of no more than 40°C, otherwise the drying can cause large changes to soil properties. Never bake the soil in an oven or in the blazing sun.

Spread the soil out on a sheet of plastic in a shaded, well-ventilated place free from dust. Clods can be broken up by gentle rubbing with a rubber stopper. *Never* crush soil samples with a sledge hammer, mortar and pestle or other harsh methods.

A sub-sample of suitable size is taken by the rolling and coning method given above.

Mailing

Place sub-samples in plastic bags or plastic jars. Follow the requests of the particular laboratory or the general instructions below.

SAMPLING PLANT TOPS

The level of nutrients in plant tops can be used as a guide to fertilizer needs. The sample taken must represent the whole population of plants from which it is taken.

For turf, mix the fresh clippings from the whole area. Take a sub-sample by the coning method given above for growing medium. The sample should be of about 500 g fresh weight. Start to dry the samples within an hour of cutting. Never allow the clippings to partly compost in a heap before taking a sample.

Dry the sample as quickly as possible by spreading it thinly on clean paper in the sun or in an oven at no more than 50°C. Put the dried sample in a labelled clean plastic or paper bag.

For other plants, the sample can be of a number of whole tops or of carefully selected leaves. Whole tops are taken for seedlings and small succulent plants. For woody plants, it is best to sample the leaves only. All the leaves taken must be of the same age and have the same position on the plants. That usually means the first fully matured leaves back from tips (Fig. 32.6)—that is, the youngest fully matured leaves. Only then will the analytical figures be able to be interpreted against the standard values known from past experience. Each sample should contain 30–40 leaves or groups of leaflets. Follow the instructions of the laboratory. Again, dry the sample quickly. Make sure your hands are clean before sampling. Some laboratories supply plastic gloves with their kits. Leaves should be carefully cleaned before drying. Wipe them lightly with a clean cloth moistened with deionised water. Do not soak the leaves in detergent or water. Follow instructions provided by the laboratory.

When some plants in an area or batch are growing poorly and others are not, two samples should be taken. Both samples must be of leaves of the same stage of growth (e.g. third leaves from tips). Differences between the samples may point to the cause of the different growth. *This is the preferred action with plant tops,* because for many species there is very little background information with which to compare analytical figures.

Figure 32.6
The usual leaves to sample for analysis are the youngest fully expanded leaves as arrowed here.
Photograph J Coppi

SAMPLING WATER, LIQUID FEEDS AND HYDROPONICS SOLUTIONS

Samples of well or bore waters, feeds and solutions must be taken only after the pump has been running for some time. Samples from dams or other deep storages should represent the whole depth of water. If possible take samples from different depths and combine them: otherwise take from mid-depth.

Collect about 500 mL. Use a plastic or glass bottle. Fill it right to the top and refrigerate. Make sure it reaches the laboratory within a few days after collection.

GENERAL INSTRUCTIONS

- Always label samples clearly. When labelling plastic bags, make sure that the marking ink will not rub off. Writing on a label stuck to the plastic is often better than writing on the plastic. Write with a felt pen on a nursery plant label and include that in the bag as well.
- Record details of the place the sample was taken from, the identification given to the sample, and the date of sampling.
- Identify each sample unambiguously, but briefly. For example, use identifications such as 'Turf A', 'Rose leaf 5', 'Green 17—bad patch'.
- Use the fastest possible means of getting the sample to the laboratory.
- Tell the testing laboratory as much about the sample as possible. Their personnel are not magicians or clairvoyants. The more you tell them, the better will be the interpretation they make. Tell them:
  - the origin of each sample;
  - what the problem area or plant looks like;
  - fertilizer history, both recent and past, including types and amounts of fertilizer applied;
  - quality of water used for irrigation;
  - when you first noticed the problem, and a description of its development.

Some laboratories insist on an on-site inspection before they interpret analytical results. This can be expensive but it is usually the surest way of solving a problem.

33 SIMPLE TESTS

This chapter gives detailed instructions for carrying out a number of simple tests on growing media. Most tests need very little equipment. The exceptions are those that need pH and salinity meters. Other tests that are given on earlier pages are:

- Determining the texture of a soil (p. 10).
- Detecting waterlogging (p. 76).
- Determining the amount of dolomitic limestone needed to raise the pH of potting mixes (p. 93).
- Using sieves to formulate potting mixes (p. 125) and to check sands for root zones for turf.
- Strip tests for diagnosing nutrient deficiencies of turf (p. 242).
- The 'can' test for sprinklers (p. 306).

Do not be put off by the length of some descriptions. We have been careful to give as much detail as possible. When regularly used, most tests take little time.

BULK DENSITY OF SOILS

Figure 33.1
Applying a drop of water to a non-wetting sand. *Photograph K A Handreck*

The bulk density of a material is the mass in grams of one cubic centimetres (or millilitre) of it.

1. Take a core sample with a golf cup-cutter (Fig. 19.5), or use a spade to cut a sample of square section.
2. Measure the volume of the sample in cubic centimetres (V).
3. Break the sample up into a large, flat dish. Do not lose any of the sample.
4. Dry the sample in the sun for several days, or, preferably, overnight in an oven set at about 100°C.
5. Measure the mass in grams (M).
6. Bulk density = $\dfrac{M}{V}$ (g/cm³). Sometimes bulk density is reported in the unit Mg/m³(megagrams per cubic metre) which is identical to g/cm³.
   This measurement is useful for detecting compaction in soils. Interpret the result according to the information given on (p. 57). You may find it easier to measure infiltration rate as a guide to the presence of compaction.

HOW WATER-REPELLENT IS MY SOIL?

There are at least four tests that can be used to assess the severity of water repellence in sandy soils. As all tests give similar results, we describe only the two easiest ones here. For all tests, first dry the soil in the air or in an oven set at no higher than 100°C.

Water droplet entry test

The water droplet entry test is useful for assessing mildly-repellent soils.

1. Fill some soil into a tablespoon whose handle has been bent so that the soil surface is horizontal when the spoon is resting on a table.

2. With an eye dropper or a Pasteur pipette (scientific supply firm), place one drop of water onto the soil surface (Fig. 33.1).
3. Record the time it takes to soak in. Times under 8 seconds indicate little or no repellence (Table 33.1); times over 4 minutes indicate severe repellence and a need to use the mini-infiltrometer test described below.

Fig. 33.2 shows how you can use this test to find out which part of a turf profile is the most water repellent.

Figure 33.2

Method of determining the location of water-repellent material in a turf root zone. *From J M Henry and J L Paul California Turfgrass Culture* 28: 9, 1978

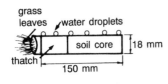

grass leaves / water droplets
soil core | 18 mm
thatch
150 mm

Table 33.1

Interpretations for water-repellence tests. (*From P M King Australian J. Soil Res.* 19: 275, 1981)

Severity of repellence	Time for droplet penetration (sec)	Infiltration rate (mm/min)
Nil	< 1	> 70
Very low	1–7	69–30
Low	8–53	24–4
Moderate	> 85	3–0.4
Severe	–	0.3–0.09
Very severe	–	0.06–< 0.02

Mini-infiltrometer test

This mini-infiltrometer test will help you determine just how severe a water-repellence problem really is.

1. Make infiltrometers consisting of 30 mm long sections of 25 mm diameter plastic water pipe.
2. Acquire a kitchen funnel of about 100 mm top diameter, and a means of holding it during the test (Fig. 33.3).
3. Place a small wad of cotton wool in the base of the funnel.
4. Fill soil into the funnel and smooth its surface.
5. Embed an infiltration ring 5 mm into the soil.
6. Gently pour 5 mL of water onto the soil within the ring. (This gives a water depth of 10 mm. If you use pipe with a diameter other than 25 mm, you should add an amount of water that gives 10 mm depth.)
7. Record the time for the water to completely soak into the soil. Interpret according to Table 33.1.

Figure 33.3

Mini infiltrometer being used to determine the severity of a non-wetting problem in a sandy soil. *Photograph K A Handreck*

HOW WATER-REPELLENT IS MY POTTING MIX?

This test (from Australian Standard AS 3743) will help you decide whether you do or do not need to use a wetting agent.

1. Dry the mix at 40°C.
2. Fill dry mix into a small dish similar to that shown in Fig. 33.4. The minimum depth is 20 mm.
3. Make a small depression in the centre of the mix with a standard light globe.
4. Add 10 mL of deionized or distilled water to the centre of the depression.
5. Record the time for the water to soak into the mix. The water is regarded as having soaked in when slight tilting of the dish gives no movement of water in the wet patch.

The Australian Standard requires soak-in times of less than 5 min (Regular) or 2 min (Premium). In situations in which the surface part of mix in pots gets very dry between waterings, you may well find that you need to use wetting agent on mixes with soak-in times of about 30 sec.

Figure 33.4
Setup for determining the wettability
of a potting mix by the method of
the Australian Standard for Potting
Mixes.   *Photograph K A Handreck*

PERFORMANCE OF A WETTING AGENT

This test ranks two or more wetting agents for their short-term effectiveness in overcoming water-repellency. To fully assess a wetting agent it is also necessary to determine the level of addition at which it becomes toxic to plants (below), and the longevity of its action (also below).

1. Dry some potting mix that is known to be water repellent.
2. Fill it into squat 100 mm pots. The weight of each pot plus mix must be the same. Allow at least four pots for control (water) and at least four for each of the wetting agents to be tested.
3. Prepare solutions of the new wetting agent and one of Aquasoil Wetter or Wetta Soil. Each is to contain 1 mL of concentrate per litre of solution.
4. Slowly pour onto the mix in a pot a volume of solution equal to the volume of dry mix in the pot. Apply water for control pots.
5. Allow drainage to finish; weigh each pot.
6. Calculate by subtraction the amount of water or solution retained by each pot. The greater the amount of solution retained, the greater is the short-term effectiveness of the wetting agent.

LONGEVITY OF ACTION OF A WETTING AGENT

Use this rather rough method to get an estimate of how long a wetting agent is likely to be effective.

1. Obtain 6 litres of potting mix known to have poor wettability.
2. Make up solutions containing a wetting agent known to be long-lasting (e.g. Aquasoil Wetter) and the new wetting agent, each at 12 mL concentrate per litre of solution.
3. Add 100 mL of solution or water to each of three 2-litre lots of the mix in plastic bags.
4. Add more water as needed to bring the mix to normal potting moisture content. Keep mixing to a minimum, because grinding of particles against one another during mixing will reduce water repellence.
5. Immediately remove about 600 mL of mix and dry it at about 40°C.
6. Store the bags at a reasonably constant temperature in the range 20–25°C.
7. Remove further 600 mL samples at 10 and 20 days after mixing and dry them.
8. Determine the wettability of the samples using the Australian Standard method given above.
9. A wetting agent with good long-term action will give a wetting time at 20 days of less than 8 seconds.

IS THIS MIX COMPONENT TOXIC?

Use this test to see if a component to be used in a potting mix is toxic to plants. It is especially useful for checking barks and sawdusts.

1. Take two samples, each of 50 to 100 mL, from the potting mix being tested.
2. Fill one sample into a kitchen sieve with very fine mesh and pour deionized water of the same volume through it. Allow the mix to drain.
3. Repeat steps 1 and 2 with a control mix that you are sure is not toxic to plants.
4. Collect at least four of the round, clear-plastic containers in which take-away food (e.g. salads or dips) is sold.
5. Place about 10 mm of each mix in each of four containers.
6. Moisten the mixes until on tilting the container a small amount of water collects in the lower part of the mix.
7. Scatter 25 radish seeds over the surface of each mix.
8. Sit the lids loosely on the containers.

9. Place them in a well-lit but shaded area that is warm.
10. Moisten the mixes as needed.
11. After 5 days, compare rates of germination. Look at the roots growing along the bottoms of the containers (Fig. 33.5).

The seeds will not germinate if the mix is extremely toxic. Better germination and/or growth in the leached compared with the non-leached mix indicates a level of salinity or something in the water in the mix that is reducing growth. Similar germination/growth in the leached sample of the mix being tested to that in the non-toxic control mix indicates that the mix will be suitable for use so long as it is leached soon after potting. You would be wise not to use mix that gives root growth that is less than 75% of that given by the control mix.

Addition: This method can be used to determine the toxicity of a wetting agent. Make samples of mix containing the wetting agent at rates of 0, 0.5, 1, 1.5 and 2 and 4 mL of concentrate per litre of mix (or equivalent weights of solid wetting agents). Run them through the test without leaching.

AIR-FILLED POROSITY OF A SOIL

One day after soaking rain or irrigation, carefully take an undisturbed sample of the soil to be tested. This can be done by hitting a metal ring into the soil, or by carefully cutting a cube with a spade or spatula. If subsoil is to be sampled, the topsoil is first carefully removed from the sampling site. Weight the soil as soon as possible after sampling (M_1 grams). Do not let it lose water.

Calculate the volume (V) of the sample in cubic centimetres (= mL). Dry the sample overnight at about 100–105°C, or break it up and dry it in the sun for a couple of days.

Weigh again (M_2 grams).

Volume of water in the sample = $M_1 - M_2$ (mL)

Volume of solids = $\dfrac{M_2}{2.65}$ (mL)

(This is for mineral soils containing only a few percent organic matter.)

Air-filled porosity = $\dfrac{V - M_2/2.65 - (M_1 - M_2)}{V} \times 100$ volume %

AIR-FILLED POROSITY OF POTTING MIXES

Those who run nurseries should know the air-filled porosity of the mix(es) they are using. The air-filled porosity of a mix is the percentage of its volume that is air just after it has stopped draining after being saturated with water.

We urge you to use the Australian Standard method, as now described.

Apparatus

1. Make the apparatus shown in Fig. 33.6. Use 90 mm UPVC stormwater pipe and matching cap.
2. Cut two 12 cm lengths and deburr the ends. Ensure that the cuts are at right angles to the length of the pipe.
3. Drill four 9 mm holes in the cap as shown in Fig. 33.7.
4. Glue the cap to one of the lengths of pipe, making sure that it is pushed *all* the way home. Apply extra glue to the upper edge of the cap on the outside to allow easy shedding of water during use.
5. Cut any raised rim from what is now the lower end of the cap and then sand smooth the whole base of the cap.
6. Heat one end of the second length of pipe with a hot-air gun and splay it out over the top of the first section. Work the heated pipe around until it fits snugly, but not tightly, over the upper end of the base.

The volume of the base of the apparatus will be close to 680 mL.

Toxic

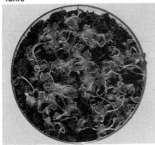

Non-toxic

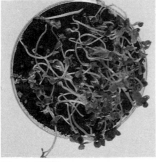

Figure 33.5
Contrasting top and root growth of radish seedlings in toxic (upper) and non-toxic (lower) potting mixes.
Photograph J Coppi

Toxic

Non-toxic

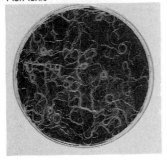

Figure 33.6
Standard AFP apparatus

Figure 33.7
Holes are drilled in the cap

Figure 33.8
Base full of saturated mix

Method

1. Place the top section firmly onto the base.
2. Moisten the potting mix to be tested until it is considered to be suitable for potting. If tested, it will have a moisture content of 50–60%. Dry mix must be moistened at least 24 hours before being tested.
3. Pour moistened mix into the apparatus up to the top of the top section.
4. Drop (free fall) the apparatus five times from a height of 50 mm.
5. Place the apparatus in a 9-litre plastic bucket and slowly run water into the bucket (not onto the mix) until the water level is just at the surface of the mix. Do not at any time allow mix components to float and separate.
6. Allow the mix to soak in the water for 30 minutes.
7. Then slowly remove the apparatus vertically from the water and allow it to drain for a few minutes.
8. Repeat the soaking and draining cycle twice more, allowing 10 minutes for each soaking period.
9. At the end of the third cycle, remove the top part of the apparatus. Slice the excess mix from that contained in the base using a kitchen knife, without exerting pressure down on the mix in the base.
10. Cover the top of the base with gauze (a piece of pantyhose will do) and secure it with a rubber band. (It may be necessary to make a 5 mm nick in some types of gauze so that air can escape as the mix is being saturated.)
11. Place the base in the bucket of water. Add water as needed to cover the base to a depth of 20–40 mm.
12. After 10 minutes, reach down with two hands into the water and cover the four holes in the bottom of the base with four fingers, two from each hand.
13. Raise the base of saturated mix vertically from the water. Allow water to drip from your hands and the base. Allow enough time for water ponded above the surface of the mix in the base to flow away through the fabric of the gauze. The aim is to ensure that the mix is completely saturated to the top of the base (Fig. 33.8).
14. Move the base to above a 4-litre icecream container (or tray of similar size). Unblock the four holes and lower the base onto plastic or wooden rods of about 15 mm square section placed on the bottom of the tray or container (Fig. 33.9). Allow to drain for 30 min.
15. Remove the base vertically from the container and measure the volume of water (V mL) that has drained from the mix.
16. The AFP of the mix is $V \times 100/680$ %.

INFILTRATION RATE

Use this test to find out how quickly water soaks into a soil. It is most useful for checking turf root zones.

1. Make an infiltrometer. At its simplest, this can be a 200 mm length of steel pipe about 300 mm in diameter; sharpen one end so that it can be easily pushed into a soil. A reasonably satisfactory alternative is to cut one from a 60 L steel drum. Leave the rim at the top and grind and sharpen the lower edge. Another alternative is to bend a piece of mild steel or aluminium sheet into a cylinder and weld the seam. Yet another alternative is to buy an infiltrometer such as that illustrated in Fig. 33.10(b).
2. Push the lower edge of the infiltrometer about 40 mm into the soil at the chosen site. This is most easily done by placing a sturdy piece of wood on the upper edge and hitting it with a sledge hammer.
3. Pour water onto the soil within the infiltrometer ring. Aim to apply a depth of about 25 mm of water. Apply more to sandy soils, less to heavy clay soils.
4. Invert a flagon of water into the infiltrometer as shown in Fig. 33.10(a). This

Figure 33.9
Draining the base

Figure 33.10
Apparatus used for measuring the rate of infiltration of water into a soil. (a) using a flagon, (b) commercial unit. Courtesy of Globe Chemicals

(a)
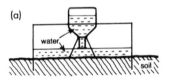

(b)

Figure 33.11
Measuring the rate of movement of water into a subsoil

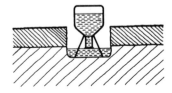

will keep a constant level of water in the infiltrometer. Have another flagon or water ready to invert as soon as the first one is empty, and so on.

5. Record the time that it takes for each of several flagons to empty. Stop when there is little change in time from one flagon to the next.

6. Use the last time recorded to calculate the steady infiltration rate of the soil.

Example: The area inside an infiltrometer ring is 700 cm^2 = 0.07 m^2.
It takes 23 minutes for 2 L of water to infiltrate the soil.

Therefore, the depth of water that has infiltrated the soil is $\frac{2}{0.07}$ = 28.6 mm.

(Two litres would cover 1 m^2 to a depth of 2 mm.)

Therefore, the infiltration rate is $\frac{28.6}{23} \times 60$ = 75 mm/hour.

An alternative is to just fill water into the cylinder to a known height of, say, 40 mm, and record the time that it takes to soak in.

Note: Some of the water will move sideways from the ring rather than straight down. The measured infiltration rate will be a little more than the actual infiltration rate for rain or irrigation water. A more accurate measurement can be made by having two infiltration rings, one inside the other. The measurement is made within the inner ring. Water poured into the space between the rings supplies that for sideways movement through the soil.

A QUICK CHECK OF DRAINAGE RATE

This test is used to see if drainage is being impaired by a part of a soil profile.

1. Dig a hole to the top of that part of the soil profile that is suspected of having a low permeability to water.

2. Deepen the hole by 20–30 mm.

3. Pour water into the hole to give a depth of about 25 mm.

4. Invert a bottle of water into the hole as shown in Fig. 33.11. For deep holes use a long cylinder of clear, rigid plastic tube, sealed at one end.

5. Proceed as in steps 5 and 6 of the 'Infiltration Rate' method above.

6. Soils having a low drainage rate (say, less than 5 mm/hour) may need to have a drainage system installed at the top of the poorly permeable layer.

WATER CONTENT OF GROWING MEDIA

Water content is expressed as a percentage of water (on a mass or volume basis) in a medium at the time of sampling.

1. Collect a representative sample. Store it in a plastic bag, and measure the water content within a few days.

2. For measurements to be on a mass basis:
Weigh a small glass or metal container (M); pyrex coffee mugs or sardine cans are suitable if weighing bottles are not available; place a sub-sample of about 20 g of medium into the container; weigh immediately if the container does not have a lid (W); place the container in an oven at 100–105°C for about 16 hours; remove the container and weigh as soon as it is cool enough to handle (S); do not delay if the container does not have a lid; calculate the water content

$$\frac{W-S}{S-M} \times 100\% \text{ (for soils); or} = \frac{W-S}{W-M} \times 100\% \text{ (for organic media).}$$

3. For measurements on a volume basis:
Weigh (in grams) a known volume (V mL) of medium as outlined under step 2 above;

calculate the volumetric volume content

$$\frac{W - S}{V} \times 100\%$$

Note: These measurements are on an oven-dry basis. When an oven is not available, drying the sample for 1–2 days under a hot sun will give an answer that is usually near enough to an oven-dry figure for practical purposes.

AVAILABLE WATER CONTENT OF SOILS

Use Table 33.2 to get a rough idea of the available water content of a soil.

1. First determine the texture of the soil (Chapter 3).
2. Then take a small sample of the soil in your hand.
3. Try to mould the soil into a ball. It is too dry for plants if it doesn't form a ball.

Table 33.2
A guide to the available water content of soils (Adapted from 'Saving water in landscape irrigation' Leaflet 2976 Division of Agricultural Sciences, University of California, 1977)

Amount of available water remaining	Feel or appearance of soils			
	Sand	**Sandy loam**	**Clay loam**	**Clay**
Zero (wilting point)	Dry, loose, single-grained, flows through fingers	Dry, loose; flows through fingers	Dry clods that break down into powder	Hard, baked, cracked surface; hard clods difficult to break; sometimes has loose crumbs on surface
50% or less	Still appears to be dry; will not form a ball with pressure	Still appears to be dry; will not form a ball	Somewhat crumbly, but will hold together with pressure	Some what pliable ; will ball under pressure
50% to 75%	Same as sand under 50%	Tends to ball under pressure but seldom will hold together	Forms a ball, somewhat plastic; will sometimes slick slightly with pressure	Forms a ball; will ribbon out between thumb and forefinger
75% to field capacity	Tends to stick together slightly; sometimes forms a very weak ball under pressure	Forms weak ball; breaks easily; will not become slick	Forms a ball and is very pliable; slicks readily if high in clay	Easily ribbons out between fingers; feels slick
At field capacity	Upon squeezing, no free water appears but moisture is left on hand	Same as sand	Same as sand	Same as sand
Above field capacity (water-logged)	Free water appears when soil is bounced in hand	Free water will be released with kneading	Can squeeze out free water	Puddles and free water form on surface

MEASURING pH

There are three ways of measuring pH. One is so inaccurate that it is useless; another is moderately accurate and is useful for quick screening or for situations where great accuracy is not needed; the other is generally considered to give the most reliable results—provided that those using it know what they are doing.

Probe meters

Probe meters consist of a probe, on top of which is mounted a small meter sensitive to electric currents. The probe consists of two different metals, insulated from one another in the probe but connected through a moving coil ammeter. The method of operation is simple. The probe is pushed into the wet medium. The needle in the meter moves to indicate the 'pH' of the medium. These meters have been found to be very unreliable. They should not be taken seriously by anyone who wants to know the pH of a growing medium.

Methods using dyes—the colorimetric methods

Many dyes are organic compounds that change colour with changes in the pH of the solution in which they are dissolved.

In the colorimetric methods, the colour produced when a solution of dyes—the indicator solution—is mixed with a medium is compared with a colour card showing the correspondence between colour and pH. There are at least two kits available in Australia (Fig. 33.12).

Colorimetric methods using indicator solutions are moderately accurate. Readings are generally within 0.5 of a pH unit of that obtained with the most accurate method.

These kits are, however, quite suitable for general landscape and garden situations. They are cheap, robust, easily transported, and quick to use. But, they cannot be used by those who are colour blind, and that's about 10% of the male population.

Colorimetric methods can be used for quick screening and checking in nurseries, but there are some problems. Potting mixes commonly contain many big particles. Large errors are easily introduced when taking the small samples used in these methods. But even if sampling is accurate, there are times when an error of 0.5 of a pH unit or more is not acceptable. For greater accuracy, it is necessary to use a pH meter.

pH meters

Meters for measuring pH have two parts: an electrode whose electrical properties change as the concentration of hydrogen ions in the solution around it changes (Fig. 33.13); and an electronics system that responds to the electrical properties of the electrode and converts them into a reading on a meter or digital display (Figs 33.14 and 33.15).

Measurements of pH are simple. The electrode is dipped into a slurry or suspension of the medium in water and the pH is read from the meter. However, there are some preliminary steps to be taken and a number of precautions that operators must observe.

- Electrodes used for measuring pH come in various shapes and sizes. All are made from glass tubing which has been blown out into a bulb at the tip. The glass in this bulb is very thin and therefore very fragile. As electrodes are expensive, care is needed when handling them. A drop of even 1 cm can be fatal. Even a scratch by a sand grain can seriously impair performance. Never touch the bulb with your fingers.
- Electrodes can become dirty. Dirtiness is indicated if it is not possible to calibrate the meter with the buffer solutions provided, or if the meter is slow to respond to changes in solution pH. Clean the electrode by immersing the

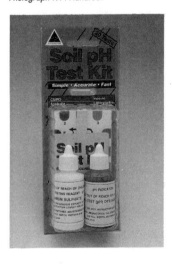

Figure 33.12
Colorimetric kit for determining the pH of soils and potting media.
Photograph K A Handreck

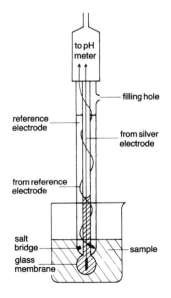

Figure 33.13
The parts of a glass electrode used for measuring pH

to pH meter

filling hole

reference electrode

from silver electrode

from reference electrode

salt bridge

glass membrane

sample

Figure 33.14

An Australian-made pH meter

Figure 33.15

Small pH meters such as this are excellent for general use in nurseries, turf, landscaping and gardening. *Courtesy of Sitest, Sydney*

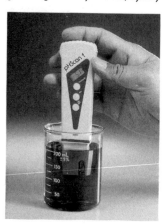

Table 33.3

Examples of inaccurate pH readings given by probe meters (*From* D R Hershey *HortScience* 23:625, 1988)

Glass electrode	Probes	
	1	2
Potting mix		
3.6	4.8	5.4
4.5	5.0	5.2
5.6	6.6	6.7
6.3	6.5	6.8
6.7	6.9	6.9
Buffer solution		
4.0	>10	>10
7.0	8.8	5.5

bulb in weak hydrochloric acid overnight (1 mL concentrated acid plus 112 mL water). Rinse thoroughly.

- Electrodes contain two chambers (Fig. 33.13). The outer chamber has to be full of saturated potassium chloride solution and free of air bubbles. *Light*, rapid tapping of the *side* of the electrode with the fingers will usually dislodge bubbles. Bubbles and insufficient potassium chloride solution will give erratic readings. Note that the level of potassium chloride solution in the electrode must be *above* the top of the suspension whose pH is being measured.
- Electrodes should be stored in a vertical position whenever possible, and with the bottom third immersed in saturated potassium chloride solution.
- Electrodes must always be rinsed with distilled water between measurements.
- The response of electrodes to hydrogen ion concentration varies with solution temperature. This is automatically taken care of in some instruments, but for most the temperature of the solution must be measured with a thermometer and the instrument adjusted accordingly.
- All pH meters must be calibrated using two buffer solutions of known pH immediately before any measurements are to be made and after every 20–30 samples.
- In nurseries, it is best that pH (and salinity) measurements be made in an area set aside for this purpose, rather than amongst the plants.

'Recipes' for measuring pH

All 'recipes' or methods of measuring pH with glass electrodes have one thing in common. Water or dilute salt solution is added to a representative sample of the medium. The resulting mixture is stirred or shaken for 15–60 or more minutes before the glass electrode is inserted into the mixture.

There are many different methods in use. A medium tested by different recipes will be shown to have a slightly different pH with each method used. Approximate equivalents are given in Table 33.4. We describe four methods.

Dilute (0.01 molar) calcium chloride

Because this method uses a salt concentration that is close to that of many soils, it eliminates the effects of salt in the soil on the measured pH. It is considered by many to give the most reliable results for soils, and to give a reading that is close to the pH experienced by plant roots. Add 5 mL calcium chloride solution (1.47 g $CaCl_2.2H_2O/L$) to 5 g air-dry soil. Stir periodically for 30 minutes with a glass or plastic rod. Measure the pH.

Saturated paste

This method is widely used in the USA for both soils and potting media. Elsewhere, many laboratories find the difficulty of deciding when a medium is saturated an encouragement to use other methods. The method does give pH values that are closer to those experienced by plant roots and the anomalies caused when larger volumes of water are added to some media do not exist with this method. With some experience, saturation point can be reasonably reliably found, but if you find this difficult for potting media, use the 1:1.5 volume method, which is the standard method used in Australia for potting media.

1. Tip about 50 g of soil or 400 mL of potting medium into a plastic container of about 1 litre capacity.
2. Slowly add distilled or demineralized water while mixing with a stainless steel spatula or a knife. The wetness to aim for is characterized as follows: The mixture will slide reasonably easily from the knife, will shift and flow when the container is tilted, yet there will be little free water coming to the surface when it is left standing for a few minutes. It's a bit like a sloppy mud pie! This is a saturated paste.

3. Cover and allow the paste to stand for at least 15 minutes but preferably for an hour or more. Dry organic materials such as peat or pine bark should be left at least overnight to wet up.

4. Check for saturation. Free water should not be standing on the surface, nor should the paste have stiffened. Add a small amount of extra water or medium to give the right consistency.

5. Mix thoroughly and measure the pH of the paste by *very gently and carefully* pushing the electrode into it.

1:1.5 volume extract (also known 1:1½ volume extract)

This method is used only for potting media. Originally developed in Holland, it is now the standard method used by Australian laboratories.

1. Take several handfuls of medium (sampled as described in Chapter 32). Add distilled or deionized water while mixing with one hand (or two—Fig. 33.16).

2. The final moisture content should be such that firmly squeezing the mix (Fig. 33.17) just expresses water from it between the fingers. The amount of 'squeeze' is like a firm handshake. It is neither a limp nor a crushing squeeze. The mix will be just a little drier than if it had just stopped draining while in a fairly tall pot.

3. Select a straight-sided, screw-top jar of about 400 mL capacity.

4. Pour into it 100 mL of water. Mark where this comes to. Pour the water out.

5. Fill about 120 mL of moist, loose mix into the jar. Firm it gently with the fingers and by light 'dumping'. Add more mix if the volume is below 100 mL, or take some out if it is above. (For more precise control, compress the mix by placing on it a weight giving a pressure of 100 g/cm². Example: If the radius of the jar is 3 cm, the surface area of the mix in it will be 3.14 × 3 × 3 = 28 cm², so the weight must be 2800 g.)

6. Add 150 mL of distilled or deionized water.

7. Shake 10 times, leave stand for 15 minutes, then shake 10 times again. Alternatively, shake for 1 hour in an end-over-end shaker.

8. Measure the pH by inserting the glass electrode into the water slurry. Gently stir the electrode in the slurry, then let it rest until the pH reading has stabilized.

1:5 (weight/volume) method

This is a main method used in Australia for measuring the pH (and salinity) of soils. It is an easy method, but it gives higher readings than do the saturated paste and calcium chloride methods (Table 33.4).

Table 33.4
Approximate equivalence of pH values of soil obtained by different methods

Method	To convert to a saturated paste value
1:5 water	subtract 0.4
1:2 or 1:2.5 water*	subtract 0.2
1:2 dilute calcium chloride*	add 0.3

Example: A soil reported to have a pH (1:5, water) of 5.9 has a reasonable chance of being measured at 5.9–0.4 = 5.5 in a saturated paste.

1. Weigh 20 g of air-dry soil into a clean screw-topped glass or plastic jar with a capacity of about 150 mL.

2. Add 100 mL of distilled or deionized water.

Figure 33.16
Wetting a potting mix up to the
correct water content prior to
measuring its pH or salinity by the
1:1.5 volume method

Figure 33.17
Squeeze the wet mix to see if it has
the correct water content

3. Shake continuously for 1 hour; or shake thoroughly every 5 minutes for 1 hour, or, shake thoroughly after adding the water, leave stand overnight, and shake thoroughly the next morning.
4. Measure the pH by dipping the electrode into the suspension immediately after it has been shaken. (In laboratories the suspension is stirred mechanically during measurement.)

Pour-through technique for mix in pots

This technique is widely used as a quick and non-destructive method of determining the pH and EC of mix in pots. It is less accurate than slurry methods but is often found to be good enough for many practical situations. It is certainly much better than guessing or not testing at all.

1. Two hours after a normal irrigation, select several pots from a batch for testing.
2. Suspend each pot over a saucer or dish of a diameter that is a little larger than that of the base of the pot (Fig. 33.18).
3. Pour onto the surface of the pot a volume of water that gives about 50 mL of drainage. Do this slowly, so as to allow time for the added water to move through the mix to displace some of the water already there.
4. Remove the pot and determine the pH and EC of the drainage water.
The EC is interpreted according to the information on p. 275.

Accuracy of pH measurements

Because of everything that can affect a measurement of soil pH, the accuracy implied in quoting figures such as 6.23 is just not possible. Quote to one decimal place only. For many situations being 'in error' by even 0.2 of a pH unit will make very little difference to what we do.

TRIALS IN NURSERIES

Use this technique when you want to check to see if a particular treatment will improve plant growth rate in a nursery. The treatment could be more frequent

Figure 33.18
Setup needed to collect pour-through
extracts from pots. *Photograph K A Handreck*

(or less frequent) watering, an increased rate of fertilizer application, an increase or decrease in the level of one nutrient element, a different pH, a new fungicide, etc. Some general comments are:

- Use at least five pots for each treatment.
- If there are already plants in the pots, select pots that have plants of closely similar size.
- Alternatively, select tubestock or rooted cuttings of as closely uniform size as is possible for transplanting into pots containing new or modified potting mixes.
- One treatment must be a control. The group of pots in this treatment will receive your usual management program, or will contain your usual mix.
- The other groups of pots will also receive your usual management program, except for the actual treatment itself.
- Label each pot carefully to show the treatment it is getting.
- Whenever possible, intermingle the pots of the different treatments. This will overcome any effect of environment that might affect growth if the groups of pots were held in different parts of the nursery.
- When intermingling is not possible (for example, when they are to be watered at different frequencies), keep the groups as close together as possible.
- Keep the pots away from the walls of glasshouses, or any other situations where the microclimate changes across the groups of pots.

In its simplest form, a trial will test the effect of just one treatment and at one level.

1. Select pots for 2 groups of plants (i.e. at least 10 pots).
2. Label one group of pots with a 'C', the other with a 'T'.
3. Apply the treatment to the 'T' pots.
4. Set the pots out in a suitable place (after planting tubestock if necessary).
5. Assess the effects of the treatment after several weeks to several months. Simply compare the height and appearance of the two groups of plants.

In its next simplest form, a trial will test the effect of just one treatment, but with several levels of that treatment. For example, the treatment could be application of a topdressing of a controlled release fertilizer to the pots. The levels could be 1, 2 and 3 kg/m³ of mix.

1. Select pots for four groups of plants.
2. Label the groups 'C', 'T', '2T', '3T'.
3. Apply the treatments to the three 'T' groups of pots. For example, if each pot contains 2 litres of mix, the amounts of fertilizer to apply will be 2, 4 and 6 g/pot.
4. Continue as in the 'simplest' trial, steps 4 and 5.

Table 33.5
The pH of a pour-through extract of medium in a pot is close to that of the lowermost part of the rootball, which can be quite different from the average for the whole rootball. *From K A Handreck Australian Hortic. in press, 1993*

	Saturated paste pH of rootball	
Pour-through pH	bottom	whole
5.58	5..48	5.03
5.48	5.45	5.15
5.95	5.94	5.52
6.89	6.46	6.24
6.93	6.86	6.24

Figure 33.19

Reading the nitrate concentration in a solution with Merck-o-Quant test strip.   *Photograph J Coppi*

A variation on this trial is to do it with two or more formulations or brands of controlled-release fertilizer, to see which gives best results under your conditions.

Somewhat more complicated is a trial in which there are two treatments, each at two levels.

1. Select pots for four groups of plants.
2. Label the pots 'T1', 'T2', 'T3' and 'T4'.
   Example: You want to check out whether you should increase the level of iron being added to your mix and/or increase the level of nitrogen nutrition. 'T1' will be your old iron and N levels, 'T2' will be the old iron level and the new N level, 'T3' will be the new iron level and the old N level, and 'T4' will be the new iron and N levels.
3. Apply the treatments as required.
4. Continue as in the simplest trial, steps 4 and 5.

For more complicated trials, you must have one group of pots for a control, one group for each treatment separately, and one group of each combination of treatments. These types of trials are too complicated for use without expert statistical help.

LEVELS OF NUTRIENTS IN POTTING MEDIA

Every couple of months, or more frequently if necessary, nurseries should check the pH and EC of a selection of pots as a guide to a need to fine-tune fertilizer applications, the amount of lime added before planting, a need to acidify water, etc. Use the pour-through method or, preferably, the 1:1.5 extraction method. Use Table 21.13 and the information on (p. 275) to interpret the readings.

You can get additional information about the fertility level in the pots by determining the concentrations of nitrate and ammonium in the extracts. Use test strips as illustrated in Figs 33.19 and 33.20. They may be bought from scientific supply firms. These strips give concentrations of nitrate and ammonium. The concentrations of actual N can be obtained by multiplying the nitrate figure by 0.226 and the ammonium concentration by 0.78.

Testing for ammonium is probably only necessary in bedding plant nurseries, as a means of preventing ammonium toxicity in winter. The way you interpret nitrate-N concentrations depends on how you fertilize. With an all-liquid program, you can compare the concentration of N in the extract with that in the feed to decide when next to apply fertilizer. When nutrients are supplied mainly by controlled-release fertilizers, it is possible for plants to be adequately fed even when there is a low level of N in the extract. Zero N probably indicates that plant growth will increase if more fertilizer is applied, but you do not need to do this if growth is already as you want it. Using the guidelines listed on (p. 275) and other information provided by research carried out at Virginia Tech., it can be concluded that maximum growth rate requires that there be at least 50 ppm N in pour-through drainage.

Concentrations of nutrients other than N can be determined only through laboratory procedures. Collect samples as described in Chapter 32.

Nitrogen drawdown index (NDI) of potting mixes and components

1. Bring the test material to potting moisture content (approx. 50% water) and maintain it at that moisture content for at least eight days prior to testing.
2. Fill the moist test material into six tubes of approximately 50 x 50 x 125 mm, or into standard nursery pots of approximately 125 mm diameter. The filling procedure must be the same for all containers and all materials. Packing is achieved by pouring the test material into the container to the brim and then settling it by gently tapping (just a little more vigorously than free fall

Figure 33.20

This strip reader increases the accuracy of reading nitrate test strips up to that of large laboratory instruments. *Photograph J Coppi*

Figure 33.21

Method of holding Victorian Forestry pots for the leaching and charging operations of determining the nitrogen drawdown index of potting mixes or materials for them.

Photograph J Coppi

Figure 33.22

Shaking excess solution from the bottoms of tubes after charging with potassium nitrate solution during determination of NDI. *Photograph J Coppi*

from 50 mm height) the base onto the bench surface five times. Packing should always be to a pre-determined weight.

3. Tubes are inserted into the holes in steel mesh so that they are held firmly about two-thirds up from the base (Fig. 33.21). Pots are sat on a free-draining mesh bench top.

4. Deionized water equal in volume to that of the volume of the material is slowly poured through the material in the container.

5. After waiting about 30 minutes, one volume of potassium nitrate solution containing 75 mg/L N is slowly poured through the material.

6. After a further 30 minutes a second volume of potassium nitrate solution is slowly poured through the material. These operations of adding potassium nitrate solution are subsequently referred to as 'charging'.

7. The containers are allowed to drain under gravity for about 15 minutes.

8. They are then sharply shaken once to dislodge any pool of solution retained in the bottom (Fig. 33.22). This is most easily achieved with tubes in a rack by abruptly stopping it after moving it down through the air for about 100 mm.

9. Allow the containers to drain for a further 5 minutes. The next three steps are referred to as 'slurrying'.

10. Within 30 minutes of the end of charging, tip the contents of three of the containers into three vessels of at least 5 times their volume.

11. Wash any residual solution and material from the container into the vessel with deionized water of 0.75 times the volume of material used (Fig. 33.23).

12. Mix the material and water and let the slurry stand for about 5 minutes.

13. Stir again. Obtain about 10 mL of the liquid of the slurry by filtration through a small kitchen strainer lined with pantyhose or through filter paper (Fig. 33.24).

14. Measure the nitrate concentration in the filtrate using Merck-o-Quant test strips (Figs. 33.19 and 33.20). If this cannot be done within 30 minutes of filtration, the filtrate must be frozen for later analysis.

15. Place each of the remaining three containers onto individual saucers, record their weights, cover their tops loosely with non-airtight covers and store them for four days in a constant temperature room at 21°C.

16. At the end of four days, repeat steps 10 to 14 for each of the incubated containers, first adding water to bring the weight of each container to that at the beginning of incubation.

17. Calculate the nitrogen drawdown index by dividing the mean concentration of nitrate in the slurries after incubation by the concentration in the slurries on the day of charging.

For example, if the slurries obtained on the first day have a mean nitrate concentration of 350 mg/L and the mean concentration at the end of incubation is 100 mg/L, the NDI of the material is 100/350 = 0.29.

AMOUNT OF FINE MATERIAL IN SANDS

Use this test to find the percentage of silt plus clay in a sand.

1. Select a screw-top jar of about 600 mL capacity. Mark it at 10 cm above the inside base.

2. Weigh out 100 g of dry sand (to the nearest 0.5 g), and tip it into the jar.

3. Add one level teaspoon of 'Calgon' or 'Aqua Soft'.

4. Add enough water to just make a slurry of the sand.

5. Paddle the sand gently with a piece of wood (Fig. 33.25) to break up any aggregates present.

6. Add water to the 10 cm mark.

7. Shake for 10 minutes.

8. Allow to settle for 5 minutes.

Figure 33.23
Preparing a slurry of the charged material during determination of NDI. *Photograph J Coppi*

9. Pour off three-quarters of the water (which now has much of the silt and clay suspended in it). Do not disturb the sand.
10. Measure the temperature of the water being used.
11. Add water to the 10 cm mark. Shake briefly.
12. Allow to stand for the number of seconds shown in Table 33.6. Pour off as much water as possible without disturbing the sand.
13. Repeat steps 11 and 12 until the water being poured off is clear. You have now removed all silt and clay from the sand.
14. Dry the sand. Weigh (S) in grams.
15. Calculate (% silt + clay) = 100–S.
16. Compare the result with the figures in Tables 17.7 and 17.8 if the sand is to be used as a topdressing or for a root zone. If the silt plus clay content is low enough, have the sand checked further by a suitable testing laboratory. Judge the sand's suitability for bunkers by using the information given on p. 207.

HEEL TEST FOR TURF

This simple test is used to check if turf soil in a wet area is too soft for play.

1. Stretch out one foot as shown in Fig 33.26.
2. Press the heel firmly as far as possible into the turf.
3. If more than half of the heel sinks into the soil, the turf will be severely damaged by play.
4. The soil has a high stability if the back of the heel no more than just penetrates into the soil.

SCREENING SOILS FOR SUITABILITY FOR CRICKET PITCHES

(*From* S. Cameron-Lee and K. W. McAuliffe *New Zealand Turf Manag. J.* Nov.: 16, 1988)

Pinch test: Knead a moistened sample into a ball of about 75 mm diameter. Squash the ball flat by hand to form a disc about 25 mm thick. A good soil should not disintegrate or crack excessively during squashing.

Tenacity test: Moist soil is rolled into a 300 mm long by 25 mm diameter cylinder. The sample is then held vertically for 15 sec. A good soil should support its own weight over this time.

Ring test: Roll a moist sample into a 100 mm long by 10 mm diameter 'worm'. Try to form a ring with the 'worm'. A soil that is suitable for first class pitches should be able to be formed into a ring without breaking.

Soaking test: Roll a moist sample into a ball of 50 mm diameter. Place it in a container of water and record the state of the ball over time. A good soil should not disintegrate within one hour.

BOUNCE TEST FOR CRICKET WICKETS

Use this test to check the pace of a cricket wicket.

1. Make from timber a 'T' with the vertical piece exactly 4.9 m long. The horizontal piece can be about 2 m long.
2. Mark the bottom metre of the long piece of wood at 10 cm intervals, starting at the junction with the short piece. Number them 10, 20, etc. from the junction.
3. To make a test, stand the 'T' upside down (⊥) on the pitch, with a tall ladder beside it. Climb the ladder with a cricket ball. Drop the ball from the top of the 'T' (4.9 m above the pitch). Ask your assistant to note the height to which the ball bounces.
4. The pace of the pitch is found by comparing this height with the figures in Table 17.11.
5. Repeat the test at several other places on the pitch.

(An alternative is to make the 'T' self-supporting (Fig. 33.27). The ball is held

Figure 33.24
Filtering the slurry during determination of NDI. (a) satisfactory method if the filtrate produced is clear. (b) apparatus sometimes needed. *Photographs K A Handreck*

(a)

(b)

Figure 33.25
Puddling a sample of sand so as to ensure that all aggregates of soil are dispersed before the particles of clay and silt size are removed from it.
Photograph J Coppi

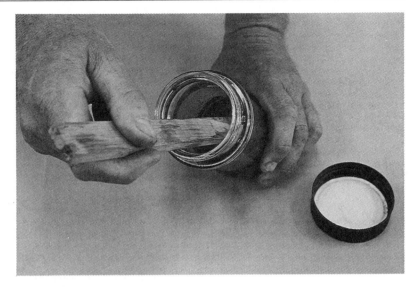

Table 33.6
Times needed for particles of 0.05 mm diameter to settle through 10 cm of water

Temperature (°C)	Time (sec)
15	52
20	46
25	41
30	37

Figure 33.26
Check to see whether a soil is too wet for play. *Photograph J Coppi*

in a tube of cloth or netting, held at the bottom with string. Pulling on the end of this string releases the ball.)

CALIBRATING SPREADERS OF FERTILIZER AND TOPDRESSINGS

For drop-type spreaders, run the spreader over a large sheet of plastic or heavy paper spread out on the ground. Measure the area covered by one pass. Weigh the amount of material deposited.

Example: A spreader delivers a band of fertilizer 600 mm (0.6 m) wide. The mass of fertilizer deposited by a 3 metre run was 45 g. Therefore, the rate of application was $\frac{45}{3 \times 0.6}$ = 25 g/m².

For spinner-type spreaders, run them in your usual way over a measured area. Weigh the amount of material in the spreader at the beginning and the end of the run.

Example: An area of 600 m² is to be fertilized. Of 15 kg of fertilizer in the hopper at the beginning, 6 kg remained at the end. The amount used was 9 kg. Therefore, the rate of application was $\frac{9 \times 1000}{600}$ = 15 g/m².

MEASURING SALINITY

The salinity of waters and growing media is measured with instruments called conductivity meters. Conductivity meters have two parts:

- A probe that is dipped into the water being tested. It has two electrodes of platinum or silver held at a set distance apart.
- A 'black box' that generates an electrical signal that passes between the two electrodes. It also houses a digital readout that gives the electrical conductivity (EC) of the water being tested (Figs 33.28 and 33.29).

General instructions

The EC of a solution will be measured to decrease as its temperature falls. We strongly recommend that you use only those salinity meters that have automatic temperature compensation (ATC) capability. At the very least, use a meter with a dial that can be adjusted to the temperature of the solution being tested. If

Figure 33.27

Simple apparatus for measuring the pace of a cricket wicket by means of the bounce test

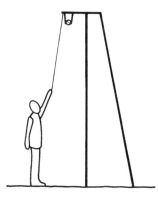

Figure 33.28

An Australian-made EC meter with Automatic Temperature Compensation. *Photograph K A Handreck*

neither is available, read the temperature of the solution and convert the reading to the standard 25°C figure by adding 2% for each 1°C that the solution is below that and subtracting 2% for each 1°C that it is above 25°C. For example, the Standard EC of a solution measured as being 1.3 dS/m at 20°C will be 1.3 × 1.10 = 1.43 dS/m.

• Read and follow the special instructions for the instrument you have, but otherwise:
• Set the conductivity meter to the temperature of the water being tested. This is important.
• Check against a standard salt solution if required by the instructions.
• Rinse the electrode with distilled water.
• Flick excess water from the electrode.
• If possible, rinse the electrode with a little of the water being tested.
• Insert the probe into the water, making sure that there are no air bubbles trapped around the electrodes.
• Read the EC from the meter.

Water, liquid feeds, hydroponics solutions

The electrical conductivities of water, liquid feeds and hydroponics solutions are measured directly as given above, without any pre-treatment. Measurements are interpreted according to the information in Table 21.2, Chapter 21 and Chapter 27.

Growing media

The electricity conductivities of growing media cannot be measured directly. The salts in them must be extracted with water and the EC of the water measured. Of course the EC will be different for different proportions of water added to a medium. To get usable results, the proportion must be kept the same for each medium tested.

What is the best proportion to use? As with pH, different people give different answers. We describe only those methods that we consider to be the best.

With all of these methods, use distilled or deionized water to mix with the medium. When other water must be used, measure its EC and subtract that from the EC of the extract.

Saturation extract

This is widely used method and there is much information on how to interpret readings obtained with it.

1. Make a saturated paste by the method described on (p. 410), but use about 250 g for soils or 250 mL for potting media.
2. Remove water from the saturated paste with a Buchner funnel and suction pump (Fig. 33.30). The funnel and catching tube must have been thoroughly rinsed with distilled water and dried before use. Use a No. 50, 42 or 576 filter paper.
3. Measure the EC of the extract.
4. Use Tables 21.4 and 21.13 to interpret the reading.

1:1.5 volume extract

This is the standard method used for potting mixes in Australia.

1. Make up a 1:1.5 mixture, as described for testing pH, steps 1–5.
2. To filter, pour some of the slurry into a small, clean plastic or glass jar as shown in Fig. 33.31. Fold an 11 cm No. 541 or 41 filter paper and push it into the slurry. Clear extract will flow into the cone formed by the filter paper. A kitchen strainer can be used for coarse potting mixes.

Figure 33.29
This small EC meter is accurate enough for most purposes.
Photograph K A Handreck

3. Measure the EC of the clear extract.
4. Use Table 21.13 to interpret the results.

1:5 (weight/volume) method

This method for determining the EC of soils will give falsely high readings if there is any gypsum in the soil. Do not use this method for potting mixes.

- Proceed as described under 1 to 3 on p. 411.
- Either allow the soil to settle for 20–30 minutes before making a measurement, or filter using the apparatus shown in Fig. 33.31.
- Measure the EC of the filtrate or of the more-or-less clear solution above the settled soil
- Use Table 21.5 to interpret the results.

IS MY SOIL SODIC?

1. Dig samples from several places across the area of soil being assessed. At each sample site, collect at least two samples—one of the topsoil and one of the subsoil. Take more samples if the subsoil has several layers.
2. Gather enough clear drinking glasses or clear plastic containers of similar size to have two for each sample. To each, add 50 mL of distilled, deionized or rain water. (Tap water is not good enough.)
3. Place the glasses where they can remain undisturbed for a day.
4. Select from each sample one small clod or aggregate about the size of a large pea.
5. At the same time, take a small portion of each soil, moisten separately, knead between the fingers and thumb, and form into small 'artificial' clods.
6. Drop the natural and artificial clods into separate glasses of water. Watch what happens from time to time over the first hour or so (Fig. 33.32). Do not move the glasses.
   You will notice several types of behaviour:

   - Some clods will remain unchanged, even after 24 hours.
   - Others will fall apart immediately or within an hour.
   - Others, whether they fall apart or not, will slowly disperse into the water, first forming a 'halo' of clay particles around the clod. This halo then spreads throughout the water.

Dispersion means that the soil is sodic and will be improved by treatment with gypsum (p. 268).

HERBICIDE RESIDUES

Use this simple test to see if dead turf or poor results on resowing a soil are due to herbicide residues in the soil.

1. Collect about 4 litres of soil from the problem area.
2. To half of the soil, add 1 teaspoon of activated charcoal. Mix.
3. Fill the soils into shallow trays or pots.
4. Sow seeds or sprigs of the species to be grown.
5. If growth is satisfactory in the soil to which charcoal has been added, but not in the other, apply charcoal to the problem soil as outlined on p. 240.
6. If there is no difference between the samples, look for other causes of the problem.

SANDS FOR CAPILLARY BEDS

Use these two tests to see if a sand is suitable for capillary beds.

Figure 33.30
Apparatus needed to remove extract
from a saturated paste. *Photograph
J Coppi*

Capillarity test

1. Choose a container that is 120 mm or more high and about 80 mm diameter. Its base must be perforated with many small (1–2 mm) holes. A 750 g baked bean can is suitable.
2. Place a layer of peat about 6 mm thick in the bottom of the container.
3. Add dry sand up to a total height (peat + sand) of 112 mm.
4. Stand container in dish of water. Final height of water should be 75 mm.
5. The sand passes the test if water appears at the surface within 24 hours. If it passes, proceed to the next test. If it fails, find a finer sand.

Porosity test

1. Remove the container of sand from the dish of water (above).
2. Pour 200 mL of water onto sand within a 4-minute period. Do not spill any.
3. If the sand absorbs all the water and it passes step 4 (below), it is suitable for capillary beds.
4. If the applied water does not drain out of the sand in another 4 minutes, the sand should be discarded, or opened up with some coarse sand.

SODIUM ADSORPTION RADIO

The sodium adsorption ratio (SAR) is a measure of the ability of a water to make a soil sodic. It is defined as follows:

$$SAR = \frac{[Na]}{\sqrt{([Ca] + [Mg])/2}}$$

Figure 33.31
Method of obtaining clear extract from 1:1.5 volume and 1:5 weight/volume mixtures of growing media and water.   *Photograph J Coppi*

Figure 33.32
Testing to see whether gypsum will improve the structure of a soil

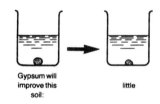

Gypsum will improve this soil: little

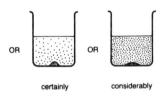

OR   OR

certainly   considerably

where [Na], [Ca] and [Mg] are the concentrations of sodium, calcium and magnesium dissolved in the water, given in m.e./L. Use Fig. 33.33 to calculate the SAR of a water.

Bicarbonate ions in the water can precipitate soluble calcium and magnesium in the soil as almost insoluble compounds. This increases the proportion of soluble and exchangeable sodium. To allow for this extra hazard, another equation is used, with the number obtained being called the adjusted SAR (adj. SAR). Use Fig. 33.34 to find the factor (F) to be used to multiply the SAR figure read from Fig. 33.33 to get the adjusted SAR figure.

Example: These calculations are for the most saline Perth water listed in Table 21.1

$$\text{Concentration of } Na^+ \quad = 140 \text{ m/L} \quad = \frac{140}{23} = 6.1 \text{ m.e./L}$$

$$\text{Concentration of } Ca^{2+} \quad = 30 \text{ mg/L} \quad = \frac{30}{20} = 1.5 \text{ m.e./L}$$

$$\text{Concentration of } Mg^{2+} \quad = 12 \text{ mg/L} \quad = \frac{12}{12} = 1.0 \text{ m.e./L}$$

$$\text{Concentration of } HCO_3^- \quad = 140 \text{ mg/L} \quad = \frac{140}{61} = 2.3 \text{ m.e./L}$$

Therefore, [Ca] + [Mg]   = 1.5 + 1.0   = 2.5 m.e./L
[Ca] + [Mg] + [Na]   = 2.5 + 6.1   = 8.6 m.e./L

From Fig. 33.33 the SAR of the water is 5.4.
From Fig. 33.34 the factor F is 1.6
Therefore, the adjusted SAR = 1.6 × 5.4 = 8.6.

A glance at Table 21.2 shows that this water will cause problems to plants and clay soils unless extra calcium is supplied.

DROPLET SIZE FROM SPRINKLERS

This simple test quickly shows you the sizes of droplets produced by a sprinkler.

1. Into a dish about 10 cm across, pour about 1 cm of SAE 90 oil.
2. Turn the sprinkler on as usual.
3. Hold a cover over the dish.
4. Walk into the area being sprinkled. Stop at the point where you want to test droplet size.
5. Uncover the dish for a few seconds. Replace the cover.
6. Walk out of your shower and look at the size of the droplets caught.
7. Compare them with the figures in Table 23.1 to decide whether to change operating pressure or nozzle size.

Figure 33.33
Nomogram for calculating the SAR of a water. Join with a ruler the figures for the concentrations of sodium (A) and the calcium plus magnesium (B). Read the SAR of the water from the point where the ruler crosses the diagonal line (C). *From 'Diagnosis and improvement of saline and sodic soils' Agric. Handbook No. 60 US Department of Agriculture 1954*

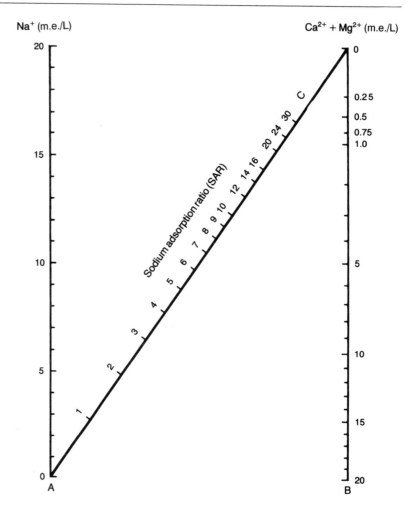

Figure 33.34
Nomogram for finding the factor F used to adjust the calculated value of the SAR of a water to allow for the concentrations of carbonate and bicarbonate ions in the water. Join with a ruler the appropriate points on the first two lines. Mark the point where the ruler intersects the tie-line. Place the ruler from this point to the appropriate point on the last line. Read the value of the F factor from the 'F' line. *Data from C A Bower et al. Soil Sci. Soc. Amer. Proc. 29: 91, 1965*

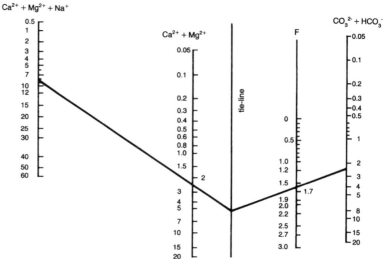

SOURCES OF HELP: ANALYTICAL SERVICES

Help is available for solving most of the problems that you will encounter, but it is often difficult to find the right sort of help at the right price. These two pages summarize the types of help on offer. We are writing this in a period of rapid change: many services once offered by government departments are being stopped or handed over to private enterprise. Amalgamations and closures are making rapid changes in the commercial scene too. Readers will often have to do some hunting before they find the help they want.

Analytical services

Most states have at least one laboratory that will analyse water, nutrient solutions, soils, potting media and plant tissue. You can use overnight courier services to interstate laboratories if necessary. We recommend that you patronise those laboratories that interpret the results for you. Most laboratories offer an excellent service. There is no need to send samples overseas for analysis. Often overseas laboratories do not know Australian conditions and so do not offer very useful interpretations.

Water and nutrient solutions

For water, the most useful analyses are for EC, pH, total alkalinity, cations (calcium, magnesium, sodium), boron, chloride, sulphate and bicarbonate. Nutrient solutions will commonly be analysed for nitrate and ammonium, EC, pH and all nutrient elements as well as most of the above. Tests to detect pathogens may sometimes be required.

Soils

The most useful analyses are those in the following list: pH, EC, available phosphorus, available potassium, chloride, exchangeable cations, CEC, total nitrogen, nitrate and ammonium, available trace elements, organic matter content, lime requirement. Some laboratories also offer particle size analysis, texture, fines in sands, water characteristic/hydraulic conductivity, bulk density, gypsum requirement, bioassay for toxicity, microbiological testing.

Turf soils

At the time of writing, three organizations were able to professionally assess the quality of materials to be used for turf rootzones and for topdressing turf. They were the Technical Services Unit of the ACT Parks and Conservation Service (Canberra), the Australian Turfgrass Research Institute (Sydney), and Turfgrass Technology (Melbourne).

They can produce specifications and designs for turf installations.

Potting mixes

All Australian laboratories that analyse potting mixes use the methods prescribed in the Australian Standard for Potting Mixes. Assessment of air-filled porosity is by the method given on p. 405. There is an assessment of ability to supply water. The 1:1.5 volume method with deionized water is used for pH, EC and soluble nitrogen. All other nutrients except molybdenum are extracted from the medium with 0.002 molar DTPA (a chelating agent that has been shown to reasonably reliably estimate the level of available nutrients in the medium). There are also tests for toxicity and for nitrogen drawdown index. Occasionally, it might be necessary to ask for tests of CEC, exchangeable cations and pathogens.

Other types of help

Most Departments of Agriculture or Primary Industries, CSIRO and such bodies as Botanic Gardens, Forestry Departments and Departments of Environment still offer help in the solution of problems encountered by those who produce plants for sale or who are engaged in planting them in landscape and other situations. Restrictions on staff numbers and changing attitudes to the provision of free advice have meant that increasingly charges are being made for the help given. Nevertheless, there is a wealth of knowledge there for the asking.

In addition, there are many private consultants who provide comprehensive or specialized services to the horticultural industries. Their names may be found in the yellow pages of telephone books or through advertisements in trade and professional magazines. While these services may not appear to be cheap, it is not uncommon for one consultation costing a few hundred dollars to save someone in the industry many thousands of dollars.

Trade, industry and professional organizations

There are many organizations in Australia to which those people in a particular industry can belong. Usually membership is restricted to people actively involved in the industry or with formal qualifications related to it. Membership of one or several organizations is considered by many to be essential to their success in their chosen trade or profession. An important part of membership is the receipt of the magazine, journal or newsletter produced by the organization. Another important part is the extra knowledge and business acquired by the contacts made through membership.

We give a listing here of some of these organizations. Addresses and telephone numbers are not included as these tend to change frequently. You may get local information from telephone books, trade journals or by asking around amongst people involved in the particular industry.

Australian Institute of Horticulture
Australian Society of Horticultural Science
Royal Australian Institute of Parks and Recreation
Australian Institute of Landscape Architects
Nursery Industry Association of Australia; and State Associations
Landscape Contractors Association of Australia; and State Associations
Irrigation Association of Australia
Flower Growers Council of Australia; and State Associations
Various greenkeepers' associations

There are also many smaller groups with specialist interests in particular crops or aspects of an industry.

FURTHER READING

Soils, general

ALLISON F E *Soil Organic Matter and its Role in Crop Production* Elsevier 1973

GLENDINNING J S (ed) *Fertilizer Handbook* Australian Fertilizers Ltd Sydney 1974

HANDRECK K A *Organic Matter and Soils* CSIRO Melbourne 1979

HANKS R J and ASHCROFT G L *Applied Soil Physics* Advanced Series in Agricultural Sciences 8 Springer Verlag Berlin 1980

MARSHALL T J and HOLMES J W *Soil Physics* CUP 1988

MINISTRY OF AGRICULTURE, FISHERIES AND FOOD, Great Britain *Soil Physical Conditions and Crop Production* Tech Bull No 29 HMSO London 1975

RUSSELL E W *Soil Conditions and Plant Growth* Longman UK 10th ed 1973

WHITE R E *Introduction to the Principles and Practice of Soil Science* Blackwell Oxford 1987

Plants

CAPON B *Botany for Gardeners* Timber Press Portland Oregon 1990

HARTMAN H T, FLOCKER W J and KOFRANEK A M *Plant Science: Growth, Development and Utility of Cultivated Plants* Prentice-Hall USA 1981

RAVEN P H and EVERT R F *Biology of Plants* Worth Publishers 3rd ed 1981

ROWELL R J *Ornamental Flowering Shrubs in Australia* UNSW Press Sydney 1992

————*Ornamental Flowering Trees in Australia* UNSW Press Sydney 1992

————*Ornamental Plants for Australia* UNSW Press Sydney 1993

WILKINS M *Plantwatching: How Plants Remember, Tell Time, Form Relationships and More* Facts On File Publications New York 1988

Australian and New Zealand soils

CHARMAN P E V and MURPHY B W (eds) *Soils: Their Properties and Management* NSW Soil Conservation Service Sydney University Press 1991

CORBETT J R *The Living Soil: The Processes of Soil Formation* Martindale 1969

DIVISION OF SOILS CSIRO *Soils: An Australian Viewpoint* CSIRO/Academic Press, Melbourne and London 1983

MOLLOY I *The Living Mantle: Soils in the New Zealand Landscape* NZ Society of Soil Science Wellington 1988

NORTHCOTE K H *A Factual Key for the Recognition of Australian Soils* Rellim Adelaide 1968

NORTHCOTE K H et al. *Description of Australian Soils* CSIRO Melbourne 1975

STACE H C T et al. *A Handbook of Australian Soils* Rellim Adelaide 1968

'Soils and Land Use' series CSIRO Division of Soils Adelaide

The CSIRO Division of Soils, state Departments of Agriculture, Primary Industries, Soil Conservation and Lands can often provide information about the properties of soils in an area.

Landscape

AUSTRALIAN PLANT STUDY GROUP *Grow What . . . series* Viking O'Neil Melbourne

CREMER K W (ed) *Trees for Rural Australia* Inkata Melbourne 1990

DOWNING M F *Landscape Construction* Spon London 1977

HARRIS R W *Arboriculture: The Care of Trees, Shrubs and Vines in the Landscape* Prentice-Hall USA 1982

NATHAN K *Basic Site Engineering for Landscape Designers* Irvington NY 1973

RECHER H F *A Natural Legacy: Ecology in Australia* Pergamon Sydney 1979

VENNING J *Growing Trees for Farms, Parks and Roadsides: A Revegetation Manual for Australia* Lothian Melbourne 1988

Composting

Biocycle (Journal of Waste Recycling) monthly journal The JG Press USA

GOLUEKE C G *Biological Reclamation of Solid Wastes* Rodale Press USA 1977

HAUG R T *Compost Engineering: Principles and Practice* Ann Arbor Science Publishers 1980

STAFF OF BIOCYCLE *The Art and Science of Composting* The JG Press USA 1991

Nurseries

Australian Horticulture monthly journal Ramsey Ware Stockland Melbourne

BALL V (ed) *Ball Red Book: Greenhouse Growing* Reston USA 1985

BUNT A C *Media and Mixes for Container-Grown Plants* Unwin Hyman UK 1988

HANNAN J J, HOLLEY W D and GOLDSBERRY K L *Greenhouse Management.* (Advanced Series in Agricultural Sciences) 5 Springer Verlag Berlin 1978

JOINER J N (ed) *Foliage Plant Production* Prentice-Hall USA 1981

NELSON P V *Greenhouse Operation and Management* Prentice-Hall USA 1991

Turf

BEARD J B *Turfgrass: Science and Culture* Prentice-Hall USA 1973

——*Turf Management for Golf Courses* Macmillan New York 1982

DANIEL W H and FREEBORG R P *Turfgrass Managers' Handbook* Cleveland Business Publ Div Harvest Publ Co 1979

DAVIS W B, PAUL J and PRATT C *Sand Green Construction and Management* University of California Div Agri Sci 1983

SMILEY R W *Compendium of Turfgrass Diseases* American Phytopathological Society St Paul Minnesota 1983

TURGEON A J *Turfgrass Management* Reston P USA 1980

WADDINGTON D V et al. Turfgrass (Agronomy Monograph 32) Agronomy Society of America 1992

Irrigation

HART B T *A Compilation of Australian Water Quality Criteria* (Australian Water Resources Council Tech Paper) AGPS Canberra 1974

McINTYRE D K and HUGHES S M *Turf Irrigation* Royal Australian Institute of Parks and Recreation Canberra 2nd ed 1988

SHAINBERG I and OSTER J D *Quality of Irrigation Water* International Irrigation Information Center Bet Dagan Israel (Publ No 2) 1978

STEWART B A and NIELSEN D R (eds) *Irrigation of Agricultural Crops* (Agronomy 30) Agronomy Society of America 1990

US SALINITY LABORATORY STAFF *Diagnosis and Improvement of Saline and Alkali Soils* USDA Agriculture Handbook 60 1954

Living things

BROWN A L *Ecology of Soil Organisms* Heinemann Educational London 1978
COUCH H B *Diseases of Turfgrasses* R E Krieger USA 3rd ed 1982
EDWARDS C A (ed) *Earthworms in Waste and Environmental Management* SPB
    Academic The Hague 1988
FORSBERG J L *Diseases of Ornamental Plants* Univ. of Illinois Press USA 1976
GOSS O M *Practical Guidelines for Nursery Hygiene* Australian Nurserymen's
    Association Sydney 1983
LEE K E *Earthworms: Their Ecology and Relationships with Soils and Land Use*
    Academic Press Sydney 1985
McMAUGH J *What Garden Pest or Disease is That?* Lansdowne Sydney 1985
PIRONE P P *Diseases and Pests of Ornamental Plants* Wiley USA 5th ed 1978
SCHALLER F *Soil Animals* Ann Arbor Science Library Univ. of Michigan 1968

Hydroponics

COOPER A *ABC of NFT* Grower Books London 1979
    Commercial Application of NFT Grower Books London 1979
DE BRUIJN F *Hydroculture: Indoor Plants on Tap* W Foulsham UK 1978
DOUGLAS J S *Advanced Guide to Hydroponics* Pelham Books 1985
FAO *Soilless Culture for Horticultural Crop Production* Rome 1990
HARRIS D *Hydroponics: Gardening Without Soil* Hydroponic Sales & Services
    Adelaide 6th ed 1982
HYDROPONICS SOCIETY OF SOUTH AUSTRALIA *Hydroponics in Horticulture and
    Floriculture* Adelaide 1984
MASON J *Commercial Hydroponics* Kangaroo Press Australia 1990
RESH H M *Hydroponic Food Production* Woodbridge USA 1981
SUTHERLAND S K *Hydroponics for Everyone: A Practical Guide to Gardening
    in the 21st Century* Hyland House Melbourne 1986

Chemistry

BUCAT R B *Elements of Chemistry* Vols 1 and 2 Australian Acad. Sci. 1984
CARSWELL D J, NEWMAN B C and MIHKELSON A E *Fundementals of Senior
    Chemistry* Heinemann 1988
GALLAGHER R and INGRAM P *Chemistry Made Clear* OUP 1987
SMITH R *Conquering Chemistry* McGraw-Hill 1987
WIECEK C *Chemistry for Senior Students* Brooks Waterloo 1989

TOLERANCE TO SALINITY

Listed here are ornamental plants, fruit trees and vegetables according to their known tolerances to salinity. Turf grasses are listed in Table 18.1. The Australian Plant Study Group's book *Grow What Where* lists other Australian native species that have a high tolerance of salinity.

For the species listed here, growth reductions will be about 25% at the EC ratings given at the top of each list.

Note, however, that tolerance to salinity can vary widely amongst varieties, selections and cultivars of a species.

Very sensitive

(EC of a saturation extract of the medium no higher than 1.8 dS/m)

Acanthus mollis	(Bear's breeches)
Adiantum spp	(Maidenhair fern)
Allium cepa	(Onion)
Antirrhinum spp	(Snapdragon)
Begonia spp	(Begonia)
Berberis thunbergii	(Barberry)
Callistephus spp	(China aster)
Camellia spp	(Camellia)
Cedrus atlantica	(Blue atlas cedar)
Cotoneaster horizontalis	(Rock cotoneaster)
Cymbidium spp	(Cymbidium orchid)
Cytisus X *praecox*	(Broom)
Dahlia spp	(Dahlia)
Daucus carrota	(Carrot)
Ensete ventricosum	(Abyssinian banana)
Euonymus alatus	(Euonymus)
Feijoa sellowiana	(Pineapple guava)
Fragaria chiloensis	(Strawberry)
Fuchsia spp	(Fuchsia)
Gardenia spp	(Gardenia)
Godetia spp	(Godetia)
Iberis spp	(Candytuft)
Ilex cornuta	(Chinese holly)
Lilium spp	(Lily)
Mahonia aquifolium	(Oregon grape holly)
Pachysandra terminalis	(Japanese spurge)
Persea americana	(Avocado)
Phaseolus vulgaris	(Beans)
Phormium tenax	(New Zealand flax)
Photinia X *fraseri* 'Robusta'	(Photinia)
Picea pungens	(Blue spruce)
Podocarpus macrophyllus	(Shrubby Japanese yew)
Primula spp	(Primula)

Protea spp	(Protea)
Pseudotsuga menziesii	(Douglas fir)
Rhododendron spp	(Azalea, Rhododendron)
Rosa spp	(Rose)
Rubus spp	(Blackberry, Boysenberry, etc.)
Saintpaulia ionanthe	(African violet)
Salix purpurea	(Blue willow)
Spiraea spp	(Spiraea)
Tilia cordata	(Linden)
Trachelospermum jasminoides	(Star jasmine)
Verbena spp	(Verbena)
Viola hederaceae	(Violet)

Sensitive

(EC of a saturation extract of the medium no higher than 3–4 dS/m)

Abelia X *grandiflora*	(Glossy abelia)
Aechmea spp	(Vase plant)
Anthurium spp	(Flamingo flower)
Aphelandra spp	(Aphelandra)
Arbutus unedo	(Irish strawberry tree)
Aster spp	(Aster)
Berberis X *mentorensis*	(Barberry)
Campanula spp	(Bellflower)
Capsicum frutescens	(Pepper)
Cedrus deodara	(Deodar cedar)
Ceratonia siliqua	(Carob)
Cinnamomum camphora	(Camphor tree)
Clivia miniata	(Kaffir lily)
Crassula argentea	(Jape plant)
Euphorbia pulcherrima	(Poinsettia)
Felecia amelloides	(Blue daisy)
Ficus benjamina	(Java fig)
Forsythia X *intermedia*	(Showy golden-bells)
Freesia spp	(Freesia)
Gelsemium sempervirens	(Carolina jasmine)
Geranium spp	(Geranium)
Gerbera spp	(African daisy)
Gladiolus spp	(Gladiolus)
Hedera canariensis	(Algerian ivy)
Hydrangea spp	*(Hydrangea)*
Juniperus virginiana	(Eastern red cedar)
Lactuca sativa	(Lettuce)
Limonium perezii	(Sea lavender)
Lonicera japonica	(Honeysuckle)
Magnolia grandiflora	(Magnolia)
Matthiola incana	(Stock)
Monstera spp	(Monstera)
Nandina domestica	(Heavenly bamboo)
Ophiopogon japonicus	(Lily-turf)
Penstemon spp	(Beard tongue)
Pittosporum tobira	(Pittosporum)
Podocarpus macrophylla	(Maki)
Prunus amygdalus	(Almond)
P. domestica	(Plum)
P. persica	(Peach)
Pyracantha koidzumii	(Firethorn)

Pyrus armeniaca	(Apricot)
Raphanus sativas	(Radish)
Rhamnus alternus	(Italian blackthorn)
Strelitzia regina	(Bird of Paradise)
Tagetes spp	(Marigold)
Viburnum tinus	(Viburnum)
Vinca minor	(Dwarf running myrtle)
Vriesia spp	(Paintbrush)
Washington robusta	(Cotton palm)
Yucca filamentosa	(Adam's-needle yucca)
Zinnia elegans	(Zinnia)

Moderately tolerant

(EC of a saturation extract of the medium no higher than 5–6 dS/m)

Agapanthus spp	(African lily)
Agave attenuata	(Century plant)
Arecastrum romanzoffianum	(Queen palm)
Brassica oleracea 'Capitata'	(Cabbage)
Brunfelsia pauciflora	(Yesterday, today and tonight)
Buxus microphylla	(Boxwood)
Casuarina equisetifolia	(Beach-oak)
Chrysanthemum spp	(Chrysanthemum)
Citrus limonea	(Lemon)
C. paradisi	(Grapefruit)
C. sinensis	(Orange)
Cucumis sativus	(Cucumber)
Cupressus arizonica	(Arizona cypress)
C. sempervirens	(Italian cypress)
Cyclamen spp	(Cyclamen)
Dianthus caryophyllus	(Carnation)
Elaeagnus pungens	—
Fraxinus pennsylvanica	(Green ash)
Hakea suaveolens	(Sweet hakea)
Ipomea batatas	(Sweet potato)
Juglans regia	(Walnut)
Juniperus chinensis	(Spreading juniper)
Lantana camara	(Lantana)
Ligustrum japonicum	(Japanese privet)
Melaleuca leucadendron	(Cajeput tree)
Philodendron selloum	(Philodendron)
Phormium tenax	(New Zealand flax)
Pinus ponderosa	(Ponderosa pine)
P. thunbergiana	(Japanese black pine)
Pittosporum phillyraeoides	(Desert willow)
Pyracantha graberi	(Pyracantha spp.)
Pyrus communis	(Pear)
P. malus	(Apple)
Raphiolepis indica	(Indian hawthorn)
Salix vitellina	(Golden willow)
Saintpaulia spp	(African violet)
Shepherdia argentea	(Buffaloberry)
Solanum tuberosum	(Potato)
Syzygium paniculatum	(Bush cherry)
Thuja orientalis	(Chinese arborvitae)
Xylosma senticosa	(Xylosma)
Zea mays	(Sweetcorn)

Tolerant

(EC of a saturation extract of the medium no higher than 8 dS/m)

Asparagus densiflorus	(Asparagus)
Beta vulgaris	(Beets)
Bougainvillea spectabilis	(Bougainvillea)
Brahea edulis	(Guadalupe palm)
Brassica italica	(Broccoli)
Callistemon viminalis	(Bottlebrush)
Calocephalus brownii	(Pincushion bush)
Casuarina glauca	(Grey buloke)
Chamaerops humilis	(European fan palm)
Crassula ovata	—
Cucumis melo	(Rockmelon)
Dodonaea viscosa	(Giant hop-bush)
Dracaena endivisa	(Dracaena)
Elaeagnus angustifolia	(Russian olive)
Eucalyptus botryoides	(Bangalay)
E. coolabah	(Coolabah)
E. occidentalis	(Flat-topped yate)
E. pileata	(Ravensthorpe mallee)
E. robusta	(Swamp mahogany)
E. sideroxylon	(Red ironbark)
Euonymus japonica	(Evergreen spindle-tree)
Ficus carica	(Fig)
Gleditsia triacanthos	(Honey locust)
Hibiscus rosa-sinensis	(Chinese hibiscus)
Lycopersicon esculentum	(Tomato)
Melaleuca cuticularis	—
M. vimenea	
Metrosideros excelsa	(NZ Christmas tree)
Myoporum spp	(Boobialla)
Nerium oleander	(Oleander)
Olea europaea	(Olive)
Ophiopogon jaburan '	(Lily-turf)
Pinus halepensis	(Allepo pine)
Pittosporum crassifolium	(Karo)
Robinia pseudocacia	(Black locust)
Rosmarinus officinalis	(Rosemary)
Spinacia oleracea	(Spinach)
Vitis spp	(Grape)

Very tolerant

(EC of a saturation extract of the medium no higher than 13 dS/m)

Acacia cyanophylla	(Orange wattle)
A. cyclops	(WA coastal wattle)
A. longifolia var. *sophorae*	(Coast wattle)
A. pendula	(Weeping myall)
A. pulchella	(Western prickly moses)
A. salicina	—
Alyxia buxifolia	(Sea-box)
Araucaria heterophylla	(Norfolk Island pine)
Arctotheca calendula	(Arctotheca)
Atriplex spp	(Saltbush)
Baccharis pilularis	(Coyote bush)
Banksia spp	(Banksia)

Callistemon citrinus	(Crimson bottlebrush)
Carissa grandiflora	(Natal plum)
Carpobrotus chilensis	(Pigfaces)
C. edulis	(Pigfaces)
Casuarina distyla	(She oak)
C. glauca	(Swamp oak)
C. obesa	—
Coprosma repens	(Mirror plant)
Cordyline indivisa	(Broad leaved cabbage tree)
Correa alba	(White correa)
Cortaderia sellowiana	(Pampus grass)
Delasperma spp	(Iceplants)
Drosanthemum spp	(Iceplants, pigfaces)
Eucalyptus astringens	(Brown mallee)
E. camaldulensis	(River red gum)
E. kondininensis	(Stocking gum)
E. occidentalis	(Swamp Yate)
E. sargentii	(Salt river gum)
E. spathulata	(Swamp mallet)
Ficus microcarpa	(Small-leaf fig)
Hibbertia scandens	(Snake vine)
Hymenocyclus spp	(Iceplants)
Lagunaria patersonii	(Norfolk Island hibiscus)
Lampranthus spp	(Iceplants)
Leptospermum laevigatum	(Tea Tree)
Leucophyllum frutescens	(Texas sage)
Lippia canescens repens	(Lippia)
Melaleuca armillaris	(Bracelet honey-myrtle)
M. diosmifolia	(Cajeput tree)
M. halmaturorum	*(Kangaroo Island paperbark)*
M. nesophila	(Western tea-myrtle)
Morea vegata	(Iris)
Pelargonium australe	(Austral storks bill)
Phoenix dactylifera	(Date palm)
Platycladus orientalis	(Oriental arborvita)
Rhagodia spp	(Saltbush)
Scaevola calendulacea	(Dune fan flower)
Tamarix aphylla	(Tamarix)
T. pentandra	(Tamarix)
Westringia fruticosa	(Rosemary westringia)
Yucca aloifolia	(Spanish bayonet)

CONVERSION TABLES

Length

Metric

1 metre (m) = 1 000 000 micrometres (microns) (μm)
    = 1000 millimetres (mm)
    = 100 centimetres (cm)
1 centimetre (cm) = 0.01 m
    = 10 mm
1 millimetre (mm) = 0.001 m
    = 0.1 cm
1 micrometre (μm) = 0.000 001 m
    = 0.001 mm
1 kilometre (km) = 1000 m

Imperial

1 inch = 0.083 foot
1 foot = 12 inches
    = 0.33 yard
1 yard = 36 inches
    = 3 feet
1 chain = 22 yards
    = 66 feet
1 mile = 5280 feet
    = 1760 yards
    = 80 chains

Multiply	by	to obtain
inch (in)	25.40	millimetre (mm)
	2.54	centimetre (cm)
	0.0254	metre (m)
foot (ft)	304.8	mm
	30.48	cm
	0.3048	m
yard (yd)	0.914	m
	91.4	cm
chain	20.12	m
mile	1.61	km
millimetre (mm)	0.0394	inch
centimetre (cm)	0.394	inch
	0.033	foot
metre (m)	39.37	inch
	3.281	foot
	1.094	yard
kilometre (km)	0.621	mile
	1094	yard

Area

Metric

1 square centimetre (cm^2) = 100 mm^2
    = 0.0001 m^2
1 square metre (m^2) = 10 000 cm^2
    = 0.01 are
1 hectare (ha) = 10 000 m^2
    = 0.01 km^2
    = 100 are
1 are = 0.01 ha
    = 100 m^2

Imperial

1 square foot = 144 square inches
    = 0.111 square yards
1 square yard = 9 square feet

1 acre = 4840 square yards
    = 10 square chain

1 square mile = 640 acres

Multiply	by	to obtain
square inch	6.45	cm²
	645	mm²
square foot	929	cm²
	0.093	m²
1000 square feet	0.93	1 are
square yard	0.836	m²
	0.0084	are
acre	0.405	ha
	40.5	are
	4050	m²
square mile	259	ha
	2.59	km²

Multiply	by	to obtain
mm²	0.0016	square inch
cm²	0.155	square inch
m²	10.76	square foot
	1.20	square yards
are	1076	square feet
	0.025	acre
ha	2.47	acre
km²	247	acre

Volume

Metric

1 litre (L) = 1000 millilitre (mL)
        = 100 centilitre (cL)
1 mL = 0.001 L
1 hectolitre (hL) = 100 L
1 centilitre (cL) = 0.01 L
        = 10 cm³
        = 10 mL

1 cubic metre (m³) = 1 000 000 cm³
1 cm³ = 1mL

Imperial and USA

1 pint (Imp.) = 0.5 quart (Imp.)
        = 1.20 pint (US)
1 pint (US) = 0.83 pint (Imp.)
1 quart = 2 pints
1 gallon = 8 pints
        = 4 quarts

1 gallon (Imp.) = 160 fluid oz (Imp.)
        = 1.20 gallon (US)

1 cubic yard (yd³) = 27 cubic feet (ft³)

Multiply	by	to obtain
gallon (Imp.)	4.546	L
	4546	mL
gallon (US)	3.785	L
	3785	mL
pint (Imp.)	0.568	L
	568	mL
bushel (Imp.)	36.37	L
	35.24	L
cubic yard	0.765	m³
cubic foot	0.0283	m³
pint (US)	0.473	L
	473	mL

Multiply	by	to obtain
mL	0.061	cubic inch
	0.035	fluid ounce (Imp.)
	0.034	fluid ounce (US)
L	0.0275	bushel (Imp.)

Multiply	0.0284 by	bushel (US) to obtain
	0.22	gallon (Imp.)
	0.264	gallon (US)
	1.796	pint (Imp.)
	2.11	pint (US)
hL	2.75	bushel (Imp.)
	2.84	bushel (US)
m³	1.31	cubic yard

Mass

Metric
1 gram (g) = 1000 milligram (mg)
$\qquad$ = 1 000 000 microgram (µg)
$\qquad$ = 0.001 kilogram (kg)
1 kilogram (kg) = 1000 µg
$\qquad$ = 0.001 tonne
1 tonne = 1000 kg
$\qquad$ = 1 000 000 g

Imperial
1 ounce = 0.0625 pound (lb)
$\qquad$ = 437.5 grains
1 lb = 16 ounces (oz)
$\qquad$ = 0.0089 hundredweight (cwt)
1 hundredweight = 112 lb
$\qquad$ = 0.05 ton
1 ton = 20 hundredweight
$\qquad$ = 2240 lb

Multiply	by	to obtain
ounce	28.35	g
pound	453.6	g
	0.4536	kg
hundredweight	50.8	kg
ton	1.016	tonne
	1016	kg
g	15.43	grain
	0.035	ounce
kg	0.0197	hundredweight
	35.27	ounce
	2.205	pound
tonne	0.98	ton

Application rates—area
Metric

L/m²	10 000	L/ha
	100	L/are
g/m²	0.1	kg/are
	10	kg/ha
	0.01	t/ha
t/ha	100	g/m²
	10	kg/are

Multiply	by	to obtain
lb/1000 ft^2	489	g/are
	4.89	g/m^2
lb/acre	1.121	kg/ha
cwt/acre	12.56	g/m^2
	125.6	kg/ha
gal (Imp.)/acre	11.23	L/ha
	1.12	mL/m^2
gal (US)/acre	9.35	L/ha
	0.935	mL/m^2

Multiply	by	to obtain
L/ha	0.089	gal (Imp.)/acre
	1.069	gal (US)/acre
L/m^2	0.18	gal (Imp.)/yd^2
	0.22	gal (US)/yd^2
kg/ha	0.0205	lb/1000 ft^2
	0.892	lb/acre
	0.00797	cwt/acre
g/m^2	0.205	lb/1000 ft^2
	0.922	lb/acre
	0.0797	cwt/acre
	0.03	oz/yd^2
kg/are	2.05	lb/1000 ft^2
	89.2	lb/acre
	0.797	cwt/acre
g/cm^2	0.228	oz/ft^2
tonne/ha	0.398	ton/acre

Application rates—volume

Multiply	by	to obtain
parts per million (water)		grains/gallon (Imp.) (water)
	0.07	
	0.001	g/L (water)
	1	mg/L (water)
		ounces/100 gal. (Imp.) (water)
	0.0160	
	0.0134	oz/100 US gal. (water)
%	10 000	ppm
oz/100 gal (Imp.)	62.4	ppm
oz/100 gal (US)	0.075	g/L
	75	ppm

Multiply	by	to obtain
kg/m^3	1.69	lb/yd^3
lb/yd^3	0.59	kg/m^3
oz/yd^3	38.5	g/m^3

Rate

Multiply	by	to obtain
litres/second (L/s)	13.2	gal (Imp.)/min
km/h	0.621	mile/h (mph)
gal (Imp.)/min	0.0758	L/s
mph	1.609	km/h

Pressure/suction

Multiply	by	to obtain
kilopascal (kPa)	0.01	bar
	10	millibar (mb)
	1	centibar (cb)
	10.2	cm water
	0.015	lb/square inch (psi)
	0.0102	kg/cm^2
bar	14.5	psi
	100	kPa
	1020	cm water
	1.02	kg/cm^2
mb	0.1	kPa
kg/cm^2	14.3	psi
psi	6.9	kPa
	0.07	kg/cm^2

Power

Multiply	by	to obtain
kw	1.34	horsepower
horsepower	0.75	kw

Salinity

See page 260.

Temperature

$°C = 0.556 (°F -32)$
$°F = 1.8°C+32$

Celsius	Fahrenheit	Celsius	Fahrenheit
105	221	25	77
100	212	20	68
95	203	15	59
90	194	10	50
85	185	5	41
80	176	0	32
75	167	−5	23
70	158	−10	14
65	149	−15	5
60	140	−17.8	0
55	131	−20	−4
50	122	−25	−13
45	113	−30	−22
40	104	−35	−31
35	95	−40	−40
30	86		

INDEX